THIS volume covers the whole field of the psychology of religion.

The author seeks to hold the scales even between the individual and society, doing justice to both but not over-emphasizing either to the disparagement of the other.

He also seeks to make an accurate estimate of the claims of both science and religion, endeavoring to maintain throughout the strictly scientific point of view without giving the religious man cause for just complaint.

Perhaps, the most important point to mention is the success which crowns the author's efforts to be thoroughly empirical and objective. He does not attempt to prove or to support any philosophical or theological or naturalistic thesis.

His one aim is to describe the religious consciousness.

This book, the result of many years of labor, is intended for both the general reader and the special student. It will be found to be suited also for use as a text-book in seminaries and universities.

THE RELIGIOUS CONSCIOUSNESS
A PSYCHOLOGICAL STUDY

THE
RELIGIOUS CONSCIOUSNESS

A PSYCHOLOGICAL STUDY

BY

JAMES BISSETT PRATT, Ph.D.
PROFESSOR OF PHILOSOPHY IN WILLIAMS COLLEGE

New York
THE MACMILLAN COMPANY
1943

Set up and electrotyped. Published June, 1920. Reprinted
August, October, 1921; February, 1923; January, 1924;
January, 1926; June, 1927; August, 1928; April, December,
1930; October, 1934; November, 1937; March, 1940;
October, 1941; October, 1943.

TO
MY DEAR SISTER
HARRIET PRATT CLARKE

PREFACE

The chief function of a preface is, I suppose, to provide information for the hurried reviewer who has not time to read further. In a sense the preface might be called the author's own book-review; or it is the book's *Apologia pro vita sua.* No apology, to be sure, need be made for a new book on the psychology of religion. The science, if such we may call it, is still young, and good books upon it are scarce. Perhaps, however, it is incumbent upon one who lays before the public so formidable-looking a volume as the present one, even within so new a field, to state at least his purpose and his point of view in writing it.

My purpose is easily stated. It is, namely, to *describe the religious consciousness,* and to do so without having any point of view. Without, that is, having any point of view save that of the unprejudiced observer who has no thesis to prove. My aim, in short, has been purely descriptive, and my method purely empirical. Like other men I have my own theories about the philosophy of religion, but I have made unremitting efforts (and I trust with some success) to describe the religious consciousness without undue influence from my philosophical theories, but merely by going to experience and writing down what I find.

I have also sought to cover the field with a fair degree of adequacy; to do justice by both religion and science; to hold the scales even between the individual and society (no easy matter in these days); and to make my book of value and (if possible) of interest to both the general reader and the technical student. I am, of course, painfully aware of the fact that in many ways I have fallen short of my aims. It is now over twelve years ago that I began writing the book; and in that length of time so many changes come over one's evaluations and one's style that in looking through the completed volume I can plainly see (though I hope the reader will not) several distinct strata of thought and language superimposed upon each other, as through successive geologic ages. These diverse elements I think are not really inconsistent with each other, though in this I may be mistaken.

In whatever else I have failed I hope at least that I have avoided provincialism, both of the geographical and of the intellectual variety. In order not to be confined to the American Protestant point of view I have seen what I could of Roman Catholicism in Europe, and of Hinduism and Buddhism in India, Burma, and Ceylon. As to the more dangerous provincialism of the spirit, none of us knows how far he succeeds in escaping it. To what extent my training in psychology has provincialized my judgment and my power of evaluation, the reader alone will be able to decide.

My thanks are due to the editors of the *American Journal of Religious Psychology* and the *Harvard Theological Review* for permission to reprint (in revised form) some of the content of this volume which first appeared in their pages; and to the following friends, former students of mine, who by the circulation of questionnaires aided me in the collection of some of my material — namely Mr. J. L. Cole, Mr. H. S. Dodd, Mr. P. W. Hammond, Mr. E. B. Hart, Mr. E. L. Hazelton, Mr. H. M. Ives, Mr. L. E. McCuen, Mr. C. B. Rogers, Mr. S. T. Stanley, and Mr. Y. Suzuki. Particularly to my wife am I indebted for increased insight into the inner nature of Roman Catholicism, for considerable assistance in the preparation of my manuscript and index, and for unfailing encouragement and keen though kindly criticism.

Williamstown, Massachusetts.
    April, 1920.

CONTENTS

THE RELIGIOUS CONSCIOUSNESS:
A PSYCHOLOGICAL STUDY

CHAPTER I

RELIGION

IT is a rather odd fact that a word so repeatedly on the lips of men and connoting, apparently, one of the most obvious phenomena of human life should be so notoriously difficult of definition as is the word Religion. None of us seem able to get along without using the word; and yet when asked just what we mean by it very few of us can tell. Nor is this unsteadiness in the employment of the term confined to those who have done but little systematic thinking on the subject. Not that the great thinkers who have written books have neglected to tell us what religion is,— Professor Leuba enumerates forty-eight definitions of religion from as many great men [1] (and, elsewhere, adds two of his own, apparently to fill out the even half-hundred). But the striking thing about these definitions is that, persuasive as many of them are, each learned doctor seems quite unpersuaded by any but his own. And when doctors disagree what are the rest of us going to do? Can we be justified in talking about religion at all?

The truth is, I suppose, that "religion" is one of those general and popular terms which have been used for centuries to cover so vague and indefinite a collection of phenomena that no definition can be framed which will include all its uses and coincide with every one's meaning for it. Hence all definitions of religion are more or less arbitrary and should be taken rather as postulates than as axioms. In this sense I shall myself propose a tentative definition of religion, not at all as a

---

[1] "A Psychological Study of Religion." (New York, Macmillan: 1912.) Appendix.

final or complete statement, nor because I think it of great importance, but because I intend ... religion and it therefore seems ... reader in advance not what the word means, but what I am going to mean by the word.

The definition which I propose is the following: Religion is the serious and social attitude of individuals or communities toward the power or powers which they conceive as having ultimate control over their interests and destinies.[2] This definition I propose for what it is worth, and if it is found in several ways defective, I shall not be surprised, nor shall I greatly care. It has, however, one or two characteristics which seem to me of some merit, and to which I wish to call the reader's attention. And its first, and perhaps its only merit, is that it defines religion as an "attitude." This word as a psychological term has received its greatest emphasis and its clearest exposition from Professor Judd,[3] and it is from him, in a general way, that I borrow it. And without accepting all of Professor Judd's views on the subject [4] I shall say briefly that the word "attitude" shall here be used to cover that *responsive* side of consciousness which is found in such things as attention, interest, expectancy, feeling, tendencies to reaction, etc. Thus it is contrasted with what Professor Judd calls "content," the relatively passive element in sensation, the accepted and recognized. It presupposes always an object of some sort, and involves some sort of content; but it is itself a relatively active state of consciousness which is not to be described in terms of the given but it is a subjective

[2] For views somewhat similar to this compare A. C. Watson, "The Logic of Religion" (*Am. Jour. of Theol.*, XX, 98), Irving King's "The Development of Religion" (New York, Macmillan: 1910), esp. p. 17, Perry's "Approach to Philosophy" (New York, Scribner: 1905), pp. 65–66, and his "The Moral Economy" (New York, Scribner: 1909), p. 218. See also Lowes Dickinson's brilliant defense of a similar view of religion in his little book, "Religion, a Criticism and a Forecast" (London, Brimley: 1906), p. 56ff, and Everett's "Moral Values" (New York, Holt: 1918), p. 382.

[3] See his "Psychology" (New York, Scribner: 1907), *passim*, esp. pp. 68–69. Also his article, "The Doctrine of Attitudes," *Jour. of Phil.*, V., 676f.

[4] His hypothesis as to the concomitant physiological processes seems particularly questionable.

respons... ... ...fined to any
one of ... Thus it is not to be co... ... ...know-
ing, fe... ... ... the mind —"
to each ... to the given. ...tional departments of ...actors that belong

RELIGION

The... ... three... ...ditional ...or defining religion as an attitude are now,
I think, sufficiently manifest. It shows that religion is not
a matter of any one "department" of psychic life but involves the whole man. It includes what there was of truth in
the historical attempts to identify religion with feeling, belief,
or will. And it draws attention to the fact that religion is
immediately subjective, thus differing from science (which emphasizes "content" rather than "attitude"); and yet it points
to the other fact also that religion involves and presupposes the
acceptance of the objective. Religion is the attitude of a self
toward an object in which the self genuinely believes.

I have qualified the word "attitude" in my definition by the
adjective "social" with considerable misgiving, for I do not
wish to suggest that religion must have a *personal* object. I
have used the word to indicate that the religious attitude toward
the Determiner of Destiny must not be "mechanical" (as, according to Mr. Watson, the scientific attitude is) nor coldly
intellectual. It must have some faint touch of that social quality which we feel in our relations toward anything that can make
response to us. It is only in this incipient way that the religious attitude need be social.

Again let me admit, or rather insist, that this, like all other
definitions of religion, is more or less arbitrary. Whoever
wishes to do so has certainly a perfectly logical right to give
a much narrower or a much broader definition of the term, provided he is willing to take the consequences. He may, if he
chooses, even confine religion to belief in Jehovah, on condition
that he will stick to his definition and consistently call irreligious all men who do not so believe. A narrow definition
based upon a particular theological belief, however, has two
patent disadvantages. In the first place, it necessarily leaves
out a great number of people and a great number of phenomena
which are by general consent recognized as religious. Thus if
we hold that belief in a personal God is the criterion of re-

ligion we not only run counter to the general view classes
Buddhism in its original form (as general view flock to
most definitions) and so on to call
irreligious many deeply spiritual souls nearer home, who certainly have something more within them than can be included
under philosophy or morality.[5]   If religion is merely this purely
intellectual and rather superficial thing it is hardly worth very
much discussion.   And, in the second place, however much it
may be worth, at any rate it is not a subject that *can* be discussed
by psychology.   One purely intellectual position does not differ
psychologically from another.   Hence the very admission that
there is such a thing as the psychology of religion presupposes
that we mean by religion something else than a theological affirmation.

For a somewhat similar reason the student of the psychology
of religion will hesitate to accept Durkheim's (much more satisfactory) view which seeks for the essential characteristic of religion in the distinction between the sacred and the profane.   A
definition of religion based on this distinction makes a very practical working hypothesis for the sociologist, as is shown in Durkheim's long and admirable work, " The Elementary Forms of
the Religious Life," [6] in which this position is maintained and
illustrated.   But the book shows no less clearly that Durkheim's
identification of religion with the idea of the sacred has notable
limitations, particularly from the psychologist's point of view.
It describes fairly enough the religion of the tribes of central
Australia; but it leaves out of account much that is of importance in the religion of the modern civilized man.   Many
religious beliefs and religious rites upon which groups or communities agree, and which may be studied objectively, come
well enough under Durkheim's formula; but the mental attitude
of the modern religious individual contains a good deal which
we should have to leave out were we to confine our study to the
limits set by Durkheim's method of stating the problem.   His
definition is devised for the use of sociology; but it is the function of the psychology of religion to describe a large number

[5] Cf. Hebert, " Le Divin " (Paris, Alcan: 1907), pp. 186–195, and the
cases there cited from Arreat's and Flournoy's and Leuba's collections.

[6] London. Macmillan: 1915.

..cts and to face a variety of problems which cannot be stated in terms of group consciousness and which have no significant relation to the distinction between the sacred and the profane.

Both the theological and the sociological definitions of religion are, therefore, too narrow to be entirely satisfactory as bases for a psychological study of religion. On the other hand it is possible to make the definition of religion so broad and inclusive as to empty it of all particular meaning. If religion is everything it will cease to be anything. If, as we are sometimes enthusiastically told, all thoughts, all feelings, all volitions of all men are always religious, then religion becomes synonymous with consciousness, and we have simply lost one good old word out of our language.

The definition I have suggested above aims to avoid both the extremes of narrowness and of excessive breadth. It does not necessarily presuppose that all men are religious — they are so only if they believe in a Power that has ultimate control over their destinies, and only if this Power is sufficiently real in their minds for them to have a conscious attitude toward it which in some faint way might be called social. I do not know that all men have this attitude. It may be that there are moments in the lives of all when they do — if so all men have religious moments. If not, then there are some completely irreligious persons. There certainly are millions who are irreligious nearly all the time and in whose lives religion plays a very negligible part. On the other hand, our proposed definition would recognize many an atheist as religious — and I do not see how we can avoid doing so if we are to regard religion as a psychological object.[7] Certainly our definition would find a great deal more religion in some agnostics than in many church-goers. A man may go to Church all his life as the conventional " thing-to-do," he may repeat the Creed every Sunday and never doubt one of its assertions, and yet the problems of Nature and Destiny may be so far removed from all his thought, and the God of whom the Creed speaks may be so unreal to him that he can-

---

[7] Whether under the proposed definition one could speak of such a position as that of Mr. Bertrand Russell as religious is indeed a question; but certainly his attitude toward the logical and æsthetic aspects of reality is closely related to religion. See his essay on " A Free Man's Worship," reprinted in " Mysticism and Logic " (London, Longmans: 1918).

not justly be said to have any conscious attitude toward Him or any other *cosmic* reality. The cosmic realities and possibilities may be completely barred from his thought by Steel Common and the price of eggs. To such a man God is not sufficiently real even to be doubted. It was something like this that Tennyson had in mind when he wrote,

> " There is more faith in honest doubt,
> Believe me, than in half the creeds."

The reference to " faith " and to " cosmic realities " which seems to have crept in inevitably, brings up the question of the relation of religion to theological belief, and it may as well be dealt with at once. And first of all it must be said most emphatically that religion is not theology. It differs from theology and philosophy and science in that it consciously cares for the ultimate cosmic problems not on their own account but from practical and personal considerations. It is not a doctrine nor a law nor an hypothesis but an attitude, and essentially an attitude of *expectancy*. Its real and basal question is not, What is the Cause or the Ultimate Nature of the World? but What is going to become of me — or of us — and what is the attitude of the Determiner of Destiny toward us and our interests?

This subjective nature of religion seems to be almost a discovery of our own times. The Eighteenth Century practically identified religion with theology, and it was not till after the psychology of Schleiermacher, on the one hand, and the evolutionary point of view on the other got well ingrained in the minds of writers on religion that the relatively subordinate position of any particular belief within the life of religion was appreciated. The origin of religion is now sought for not in any external revelation but within the subjective needs of human nature, and its development is to be traced through purely human influences, as is the case with language, morality, and art. Thus we have come to see that religion is essentially a human thing, a biological product and instrument, that it is to be understood better by observing its functions than by analyzing any of its particular doctrines, and that it is to be judged by the way it works rather than to be tested by logical canons

..s an intellectual system.[8] Religion is not so much theology as life; it is to be *lived* rather than reasoned about.

In short, religion is not a theory about reality; it *is* a reality. And yet we must not forget that it is a reality which includes a theory. The fact that it has had a subjective origin and growth of much the same nature as language, morality, and art, must not hide from us the other fact that it involves an outer reference of a sort that these do not. It is an attitude toward the powers in ultimate control of one's destiny, and hence involves a belief in such powers. This belief need not be explicit — often, especially in early times, it is not so. But if it is not explicit it is at any rate implicit; and inevitably for most of us moderns it is to a considerable extent actually explicit.[9] In one way or another, then, religion always and necessarily involves some sort of theology, some sort of belief about the ultimate Determiner of Destiny. Religion is not merely a feeling; it is, as Professor James says, "a postulator of new facts as well." It takes itself seriously, and is not satisfied with being simply comforting and "useful"; it means to be also *true*. The religious consciousness inevitably considers its religion objective as well as subjective. And if it be said that the *value* of religion at any rate is subjective only, then at least religion must not know that this is the case; for if it learned the secret both its value and it would cease to be even subjective.

This fact that religion is an attitude that involves a belief differentiates it from morality. No one indeed can deny that the two are very closely related, that in origin they were hardly distinguishable and in development have gone side by side, nor that the two may and should command the same things. This almost inextricable relation of morality and religion has been influential in determining much that is loftiest and best in the messages of all the prophets and great religious leaders of every religion, and it was this upon which Jesus laid peculiar em-

8 Cf. Prof. Foster's admirable little book, "The Function of Religion in Man's Struggle for Existence" (Chicago, University of Chicago Press: 1909).

9 This is true of all religions that have reached the stage which Bousset calls "Religions of the Law." See his "What Is Religion" (London, Fisher Unwin: 1907), Chap. V.

phasis. The different " historical religions," in fact, are differentiated from each other largely by the moral ideals they uphold, and hence may be said to be characterized chiefly by their ethical teachings. In fact these " historical religions " regularly contain two quite distinguishable, though also quite inseparable, moments: an attitude toward the Controller of Destiny and a system of teachings about the conduct of life. In every well formed religion, indeed, each of these is the natural or inevitable correlate of the other, but they are still theoretically distinguishable. Hence each of these religions may be said to be both a religion and a system of ethics. With this explanation I trust it will not seem paradoxical if I say that while every " religion " is in part morality, religion and morality as such are not identical.

The fact that both religious and moral elements are to be found in every great religion and are always closely associated will explain why so many writers have almost completely identified the two. From the time of St. James to the appearance of the latest book on the subject we have been told that pure religion consists in visiting the orphan and widow in their affliction and in keeping oneself unspotted from the world—in other words, in personal and social morality. This identification of religion with morality — especially with social morality — is defended at length in Professor Ames's admirable " Psychology of Religious Experience." Religion is there defined as " the consciousness of the highest social values " [10], and throughout the book this view that religion is simply social righteousness is continually restated and freshly illustrated. Thus " non-religious persons," to whom Ames devotes a chapter, are those who, for lack of some mental endowment, are not interested in the welfare of society, whereas the typically religious people are those who work for social improvement. More explicitly his position is expressed thus: " The term moral has been used to designate those ideals which pertain particularly to human social welfare, in distinction from the claims of religion which seeks authority for conduct in the will of a Deity. The contrast between moral and religious conduct belongs to that con-

[10] " The Psychology of Religious Experience." (Boston, Houghton, Mifflin: 1910) pp. VII. 168. 169, and in fact throughout.

⸺eption of the world which makes a rigid distinction between the natural and the supernatural, between the human and the divine. But if religion is identified with the most intimate and vital phases of the social consciousness, then the distinction between morality and religion is not real. . . . All moral ideals are religious in the degree to which they are expressions of great vital interests of society. . . . The attempt to delimit the field of natural morality from religion presupposes in the older writers a dualism between human and divine, natural and 'regenerate' natures. Without the definite assumption of this dualism the line between morality and religion becomes obscure and tends to vanish completely." [11]

As was said some time ago, every one, in a sense, has a right to make his own definitions for his own terms, provided he will take the consequences. But while this is true abstractly, it would seem that something is due to the traditional uses of the language in which one happens to be writing. No one can be logically restrained from defining religion as morality. But it should at least be pointed out that to do so is to depart from the usages of the English tongue. And it would seem that before appropriating a common and useful though somewhat indefinite, old word such as religion, and making it exactly synonymous and interchangeable with another common word, morality, Professor Ames and the numerous writers who agree with him should at least coin for us a new word which we might use in place of the old one. For, call it what you will, there is in most human lives an attitude toward the Determiner of Destiny which simply is not to be identified with social righteousness or any other kind of morality. And this attitude certainly approaches much more closely to the common meaning of the English word *religion* than does the very admirable thing which Professor Ames has suggested as the equivalent of the term. It is this attitude — not morality — that one expects to read about in a book on religion. And if religion be the sort of attitude I have suggested, then it is perfectly possible that a religious man may be immoral and that a moral man may be irreligious. A deeply religious man indeed is not likely to sin greatly against his own code of morality, and his religion will,

[11] Pp. 285–87.

in fact, be his greatest help toward righteousness. Religion and morality may and often do and always should lay down the same commands. But though thus intimately connected, they are for all that quite distinguishable. Religion if taken seriously and rationally will be deeply moral; but it *is* not morality.[12]

One of the sentences quoted above from Professor Ames is certainly irrefutable — namely this: "If religion is identified with the most intimate and vital phases of the social consciousness, then the distinction between morality and religion is not real." Surely this is so. *If* religion be so identified then it becomes thereby morality. Hence the question of the relation of religion and morality is seen to be closely connected with the further question of the social nature of religion. The definition I have suggested would of course make it something more than the "consciousness of the highest social values"; but beyond this there arises the farther consideration of the part played by society and by the individual in religion.

The last twenty-five years have witnessed one of those remarkable intellectual epidemics to which the human race is so notably subject. If this were a book, not on the psychology of religion, but on the psychology of philosophy, several chapters might very well be devoted to the very striking way in which the "cold intellect" gets innoculated with abstract and academic theories — a way quite comparable to that in which fevers, slang, styles of dress and religious enthusiasms spread. In the Eighteenth Century it was the idea of the individual that was contagious. The Twentieth Century is soundly cured of that excess (fortunately for us) and the importance of the "social" is to-day receiving at last its due.[13] Especially is this the case with the study of religion. The Eighteenth Century regarded religion as purely an individual matter, and even such recent writers as Max Müller and C. P. Tiele speak of the religion of primitive men as though it were purely a relation between the individual and the "Infinite" whom he

---

[12] Cf. further Professor Palmer's "The Field of Ethics" (Boston, Houghton, Mifflin: 1902) Chap. IV, esp. pp. 177–82, and Hebert, op. cit. pp. 178–86.

[13] Cf. Warner Fite, "The Exaggeration of the Social," *Jour. of Phil.*, IV, pp. 393–96.

perceives," [14] or "apprehends." [15]   The present reaction
against this view is so violent that perhaps I may be excused
for having referred to it as an " epidemic."   Professor Ames's
view of religion as a form of social consciousness, quoted above,
is typical of nearly all the recent treatments of the subject.
Professor Irving King [16] expresses himself in almost the same
way as Professor Ames.   Mr. Jevons distinguishes religion
from fetichism and from magic purely by its social nature.
" Religion is social, an affair of the community; fetichism is
anti-social, condemned by the community."   " A god is not
merely a power conceived of intellectually and felt emotionally
to be a personal power from whom things may be hoped and
feared; he must indeed be a personal power and be regarded
with hope and fear, but it is by a community that he must be so
regarded." [17]   From a different point of view but in essential
harmony with the authors cited, Professor Patten begins his
recent work on " The Social Basis of Religion " [18] with these
words: " This book . . . identifies religion, not with morality, but with the social reaction against degeneration and
vice."   And Professor Durkheim defines religious beliefs and
practices as those which carry with them social obligation, and
insists that religion is altogether a social phenomenon.[19]

It was, indeed, high time the social element received its
proper emphasis, and that religion was seen to be as much a
matter of the community as of the individual.   Especially from
an historical point of view are the authors quoted, and others
like them, justified in their insistence that religion has always
sprung out of a social background and has never been the product of a single individual.   Among primitive peoples particu-

[14] Max Müller, " Lectures on the Origin and Growth of Religion." (London, Longmans: 1901.)   Lecture I.

[15] C. P. Tiele, " Elements of the Science of Religion."   (Edinburgh, Black-
wood: 1897 and 1899) Vol. II, pp. 230–231.

[16] " The Development of Religion," passim.

[17] " Introduction to the Study of Comparative Religion."   (New York,
Macmillan: 1908), pp. 126, 136–37.   See also pp. 95, 121, 217 and his " Introduction to the Study of the History of Religion."   (London, Methuen:
1904), pp. 101, 166, 177–78.

[18] New York, Macmillan: 1911.

[19] " De la Definition des Phénomènes religieux."   L'Année Sociologique,
Vol. II, pp. 1–28.   See also his " Elementary Forms of the Religious Life,"
passim.

larly is the social nature of religion marked. The lonely savage — the "poor Indian" — on his lofty mountain top "perceiving the Infinite" is a myth. "Individual religion" is simply not to be found among primitive races and is, in fact, among them almost unthinkable. Later on I hope to deal more at length with the influence of society upon religion, but here, at the very start, it must be recognized that religion in all its actual historical forms is always to a great extent a social product.

Our recognition of this fact, however, need not and should not carry us to the extreme of forgetting that religion has often been *in part* also a product of the individual. Upon the more primitive forms of religion the individual has probably had only microscopic influence — just how much influence he has had in any given case it is simply impossible for us to calculate. But certainly in the great prophetic religions, the individual has had a great deal of influence. Buddhism without Gautama and Christianity without Jesus would resemble strikingly Hamlet without Hamlet. Of course the religion even of the founders has been largely the product of social forces. But this is true of poetry, art, invention and every human product, and it is therefore quite misleading to speak of religion as peculiarly social in its nature. Very often, on the contrary, a man's religion is the most "individual" thing about him. And it is particularly important to note that as culture and thought advance religion becomes more and more individual and constantly less dependent on social forms and sanctions. The modern American and European have a direct sense of their individual relation to the Determiner of Destiny which, though in a sense (like everything else) largely the product of society, it would be misleading to call social. *Primitive* religion, which is to-day receiving so much careful study is, indeed, predominantly social, and its nature certainly throws considerable light on religion as such. Yet we must not forget (as the students of primitive religion seem often to do) that the modern man is as genuinely religious as the savage; and that the real nature of religion may be as truly seen in one's next door neighbor as in the Toda of Central India or the Semite of 1500 B. C.

Religion is the product both of society and of the individual.

ιτ also gets itself expressed both in society and in the individual. The social expression of religion so far forth as it is a matter of externals belongs not to the psychology of religion but to history, anthropology, and allied sciences. As psychologists we are interested primarily in the way religion manifests itself in the thoughts and feelings and activities of individuals (i. e. of individuals in society). It may therefore not be out of place to close this chapter, which aims to give a general view of the nature of religion, with a consideration of certain types of religion as it gets expressed in individual men and women. This relatively concrete manner of treatment should, I think, show much more clearly what sort of thing religion is than any amount of abstract discussion.

In an earlier work [20] I divided religious belief into three chief types,— " primitive credulity," " intellectual belief " and " emotional belief." The first two of these terms explain themselves, while the last was made to include " the will to believe " and Mysticism. In his great work, " The Mystical Element of Religion," [21] Baron von Hügel makes use of practically the same division, applying it, however, not simply to belief, but to religion as a whole. This triple division, in fact, he regards as ultimately based upon the structure of the ideo-motor arc which begins with sense-impression, moves through the central process of reflection, and ends in the final discharge of the will in action.[22] Religion has thus three aspects, (1) the " traditional " or " historical," (2) the " rational," and (3) the " volitional " or " mystical."

The tendency to divide things into threes is certainly one of the curiosities of human nature. We may seek to justify it according to our taste by appeal to the Reflex Arc, the Hegelian Dialectic, or the Holy Trinity. But whatever its origin, I believe an unprejudiced empirical study of the facts will show that both von Hügel's triad and mine are too simple and that the last member in both cases will have to be expanded, giving us (alas!) four types or aspects instead of three. For certainly the " will to believe " and the active, volitional, practical ex-

20 " The Psychology of Religious Belief " (New York, Macmillan: 1907).
21 London and New York, Dent & Co.: 1909.
22 Vol. I, pp. 52 and 57.

pression of religion are as far removed from the mystical form of religion and belief as they are from the intellectual.

I think, therefore, we shall be justified in saying there are four typical aspects of religion, or, if you like, four temperamental kinds of religion: — (1) the traditional which takes its attitude from the authority of the Past — from parents, teachers, tradition, the Church, etc; (2) the rational, which seeks to free itself altogether from authority and to base itself purely on reason and the facts of verifiable experience; (3) the mystical which appeals solely to a particular kind of experience and a kind that is peculiarly subjective and hence not scientifically verifiable; (4) the practical or moral which lays the emphasis upon the thing that must be done rather than upon the thing that must be believed or felt. All four of these aspects of religion are to be found in every genuinely religious person and in varying degree according to circumstances and particularly according to age. Thus the child is characterized almost entirely by traditional religion, the adolescent is an especially good example of the rational and sometimes of the mystical aspects, while in middle life any one of the four aspects may be most prominent, and here the practical or moral element certainly gets its best development.

(1) The traditional aspect manifests itself under many forms. It first appears in the religion of the child who accepts everything that is told him because it is as yet out of the question for him to doubt anything. It characterizes most unthinking adults who have little or no religious feeling and who if still religious at all are so largely from habit and by inertia. A very different class of persons whose religion is chiefly traditional is constituted by those very earnest and genuinely religious souls who find in the traditions and forms of their Church something so august or so beautiful, and withal so authoritative, that they have only a deaf ear for any protests their intellects may offer, and their own, sometimes well-developed, mystical tendencies are made subservient to the dominant demands of the Tradition which they love.

We all start in as formalists and all historical religions inevitably contain and probably always will retain a good deal of the purely traditional. Man never has been, and presumably never will be, a mere reasoning being, and even if he were he would have to accept from the accumulation of social tradition most of the material about which he is to reason. And the traditional aspect of religion constitutes a large part of its social nature. As Father Tyrrell said in commenting upon von Hügel's book: " Religion is institutional just because it is social; because it is only through the educational influence of society that the communised religious experience and reflection of the past generations are brought to bear upon us so as to waken, guide and stimulate our religious faculty, which else might remain dormant, or at best only reach a rudimentary development." " The legitimate end of institutionalism is to reproduce the common and traditional type of religion in the individual soul; and this, not by way of violent insertion from the outside, but by stimulating and guiding the natural process of spiritual growth." [23]

Such are the uses and such the normal development of institutional or traditional religion. It probably reaches its highest sane and healthy condition in the Protestant Episcopal Church. Its dangers are equally obvious. The traditionalist is so in love with his own lovely form or glorious tradition that he is sadly liable to blindness for all else. Institutionalism if left to itself tends to develop a narrow exclusiveness and intolerance which sees no good in anything but its own form and tradition. And worst of all it is so bound to the past that further development through reason and personal experience are made almost impossible. The old is so fine that the new cannot be good. God having spoken once for all need never speak again. Hence it has ever been the priest who has most opposed the prophet. The mystic who trusts his vision and the thinker who dares follow his reason have no place within the fold of a stiff ecclesiasticism. " Its object is not merely to give a certain bias — that is the object of every educational institution — but to make the subject immune against all other influences to which he may be exposed in the course of his life. It is not so much the more or less unconscious giving a bent that is in question; it is the giving a bent which is, so to speak, itself a bent to a

[23] George Tyrrell, " The Mystical Element of Religion." *Quarterly Review*, CCXI, 101–126.

bent. It is the deliberate effort to prevent a man ever coming into the rights of his reason on the assumption that, in the most important matters, the reason is incompetent." [24]

Thus the religion of traditionalism if left to itself, without the fresh air of the reason and the warm life of the mystic experience, becomes cold, dead, and untrue. It inevitably dwarfs, dries up, and stultifies those who yield themselves altogether to it. And when carried to its extreme form it ceases to be religion; for it becomes so preoccupied with the sacred rite or the pious form of words handed down and sanctioned by the Past, that both cease to have any meaning. Examples approximating to this extreme are to be found in the Christianity of the Greek Church and the Buddhism of China in their worst forms. When the cosmic background is thus lost from sight the performance ceases to arouse or to imply any attitude toward the Determiner of Destiny, and thus becomes merely traditional mummery and ceases to be in any sense religious.

(2) The great foe of excessive institutionalism is rationalism. It is largely by means of the constant exercise of the reason upon matters religious that religion is kept young and in touch with the rest of the life of man. The Eighteenth Century regarded religion altogether as a matter of reason and, while not every one would admit that we have swung too far in the opposite direction, there certainly is a tendency in many contemporary writers to undervalue the position which the intellect does and should hold in the religious life. Though many deeply religious people do very little reasoning upon their beliefs, there is a type of mind equally religious and equally admirable for whom religion is very largely a rational matter and one which could hardly be prized were it otherwise. [25] Such a condition do we find, for instance, in St. Augustine, in Spinoza, and in Martineau. The religious body which most manifestly displays it is probably the Unitarian.

[24] Lowes Dickinson, " Religion; a Criticism and a Forecast," pp. 16–17; Cf. also von Hügel, pp. 70–72; and Tyrrell, p. 108.

[25] This very real aspect of the religious consciousness, so often neglected nowadays, is admirably set forth in Professor Hebert's little book " La Forme Idealiste du Sentiment Religieux " (Paris, Emile Nourry: 1909.)

But like ecclesiasticism, rationalism also has its dangers and may be carried too far. Not indeed that one can ever be too rational. The danger from rationalism comes not from its positive but from its negative characteristics. Human nature is such that if any one part is excessively emphasized some other part tends to be dwarfed and negated. Moreover the tools with which the intellect works — concepts, hypotheses, etc. — may prove harmful as well as helpful; for so serviceable are they that the intellectualist may come to confuse them with the realities to which they should simply lead him. "The Analytic and Speculative faculty," says von Hügel, "seems habitually, instinctively to labor at depersonalizing all it touches, and thus continually both to undermine and discrown the deeply personal work and world of the experimental forces of the soul. Indeed the thinking seems to be doing this necessarily, since by its very essence it begins and ends with laws, qualities, functions, and parts — with abstractions which at best can be but skeletons and empty forms of the real and actual, and which of themselves ever tend to represent all Reality as something static, not dynamic." [26] Your purely conceptual thinker is ever at one remove from reality. And when rationalistic religion reaches its extreme form — as it does in an occasional theologian or philosopher here and there — it gets altogether out of touch with human life and becomes merely a speculative and academic theory or else a cold and thoroughgoing skepticism. A philosophical hypothesis is in itself no more an attitude toward the Universe and toward man's destiny than is the binomial theorem; and when rationalism comes to be merely such an hypothesis it is religious no longer. In the words of Jonathan Edwards, "he that has doctrinal knowledge and speculation only, without affection, never is engaged in the business of religion." [27]

(3) Against this devitalizing of religion, mysticism (in the large sense of the word) is the constant protest and the un-

[26] Op. cit. Vol. I, p. 76.
[27] "A Treatise Concerning Religious Affections." Part I, Section II. It will be found in Vol. III of Edwards' collected "Works" (New York, Leavitt & Trow: 1844).

failing antidote. Whatever else mysticism may become it is at any rate always alive and always very real and concrete. And while it would indeed be untrue to assert that only the mystical are genuinely religious, it is safe to say that all intensely religious people have at least a touch of mysticism. For the mystic's attitude toward the Determiner of Destiny is one of intense, or at least, very real emotion. The individual's relation to the Beyond not only is believed in but seems actually to be experienced; and this experience is one of the most solid bits of concrete fact that ever comes into human life. Later on in this book I mean to give the subject a rather exhaustive study, and therefore instead of describing it further here I shall simply refer the reader to the chapters in which it is treated (XVI–XX). Here, however, let me point out the relations of mysticism to rationalism and institutionalism. Mysticism has something in common with each of these and it also differs from each. Hence one finds it at times at war with one and in alliance with the other, and then suddenly changing front and opposing its old ally by the aid of its old enemy. Neither of the two does it heartily care for, but of the two it has most often chosen institutionalism as its mate. This, as von Hügel says, is perhaps " not hard to explain. For if external, definite facts and acts are found to lead to certain internal, deep, all embracing emotions and experiences, the soul can to a certain extent live and thrive in and by a constant moving backwards and forwards between the Institution and the Emotion, and can thus constitute an ever-tightening bond and dialogue, increasingly exclusive of all else." [28] And perhaps even more important as an explanation of this rather strange alliance is the common antipathy of both the mystic and the priest for the abstractions of the thinker, and for the deadening and skeptical effect which rationalistic analysis often has alike upon the glory of tradition and upon the joy of ecstasy.

Yet mysticism has in common with thought the love of liberty. Its truth is based upon an immediate, personal experience, and hence it unites with rationalism in resenting the claims of every other authority than its own. Not without reason has the Church always feared every popular outbreak of mys-

[28] Op. cit. Vol. I, p. 75.

ticism. He who has experienced the Divine within his own heart is likely to hold all formalism and tradition unnecessary or cheap if not misleading or even diabolic.

This confidence in its own all-sufficing inner light and the intense joy of the experience have been the two great dangers of excessive mysticism, when not balanced by a suitable respect for the inherited wisdom of the race and never inhibited by the restraining hand of a cool and sober reason. The mystic inevitably and rightly trusts his own experience. But when he ceases to criticize it and ceases to trust anything else his mysticism becomes the most misleading form of subjectivism and superstition. And when this inner joyous experience is nourished and coaxed for its own sake exclusively, the mystic becomes little better than the sensualist. This has been the case not infrequently in India and sometimes also among the neurotic ecstatics of Christendom. When this happens exaggerated mysticism becomes a psychological method of self-gratification and no longer an attitude toward the larger Beyond. Hence it too ceases to be in any real sense religious.

(4) But very few of the Christian mystics have carried their mysticism to the extreme just described. And this not because they have been less mystical than the Indian mystics but because they have been better balanced. Some of them have added as an antidote a great reverence for the objective teachings and institutions of the Church. Some of them have been thinkers and have been saved from the extremes of mysticism by their reason. And some have found in the practical activity of a life of service the counter-balancing interest needed to keep them healthy and sane. The effort of the will in the service of a moral ideal is one of the great expressions of religion; and to a certain type of person, religion presents itself chiefly as a moral matter. These people have seen the futility of any one of the aspects of religion thus far studied when taken alone, and with one voice they insist that faith without works is dead. Religion they define in the words of Kant as the viewing of all our duties as divine commands. The long line of the Prophets of Israel, culminating in Jesus himself, while recognizing the importance of the three other aspects of religion, put the emphasis here. Throughout the Middle Ages

this view of religion was in part forgotten; but we of the Twentieth Century seem to be working back toward it — or up to it
— at last.

The importance of morality is being emphasized not only
in a positive but in a negative fashion. The attacks of criticism upon " revealed theology " and of science and philosophy
upon " natural theology " are every year weakening traditional
and " rational " religion. Thus there has arisen a very common feeling, which would have been almost incomprehensible
to many scholastics of the Middle Ages, that one's faith, so far as
he has any, must be based on " the will to believe," and that
to know much about " God " — or even to be sure that there
is any God — is quite beyond our power. As Leuba puts it,
the religious consciousness cares very little who God is but
wants to use Him for various purposes.[29]   And many deeply
serious minds, who in the Middle Ages would have been among
the great doctors and saints of the Church, are turning away
from creeds of every sort to purely ethical effort. The Society
for Ethical Culture with its several branches and its large appeal is typical of this tendency. Nor is this aspect of the earnest mind limited to our generation or to Christian lands. The
teaching of Buddha was quite comparable to it. Wearied with
the many gods and the many ways of supernatural salvation,
Gautama sought — and claims to have found — a method that
is both thoroughly natural and human and thoroughly verifiable. The evil from which his teaching saves is a very concrete and present one, and the methods he uses ask nothing
of the divine and are at the command of whoever will try
them. His last words were typical of his whole teaching, and
fundamental to it — " Work out your own salvation with diligence."

When one reaches this position one is on the very outer edge of
religion or frankly over the line. If the Buddhism of Gautama
is to be classed as a religion at all, it is because the Founder
maintained and inculcated not only a manner of life but a
very definite and earnest attitude toward the Universe. Our
destiny is not merely in our own hands but is dependent also
upon the inexorable Law of Karma. And a very conscious atti-

[29] " The Contents of the Religious Consciousness," Monist XI, 571.

tude toward Karma and toward this evil world and this miraculously moral Universe is the thing which the Buddhist monk most persistently seeks to cultivate.[30] Were this attitude toward the Universe and its laws, toward the ultimate Determiner of Destiny, altogether lacking (as with some practical men it may be) and were Buddhism merely a manner of life and a practical way of avoiding sorrow, then it is hard to see how it could in any sense be called a religion.

The moral aspect of religion, unlike the other types, retains a great deal of its value even when unaccompanied by the rest. The purely abstract intellectualist may be of no great service to the community and both the extreme formalist and the pathological ecstatic may do real harm; but the moral man is always so far forth an asset of the highest sort. If, however, in his emphasis on moral activity he has completely cut himself off from the other aspects of religion he cannot be called a religious man. And if religion has any value, his life is just that much the poorer for its loss.

Doubtless other aspects of religion could be named beside the four I have been dealing with. But I am inclined to think that any such additional aspects would really be found to belong with some of my four. As I have pointed out, between these four religious tendencies there is likely to be more or less conflict. And yet each needs the others to such an extent that without them it would cease to be religious at all. At least two of them must be present in every person who is in any sense religious. Probably all four are to some extent present in nearly all of us. And the ideal both for the religious individual and for the religious society, church or community is the harmonious development and coöperation of all four.

[30] In another connection I have pointed out how the Karma of Buddhism makes a very pragmatic God. See my "India and Its Faiths" (Boston, Houghton Mifflin: 1915). Chap. XIX.

CHAPTER II

THE PSYCHOLOGY OF RELIGION

RELIGION has been studied in many ways and from many angles, and of these many forms there are three that deserve our special attention. The first, the philosophy of religion, goes back to the very beginning of human thought and is, in fact, the oldest form of human reflection. For though our "Histories of Philosophy" usually begin with Thales and water, Greek philosophy has its source nowhere this side of Hesiod and the gods; while genuinely philosophical reflection was busy long before that, in the Upanishads and the Vedas, with Brahman and the Devas. The history of religion — the second of the three forms of the study of religion — though not so old as its philosophy, goes well back into the historical times of Greek antiquity. The psychology of religion, on the other hand, the youngest of the three sisters, was born only within our own times and is still hardly beyond her lisping infancy.

The aims and methods of these three pursuits are, in a general way, clear from the names they bear. The philosophy of religion, the most ambitious of the three, is not so much a study of religion as a study of Reality and an attempt to determine the truth about the Determiner of Destiny. The history of religion is much less ambitious, takes religion as it finds it, whether true or false, and seeks merely to discover how, as a human institution, it has developed. The psychology of religion is more akin to the second of these than to the first, both in the object of its study and in the humbleness of its aim. Like the history of religion, it takes religion as it finds it, is interested in it primarily as a great human fact, and quite leaves out of account the question whether or not the concepts of religion are true. It differs from the history of religion, just as psychology differs from history. It seeks, in short, to be a science. Before going farther with its aims and methods, therefore, it will be best to consider briefly what a science means to be.[1]

The alpha and omega of science is art. Art is its source and art its goal. And art is here to be understood in its widest sense as practice or reaction. Necessity is the mother of invention, and the need of reacting wisely upon the environment goes before man's earliest search for knowledge, rewards and justifies his latest scientific achievement, and (what just now is more to the point) determines the very nature of science through all its history. This general need of wise reaction shows itself especially in two forms,— the necessity of manipulating nature and predicting its course, and the necessity of communicating with one's fellows. If one is to live successfully one must *use* nature — or at least *look out for* her — and this requires a knowledge of how things act and of what one may properly expect. This means *learning,* the guidance of one's actions through the influence of past experience. And intelligent learning means the *identification of situations.* My past experience does me no good if on the recurrence of a previous situation I fail to recognize it and to use it as a sign of what I am to look out for next. Hence the necessity of more or less exact observation of conditions and the more or less explicit formulation or description of them for future guidance. The need for communication with one's fellows is hardly to be separated, even in the abstract, from this need of prediction and manipulation, and it leads to the same attempt at relatively exact description. In the face of an indifferent or hostile Cosmos I am helpless if alone, and the coöperation of my fellows is indispensable. But if we are to coöperate we must have common objects and must describe them in terms that shall not be subjective but intelligible to all because common to all; and if our objects are to be common to all they must be verifiable by all.

These two fundamental needs, prediction and communication, determine the whole nature of science. And, first of all, they determine the scientific fact. Not every fact is neces-

[1] In the following discussion of science I do not mean to be dogmatic; I am simply expounding the view which seems to me the proper one. There are, of course, other views, and one's choice between them is in some sense arbitrary.

sarily an object of science. A fact out of all relation to other facts would not be a scientific fact, both because it would be unverifiable and because it would be useless so far as prediction, manipulation and coöperation were concerned. Hence science can be justified in taking cognizance of a proposed fact only on condition, firstly, that it be verifiable by other men under similar conditions, and secondly, that it be in some relation to other facts which science is able to verify and state in general terms.

Though the chief end of science is art in the sense in which I have used that word, and though this end dominates the course of science and determines its nature, it must not be forgotten that the instinctive human *desire to know* is a contributory cause and prompts much of the progress of science through all its history. "All men by nature desire knowledge," said Aristotle, and this desire is not confined to the more intellectual but is found incipiently in all; it is, in fact, one of the instincts of the race, inherited from our brute ancestors,— the " instinct of curiosity " as most psychologists call it. It exists alike in the scientist and in the savage, in the monkey and in the dog. Biologically it is to be explained by the practical utility of knowledge, and hence it is ultimately only another illustration of the guidance and determination of knowledge by practice. Yet as found in ourselves this instinct has a relatively independent position. Hence it is certainly true that knowledge is valuable for its own sake, irrespective of its practical consequences, and valuable for the same reason that gives value to other things, — namely, because we want it. Thus, from more motives than one, science seeks to build up a systematic view of the objects of human experience that can be expressed in communicable terms and that can be verified by any human being under the proper conditions.

The three methods used by science to achieve this systematic view of our world are commonly said to be Description, Generalization, and Explanation. Description starts with the particular but only for the sake of the general. It starts with the particular because it can find only particulars to start with. But as Arisotle pointed out, science aims always at the general. The reason for this is plain enough from what has been said of the practical aims of science. The particular situation could be no guide to action unless it were a case of some general kind of situation which had been observed before or which might be expected again. Hence the need of general descriptions. It is largely in this that the difference between science and history consists;— history is interested in the particular for its own sake, science cares for it only as it represents a general condition.

Especially important for our practical life is the knowledge how different kinds of objects act on and affect each other. Hence particular observations of such actions or events are accumulated and formulated into generalizations or laws. These, be it noted, are only descriptions of the way in which things act. " Generalization," therefore, does not differ in principle from " description " — it is, in fact, nothing but a general description rather than a real second method of scientific procedure.[2]

Causal explanation may seem, on a superficial view, to be different in kind from description and generalization, but in essence it is merely an application of their results, and is, therefore, ultimately, only abbreviated description. This is plain the moment one grasps the meaning of causation as used in science. Since the days of David Hume, " causation " has ceased to mean the action of a mysterious " force " or " power " or " essence," and (in science at any rate) it stands simply for the fact of regular or invariable connection between phenomena. The particular " causal laws " are, therefore, simply descriptive generalizations, and a " causal explanation " consists merely in the application of one of these generalized descriptions of past experience to the particular case in hand. Scientific explanation is thus nothing more than classification — it consists in saying, This is a case of that. The new and particular event is " explained " in the sense of being better understood by being subsumed under a type or genus of events previously experienced and well recognized. We " understand " the strange or wonderful by learning that it is not exceptional, that it belongs to a group whose members always act in this same fash-

----

2 It differs, of course, from the description of a single fact in that its object never can be directly observed but is a creature of the scientific imagination.

ion,— the single wonder being explained by a million. A native of the tropics seeing for the first time very cold water turn into ice is astonished. The scientist "explains" it to him by saying that very cold water *always* turns into ice. It is, if you like, a mystery still,— in one sense, an infinitely greater mystery. Yet in another sense the phenomenon is now better understood, since it is put in its setting, and the particular shown to be a case of the general. It may be even further explained by reference to other substances which are known to be harder in cold weather than in warm. The unknown has now been reduced to the known, the new described in terms of the old.

The causal explanation of an event is, therefore, nothing but the short-hand, abbreviated description of that event. Instead of describing it in detail with all its antecedents and consequences, we refer it to an already well-known class, just as one may describe an individual animal by referring it to its species. The already known class, moreover,— the scientific law, of which this particular event is an instance — is itself only a general description of observed past experience. Hence causal explanation as well as generalization reduces in principle exactly to description, and in this broad sense description may be called the one method — and the one immediate aim — of science.

Causal explanation, however, though thus shorn of its mystery, is not a thing that one can afford to slight; nor does its reduction to description open the door to miracle. No doubt it can never be proved that everything is related to other things by definite laws, that there is regularity in the way all things act. Conceivably there may be spheres of reality in which this regularity ceases; in which the effect is not given with its proved conditions. It can never be proved that no such spheres exist. Science can give no reason why things *must* happen regularly. In fact science knows the word *must* no more than she knows the word *ought*. With the *is* alone is she concerned. She merely records the facts—and gives advice. A miracle would be only an irregularity in nature, and prior to experience an irregularity is no more unlikely than a regularity. To the unsophisticated mind, in fact, universal regularity would seem by far the more astonishing. The only miraculous thing about miracles is that they happen so seldom. In itself, the turning of water into wine is no more wonderful, no more inexplicable in the deeper sense, than the turning of water into blood. Only the one we have never known to happen; the other happens constantly within our very bodies. It is perfectly possible that there are miracles. But if there are, science is so far forth and in that particular sphere impossible; and wisely guided action within that sphere is equally impossible. The regularity which is undemonstrable is the presupposition of both science and action. Hence science rightly makes the postulate that there are no miracles,—which is no more than saying that science goes at her task in a courageous spirit and with a sense of responsibility. She means to do her best. She means to puzzle over every problem to the very end, instead of giving up weakly at the first difficulty and saying, This is doubtless a miracle and hence insoluble, so pray excuse me, and give me something easy! The practical aims of science forbid its taking cognizance of anything which is not ultimately explicable by the causal law, of anything which will not fit into a general description of human experience.

For be it noted that science is forever limited to the data derivable from human experience. The very necessity for verification and communication demands this. Inasmuch as nothing can be communicated to other men or verified by them but that which is presented to common human experience, science is limited to describing the experience data of human beings and the relations between them. Now human experience is not only limited; it is fragmentary. It is best represented, as Professor Ward has suggested, not by an island but by an archipelago. There are gaps within it, or, at least, so it seems; and these gaps are very possibly filled out by events not experienced by any human being. Of course the impulse is natural to fill in these gaps with creatures of the imagination — to construct hypotheses as to unexperienced realities conceived of as " really " connecting the parts of our sundered experience. Such guesses may be useful in aiding our poor minds to hold together the loose ends of our actual experience; but it must be remembered that so far forth as they are unverified they are not a genuine part of scientific knowledge. They can become such only by being actually experienced by true representatives of the race. For one can never prove that an unexperienced hypothetical entity is the *only* solution of a given problem — that no other guess is possible. Hence when a scientist proposes any such unverified entity as a gap-filler, he is simply inventing aids to the imagination and the memory, or else he is writing metaphysics. It may be perfectly good metaphysics, but it is metaphysics, not science. Here is the true line between the two subjects,— the line dividing verifiable human experience, on the one hand, from the hypothetical reality back of it.

Metaphysical hypotheses may be of various sorts, and historically are divisible into two chief classes, the materialistic and the spiritualistic. While neither of these hypotheses belongs to science, both are consistent with scientific aims and methods so long as the hypothetical, ultra-empirical reality is not conceived as interfering with our experienced world in ways that are necessarily incalculable by science. Judged by this test, the materialistic hypotheses have usually had the advantage over the spiritualistic. Unthinkable and self-contradictory as they often have been, they are framed expressly for the satisfaction of scientific aims and hence fit into the scientific scheme better than the spiritualistic hypotheses usually do, made as they usually have been for very different purposes. Probably the one or the other of these hypotheses is true. If so then the *ultimate* explanation of the phenomenal world — the explanation of our experience as a whole — would be found in this ultimate reality. But this ultimate kind of explanation is a matter for philosophy, not for science. Her task is much more modest than this. Her only sphere is human experience and her only aim description.

The fact that the practical aim of science determines its nature has often been taken in such rigid fashion as to make natural science almost impossible. Obviously prediction that shall be both absolutely exact and absolutely certain is out of the question until quality shall have been reduced to quantity and all the relations between phenomena shall be expressed in mathematical terms,— until, in short, induction shall have given place to deduction. This was what Kant had in mind when he despaired of psychology because its object could not be expressed mathematically, and what Locke meant when he despaired of physics because, in our ignorance of the " real essence " of any given " substance " we could not deduce from it its various qualities.   For if the word science be taken in this strict sense, physics no less than psychology would have to forego the honored title; there would be no " natural sciences " and the only science left us would be mathematics.   Abstract mechanics and abstract dynamics would indeed still be sciences, but only because they would be branches of mathematics, and the moment they were applied to the facts of actual experience they would cease to be scientific.   Hence it seems best to take the word science in a larger and, I confess, a looser way, so as to cover any systematic description of the verifiable facts of human experience.   This does not mean that the aim of prediction is given up, but only the pretense of perfectly exact and absolutely definite prediction.   These will still be the ideal and the " limit " of all science, and different sciences will differ in the degree to which they approximate to these ideals.

If this be admitted, then psychology is a genuine, though not a very exact science.   Its aim will be to *describe mental processes*.   And I use the word *describe* here in the same broad sense as before.   Psychology will describe in the sense of putting its observations into communicable terms, generalizing them into empirical laws, and explaining the particular by the general.   In explanation it will make use of any known scientific generalizations that it needs.   Some of these will be its own records of psychical events, others will be furnished it by other sciences.   Particularly will physiology be of service here.   Within the purely psychical field there are gaps which may be filled out by known physiological events.   And, moreover, where no such known physiological events have been found it is often useful, for the purpose of helping out our " understanding " (i. e. our imagination) of the matter, to devise or picture a series of physiological events made to order to fill the gap.[3]

[3] Cf. Prof. Titchener: " If we attempted to work out a merely descriptive psychology we should find that there was no hope for a true science of mind. . . . There would be no unity or coherence in it. . . . In order to make psychology scientific we must not only describe, we must also explain mind. . . . If we refuse to explain mind by body, we must accept one or the other of two equally unsatisfactory alternatives: we must

Sometimes a series of " unconscious mental phenomena " are invented for the same purpose. In a sense it is almost indifferent whether such hypothetical events are really *there* or not, so long as the concept of them is useful in connecting the actually experienced series, and thus making regularity and prediction at least theoretically possible.

For prediction is to a very considerable extent possible even in psychology. To be sure it cannot predict with absolute certainty nor with mathematical exactness, but it often can tell us what in a given situation we may reasonably expect, and thus enable us to utilize past experience for future action. Beyond this psychology cannot go, and beyond this it need not go in order to be a science. If, forgetting its limited powers, it stakes its reputation on exact and unfailing prediction, or on its ability to " explain " in any other and deeper sense than that outlined above, it may well be called " hopeless." [4] But its

either rest content with simple description of mental experience, or must invent an unconscious mind to give coherence and continuity to consciousness. Both courses have been tried. But if we take the first we never arrive at a science of psychology; and if we take the second we voluntarily leave the sphere of fact for the sphere of fiction." (" A Text book of Psychology," New York, Macmillan: 1910, pp. 38–40.)

Dr. Morton Prince comments upon this passage as follows: " If he [Prof. Titchener] means that we should explain mind by specific parallel nervous processes, we certainly are entering the ' sphere of fiction,' indeed of romance, for we cannot correlate the simplest conscious process with any specific physiologic process nor have we even a glimpse of the data which will allow us to approach the problem. If on the other hand he means a physiologic process as an abstraction or concept, we are still entering, but justifiably, the sphere of fiction, though I would rather phrase it, of imagination, as much so as when we ' invent an unconscious mind.' Unconscious mental processes belong no more to the sphere of fiction than to unconscious physiologic processes. Both are simply concepts which we postulate to explain the facts. We simply say the phenomena occur as if the concepts were true. . . . So far as such concepts satisfactorily explain the phenomena and allow us to predict events we may treat them as true and as the cause of phenomena. To my way of thinking it does not make the slightest difference, so far as the purposes of explanation are concerned, whether we treat unconscious processes as physiologic or as mental — both are concepts and in this sense only belong to the ' sphere of fiction.' " (" The New Psychology and Therapeutics," *Jour. of the Am. Medical Assn.*, March 30, 1912.)

[4] Cf. Möbius, " Die Hoffnungslosigkeit aller Psychologie," (Halle, Marhold: 1907). Psychology is " hopeless " for Möbius because he identifies natural science with physical science and because psychology cannot answer the most important questions without calling in the aid of metaphysics.

humbler task is by no means hopeless, and it is one well worth while, and large enough to occupy all who are interested in it to the end of time. Hence it seems to me a mistake to call psychology, as Prof. Münsterberg does,[5] only a stop-gap for physiology, or to limit its permanent function, as Prof. Taylor does,[6] to " providing Ethics and History with an appropriate terminology." To describe the workings of the human mind is a perfectly definite and independent task and one in itself well worth while.

To describe the workings of the human mind so far as these are influenced by its attitude toward the Determiner of Destiny, is the task of the psychology of religion. As its name implies, it means to be psychology — that is, it means to be a science. Human experience is the subject of its investigation. It aims at nothing metaphysical or transcendental.[7] The reader, of course, will decide for himself the question whether its aim should be thus humble; but to me at least it seems plain enough that transcendental analysis belongs rather to the philosophy than to the psychology of religion. The true task of the latter is, in my opinion, simply to study the religious consciousness just as any other science studies its object. Nor is there any good reason for setting up any bounds within the religious consciousness which the psychologist shall not be allowed to pass if he can. Certainly it is very sacred ground that the psychol-

This, of course, is a possible position, but the special meaning it gives to " hopeless " should be carefully noted. Whether or not psychology turns out to be hopeless will depend on the kind of hope you cherished for it in the beginning.

[5] " Grundzüge der Psychologie " (Leipzig, Barth: 1900) pp. 415–435.

[6] " Elements of Metaphysics " (London, Methuen: 1903) p. 305.

[7] This, at least, is the opinion of nearly all investigators in this country, and it is from this point of view that the present book will proceed. It is only fair to say that this view is not absolutely universal. In Germany in particular a few prominent writers, approaching the subject from the theological side, insist that the psychology of religion must seek and find in the religious experience a *metaphysical somewhat* — " *ein metaphysisches Etwas*." And Wobbermin (the translator of James's " Varieties ") asserts that the scientific method of American investigators can produce no important results and that we should rather make use of " transcendental analysis." Cf. Dr. Roland Schutz in the *Zeitschrift für Religionspsychologie*, Vol. V, pp. 246–247. See also Bauke's exposition and criticism of Wobbermin's position in the *Zeitschrift* for June, 1911 (Vol. V), pp. 97–104.

ogist is here studying, but, for that very reason, it is all the more worthy of study.   Hence the psychologist will be justified in making use of any material that seems to him promising. He will probe the most sacred depths of the private experience of individuals as thoroughly as he can; he will ransack the public records of social religious practices and common religious ideas; and the results of these various investigations he will describe, compare, and generalize as completely as is possible.

When stated in this abstract fashion, the task of the psychologist may seem relatively simple; but if one seriously undertakes it, he will be met at the outset with certain difficulties peculiar to this field.   He must, namely, face the questions how he is to get at the material for his study, and how much it will be worth when he has got it.   Three methods for obtaining material naturally present themselves, and have in fact been followed by leading psychologists.   The first is a study of individual experiences as portrayed in autobiographies, letters, and other spontaneous expressions of religious persons.   The second method is the collection of answers to definite questions from a number of persons through the use of a *questionnaire*.   The third method investigates the relatively objective expressions of social religion furnished by history, anthropology, and the sacred literature of various peoples.

The first two of these methods have the advantage of studying religious experience at its source, that is, in the individual soul.   They are open to the obvious danger, on the other hand, of emphasizing a type of character that is ready to expose to view its most sacred experiences.   The *questionnaire* method is particularly open to suspicion, both because of this unfortunate selective tendency, and also because it almost inevitably puts the respondent into a slightly unnatural attitude by the very fact of setting him down to answer deliberately some one's questions concerning his religious life.   The respondent is often quite incapable of giving an exact or even significant psychological description; and if he is able to do so he is usually unwilling to take the requisite time and trouble, and so writes a short answer too superficial to have any real value.   Moreover if the results of such answers are tabulated and an effort made to get statistics and percentages from them, the result is quite likely to be misleading; because by a process of natural selection the great majority of the answers will be from those who have something startling to relate and rather enjoy relating it.[8] To avoid difficulties like these, some writers turn to the more objective and impersonal records of social religion, such as rites, ceremonies, and theological concepts or primitive superstitions. And here indeed we get all the advantages of objectivity,— with all its dangers. For, after all, it is psychology, not sociology nor theology nor history that we are studying, and psychology is the science of subjective states and processes which in the last resort are to be found only in the individual. It is the real " inwardness " of religion that we want to know about; and to throw aside the subjective altogether because of its attendant dangers will be like pouring out the baby with the bath.[9]

And, after all, the difficulties of the first two methods are not so great but that they may, to a considerable extent, be overcome. Doubtless it is true that many who regard their religious experiences as very sacred will refuse to describe them to the psychologist for coldly scientific purposes. But these same people will often relate them or write them out in detail for the edification of the faithful; and there is no law against

[8] For an admirable criticism of the *questionnaire* method as ordinarily used see Stählin, " *Die Verwendung von Fragebogen in der Religionspsychologie,*" *Zeitschrift für Religionspsychologie,* V, 394–408 (March, 1912). Cf. also my " Psychology of Religious Belief," pp. 232–234.

[9] Prof. Billia goes so far in criticism of the historical method as to insist that it has no value. (See his paper " On the Problem and Method of the Psychology of Religion " in the Monist, XX, pp. 135–139.) It " gives the illusion of describing and cognizing a mental fact while remaining outside of the fact itself." The outer expression, which the historian and anthropologist see, gives, in Billia's opinion, very little inkling as to the inner fact which alone should interest the psychologist. This question goes hand-in-hand with another that is of interest in this connection,— a question that was raised at the 1909 International Congress of Psychology — namely whether the non-religious psychologist can effectively study religion. Prof. Billia answered this in the negative, while the majority gave an affirmative answer. It is hard to see why the non-religious psychologist, if there be such a person, cannot throw some light on the religious consciousness by a careful collection and comparison of the ways in which it expresses itself; just as a blind man may be learned in the laws of colors, and just as a psychologist may study the physical processes of the dancing mouse without being one. None the less, he would be at a distinct disadvantage and could hardly expound the real inwardness of the experience as could a psychologist who could interpret his data by his own introspection.

the psychologist studying these acounts. Nor is it true that
those who thus describe their inner lives are necessarily superficial. The very names Augustine, Teresa, Fox, Tyrrell, are
enough to disprove any such idea. Even the *questionnaire,*
moreover, if carefully used, may bring considerable very reliable information. Thus the " *Religions-psychologische Arbeits-
gemeinschaft,*" recently organized in Germany, though very
skeptical of the value of the *questionnaire* as ordinarily employed, is making a limited and trustworthy use of it by directing its questions only toward the externals of religion rather
than toward inner experiences, and by insisting that the respondent shall never see the questionnaire nor be asked for
categorical answers, but that all information from him shall be
drawn out by the collector through informal conversation.[10]
These two safeguards certainly avoid practically all of the difficulties which tend to make the *questionnaire* method untrustworthy; and, personally, I am not convinced that the method is
altogether useless even without such limitations. The relia-
bility of the method will depend in each case upon the particular
subject investigated and upon the care of the editor in interpreting the results. The collector should certainly talk with
his respondents whenever possible, and should always interpret
their answers in the light of each other and throw out whatever
seems in any way suspicious; and if all this is done the material collected can hardly be considered altogether worthless.[11]
Finally, if the biographical and *questionnaire* methods be supplemented by the more objective study based on public and
social religious expressions, beliefs, rituals, and the like, the
psychologist will have at his disposal a very respectable body of
facts as the raw material for his work.[12]

[10] See the article by Stählin cited above, esp. pp. 403–407; and also the
same author's account of the founding of the *Religions-psychologische Ar-
beitsgemeinschaft*, in the *Zeitschrift für Religspsy*, IV p. 222.

[11] A further argument for its use is the fact that the biographical method
is in great need of supplementation. Religious material from biographies
emanates almost invariably from somewhat extraordinary religious souls,
and if one's description of the religious consciousness is based upon this
source alone, the picture is likely to be over-colored. This, for example, is
the one fundamental weakness in James's great book.

[12] These different sources vary in their value according to the problem to
which they are applied; and in this book I shall attempt to utilize them
accordingly.

Having collected his facts, the psychologist will proceed as other scientists proceed with their data. That is to say, he will group his facts and note general relations between them, thus seeking a systematic and general description of the various facts in the religious consciousness. Whenever possible, he will " explain " these facts by subsuming them under the laws of general psychology. That is to say, he will proceed on the assumption that, for the purposes of science, religious facts are not different in kind from other psychic facts. Thus he will seek to build up a scientific view of the religious life, interpreting and explaining it by itself and by the known facts and laws of the human mind, "expounding nature by nature," as Höffding says, " just as a passage in a book is expounded in such a manner as to connect it with other passages in the same book." [13]

The reader may perhaps question whether such a procedure is justifiable. He may insist that it builds upon an assumption that is at least uncertain and seems in some respects very dubious. And he may assert that in the religious consciousness at its best we have something that is very difficult to explain by the laws of general psychology. Certainly no one will appreciate the force of this last statement more fully than the psychologist. When one compares the deeply religious and spiritual person with the best and bravest of those who are not religious, one sees, it must be confessed, that the former possesses something which the others lack. It is not that he is any better morally than his non-religious brother, nor any more appreciative of beauty and love nor any braver. It is, rather, that he has a confidence in the universe and an inner joy which the other does not know. He is, perhaps, no more at home in this world than the other (perhaps he is not so much at home here), but he seems more at home in the universe as a whole. He feels himself in touch, and he acts as if he were in touch, with a larger environment. He either has a more cosmic sense or his attitude toward the cosmos is one of larger hope and greater confidence. Besides this, or as a result of this, he has an inner source of joy and strength which does not seem dependent on outer circumstance, and which in fact seems greatest at times

[13] " The Philosophy of Religion."   (London, Macmillan: 1906) p. 20.

when outer sources of strength and promise fail. He is, therefore, able to shed a kind of peace around him which no argument and no mere animal spirits and no mere courage can produce. Whence comes this difference? On what are these values, which we all recognize, founded? Evidently, the immediate answer can be put in psychological terms. The peace and power in question follow, by regular psychological laws, from a certain form and intensity of belief and a certain emotional experience. Whence comes this belief and this experience? Doubtless it will be much more difficult to trace these back to some precedent situation, for the conditions here envolved,— social, psychical, physiological — become now very complex. Yet conceivably this might be done. But the reader may continue his questioning and ask: Is the belief here involved illusory, and is the experience deceptive? Can a complete and ultimate explanation of them be given in psychological terms, and if so would not such an explanation if known destroy its object?

Certainly the psychologist who started out on the assumption that every religious phenomenon is to be completely and ultimately explained by psychological laws, that we have in our hands — or at least can some day get into our hands — all the data needed for such an ultimate explanation, would be like a physicist who failed to recognize that there might be gaps within his field — that there might be links in the chain of causes which, from the nature of the case, could never be directly experienced by human beings. It is the recognition of such gaps that has led the physicist to the invention of the many atoms and the many ethers. These, as I have said, are not scientific objects; they are devices to enable him more easily to put together the parts of his fragmentary experience. The two ends of the cable he sees; he grasps them at the points where they plunge beneath the surface. His imagination depicts what the submerged links may be like. This is all mythology and metaphysics except so far as it enables him to think together the two parts which he actually holds and to explain them in terms of each other.

Are there such gaps in the field of religious psychology? This is a question of fact. There are for us as many gaps as

we find.   There is for us a gap wherever we cannot see a connection.   These gaps we must seek to fill as best we can;— if
possible by discovering actual experience, verifiable objects, that
make the desired connections;[14] where this is not possible, we
must recognize the fact, note how the several parts vary in relation to each other, and write down our resulting generalizations.
General psychology, as has been pointed out above, has numerous gaps of this kind, and usually seeks to fill them by some
more or less ingenious hypotheses of brain physiology.   The
theologian and the religious man frequently insist that similar
gaps exist among the phenomena of the religious consciousness
— as seen, for example, in conversion, the answer to prayer, the
mystical experience.   But just as the general psychologist who
knows his business will remember that his physiological hypotheses, no matter how useful, cannot be genuine objects of
his science until empirically verified, so the psychologist of religion must remember that explanation through the Supernatural, though quite possibly true, is not psychology, and that he
must confine himself to the verifiable facts of human experience.

The question of the Supernatural so frequently confronts one
in the study of the psychology of religion that a word more
should be added concerning it here.   In brief, there are two
chief views of it and of its relation to the natural, one of which
may be called the phenomenal view, the other the noumenal.
According to the first, the Supernatural, or the Will of God, is
to be regarded as a cause among other causes, and it is usually
depicted as also acting in ways that are to the human mind
forever incalculable.   Its ways are not regarded as *altogether*
incalculable, to be sure, but frequently as dependent upon certain well-known conditions of a moral nature.   With all this,
however, there still remains a considerable residuum of uncertainty and inexplicability about its actions, and it is depicted
as interfering at unexpected times with the ordinary and regular
course of events.   Such a statement makes the view sound crude,
possibly, but however that may be, it is the position actually
held by very many religious people.[15]   And a good deal may be

---

14 A good example of this is seen in the explorations of the subconscious
by Freud, Prince, and others, by which facts are brought to light which
connect and hence " explain " much that before was unconnected.

15 The frank acceptance of the Supernatural as a phenomenon by the

said for it. It has a pragmatic value which the larger, " noumenal," view retains only with some difficulty; for according to this " phenomenal " view it is plain that the Supernatural, in pragmatic terms, *" makes a difference."* The religious soul usually wants a God who will do something for him. And a Supernatural which made no difference to our experience might be called " divine " or materialistic with indifference.

I do not see that this view of the Supernatural can be proved false. There are too many seeming gaps in our experience, too much that is unexpected and unaccountable in our lives, for us to be able to demonstrate in them an unbroken causal chain. As a fact, to be sure, this view of the Supernatural so far as it concerns the outer world has been largely given up;— and, it must be added, with no great harm to the cause of religion.[16] In the inner world, however, it is still defended, and the theologian and philosopher are perfectly free to accept and vindicate it. But the psychologist is not free to do so. If the Supernatural breaks in upon the natural, psychology as a science is *so far forth* impossible. The theological explanation is no explanation for the psychologist, because it is not capable of being confirmed by experience.[17] And for psychology, or

popular view is not always recognized by psychologists in arguing this point — e.g. Irving King, " The Development of Religion," p. 9.

[16] One still meets with it occasionally, even in very intelligent circles,— witness, for example, the not uncommon explanation of the Sicilian earthquake in 1909 as due to God's anger over the wickedness of the Sicilians.

[17] From the point of view maintained in this chapter it will plainly be impossible to consider theology a science. It cannot be called a science (in our use of the term) for the same reason that the theory of the ultimate nature of matter cannot be called a science. Professor Macintosh in a most original and suggestive book (" Theology as an Empirical Science "— New York, Macmillan: 1919) maintains that theology has the same right to the name science as physics or chemistry; that God may be directly perceived; and that if we deny this second proposition on the ground that we can perceive only our own mental states, we thereby destroy not only theology but all objective science, and have nothing left but a false psychologism. With the latter part of this argument I am in fullest sympathy; but I still cannot feel that " God " is *verifiable* in the same sense in which the objects of physics and chemistry may be verified, and hence cannot see my way to considering theology a science. Even on the hypothesis that God is as directly experienced by a certain gifted few as other persons are, theology would still be in another category from science. Nor do I think that such a position as mine leads one to psychologism, for one may and should distinguish between the data

any science, to admit that there are any facts incapable of being explained, incapable of being regularly connected with the other facts of experience, would be a surrender of its fundamental presuppositions. For its own protection science must *act as if* this view of the Supernatural and its interruptions of the natural were false. It cannot take cognizance of interruptions.

The second view of the Supernatural referred to above regards it as the noumenal side, the inner being, of all Reality,—the *" Natura Naturans "* of Spinoza. It is immanent within the phenomenal world and is expressed by it as really, though probably not so completely, as by any transcendent world. It is a *Super*natural not in that it interferes with nature but in that it includes and transcends nature. The upholders of this view usually deny miracle, and at any rate, no miracle is necessary to it. The regularity of the causal law is regarded as being merely *the way God acts.* It sees God in order rather than in disorder, in the dependable working of law rather than in incalculable interferences with law. Thus there is no possible quarrel between it and science. An extension of this view might suggest that some of the gaps in the religious experience may possibly be filled by realities and forces in another spiritual world which act according to regular laws, so that the results of their action are as certain and (conceivably) as predictable as the performances of the atoms. In this way the pragmatic value of the phenomenal view would be retained, for the Supernatural would thus " make a difference." Such an hypothesis would, of course, be metaphysical in the extreme, but it would be perfectly consistent with a scientific view of the religious consciousness.

Three different attitudes are possible toward the breaks that we find in experience, both of the outer and of the inner world: (1) We may make the theological hypothesis of supernatural

given us in perception together with their objective interrelations, and the subjective mechanism (sensational, ideational, etc.) by means of which we perceive. Both of these groups are verifiable in human experience (in a direct way that neither God nor the ultimate nature of matter are), yet the former belongs in a peculiar sense to the physical scientist, the other to the psychologist. For further exposition of the epistemological view here involved, see " Essays in Critical Realism."

interference.   (2) We may invent some other hypothetical intermediary to help us think over the break — e. g. atoms, ether, brain action, the " Unconscious."   (3) We may frankly recognize the fact that any such stop-gaps are purely hypothetical and beyond our experience, and content ourselves with simply describing the phenomena as we find them, leaving the guesswork, for the time being, to others.

This third attitude, as it seems to me, is the proper one for the psychology of religion.   It is essential to a right understanding of any of the great questions of religion and philosophy, as well as of those of science, which we shall meet in the course of our study, to recognize at the beginning the relatively limited aims and pretensions which the psychology of religion, justly understood, should maintain.   I cannot help thinking that it would ultimately lead to great disappointment, if not to positive skepticism, if we should sanguinely expect, as I fear many cultured religious people have been led to expect, that the psychological study of religion can demonstrate any of the truths of theology.   And equally misleading does it seem to me to suppose, as some leading " functional " psychologists seem to do, that the psychology of religion can ever so develop as to be in any sense a substitute for philosophy or theology.   In the opinion of this school, ethics, æsthetics, logic, epistemology, and metaphysics, are ultimately nothing but functional psychology. As a result, the psychology of religion " becomes " in Professor Ames's words, " the conditioning science for the various branches of theology, or rather, it is the science which in its developed forms becomes the theology or the philosophy of religion.   If reality is given in experience (and where else could it be given?), then the science of that experience furnishes the reasonable and fruitful method of dealing with reality, including the reality of religion.   The psychology of religion possesses, therefore, the greatest possible significance.   It does not merely prepare the way for theology, but in its most elementary inquiries it is already dealing with essentials of theology and the philosophy of religion.   On the other hand, the philosophy of religion in its most ultimate problems and refined developments does not transcend the principles of psychology.   The idea of God, for example, which is the central conception of theology, is subject to the same laws of the mental life as are all other ideas, and there is but one science of psychology applicable to it.[18]

On reading passages like this from enthusiastic representatives of the new functional psychology one comes away wondering not that they have included so much but that they have included so little within their capacious science. Why stop with the various branches of philosophy? Why not also reduce physics, chemistry, astronomy to functional psychology? What, indeed, are the physical sciences but formulations of experience — and is not psychology the science of experience? The same arguments hold in the case of physics that held for metaphysics. Surely if " the idea of God is subject to the same laws of the mental life as are all other ideas," the same may be said with equal truth of the idea of the solar system. And this, I think, makes clear both the fallacy and the danger of this " pragmatic " view. Psychology studies the *idea* of God and the *idea* of the solar system and stops there. But neither astronomy nor theology means to limit its study to our ideas. They both mean to be objective — and it is hard to see why one should be denied this privilege if it be granted to the other. And if objectivity be denied to theology, the dangers that inevitably result are evident. Theology becomes purely subjective,— a description of the way we feel; the idea of God is substituted for God and hence becomes the idea of an idea, or a confessed illusion; and the psychology of religion, having absorbed all that was objective in religion, finds it has nothing left to study, or at best becomes a branch of abnormal psychology. " This method," writes Boutroux, " if it succeed, will lead sooner or later to the abolition of the fact itself, while the dogmatic criticism of religions has striven in vain for centuries to obtain this result. . . . Contrary, then, to the other sciences which leave standing the things that they explain, the one just mentioned has this remarkable property of destroying its object in the act of describing it, and of substituting itself for the facts in proportion as it analyzes them." [19]

The psychology of religion must then, in my opinion, take a

[18] " The Psychology of Religious Experience," pp. 26–27.

[19] " Science and Religion " (English translation, New York, Macmillan: 1911), pp. 196–197.

much humbler position than that which some of its devotees desire for it. It must content itself with a description of human experience, while recognizing that there may well be spheres of reality to which these experiences refer and with which they are possibly connected, which yet cannot be investigated by science. From this less ambitious view of its task, however, one must not conclude that the psychology of religion is either valueless as an end or useless as a means. Sharing in the limitations of science, it shares also in its values. If religion is worth a tenth part of what its believers claim for it, it is worth cultivating as a human possession; and if it is to be wisely and fruitfully cultivated, it should be carefully and scientifically studied. If the religious values are to any extent bound up with each other and with the rest of life by laws of relationship, it is of great importance for us to know what those laws are. The psychology of religion is still too young to have accomplished a great deal in this practical direction. The field has been surveyed only in its outlines, and only in a general way can the practical religious worker gain from psychology a knowledge of what to expect in any given case. Exact and perfectly certain prediction is, of course, out of the question. But it is not too much to say that he who would systematically cultivate the religious life can already find a good deal of practical help from the psychology of religion; and as our knowledge of it increases we may confidently look to it for more and more assistance.

But even aside from its practical application, the psychology of religion has a value as an end in itself for all those who, in Aristotle's phrase, " desire knowledge." To know the truth is worth while for its own sake,— Francis Bacon, in fact, went so far as to call the search for truth and its attainment "the sovereign good of human nature." And surely few things are so worthy of man's study,— just because few things are so thoroughly and deeply human — as is religion. It dominates the life of the lowest savage and fills the thought of the most transcendental philosopher. It is the central power of the primitive community and it animates the ideals of the most advanced civilization. In it the king and the peasant, the rich and the poor, the saint and the sinner too, feel bound together. As much as anything else, it is that "one touch of nature" that "makes the whole world akin." It is the first thing the child learns at his mother's knee, as it is the last to fill his mind as he enters the great unknown.

It will, then, be the aim of this book to describe some of the facts of the religious consciousness as it expresses itself in various forms. No fundamental thesis will be defended and no unitary law will be laid down or traced out. The study will be frankly inductive and empirical and therefore perhaps somewhat fragmentary. We shall seek to follow where the facts lead, believing that religion is so great a thing that the mere aim to describe some of its forms and expressions is an ideal high enough to justify any amount of patience and labor.

NOTE. The subjects discussed in the preceding chapter are of such fundamental importance that the reader who is not acquainted with the literature of the subject should consult some of the following references:

Boutroux, "Science and Religion" (New York, Macmillan: 1911), Part I, Chap. IV, Part II. Chap. II.

Bradley, "Appearance and Reality" (London, Sonnenschein: 1897), Chaps. 11 and 22.

Coe, "The Psychology of Religion" (University of Chicago: 1916), Chaps. I, II, and III.

Foster, "The Finality of the Christian Religion" (Chicago, University Press: 1906), Chap. 6.

Höffding, "The Philosophy of Religion" (London, Macmillan: 1906), pp. 14–57.

Holt, "The Concept of Consciousness" (New York, Macmillan: 1914). Holt's view is quite different from that presented in the text.

Mach, "Science of Mechanics" (Chicago, Open Court: 1893), Chap. 2.

Macintosh, "Theology as an Empirical Science" (New York, Macmillan: 1919), Introduction.

Möbius, "Die Hoffnungslosigkeit aller Psychologie" (Halle, Marhold: 1907).

More, "Atomic Theories and Modern Physics," Hibbert Journal, VII, 864–881; "The Metaphysical Tendencies of Modern Physics," Hibbert Journal, VII, 800–817.

Münsterberg, "Grungzüge der Psychologie" (Leipzig, Barth: 1900), Chap. 2.

Pearson, "The Grammar of Science" (London, Black: 1900), Chaps. 2, 3, 4.

Perry, "The Approach to Philosophy" (New York, Scribners: 1905), Chap. 5; "Present Philosophical Tendencies" (New York, Longmans: 1912), Chap. 3.

Poincaré, "Science and Hypothesis" (New York, Science Press: 1905), Parts III and IV; "The Value of Science" (New York, Science Press: 1907) Part III.

Royce, "The World and the Individual," Vol. II. (New York, Macmillan: 1901); Lectures 1, 2, 4, and 5.

Taylor, "Elements of Metaphysics" (London, Methuen: 1903), Book III,
    Chap. 6.   Book IV, Chap. 1.
Ward, "Naturalism and Agnosticism"(London, Black: 1906), Lectures
    1, 2, and 3.

CHAPTER III

RELIGION AND THE SUBCONSCIOUS

THE aim of science is to make out a complete general description of human experience in the form of laws of regular and predictable sequence. But, as was pointed out in our last chapter, the perfect realization of this ideal is impossible because there are breaks or gaps in this experience as we know it; not all the sequences which we experience are complete. Evidently there are two ways conceivable in which this difficulty may be met. One is by discovering new events, actually experienced but hitherto unknown, which will help to fill up the gaps. The other is to make the hypothesis of unexperienced events which cannot be genuinely verified but which are nevertheless useful in enabling us to think together the sundered strands of our unconnected experience. Now when such gaps occur in mental sequences, the psychologist has two possible sources to which he may look for gap-fillers. One of these is the physical world, especially that part of it known as the nervous system of the individual. The other is the " subconscious." Each of these sources furnishes the psychologist with both the kinds of assistance mentioned above:— from each, that is, he derives new experienced events and unverified but useful hypotheses. Upon the facts and fictions of physiological psychology, I shall not dwell; but the subconscious looms so large in recent discussions of the psychology of religion that I feel justified in devoting the present chapter to a consideration of it.

The conception of the subconscious or the unconscious originated, I suppose, with Leibniz.[1] It was made popular as a philosophic doctrine by von Hartman in his dangerously fascinating work, " Die Philosophie des Unbewussten." [2] But it was not until relatively recent times that it was imported from

[1] Cf. the Monadology (*passim*), and the New Essays.
[2] English Translation by Coupland (London, Paul, Trench, Trübner: 1884.)

philosophy into psychology in the stricter sense of the term.
This was done partly by F. W. H. Myers and his followers,
partly by various neurologists and medical men whose researches
and practice led them into the field of pathological mental phenomena.   Coming into psychology through this double doorway, the conception of the subconscious has had a rather varied
development.   The physicians have groped and grubbed and
worked their way through a mass of abnormal and often very
unpleasant cases, mining what facts they could; while the
Myers school has been borne, often on the wings of intuition, to
conclusions far more interesting, and, if true, metaphysically
far more significant.

Myers's hypothesis was that the conscious self of each of us
is only a small part of the real self; that underneath the conscious personality there extends a much larger "subliminal"
self, below the threshold of our immediate awareness, behind
the door, dominating many of our actions and our thoughts by
powers not known to us, and constituting the real and essential
personality, of which the conscious self is but a broken gleam.
He writes: "The conscious self of each of us, as we call it,—
the empirical, the supraliminal self, as I should prefer to say,—
does not comprise the whole of the consciousness or of the faculty
within us.   There exists a more comprehensive consciousness,
a profounder faculty, which for the most part remains potential
only so far as regards the life of earth, but from which the consciousness and the faculty of earth-life are mere selections, and
which reasserts itself in its plenitude after the liberating change
of death." [3]   This does not mean that we have two selves; it
means that the one true self is the totality of which the supraliminal part is but a fraction.   "I mean by the subliminal
self that part of the self which is commonly subliminal; and I
conceive that there may be, not only coöperations between these
quasi-independent trains of thought, but also upheavals and al-
ternations of personality of many kinds, so that what was once
below the surface may for a time, or permanently, rise above it.
And I conceive also that no self of which we can here have
cognizance is in reality more than a fragment of a larger Self —

[3] "Human Personality and Its Survival of Bodily Death" (London,
Longmans: 1903).   Vol. I, p. 12.

revealed in a fashion at once shifting and limited through an organism not so framed as to afford it full manifestation." [4]

Within this subliminal part of us, as within the supraliminal part, there are various kinds of phenomena, some lofty, some "dissolutive." To illustrate this, Myers uses a simile which has become famous, the comparison, namely, of our empirical consciousness to the visible spectrum and of our subliminal faculties to the ether waves which we cannot see. "At both ends of this spectrum, I believe that our evidence indicates a momentous prolongation. Beyond the red end, of course, we already know that vital faculty of some kind must needs extend. We know that organic processes are constantly taking place within us which are not subject to our control, but which make the very foundation of our physical being. We know that the habitual limits of our voluntary act can be far extended under the influence of strong excitement. It need not surprise us to find that appropriate artifices — hypnotism and self-suggestion — can carry the power of our will over our organism to a yet further point. The faculties that lie beyond the *violet* end of our psychological spectrum will need more delicate exhibition and will command a less ready belief. The actinic energy which lies beyond the violet end of our solar spectrum is less obviously influential in our material world than is the dark heat which lies beyond the red end. Even so, one may say, the influence of the ultra-intellectual or supernormal faculties upon our welfare as terrene organisms is less marked in common life than the influence of the organic or subnormal faculties. Yet it is *that* prolongation of our spectrum upon which our gaze will need to be most strenuously fixed. It is *there* that we shall find our inquiry opening upon the cosmic prospect, and inciting us upon an endless way." [5]

It is, according to Myers, from this violet end of the spectrum, so to speak — from the supernormal part of our subliminal selves — that come the insight of the poet and the intuition of the prophet. Art and religion, mysticism, love, invention — these and many other striking facts of human nature are thus made intelligible by one hypothesis. "An 'inspiration

[4] Ibid. p. 15.
[5] Ibid. Vol. I, p. 18.

of genius' will be in truth a *subliminal uprush,* an emergence into the current of ideas which the man is consciously manipulating of other ideas, which he has not consciously originated, but which have shaped themselves beyond his will, in profounder regions of his being." [6]

All readers of the " Varieties of Religious Experience " will remember how much Professor James was influenced by these views of Myers.[7]   Not that he accepted Myers's hypothesis in its totality.   James was too keen a psychologist and too empirical a philosopher to consider Myers's view a demonstrated truth. Nor did he feel at all sure that the subconscious part of the mind had sufficient unity to be regarded as a personality.   The evidence, in his opinion, was as yet far too scanty to justify us in coming to any conclusion on the exact nature and organization of these subliminal facts.   But he was convinced that the conscious self came into touch with, and was influenced by, psychic forces that psychology had as yet hardly recognized. This he regarded as of prime importance to the subject of psychology.   " We have," said he, " in the fact that the conscious personality is continuous with a wider self through which saving experiences come, a positive content of religious experience which, it seems to me, is literally and objectively true as far as it goes."   And his own " over-belief " was that our being upon its further side plunges " into an altogether other dimension of existence from the sensible and merely 'understandable'" world.[8]

It is not surprising that a view in itself so romantic as Myers's hypothesis of the subliminal self, presented with such charm of style, and having the sympathy, if not the positive support of our greatest psychologist, should make a very strong appeal not only to that large class which is ever eager for the mysterious, but to many serious thinkers, theologians, and religious men, who have found in the works of Myers and James a new source of religious hope and faith.   Had not this dis-

[6] Ibid. p. 71. For an able criticism of Myers's theory see Prof. Stout's article on it in the *Hibbert Journal* for October, 1903.

[7] See also his paper on " Frederick Myers's Services to Psychology," in " Memories and Studies."   (N. Y., Longmans: 1911.)

[8] " The Varieties of Religious Experience " (London, Longmans: 1903) p. 515.

covery of the subconscious self come, indeed, in the very nick of time, when the old foundations were being undermined by criticism and thrown down by science? What an unforeseen, unhoped for, reversal of the rôle of science this was! No longer the foe, science was now become the ally of faith. Hereafter, Higher Criticism and Rationalism and Naturalism might do their worst. Only the outworks of religion were open to their attack, and the man of faith might when he chose retire to the impregnable fortress of his Subconscious Self.

The rapidity with which this view has spread is one of the most interesting facts in the intellectual history of recent years, and a witness to the wide-felt need of a belief in something somehow supernatural. The popular magazines have got hold of it, and the man in the street knows that there are two of him. Preachers have made their congregations familiar with this new basis for religion, and books written by scientific — and by unscientific — men have taken it for granted. I quote a typical passage from one of them:

"The subconscious mind is a normal part of our spiritual nature. There is reason to believe that it is purer, more sensitive to good and evil, than our conscious mind. . . . Though it is doubtless more generic and in closer contact with the Universal Spirit than reason, yet its creations bear the imprint of individual genius." [9] Another writer puts it thus: "Man's mind is something far larger than he is conscious of: his consciousness is but a speck of light illuminating one part of his whole self. . . . Or, to put the matter in a still simpler metaphor, the mind is like an iceberg of which the greater part is hidden under the sea." [10] A distinguished theologian varies the figure, likening the mind not to an iceberg, but — as near as I can make it out — to a sort of bottle with a narrow neck and no bottom. The narrow neck is our consciousness, the main part of the vessel is our subconscious, and from it "filters" up the contents of our minds. Moreover, "the narrow-necked vessel has an opening at the bottom, which is not stopped by any sponge. Through it there are incomings and outgoings,

[9] Dr. Worcester, in "Religion and Medicine," (New York, Moffat Yard: 1908), p. 42.
[10] Dreamer, "Body and Soul," (New York, Dutton: 1909), p. 39.

which stretch away into infinity, and in fact proceed from, and are, God Himself." [11]

It is evident that we are here dealing with a question of prime importance for more things than psychology. If the mind is the sort of thing described above, we ought to know it; and we ought to consider carefully the evidence on which the conclusion is based. To get at the evidence, however, on which the belief in the subconscious rests is made doubly difficult by the fact that the term in question is exceedingly ambiguous. Like other amiable beasts of burden, it has been so overworked that it is now good for little but a vacation — a reward which it might be well to grant. The many meanings which it has had to bear can, however, be reduced to three or possibly four principal ones, which we shall now examine in turn.

The first of these uses of the word " subconscious " makes it synonymous with the *fringe* or *background* of the mind.[12] This is, of course, a part of our immediate experience, of our direct awareness, with nothing subliminal or supernormal about it. If our consciousness be represented by a series of concentric circles, the innermost of these will stand for the center of closest attention, and the outermost zone for the fringe-region or background. Between the two there is no break, no " dissociation," but one shades off into the other by a gradual decrease in vividness of content. This outer zone of our con-

[11] Sanday, " Christologies Ancient and Modern," Oxford U. Press, 1910. See also the comments upon Dr. Sandy's book by the Bishop of Ossory in the *Hibbert Journal*, IX, 235.— Other figures beside that of the iceberg and the bottle are often met with among enthusiastic expounders of the wonders of the Subconscious. Edward Lewis, in a rather beautiful passage, uses the illustration of the pool communicating with the ocean. (" Edward Carpenter," N. Y., Macmillan: 1915, pp. 7–8.) Rev. Dr. Snowden likens the Subconscious to the five or six story cellar of a skyscraper (" The Psychology of Religion," Revell: 1916, pp. 68–69). Miss Sinclair finds that the subconscious or " the country of abnormal consciousness, stretches forwards as well as backwards, and belongs every bit as much to our future as to our past." (" A Defence of Idealism," New York, Macmillan: 1917, p. 259.)

[12] E.g. Prof. Joseph Jastrow — this at least is at times the meaning he gives the word. Cf. his work on " The Subconscious " (Boston, Houghton, Mifflin: 1906). Marshall takes a similar view, using *the subconscious* to mean " the undifferentiated mass of unemphatic psychic parts which constitutes what we may well speak of as the *field of inattentive or sub-attentive consciousness.*" See " Consciousness " (N. Y., Macmillan: 1909), p. 20; and also his articles in the *Journal of Phil.*, Vol. V, nos. 4 and 18, and in the *Hibbert Journal*, Vol. VII, p. 307.

sciousness, however, though not attended to, is often of decisive importance in guiding both our thought and our action. We seldom realize all the factors that go to determine our decisions and our judgments. The syllogism is really a very poor representative of the way we think. There is a great deal more in our consciousness at any moment than we pay attention to; and this great, vague, unanalyzed mass of what Marshall calls our "sub-attentive consciousness" furnishes a large part of the data for our judgments, and often forms our opinions when we think we have reasoned our way to them. "The inventor, in working on his particular invention, has a mass of accumulated material and experience, indispensable for the development of the invention, but which is in the background of his consciousness. Similarly, the mathematician, in solving his problem, which forms the focus of his consciousness, possesses a body of knowledge or a mass of material which, though it lies in the periphery of his consciousness, still forms the mainstay of his particular investigation." [13] Both our rougher and more general opinions and our more exact discriminations depend in large measure on what Jastrow calls "mass impressionism"— the total unanalyzed effect which the object in question has upon the background of our minds.[14]   The bank-cashier may be able to detect the counterfeit bill with unfailing certainty, and yet be quite unable to tell you how he does it, or to describe with any exactness the ear-marks of genuine paper money.

The influence of the background upon life and action is no less marked. In Professor Ward's opinion, the background or "continuum," as he calls it, is the original form of psychic life, and it is from it as a matrix that all the more sharply defined forms of consciousness have developed.[15]   It is not at all to be considered as a mere reservoir of sensations unattended to. Besides the sensations and the hazy ideas — and more primitive and fundamental than they — there are in the fringe all manner of latent and incipient impulses, attitudes, tenden-

[13] Sidis and Goodhart. "Multiple Personality" (New York, Appleton· 1905) p. 241.

[14] For many excellent examples see "The Subconscious," pp. 425–429.

[15] See his article "Psychology" in the Encyclopedia Britannica, eleventh Ed. (1911), Vol. XXII, esp. pp. 555–556.

cies to reaction, partially suppressed feelings, wishes, volitions. " The instinctive desires and impulses have their roots in it, and get their power from it; the inborn reactions upon the environment, so far as they are conscious, the native antipathies and tendencies, our deepest loves and hates — all these are parts of it and grow up out of it." Moreover, " it is the inheritor of our past, and forms what might be called a feeling memory. At every moment our whole outlook is colored by our past impressions and ideas. These are not present as such — they are not distinctly remembered — but a general feeling-tone and tendency to reaction is established by them and is modified by each event of life; in short, the total feeling background is affected by all our thoughts and experiences in such a way that they influence every passing moment. Our total past experience is in a sense summed and massed in the background, and thus becomes a compendium of our history. But it is much more than that; it is largely the store-house of heredity as well. It is in the line of direct descent and inherits an endless amount of wisdom gained with so much toil by our entire ancestry." Thus it has a kind of *" racial* or *instinctive* wisdom which seems to put it in touch, in a perfectly natural manner, with forces hidden from the clearly conscious personality and which makes it wiser in many ways than the individual." [16]

There is nothing mysterious about this, nothing supernatural, nothing that is in any sense a discovery. The fringe region is in no way " higher " or " purer " than the center of consciousness. It contains evil as well as good, or rather, it contains neither the one nor the other, but the materials for both. Only conscious personality is moral — nothing is morally good except a good will. The background is only a background; it is there not for its own sake but for the sake of the total personality. The best and purest aspect of the mind, the aspect of it most highly developed and the most nobly human, is to be found not in the obscure shadows of the background, but in the clear sunlight of full consciousness.

[16] Pratt, " The Psychology of Religious Belief," pp. 15 and 23. I take this opportunity to acknowledge the justice of certain criticisms of Chapter I of the book referred to. There is no doubt that in that work I identified

A second meaning sometimes given to the term "subconscious" makes it identical with the unconscious, and interprets the unconscious as the purely physiological. It is a generally accepted hypothesis that brain facts accompany mind facts, either as a causal substratum or as correlates. While it has not been absolutely demonstrated, it seems most probable that certain brain events are so correlated with certain mind events that the former are regularly followed or accompanied by the latter. If this is true, then many of the phenomena of consciousness are to be explained (in the sense indicated in the preceding chapter) by reference to the unconscious, that is, to physical phenomena in the nervous system. Moreover, the physiological mechanism of the body performs many purposeful acts without direction of consciousness, such for example as the numerous organic, reflex, and instinctive movements. May we not, therefore, explain the various phenomena commonly attributed to the action of the "subconscious" as due to the unconscious, that is, to the automatic activity of the nervous system? Many of these phenomena were thus explained by Dr. Carpenter over sixty years ago as due to "unconscious cerebration";[17] and a large number of psychologists [18] to-day insist that there is nothing in the facts that have come to light since Carpenter's "Mental Physiology" was written to force us to any other principle of explanation.

It is plain enough, however, that this explanation will suit neither the Myers school nor the majority of the pathologists. Nor are these gentlemen any better satisfied with the first meaning of the word "subconscious" suggested above. They will insist that the subconscious is not merely the physiological, and that it is not to be identified with the content of the fringe.

feeling too closely with the background and gave it too preponderating a position over thought.

[17] See his "Mental Physiology" (Fourth Ed. N. Y., Appleton: 1887.) Chap. XIII. The famous phrase quoted above appeared first in the 4th edition of his "Human Physiology," published in 1853.

[18] E.g. Münsterberg, Ribot, Pierce, Kirkpatrick.— See "A Symposium on the Subconscious," papers by Münsterberg and Ribot, *Journal of Abnormal Psychology*, II 25–37; Pierce's paper "An Appeal from the Prevailing Doctrine of a Detached Subconsciousness" in the Garman "Studies" (Boston, Houghton, Mifflin: 1906); and replies to Morton Prince by Pierce and Kirkpatrick respectively in the *Journal of Phil.*, V., 269 ff. and 421 ff.

For them the real question of the subconscious, therefore, is whether this fringe material is the last thing in the way of psychic stuff, or whether there is genuine consciousness not felt by the personal center and yet connected with the same physical organism. Does the consciousness of which we are aware exhaust all the psychical phenomena centering in our bodies, or are there pulses of consciousness entirely outside the circle of our awareness? In other words, to use at last an unambiguous term, is there such a thing as a *co-consciousness?*

I said above that there were three or possibly four meanings which the word " subconscious " at times bore. Its interpretation as a co-consciousness is, of course, the third of these. The fourth, if there be a fourth, is very hard to state. We sometimes find the word " subconscious " — or more commonly the word " unconscious "—" *das Unbewusste*," " *l'inconscient* "— used to mean some kind of psychic state which is yet unconscious. Bergson, for example, appeals at times to such unconscious mental states.[19] Freud, in some parts of the " Traumdeutung," insists upon unconscious psychic states in no uncertain terms, and in one passage (part of which I reproduce in a note [20]) quotes Professor Lipps as an upholder of the same view. Just what can be meant by " unconscious psychic states " it

[19] See " Matière et Memoir " (Paris, Alcan: 1903), Chaps. II and III, esp. pp. 152–161.

[20] " Die Frage des Unbewussten in der Psychologie ist nach dem kräftigen Worte von Lipps weniger eine psychologische Frage, als die Frage der Psychologie. So lange die Psychologie diese Frage durch die Worterklärung erledigte, das " Psychische " sei eben das " Bewusste," and " unbewusste psychische Vorgänge " ein greifbarer Widersinn, blieb eine psychologische Verwertung der Beobachtungen, welche ein Arzt an abnormen Seelenzuständen gewinnen konnte, ausgeschlossen. Erst dann treffen der Arzt und der Philosoph zusammen, wenn beide anerkennen, unbewusste psychische Vorgänge seien ' der zweckmässige und wohlberechtige Ausdruck für eine feststehende Tatsache.' Der Arzt kann nicht anders, als die Versicherung, ' das Bewusstsein sei der unentbehrliche Character des Psychischen,' mit Achselzucken zurückweisen. . . . Die Rückkehr von der Überschätzung der Bewusstseinseigenschaft wird zur unerlässlichen Vorbedingung für jede richtige Einsicht in den Hergang des Psychischen. Das als allgemeine Basis des psychischen Lebens angenommen werden. Das Unbewusste muss als allgemeine Basis des psychischen Lebens angenommen werden. Das Unbewusste ist der grössere Kreis, der den kleineren des Bewussten in sich einschliesst; alles Bewusste hat eine unbewusste Vorstufe, während das Unbewusste auf dieser Stufe stehen bleiben und doch den vollen Wert einer psychischen Leistung beanspruchen kann."—" Die Traumdeutung " (Leipsig und Wien, Deuticke: 1909), p. 380.

is a little hard to see. The term, of course, immediately suggests round squares and true falsehoods. Freud's own explanation of the anomaly seems to be that it is " something, I know not what." It is, he insists, " the genuinely real psychic [das eigentlich reale Psychische], as completely unknown to us as to its inner nature as is the reality of the outer world, and given to us through the data of consciousness just as incompletely as the outer world is given through the sense organs." [21]

This appeal to the unknowable to explain the contradictory is not very enlightening. Hence some of his admirers insist on other interpretations of the *Unbewusste*. Dr. Bernard Hart suggests that the word as used by both Freud and Jung should be taken merely as a concept, a short-hand expression for the manipulation of our experience, rather than as a name for anything thought of as really existing. [22] Other readers of Freud, in spite of the passage referred to above, will insist upon interpreting his " Unbewusstes " in terms of co-conscious mental states. [23] And, in fact, if the term is to be taken as referring to anything real and psychical it is hard to see what else it can mean. Hence we shall now turn to the question of the existence and the nature of the co-conscious.

The facts to which appeal is made to prove the existence of a co-consciousness are of two general classes: *First,* those found in normal subjects; and, *second,* those found in abnormal subjects, whether their abnormal condition be natural or induced temporarily by artificial methods. Limits of space make

[21] Op. cit. p. 381.

[22] " The Conception of the Subconscious," *Jour. of Abnormal Psy.,* IV, 354–62. Dr. Beatrice Hinkle in the Introduction to her translation of Jung's " Wandlungen und Symbole der Libido " expresses the view that for Freud — and apparently also for Jung — the " Unconscious " means the " realm " where various unknown but disturbing emotions lie hidden, and that it is also " a name used arbitrarily to indicate all that material of which the person is not aware at the given time — the not conscious." She adds: " This term is used very loosely in Freudian psychology and is not intended to provoke any academic discussion but to conform strictly to the dictionary classification of a ' negative concept which can neither be described nor defined.' " (Jung-Hinkle, " Psychology of the Unconscious," New York, Moffat Yard: 1916, p. xv.)

[23] Dr. Prince, among others, often refers to Freud's views in this way. A very clarifying discussion of the terms Subconscious, Unconscious, and Co-conscious will be found in Chap. VII of Prince's " The Unconscious " (New York, Macmillan: 1914.)

it impossible to present here a critical exposition of the facts in question, and we must, therefore, content ourselves with the conclusions (so far as there are such) to which the weight of scientific opinion inclines. In brief, then, the evidence does not seem to be such as to force us to the hypothesis of a co-consciousness in normal human beings. Many facts, indeed, have been adduced which strongly suggest such a view, but none that make it indispensable. They can, I think, invariably be explained in terms of the fringe or of the nerve processes, or by the accepted laws of psychology. Several competent psychologists, to be sure, would not concur in this view, and further investigation may yet show that their position is preferable to the one presented above. The fact, however, that these psychologists regard the split-off states of normal persons as of rare occurrence and of slight importance, and the difficulty of drawing any hard and fast line between normal and abnormal subjects make the difference between the two positions relatively unimportant. It is almost indifferent whether we say that normal persons may occasionally have fleeting, split-off conscious states, or that normal persons never have such states, but that many or most of us are occasionally abnormal.

When we turn to the plainly pathological cases, we meet a very different state of things. The evidence here for co-conscious mental life is so strong that, if one adopts an empirical point of view and refuses to decide the matter on *a priori* considerations, it is very difficult to resist the conclusion that within the same mind there may exist at the same time both a principal and a subordinate center of conscious life, split off from, though mutually influencing, each other. I must hasten to add that this conclusion is not shared by all psychologists. It is, however, the opinion of the majority of those who have had first-hand experience with these pathological phenomena. The facts which they cite seem to show striking marks of the presence of consciousness and of some consciousness other than that of the patient's leading personality. The favorite alternative explanation is unconscious cerebration; and the ascription of so much intelligence to purely physiological processes as that hypothesis would require would be enough to make one seriously doubt the consciousness of one's fellow-beings.

It may indeed very well be, as suggested above, that even in some of us so-called normal persons there are at times fleeting gleams of conscious life split off from the main psychic stream; or, if we prefer another way of putting it, that any of us may occasionally become temporarily abnormal. After the investigations of Prince and other alienists, it is difficult to doubt that mental shocks and emotional excitement tend not only to confuse but to dissociate consciousness. If this be the case, there will be all degrees of dissociation, ranging from cases of complete or approximate mental unity down through greater and greater degrees of dissociation, until at last we find several fairly independent and fairly unified separate " personalities " or " complexes " functioning in one body, or until even these are disintegrated into more elementary groups of psychic states, each narrower, less unified, and less stable than the last.

The nature and content of the co-conscious states of persons only incipiently abnormal (and of normal persons, if normal persons have them) can be pretty well made out from some of Prince's and Sidis's investigations. They are invariably limited and disintegrated, and usually quite unimportant and unrelated to any purpose — sensations, feelings, impulses, unconnected and simply flickering into life and out again, like the light of the fire-fly in the dark. They are seldom combined into anything that can be called a *thought*. They are without self-consciousness, and there is " no evidence to show that the dissociated consciousness is capable of wider and more original synthesis than is involved in adapting habitual acts to the circumstances of the moment." " There is no hard and fast line between the conscious and the subconscious, for at times what belongs to one passes into the other, and vice versa. The waking self is varying the grouping of its thoughts all the time in such a way as to be continually including and excluding the subconscious thoughts." The split-off states, except in thoroughly pathological cases or in artificially produced abnormal conditions, give rise to no " automatisms " or independent and disconnected actions and hallucinations.[24]

24 The substance of this paragraph and the quotations in it are taken from Prince, " Some of the Present Problems of Abnormal Psychology," *Psychological Review*, XII, 135–139. See also Sidis and Goodhart," Multiple Personality," *passim*.

In extreme cases, such as that of Miss Beauchamp and B A reported by Morton Prince, we have, indeed, in the co-conscious, something approximating much more closely to the popular notion of the " Subconscious Self." Miss Beauchamp's third alternating " complex " (known as " Sally ") not only claimed to be co-conscious — and proved it to the satisfaction of Dr. Prince and most of his readers — but developed also a very definite character, which she retained with consistency from her first appearance until finally " squeezed." [25] She was, namely, throughout, a rather pert, interesting, immature young girl, differing noticeably in tastes and manners from both the other personalities, considerably inferior to both in knowledge and intellectual power, and markedly inferior to one of them in conscience and character. In another of Dr. Prince's cases, B, who has given pretty conclusive evidence of being co-conscious with A,[26] maintains, like Sally, a perfectly distinct and consistent character throughout. She does not resemble Sally in immaturity, but is decidedly inferior to the complete and normal integrated personality. It should be added that both these co-conscious " personalities " have written their autobiographies, that of B in particular being highly intelligent and instructive.[27] It is, to be sure, questionable whether either " Sally " or " B " is as much of a personality as each claims to be. No doubt they are well-developed, *alternating* personalities, but it is far from clear that as co-conscious entities they have sufficient unity and completeness to deserve the title *personality* or *self*. My late colleague, Professor John E. Russell, made the suggestion that in the co-conscious state such " personalities " are merely " complexes " or groups of ideas, and that the claim of each to unbroken co-conscious *personal* life is due to an illu-

[25] See " The Dissociation of a Personality," (N. Y., Longmans: 1906), *passim*.

[26] See Prince, " Experiments to Determine Co-conscious Ideation," *Journal of Abnormal Psychology*, III, 33–42. Prince and Peterson, " Experiments in Psycho-galvanic Reactions from Co-conscious Ideas," Ibid., III, 114–131. Three more recent but less persuasive cases of seemingly co-conscious activity are reported by Dr. Prince in a paper on " Co-conscious Images," in the *Jour. of Abnormal Psy.*, XII (1917), 289. See also a criticism of their evidential value by Professor Chase. Ibid., XIII (1918), 29–32.

[27] For Sally's autobiography see " The Dissociation of a Personality," Chap. XXIII. For B's see " My Life as a Dissociated Personality," in the *Jour. of Abn. Psy.*, III, 314–334.

sion of the memory.[28]   However this may be, it is interesting
to note that " Sally " and " B," the only " co-conscious selves "
whose histories have been investigated, have originated out of
" complexes " or groups of feelings, ideas, and impulses within
the central consciousness, complexes of the same sort as are to
be found in any of us.   Who is there that has not noted in his
own experience how the emotion due to some insult, slight, or
injury can gather to itself special ideas and tendencies and become a little center of relative independence within the mind?
It is in some such general way that a dissociated " personality "
originates.   It does not start as a " subconsciousness."   It was
not there in the beginning like the submerged two-thirds of the
iceberg, nor like the bottom of the " narrow-necked vessel "
which is " not stopped by any sponge."   It originates as other
ideas originate, and is as much a matter of the common day
as they.   There is nothing mysterious or supernatural about its
origin — unless, indeed, disease be supernatural.   And this is
true, not only of its origin but of its content and its powers.
The co-conscious ideas, complexes, etc., that have been investigated show little evidence of being in any way " higher " and
" purer " than those of the normal personality.   It was perhaps natural to suppose that the subconscious was wiser and
better than the normal self — until it had been seen.   But now
at length we have two subconscious selves " flowering " and
walking out upon the scenes and writing their autobiographies;
and they turn out to be nothing very wonderfully wise, but just
B and Sally.

I have dealt thus at length with the co-conscious because it is
as a co-conscious that the " subconscious " is usually interpreted
by popular writers, preachers, and lecturers.   It is important
for the serious student of this subject not to be misled by
glowing pictures of the " Undermind," but to realize that the
co-conscious, so far as the evidence goes, is either non-existent
or practically negligible in normal persons; while in pathological subjects, though sometimes, indeed, the source of valuable
ideas and useful actions, it is always limited and inferior to
the waking self, and likely to be very far from beautiful or

[28] This view is also held by Janet.— See his " L'Automatism psychologique " (5th Edition. Paris, Alcan: 1907) p. 336.

sublime. What I have said of the co-conscious, however, must not be taken as a failure to recognize the immense importance and the unquestionable value in each of us of the "subconscious" in the broader sense. And in this broader sense the word "subconscious" may still be of use. If we put together under this term all those factors of ourselves which are not to be identified with the attentive consciousness — the physiological, the fringe, and the co-conscious in those who possess it — we cannot fail to be impressed with the enormous influence exerted by these upon our lives. I have already spoken of the importance of the fringe region and I need add nothing here; nor need I point out how our nervous systems unite us to the distant past of the race and to our own past, preserving for us both instincts and habits, and enabling us to utilize our memories without distinct recall and thus apply our past experience. If we interpret the subconscious as meaning both the fringe and the nervous system, we may say that it is largely this that makes us what we are. "The whole of our past psychical life," says Bergson, "conditions our present state, without being its necessary determinant; while also it reveals itself in our character." [29] It is plain, therefore, how important an influence the subconscious in this broader sense exerts upon each man's religion. To the work of Starbuck and James, in particular, we owe a great deal for the insight they have given us in this matter. A man's religion is not merely a matter of his clear-cut conscious processes: it is bound up with his whole psycho-physical organism. Truly, he who loves God loves Him with all his heart and soul and mind and strength. He loves God not only with his soul and mind, but with his body too. Our religion goes deeper down into our lives than most things, and is knit up with all that we are. It springs out of our connection with the past; it involves our individual, and even our racial, history, it is one aspect of what we are and all we hope to be. This is the truth at the heart of much modern writing about the subconscious and religion — only in "ein bischen andern Worten."

The influence of the subconscious upon the religion of most of us is due to our racial inheritance and our individual history.

[29] "Matière and Memoire," Chap. III.

By nature and heredity we come into the world with certain instincts and needs and ways of reacting which respond to our condition of dependence in such a way as to make most of us " incurably religious." Here, then, is one of the " subconscious " roots of our religion.   The other root of it, as I have said, is to be sought in the particular environment and experience of the individual.   We are born as babies into a world of grown ups, and our parents and teachers, and, in fact, society as a whole bring the irresistible might of their combined influence to bear upon our pigmy selves to make us religious.   This influence is never outgrown.   Though in our later reasonings we may think we have freed ourselves from it, it is present and ineradicable in our subconsciousness, influencing our conscious lives in ways that we do not recognize.   The whole drama of our maturer years is presented before a background determined almost entirely by our social inheritance and our early experiences. Freud has recently shown how very large a part of the material of our dreams is made up of childhood memories — memories, some of which had seemed to be quite forgotten.[30]   Sir Francis Galton years ago pointed out the fact that even in our waking hours our minds are incredibly full of ideas to which we pay little or no attention, a large part of which are memories drawn from childhood and youth.[31]

[30] " Traumdeutung," pp. 132–155; " The Origin and Development of Psycho-Analysis," *Am. Jour. of Psy.*, XXI, pp. 181–218.   See also Prince, " The Mechanism and Interpretation of Dreams," *Jour. of Abnorm. Psy.*, V. 146–150.

[31] After his first successful introspection of the matter he writes: " I saw at once that the brain was vastly more active than I had previously believed it to be, and I was perfectly amazed at the unexpected width of the field of its every-day operations." Upon repeating the experiment he was again amazed at the number of ideas found in the background or ante-room of consciousness, but, he adds, " my admiration at the activity of the mind was seriously diminished by another observation which I then made, namely that there had been a very great deal of repetition of thought.   The actors in my mental stage were indeed very numerous, but by no means so numerous as I had imagined.   They now seemed to be something like the actors in theaters, where large processions are represented, who march off one side of the stage, and, going round by the back, come on again at the other." Upon careful investigation Galton succeeded in locating the origin of many of these recurrent ideas, and found, as I have said, that a large proportion of them came from the impressible years of early life.   " Inquiries into Human Faculty."   In the " Everyman " Edition of Dent & Co., the passages referred to above will be found on pp. 134–141.

It is not merely ideas and visual and verbal images that fill the backgrounds of our minds. More important and influential are the moods, emotions, impulses and prejudices, the "complexes" which have their roots in some half-forgotten past, and twine themselves all through our mental history. Their abiding place is in the darker region of the fringe, or possibly in the quite unconscious cells of the nervous system, but they influence our sentiments, our creeds, our actions, in ways that might surprise us were they fully recognized. Especially influential in determining the background of our lives are our desires and early ideals. Freud has shown (with great exaggeration, to be sure) how large a rôle desire plays in forming our dreams, and it is certain that not only in dreams but in our waking moments desire, whether suppressed or recognized, has a leading part in shaping our whole subconscious or unconscious life. Thus it comes about that the ideals, the longings, the ardent wishes of youth sink into the subliminal region and constitute a large part of its ultimate return contribution to conscious life. Hence the ideal nature of much that springs from the subliminal region of lofty souls. Hence also much of the religious trend that most of us find shaping so large a part of our lives. The religious ideas, promptings, emotions, and ways of viewing things, impressed upon us during youth, or resulting naturally from inherited tendencies, become so ingrained into the very texture of our minds that we can never get away from them. They tinge and influence our feelings, our opinions, and our total reaction upon the world in ways that we know and in ways that we know not.

This is another way of saying that the subconscious is eminently conservative. And in whatever way you interpret the "subconscious" this remains true. The conservative nature of the physiological is painfully evident to every one who has tried to break a habit. And after what has been said on previous pages of this chapter, nothing need be added to show how the fringe-region and the co-conscious treasure up the past, and use it to influence the present and predetermine the future. This is the ultimate explanation of religious conservatism. Theology, the explicit formulation of religious belief, usually lags behind science and philosophy because the two latter make sense perception and clear reason their criteria, whereas religion is a matter of the whole man, and is determined to a very great extent by the racial and personal past, by the ideas that have become ingrained and are now revered, and by the feeling of profound respect for tradition, all of which, though they are at times matters of attentive reasoning, have their roots very largely in the background of the mind or even in the purely habitual reactions of the nervous system.

The great source of the content of the subconscious is, then, the conscious — the experience of the past, both the race and the individual being taken into account. Is there any other source for this content — some supernatural source, different in kind from that already described? I do not see that psychology can answer this question with any definite proofs. It will, of course, proceed on the assumption that there is no such source, until the necessity of the hypothesis has been demonstrated. A superhuman source of revelation, though something in which the philosopher may well believe, is not something which the man of science can ever verify. Leaving aside hypotheses that involve the supernatural, he must seek — very likely in a plodding and prosaic fashion — to find out what can be done with the natural. And in our particular problem his methods have not as yet proved inadequate. The prophets and mystics have, indeed, been greatly influenced by the subconscious, but it is far from clear that there is anything mysterious about the ultimate source of this subconscious influence. The highest ideals of the community or of the nation, accepted with enthusiasm and emotion by the youthful mind, " apperceived " by the great mass of the man's instincts and inherited impulses, pondered over carefully and repeatedly, and allowed to continue their activity in the fringe or in the form of unconscious cerebration — these certainly go far towards explaining so much of the message of each of the prophets as need be attributed to subconscious origin. Nor does this view necessarily exclude the possibility of divine influence, inspiration, and communion with God: for it is difficult to see why God should choose to communicate with a split-off complex or a brain cell rather than with the man himself.   What is highest in the religious genius is to be sought in his conscious states rather than in some form of insensibility.

It has often been suggested that telepathy is one source of the subconscious, and this is of course quite possible.   The evidence in favor of the existence of telepathy is strong, and if there really is such a thing, the subconscious — however interpreted — would very likely be influenced by it.   There is, however, no good reason for regarding the subconscious as the exclusive channel of such influence.[32]   In advance of empirical data on the subject, telepathy, if it exist, is as likely to affect one mind state as another, and the " conscious mind " seems as likely to be directly open to its influence as the subconscious. And, of course, even though it should be proved that telepathy from other minds is one source of the content of the subconscious, it would still remain true (in default of evidence to the contrary) that the *ultimate* source of this content should be sought in the social environment — that is, in the past experience, the ideas, ideals, impulses, and longings of the race.

Though the ultimate source of the content of the subconscious is thus perfectly natural, its influence upon the mind of the individual often makes itself felt in ways that inevitably seem to him extremely mysterious, and that are consequently interpreted by him and by those who know him as tokens of some supernatural power.   Particularly is this true in the case of those who have a tendency toward abnormality.   The phenomena which I have here in mind are such things as violent but unaccountable impulses to do certain things, fixed ideas whose source cannot be traced, " inspirational speaking," so far as this is not to be accounted for by the ordinary laws of association, motor automatisms, visions, and the like.   These all bring with them the sense of external origination — of being *given* or imposed from without.   Now, this feeling is a well recognized characteristic of the working of the co-conscious wherever found.   Moreover, all the phenomena above referred to have parallels in non-religious cases, where the explanation is plainly to be had in terms of a dissociation of consciousness.   The impulses and fixed ideas found in many religious persons are not

[32] As, for instance, Myers does.

different psychologically — though they be ethically at the antipodes — from the " phobias " that Freud is finding in the " unconscious " and Sidis in the " co-conscious." The " inspiration " of the prophet, like that of the poet or of the inventor, often seems to have its immediate source in the deeper and unconscious parts of his being. Just how the subconscious acts in these cases is of course not certain,[33] but that there is some subconscious mechanism here at work, as even in our every-day search for a forgotten name, seems evident. The prophet ponders long over the condition of his people, the will of God, and the problem of his own duty. Then some day suddenly the sought-for solution rushes into his mind — he finds a message ready-made upon his tongue, and it is almost inevitable that he should preface it with the words: " Thus hath Yahweh showed me! " As for the extreme cases of religious visions and motor automatisms, one has only to look at a single page of the *Journal of Abnormal Psychology* for parallels to both.[34]

[33] How it acts in some cases is shown by one of Dr. Prince's co-conscious subjects. See " Problems of Abnormal Psychology." *Psy. Rev.* XII, 137–138.

[34] Thus " B," the co-conscious personality, in her autobiography writes: " C [the dominant personality who was, however, unconscious of B] was asked to go for a long automobile ride and dine in the country, coming home in the evening. I was very anxious to go, but I had promised Dr. Prince not to interfere with C. I did not try to " come " [i.e., to become the directing personality], but I could not help *wanting* to go, and I thought to myself, " O! I wish she would go! " C. declined at first as I knew she would, but as my longing increased she began to waver, hesitated, and finally said she would go. . . . C. once had a visual hallucination of Dr. Prince, because I was thinking of him. She was thinking of entirely different matters, but I was thinking that if it were not for Dr. Prince I might, perhaps, stay all the time, etc. As I was thinking all this, C suddenly saw Dr. Prince standing before her. He was so real that she spoke his name, saying: " Why, Dr. Prince! " She was not asleep, but was lying in bed looking at the fire when she had this hallucination. She knew it was a vision, but it was very distinct." (" An Analysis of Co-conscious Life." *Jour. of Abnor. Psy.* III, 332.) Several cases in which " Sally " influenced Miss Beauchamp in ways similar to this are to be found in the " Dissociation of a Personality." I do not mean by quoting the above to imply that all visions are due to the presence of a co-consciou‾ personality. I mean simply to show that the presence of a dissociated complex is sufficient to explain a vision and that doubtless many religious visions are due to some such cause. Dr. Prince's most famous patient, Miss Beauchamp,— a deeply religious young woman — frequently had visions of Christ and of the Madonna, all of them explicable on the theory of the

I would not be understood by this to imply that the religious geniuses who have been slightly psychopathic are *mere* " psychopaths." I have said, indeed, that dissociation probably is an abnormal state; but this means simply that it differs from the common human condition. It does not mean that such dissociation is always an impediment to human usefulness. That the ordinary man should be without this characteristic is doubtless best for the race, just as it is best we should not all be poets or have the " artistic temperament." But that does not mean that we should be better off with no poets or artists. Dr. Prince seems to be coming to the conclusion that, though the dissociated states (except of a most elementary sort) are abnormal, the susceptibility to them under quite common conditions is normal.[35] It may very well be that for certain purposes dissociated mind states have their special value; they may, for instance, function more readily than purely physiological formations, thus enriching the controlling consciousness with more possible ideas from which the laws of association may choose, or possibly endowing the psycho-physical organism with more immediately available force. The value of such mental conditions, in any event, must be determined not by asking ourselves whether they are usual or result from usual physical or psychical conditions, but by looking to the results which they achieve. As James puts it, the true criterion of value is expressed in the words, " By their fruits ye shall know them, not by their roots." Now if we examine the fruits of such psychopathic dispositions we find that they are varied. In the great majority of cases they are bad; hence the emphasis I have put on the absurdity of looking to the " subconscious " as nobler and purer than the conscious self. But in the case of some noble but psychopathic personalities the split-off states do seem to be of real use; though even here, it must be remembered, the highest and noblest part of the man is his conscious personality. Especially in the case of many great religious leaders, do we find psychopathic conditions that seem to have contributed a good deal toward making them the useful men they were.

functioning of a subconscious complex. (" The Dissociation of a Personality," Appendix L, pp. 548–550.)

[35] See " Problems of Abnormal Psychology." *Psy. Rev.* XII, pp. 131 and 140–143.

Consider for example Ezekiel, Mohammed, George Fox, St. Paul — the reader will be able to add to the list many other names. In these men and women much of the force which made them great and useful seems to have been connected with their psychopathic disposition. Prof. James writes:

" In the psychopathic temperament we have the emotionality which is the *sine qua non* of moral perception; we have the intensity and tendency to emphasize which are the essence of practical vigor; and we have the love of metaphysics and mysticism which carry one's interests beyond the surface of the sensible world. What, then, is more natural than that this temperament should introduce one to regions of religious truth, to the corners of the universe, which your robust Philistine type of nervous system, forever offering its biceps to be felt, thumping its breast, and thanking Heaven that it hasn't a single morbid fiber in its composition, would be sure to hide forever from its self-satisfied possessor." [36]

In quoting thus from Professor James, however, I am going beyond the immediate subject of this chapter, for the psychopathic state is not synonymous with the dissociated state, and a psychopath with all the advantages claimed for him in the passage just quoted need not possess a co-consciousness. The converse is certainly true — the great majority of those possessing dissociated mind states have none of the superiorities set forth by James. Moreover, while some kind of co-consciousness has probably characterized many of the religious leaders of the race, and while they have owed much of their influence to it, it still remains true, as it seems to me at least, that such dissociations can be of advantage only under special and unusual conditions; and, I may add, under conditions likely to recur less often in the future than they occurred in the past. Split-off states are never an end, but are at best a means only. At best, they are sources of weakness as well as of strength. The highest type of man, in the religious life as well as elsewhere, is the unified and rational self. For our ideal we look not so much to Ezekiel as to Amos, not so much to Fox as to Luther, not so much to Paul as to Jesus.

[36] " The Varieties," p. 25.

CHAPTER IV

SOCIETY AND THE INDIVIDUAL

In our first chapter we found ourselves confronted with the conflicting claims of the individualists and the collectivists, the one party implying that religion was essentially a matter of the individual, the other insisting that it is altogether a social phenomenon. And we found reason to believe that both parties were wrong and that both were right or (more exactly perhaps) that the two views did not disagree so fundamentally as the expressions of them would indicate. For, as a matter of fact, there is no doubt in any one's mind that religion is both a social and an individual matter. It is the aim of this chapter to work out in a general way the contributions made to religion by each of these great sources of spiritual life — society and the individual.[1]

The question is by no means simple. For consider: society is altogether made up of individuals, and all individuals are the products of society. We seem faced with a " circle " which if not " vicious " is at least recalcitrant and resists our efforts to trace its course — a line with no beginning and no end. The circle, however, is not so vicious as it seems, for the problem may be stated in terms that permit of a definite answer. Let us ask then first of all, What is the source of the individual's religion? The answer to this question will evidently depend in part on the answer to the more general question: Whence does the individual get his ideas, his emotions, his desires, his motor tendencies, his character and disposition? To this question psychology answers without hesitation: There are two sources for these things, namely heredity and expe-

---

[1] I am aware of the misleading nature of these terms when taken abstractly, and of the truth lurking behind Miss Follett's equally misleading assertion that " there is no individual and there is no society " (" The New State "— New York, Longmans: 1918 — p. 19). The words do mean something, however, and I trust my use of them as explained below will mislead no one.

rience.   If now we return to our first question we may answer
it by saying that the individual's religion has two sources,
namely the abilities, tendencies, and disposition which he brings
with him into the world, and the experience, largely of a social
nature, which he acquires by his intercourse with the world and
with his fellow beings.

Doubtless there are no " innate ideas "— religious or other;
John Locke was right about that.   But the fact that man is a
" rational animal " is not to be explained by any experience of
his, social or non-social.   Rather is his possession of reason the
condition of his having experience of the human sort at all.
Leibniz's dictum about the intellect [2] is here in point.   Using
the word in a large sense, the intellect, or reason, is one of the .
things which the individual brings with him into the world and
with which he meets and appropriates his social experience.
Here then is one individualistic factor, and an important one, in
his religion.   For be it remembered, religion is to mean for
us not a particular creed or set of ceremonies,— not a " *croyance
obligatoire,*" [3]— but an *attitude toward the Determiner of Destiny.*   And certainly the possession of intelligence is one of
the conditions of such an attitude.

But we may go farther than this.   The individual brings
with him into the world (prior to any social influence) certain
innate tendencies and instincts which determine to a considerable extent what his religious attitude shall be.   And here we
come upon the question of the so-called " religious instinct."
The phrase is common enough.   References are made to it not
only in the pulpit and in popular literature but in much
scholarly writing also.   But when the question is seriously
raised of the existence of such an instinct, most psychologists
will have no hesitation in answering it in the negative.   To be
sure, psychologists are not fully agreed as to the exact number
of human instincts, nor as to the details of the definition of the
term; but in spite of many disagreements there is pretty complete unanimity among them in denying the existence of a
" religious instinct." [4]   In general it may be said that an in-

[2] " Nothing in the intellect that was not first in the senses except the
intellect itself."

[3] One of Durkheim's definitions.   See Chapter I, p. 11, of this book.

[4] The unanimity is not absolute.   Professor Morris Jastrow writes as if

stinct is an inherited tendency to act and feel in a specific and characteristic fashion upon the perception of a specific stimulus. Now if this very general definition be so stretched and interpreted as to make religion instinctive it will become so general as to lose all special meaning and hence all psychological usefulness. If religion be an instinct, then it will be hard to name any common human way of thinking or feeling which is not instinctive, and our good psychological term (like so many others) by being used to mean everything will cease to mean anything. Certainly the tendency of psychologists to-day to narrow rather than to broaden their terms is not only justified but absolutely essential to the perfection of a truly scientific psychology. And there can be little question that we shall do well to limit

the existence of a religious instinct were almost axiomatic. ("The Study of Religion," New York, Scribners: 1902, pp. 101, 153.) Mr. Henry Rutgers Marshall has long maintained that religion is instinctive, or is at least an instinct in the making. ("Instinct and Reason," New York: Macmillan: 1898, Chap. IX.) More recently Professor Starbuck has advanced a similar view. The original and instinctive religious element has, he tells us, two phases which he calls the " cosmo-æsthetic sense " and the " teleo-æsthetic sense." These two together form the ultimate religious element of human nature which he describes, in its most primitive form, as " a delicate sense of proportion or relation or fitness or harmony that directs consciousness and determines at each point the particular advantageous response or emphasis." ("The Instinctive Basis of Religion," a paper read before the Nineteenth Annual Meeting of the American Psychological Association in 1910, and reported in brief in the *Psychological Bulletin*, VIII, 52–53.) See, however, his paper on "The Child Mind and Child Religion," in the Biblical World, XXX, 191–201, for September, 1907, in which he gives a view of the subject, approaching more nearly that presented in this book. Professor Hocking seems to hold a position somewhat similar to that expressed by Starbuck in 1910, insisting that " there must be a distinct place in the economy of life for the cult of the Absolute in its contrast with life, and if religion is the name of this place the instinctive motive of religion would be a specific craving due to the atrophy of social and æsthetic values, a *craving for restoration of creative power*." ("Human Nature and Its Remaking ": — Yale University, 1918, p. 331 note.) At the same meeting of the Psychological Association at which Starbuck's paper was read Dr. King presented a paper on "The Question of an Ultimate Religious Element in Human Nature" (*Psychological Bulletin*, VIII, 51–52) in which the purely social origin of the religious sentiment was maintained. Neither of these views appears to me satisfactory, for reasons which I trust have been made clear in the text. The true explanation of the religious sentiment must be sought in a combination of instincts which originally are too simple to be called religious. Religion would thus have an instinctive basis without our having to postulate any religious instinct.

the term instinct (in the case of man) to something like the dozen innate and *specific* tendencies worked out so carefully by McDougal,[5] or to the sixteen given by James,[6] or the twenty or more suggested by Hocking;[7] if we go beyond that number it should be by a process of analysis such as that of Thorndike[8] rather than by widening the field of instinct and thus making the term quite indefinite.

There is, then, no specific " religious instinct." Yet there is a real truth behind the phrase. None of man's religious acts and feelings are instinctive in the sense in which anger and love are; and yet we may say that given a being endowed with intelligence and with the dozen or more specific instincts and tendencies of man, such a being is bound to be religious, at least potentially, or incipiently, in the sense of our definition. He is bound, that is to say, to possess at least the possibility or the beginning of some kind of conscious attitude toward the Determiner of Destiny. And be it noted that the character of this attitude will be largely determined for man by his instincts — by the specific inborn tendencies which he, the individual, brings with him into the world. Some of these instincts (and their correlative emotions) are more important for the religious attitude than others. Thus fear has from very early times been recognized as one of the constituents of religion,[9] and among contemporary writers Ribot,[10] Leuba,[11] and McDougal,[12] have emphasized its importance. Fear, however, is not the only instinct that affects the religious attitude. Ribot recognizes " the tender emotion " as equally important,[13] and both Leuba,[14]

[5] " Social Psychology " (Eleventh Ed., Boston, Luce & Co.: 1916), Chapters 2 and 3.

[6] " Principles of Psychology " (New York, Holt: 1896), Vol. II, Chapter 24.

[7] " Human Nature and Its Remaking," Chap. IX.

[8] " The Original Nature of Man " (Columbia University: 1913), II, V–X.

[9] Cf. the oft-quoted line of Petronius, " Primus in orbis timor fecit deos."

[10] " La Psychologie des Sentiments " (Paris, Alcan: 1897), Deuxième Partie, Chap. 9, esp. pp. 311–312, and 317.

[11] " Fear, Awe, and the Sublime in Religion." *Am. Jour. of Religious Psychology*, II, 1–13; " A Psychological Study of Religion," Chap. VII.

[12] " Social Psychology," Chap. 13.

[13] Op. cit., pp. 311, 317.

[14] Leuba defines awe as " arrested fear in the presence of objects whose greatness is apprehended." Op. cit. p. 15.

and McDougal either add awe to fear, or admit fear only under the form of awe. According to McDougal's analysis, the religious emotions are ultimately based upon the instinctive emotions of wonder, negative self-feeling, fear, tender emotion, and curiosity. Dr. Wright would add to these the gregarious, reproductive, and food-seeking instincts; [15] Mr. A. S. Woodburne would make still another addition — namely an instinctive effort at self-preservation; [16] in a highly developed religion, in fact nearly all the instincts may be involved.

Whatever the exact list of man's instincts, and whatever the innate emotions on which his religious life is ultimately based, certain it is that his inborn tendencies and needs when combined with the power of thought and the will to think are quite enough to account for some kind of religious attitude or sentiment, even aside from the influence of society upon him. And it must be remembered further that the very fact that society is able to influence him is itself based upon an innate characteristic of the individual — namely his ability to be influenced. Sensitiveness to social influence, suggestibility, sympathy, and the power of imitation are among the inborn tendencies which the human being brings into the world with him — he does not acquire them from society. If society molds the individual it is because the individual human being (unlike the animal) is capable of being molded by society. This is of course a redundant assertion, but it is one that is worth making none the less.

The rise of religious ideas and feelings in the individual without the intervention of social influence is illustrated in the cases of two deaf mutes, Mr. Ballard and Mr. D'Estrella, each of whom has given an account of his earliest religious notions and of the way in which they originated.[17] The former, indeed, never came to any conclusion which satisfied him until he entered the school for the deaf and learned the theology of his teachers, but his restless search for an answer to the question,

---

[15] " Instinct and Sentiment in Religion " (*Phil. Rev.*, XXV, 1916, p. 34).

[16] " The Relation of Religion to Instinct " (*Am. Jour. of Theol.*, XXIII, 1919, 319–44.)

[17] Mr. D'Estrella's account is reported in an article entitled " Is Thought Possible without Language " by Samuel Porter, in the *Princeton Review* for January, 1881 (pp. 104–128). For Mr. Ballard's story see James, " Thought Before Language," *Phil. Rev.*, I, 615.

"How came the world into being?" which he was constantly asking himself, is sufficiently significant. The orderly motion of the heavenly bodies and the shock of a thunder storm were the first things to suggest this question to him. Mr. D'Estrella was more successful in his lonely search. Quite early he came to the conclusion that the moon was alive and was somehow related to his moral life, while the sun he regarded as a ball of fire which some "great and strong man, somehow hiding himself behind the hills," tossed up every morning and caught every evening for his own amusement. The idea of this "great and strong man" also explained for him the lighting of the stars and many other natural phenomena.

But if a deaf mute, of average mentality, can develop for himself some sort of religious view, *a fortiori* can the religious genius, taking the materials which society furnishes, work them over into new forms, put upon them his personal impress, and adding his own intuitions give back to society points of view, concepts, and plans of action which it never had before and which it never would have attained to but for him or for some one like him. Taine's absurdity of discounting the individual is not often repeated in its extreme form to-day; but our present popular emphasis on the "social aspect" of pretty much everything is somewhat in danger of making us overlook or forget the tremendous importance of the individual's contributions, particularly in art, morality, and religion. Truly poetry is in one sense a social product; yet if Chaucer, Shakespeare, and Milton had died in their cradles, English Literature would be much less worth the reading. And while religion is "a social phenomenon," its actual historical course would be very considerably modified if we could go back and take out of it simply these five men: Zarathustra, Buddha, Amos, Jesus, and Mohammed.

But it is not merely the prophet or religious genius to whom religion is indebted and on whom it depends. We too easily overlook the fact that even the most "social" of ideas are the products of coöperation between many individual minds, each of which has thus contributed its mite to society.[18] And while

18 Cf. Miss Follett's insistence that "interpenetration" (i. e., intelligent coöperation) is a much more important social process than imitation.— "The New State." Part I.

from one point of view it is unquestionable that the content of religion is a social matter, if religion is to live it must be not only accepted but realized and reborn in the hearts and lives of the individual members of each new generation. It is not only man but religion also that *must be born again;* and born again it is with each person who takes up a serious and reverent attitude toward Destiny. It is this that makes it a matter not only of sociological but of psychological interest. And no prophet or God's messenger can bring to religion this living realization for any other soul. Each one of us must do it for himself.

Thus the inborn nature of the individual determines what might be called the *form* of his religious life. The *matter* is chiefly the contribution of society.[19] The particular content of each man's religion, the cognitive aspect of his religious sentiment,[20] his ideas and activities, together with the sense of au-

[19] It is here that the question of individualism versus ecclesiasticism centers. The discussion of this has been endless but the reader will find an instructive and interesting example of it in pages 28–31 of James's "Varieties," and Chapter I of Stanton Coit's "National Idealism and a State Church" (London, Williams and Norgate: 1907). Dr. Coit exaggerates James's individualism and seems also to make the mistake of attributing to ecclesiastical institutions all that really belongs to social influence in general; yet he has done well in insisting upon the social roots of much that James is satisfied in tracing only to the individual. An attack upon the individualist view of religion somewhat similar to that made by Dr. Coit is to be found in Wundt's "Völkerpsychologie." Religion, according to Wundt, can be understood only by studying its origin in primitive society, and a method such as that of James which trusts to individual cases, quite out of their setting and taken unsystematically, is hardly superior to the unscientific abstractions of the 18th Century enlightenment. Religion is therefore not a problem for individual psychology but for *Völkerpsychologie.* See pp. 729–34 of the "Zweiter Band, Dritter Teil" (really Vol. V) of the "Volkerpsychologie" (Leipzig, Engelman: 1909). It is needless for me to add that while recognizing the pertinence of Wundt's criticism upon the *merely* individualistic study of religion, I cannot agree with him that our study should be *merely* social.

[20] I use the word "sentiment" here as practically synonymous with "attitude." Strictly speaking, a sentiment is a relatively permanent tendency to emotion and action crystallized about some central idea. See the excellent discussions of Sentiment by Shand (*Mind,* New Series V, 203–226), and McDougal ("Social Psychology," Chap. 5). These psychologists have pointed out how a large number of varied and even opposing instincts and emotions may be united within one sentiment or group of *potential* emotions. The religious sentiment thus includes at once in potential form all those ways of feeling and acting which the thought of the Determiner of Destiny may, at different times and in various circumstances, arouse.

thority which gives them their peculiar tone, will be determined for him almost entirely by his social milieu.[21]   Not entirely; for his reason and his native tendencies largely determine his *selection* of content, and also may contribute their share toward the formation of new ideas in his group.   To put it in another way, the *application* which the individual shall make of his instincts, so far as they enter into his religion, is directed *chiefly* by his fellows.   He can fear, but he must learn from society what to fear; he can love, but he must learn what to love; he can think, but he must learn what to think.   Conceivably, indeed, he might stand alone on his coral island or his mountain peak, as Max Müller pictures him, and if so he might no doubt have some kind of conscious attitude toward the powers that seemed to determine his welfare.   He might even form for himself the image of a great man tossing the sun up every morning and catching it at night, as Mr. D'Estrella, the deaf-mute, actually did.   But his ideas, feelings, and reactions would be very different from those of men in touch with their fellows.   It is not likely you would find him " perceiving the Infinite."   The Infinite is a concept that is worked out actually through social intercourse.   And whatever the hypothetical lowly savage might think or feel, the important thing for the student of religion to investigate is what actual men as a fact do think and feel in their religious moments, and how it is they come to think and feel as they do.   And the answer to these questions is to be found only in social terms.   Religion in the only forms in which we know anything about it, is the religion of men born and brought up among their fellows and forming a constitutent part of some human group.   And once we have recognized the original psychical endowment of the individual, the influence of society in making him what he is can hardly be exaggerated.   If we may trust Professor Boas,[22] and most other anthropologists for that

21 This fact that the *content* of religion is a social product explains to a great extent the tendency of those who study religion from the historical point of view to minimize the contribution of the individual.   History, development, is a matter of changing content, and the content of *a religion* is always social in its bearings.   Individualism has no history.   The historian's interest even in the most individualistic of the prophets is centered chiefly in discovering the social origin of some of his ideas, or in tracing his influence upon society.

22 See, e.g., "The Mind of Primitive Man" (New York; Macmillan: 1911).

matter, neither primitive man nor the present-day savage differs radically in mental endowments and powers from members of the most highly civilized races. The enormous chasm which separates the Australian or the cave-man from the Twentieth Century European is very largely a matter of social heredity. The Christian theologian and the Siberian Shaman have different religions not because of different individual endowments but because of different social surroundings.[23]

Society is able to have this enormous influence upon the individual because it not only instructs him but to some extent genuinely constitutes him. Cooley expresses very well the great trend of contemporary thought upon this subject when he writes: "A separate individual is an abstraction unknown to experience, and so likewise is society when regarded as something apart from individuals. The real thing is Human Life, which may be considered either in an individual aspect or in a social, that is to say a general, aspect; but is always, as a matter of fact, both individual and general." [24] Baldwin [25] and Royce [26] have shown in great detail how self consciousness

---

[23] Not only does society furnish the individual with his theological beliefs; these theological beliefs are largely determined by the structure of society. The supernatural world of most religions has been modelled to a considerable extent upon the social and political institutions familiar to the believers. See Durkheim, "Elementary Forms of the Religious Life" *passim;* Cornford, "From Religion to Philosophy" (New York; Longmans: 1912) *passim;* King, "The Development of Religion," Chaps. IV, V, IX, X. These authors express the view in question in an extreme, not to say an exaggerated form; but there can be no doubt that the influence of social structure upon the content of religious belief is considerable.

[24] "Human Nature and the Social Order" (New York, Scribners: 1902) p. 1.

[25] "Mental Development" (Third Ed., New York, Macmillan: 1906), 319–324; "Social and Ethical Interpretations" (Fourth Ed., New York, Macmillan: 1906), Chap. I; "The Individual and Society" (Boston, Badger: 1911), Chap. I.

[26] "The External World," *Phil. Rev.,* III, 513–545; "Some Observations on the Anomalies of Self-Consciousness," in "Studies of Good and Evil" (New York, Appleton: 1898), 169–197. What we may call the social view of the self has been admirably summarized by Prof. Robert MacDougal thus: "The self of psychology is historically and socially conditioned. From the outset its milieu is a spiritual community. It can neither exist nor be developed apart from the vital protoplasm of human association . . . It [the self] is thought in terms of certain possessions and ideal aims, of characteristic attitudes and reactions, of relations with the objective world and their modifications. In chief part these are interpersonal relations

and consciousness of physical nature is conditioned upon social intercourse. In short each one of us is what he is in virtue of his relations to his fellows. His place in the social net-work is a genuine part of him.

The process by which the individual takes on the impress of society is generally known as *imitation,* although it might be serviceable to reserve that term, as McDougal suggests, for the active part only of the total process, using the words suggestibility and sympathy for the cognitive and emotional portions. Taking the word imitation in the wider and commoner sense, we may then say that it is in part this ability to think or believe something, to feel somehow, and to act in some way not prompted by instinct but merely by observing others do it, that differentiates human society from animal "companies." [27] Animals seem to "imitate" only those activities which are already instinctive to them: human beings can and do imitate actions of other human beings — or even of animals — in which they are interested but for which they possess no specific instinct.[28] Imitation, however, must not be considered itself an instinct. Insofar as it is something more than the social instigation of some of the specific instincts, or something different from deliberate and volitional copying, it is explicable by the general laws of primitive credulity, dynamogenesis, and ideomotor action.

. . . These active programs and permanent sources of stimulation are not properly things which the self possess; they are the very tissue of its living body." "The Social Basis of Individuality," *Am. Jour. of Sociology,* XVIII, 12. While the truth in what may be called the social view of the individual as thus stated is both unquestionable and of fundamental importance, one should be on one's guard against the exaggeration of this truth which many of its upholders often fall into. Society, it must be remembered, does not *constitute* the individual in the same sense nor to the same degree that individuals constitute society. A needed corrective to the extreme "social" view is to be found in Fite, "The Exaggeration of the Social" (*Journal of Philosophy,* IV, 393). "Individualism" (New York, Longmans: 1911); and Sellars, "Critical Realism" (Chicago, Rand McNally: 1916), pp. 172–75.

[27] Baldwin's term, adopted from Tonnies and Durkheim. See "Social and Ethical Interpretations," pp. 503, 524–26.

[28] This view of human imitation is not universally accepted. For arguments against it see Thorndike, "Animal Intelligence" (New York, Macmillan: 1911; p. 250ff), and Wallas, "The Great Society" (New York, Macmillan: 1914), pp. 121–24.

Sociologists of the Tarde school make a somewhat useful distinction between two kinds of imitation, according as it tends to preserve an old custom or to establish a new one. These they call respectively custom or tradition, and convention or fashion.[29] The two of course overlap and are not always separable, but the distinction is practically helpful, and the influence of both kinds of imitation can be seen very plainly in religion. And here the stronger of the two is, of course, tradition. The reason for this is not far to seek. It is to be found in the prolongation of human infancy and childhood and in the fact that the generations over-lap. The individual is born into the world in a perfectly helpless condition, with a mind which is both entirely empty and exceedingly impressionable, and he finds himself in a society of older persons all of whom, in religious matters, think, feel, and act pretty much alike. It seems as if the adult world had entered into a conspiracy against the tender infant mind, to force it into the old approved social grooves. And indeed it has. The conspiracy, in fact, is both implicit and explicit. The child finds all its world worshiping and believing in practically the same ways, and hence inevitably imitates these ways; and not only so, but when he reaches a teachable age all the forces of home and school and church (or whatever corresponds to these in lower forms of society) are deliberately brought to bear upon him to make him like every one else.[30] The torch of custom is forced into his hand and he is compelled to carry it and pass it on but slightly changed to the next generation. Thus the religious feelings, ideas, and ways of acting

---

[29] See especially Tarde, "The Laws of Imitation" (Eng. Trans.; New York, Holt: 1903); and Ross, "Social Psychology" (New York, Macmillan: 1909).

[30] The preservation of something like the Puritan attitude toward the Sabbath and the Church or "Meeting-house" is an excellent example, and in it we see the process of religious conservatism in a rather interesting and striking form. I say this because here we have an extreme case of the deliberate inculcation of a religious view. No matter how the parent has come to feel about Church and the observance of Sunday, he is pretty likely to bring up his child with something like the same respect for them that he himself was brought up to have. Thus it often happens that when the children begin to grow out of infancy the father takes a new interest in church attendance and is suddenly careful to remember the Sabbath day, in order to "give a good example to the children." The fact is we are careful to instill into our children, not so much our own feelings, but the feelings we think we ought to have and want them to have.

which the social group has been centuries in evolving are assimilated by the individual in a few years; and in such thorough fashion is the work done that his acquisitions of this sort deserve the name " social heredity," they being comparable often, in the hold they have over him, to those products of physical heredity which he brought into the world with him.

In our last chapter we saw how this impression made by society upon the child accounted for the marked conservative tendencies of religion. Modes of feeling, thinking, and acting in religious matters are ingrained by one generation into the mental fringe or background (possibly even into the nervous system) of the next, so that they become " secondarily automatic." These habitual reactions are *learned as things to be revered*. Their sacredness is their most striking characteristic, so that one learns to reverence them in the very act of learning them at all. Sacred is what these traditions are, and one does not know them until he recognizes them as things to be maintained and scrupulously observed. It must be noted, moreover, that the distinction between the sacred and the profane is essentially a social distinction. The sacred is that which society protects and isolates by its interdiction; the profane or secular is that " to which these interdictions are applied and which must remain at a distance from the first." [31] As was pointed out in our first chapter, Durkheim even goes so far as to erect this distinction into the essential characteristic of religion and to insist, also, as a consequence, that Society from whose sanction the sacred takes its rise is itself our real object of worship and of religious faith. " In a general way it is unquestionable that a society has all that is necessary to arouse the sensation of the divine in minds, merely by the power it has over them; for to its members it is what a god is to his worshippers." [32] The power which it exerts is not only physical but moral. Its members recognize its spiritual authority and feel toward it the emotion of *respect*. Hence the conclusion that " the reality which religious thought expresses is society." [33]

In commenting upon Durkheim's view in our first chapter, I pointed out that his thesis, while workable enough for so-

[31] Durkheim, " The Elementary Forms of the Religious Life," p. 41.
[32] Ibid. p. 206.
[33] Ibid. p. 431.

ciology, leaves a large part of individual religion, and even much of modern social religion, out of account and hence is quite insufficient for the psychologist. The object toward which the religious man maintains his characteristic attitude is not the historical source of " the sacred " but rather the hypothetical power which he considers the Determiner of Destiny. Still though it is impossible for us to accept Durkheim's view in its extreme form, there can be no doubt that many aspects and characteristics of the " historical religions " are to be explained by the important distinction between the sacred and the profane. And it must never be forgotten that, however this distinction, once it has arisen, may be interpreted, and whatever it may mean to individuals, it invariably has its source in the taboos and interdictions of society.

This is perhaps as good a place as any to consider a view held by several members of what may be called the Durkheim school, closely related to the facts and theories just considered. Religion, it is held, is altogether a social product; it originated as a mass of beliefs, feelings, and actions enforced upon the individual by the group; and the " collective representations " which constitute its ideational side have been handed down to more intelligent times, thus carrying into scientific ages and among civilized peoples beliefs and feelings which should long ago have been discarded. The social origin of religion is thus used as a proof that religion to-day is an anachronism. M. Levy-Bruhl, who is the chief upholder of this view, maintains that the intelligence of primitive man and of the primitive societies in which religion had its birth, must not be judged by what we know of intelligence to-day. It was as yet at a prelogical stage, quite innocent of the principle of contradiction, and it operated by a category of its own, entirely unscientific and illogical in its nature, which M. Levy-Bruhl calls " participation." Religion then had its origin in this pre-logical state, in which the individual merely accepted the beliefs of the group without question or analysis; and the " collective representations " of which religion consists are, consequently, quite out of place in a logical age like our own in which the principle of contradiction has taken the place of the vague and mystic category of participation.[34]   That the collective consciousness in which religion originated is on a plane much lower than reason and that reason belongs only to the individual, is maintained in another connection by MM. Hubert and Mauss [35] — with the natural inference as to religion.   This same point of view is taken up by Mr. Cornford and applied in particular to the Greek religion.   The two underlying conceptions of both the religion and the early philosophy of the Greeks were, according to him, *physis* and *Moira* — nature and destiny.   The former of these is, in its origin, social custom, the latter social restraint.   Thus both have their source in the universal sense of the collective consciousness and the feeling of its authority over the individual.   " Out of this primitive representation arose, by differentiation, the notions of group-soul and daemon, and finally the individual soul and the personal God.   These imaginary objects, souls and Gods, are made of the same stuff; their substance is simply the old sympathetic continuum, more or less etherialized." [36]

This is not the place to consider the question of the origin of religion, but a word or two should be ventured in comment upon the view maintained by the authors we have been considering on the social origin of religious concepts and their consequent irrational and untenable nature.   There can be no doubt that a large portion of the concepts even of the higher religions is of social origin, and that all of them are forced upon the individual members of the group by the influences which social psychology studies.   From the fact, however, that a given concept or belief is the product of the group consciousness it does not necessarily follow that it is irrational and untenable.   M. Levy-Bruhl's picture of a pre-logical intelligence producing religion in the collective consciousness before the principle of contradiction was made use of in thinking, is quite as unjus-

[34] " Les Fonctions Mentales dans les Sociétés Inférieure " (Paris, Alcan: 1910).

[35] " Esquisse d'une Theorie Général de la Magie," L'Anée Sociologique, Vol. VII, (1902–03), p. 122.

[36] " From Religion to Philosophy," pp. 124–25.   A view more sympathetic toward religion but in the last analysis not essentially different from that of Levy-Bruhl is to be found in Miss Harrison's " Themis " (Cambridge University Press: 1912).   See especially the Introduction.

tified by anything we can call science as is Rousseau's description of the "State of Nature." Mr. Clement Webb, in fact, has pointed out that M. Levy-Bruhl does not seem to know what the principle of contradiction is.[37]   And aside from this, it seems odd to find the school of sociologists who regard all the categories of logic as the developments of "collective representations" insisting that religion is illogical because it has the same social source.   Much more sound, surely, is the view of Durkheim himself who finds in the social origin of religion the strongest evidence for considering its fundamental beliefs, when properly interpreted, profoundly true.   The historical student of religion, moreover, will hesitate before making the easy generalization that because many of the elements in the higher religions are of primitive and social origin, therefore *all* the elements of these religions are due to the same source. He knows too well that there is such a thing as religious development, that in the course of this development new ideas and practices are evolved, that some at least of these new elements are plainly due to the influence of religious geniuses, and that many of them are due to intelligent coöperation on the part of innumerable nameless individuals.   The fact therefore that religion gets much of its content and all of its authority from society cannot be regarded as a demonstration that it is to be classed with magic and other out-grown superstitions which advancing scientific generations must soon slough off.

The consideration of this point of view has taken us somewhat out of our course and we must now return to the point we had reached before our digression.   We had seen that the authoritative nature of religion and its conservative and traditional elements must be put down to the score of society rather than to that of the individual.   But between different kinds of religious tradition there are differences in the strength of conservatism.   Especially is this seen to be the case if one compares religious beliefs with rites or customs.   Approved ways of acting have been historically much more tenacious of life than approved ways of thinking.[38]   A curious example of this is the following instance related by Höffding:

[37] See his "Group Theories of Religion and the Religion of the Individual" (London, Macmillan: 1916), especially Chaps. II and VI.

[38] This is the truth at the heart of Tarde's famous "Law," that "imita-

" In a Danish village church the custom of bowing when passing a certain spot in the church wall was maintained into the nineteenth century, but no one knew the reason for this until, on the whitewash being scraped away, a picture of the Madonna was found on the wall; thus the custom had outlived the Catholicism which prompted it by three hundred years; it was a part of the old cult which had maintained itself." [39]

Illustrations of the conservatism of rites, ceremonies, and sacred ways of acting in general might be cited in endless number from all the historical religions of the world. In low and primitive races they constitute the great bulk of the peoples' religion. For these tribes beliefs are few, indefinite, and relatively unimportant; you may *think* what you like, for you are not expected to think at all, but you must *act,* in sacred matters, as the group acts. Down through the centuries go the old rites, serenely oblivious to changing thoughts and changing needs. The earliest Egyptians placed stone implements in the graves of their dead. Ages pass, and eventually metal instruments are invented. The living now lay aside the stone tools of their fathers because in practical life utility is stronger than custom. But stone implements are still made for the use of the dead, because the dead have always had them, and burial is a religious rite." [40] The Buddhist monks, and for that matter the monks of almost every religion, still read their Scriptures in the ancient tongue. It may be that not one of them can understand a word of what he reads, but that matters not. The thing to which the sacredness of tradition has attached is the *rite,* the *reaction,* the making of those sounds in that way, at such a time and so often,— not the thinking of any special

tion proceeds from the inner to the outer man." (" Laws of Imitation," p. 199.) It is a more tenable " law " when expressed from the point of view of conservatism than from that of change. As Tarde expresses it, it is open to Baldwin's criticism, that, as a fact, " the relatively trivial and external things are most liable to be seized upon. A child imitates persons, and what he copies most largely are the personal points of evidence, so to speak: the boldest, most external manifestations, not the inner essentials mental things." (" Mental Development," pp. 336–337.) This of course is true. But it is also true that though ways of doing may be easily imitated they are particularly difficult to uproot.

[39] " The Philosophy of Religion," p. 148.

[40] Reisner, " The Egyptian Conception of Immortality " (Boston, Houghton, Mifflin; 1912) pp. 12–13.

thoughts. In like manner the Abyssinian Christians retain the Koptic in their liturgy and the modern Parsee retains the language of the Avesta, the non-Arabic Mohammedans cling to the Arabic in their Scriptures, the Jaina to his Prakrit and Sanskrit Sutras, the Jew to his Hebrew and the Catholic Christian to the Latin of the Vulgate and the Mass. In short, every religion and every church that has a ritual trains its members to do the old things in the old ways, and to permit but little change.

This conservatism of custom is specially noticeable in cases like that quoted from Höffding in which an actual change in belief has taken place. And cases of this sort are to be found wherever a new creed replaces an old one. Zarathustra may preach a relatively spiritual monotheism and destroy the polytheism of his country, but the old Aryan sacred customs must be maintained. Mohammed may cast down all the idols of the Caaba, but the Caaba and its black stone remain sacred, pilgrims must still come annually to Mecca, run the ancient naked race about the now empty shrine, drink of the sacred well Zem Zem and act very much as their ancestors did before they learned there was no God but Allah. And the converts to Islam in every part of the world will be found accepting Mohammed and the Koran with eagerness, but still decking out the sacred tree with all manner of gay rags just as their pagan fathers did, or carrying on some other hoary custom that was old before the Prophet was young. Nor has it been otherwise in our own Christianity. Antiquaries can cite us endless instances of customs of pagan Rome incorporated in Catholic observance or of old Germanic or Saxon or Celtic spirit-mongery retained by the Christians of northern Europe long after the beliefs which at first went hand-in-hand with them had been not only discarded but clean forgotten. And in our own day upon the "foreign field," the enthusiastic Christian convert, brown, yellow, or black, who accepts the creed with stronger faith and more avidity than two-thirds of the American or European Christians who sent his missionary to him, must still cling to some of the old rites and many of the old feelings which his heathen fathers nourished in the dark forests through the dark centuries.

This superior strength of custom over belief in resisting the inroads of change is more noticeable in the lower than in the higher religions, and it is so because in the latter belief has a greater relative importance than in the former. Especially in Christianity has effort been made time and again — and in fact quite constantly — to keep unchanged the theology of the past. The ideal of belief is expressed in the formula, " *Quod semper, quod ubique, quod ab omnibus.*" And mechanisms of various sorts such as the Holy Inquisition of the Roman Church and the Heresy Trial of the Presbyterian have been invented to keep pure the faith once delivered to the Fathers by the Prophets. And of course it would be a mistake to fail to recognize the strength of conservatism in doctrine as well as the conservatism of action and feeling. Each generation starts in believing what its predecessor believed, and a faith once thoroughly grounded is not easily disturbed. Fundamental beliefs, in fact, are sometimes more conservative than superficial acts, and it not infrequently happens that the basal concepts of an old religion are retained after its rites have been exchanged for those of some new faith. Though this is true, however, it cannot be doubted that religious customs in general are much more conservative than are creeds and dogmas, and it may be worth our while to note briefly some of the causes for this fact.

One of the explanations, often pointed out by sociologists, is that beliefs are subject to rational discussion and refutation in a way that customs are not. A new conception of things, at first adopted by the thinkers of a group and gradually made common property, may after a while be generally recognized as inconsistent with some ancient dogma, but there is no way in which it can come into such immediate conflict with a rite or consecrated way of acting. A breach, moreover, of a religious observance is patent to all the community and arouses more general and more violent indignation and social disapproval than does an heretical idea. One's thoughts are private and subjective things, and a man may well feel that both he and his neighbor have a right to believe as they like provided they observe the external and objective customs of their tribes. Within the savage church a " freedom of thought " may be permitted which would have shocked a 17th Century Puritan —

or even a 19th Century Scotch Presbyterian ; and the " free thinker " will go unscathed and probably unnoticed provided he does not offend the taste of the community by original modes of acting. Religious customs, moreover, are absorbed by the individual in earlier and more impressible years than are beliefs, and thus become more ingrained into his nervous system. And I think there is also a more fundamental physiological reason still, bound up somehow with the working of the nervous system, though just how we can hardly be sure. The difference between a creed and a religious custom is, namely, the same as that between an idea and a habit. Now it is a psychological common-place that ideas may be changed with relative ease but habits can be broken only with the greatest difficulty. The explanation of this fact is, I say, ultimately to be sought in the nervous system. Few things are so fundamental in our lives as the law of habit, by which a given precept becomes so inextricably associated with a given reaction that the latter follows almost inevitably upon the appearance of the former. Just what the nervous mechanism is that underlies this law cannot be said with both definiteness and certainty. But there can be no doubt that the nerve paths involved greatly exceed both in simplicity and in stability those which underlie the process of ideation and thought — which, whatever else they may be, are certainly very complex and exceedingly unstable. The conservatism of religious customs as compared with religious beliefs is therefore to be explained ultimately in both psychological and physiological terms.

The law of habit, moreover, working in connection with social approval and disapproval will enable us to understand the sacredness and authority of both religious customs and religious beliefs. The force of habit and the very inertia of a long-standing belief give belief and custom a coloring of self which forces one to respect them. They are a part of oneself — they are the ways I have always acted and always believed. Still more important in giving sacredness and authority to ideas and actions is the impressive source from which they come to us — namely our parents, the elders of the community, Society itself. Since in every individual the *ought* grows out of the *must,* and the earliest sense of duty grows out of the reaction to the commands of one's elders, the *forbidden* tends always to seem wrong, and the *commanded* to seem right. Durkheim is therefore justified in insisting that the sense of obligation which attaches to so many of the beliefs and observances of all historical religions is due to their social origin. " Everything obligatory is of social origin. For an obligation implies a command, and consequently an authority who commands. If the individual is to be held to conform his conduct to certain rules it is necessary that these rules should emanate from a moral authority which imposes them on him, and which dominates him." [41] This authority is society, the only power we can empirically verify that can dominate the thoughts and the will of the individual. The fact that its commands seem to him mysterious is what we should expect. For its customs and its ideas are not spontaneous with him, but originating in an age long antedating his birth and under conditions of which he has no inkling, they are forced upon him in a manner that he cannot resist. And their very mystery adds to their authority and increases their sacredness. All authoritative religion is a social phenomenon.

After our long discussion of tradition, little need be said of the other branch of imitation, namely convention or fashion. That it exists in religion as elsewhere is plain enough. The great change that has come over the theology and worship of Europe and America in the last fifty years is an impressive example of it. For the reason why most of us individuals (taken separately) do not believe as our grandfathers did is not to be sought for in any great originality or strength of intellect on our part. Our grandfathers copied their grandfathers to be sure, and we do not so faithfully copy ours; but the reason for it is that we copy other people instead, namely some of our more advanced contemporaries. We are all imitators; it is only a question of whom we shall imitate. At the same time, of course, we must not forget that most of us, in some slight degree, are also originators.

The yielding of tradition to a kind of imitation that involves change is due to two principal psychological causes: the first is that man is a suggestible being, and the second that

[41] " De la definition des phénomènes religieux," p. 23.

man is a rational being. When we find a number of those around us who possess prestige cherishing religious views at variance with those taught us at our mother's knee, it is difficult to retain the old beliefs unchanged, even though we refrain from all theological discussion. There is such a thing as a psychological atmosphere which all but the most thick-skinned feel. And just as the northerner who goes to live in the south usually becomes an ardent advocate of the " White Man's Government," so the orthodox youth who goes to the heretical college, or settles in a " liberal " community usually becomes innoculated with the new ideas.[42] Nor is this true only of ideas for which rational justification can be given; superstitions and absurd ideas, if held by the community as a whole, have much the same power. Bagehot speaks of the force which even the belief in witchcraft may come to have over those who at first laugh at it. The European resident in the East often ends by feeling that there " really is something in it." " He has never seen anything convincing himself, but he has seen those who have seen those who have seen. In fact he has lived in an atmosphere of infectious belief, and he has inhaled it." [43]

The power of rational ideas to force their way even against tradition needs no illustration. It is to this, of course, that the many changes of Christian theology in modern times are largely due. It must be remembered, however, that even here the rationality of the ideas in question plays only a small part in their popularization. Not their intrinsic rationality but the fact that they are accepted and taught by *people who ought to know,* by those who have a peculiar *prestige,* this it is that gives them their hold over the popular mind. So far as Darwin has triumphed over Genesis, and the higher criticism over the infallibility doctrine of the Scriptures, in popular theology, the cause must be sought chiefly in the fact that the preachers

[42] Another instance of the power of convention is to be found in the attitude of a large proportion of the religious people from eastern communities who settle in western towns where institutional religion has found no footing. The ease with which they lose their religious ways of thinking and of acting is very notable.

[43] "Physics and Politics " (New York, Appleton: 1873), p. 93. The more immediate and, I may add, pathological strength of suggestion in religious matters will be studied at length in our chapter on Revivals.

and professors have taught the newer views and *are known to accept them.* Here as elsewhere faith is largely a matter of faith in some one else's faith. There is no doubt that a great number of those who hold most enthusiastically to the " latest results of modern science and criticism " as applied to religious questions would be unable to give you a single good reason for their belief.

The inability of traditional belief to maintain itself altogether unchanged is, of course, the condition of there being any history of religion or religions. Religion is not always merely on the side of conservatism. The religious genius, in fact, is always regarded as an innovator. His formula, if such a term may be used of him, is: " Ye have heard that it hath been said by those of old times. . . . but *I* say unto you." And the enthusiastic religious soul often sets himself against the old for the sake of the nobler vision of that which never yet has been. " It would be absurd," say Dewey and Tufts, " to attribute all the individualism to science and all the conservatism to religion. . . . The struggle for religious liberty has usually been carried on not by the irreligious but by the religious. . . . The history of the noble army of martyrs is a record of appeal to individual conscience, or to an immediate personal relation to God, as over against the formal, the traditional, the organized religious customs and doctrines of their age." [44] Unfortunately we must add it is not only the ideal that prevents the perfect maintenance of religious beliefs and customs; it often happens that the dead weight of human infirmity hangs like a chain upon the more ideal religious traditions, and unless they are sustained by the enthusiasm and the unremitting vigilance of a spiritual minority, it drags down the finer elements of the faith to the earth again, turns prayer into formula, and religion into magic. The maintenance of lofty ideals, even if they be traditional, requires effort, and the sheer inertia of the mass of mankind tends ever to fall below the higher standards and to carry the noble religious tradition down with it. Social heredity no less than physical has its law of atavism. In religion as elsewhere " *facilis descensus Averni.*"

[44] " Ethics " (New York, Holt & Company: 1909), p. 85.

Whether the force operating against the religious tradition be ideal or degenerating, in the long course of the years it tells, even against so strong a resistance as that of religious conservatism. This fact is no new discovery. It was observed by Mohammed and gave rise to his belief in a primitive pure revelation, regularly forgotten by the passing generations of men, and regularly renewed by the succession of the Prophets. And much earlier than Mohammed's time, it formed the basis of the early Buddhist view that the Dhamma was regularly forgotten and had to be brought back to earth again every 4000 years by the series of Buddhas, of whom Gautama was the latest. This Buddhist and Mohammedan view is based on a sound psychology. And it is a fact which Christians no less than others must recognize and with which they should reckon. Certainly the history of Christianity is as striking — and almost as sad — an illustration of the fact as is the history of Buddhism. And this fact of the certainty of change, for better or for worse, is not confined to the past but is bound to hold true in the future as well, since it is based on the very laws of the human soul.

The present chapter and the three preceding it have dealt with religion in rather general terms. We must now come to closer grips with our subject and study the religious consciousness in greater detail — its nature and content, its activities and expressions, its development. While the influence of society must ever be kept vividly in mind, the immediate object of our study — as the present chapter has indicated — must be the religion of the individual; for we are here concerned not with sociology or anthropology or history, but with psychology. In the following chapter we shall, therefore, consider the earliest form of the individual religious consciousness as found in the soul of the child, tracing its development thereafter through youth into the mature years.

CHAPTER V

IT is seldom that the psychologist can be more optimistic than the poet. But, strangely enough, he sometimes has the opportunity, and nowhere is this more evident than on the question of the development of the individual mind. According to Wordsworth,

> "Heaven lies about us in our infancy!
> Shades of the prison-house begin to close
> Upon the growing Boy,
> But he beholds the light, and whence it flows,
> He sees it in his joy;
> The youth who daily farther from the east
> Must travel, still is Nature's priest,
> And by the vision splendid
> Is on his way attended.
> At length the man perceives it die away,
> And fade into the common light of day."

In this decidedly somber view of the development — or degeneration — of the individual, the psychologist cannot follow the poet. Indeed the genetic study of mind results in a description of human life almost the reverse of that presented by Wordsworth. In the first place, if we may believe the psychologist, it is not true, (at least not true in any special sense) that heaven lies about us in our infancy. This view is a poetic idealization of babyhood which finds no support from the scientific study of babies. *Earth* lies about us in our infancy — that is the plain, prosaic fact. The baby is a little animal and hardly more. Nothing more in truth, except in promise and potency; and the promise and potency exist only for the on-looking mature mind. The baby knows nothing of them nor of the Heaven which lies about us all. The shades of the prison-house begin to *break* about the growing boy. And it is only by the complete man in his hours of greatest maturity and insight that Heaven is seen and felt to lie about us.

The baby, as I have said, is born into the world a little animal, with an equipment of senses, reflexes, instincts, and incipient intelligence. The world he is born into is admirably adapted to exactly his needs and potentialities. It has been humanized for him by a thousand centuries of human life and thought and effort. Preëminently it is a social world, a world of people older than he who not only are themselves stamped with certain traditional ways of action and thought but also insist upon impressing, directly or indirectly, the same stamp upon him. In the preceding chapter we have seen that the child is like soft clay in the hands of the older generation, and that his innate tendency to imitation necessitates his copying the models which he finds. These words " imitation " and " copying," however, must be taken in a broader sense than that given to them in common speech. The imitation of which child psychology speaks is mostly quite involuntary, and in a sense passive as well as active. The child is, as it were, submerged in a medium in which he soaks till it permeates his entire being. This medium is constituted by the social heredity,— the customs, attitudes, feelings, ideals,— of that part of the race to which he belongs. He breathes it with the air and drinks it in with his mother's milk. It is all natural to him, in the sense that it is thoroughly human and is adapted marvelously well to all that he is and may be; yet he did not bring it with him, but simply finds it waiting for him and inevitably his whether he will or no.

Part of this racial inheritance is the child's religion. It would be as impossible to say when he begins to acquire it as it would be to say when he begins to learn his mother tongue. And, once started, its growth is as natural as it is gradual. It is not something that depends upon teaching, as a foreign language does. If you ask the good and wise mother how she taught her children to be religious she will not be able to tell you. Theology has to be taught; religion cannot be. When the mother gives her child his first lesson in theology she finds that he is already incipiently religious.

When I say that the child is incipiently religious I am, of course, using religion in the broad sense defined in the first chapter. The child, I mean, is beginning to have some sort of attitude, extremely indefinite and lacking in self-consciousness, to be sure, toward the powers determining his destiny. This truly religious attitude is natural for him because he possesses those instincts which in their combination make the adult man religious.[1] The particular objects and ideas about which these instinctive tendencies center are varied and of no special significance. The powers which the child at first envisages as determining his destiny are confined to his immediate social circle; and the beginnings of his religious sentiment are to be found in, and grow up out of, this net-work of personal relationships in which he finds himself lying, as in a cradle. "The child's earliest expressions of reverence, love, devotion, trust, dependence, are directed to the actual persons of his environment. It is impossible, in these early manifestations, to distinguish what is ethical from what is religious; that is, it is impossible to see any marked phase of the expressive attitudes of the child which can be called religious in a distinctive sense . . . . He reaches a constantly enlarging sense of the richness of personality by growing up into the lessons set by the actions of others: and he attains greater intimations of the depth and possible meaning of the persons about him through his own reactions to them. So the great line of development of his personal self, with its more and more refined sense of personal character in others — this is his one and only source of sentiment "[2] — whether the sentiment be ethical or religious.

The young child's mind is like a garden in May. All the things in it are growing at once, and nothing waits for anything else. Language, morality, and religion, feeling of all sorts and every kind of knowledge are all shooting upward at a furious rate, and all seemingly dependent on the prior appearance of each of the others, to the logical confusion of the recording psychologist. Of special importance for the growth of religion at this period is the development of self-consciousness and of social consciousness; for these are the presuppositions of religion's becoming explicit. And as Baldwin and Royce have

[1] Professor Coe discusses this point very instructively, although with his usual over-emphasis upon the social. See "The Origin and Nature of Children's Faith in God." *Am. Jour. of Theology,* XVIII (1914) 169–90.

[2] Baldwin, "Social and Ethical Interpretations," p. 337.

so well pointed out,[3] each of these is, in a sense, the presupposition of the other. In short the child's consciousness of himself and his consciousness of other people as selves, grow up together out of a social milieu; and only as his experience becomes thus gradually differentiated do his first half-conscious attitudes toward the sources of pleasure and pain, his vague sense of dependence and of wonder, take on a more definite and explicit form. At first they attach themselves inevitably to the most prominent factors in the child's universe, namely father and mother, or possibly nurse. It is from them that all blessings flow and about them that most mystery centers. The child's attitude toward them is not usually called religion; but (allowing for its simplicity and indefiniteness) it is psychologically the same in nature as the attitude which he will in future years come to have toward God. "It is a tolerably safe assertion," says Tracy, "that a child who, for any reason, has never worshiped his mother, will be by so much the less likely ever to worship any other divinity." [4]

The origin of the child's religion out of a complex of inherited social tendencies and personal relations makes it inevitable that its first explicit formulation should be crassly anthropomorphic in form. His God, growing directly out of his father or his mother, is made in the image of man. The process by which the God-idea gets formed is influenced and complicated by all the factors of the child's complex mental environment. Among these we may point out three which are particularly potent — namely (1) the indirect influence of the actions of older persons, (2) direct teaching on religious subjects, (3) the natural development of the child's mind. All three of these influences should be treated at once, for they all act together through a period of years, and every step in each aids in the forward movement of the others.

Of these three influences the first in point of time, and perhaps the first in pervasiveness, is the indirect influence of those who surround him. The child is intensely interested in peo-

[3] Baldwin, op. cit. Chaps. I and II. Royce, "The External World and the Social Consciousness." Phil. Rev. III, 513–45.

[4] "The Psychology of Childhood" (Boston, Heath & Co.: 1909), p. 190. On the same point cf. Baldwin, op. cit. pp. 343–44.

ple and is a close observer of what they do, and by an unescapable law of the human mind he imitates their actions and thus indirectly comes to share in their mental attitudes and feelings. I speak of this law of imitation as unescapable for it is founded on one of the most fundamental facts of psychology and physiology. In psychological terms, we may call this the law of sensory-motor or ideo-motor action, or in physiological language we may refer to the reflex arc. Not only the human child, but all conscious beings that we know anything about — at any rate all those with nervous systems — are built upon a plan which may be described by the words *stimulus-reaction*. A process once perceived *and attended to* tends to be set up or imitated in the muscles of the percipient,[5] the tendency being stronger or weaker according to the absence or presence of inner inhibitions or of rival stimuli and according to the freshness and suggestibility of the mind. Now the mind of the child, so lacking in inhibitions, so unspoiled by previous experience, is peculiarly suggestive, hence the vivid perception of another's interesting act tends to initiate motor processes towards both his voluntary and his non-voluntary muscles. And so close is the relation between reaction and feeling, between bodily expression and inner state, that he who imitates another's act, posture, or expression is likely to share at least incipiently in the mental attitude thus expressed. Here we have one of the most subtle, far-reaching, and long-enduring of all the influences that mould the religion of the child. The boy may be taught all the thirty-nine Articles or howsoever many there be, but if he sees in his parents and those about him no expression of reverence for a Power greater than themselves, no sign of worship or of religious feeling in their conduct or their conversation, his religion will probably be of a very superficial sort. It is more important that he should imitate actions which are expressive of religious feelings and thus come to wonder, think, and feel for himself, than that he should learn any amount of pious words. Carlyle makes Teufelsdröckh refer to this indirect influence of his foster-parents as the great power in his own early religion. " The

---

[5] The almost total absence of imitation in the sub-human world, except in the case of actions already prompted by instinct is due to the facts that animals seldom pay attention to objects or actions not connected with their specific instincts, and that they are incapable of free ideas.

highest whom I knew on earth I here saw bowed down, with awe unspeakable, before a Higher in Heaven: such things, especially in infancy, reach inwards to the very core of your being."

The pedagogical inferences from these facts, I think, are plain enough. The wise parents who wish their child's religion to be more than skin deep will take pains to let the little one see the expressions of their own religion, and will make these expressions more obvious than they would otherwise be. The psychology of religion might have a good deal to say in favor of the resumption of the old customs of family prayers, the saying of grace at meal time, and other modes of religious expressions which, our fathers practiced and which so many of us have outgrown. Wherever children are growing up, the outward expression of the religious attitude is simply not to be replaced by anything else. The child's observation of these actions and his spontaneous attempts to imitate them will moreover make the best possible preparation for the more explicit inculcation of religious ideas. This direct teaching should be given only in connection with the indirect influence just described, and should at first be based as much as possible upon the child's own curiosity concerning the significance of his parents' acts and attitudes. Doubtless the seed is the word; but there is little use in sowing the seed before the soil has been prepared for it.

Yet I would by no means minimize the importance of direct teaching. Religion if it is to be a real force in life, must be more than implicit. And of course, as a matter of fact, religious instruction cannot be withheld from a child to-day, unless he be stone deaf, and perhaps blind also. If his parents do not teach him religious conceptions, his companions will, and if these hold their peace, the very labels on canned goods will break forth into theology.[6] And so we find that the child's explicit ideas on religious matters are simply a compound of what he has understood from the various sources of his instruction, modified unintentionally by the working of his own

[6] "One boy says he got his ideas of the devil from a Punch and Judy show, two say their ideas of the devil came from the pictures on deviled ham, several mention the hired girl as authority, and a large number say their ideas came from pictures."— Earl Barnes, "Theological Life of a California Child." Pedagogical Seminary II, 448.

imagination. The importance of the latter is often much greater than is commonly supposed. Where, for instance, did a six year old friend of mine get this notion? — that " God is a face of a man with big ears. He doesn't eat anything but only drinks dew " ? The possibility that the child may misunderstand absolutely anything that is told him, no matter how simple it may seem to his older instructors, must also be taken into account in explaining the strange ideas that get mixed up in his theology and the incomprehensible nature of some of his ritual of worship. Father Tyrrell, speaking of his own childhood, says, in his Autobiography, " ' *Jesus-Tender; Shepherd-hear-me* ' were two polysyllables for me for many years, and it is even now an effort to analyze them; and *Rocka Vages* has associations that ' Rock of Ages ' can never have. I like the old readings better," he adds; " sentiment is more precious than sense." [7]

If we take into account the instruction which the child receives in theological matters from parents, servants, playmates, teachers, preachers, books, and pictures, and add to that his inevitable misunderstanding of much that is taught him, and his own imaginative contribution produced in the process of mental digestion, we shall understand the strange mixture of commonplace ideas and fantastic imagery which characterizes the child's theology. It will, therefore, be quite unnecessary here to describe at length children's ideas of God or to quote particular statements of particular children concerning Heaven, Hell, etc.; the reader who so wishes may read long and interesting compilations of them in many places, references to the most important of which he will find in a note at the foot of this page.[8]

[7] " Autobiography and Life of George Tyrrell," arranged by M. D. Petre, (New York, Longmans: 1912). Vol. I, p. 16.

[8] Barnes, Earl, " Theological Life of a California Child," Ped. Sem. II, 442–448.

Bergen, F. D., " Notes on the Theological Development of a Child," *Arena*, XIX, 254–266.

Brockman, F. S., " A Study of the Moral and Religious Life of 251 Preparatory School Students in the United States," Ped. Sem. 255–273.

Brown, A. W., " Some Records of the Thoughts and Reasonings of Children," Ped. Sem. II, 358–396.

Chrisman, O., " Religious Ideas of a Child," *Child Study Monthly*, March, 1898.

I have spoken of the development of the child's own mind as one of the three great factors in the formation of his theology. The instinct of curiosity with which Nature has endowed him sets him very early to wondering and to questioning himself and others, and increasing experience and intelligence soon make it impossible for the answers to his questions and the solutions of his problems to be stated in terms of father or mother or of the social circle immediately open to his perception. His dependence upon his father and mother is no longer felt as *ultimate;* there is a sense of a Beyond, a farther power or group of powers on which they too, with him, depend. This sense of something more is at first implicit only, but quite early it becomes explicit — being hastened in its growth by the influence and teaching of others. Just when thought in this form makes its first appearance, it is of course impossible to say with exactness, but in an incipient form it may be present by the end of the third year. And theology is often the child's first science. His persistent questioning repeatedly drives his interlocutor back to God as the ultimate explanation of most things, and so the little mind, now very alert, finds in God a new and intellectual satisfaction. To be sure, even God is often not really ultimate for the child, for he must be told who made God: yet on the whole he finds in Him the most

Coe, G. A., "Origin and Nature of Children's Faith in God," *Am. Jour. of Theol.*, XVIII, 169–90.

Ebell, "Der Himmel in der Gedankenwelt 10–und 11–jähriger Kinder," Monatsblätter für den Evangelischen Religionsunterricht, Aug.–Sept., 1911, pp. 252–254.

Hall, G. Stanley, "The Contents of Children's Minds," *Princeton Rev.*, N. S., XI, 249 ff.

Pratt, J. B., "The Psychology of Religious Belief" (New York, Macmillan: 1907), Chap. VII.

Schreiber, H., "Der Kinderglaube" (Langensalza, 1909) pp. 29–39.

Shepherd, "Concerning the Religion of Childhood," *Jour. of Relig. Psy.*, VII, 411–16.

Shinn, Millicent W., "Notes on the Development of a Child" (Berkeley, Univ. of California: 1894).

Shinn, "Some Comments on Babies," *Overland Monthly*, N. S., XXXII, 2–19.

Street, J. R., "The Religion of Childhood," *Zion's Herald* (Boston) LXXVIII, 108–109, 118–119. See also Homiletic Review, LV, 371–375.

Sully, J., "Studies in Childhood" (New York, Appleton: 1896).

Tanner, Amy E., "Children's Religious Ideas," Ped. Sem., XIII, 511–513.

satisfactory answer to his questions. Thus the cosmological argument comes to be the one great theological argument of childhood. This is due not only to the development of the child's intelligence but also to the fact that at the same time with it his activity and his interest in activity are rapidly growing. He wants to know how things are made and who made them and why. The two great categories of explanation — the causal and the teleological — are now developing (from the third year onward) *pari passu*,[9] and both of them are important factors in leading the child's mind to the conception of a Creator who made things and people for various purposes.

But while thought plays a rôle of more or less importance in coloring the nature of the child's religious belief, it is extremely seldom that it adds very much to the strength of his conviction. The child's theology, like the rest of his store of beliefs, is emphatically based on authority. The reason for this is of course plain enough, and is to be sought in the very nature of the child's mind — in fact in the nature of mind as such. Implicit belief, the unquestioning acceptance of the presented, is the natural reaction of the virgin mind. It is as important a characteristic of it as is the tendency to imitation, discussed a few pages back. In fact these two qualities of the mind before it has been moulded and re-formed by experience,— its " suggestibility " and its " primitive credulity," — are in a large sense aspects of the same thing. Just as the human being tends to imitate every process which he perceives and attends to, so he tends to accept as real everything presented to him and to believe as true whatever he is told. Doubt is necessarily a secondary phenomenon — it presupposes at least two rival claimants for belief both of which cannot be accepted as true. That there can be such discord is something which the child learns only after bitter and surprising experience. His mind at first offers no resistance to new ideas nor ever asks their credentials. Whether they come from parent, hired-girl, or Punch-and-Judy show, they are admitted as " Gospel Truth." Hence

[9] According to Baldwin the causal develops before the teleological, but the causal explanation is usually given in terms of personal activity. See " Social and Ethical Interpretations," pp. 346–49. In Leuba's opinion the child's category of causality has not necessarily anything to do with personality. See " A Psychological Study of Religion," p. 79.

the religion of childhood is based on authority in a perfectly absolute sense.[10]   And so it continues to be until at length the child's attention is called to the fact of conflict between two entering ideas, or more likely between some new idea and some old belief.   When this day comes, the child begins to say Farewell to his childhood.   He has tasted of doubt, and he must now begin to add thought to authority in his religion and in all his knowledge.

In religious matters many reach adolescence without any doubts.   In the case of others doubt begins quite early.[11]   A. W. Brown cites a boy of three who had already developed enough of the questioning spirit at least to wonder whether his father was correct in saying that God could do everything: " If I'd gone upstairs," he asked, " could God make it that I

[10] Father Tyrrell writes of his own early religion: " To say that I either believed or disbelieved in God, or in anything else at that age would be to forget that for children the difference between fact and fiction is of little or no interest.   In religious, as in other matters, I dutifully repeated the prescribed formulæ, and if I knew that God existed and that Jack the Giant-Killer did not, it was only because I was told so.   It was only this passive faith in the words of others that made me afraid of ghosts and banshees and of the dark.   The notions that any beliefs, opinions, or professions, different from ours, could be tenable was quite unthinkable; the critical and reasoning faculty was as yet wholly dormant." Op. cit., Vol. I, p. 48.

[11] Perhaps earlier and more often than we commonly think.   The child's replies to the questions of grown-ups may be merely verbal answers and hide his own real beliefs.   Fräulein Barth discovered that the conventional descriptions which the children in her school (of ten and eleven years) gave of Heaven, God, etc., were regarded by them as only " Märchen."   A little girl who had just described Heaven in the usual way added, " Aber in Wirklichkeit giebt es keinen Himmal, dort oben ist nur Luft und Wasser." This position was found typical of a goodly proportion of the children. One little girl gives the following rather pathetic confession of faith: " Als ich klein war, habe ich nie an die Hölle geglaubt.   Aber an den Himmel desto mehr.   Ich habe gemeint, Gott sässe auf einem Stuhl, und um ihn alle Engel.   Gott habe ich mir vorgestellt, er habe an allen Seiten Augen, weil es immer heisst, er würde alles sehen.   Aber jetzt weiss ich ja, dass das Blaue alles nur Luft ist, aber wo der Liebe Gott hingekommen ist, weiss ich nicht."   Another child answered to the question, " What do you yourself really believe about heaven ? " as follows: " Wenn man tot ist, dann ist man auch fertig mit allem Leben.   Sonst interessiert mich alles nicht."   Fräulein Barth believes that if this child had simply been asked to describe heaven, she would have given a vivid and proper account. (" Der Himmel in der Gedankenwelt 10–und 11–jährigen Kinder," Monatsblätter für den evangelischen Religious-unterricht.   Nov., 1911, pp. 336–338.)

hadn't?" Once started, this unwillingness to accept all that one is told, grows with increasing experience. According to Earl Barnes it culminates with most children between the ages of twelve and fourteen, after which comes a period of diminished critical activity in religious questions, lasting until the great upheaval of adolescence.

Childhood doubts are of course of many sorts: but the great majority of them are due to one or the other of two great causes. These are conflict between authoritative theology and the child's own experience, and contradiction between the theological ideas taught him and his own growing sense of morality and justice. I quote a few illustrations from my respondents. One of them writes: "I doubted very much God's answer to prayer. I wanted very much a baby sister, so I prayed for one every night. None came and for several years I doubted the power of prayer." Another tells me that having been taught that the prayer of faith would move mountains, she attempted at eight to make use of it. At that age she went with her parents on a trip to the White Mountains, and one evening prayed for three hours that Mt. Washington might be removed into the sea. The disappointing result shook her faith to such an extent that she did not pray again all summer.[12]

[12] The question of prayer probably causes more childhood questionings and doubts than any other theme, for here the child has a very practical piece of theology which if true should be utilized, and one also very easily tested. Edmund Gosse has some charming reminiscences from his boyhood upon the subject. "My parents said: 'Whatever you need, tell Him and He will grant it, if it is His will.' Very well; I had need of a large pointed humming-top which I had seen in a shop-window in the Caledonian Road. Accordingly I introduced a supplication for this object into my evening prayer, carefully adding the words: 'If it is Thy will.' This, I recollect, placed my Mother in a dilemma, and she consulted my Father. Taken, I suppose, at a disadvantage, my Father told me I must not pray for 'things like that.' To which I answered by another query, 'Why?'. And I added that he said one ought to pray for things we needed, and that I needed the humming-top a great deal more than I did the conversion of the heathen or the restitution of Jerusalem to the Jews, two objects of my nightly supplication which left me very cold." This was during his sixth year. At about the same time, he decided to test his father's statement that God would be very angry and signify his anger if any one in a Christian country should commit idolatry. This he tested by deliberately committing the sin — hoisting a chair onto the table and bowing down before it in prayer. "Father and Son." (New York, Scribners: 1908) pp. 49 and 53.

A third respondent — also at the age of eight — determined to put God's *foreknowledge* to the test. "I often tried to fool God. I would say I would do one thing and then suddenly change and do something else: start down one side of the street and suddenly cross and go down the opposite side, etc."

It is not this conflict between authority and experience, however, but the inconsistency between the teachings of theology and the growing sense of the real nature of goodness and justice that gives rise to the more serious doubts in the minds of the thoughtful child. A typical expression of this sort of questioning is the following response: "It didn't seem to me possible that a God who had made us so prone to sin could punish us so severely as was taught." And this (from a girl of ten): "Mama, God must have known that Adam and Eve would eat that apple, and they couldn't help doing it if He planned to have them do it. So why did He blame them?"

Doubts like these in early childhood we can perhaps afford to smile at. But when the breech between theology, on the one hand, and experience and moral intuition on the other is permitted to continue into adolescence it becomes a serious matter. Here is a subject for careful thought on the part of parents and all those who have to do with the religious instruction of the young. Is there not enough in our Christian theology that we can teach our children without mingling with it assertions which their own experience can speedily refute, or characterizations of God which their dawning sense of righteousness finds strange or intolerable? But even aside from theological lessons of this sort, the attempt to teach doctrine to children before they have reached the age of conceptual thought is of very questionable wisdom. Surely there is need enough for religious instruction in other fields to keep both teacher and learner busy. Especially should it be impressed upon children of all ages that religion and morality are inseparable and that religion therefore has to do with every moment of their waking lives and with every act and thought and word. It is perhaps in failing to do this that our religious instruction is found most sadly wanting. To the ancient world religion was a serious business; to us moderns it is in danger of becoming a kind of epiphenomenon. It is a sad picture which the Rev. R. Emlein, Stadtvikar in Mannheim, presents in the *Zeitschrift für Religionspsychologie—*. One hundred and four boys, from twelve to fourteen in age, after eight years of religious instruction, are set to answer the question: "What value has religion?" "Out of the one hundred and four, sixty-six begin: '*Religion has absolutely no value.*' Fifty-eight subjoin the reason: '*Because we can't use it in our business.*' Twenty-five see in religion some sort of ideal value, to be sure, which yet is minimized by all sorts of limitations, since religion is useful only ' when you are old,' or ' when things are going wrong with you,' or ' when you are away from home.' Finally a few, thirteen in number, regard religion as something which ' you must know because it is God's word,' or ' because you can't go to Heaven without it.' "

These last years of childhood are critical for religion, and as Herr Emlein so well points out, the kind of religious instruction which the child gets at this time may be decisive for the rest of his life. " It is the time when the childish fancy gradually sinks and is replaced by the critical, reflective understanding. It is the time of transition from the Old to the New. Hence the enormous importance of this period to the teacher, for it is his task to lay the foundations of this New which is to be. It is for to him to say what stones of the old building may be used for the new, and above all to determine how the new building-material — the understanding — is to be utilized. . . . It would be interesting to discover how often theoretical and practical atheism has its ultimate source exactly in religious instruction itself which has neglected to make a bridge between critical understanding and religion." [13]

We often fail to realize how critical and still more how complex these years at the end of childhood are. We have both idealized and simplified childhood, and neglecting both our own memories and any careful investigation of children's minds,

[13] " Vom Kinderglauben," *Zeitschrift für Religionspsychologie*, V, 141–148. For some excellent observations on the subject of religious instruction see: Coe, " Education in Religion and Morals;" Dawson, " Children's Interest in the Bible," Ped. Sem., VII, 151–178 (esp. pp. 176–178); Hall, " Educational Problems " (New York, Appleton: 1911), Chap. IV; Röttger, " *Die Religion des Kindes,*" *Zeitschrift f. Relspsy.* VI, 298–302; Starbuck, " The Child-mind and Child Religion," Part IV. " The Development of Spirituality," *Biblical World*, XXX, 352–60; Willuhn, " *Die Psychologie der Kinderpredigt,*" *Ztsft f. Relspsy.* II, 334–340.

we have constructed an idylic picture, which we name " Childhood," out of children's unwrinkled faces and their lively games. Thus happiness, innocence, and a purely objective consciousness are thought to be the peculiar characteristics of the child up to, say, his fourteenth year. This grown-up view of the child is probably about as accurate as the child's notion of the grown-up. Children are often very unhappy; in fact a sensitive child may be as utterly wretched half a dozen times in one day as his father is during the course of a year. He believes his father is never unhappy, because his father never cries; and his logic is at least as good as ours. Nor are children, say from eight to fourteen, by any means so innocent as we like to think them. Many of them consciously break more moral laws than they ever will in mature life. And, accompanying these actions, goes often a sense of sin and an inward tumult which we never guess because they are deliberately hidden from all of us outsiders. " My outside life," writes Prof. Jones of his own boyhood, " was just like that of any healthy growing boy. I played boy's games, learned to swim and dive, and in the times between I went to school and worked on the farm. It looked from the outside as though this made up the whole of my life. But looked at from within, my life was mostly an invisible battle. More real than the snow fort which we stormed amid a flight of snow-balls until we dislodged the possessors of it, was this unseen stronghold of an enemy who was dislodged only to come back into his fort stronger than ever, so that my assaults seemed fruitless and vain. . . . I never talked with anyone about my troubles, and I do not believe those nearest me realized that I was having a crisis, for there was no outward sign of it. This whole situation, now so hard to describe clearly, would hardly be worth telling about, and would certainly not here come to light, if it were not for the fact that it is an experience which is well-nigh universal, and one which needs more attention than it usually gets. Boys are much deeper, much better, than even their *mothers* know, and down below what they say, is a center of life which never is wholly silent." [14]

[14] " A Boy's Religion from Memory " (Philadelphia, Ferris and Leach: 1902), pp. 102, 109, and 141.

This inner life of the boy and girl is of peculiar importance in relation to their religion. The question of the presence of religious feeling in children is extremely difficult. Anything like statistical conclusions is here of course quite inconceivable, and one can only say, in the vaguest terms, that while perhaps the majority of children have relatively little that is subjective about their religion, a good many girls and boys of eight or ten have an inner life of intense and genuine religious feeling. This does not mean that children are mystics; the feeling in question may be one of fear or awe toward a distant and rather dreadful Ruler. But even so it makes the child's religion something more than mere " primitive credulity." God becomes a reality and a power in life quite comparable with father and mother. " Thou, God, seest me " is a very impressive thought to many little children. And between the years of ten and thirteen or even eight and thirteen, many a child goes through one or more violently emotional religious upsets. I quote at length one example, from one of my respondents:

" The first real self-conscious experience of this kind was connected with the realization that I, actually myself, would some day die and give an account of myself before God, whom I pictured to myself with great realism. I had taken the whole thing for granted before, but never actually felt that I myself would have this experience, and it gave me a feeling as if I were suddenly having my very soul laid bare. I think this was when I was about eleven or twelve years old. This was the first ' experience ' I can remember, and was not at all of the comforting, but rather of the fearful order,— the whirlwind instead of the still small voice. I was old for my age in many respects, which may explain its coming so young. The experience came in the weekly church prayer-meeting, which I attended since I was the minister's daughter, but I was not in the least in a religious mood at the time. I remember *everything* about it — the warm, sultry summer evening, the subject of the service, ' Profanity,' the old deacon who was speaking and to whom I had not been paying attention, the girl with whom I was sitting and with whom I had been whispering. I remember even the color and pattern of her dress — and how in the first dazed feeling of the experience I wondered how anyone could care about having a pattern of roses on a dress, when she was really only a skeleton inside! The gloom of this sudden revelation of the shortness and unsatisfactoriness of life hung over me for some time, and although I look upon the whole period as a morbid and even superstitious one, it did bring me up standing and threw me into a search for something that *would* satisfy, and in time my healthy temper reasserted itself. The facts of my whole early training and habits of course determined the method that I sought for escape from such a struggle of mind, but this was certainly the turning point when I began to take, in a voluntary serious manner, what before had come with no will or consideration on my part at all."

Besides feelings of the more fearful order, religion produces in many children a sense of quiet joy and confidence and of friendship toward God. In some ways this is easier for children than for their elders. The imagination in these early years is extremely vivid, and everyone knows children who have imaginary friends and spend much of their time playing and talking with them. Now for many a child God is simply one of these friends. " God was just as real a being to me," says Professor Jones, in the little book already cited, " all through my boyhood as was any one of the persons in our nearest neighbor's house." [15] The result of this ideal intimacy with God is inevitably a very genuine if child-like love for Him, and a feeling of confidence, since He is near. A lady of my acquaintance recently overheard a conversation between her two boys in which the younger asked his older brother (aged eight) how he knew that God heard his prayers. The boy answered, " Because I feel Him in my heart." There was nothing mysterious about this; he had always been told that God was in him, and his first lesson in religion from his mother had been that God was the part of him that loves. It is from perfectly natural beginnings like this — the product of instruction and of the child's own nature — that something like an incipient mystic sense takes its rise in some children. I mean by this what might be called a sense of God's presence resulting naturally (in thought-

[15] P. 97.

ful and sensitive children) from the *belief* in God's presence but quite distinguishable in intensity and feeling tone from mere belief. Out of fifty of my respondents who claim to be able to date the origin of this experience in their own lives, twenty-nine insist that it goes back to the twelfth or thirteenth year or earlier. Nearly all say that it was a gradual growth, though with a very few it appeared suddenly. The descriptions of this experience offer nothing striking but show merely a natural development out of what was there before. " At eight I felt that God was with me. It was much the same feeling as toward a very dear and trusted friend. I thought God was watching my life and helping me." " One morning when I was praying I felt aware that I was talking to a real Presence in quite a different way from anything I had ever felt before. It was not like a vision but just a sense of infinite Presence. It comes since, more strong, but only at times: I was twelve then." [16]

Many children, probably a large majority, grow out of child-hood with no such religious feeling as that described. For them God is a reality in the way the President is, but in no more intimate sense. This may be true even of those who after-wards become men of intense religious feeling — as for instance Father Tyrrell, who simply " repeated dutifully the prescribed formulæ," and who " knew that God existed and that Jack the Giant Killer did not," only because he was told so. And even for those children whose religion is of a more inward na-ture, religious feeling is still far from attaining its climax. The beauty of the religion of childhood lies chiefly in its prom-ise and potency. It looks for its fulfillment to adolescence and maturity, which we shall study in our next chapter.

[16] See also the much more instructive case cited at length in my " Psy-chology of Religious Belief, pp. 225–226.

CHAPTER VI

ADOLESCENCE

The period extending from approximately the twelfth to the twenty-fifth year, commonly called adolescence, is the flowering time for religion, as for most other things in human life. It is not the time of fruitage; that comes later on. But much that is most fragrant and attractive in the religious life comes out for the first time in these youthful years. The transition from childhood to adolescence, though not sudden enough to be capable of an exact date, is the most momentous change in the whole life of the individual. It is, in fact, nothing less than a new birth into a larger world. The child is made over physically and spiritually. For the first time he comes into possession of all his bodily functions, and at the same time new vistas open out before his intellect and his imagination, and he discovers within himself unguessed intensities of emotion and desire. The result is that strange mingling of vision and confusion, of the sense of power and the despair of weakness, of noble aspirations and undreamed of temptations, that conflict of joy and pain, of sin and exaltation, which make youth a period of never-failing fascination for the student of human nature.

No other period is so fateful in its influence upon the whole of life. The line of direction which the individual is to follow through all his years is usually determined in this critical period. All sorts of things are to be done at this time or not at all: but these many things may perhaps be subsumed under the four following great tasks which nature sets each youth during these busy years; (1) to develop to the full the powers and functions of his body, (2) to come into possession of his intellectual heritage and make it over into his own property, (3) to adapt himself to the society of which he is now (for the first time) a real member, and — what in a sense includes all the others — (4) to grow out of thinghood into selfhood.

The religious life of the adolescent is as full of ups and downs as is the rest of his experience during these tumultuous years. Starbuck, whose treatment of adolescence and its religion is in most respects admirable, has attempted to classify these conflicting experiences and determine the approximate average age at which each appears. Thus a period of " clarification " often comes at the end of childhood, followed by " spontaneous awakening " at about fifteen. Confusion and struggle manifest themselves not chiefly at any one point but through a period of years, a period which Starbuck refers to as " storm and stress," and which in girls begins at thirteen and a half, in boys three years later. After " storm and stress " comes a period of doubt, which begins oftenest at fifteen or sixteen with girls [1] and at eighteen with boys. Doubt, in turn, is followed, in the majority of cases, by a period of " alienation," lasting usually for five or six years.[2] Starbuck's classification was worked out carefully from the responses to a questionnaire; yet it is doubtful whether so clean-cut a division of the phenomena of adolescence gives a true picture of the reality. It is too simple, too diagramatic. We shall better understand the fluid and varying processes of adolescent religion if we resign the ambitious task of schematizing it, and content ourselves with the more blurred and vaguer picture of the young being moving about in worlds not realized, and going through two great sets of experiences which tend to alternate with each other, one of increasing insight, power, and joy, one of bewilderment, passivity, and depression. The more positive and joyous of these two types of experience may be said, in a general way, to consist in an immediate realization and appropriation of the facts of religion which during childhood had been quite unknown to him or at best had been accepted quite externally.[3] God now ceases to be

[1] See also Latimer, " Girl and Woman " (New York, Appleton: 1910) pp. 41–45.

[2] It should be stated that this classification, with the various ages indicated, is given by Starbuck only for the non-conversion cases. As we shall see, conversion, in his opinion, shortens up the process. His figures, etc., as quoted in this paragraph, are from Part I of his " Psychology of Religion " (New York, Scribners: 1903).

[3] For example, a respondent of Lancaster writes: " At fourteen or fifteen I became a Christian. I can give no cause for the change. I then seemed to realize for the first time all the truths that had been presented before."

on a par with the President, and to many a youth becomes indeed the great Companion. This heightened reality and inwardness of religion expresses itself to some extent both emotionally, intellectually, and morally, though of course the place of emphasis will vary with the individual. Naturally this is a point on which the sexes tend to differ. " It is significant," writes Starbuck, " that girls first awaken most frequently on the emotional side and least often to new insight into truth. The boys, on the contrary, have the emotional awakening least frequently, but organize their spiritual world most often as a moral one." [4]

This enlargement of horizon characteristic of the adolescent period is in part the direct outgrowth of a new sense of self and a new interest in other persons. The youth has now for the first time become a complete person, and as he himself has changed, all the world has changed to him. All the factors of developing manhood and womanhood contribute toward this deeper interest in persons, but especially notable are the indirect influences of the sexual instinct, now for the first time fully developed. It is very easy to overemphasize the importance of this instinct in the religious life, and I would not, therefore, dwell upon it here at length; but that its indirect influence during adolescence is considerable there is no denying. I would, however, stress the fact that its influence is chiefly indirect and unconscious, and as such it adds much that is fine and spiritual to the brighter side of adolescent development.[5]

This is a very typical case. See Lancaster's " Psychology and Pedagogy of Adolescence," (Ped. Sem. V, July, 1897, p. 96). For further study of adolescent religion, in addition to Starbuck and Lancaster, the reader will find the following references useful: Brockman, " A study of the Moral and Religious Life of 251 Preparatory School Students in the United States," (Ped. Sem. IX, 255–273) ; Coe, " The Spiritual Life," (New York, Eaton and Mains: 1900) ; Coe, " Education in Religion and Morals," (Chicago, Revell: 1904) ; Daniels, " The New Life: A Study in Regeneration," (*Am. Jour. of Psy.* VI, 61–103) ; Gulick, " Sex and Religion," (*Association Outlook*, 1897–98) ; Hall, " Adolescence " (New York, Appleton: 1904) ; Vol. II, Chaps. 13 and 14; Leuba, " The Psychology of Religious Phenomena," *Am. Jour. of Psy.* VII, 309–385.

[4] Op. cit., p. 198.

[5] The reader will find an excellent analysis of these indirect influences of sex upon the brighter side of adolescence in Coe's " Psychology of Religion," pp. 163–66.

The negative and painful experiences of adolescence are more complex than the joyous ones. As we have seen, Starbuck classifies most of them under two heads — "storm and stress" and "doubt"; and while it is misleading to make this a sharp division and to assign definite dates to each so as to imply that one is finished before the other begins, still the distinction is useful for purposes of presentation — as indeed Starbuck's admirable presentation most abundantly shows. The term "storm and stress" is used to indicate the less intellectual forms of the adolescent turmoil. It includes such mental states as a vague sense of incompleteness, indefinable aspirations and dissatisfactions, a sense of sin sometimes exceedingly vague, sometimes quite definite, varying from the consciousness of some particular offense to the indefinite conviction of having committed "the unpardonable sin," exhausting struggle between high ideals and tempestuous passions, morbid depression, and fear of eternal damnation.

The causes of these tumultuous religious experiences are varied. One school of psychologists — or rather of alienists — would explain them entirely by reference to sexual influences. The fact that the sexual life and the religious life get most of their development during the same years is pointed to as evidence of the erotogenesis of adolescent religion. Dr. Theodore Shroeder, one of the most enthusiastic advocates of this view, would in fact go so far as to insist that all religion is ultimately reducible to sexual excitement and sexual ideas,[6] and

---

[6] "The differential essence of religion is always reducible to a sex ecstasy." ("The Protogenetic Interpretation of Religion," *Jour. of Rel. Psy.*, VII, 23.) "Religion came into being by ascribing to the sexual mechanism a separate, local intelligence, which, coupled with a seeming transcendence of the sex-ecstasy, resulted in the apotheosis of the sex-functioning and the sexual organs, and all the manifold forms of religion are to be accounted for only as the diversified products of evolution, resulting wholly from physical factors and forces, operating upon man under different conditions." ("Erotogenesis of Religion," *Alienist and Neurologist*, XXVIII, August, 1907.) Dr. Shroeder has reinforced his argument in numerous other articles on the subject, among which are the following: "Religion and Sensualism" (*Jour. of Relig. Psy.*, III, 16–28). "Erotogenesis of Religion," (*Jour. of Relig. Psy.*, V, 394–401). "Adolescence and Religion," (*Jour. of Relig. Psy.*, VI, 124–48). There are many admirable criticisms of this extreme view; for example, P. Naecke, "Die Angebliche Sexuellen Wurzel der Religion," (*Zeitschrift f. Relig. Psy.*, II, 21–38), and (perhaps best of all) Prof. James's famous footnote on pages 11 and 12 of the "Varieties"

much the same position (though not quite so extreme) seems to be held by Freud and many of his followers.   So extreme a position as this will hardly need any refutation for the average reader, and if it does the whole of this volume should serve as a better refutation than any explicit examination of the thesis I could give here or elsewhere.   For if this book proves anything it should show that religion has not one but many roots, and that even if sexual influences have an important bearing upon it, they are by no means the only causes that are to be reckoned with.   But of course one who recognized the absurdity of extreme generalizations such as that of Dr. Shroeder might still insist that certain aspects of the religious turmoil of adolescence were due solely to sexual causes.   Particularly does the sense of guilt, so commonly expressed by religious adolescents, seem to be closely related to the psychological manifestations of the developing sexual life.   Many an alienist, on general pathological grounds, considers the sexual explanation of these phenomena the only one needed.[7]   Nor are we limited to considerations of a general nature for evidence of the great influence of sexual passion in the production of the sense of guilt so characteristic of this period.   The responses to questionnaires such as those of Starbuck and Brockman show that in a large proportion of young men the sense of guilt is in no

[7] " Ich kenne bis jetzt nur eine Quelle eines Schuldgefühles, das man meinetwegen religiös oder transzendent nennen mag; die Onanie und event. einige ähnliche sexuelle Verfehlungen.   Wo ich bei den Kranken ein solches Gefühl der Verschuldung analysieren konnte, kam ich auf sexuelle Selbstvorwürfe.   Ob noch anderes dazu gehört, und event. was, das weiss ich nicht. Sicher aber ist mir, dass, was bei den Kranken eine so gross Rolle spielt, beim Schuldgefühl des Gesunden nicht nebensächlich sein kann; denn unsere psychische Krankheitssymptome sind nur Verzerrungen oder Uebertreibungen normaler Phänomene."   Professor Bleuler — quoted on page 5 by Dr. Friedmann in his symposium on " Das religiöse Schuldbewusstsein," *Ziscft f. Relspsy.* III, 1–16, April, 1909).   In the same article Dr. C. G. Jung is quoted as follows: " Im Grunde genommen ist das Phänomen (das religiöse Schuldfühl) wohl aufzufassen als eine nur partielle, d.h. zum Teil misglückte Sublimation der infantiler Sexualität.   Ein gewisser Betrag an verdrängter Libido, dargestllt durch entsprechende Phantasien, ist stehen geblieben und nach bekanntem Muster in Angst konvertiert.   Die Natur des nicht sublimierten Restes geht mit Evidenz hervor aus den bekannten Versuchungsszenen der Heiligenlegende.   All das ist durch die Freudsche Psychoanalyse übrigens schon längst nachgewiesen."   (P. 7.)

sense imaginary or "constitutional," but is merely the consciousness of very real sexual temptations and sins.[8]

It is, however, a mistake to attribute all the depression and "conviction of sin" so common among adolescents, particularly in Protestant communities, to this cause alone. In fact it is doubtful whether it has any great influence in producing the sense of uneasiness, depression, and "conviction" among adolescent females. Ill health of any sort is likely to produce depression, and this is probably the explanation of much of the morbidity and religious anxiety found among young people of both sexes, but particularly among girls. The new and lofty aspirations of youth, combined with the weakness and weariness that often accompany rapid growth, are enough to account for a great deal of the sense of guilt. But one of the chief causes of this striking phenomenon of adolescent religion as found in Protestant countries is yet to be mentioned. It is, namely, the theological prepossessions with which our youth are so often brought up. This influence, in my opinion, has been pretty generally underrated by nearly all the writers on the psychology of religion who have treated the subject. The tendency has been to make "conviction of sin" a more normal adolescent phenomenon than it really is. The psychological literature on this subject gives the reader the impression that the sense of guilt belongs naturally to human nature in these youthful years; and one is seldom reminded that this literature is very largely based upon the biographies of "evangelical" theologians, and on the results of questionnaires which have been answered chiefly by people brought up to believe that they were by nature poor sinners and that "conviction of sin" is the primary condition of salvation. That the earnest youth possessed of views like these and looking in vain within himself for a certain sort

[8] See Starbuck, op. cit., p. 220, and Brockman, "A study of the Moral and Religious Life of 251 Preparatory School Students in the United States," particularly pages 266–71. These pages make very painful reading and should give food for thought to every one who has at heart the welfare of our American boys and young men. The late age of marriage in America and our comparatively high ideals on sexual matters, probably make the struggle for the control of passion that goes on in the lives of our American youth more intense and more painful than it is anywhere else in the world.

of ill-defined experience as a token of his own "change of heart," should regard as sinful many of the thoughts, feelings, and impulses natural to his years and should describe the vague dissatisfactions of adolescence in the conventional phrases of a somewhat mechanical theology, is exactly what we should expect. The following response, for instance, taken from Starbuck is very typical: "When about eighteen I studied and thought long on the question of sanctification. The experience I sought was not in the conquest of marked evil habits, and on the whole was rather vague. Two or three times with fear and nervous apprehension I took the start, saying, ' Now I claim as mine perfect holiness'; but I found nothing different save a trying nervous strain of anxiety and painful scrutiny lest some shade of thought should prove false my claim to perfect sanctification." [9]

As a fact, in those religious communities in which there is no theological emphasis upon " conviction," the intensity of " storm and stress " is greatly diminished and the nature of the struggle considerably modified. Take, for instance, religiously educated Catholic girls. They are as intensely interested in moral and religious questions as any group of Protestant girls, they are as introspective, their attention is probably even more constantly directed toward the development and culture of their souls; but there is among them little of that *general* sense of sinfulness which plays so large a part in " evangelistic " experience — and in contemporary religious psychology. Catholic girls recognize perfectly well their own imperfections and they struggle constantly for moral improvement; but both the short comings which they realize and the goal which they seek are perfectly definite things. They are struggling not for " peace of mind " or any other emotional state, nor for " sanctification " or any other ill-defined theological condition of soul, but for the overcoming of some particular weakness or the acquisition of some particular grace. The contrast is, to be sure, in part one of *relative* emphasis, the evangelical youth thinking mostly about his feelings, the Catholic mostly about his character and " works." But it is also a contrast between the vague and the definite. And hence it comes about that

[9] Op. cit., p. 215.

the youth brought up in evangelical circles is the subject of much painful emotion which is almost entirely spared the young Catholic. Still more light is thrown upon the adolescent sense of guilt if we turn from Christendom altogether and examine the experience of religious youths in such a deeply religious land as India. In Max Müller's biography of Ràmakrishna, for example, and in the autobiography of Devendranath Tagore, are to be found vivid accounts of the religious storm and stress of adolescence, full of dissatisfaction, longing, and other experiences common to the adolescent of Protestant Christendom; but in spite of the sensitive conscience of these truly saintly men there is no evidence of any sense of sin.[10]

According to the figures collected by various writers on adolescence, the period of "doubt" follows that of "storm and stress." And though as a fact incursions of doubt are likely to appear at almost any time in adolescence, it is true that the climax of adolescent doubt usually begins after the more emotional pertubations of "storm and stress" have got well under way. This indeed is natural, since the more serious kind of doubt presupposes greater intellectual development than is to be found in the years when "storm and stress" begins. Yet it would be a mistake to regard the intellectual influences as the only causes of doubt. For doubt is a peculiarly adolescent phenomenon and must be explained by a combination of inner as well as of outer influences. "Looking through the cases," writes Starbuck, "we find that almost all of the doubts begin between eleven and twenty. There are a few scattered ones during the twenties, and almost none after thirty. The scattered ones that come after twenty-six are so few as to tend to establish the law that doubt belongs almost exclusively to youth. If the person is thrown into constantly changing environments during the whole period after adolescence one would expect, if the external influences were the only occasion for doubt, that there would be throughout life a continual turmoil and upheaval. Since this is not the case, one must look for deeper causes than

10 Max Müller, "Ramakrishna, His Life and Sayings" (London, Longmans: 1910), esp. pp. 33–42. "The Gospel of Ramakrishna" (New York, Vedanta Society: 1907). Devendranath Tagore, "Autobiography" (Calcutta, Lahiri: 1909), esp. pp. 4, 15 f., 36 f.

the sociological and historical ones, and these are to be found again in the psycho-physiological organism." [11]

I am not sure it is perfectly correct to say religious doubt is a regular and inevitable product of adolescence, but certainly the tendency to question authority and to ask the reason for things is natural to the growing mind, and the combination of an enquiring intellect which has not yet got its bearings, and an authoritative religion which insists upon an unreasonable acceptance of dogma is almost certain to breed religious doubt, sometimes of a painful character. But the pain that sometimes accompanies this skeptical period should not blind us to its value as a discipline for the sincere and earnest mind. Havelock Ellis has pointed out this aspect of adolescent doubt in words somewhat exaggerated, to be sure, yet well worth repetition. " The man who has never wrested with and overcome his early faith, the faith that he was brought with and that yet is not his own, has missed not only a moral but an intellectual discipline. The absence of that discipline may mar a man for life and render all his work in the world ineffective. He has missed a training in criticism, in analysis, in open-minded-ness, in the resolutely impersonal treatment of personal problems, which no other training can compensate." [12]

The great cause for adolescent doubt is the inner discord roused by some newly discovered fact which fails to harmonize with beliefs previously accepted and revered. I have called it an inner discord, and by that I mean to emphasize the emotional as well as the intellectual nature of the experience. The young man is often very rationalistic, but the peculiar nature of his religious doubts is not to be explained merely by an intellectual apprehension of logical inconsistencies. The youth who has been brought up with no reverence or love for a religious belief may become as skeptical as you like yet never know the intense and painful upheaval of " adolescent doubt." The doubt experience here in question is something very different from intellectual denial or intellectual uncertainty. It involves on the one hand a dearly loved and highly prized faith, and on the other a very real though possibly vaguely defined loyalty to

[11] P. 234.

[12] " Science and Mysticism," *Atlantic* for June, 1913, p. 778.

truth. The will to believe is rather too sophisticated (or timid) a doctrine for most earnest youths, and thus they lack the refuge to which their elders often flee for peace. Hence when the new studies of their high school and college days are found inconsistent with the religion of their childhood, or when their growing sense of justice or goodness or reality makes some hitherto reverenced dogma seem unworthy or absurd, or when religious people previously respected are found living evil lives, or when one's faith in prayer is shaken by the failure to get an answer which childhood's training had led one to expect — in any or all of these cases the gates of doubt are opened, and often the doubt of one thing leads to doubting all.

A second great cause for doubt is probably to be found in various obscure physical conditions which have little enough to do with intellectual matters. Especially is this true of girls. Many of the female respondents to questionnaires on this subject seem to have doubted nothing in particular but simply "everything." Their "doubt" is an expression not of intellectual questioning but of an emotional disturbance which is merely a part of the storm and stress upheaval. It is the exceptional young woman whose doubts are of a serious and intellectual nature. As Starbuck puts it, "Men are more apt to have doubts without storm and stress, while women are more apt to undergo a ferment of feeling in the absence of doubt. . . . That is, one might say that adolescence is for women primarily a period of storm and stress, while for men it is in the highest sense a period of doubt." [13]

The conventions of theology which have been so influential in inducing "conviction of sin" have done much less to encourage doubt. Yet they have done something, and the conventional notions of the public in general, especially in the last thirty or forty years, have had a considerable influence in spreading among the young an expectation of doubt. This was not always so. The youth of the Middle Ages as a rule was not expected to go through a period of doubt. But to-day things have changed. Youthful skepticism is one of the natural products of our age, and this fact has been advertised in sermons, theological treatises, popular novels, and learned works on the

[13] P. 241.

psychology of religion, till everyone knows it. Unquestionably doubt is natural and inevitable for a certain conspicuous number of our young men, and this fact being known acts as a stimulus to doubt upon a number of others who might never have realized that they were skeptical if they had not known that they were expected to be. Thus social conventions extend a perfectly natural phenomenon beyond its natural boundaries. Just how important this influence is there is no means of telling, but I have little question that with many a young man of the less serious sort doubt is largely imitative, and that in many of the genuine and spontaneous cases it appears earlier and is probably more violent because of the auto-suggestion and hetero-suggestion on the subject. Others are watching to see the youth go through a period of strain and he is watching himself to see it come, so it comes. The psychological mechanism involved is not essentially different from that involved in reading a popular medical book of " symptoms," and discovering that one has all the diseases described. It would probably have been instructive had some circulator of a questionnaire in the early nineties calculated the rise in the curve of adolescent doubt following the publication of "Robert Elsmere." That was twenty-five years ago, and since then "Robert Elsmere" has been followed by a large family of spiritual children who have not lived in vain.— Note, for example, the conventional tone of the following, which I take from a thesis of one of my students: " A college youth passes through a wretched period of doubt and disbelief, he falters, the old dogmas seem mere rubbish — he sees the folly of it all, yet he yearns after the old, the grand, the awe-inspiring," etc., etc.

I would not be understood as denying the reality and intensity and spontaneity of doubt in the mind of many an earnest youth, but I do believe that the expectation of it has much to do with the rise of a superficial kind of doubt in many a less earnest mind, and also that the phenomenon of adolescent doubt is not nearly so wide-spread as a great deal of the literature on the subject would have us believe. So far as I can discover, the majority of the students in my college classes have passed through none of the painful skeptical experiences so commonly pictured as normal, and there is of course every reason to suppose that youths outside of college are even less troubled with religious doubts than are those who have a college education.

When the emotional and intellectual and moral turmoil of adolescence are over, the young man or woman settles down, somewhere in the middle twenties, into the relatively stable condition of mature life. Not that struggles and doubts and changes are forever past; but the doubts, if they come, are of a more purely intellectual nature, the struggles seem, as a rule, less intense and much less important. One's theology may, and often does, undergo considerable alteration in these mature years; but after thirty one's *attitude* toward the Determiner of Destiny is pretty well settled. The quieting of the emotional life, and the change from the romantic, imaginative viewpoint of youth to the more classical preferences and the practical tendencies of middle age have their effect upon the mystical as well as upon the turbulent side of the individual's religion. With some of the greater mystics, to be sure, who made a life business of cultivating the ecstasy, the acme was not reached until youth was well past.[14] But with the rank and file of slightly mystical individuals, who make no systematic attempt at the cultivation of their religious feelings, the approach of middle life tends to calm the religious emotions and to transform religious romanticism into something much more quiet and in itself less absorbing. The acme of the mystical tendency toward violent emotion is probably reached with most people by twenty-two or thereabouts, and soon thereafter begins to decline, getting itself translated into calmer, more diffused and steadier feeling and into active practice. Ignorance of the fact that this is the normal course of religious development is often a cause of surprise and depression. Many a religious young man or woman between twenty-five and thirty feels a sense of sadness and even of self-accusation on noticing this partial dying out of the more intense and emotional mysticism of his younger days, as though he were travelling ever farther from the East, and beholding the vision splendid " fade into the common light of day." But while religious feeling should never and probably need never completely die out, it is normal and proper that it should be less intense and less recurrent in the

14 St. Tersea, e.g., had her first great ecstasy at 43.

hardworking years that are ahead.   Youth is the time for hailing the vision and coming to love the light; the religious task of the great middle years is to live and act in the light that has been seen.   The chapters that are to follow will be devoted chiefly to the religion of mature life in its varied aspects; hence this subject need not detain us here.

As maturity sinks imperceptibly into age, many, perhaps most, of the interests of active life begin to lose their hold upon the mind.   But religion seldom loses its hold.   Nearly all those who have ever been religious remain so to the end. There are several fairly obvious reasons for this.   In the first place it is undoubtedly one aspect of the familiar fact that the earliest faculties, interests, and memories survive the longest. Those brain centers which are the last to be built up in the course of education are the first to be broken down when the decline of approaching senility begins.   And the old man who forgets the events of yesterday in recalling the stories of his childhood, loses interest in the achievements of science and forgets its facts, but clings to those views and hopes which he learned at his mother's knee.   The weakening of the critical faculty, moreover, and the loss of ability to assimilate new ideas, makes the elderly mind less open to the subtle influences of the skeptical spirit, which in middle life as well as in adolescence is one of the greatest foes of established religious belief.   The old faith thus comes to be cherished as a matter of course and never any longer questioned.   Moreover, quite aside from these quasi-physiological reasons, the elderly individual, conscious that death cannot be very far off, finds his religious faith growing in value to him as most of life's other interests decline, and he deliberately clings to it as the most precious of all his possessions. Thus around his religion he finds clustering all the lively impressions and the pleasant pictures of his childhood, and all his hopes and longings for the mysterious Beyond.   So religion becomes the storehouse of the values of the Past and of the Future, and stands to him for life itself.   It is not strange, therefore, that he should cling to it with increasing tenacity as his one really important possession, the surety of his only lasting hope, amid the downfall or gradual crumbling away of nearly everything else.

In looking back over the life history of the individual's religion from birth to death, one is struck by its amazing elasticity and adaptability. The child's religion, the youth's, the religion of maturity, the religion of age — how widely they differ, yet how genuine, how intense and serviceable each in its own place is! There is hardly an aspect of our changing life with which religion does not come into touch and which it may not bless and consecrate. The two most elaborately complete of the historical religions — Roman Catholicism and Hinduism — have expressed in external institutions this inner fact of the parallelism of religion with life itself. Confirmation, Holy Communion, Marriage or Holy Orders, Extreme Unction, and Burial in the Catholic practice, and the various solemnities of the Hindu Dharma beginning at conception, and, in theory at least, never ending so long as a male descendant of the family survives to offer the ancestral *shraddha* — these are but practical applications and noble symbols of the fact that religion is almost as many-sided and inclusive as life. When we come to this realization, how pitifully narrow and unaccountably blind seem the various attempts that are always being made by enthusiastic and scholarly doctrinaires to deduce the whole of religion from some single human influence!

CHAPTER VII

TWO TYPES OF CONVERSION

IT may seem strange that in an entire chapter on adolescence not a word should have been said concerning that most striking of adolescent religious phenomena, conversion. I hasten, therefore, to reassure the reader that the omission was due to no lack of realization of the importance of conversion but rather to a desire to treat so important a subject more adequately than was possible within the limits of a chapter devoted primarily to something else; although it is only frank to add that I was also influenced by the conviction that violent and sudden conversion has played an altogether exaggerated rôle in the descriptions of the adolescent religious life as given by most writers on the subject, and that the reader would, therefore, carry away a truer conception of adolescence if the conversion experience, whether sudden or gradual, should be reserved for a separate chapter.

In one sense, indeed, the whole moral and religious process of the adolescent period may well be called conversion. Early in the last chapter the statement was made that the great task of the adolescent was to grow out of thinghood into selfhood. Now the essential element in conversion is nothing else than this new birth. In the whole history of ethical discussion there is no saying more full of insight into the nature of the moral life than those words of Jesus, " Ye must be born again." The physical birth is not a moral birth. The child comes into the world a little animal, and for several years he remains hardly more than a psychological thing. His impelling motives are still chiefly his unmodified and uncontrolled instincts, which play upon him and dominate his life. In fact one can hardly say that there is any " he," any self there to be dominated. And the great task of his youth consists in the formation of a true self, which shall be the master and not the tool of his instincts and impulses. If he is to be a full-rounded human being he must " put off the old man " and put on the new. In short he must become a moral self.

Whatever may be our views of the metaphysical or the psychological nature of the self, there will, I think, be little disagreement if for the purposes of our present discussion I define the moral self as a group of powers united in the service of a harmonious system of purposes.[1] A moral self, as distinguished from an animal, a child, or a psychological specimen, is not merely the mechanical toy of an external environment or an inherited group of instincts, but is self-guided in the sense that its activity is, at least in part, determined by purposes or ideals. The establishment of fairly settled purposes is therefore the first step in the achievement of moral personality. But purposes may and often do conflict with each other quite as much as with temporary gusts of passion and impulse. Hence the other great step in self-making is the victory of one group of harmonious purposes over all others, and the complete subordination of everything else in life to these best-loved ends. This victory will have all degrees of finality; with none of us human beings is it ever absolutely complete. But the measure of a man's moral selfhood is exactly the degree of this victory.

Now as I understand it, the essential thing about conversion is just the unification of character, the achievement of a new self, which I have been describing. The process may have many by-products of an emotional nature, it may express itself in varying intellectual terms, it may be gradual or seemingly sudden, but the really important and the only essential part of it is just this new birth by which a man ceases to be a mere psychological thing or a divided self and becomes a unified being with a definite direction under the guidance of a group of consistent and harmonious purposes or ideals.

This new birth involves the whole man. It is, indeed, primarily a moral matter, but that does not mean that it is a matter of " will " as distinct from emotion or thought. Psychology is unable to find any such thing as " pure " will.

[1] A similar though somewhat different view of the self will be found in Taylor's " Metaphysics," Book IV, Chap. 3; Royce's " The World and the Individual," Vol. II, Lecture VI.

It is simply impossible for the " divided self " — the man torn between conflicting loves — to bring unity into his life by merely saying, Go to, now, I choose this set of purposes and give up the others. Long continued determination of this sort must indeed have its effect, but before the man can really will one set of ends in preference to the other he must have already come to love them best. Thus willing involves feeling as a very part of itself. Before the new ideals come to unify and dominate the life they must be *accepted* and *loved;* they can subjugate the old purposes and passions only by a change of emotional values. This done, " will " (however one may interpret that term) may reinforce the new ideals by constant control of the attention. Nor is the intellectual side of the process to be neglected, though it is frankly the least noticeable of the three. In most cases it seems to play but a negative part; yet it always holds some degree of veto power; and in many individuals that combination of the emotional and intellectual which we call the love of truth forms the very central core around which the new character is crystallized and which guides the entire process of conversion.[2]

Adolescence, as I have said, is the normal period for this re-formation of the individual's life, though if the task has not been done then it may sometimes be achieved later on, and occasionally a fairly unified self may be overthrown and replaced by a new combination of impelling and harmonious ideals. With most young people the process goes on so gradually as to be largely unconscious. The new ideals grow rather silently, at times break out into somewhat noisy conflict with each other and with the more primitive powers of unmodified impulse, but in the main they win their victories by the subtle modification of values, and by the end of the adolescent period the young man finds himself a fairly unified person. Not always is this the case. Peculiarities of temperament[3]

---

[2] Cf. G. Truc's analysis of the " state of grace," as a harmony of the intellectual and emotional factors.—" La Grâce " (Paris, Alcan: 1918), Chap. II.

[3] James's well-known distinction between the " healthy-minded " and the " sick soul " is here in point. The former grows into that unity of feeling and of will which we have been considering by a peaceful and imperceptible

or unfortunate environmental conditions may make the conscious struggles sharper or the final victory more sudden and dramatic. But whether the change be spectacular or come like the Kingdom of Heaven, " without observation," the essential thing in it is the same: the " natural man " is replaced by the " new creature."

The emotional turmoil of adolescence described in the last chapter is of course an outcropping or expression and sometimes a genuine part of the conversion process. For, as indicated above, though conversion is often so gradual as to be almost imperceptible, it may rise into consciousness in the form of a long and painful struggle or a short, sharp and sudden crisis or transformation. It is these visible and striking forms of the new birth that commonly go by the name conversion. And though from the ethical point of view they surely are of no greater importance than is the quieter form of self-unification, they unquestionably do possess great psychological interest and for many reasons are worthy of close study.

The best way to study conversion is to go directly to typical examples of it and let them speak for themselves, before

process: it is to him the most natural thing in the world. The sick soul, on the contrary, is painfully conscious of division and conflict. (See the " Varieties," Lectures IV–VIII inclusive.) A similar distinction is that made by Höffding between the " *expansive* " and " *discordant* " natures. The latter are " tortured by the opposition offered within their own breasts to their ideal, the effect of which is heightened by the close proximity of the ideal." The expansive natures feel no such inner struggle and division. Another distinction made by Höffding is that between what he names the " affective " and the " continuous " types. " Some natures are inclined to vehement fermentation. The transitions from one state to another, or one period of life to another, take place for the most part by sudden crises and visible leaps. They differ from the discordant natures already described in that the oppositions succeed one another in time, while with the discordant ones the conflicting tendencies are contemporaneous . . . Where development proceeds by leaps, and where there is a tendency to emotional states, we get a type which might be called the *affective*. The peculiarity of other natures causes their development to proceed by small steps, and hence it presents the character of continuity. The life of feeling and will has, in such cases, a more divided, more interior character, while in affective natures there are momentary concentrations, and they are characterized by the stamp of violence rather than of inwardness. The *continuous* type (as we will call this type), has a certain kinship with the expansive type." (" Philosophy of Religion," pp. 284–288.)

consulting the opinions of others, whether theological or psychological, on the interpretation of the phenomena. The cases I have chosen to present first of all are from fields as far removed as possible from our usual sources of information, and are only slightly or not at all influenced by any preconceived notions derived from Christian theology. Professor James pointed out in his " Varieties " that falling in love and falling out of love are experiences in many ways psychologically parallel to conversion; and he has also shown that " counter-conversion " [4] — or the sudden and emotional turning away from Christianity and religion — may follow much the same psychological course as the conventional conversion experience. The first case I shall cite is of a sort that might be called counter-conversion. It is, namely, the conversion of the Italian philosopher Roberto Ardigo,— a conversion away from a traditional authoritative theology to a new unification of character brought about by an all-dominating love of truth. Ardigo had from birth a reflective and also a religious nature, and was brought up in orthodox Catholic surroundings and became a priest,— in fact was appointed prebendary of Mantua Cathedral. At times throughout his youth doubts as to the truth of the teachings of the Church had presented themselves to his mind, but had resolutely been put aside. He now devoted himself more closely than ever to the study of the scholastic philosophy and also to science, convinced that the two were perfectly consistent, and eager to champion Catholicism against Protestant and other attacks. But he came to perceive that scholasticism and science took different ways and there ensued a struggle of two loyalties combined with a gradual process of thinking his way out, which finally resulted in a rather sudden discovery that his scientific ideas had already definitely conquered his theological views and his loyalty to the Church. In his own words:

" I dedicated myself heart and soul to theology — as well as to the study of natural science and of philosophy, to which I have been ever true — especially to the dogmatic and apologetic. I collected for myself a library of the Old Fathers and

[4] Cf. the " Varieties," pp. 176–179.

the theologians, devoting the best of my young years to their study, especially that of St. Thomas. At length I wrote and published a book on Confession, directed against the Protestants. But the outcome of my study was wholly contrary to its aspiration and expectation. Gradually it came to a point at which the doubt, which had already presented itself to me from all sides in my earlier years, against which I had struggled with unceasing reflection and study, and which I had long regarded as conquered, cropped up unopposed. And, one fine day, to my immense astonishment, it stepped forward as a definite conviction and an incontestible certainty. Marvelous! Up to that day I had devoted myself to the effort to remain firm in my old religious beliefs, and yet, within me, and without my knowing it, the Positivist system had become freely developed in the midst of the system of religious ideas which was the fruit of an effort so great and so protracted. The new system I found, to my very great amazement, already complete, and unshakably settled in my mind. At that moment I had observed, as I sat on a stone under a shrub in the garden which I had laid out near my canonical residence, how my last reflections had snapped the last thread that still held me bound to belief. Now it suddenly came to me, as though I had never in my life believed, and had never done otherwise than study, to develop the purely scientific tendency in myself. This arose, as I believe, out of the zeal with which I had sought to experience as far as possible all the conflicting grounds of religion, to be able to believe on good security, and to defend my belief against all attacks." [5]

Ardigo's conversion was complete and permanent, and he remained to the end of his life an ardent servant of the scientific ideal, although at times it cost him considerable sacrifice. The reader will note, without lengthy comment of mine, how completely this case parallels the more familiar religious type of conversion. The process was gradual, the discovery of its finished work sudden, the unification of character brought about was complete. The intellectual factor was, to be sure, more prominent in Ardigo's case than in the common type of

[5] Quoted by Höffding in his "Modern Philosophers" (London, Macmillan: 1915), pp. 42–43.

conversion, yet even here the process was by no means one of mere intellectual illumination.

That conversion is a natural human phenomenon, independent alike of supernatural interference and of theological prepossession, is evident from Ardigo's experience. This fact, however, will come out more distinctly if we turn from Christendom altogether and consider two rather illuminating cases of conversion furnished us by Hinduism,[6] — to both of which reference was made in the preceding chapter.

[6] Examples of conversion might be cited from many other religions. To the Greeks, for instance, it was a well known experience. Thus Plutarch cites a case of sudden conversion in the story of Thespesius of Soli, whose remarkable dream of the punishment of the wicked in the next world is said to have wrought in him so radical a revaluing of all values that the whole course of his life was altered ("On the Delay of the Divine Justice," section 22). If Thespesius be a fictitious character, the story is all the better evidence of the belief of the ancients in sudden conversion. During Nero's century, in fact, and later, conversion had a prominent place in the belief and experience of earnest religious pagans, such as Seneca, Apollonius of Tyana, etc. (See Dill's "Roman Society from Nero to Marcus Aurelius," London, Macmillan: 1905; Book III, Chaps. I and II.) In the February, 1910, number of the *Zeitschrift für Religionspsychologie*, Professor Heidel cites several ancient cases of what seems to be conversion — from the Mysteries of Eleusis, from the philosophic schools, and from the Mithra cult. ("*Die Bekehrung in klassischen Altertum*," loc. cit., Vol. III, pp. 377–402.) The Moslem Sufis very early recognized and even systematized the phenomenon of conversion, (Nicholson, "The Mystics of Islam," London, Bell: 1914; pp. 30–32). Al Ghazzali, the greatest of the Moslem mystics, had a marked conversion experience, lasting through many years. From India also several examples of conversion might be cited besides the two described in the text. Gautama's six years of search and struggle, culminating in the famous victory under the Bo tree, with its subsequent unbroken peace, is too mythical in its details to warrant close examination here, yet the large outlines of the story are so true to the usual course of human nature in the conversion process that they gain new credibility from modern psychology. The conversion of Chaitanya, the famous Apostle of Krishna to the Bengalese, might well repay close study, — a conversion resembling in many ways that of St. Francis. Chaitanya, indeed, had always been interested in philosophy, but his religion was of a relatively cold, intellectual sort, and he was filled with the pride of learning. On a pilgrimage to Gaya he met a Krishna devotee who impressed him very deeply, and finally succeeded in converting him to *bhakti*, — the emotional devotion to the personal Krishna. The change in Chaitanya's character and his life purpose was even more complete than it was sudden, and he became for the rest of his days the inspired and ecstatic worshiper and preacher and (as his disciples believed) the incarnation of the personal deity whom he had come to love. There are several lives of

The first of these is that of Ramakrishna, the famous Bengalee saint and mystic and the founder of the Order which bears his name. Ramakrishna was born in 1833, and from boyhood evinced that intense religious nature which characterized him through life. He belonged to a poor but very high-caste Brahmin family, and pride of birth, mingled with an unyielding religious orthodoxy, was impressed upon him through all his boyhood and youth. His psychopathic disposition was also early in evidence. We have a story of his falling into a trance at the sight of a flock of white cranes against a blue sky, when he was a lad of ten or eleven. His great interest in religion brought him at the age of twenty to a new temple of Kali at Daksineshvara, at which his elder brother was acting as priest. But though he frequented the place he persistently refused to accept any cooked food within the temple precincts because the founder of the temple was a Shudra woman. I mention this because his religious pride of caste seems to have been one of the most difficult things for him to overcome in his subsequent conversion.

The first stage in Ramakrishna's conversion dates from the time when he began to frequent the shrine of Kali. The thought of the Mother Goddess got hold of his imagination and his emotions and mastered his attention to the exclusion of everything else. " He now began to look upon the image of Kali as his mother, and the mother of the universe. He believed it to be living and breathing and taking food from his hand. After the regular forms of worship he would sit there for hours and hours, singing hymns and talking and praying to her as a child to his mother, till he lost all consciousness of the outward world. Sometimes he would weep for hours, and would not be comforted, because he could not

Chaitanya, one of the most available of which is Professor Sarkar's translation of the " Chaitanya-charit-amrita." (Calcutta, Sarkar and Sons: 1913.) Chaitanya was born in 1485, and converted at about 22. For the conversion of Nichiren, the reformer of Japanese Buddhism of the 13th Century, see Anesaki, " Nichiren, the Buddhist Prophet," (Harvard University Press: 1916), Chap. II. For a description of the process of conversion in Mahayana Buddhism, as portrayed in the life of the ideal Bodhisattva, see Suzuki, " Outlines of Mahayana Buddhism" (London, Luzac: 1907), p. 313 f.

see his mother as perfectly as he wished." [7]   This sense of unsatisfied religious longing, connected evidently with a recognition of his own incompleteness, continued for years. " His
whole soul, as it were, melted into one flood of tears, and he
appealed to the Goddess to have mercy on him and reveal herself to him.   No mother ever shed such burning tears over the
death-bed of her only child.   Crowds assembled round him
and tried to console him, when the blowing of the conch-shells
proclaimed the death of another day, and he gave vent to his
sorrow, saying, ' Mother, oh my mother, another day has gone
and still I have not found thee.' " [8]   Visions of the goddess
were granted him at this time but though they brought some
degree of calm they were far from satisfying his longing.   The
trouble under which he was suffering was far too inward for
any visions to allay.

Max Müller's account, drawn as it is from the descriptions of the mystic's disciples, is here insufficient to enable
us to make out in detail the exact nature of Ramakrishna's
spiritual malady, but it is plain that it was some form
of what James calls the " divided self."   In fact two points
upon which Ramakrishna was as yet lacking in the inner
unity of perfect moral selfhood come out plainly enough
in the account (though seemingly without the intention of the
recounters) : he still retained something of the old Brahmin
pride of birth, and something (though surely very little) of
the common human love of things.   From both of these he
felt it absolutely essential that he should free himself; and
it is interesting to note that his method was that of earnest
and direct attack, believing, evidently that God helps those
who help themselves.   Recounting these struggles, in later
years, he said, " Sometimes I used to go to the closets of the
servants and sweepers [the lowest caste in India] and clean
them with my own hands, and prayed, ' Mother! destroy in
me all idea that I am great, and that I am a Brahmin, and
that they are low and pariahs; for who are they but Thou in

[7] Max Müller, " The Life and Sayings of Ramakrishna," p. 36.   Most of
my account of this phase of Ramakrishna's life is taken from this book.
[8] Op. cit., p. 38.

so many forms?' Sometimes I would sit by the Ganges with
some gold and silver coins and a heap of rubbish by my side,
and taking some coins in my right hand and a handful of rubbish in my left, I would tell my soul, 'My soul! this is what
the world calls money. It has the power of doing all that
the world calls great, but it can never help thee to realize the
ever existent knowledge and bliss, the Brahman. Regard it
therefore as rubbish!' Then mixing the coins and the rubbish in my hands, while repeating all the time, 'money is
rubbish, money is rubbish!' I lost all perception of difference
between the two in my mind, and threw them both into the
Ganges." [9]

On one other thing besides Brahmin pride and love of possession Ramakrishna felt himself still a divided self, although
one would gain no hint of this from the accounts that have
emanated from his disciples. I have it on the authority of
a prominent and very well-informed Indian gentleman, Mr.
Bipin Chandra Pal of Calcutta, that through these years of
adolescent storm and stress, Ramakrishna was greatly troubled
by the solicitations of the flesh, and, though he never yielded
to them, it cost him an intense struggle to overcome them. In
three particulars, then, that can be clearly made out Ramakrishna found his ideal self in conflict with "the old Adam,"
and the struggle between the two was psychologically not unlike that of many a Christian saint. It should be added, however, that with him the emphasis of conscious attention seems
always to have been placed upon the ideal toward which he
was striving rather than upon the old and lower self which he
was seeking to outgrow. There was little if any "conviction
of sin" in Ramakrishna's storm and stress. In later years
he expostulated with his friend Keshab Chunder Sen for having adopted into the Brahmo Samaj the Christian custom of
centering the attention upon sin,— a custom which he regarded
as very detrimental to spiritual growth. "Someone," he said
to Keshab, "gave me a book of the Christians. I asked him
to read it to me. In it there was only one theme — sin and
sin, from the beginning to the end. The fool who repeats

9 Op. cit., p. 42.

again and again, 'I am bound, I am bound,' remains in bondage. He who repeats day and night, 'I am a sinner, I am a sinner,' becomes a sinner indeed." [10]

Ramakrishna's storm and stress lasted for twelve years. Looking back at this period later on in life he said that " a great religious tornado, as it were, raged within him during these years and made everything topsy-turvy." " In his despair he cried out, ' Mother, oh my mother, is this the result of calling upon thee and believing in thee?' And anon a sweet voice would come and a sweet smiling face, and say, ' My son, how can you hope to realize the highest truth unless you give up the love of your body and of your little self?' " [11] The thought of " the little self," and the love of it were, in his opinion, the greatest evils in the way of complete religious conversion. In later years he taught his disciples: " The sense of ' I ' in us is the greatest obstacle in the path of God-vision. It covers the Truth. When ' I ' is dead, all trouble ceases." [12] This view, which formed the burden of much of his preaching, was evidently the outcome of his own experience during the long years of struggle. But at length the victory was won,— not by any sudden insight or reformation, but by a gradual process, in which both increased self-control, intellectual illumination, and (most important of all) an absolute unification of values, played important and mutually helpful parts. [13] The moral and intellectual and emotional unification thus attained, together with the peace and joy that flowed from it, were now permanent. The flesh no longer felt any incitements to insurrection, love of things and Brahmin pride were gone for ever. He lived to the end of his days in complete poverty, and in never failing intuition of the presence of God in low and high, in himself and in everything. " I have now come to a stage of realization," he said toward the close of his life, " in which I see that God is walking in

---

[10] " The Gospel of Ramakrishna," pp. 159–60.

[11] Max Müller, op. cit., p. 41.

[12] " Gospel of Ramakrishna," p. 51.

[13] The intellectual element in his conversion came largely from the influence of two traveling garus, who gave him new insight into Indian philosophy. The manner in which the intellectual coöperated with the emotional in Ramakrishna's conversion recalls the similar case of Ardigo.

every human form and manifesting Himself alike through the saint and the sinner, the virtuous and the vicious.   Therefore when I meet different people I say to myself: ' God in the form of the saint, God in the form of the sinner, God in the form of the unrighteous and God in the form of the righteous!'   He who has attained to such realization goes beyond good and evil, above virtue and vice, and realizes that the Divine is working everywhere." [14]

The other conversion case which I take from India is far less striking, but it has the one advantage of being described for us by the subject himself.   I refer to Maharshi Devendranath Tagore, the father of the famous Bengalee poet. Devendranath was brought up in a rich and orthodox Bengalee family which, though in some ways liberal, clung devoutly to the worship of Kali and the use of images.   Most of his childhood's religious instruction and inspiration came from his grandmother, a deeply religious and devout worshiper of Kali and Vishnu.   This rather primitive religion seems to have sufficed him until his grandmother's death, when he was eighteen.   His love for her was very great and he spent with her the three days that the old lady took to die, by the side of the Ganges.   The impression made upon his deep and sensitive nature was very considerable and resulted in what Starbuck would call " spontaneous awakening."   As the attendants were singing a hymn in the ears of the dying woman, on her last night, after he had left her, the solemn strains awakened within him a new experience.   " The sounds," he tells us, in his Autobiography, " reached my ears faintly, borne on the night wind; at this opportune moment a strange sense of the unreality of all things suddenly entered my mind.   I was as if no longer the same man.   A strong aversion to wealth arose within me.   The coarse bamboo mat on which I sat seemed to be my fitting seat, carpets and costly spreadings seemed hateful; in my mind was awakened a joy unfelt before. . . . Up to that time I had been plunged in the lap of luxury and pleasure.   I had never sought after spiritual

14 " Gospel of Ramakrishna," p. 88.   I should add that Ramakrishna gave up all the remainder of his life, after his conversion, to preaching and teaching, and that his influence seems to have been a great force for righteousness and true religion.

truths. What was religion, what was God? I knew nothing, had learned nothing. My mind could scarcely contain
the unworldly joy, so simple and natural, which I experienced
at the burning ghat. Language is weak in every way; how
can I make others understand the joy I felt? It was a spontaneous delight, to which nobody can attain by argument or
logic." [15]

The new-found delight soon passed. The next few days
were filled with the excitement of the grandmother's funeral,
and when this was over, young Tagore sought to recover the
strange joy which had come to him so mysteriously. But it
would not return. "At this time," he writes, "the state of
my mind was one of continued despondency and indifference
to the world. On that night the indifference had been coupled
with delight. Now, in the absence of that delight, a deep
gloom settled on my mind. I longed for a repetition of that
ecstatic feeling. I lost all interest in everything else." [16]

Tagore now entered upon a period of depression and at times
almost of despair, in which emotional and intellectual factors were inextricably interwoven. He was very wretched,
but not with any sense of sin. The thought that he himself
was guilty seems never to have entered his mind. He was
ignorant,— that was the depressing fact. He wanted insight,
he wanted relief from the weary weight of all this unintelligible world. And he wanted a renewal of that strange joy
which for a moment had given him a taste of a new kind of
being. He tried earnestly to free himself from his depression,
not by inducing pleasant emotions but by pondering on the
mystery of things, and searching for the truth. The polytheistic and idolatrous religion of the family had little for
him, and no one helped him to anything better. "I knew not
where to turn for solace," he writes. "Sometimes lying on
a sofa and pondering over problems about God, I used to become so absent minded that I did not know when I had got
up from my couch and taken my meals and lain down again.
I used to feel as if I had been lying there all the time. I

[15] "Autobiography of Maharshi Devendranath Tagore." Translated from
the Bengalee by Satyendranath Tagore, p. 3.
[16] Op. cit., p. 4.

would go alone to the Botanical Gardens in the middle of the day, whenever I got a chance. It was a very secluded, solitary spot. I used to take my seat on a tombstone in the middle of the gardens. Great grief was in my heart. Darkness was all around me. The temptations of the world had ceased but the sense of God was no nearer,— earthly and heavenly happiness were alike withdrawn. Life was dreary, the world was like a graveyard. I found happiness in nothing, peace in nothing. The rays of the midday sun seemed to me black. . . . At that time this song suddenly broke from my lips: 'Vain, oh vain is the light of day, without knowledge all is dark as night.' This was my first song. I used to sing it out loud sitting alone on the tombstone." [17]

Young Tagore's search was, therefore, largely an intellectual one, and I am glad to have another example besides that of Ardigo to emphasize an element in the conversion experience usually quite neglected. But it would be a great mistake to regard Tagore's search as purely intellectual. It was his heart more than his head that felt unsatisfied. He was looking for — or waiting for — a view of God and of human destiny that should both satisfy the demands of an increasingly critical intellect and also appeal so strongly to his emotional nature as to rouse all his slumbering enthusiasms and loyalties. The universe seemed barren to him and life empty and worthless. What he needed chiefly was not merely an answer to intellectual puzzles, and much less a succession of pleasing and peaceful feeling states, but a new and intense value, a pearl of great price, around which he might unify his life and by the aid by which he might realize his moral self. Tagore cannot be described as a divided self, as are so many subjects of conversion; but he lacked the unity of developed moral selfhood because he had as yet found nothing big enough to appeal to his big nature. Life was stale, flat, unprofitable. His disposition might be described as essentially *metaphysical*: his interests were cosmic, and so long as the cosmos seemed to him either dark or unworthy he must continue to be not only unhappy but irresolute, inactive, with dissipated and unused powers, and lacking in that concentration of interest

[17] P. 7.

and purpose which is necessary for a fully developed moral self. What he needed was a new center of loyalty; and he could be utterly loyal to nothing short of an all-inclusive yet spiritual God.

He found Him at last. As in so many conversion cases, the process was gradual and the final consummation sudden. The process of thinking out the world riddle, with some help from English philosophical books and from childish memories of Ram Mohun Roy, continued about four years without bringing any noticeable satisfaction. Considerable intellectual insight indeed was gained, and the young thinker resolutely gave up all sanctioning of idolatrous worship, and became convinced, so far as his intellect was concerned, of the probability of the existence of one God. More, therefore, had probably been accomplished below the surface than he himself knew. Gradually the emotional forces of his nature were being prepared for the complete unification and satisfaction that seem now, as we look upon the case, to have been almost inevitable for a nature such as his. The needed touch which brought the spiritual forces at last into a state of stable equilibrium and made evident upon the surface what for so long had been going on in the depths, came about (as in the case of St. Augustine [18]) by what most of us would call a mere chance. But however we may interpret events of this sort, the pious souls who experience them — the Augustines and Tagores — inevitably see in them the hand of God. Let Devendranath himself describe what occurred:

" When I was in this depressed state of mind, one day all of a sudden I saw a page from some Sanskrit book flutter past me. Out of curosity I picked it up, but found I could understand nothing of what was written on it." Taking it to a learned Sanskrit scholar, he got it translated. It was a page from one of the old Upanishads, the most sacred and authoritative of the philosophical books of India, and it expounded the omnipresence of the Divine and its unity with the human spirit. " When I learned the explanation," Tagore continues, " nectar from paradise streamed down upon me. I had been eager to receive a sympathetic response from men, now a di-

[18] See the Confessions, Book VIII, Chap. 12.

vine voice had descended from heaven to respond to my heart of hearts, and my longing was satisfied. I wanted to see God everywhere, and I found just what I wanted. I had never heard my inmost thoughts expressed like this anywhere else. Could men give any such response? The very mercy of God Himself descended into my heart, therefore I understood the deep significance of the words. Oh what words were these that struck my ears! Enjoy that which He has given unto thee! What is it that He has given? He has given Himself. Enjoy that untold treasure, leave everything else and enjoy that supreme treasure. Cleave unto Him alone and give up all else. Blessed beyond measure is he who cleaves unto Him alone. This tells me that which I have long desired.

" The keenness of my sorrow had lain with this, that I was dead to all happiness, earthly or divine: I could take no delight in the things of this world. I could feel no joy in God. But when the Divine voice declared that I should renounce all desire of worldly pleasure and take my delight in God alone, I obtained what I had wished for, and was utterly flooded with joy. It was not the dictum of my own poor intellect, it was the word of God Himself. Glory be to that *Rishi* in whose heart this truth was first revealed! My faith in God took deep root; in lieu of world pleasure I tasted divine joy. Oh! what a blessed day was that for me — a day of heavenly happiness!" [19]

And this time the happiness and the peace were destined never to be lost. Throughout a long life Devendranath Tagore carried them with him and lived in the light of them. His slumbering loyalties were now enlisted in the cause of spreading the knowledge and the worship of the true God; and life, previously so empty, became full and rich and satisfying. He rejuvenated the moribund Brahmo Samaj and made it a power for righteousness and for religion throughout Bengal; and all who knew him came to recognize in him one of those rare souls who live as in the presence of a spiritual world.

There is nothing peculiar in these Indian cases. They follow lines of development psychologically identical with those traceable in many a Christian conversion. Tagore's case, for

[19] Pp. 14–16.

example, is paralleled in most essentials by Tolstoi's. Like Tagore, Tolstoi found the external and superstitious religion of his childhood and of those about him quite insufficient for his needs. For a time, therefore, (and in this detail he is unlike Tagore) he lived without religion of any sort, putting the ultimate questions out of his mind by a life of excitement and pleasure. But the questions returned, and with them came the sense of the emptiness of life which had so afflicted the young Tagore. " I had moments of perplexity," he writes in his " Confession," " of a stoppage, as it were, of life, as if I did not know how I was to live and what I was to do, and I began to wonder and was a victim of low spirits. These stoppages of life always presented themselves to me with the same questions: ' Why ? and What after ? ' . . . . I became aware that this was not a chance indisposition, but something very serious, and that if all these questions continued to recur, I should have to find an answer to them.

" Before occupying myself with my Samara estate, with the education of my son, with the writing of books, I was bound to know why I did these things. As long as I do not know the reason ' why ' I cannot do anything, I cannot live. . . . I could find no reply. Such questions will not wait: they demand an immediate answer: without one it is impossible to live: but answer there was none.

" I felt that the ground on which I stood was crumbling, that there was nothing for me to stand on, that what I had been living for was nothing, that I had no reason for living. My life had come to a stop. I was able to breathe, to eat, to drink, to sleep, and I could not help breathing, eating, drinking, sleeping, but there was no real life in me because I had not a single desire the fulfillment of which I could feel to be reasonable. . . . The truth was that life was meaningless." [20]

Tolstoi's case can hardly be described as that of a " divided self." No struggle between discordant forces is to be detected in his experience. Rather is his case, like that of Tagore, one in which no center of loyalty capable of arousing his enthusiasms and enlisting his energies had as yet been found. " The truth is that life was meaningless." Two things here are es-

[20] " My Confession," Chaps. 3 and 4.

pecially worthy of note.   Although Tolstoi had previously given himself up for years to a life of dissipation there is no trace in all his five years of depression of anything remotely resembling the " conviction of sin " so prominent in the conventional conversion.   Instead of being fastened upon his past sins, his attention was fixed upon the world problem and was busied searching for a solution.   And this brings us to the second characteristic in Tolstoi's conversion process that I wished to point out,— namely that it was a process of active search, and that the effort he made played at least a very important rôle in the final victory.   As in Tagore's case, the process was in part an intellectual one; and though, indeed, Tolstoi's pondering over the problem was for a long time quite barren, so far as immediate results were concerned, in the end the rational process proved a helpful guide, and — what was more important still — the very effort to think the thing out kept the faculty of effort alive and with it some sparks of courage and self-trust.   In spite of his temporary intellectual conviction that life was naught, in spite of his despair and depression, he kept up the struggle, and the living energy within him,— unaided by any happy chance such as those that brought succor to Augustine and Tagore — together with a new and slowly dawning rational insight, finally and gradually brought him the new center of loyalty which made him over into complete moral selfhood. By consulting his own experience and by watching the simple and happy and successful lives of pious peasants about him who lived by the aid of an unfaltering religious belief, he came to see and to feel — to understand from within — that faith in God was not only defensible but that it alone could give ultimate meaning to life.   In it he therefore found at last something that enlisted all his loyalties, and to the end of his days he lived and worked unperturbed and with unified energies in the light of this apprehension.

The four cases we have considered — one from Roman Catholicism, two from Hinduism, and one from the Russian Church — differ considerably in detail, yet have many important points in common.   For one thing, all four of the men we have studied knew more or less clearly what they wanted and exerted all their energies, in very direct and manly fashion, toward attaining it.   Although in each case the question of life's chief values was the center of the struggle, none of them was satisfied, or would have been satisfied, with any sort of merely emotional state.   They were not seeking for some change in their feelings but for something very much more objective.   And the outcome of the process in each case not only brought the man a new sense of calm and satisfaction,— that to each of them was the smallest part of it; it made him over into a new creature.

From these very intelligible cases of conversion we turn now to a quite different type — the type namely that has served as the conventional model in a large part of Christendom for several centuries.   Probably it would be hard to find two better and at the same time more influential examples of this type than the cases of John Bunyan and David Brainerd.   We are fortunate, moreover, in having both these cases described for us in the words of the subjects themselves.

Bunyan's childhood was passed in the years when English Puritanism was approaching its height,[21] and the pietistic views of those about him concerning sin, damnation and the rest, sank deep into his tender mind.   At the age of nine he was already having dreadful thoughts and still more dreadful dreams of the Day of Judgment and the Torments of Hell. His besetting sin seems to have been swearing, but before long he gave this up — as well as dancing and looking at the church bells in the " Steeple house " and other equally heinous amusements.   He took, moreover, to reading his Bible and discoursing on religion, and came in fact to believe that God was pleased with him.   Then one day, from the discourse of certain pious women to which he listened, he learned that one's own righteousness was worthless and that instead of regarding it as something noble and worth striving for one should " contemn, slight and abhor it as filthy and unsufficient to do any good." [22]   He also learned from these women that a conversion experience was necessary to salvation and that the saved soul had certain emotional experiences which he had never tasted.. " At this,"

[21] He was born in 1628.
[22] See section 37 of Bunyan's " Grace Abounding."

he tells us, " I felt my own heart begin to shake, and mistrust my *condition* to be naught; for I saw that in all my thoughts about Religion and Salvation the new Birth did never enter into my Mind, neither knew I the Comfort of the Word and Prom- ise, nor the Deceitfulness and Treachery of my own wicked Heart. . . . I was greatly affected by their words, both because by them I was convinced that I wanted the true Tokens of a truly Godly Man, and also because by them I was convinced of the happy and blessed Condition of him that was such an one." [23]

With convictions of this sort deep in his heart Bunyan went through many wretched years, seeking for nothing in particu- lar, for he knew of nothing definite for which to seek, striving for nothing in particular, because striving and self-help he had been taught were useless and worse than useless, but chiefly wondering whether he were saved or not and gradually coming to the conclusion that he was probably damned. Salvation, he knew, came by faith; but " faith " did not mean the intellectual acceptance of a doctrine nor anything else that was definite: it meant apparently some kind of mental state and inner assur- ance, of so vague a character that the poor young man was quite at a loss to know whether he had it or not. Forever, he tells us, there was running in his mind the question, " But how if you want Faith indeed? But how can you tell if you have Faith? And besides I saw for certain, if I had it not, I was sure to perish forever." [24]

Thus " the sight and sense and terror of his own wickedness " grew upon him and the dreadful fear lest he were damned. And then came a new fear, namely the fear of losing his fear and his depressing sense of guilt. " For I found that unless guilt of conscience was taken off the right way, that is by the Blood of Christ, a man grew rather worse for the loss of his troubles of Mind than better. Wherefore if my guilt lay hard upon me then I should cry that the blood of Christ might take it off: and if it was going off without it (for the sense of Sin would be sometimes as if it would die, and go quite away) then I would also strive to fetch it upon my heart again." Thus

[23] Sections 39 and 40.
[24] Section 49.

for years Bunyan did his best to cultivate the sense of sin and make it habitual; and with remarkable success.[25]

It would take too long to follow Bunyan through all the ups and downs of his spiritual sickness,— for there were ups as well as downs; all of them due to no act of his but simply matters of unreasoning feeling.   One of these breathing spells lasted for some time, and came about apparently because certain comforting Biblical verses got to running in his head.   Bunyan was all his life subject to auditory obsessions of verses of scripture, and his mood seems to have been more often determined by these than by anything else.   If a comfortable verse came into his mind he would be happy and conclude that he had " Faith " and was saved, until some threatening verse took the place of the pleasant words, whereupon he would fall into the depths of misery and conclude that he was lost.   For the whole struggle with him was subjective to the extreme — a matter of the way he *felt*.   He was a spiritual hypochondriac, always feeling his hedonic pulse.   He was, moreover, extremely suggestible and peculiarly subject to the fascination of the terrible.   The thought how dreadful it would be to say certain words would automatically bring these words and their comrades to his mind; and it was apparently in this that his " temptations " and " sins " chiefly consisted.   It was, in fact, in this way that he fell again — after his one fairly long period of comparative peace — into a fit of despair longer and more dreadful than anything that had preceded it.   He had really persuaded himself that he loved Christ, when the Tempter crept into his mind with the words, " Sell Christ for this, sell Christ for that, sell him! sell him! "   These words, for ever running through his head, became, in fact, a veritable obsession.   " But, to be brief, one morning as I did lie in my bed, I was, as at other times,

[25] Especially was it " the unpardonable sin " that he either thought he had (unwittingly) committed, or else — from the vertiginous fascination of the terrible — felt bound to commit, with no definite notion as to what this sin might be except, apparently that it was somehow to be committed by saying certain words (though what words does not appear). " And in so strong a measure was this temptation upon me that often I have been ready to clap my hand under my chin to hold my mouth from opening, and to that end also I have had thoughts other times to leap with my head downward into some muck-hill hole or other, to keep my mouth from speaking." (Section 103.)

most fiercely assaulted with this temptation, to sell and part with Christ; the wicked suggestion still running in my mind, *Sell him, sell him, sell him, sell him,* as fast as man could speak. Against which also, as at other times, I answered, *No, no, not for thousands, thousands, thousands,* at least twenty times together. But at last, after much striving, even until I was almost out of breath, I felt this thought pass through my heart, *Let him go, if he will!* and I thought also that I felt my heart freely consent thereto. Oh the diligence of Satan! Oh the desperateness of man's heart! Now was the battle won [i. e. by Satan], and down fell I, like a Bird that is shot from the top of a tree, into great guilt and fearful despair. Thus getting out of my Bed I went moping into the field; but God knows with as heavy a heart as a mortal man, I think, could bear; where for the space of two hours I was like a man bereft of life and as now past all recovery and bound over to eternal punishment. And withal that scripture did seize upon my soul, ' Or profane person as Esau who for one morsel of meat sold his birthright; for ye know how that afterward, when he would have inherited the blessing, he was rejected; for he found no place of repentance, though he sought it carefully with tears.' " 26

This state of utter depression lasted for two years, during which Bunyan felt almost continuously the mental sufferings of the damned, being convinced that he had committed the unpardonable sin. Occasionally he would get a little respite through the entrance into his mind of the words of some scriptural verse, such as " The blood of Jesus Christ, His Son, cleanseth us from all sin." But as soon as the verberations of these words died out of his mind the old misery returned; and ever like a refrain, driving out all other thoughts, would come back to him the dreadful words about Esau,— " for he found no place of repentance, though he sought it carefully with tears." 27

26 Sections 139–141.

27 The extremes to which his mental suffering went are to be seen in passages like the following: " Then was I struck into a very great trembling, insomuch that at sometimes I could, for whole days together, feel my very body, as well as my mind, to shake and totter under the sense of the dreadful Judgment of God, that should fall on those that have sinned that most fearful and unpardonable sin. I felt also such a clogging and heat at my stomach, by reason of this my terror, that I was, especially

Poor Bunyan eventually got out of his trouble in the same way he got into it,— that is to say by the obsession of scriptural verses.   The decisive struggle — so far as there was any really decisive struggle — occupied about seven weeks at the close of his two years of " conviction."   Nothing happened, apparently, except that the comforting verses came into his mind more often and stayed longer, and the terrifying ones gradually lost their hypnotic power.   Yet they did not yield to their rivals without many a fierce battle.   " My peace," he writes, " would be in and out, sometimes twenty times a day: Comfort now, and Trouble presently: Peace now, and before I could go a furlong as full of Fear and Guilt as ever heart could hold: and this was not only now and then, but my whole seven weeks of experience; for this about the *sufficiency of Grace,* and that of Esau's parting with his Birthright, would be like a pair of scales within my mind; sometimes one end would be uppermost, and sometimes again the other: according to which would be my peace or trouble." [28]

Peace at last got the better of trouble, as I have said, but the *victory,* if so we may call it, was utterly devoid of moral significance.   Bunyan himself, in fact, had nothing to do with it (which, indeed, according to the received view of conversion seems to be quite the orthodox and proper thing) ; he was merely the passive battle ground between the Esau verse with its allies, and the Sufficiency verse with its reinforcements.   The victory, therefore, was not his, but merely that of one mental obsession and its feeling tone over another, and is of real interest only as a psychological and even pathological phenomenon. No new insight was gained, no new resolve was made, no change of values was brought about, no new birth was effected, no moral selfhood was achieved.   Bunyan's real conversion was the inner change of values that took place somewhere between his self-centered youth and his truly Christian years in Bedford

at sometimes, as if my breast bone would have split asunder.   Then I thought of that concerning *Judas, who, by his falling headlong, burst asunder and all his bowels gushed out* . . . Thus did I wind and twine and shrink under the burden that was upon me; which burden also did so oppress me that I could neither stand, nor go nor lie, either at rest or quiet."   (Sections 164, 165.)

[28] Section 205.

jail. But of this process we get scarcely a suggestion in all his long account. The " conversion " which he has described to us and which has been held up as a splendid example by all the generations of evangelical teachers from his day to ours is almost entirely a matter of feeling, and has little more moral significance than the struggle, which most of us have experienced, between two haunting and obsessing tunes which go running on in a man's mind till one drives the other out.

I have gone thus into detail in Bunyan's case (in spite of its pathological characteristics) because of the marked influence of preconceived ideas of conversion in determining most of its course, and also because of the influence it has had in fixing and strengthening the outlines of the conventional conversion experience ever since. Our second orthodox case of conversion is much less extreme, and in fact is quite common place and usual, yet follows the same general outlines as Bunyan's. For this reason it may be treated in much less detail. David Brainerd (who was born in Connecticut in 1718) was brought up under most orthodox and pious influences and was, apparently, always a serious and model boy and youth — although up to the advanced age of eight he had experienced no conviction of sin. At nineteen he " imagined " that he did dedicate himself to the Lord, though he came to recognize later on that he had not really done so and as yet was ignorant of the real nature of the new birth. About a year thereafter, while a student at Yale College, he experienced his first real " conviction of sin." It was, of course, not any sin in particular, but sin in general of which he was convicted: and as was the case with Bunyan (and as, indeed, is almost inevitable for one confronted by so terrible but illusory a difficulty) he went through a period of great depression. For, according to the established theory of conversion prevalent at the time, the sinner can do nothing at all to get rid of his sin or to help himself; he can in fact do nothing at all but wait and watch his feelings and cultivate conviction and despair. The difficulty, in fact, consists just in the natural tendency to strive to do something, a tendency which has to be overcome before real conversion is possible. It was a long time before young Brainerd could really bring himself into this passive and desperate state of mind. " Hundreds of times I renounced all pretenses of any worth in my duties, as I thought, even while performing them; and often confessed to God that I deserved nothing for the very best of them but eternal condemnation; yet still I had a secret hope of *recommending* myself to God by religious duties. . . . Sometimes I was greatly encouraged and imagined that God loved me and was pleased with me, and thought I should soon be fully reconciled to God. But the whole was founded on mere presumption, arising from enlargement in duty or warmth of affections, or some good resolutions or the like. And when, at times, great distress began to arise on the subject of my vileness and inability to deliver myself from a sovereign God, I used to put off the discovery, as what I could not bear. . . . Thus though I daily longed for greater conviction of sin; supposing that I must see more of my dreadful state in order to remedy; yet when the discoveries of my vile, wicked heart were made to me, the sight was so dreadful and showed me so plainly my exposedness to damnation, that I could not endure it." [29]

Thus Brainerd found himself in the same desperate dilemma which had confronted Bunyan: his conviction of sin and fear of damnation were his torment, yet the one thing he feared most was the loss of fear and of conviction, for only by them had he any hope; and at the same time if he took any comfort out of the hope arising from his fear this hope seemed sinful and a new obstacle in the way of salvation.[30] It is significant that in all his detailed description of his "conviction of sin" he does not mention any particular sin, whether positive or negative, of which he was guilty. "Conviction" for him, as for Bunyan, was the *sense* of sin rather than any recognition of definite acts or negligences, and this *sense* he diligently fostered and hugged, exactly as the Catholic ascetic or Indian sadhu

[29] See the extracts from *Brainerd's Journal* in Jonathan Edwards's "Life of the Rev. David Brainerd," Chap. I, (to be found in Vol. I of Edwards's Works; New York, Leavitt; 1844).

[30] "When at any time I took a view of my convictions and thought the degree of them to be considerable, I was wont to trust in them; but this confidence and the hope of soon making some notable advances toward deliverance, would ease my mind, and I soon became more senseless and remiss. Again, when I discerned my convictions to grow languid and thought them about to leave me, this immediately alarmed and distressed me," etc., etc.

hugs physical sufferings. The nearest approach to a definite statement of a definite sin to be found in this section of Brainerd's account is a reference to thoughts which, against all his efforts, would slip into his mind by the sheer fascination of the hateful — as was the case with Bunyan; and though neither Bunyan nor Brainerd consented to these thoughts, the mere fact that they ever got entrance seemed to prove them exceeding sinful.

Finally, as in Bunyan's case, the miserable period came to a close of its own motion. Wearied out by the effort to realize his own utter helplessness he came to feel helpless indeed and desperate and damned, and hence stopped trying to make any efforts. " I had thought many times before that the difficulties in my way were very great; but now I saw, in another and very different light, that it was for ever impossible for me to do anything toward helping or delivering myself." A few days after this state of utter dejection and effortless desperation had come upon him, the feeling of oppression gave way suddenly and without any apparent reason to a feeling of great joy and peace, and Brainerd began to hope that he was saved. Thus as in Bunyan's case, the whole drama was one of feeling, and all that was accomplished was the substitution of one feeling for another. No new insight had been gained, no change of will or of character had been wrought, no new ideals had been revealed, no new unification of purpose, no new devotion of self and its energies brought about. He had merely gone through the conventional and approved triad of emotions — (1) neutral, (2) depressed, (3) elated.[31]

[31] Mrs. Burr makes reference to over a hundred cases of depression similar to that of Bunyan and Brainerd, " Religious Confessions and Confessants " (Boston, Houghton, Mifflin: 1914), pp. 250–62.

CHAPTER VIII

THE FACTORS AT WORK IN CONVERSION

In the preceding chapter I have tried merely to describe the phenomenon of conversion by the presentation of six typical cases. These cases, however, as the reader will remember, fell naturally into two quite distinct groups. It will be the aim of this chapter to investigate the causes of this difference, and then to explain so far as I can the more important phenomena of conversion as such.

When we compare the cases of Bunyan and Brainerd with the four other cases described in the preceding chapter, the contrast is very striking; and the explanation of the contrast is not far to seek. One cannot read an account of a conversion of the Bunyan-Brainerd type without seeing that its whole course is laid down along conventional lines predetermined for it by an accepted and unquestioned theology. The tap root of this set of ideas concerning the necessary development of individual religion is to be traced back at least as far as Martin Luther — if indeed it does not go back to Augustine and St. Paul. In his attack upon the Roman Catholic view that religious merit may be acquired by penances and other " works," Luther laid great emphasis upon his new insight that true salvation is an inner matter and can never be attained by mere obedience to the Law. He saw, moreover, that few things stand more in the way of true spiritual regeneration than the kind of self-righteousness which partial obedience to the Law naturally induces. The great value of the Law, he therefore taught, consists in setting up a standard which it shall be impossible for us to reach and thus bringing home to us our own imperfection and our need of divine Grace — which comes to us through faith. Thus we shall come to realize that we can really do nothing for ourselves; and the first step towards salvation is the recognition of our own helplessness.[1] Natu-

[1] This view is perhaps most clearly expressed in Luther's Commentary on

rally enough in nearly all evangelical sects after Luther's time, the uselessness of voluntary effort, our own utter worthlessness, and the entirely supernatural quality of conversion and salvation came to take on more and more importance.   Calvin's great emphasis upon sin, moreover, reinforced the influence of Luther's denunciation of self-help.   Absolute acceptance of the teachings of theology was, of course, presupposed as a necessity for salvation, but beyond that intellectual insight was considered of no more avail than voluntary effort or virtue or "works." Hence the attention of every one desiring salvation — since it was vain to center it on thought or deed or will — was inevitably fixed upon feeling.   Feeling indeed could help — the feeling of one's own "devilishness" and despair — and nothing else could.   Moreover by feeling alone could one come to be aware of the miraculous action of Grace in the processes of Adoption, Sanctification and the rest.   Hence the gaze of the young evangelical who earnestly desired his soul's salvation was turned intently inward; and more and more some violent affective experience came to be regarded as the invariable sign, if not as the very essence, of conversion.   The view of the new birth as a long process of moral development was spurned, and instead it was thought to be always something catastrophic and miraculous.   According to Macaulay, " the young candidate for academical honors [at Cambridge and Oxford, in Cromwell's time]

the Epistle to the Galatians; from which I take the following scattered sentences:

"Verum officium et principalis ac proprius usus legis est, quod revelat homini suum peccatum, caecitatem, miseriam, impietatem, ignorantiam, odium, contemptum Dei, mortem, infernum, iudicium et commeritam iram apud Deum."   "Quare magnum et horrible monstrum est Opinio justitiae. Ut ergo Deus eam contundat et conterat, opus habet ingenti et forti malleo, lege scilicet, quae malleus est mortis, tonitru inferni et fulmen irae divinae. At quid? ad collidendam iustitiae opinionem quae rebellis, pertinax ac durissimae cervicis bestia est."   "Sed hoc opus, hic labor est, ut sic exterritus et contusus lege possit sese interum erigere et dicere: Iam satis contritus et contusus sum, satis misere afflixit me tempus legis.   Iam tempus est gratiae et audiendi Christi . . . Ego, inquit, si diutius vixero, emendabo vitam meam, hoc et hoc faciam; vel: ingrediar monasterium, parcissime vivam contentus pane et aqua, nudis pedibus incedam, etc.   Hic nisi omnino contrarium feceris, hoc est, nisi ablegaveris Mosen cum lege sua ad securos et induratos et apprehenderis in istis pavaribus et horroribus Christum possum, crucifixum, mortum pro peccatis tuis, actum est plane de salute tua" (Luther's *Werke*, Weimar, Hermann Böhlans: 1911, Vol. 40, pp. 479–90 — namely the comment on Gal. III, 19).

was strictly interrogated as to the day and hour when he experienced the new birth." [2]   And, as we all know, John Wesley and the early Methodists made more of this than even the earlier Puritans.   As a matter of course this view of the nature and necessity of conversion was brought to America with the rest of the Puritan theology; and in the early 18th century it found great reinforcement at the hands of Jonathan Edwards, whose large influence in evangelical theology has made it dominant in certain orthodox circles ever since.[3]

The important difference between our two groups of conversion cases, and the reasons for this difference, must now be perfectly plain.   It is an odd fact, however, that some of the leading writers on the psychology of conversion have been only dimly aware of this difference or its cause, and in fact have built up their norm and based their descriptions on the second type rather than on the first.   Coming thus to the aid of Luther, Edwards, and Bunyan, they have accepted the conventions of theology as the principles of human nature.[4]

[2] History of England.   Volume I, Chap. III.

[3] Edwards's sermons were full of the need of conversion and of emphasis upon its emotional nature, and his practice was to work upon the feelings as strongly as possible.   This method he defended at length in his "Thoughts on the Revival of Religion in New England" (see esp. Part III), and in more systematic and theoretic fashion in his "Treatise concerning Religious Affections."   In this work he devotes twenty-five pages to showing that "religion consists much in holy affection," and especially emphasizes the view that the true feelings of conversion are of a purely supernatural sort and are entirely different from any other experiences.   See pp. 137–38 of the 1821 Edition of the "Treatise" (Philadelphia, James Crissy).   Mrs. Burr points out that "in the mediæval cases of conversion the mystical and visionary manifestations are nearer to the normal life and the conversion crisis itself is less easily defined."   A marked change comes with the seventeenth and eighteenth century pietists.   The contrast is due, in her opinion, to the change that had taken place in men's views of the natural and the supernatural worlds in the interval —"Religious Confessions and Confessants," 296–97.

[4] Starbuck, indeed, acknowledges the fact that conversion is really "spontaneous awakening and storm and stress crystallized into a dogma." But the reader of our chapter on Adolescence will remember how *natural* Starbuck regarded the "conviction" period of storm and stress — quite in line with the evangelical dogma of Original Sin; and after the sentence concerning conversion just quoted from him he adds: "Theology takes these adolescent tendencies and builds upon them; it sees that the essential thing in adolescent growth is bringing the person out of childhood into the new life of maturity and personal insight.   It accordingly brings those

Not only have some influential writers on the psychology of religion pronounced what we may call emotional conversion perfectly normal; following the lead of theology and basing their analysis chiefly on cases whose course has been determined by theological preconceptions, they have systematized the emotional conversion process into regular stages and have taught the normality of " conviction " and the necessity of " surrender." Starbuck's respondents had a great deal to say of their sense of sin, and it naturally plays a large part in his description of the pre-conversion experience.   While he emphasizes the fact that voluntary effort if used before the conversion is often helpful, he insists in quite orthodox fashion that in the majority of cases it must be given up at last if conversion is to be achieved; one's efforts at that time being worse than useless.   James seems to go farther than Starbuck.   While he recognizes two types of conversion, the voluntary and the involuntary, he regards the former as relatively unimportant (apparently because it is " less interesting "), and also relatively rare.   In the following passage he has sought to condense his own view and Starbuck's on the process of conversion:

" Of the volitional type of conversion it would be easy to give examples, but they are as a rule less interesting than those of the self-surrender type, in which the subconscious effects are more abundant and often startling.   I will therefore hurry to the latter, the more so because the difference between the two types is after all not radical.   Even in the most voluntarily built-up sort of regeneration there are passages of partial self-surrender interposed; and in the great majority of all cases, when the will has done its uttermost towards bringing one close to the complete unification aspired after, it seems that the very last step must be left to other forces and performed without the help of its activity.   In other words, self-surrender becomes then indispensable.   ' The personal will,' says Dr. Starbuck, ' must be given up.   In many cases relief persistently refuses to come until the person ceases to resist, or to make an effort in

means to bear which will intensify the normal tendencies that work in human nature.   It shortens up the period of duration of storm and stress." (Op. cit., p. 224.)   The work of theology in producing conviction and conversion is thus regarded as a perfectly normal process and one that merely hastens the regular processes of Nature herself.

the direction he desires to go ' . . . . Dr. Starbuck gives an interesting, and it seems to me a true, account — so far as conceptions so schematic can claim truth at all — of the reasons why self-surrender at the last moment should be so indispensable. To begin with, there are two things in the mind of the candidate for conversion: first, the present incompleteness or wrongness, the ' sin ' which he is eager to escape from; and, second, the positive ideal which he longs to compass. Now with most of us the sense of our present wrongness is a far more distinct piece of our consciousness than is the imagination of any positive ideal we can aim at. In a majority of cases, indeed, the ' sin ' almost exclusively engrosses the attention, so that conversion is *" a process of struggling away from sin rather than of striving towards righteousness."* A man's conscious wit and will, so far as they strain towards the ideal, are aiming at something only dimly and inaccurately imagined. Yet all the while the forces of mere organic ripening within him are going on towards their own prefigured results, and his conscious strainings are letting loose subconscious allies behind the scenes, which in their way work towards rearrangement; and the rearrangement towards which all these deeper forces tend is pretty surely definite, and definitely different from what he consciously conceives and determines. It may consequently be actually interfered with (*jammed,* as it were, like the lost word when we seek too energetically to recall it) by his voluntary efforts slanting from the true direction." [5]

Not all the psychologists who have written on conversion have gone so far as James and Starbuck in justifying the conventions of evangelical theology; but as none of them have drawn any sharp distinction between what may be called the moral and the merely emotional types, the upholders of the Bunyan-Brainerd process have, for the last dozen years, (whether justifiably or not) been jubilantly hailing the psychology of religion as their loyal ally in support of the necessity of conviction and helplessness.[6] It is for this reason that I have treated conversion at

[5] " The Varieties of Religious Experience," pp. 207–09.

[6] The Rev. R. H. K. Gill, Ph.D., combines this point of view with the popular notion about the " subliminal " in the following remarkable sentence, explanatory of conversion:

what must seem to the reader such tedious length. For I do not in the least share the view indicated above. In the first place I believe conversion of the violent type is by no means so common or so normal an experience as most treatises on the psychology of conversion would lead one to suppose. It is, of course, a perfectly genuine phenomenon but its occurrence is confined chiefly to certain exceptional individuals whose personalities have become incipiently " divided " either because of real moral delinquencies, or unusually high ideals, or unfortunate surroundings, or because of some native nervous instability. In the great majority of cases detailed by religious writers or reported from questionnaires, the violence of the experience is in part induced by the suggestions of a conventional theology and in part is purely imaginary, existing in expression rather than in experience. I venture to estimate that at least nine out of every ten " conversion cases " reported in recent questionnaires would have had no violent or depressing experience to report had not the individuals in question been brought up in a church or a community which taught them to look for it if not to cultivate it. With most religious people conversion (of the genuine moral sort) is a gradual and almost imperceptible process, with an occasional intensification of emotion now and then during adolescence. Many, perhaps most, religious adolescents have a number of these emotional experiences which may last for a few moments only or for days and weeks. In churches which lay no special emphasis upon conversion, such as the Roman Catholic, the Greek, the Unitarian, and the Episcopalian, as in most non-Christian religions,[7] no great notice is taken of these periods of excitement. The emphasis in the Catholic Church is on outer acts and on character building, and as the young person is not directed to watch his emotional

" The anxiety about the intended moral reform and the continued agony of penitence, filling the mind for a period of time, helps the consuetudinary evil-mindedness to be lost in the subliminal self," (" The Psychological Aspects of Christian Experience," Boston, Sherman, French: 1905, p. 41).

[7] Bhagavan Das. for example, in treating of conversion in his own religion (Hinduism) makes but little of the emotional crisis. For the Hindu the one great thing is apprehension of the truth.— " The Psychology of Conversion " (Adyar, T. P. H.: 1917).

experiences he seldom finds any of striking importance. Sometimes the first communion rouses an emotional excitement, but both the Church and the individual regard this as precious indeed but only incidental, and as merely one of many religious experiences. In those denominations, on the other hand, in which the subjective is emphasized as against the objective, and which teach the necessity of " a conversion experience," some one of the many emotional stirrings of adolescence is singled out as *the* conversion, and the others are ignored and largely forgotten.[8]

One word more concerning "conviction of sin" and surrender of effort — two factors of conversion which have been so enthusiastically championed by both evangelical theology and popular psychology. By both, I say, for the truth is that the theologians and certain writers on the psychology of religion have coöperated unknowingly to form a vicious circle which it is difficult to avoid. The theologians by their teachings have induced a largely artificial form of experience; and the psychologists coming after, have studied the experience thus induced and formulated its laws, thus making Science verify Theology. There is little really good evidence for the assertion which James quotes approvingly from Starbuck that conversion is " a process of struggling away from sin rather than of striving toward righteousness." In cases of the Bunyan-Brainerd type, to be sure, the James-Starbuck view holds: in fact it was reached exactly on the basis of the Bunyan and Brainerd cases and those influenced by them. But in cases of

[8] Starbuck's assertion that though conversion is often induced by theology " it shortens up the period of storm and stress," is in one sense borne out by his figures, and corroborated to some extent by the fact that in Hinduism (according to Bhagavan Das) the age of emotional crisis if it comes at all is later than in Christianity. But this by no means establishes the normality and desirability of the methods by which conversion is induced, for it must be remembered that the storm and stress period which conversion shortens is itself often induced by the same conventional theological ideas which bring about the final emotional experience. The unreasonableness of singling out one emotional crisis as the supreme and decisive turning point of life and *insisting that this represents the normal process* comes out plainly when one considers how commonly depression and other symptoms of "storm and stress" return after "conversion," even among orthodox cases. See Mrs. Burr's enumeration, op. cit., p. 318 f. The choice of one emotional seizure among many is usually almost arbitrary.

really significant conversion it is rare indeed that the attention of the individual is riveted on his own sinful nature or his gaze turned chiefly upon the past.   There are a number of cases of conversion in the New Testament but in not one of them does the sense of sin play an important part.   No better record of real conversions is perhaps anywhere to be found than Harold Begbie's " Twice Born Men," [9] and in not a single case there reported is there anything really comparable to the " conviction period " of theology — and psychology!   These men had all been great sinners, but most of them seemed to think very little about their sins — surprisingly little from the reader's point of view.   The reader invariably has a much deeper sense of their sin than they have themselves.   And in the few cases where they are conscious of guilt it is always some particular crime that they have in mind, and never that indefinite sense of having done they know not what which so troubled poor Bunyan and his modern imitators.   It is not sin that troubles them but misery, and the chief thing that fills their consciousness and brings about the change is not a struggle away from sin but a striving toward something new.   They want to be respectable

---

[9] New York, Revell: 1909. One might add to the cases cited many of the most famous conversions of Christian history to show how unimportant a rôle the " conviction " phenomenon often plays. There is no trace of it, for example, in St. Paul's conversion. Undoubtedly much was going on in the background of Paul's mind which does not come out in the account and which is hinted at by his subsequent descriptions; but this seems to have been a questioning of his own position and a seeking for new light, rather than anything that can properly be described as " conviction of sin " as that term is used by the theologians who have formulated the evangelical type of conversion. George Fox's case may be held up as one in which conviction led to real conversion: but it will be noted that the " troubles " to which Fox refers in his Autobiography, so far as they were more than physiological, were concerned with the evil condition of the world quite as much as with the sins and dangers of his own soul. Moreover his rescue came about not through the intensification of the feeling of guilt nor by the resignation of effort, but chiefly through an " opening " which gave him a new insight into the possibility of a perfect moral life through the help of Christ. (See Professor Jones's edition of his " Autobiography," Philadelphia, Ferris and Leach: 1903, Vol. I, esp. pp. 68–85.) But the conviction doctrine relies most of all, after Bunyan's case, upon St. Augustine. In this, however, it is trusting to an untrustworthy support. For while Augustine felt " conviction of sin," it was not of the Bunyan-Brainerd type, but the recognition of a perfectly real and definite form of indulgence which for a long time he could not bring himself to give up. See the Confessions, esp. Book VIII, Chapters 5–12.

and decent. Begbie gives it as his opinion and as the opinion of the most experienced workers of the Salvation Army that desire for good is absolutely essential to conversion.[10]

A study of Begbie's cases, moreover, shows no less conclusively that the surrender of effort is by no means an essential to conversion. It is plain indeed that such a passive attitude may be very helpful in cases of the Bunyan-Brainerd type where the whole question is one of achieving a certain desirable feeling state: the wished-for calm can often best be attained by giving up all effort, quite on the analogy of the process of falling asleep. But when the aim to be achieved is the giving up of old evil habits, the acquisition of new insight, the revolution of one's ideals, purposes, values, and character, then effort is of the utmost importance. There must indeed be *surrender* — surrender of the old purposes and loves, the old self; surrender in this sense is the very essence of conversion. But while effort alone can seldom bring this about, it is, (as Starbuck points out [11]) one of the most important means of bringing about the new insight or the revolution of values which makes surrender possible. This was seen in the cases of Ardigo and Tolstoi and of the two Indians, and it comes out very plainly in Begbie's men. Here there is no suggestion of what one occasionally finds so emphasized in the conventional report: " I had to stop trying first." The important thing in almost every case was not to stop trying but to *begin* trying. I emphasize this as I do because the notion that he who aspires to conversion must give up trying to help himself seems to me one of the most dangerous fallacies that theology has ever slipped into. It is perhaps the most deplorable aspect of that whole view of conversion that has tended to hold up the artificially induced misery of the Brainerd

[10] P. 185. This is also the conclusion of the workers at Briar Brae Lodge, New York. It is a long cry from Briar Brae Lodge to the Buddhism of Japan, yet it is interesting to note that in the process of conversion as laid down in the Mahayana, the emphasis is all upon joy, intellectual enlightenment and moral progress, with practically no reference to the sense of sin. The moral elements stressed are all positive, and consist in self-training, unselfishness, and lofty aspiration.

[11] Starbuck, though insisting that at the final crisis effort is harmful, recognizes fully the value of effort before the crisis.

type, and even the pathological morbidity of the Bunyan type, as norms for the imitation of earnest Christians.

It is of course true that effort alone is not sufficient; the man must *want* to be saved before he makes the effort. The attainment of moral selfhood means the acquisition of new purposes and new *tastes;* and as it is perfectly plain that there is no forcing of tastes, it follows that no amount of effort alone will bring one the new love that is needed. Chronologically speaking, therefore, effort is a secondary factor. But when the new tastes and purposes are acquired much still remains to be done. New insight, perhaps, must be gained or old habits overcome, and here effort is of great importance. In some cases of conversion the renewed and persistent effort of the individual who has had just one fascinating glimpse of the possible new life, is the really dominant factor in the explanation of the great change that comes about in his character. A case of this sort will be found in a note at the foot of this page.[12]

Effort, of course, is not the only helpful factor at this stage. Quite as often the explanation of the moral transformation brought about is to be sought for in physical and environmental changes — provided always that the desire for a better life is really present. The workers in Briar Brae Lodge, New York, report transformation of lives chiefly by these means. The vic-

[12] The following account was given me by the Rev. Ernest B. Hart, a young minister and former student of mine who preached at the meeting at which the subject was converted:

"The subject, a worthless, good-for-nothing drunkard, about forty-two years old, was looked upon by all who knew him as about the poorest specimen of manhood. He 'happened' into a meeting one Sunday evening and went out a converted man. He took with him a clear vision of what might be in his life if he let God enter it. But (and this was his peculiar attitude) he realized that his life was bad, and the first thing for him to do was to overcome his bad habits before having anything to do with God. He therefore swore off the drink habit, and *after* a long struggle entirely overcame the desire for drink. (He has never drunk a drop from the time he left the church that night, and it has been nearly three years.) He did this entirely by his own efforts, not once asking God to help him. It was up *to him* to overcome. And he did it. He tells me that after he had, by force of will, conquered the bad habits, he then allowed God to enter his life. But he felt that before he could ask God to be his God, he must rid himself of his bad habits. To-day he is an upright, exemplary citizen, looked up to and respected by people in general."

tim of drink who has been permitting his family to starve is taken from his evil surroundings, sent for a while to the hospital, then invited to the Lodge for a few weeks of rest where he comes to feel that some respectable people respect and care for him; and then after a month or two in the country he is sent back to work at a new job and reunited with his family; and after the process he is often a new creature.

But, as has been said, if the amelioration of physical conditions is to be useful, and if effort is to be even thinkable, there must be on the part of the individual himself a genuine desire for a new life. The problem is therefore to make the new life seem to the sunken man or woman both desirable and possible. Sometimes the misery that results from poverty and crime is enough to make the man long for something better. And if at such a time he falls in with kind people, like the Briar Brae Workers, the new life may seem to him within his reach and he may, consequently, make the necessary effort toward his own reform. In such cases we may and do have real conversion without the assistance of anything specifically religious.[13] With the hardened sinner things are seldom so simple and some stronger influence must be appealed to if the man's life and character are really to be turned round. Falling in love at a critical moment can sometimes do this; patriotism may; but as a fact the great power for the transformation of life that dwarfs all others combined is religion. For religion deals with the deepest questions and the most abiding values, and it holds out to the desperate man who has lost all hope in himself or in human help, the promise of supernatural and unfailing assistance. This fact comes out most strikingly in Begbie's cases. Especially does religion make real to these men the possibility of a better life. Among most of them dissatisfaction with their old life had already been roused by the sufferings of poverty or the hard hand of the law,[14] but they had no hope in anything better till they saw with their own eyes what religion had actually done for some of their number, or were con-

[13] Cf. also the case of Mr. Fletcher in James's "Varieties." Mr. Fletcher got rid of the evil habits of anger and worry by being convinced in an argument that it was possible to do so. (P. 181.)

[14] In several of Begbie's cases it seems to have been the misery of imprisonment that gave the first impetus to their conversion.

vinced in some way that God — and certainly God alone — could save them. Thus " Jack " the drunkard is induced, on some pretext, to go to the Salvation Army meeting. " He stood in the front of the standing pack which occupied the back of the hall, listening. He saw men who had been prize-fighters, criminals, tramps, and petty thieves standing clean and happy on the platform, speaking of the joy that had come to them with conversion, and explaining that conversion meant a surrender of man's mutinous will to the will of a God all-anxious to care for them. Again and again came the assurance: ' However bad any man here may feel himself to be, however hopeless and ashamed and lost he may feel, he has only to come out publicly to this penitent form, kneel down and ask God for His mercy, to have the load lifted off his soul and to feel himself strong in the strength of Almighty God to overcome all his temptations.' " [15]

The " Army " insists on a public declaration of one's determination to lead a new life; and wisely. For this act helps to clench the self-surrender which, if it were purely subjective and secret, might well be disregarded at the next temptation. The public avowal both brings to the new convert the encouragement and moral support of the community, and also holds constantly before his mind the fear of its censure should he give up the struggle. " You must come to the meeting to-night," says the old convert to the new, " and you must go to the penitent form and *say out loud* that you're sorry, that you want new life." [16]

It is no wonder that when the new convert has taken this public stand and feels himself, society, and God all united in the struggle for the better life, there should come into his heart a great joy and peace. It is in part the peace of passing out of a state of indecision into the assured stability of having everything settled.[17] To have one's mind " made up " after long uncertainty is always a relief, and when there goes with it the conviction that refuge is now to be found from the worst mis-

[15] PP. 251–52.

[16] P. 204.

[17] Few better examples of this are to be found than among the exulting expressions of the early Buddhist monks — many of whom were, in a sense, atheistic. See Mrs. Rhys David's translation of the " Psalms of the Early Bud hists " (London, Frowde: 1913), *passim*.

eries of sin, that freedom from the devil of drink, and supernatural help in keeping on the straight and happy path, are
now assured, great joy is the inevitable result.   But in the really
religious cases there is often still more reason for joy, for the
convert feels the presence of a new friend who loves him and to
whom he is endlessly grateful and whom he is coming to love
passionately.   In many cases getting converted means falling
in love with Jesus.

Many entire cases of conversion, therefore, and many of the
details of all conversions are to be explained by familiar facts.
There are some aspects of conversion, however, not so easily disposed of.   The transformation is sometimes so sudden as to be
startling,[18] and so complete as to suggest some physiological
change in the organism.   Begbie cites several cases in which
drunkards of years' standing become free from the drink habit
seemingly at one stroke, and turn from lives of criminality to
eager service of others.   Cases of this sort have driven both
theology and psychology to search for explanations somewhere
outside the field of ordinary mental occurrences.   Theology has,
of course, had recourse to the supernatural, and psychology to
the subconscious.   And there is no doubt that if the subconscious be given a sufficiently wide interpretation, psychology is
justified in looking to it for the explanation of these striking
phenomena.   Experiments with anæsthetic subjects,[19] experiments in post-hypnotic suggestion and with those pathological
cases which Freud, Prince, Sidis and others have made so
familiar, where a buried complex produces various psychical
disturbances,— experiments of these and other types show much
the same sort of sudden rise of ideas, convictions and emotions
not to be accounted for by the normal consciousness as is to be
found in the conversion of St. Paul or of Alphonse Ratisbonne.[20]   Writers on the psychology of conversion are therefore pretty well agreed that cases of this sudden sort always involve subconscious influence.[21]   The most generally accepted

[18] James gives a number of striking examples in Lecture X of the
" Varieties," and Mrs. Burr adds a great many more (op. cit., Chap. VII).

[19] See almost any treatise on abnormal psychology, e.g., Binet's " Alter-
ations of Personality " (New York, Appleton: 1903), esp. Chap. VIII.

[20] See pp. 223–226 of the " Varieties."

[21] Cf. for example, James's " Varieties," pp. 233–41; and Starbuck,

theory is that ideas and emotions coming into one's mind by ordinary channels and soon forgotten sink into the subconscious — whether we regard this as a co-conscious or merely as the back-ground and marginal region of the mind, or even as the purely physiological and unconscious — and there germinate, associating with themselves increasing emotional complexes and tendencies to action, and gradually transform one's tastes and values, until the day of ripening comes, when suddenly the complex rises to consciousness and dominates it, and the man finds himself a new creature, and loves what once he hated.[22]

But though psychologists are pretty well agreed in attributing cases of this sort to the action of the subconscious, they are, as we have seen, far from united on the question how this " subconscious action " should be interpreted.   A large number (e. g. Coe) use the term subconscious here to mean the frankly unconscious mechanism of the nervous system.   Others (e. g. James) seem to regard the subconscious as a co-consciousness — a genuine doubling of the stream of thought being here involved, either as a normal condition or as an incipiently abnormal disaggregation of consciousness due to emotional excitement.   On this interpretation one may picture the ideas and emotions of the primary consciousness acting by suggestion on the secondary stream and there germinating and growing till at last they force themselves into the primary stream once more.[23]   Dr. Morton Prince has still another explanation for striking and sudden conversions, which calls for no doubling of consciousness but merely for a lapse of memory and a retention of emotion.[24]

" Psychology of Religion," Chap. VIII.   Professor Coe has shown that sudden conversion is much more likely to take place in subjects with an active "subliminal" than is the case with more normal persons.   See "The Spiritual Life," Chap. III.

[22] Many of our most important decisions are made for us in this way. A friend of mine, for example, tells me of his choice of a profession which came about quite in the style of a sudden conversion.   For two years he had pondered the question and could not come to a decision.   One night after going to bed it came into his mind " like a shot " that he was going to be a lawyer, and after that the question was never raised again.

[23] Popular writers, carrying suggestions from James much farther, surely, than he would have approved, have made much of this view, and given it a new theological interpretation by connecting the subconscious with the Divine.

[24] His famous patient, Miss Beauchamp, in a state of ill health and

Cases such as that of Miss Beauchamp and M. Ratisbonne are, of course, rare; hence whether or not we are ever justified in appealing to a doubling of consciousness, one can at any rate get on very well without it in interpreting most cases. As a rule, if not invariably, an interpretation of the subconscious which identifies it with the marginal and the unconscious is ample for purposes of explanation.

But the suddenness of conversion is not the only difficult thing to explain. The striking victory over evil habits of long standing which sometimes comes about through conversion is perhaps quite as hard to understand,— as it is certainly very much more important. James's suggestive essay on the "Energies of Men," [25] and Sidis's experimental investigations with neurotic patients [26] points toward the presence in each of us of

despair, went into a church to pray. While praying all was suddenly changed, without her knowing why. "She became filled with a great emotion of joyousness and well-being. A great feeling of peace, restfulness, and happiness came over her." She came away feeling strong and believing herself well, and above all convinced that she had had a Visitation, and so determined to enter a convent and become a nun. By hypnotizing her Dr. Prince was able to discover what had really happened, which was this: "While Miss Beauchamp was communing with herself (and in her depressed state) her eyes became fixed upon one of the shining brass lamps in the Church. She went into a hypnotic or trance-like state of which she has no memory. In this state her consciousness was made up of a great many disconnected memories, each memory being accompanied by emotion. There were memories of a religious character; and these memories were accompanied by the emotions which they had originally evoked (all being of a peaceful and joyous character). . . . After a short time Miss Beauchamp awoke and on waking all the memories which made up the consciousness of the hypnotic state were forgotten. At first her mind was a blank so far as logical ideas were concerned. She thought of nothing definite and yet she was filled with emotions. They were the same emotions which belonged to the different memories of the hypnotic state. These emotions persisted." Soon after, they began to call up congruent ideas of a religious nature, and, knowing nothing of the time gap and the trance-state or of the memories which had produced her new emotions, she naturally regarded the great contrast between her former depression and her present joy as of supernatural origin, and felt herself converted and cured. (Op. cit., pp. 344–50.) This explanation of Miss Beauchamp's sudden conversion, it will be noted, might apply perfectly well to many a case like that of M. Ratisbonne. And if this interpretation be the true one, it is plain that we shall have substituted *alternating* conscious states for co-consciousness ones, and no *doubling* is therefore required.

[25] *Philosophical Review*, XVI (1907), 1–20. Reprinted in his posthumous "Memories and Studies" (New York, Longmans: 1911).

[26] See esp. "The Psychotherapeutic Value of the Hypnoidal State." *Jour. of Abnormal Psychology*, IV (1909–10), 151–71.

reservoirs of energy not ordinarily used, which at times of crisis
or by means of psychological devices may be " tapped " — with
results that are to say the least very striking.   The letters which
Sidis prints from former patients whom he has cured by his
" hypnoidal " process read very much like the testimonies of
converts at an " experience meeting."   And it is quite com-
prehensible that the new confidence and peace which a religious
conversion brings might act upon tired nerves in much the same
way as the resting and recuperating influence of the hypnoidal
state.

But the most important thing about conversion is of course
the change of character that so often results — the change, in
fact, which invariably results in every genuine conversion.
And, this too, as a rule, perhaps always, requires reference to
the subconscious or the unconscious for full explanation, whether
the conversion be sudden or gradual.   But the subconscious
process which brings about the truly new birth is seldom of the
sensational sort so dear to popularizers of psychology and certain " up-to-date " theologians.   It does not consist in the bur-
rowing and mining of subconscious ideas and the splitting and
doubling of consciousness; it is, instead, merely the undramatic
change of values which the most normal and common-place
of us notes at work within himself in almost every epoch of life,
but particularly during the period that leads from childhood to
maturity.   When you were a child your favorite music was
Dixie played by a brass band; and Beethoven from a symphony
orchestra seemed painfully stupid.   Now Dixie and the band
leave you indifferent, but to hear an orchestra rendering the
Fifth Symphony is one of the great delights that life has
to give.   When and how did the change come?   You may be
able to tell when was the first time you enjoyed Beethoven; it
may have come to you at some concert as a revelation.   But
more likely you can give no fixed date, and certainly you can
name no one special cause.   The great cause was the whole of
your musical education and still more the whole of your mental
development.   It was an unconscious process certainly — if you
like, a " subconscious " one; but it involved nothing mysterious
and Freudian.   There was no idea of the beauty of Beethoven
that lodged in your subliminal, dug its way down, germinated.

caused occasional uneasiness on the surface, flowered below ground, and suddenly shot up into the primary consciousness in an explosion, like a torpedo from a submarine. And yet the new taste for Beethoven was certainly the product of subconscious forces.

The same thing is true of religious conversion. It follows the same laws as the change of taste; because, in the last analysis it is itself a change of taste — the most momentous one that ever occurs in human experience. It is an "*Umwerthung aller Werthe*"; and all the processes and experiences and lessons of life are involved in it.

CHAPTER IX

CROWD PSYCHOLOGY AND REVIVALS

THE phenomena known as religious revivals are among the most interesting facts of crowd psychology. The complex and varied forms which they take, the striking and at times momentous results which they achieve, as well as the skillful methods employed by the master artists who occasionally direct their course, naturally attract the attention of the psychologist and whet his curiosity as to the psychological principles of their explanation.

This explanation, if I am not mistaken, is to be found in the laws of rhythm, on the one hand, and what is known as crowd psychology on the other. Rhythmic action is one of the most fundamental characteristics of the human mind. In fact, as Herbert Spencer has pointed out, it is not confined to the mental sphere but dominates all life and much even of the action of inorganic nature.[1] The processes of the human body are a series of complex and interrelated rhythms, and these affect the whole background of consciousness and color all our thoughts and feelings. They range all the way from regular and rapid processes such as the heart beat up to more or less irregular recurrences with time spans of weeks or months. Our mental life not only is deeply affected by all of these physiological processes, but carries the principle of rhythm (with or without bodily correlate) still farther, imitating constantly the swing and return of the pendulum as long as life lasts. Hunger and satiety, sleep and waking, exertion and repose, excitement and relaxation, enthusiasm and indifference, follow each other with almost the certainty, if without the exact regularity, of day and night and the revolving seasons. It would be odd, therefore, if so fundamental a human characteristic as religion should fail to be influenced by this

[1] See chapter X of Part II of his " First Principles " (4th Ed.) esp. sections 85, 86, and 87.

deep-seated human characteristic; and as a fact, the religious consciousness is as rhythmic in its action as any other aspect of the human mind.   The truth of this is confirmed by the experience of nearly every religious man and woman whose religion is something more than the performance of conventional acts and the acceptance of a conventional creed; and the more intense one's religious experience the more is its rhythmic nature likely to be felt.   The mystic life as a rule oscillates from times of inner emotional warmth to periods of outer activity or even of emotional " dryness."   And, not to speak of the mystics, all those who have known what it means to be " on the heights " in any sense or to any extent, know also that one cannot remain there long.

The historical religions have been quite aware of these psychological facts and have often acted upon them in seeking to direct the religious life.   One of the books that make up that collection of rules of the ancient Chinese, the Li-ki, going back no one knows how far into antiquity, prescribes a semi-annual retirement for religious reflection, and inculcates the lesson that the rhythms of human life should imitate the rhythms of the Universe (the " Tao ").[2]   In similar fashion the Buddha divided the year into two periods, during one of which he and his disciples went forth on missionary journeys, while in the other they retired and spent the months in meditation.   The " Christian Year," with its great emotional seasons and sacred days for recollection and contemplation, is the expression given by the Christian Church to the rhythmic needs of the human heart; and the recurrent holy seasons and holy days of Hinduism express the same universal demand.   Perhaps the most obvious illustration of this pendulum-like oscillation of the religious consciousness is to be found in the Christian Sunday, the Jewish Sabbath, and the Mohammedan observance of Friday.   A further testimony to this human need for religious refreshment at recurrent intervals for society as well as for the individual, is the belief so fundamental to Buddhism, Jainism, and Mohammedanism that new revelations of the truth have been needed and have come historically at more or less regular

[2] Book V, *passim*, esp. Part II, § 15, translated in S. B. E. Vol. XXVII (Oxford Univ.: 1885).

periods, because of the gradually failing faith of men.   It is
to be noted that these revelations, brought by successive Buddhas, Tirthankaras, or prophets, are not regarded as revelations
of new truth, but as the rejuvenation of men in their living
belief in the old truth and in their practice of it.

But the religions have not been satisfied with making a place
for the rhythmic recurrence of religious sentiment in the
hearts of their individual followers.   Many of them have made
use of the forces of social suggestion to reinforce nature, and
hence has resulted not merely the religious refreshment of
lonely individuals, but group movements in which many individuals have joined, each one influencing the other so as to
make the religious revival much more intense than could be the
case if the individual were left to himself and to the ordinary
rhythms of the religious consciousness.   Even very primitive
peoples furnish excellent examples of this.   In his admirable
work on revivals Davenport has given a detailed description
of the phenomenon as found among the American Indians.[3]
The ancient Greeks,— who were surely far removed in culture
from the primitive natives of North America — showed an
equal propensity to revivals of an exceedingly emotional type.
The cult of the Thracian Dionysos seems to have been introduced into central Greece and nourished there largely through
the use of what might be called " revival meetings "— and these
of a very emotional and exciting sort.[4]   The annual celebration

[3] " Primitive Traits in Religious Revivals " (New York, Macmillan:
1906).   Chap. IV.

[4] They are described by Rohde as follows: " Die Feier ging auf Berg-
höhen vor sich, in dunkler Nacht, beim unsteten Licht der Fackelbrände.
Lärmende Musik erscholl, der schmetternde Schall eherner Becken, der
dumpfe Donner grosser Handpauken und dazwischen hinein der ' zum
Wanhsinn lockende Einklang ' der tieftönenden Flöten, deren Seele erst
phrygische Auleten erweckt hatten.   Von dieser wilden Musik erregt, tanzt
mit gellendem Jauchzen die Schaar der Feiernden.   Wir hören nichts von
Gesängen: zu solchen liess die Gewalt des Tanzes keinen Athem.   Denn
dies war nicht der gemessen bewegte Tanzschritt, in dem etwa Homers
Griechen im Paean sich vorwärts schwingen.   Sondern in wüthenden, wir-
belden, stürzenden Rundtanz eilt die Schaar der Begeisterten über die
Berghalden dahin.   Meist waren es Weiber, die bis zur Erschöpfung, in
diesen Wirbeltänzen sich umschwangen; seltsam verkleidet: sie trugen
' Bassaren,' lang wallende Gewänder, wie es scheint, aus Fuchspelzen
genäht; sonst über dem Gewande Rehfelle, auch wohl Hörner auf dem
Haupte.   Wild flattern die Haare, Schlangen, dem Sabazios heilig, halten

of the Eleusinian Mysteries had certain features of a decidedly revivalistic nature,[5] and the intensity of religious feeling thus deliberately aroused in a large group of believers brought spiritual refreshment to the individual, who was able to go in the strength of it many days.   The modern Vaishnavism of India, and especially of Bengal, has repeatedly been characterized by the deliberate arousing of group emotion through revival methods.   Chaitanya, the Vaishnava reformer and missionary of the 16th Century, was a master in the art of producing religious excitement, through the use of exhortation, song, and even dance,[6] and the sect founded by him, which is to-day perhaps the most popular and enthusiastic religious body in Bengal, still makes use of the emotional methods of revival which he so skillfully practiced.[7]   Judaism, like so many other vital religions, felt the need of occasional periods of special religious refreshment, a need to which there was ever found some John the Baptist ready to respond with his exhortation, " Repent, for the Kingdom of Heaven is at hand."   It is hardly necessary to add that within Christianity even so non-evangelical a body as the Roman Catholic Church, at more or less regular intervals, carefully conducts deliberately planned revival meetings, (known as " retreats "), in which both the rhythmic demands of human nature and the forces of social psychology are laid under contribution to stimulate the religious life of the community and of its individual members.

As I pointed out in the beginning of this chapter, the psychological explanation of these violent movements of social religion is to be sought not only in the rhythmic nature of the human

die Hände, sie schwingen Dolche, oder Thyrsosstäbe, die unter dem Epheu die Lanzenspitze verbergen.   So toben sie bis zur äussersten Aufregung aller Gefühle, und im ' heiligen Wahnsinn ' stürzen sie sich auf die zum Opfer erkorenen Thiere, packen und zerreissen die eingeholte Beute, und reissen mit den Zähnen das blutige Fleisch ab, das sie roh verschlingen." (" Psyche," Tübingen, Mohr: 1903; Dritte Auflage, Vol. II, pp. 9–10.)

[5] Cf. Prof. Heidl's article referred to in a preceding chapter, " Die Bekehrung in klassischen Altertum," (Zeitschrift f. Relspsy. III), esp. pp. 384–89.

[6] See Sarkar's " Chaitanya's Pilgrimages " taken from a 16th Century biography, the Chaitanya-charit-amrita.   Translated by J. Sarkar, pp. 165, 308–09.

[7] See Macnicol's " Indian Theism " (Oxford University Press: 1915), p. 132.

mind but also in the general principles of crowd psychology. It is necessary, therefore, at this point to say a few words upon the latter subject. Since the appearance of Tarde's " Laws of Imitation " [8] it has been customary with many writers to treat of the psychology of the crowd as if it were essentially different from the psychology of the individual, and to refer to imitation or suggestibility as if it were almost created by the presence of the mob. If we examine these phenomena, however, we shall see that they are plainly characteristic of the individual out of the crowd as well as in it, and that they are, moreover, by no means so simple as much mob psychology takes them to be. It will hardly do, therefore, merely to say that man is endowed with an instinct of imitation or suggestibility, and stop with that.[9] For, as a fact, we can go further. As we have seen, there is no specific instinct of imitation : both imitation and suggestibility themselves are complex phenomena into which several factors enter. Perhaps the most fundamental of these, as was pointed out in a previous chapter, is the tendency of every mental content which holds the attention to get control of the motor centers and thus to work itself out into the action of the voluntary muscles — a tendency commonly referred to as dynamogenesis and ideo-motor action.[10] Another factor in sug-

[8] 1892.

[9] As Prof. Bentley has well said, " Suggestion, domination, etc., are — until they are empirically defined — sheer abstractions used as agents or forces. They are precisely analogous to the *faculties* of the eighteenth century." (" A Preface to Social Psychology." Psychological Monographs of the *Psy. Rev.*, June, 1916, p. 11.)

[10] Is is only fair here to point out that the very existence of such a thing as ideo-motor action has recently been denied by competent psychologists — notably by Professor Thorndike in his presidential address before the American Psychological Association in 1913, (" Ideo-Motor Action," published in the *Psy. Rev.* for March, 1913, pp. 91–106). This is, of course, not the place for a detailed discussion of the subject, but I may at least say that Professor Thorndike's presentation of his side of the case has left me quite unconvinced. If we maintain ideo-motor action in reference to the voluntary muscles only and if we refrain from insisting that the idea which prompts the movement must be *like* the movement, Professor Thorndike's criticism of the doctrine will be robbed of most of its weapons. Certainly the weight of authority is still greatly upon the side of the doctrine as propounded by James. (See the " Principles of Psychology," Vol. II, pp. 522–28.) I am not sure, moreover, that the difference between Professor Thorndike and the majority of psychologists on this subject is so great as he thinks it; for by admitting what others

gestibility is the tendency of the mind to accept as true every un-contradicted idea which stands before it — in other words, the phenomenon of "primitive credulity." [11]   So far as I can see, these related modes of mental action are hardly further analyza-ble, and depend directly upon the structure of the nervous sys-tem and the very nature of the human mind.   But they do not fully account for what crowd psychology calls imitation or sug-gestion.   For not all the ideas or actions suggested to the mind get an equally powerful hold over the attention.   To understand fully the force of suggestion and imitation we must refer to the additional fact that man is by nature and instinct a social being.   He is so made that suggestions coming to him from his fellows possess a peculiar power over his attention and hence master his beliefs and his actions as no others can.   Based as it is on forces so fundamental as those we have been considering, the power of social suggestion is very great over all minds.   In more developed and complex natures, however, it seldom seems dominant, because in a sense it defeats itself.   Within an edu-cated mind no one idea or motor impulse is long without rivals for the control of attention.   The rival ideas thus tend to in-hibit each other, and either to prevent action altogether, or to give time for cool consideration of all relevant issues before action is taken or adherence to belief finally given.   In more primitive minds this inhibitive power is largely lacking, and any idea that comes from a source possessing prestige or power over the attention is likely to master the entire mind and control the muscles of the body.[12]

call ideo-motor action in cases where instinct or habit are involved he has left room for something very like conciliation.   At any rate, the kind of ideo-motor action which he has left standing by this admission is prob-ably quite as much as is needed for the purposes of our chapter.

[11] For a discussion of this see Chapter X of this book.

[12] Animals are, of course, particularly good examples of the power of a certain limited kind of suggestibility, obeying as they do quite automati-cally and obviously any suggestion in line with their instinctive interests. The hypnotized person is a better example of *social* suggestion.   Certain very primitive and ill-organized individuals, especially among the lower races, are almost equally suggestible.   An excellent example of this as found among the Malays is given by Sir F. A. Swetenham in his "Malay Sketches" (New York, Lane: 1899), in which (among other striking cases) he describes the hypnotic effect produced upon some of the natives by the sight of stones being thrown into the water.   So great was the force of

It hardly needs saying, therefore, (although, considering the past history of the " suggestion " doctrine, it perhaps had better be said) that human nature in a crowd is the same as human nature everywhere else, and that there are not really two psychologies, the individual and the social. The acts which men perform when in association with others grow out of the fundamental forces that control their action when alone.[13] What the presence of the crowd does is to emphasize certain factors already present, which it is able to do because of man's peculiar sensitiveness to social stimuli. It does not create suggestibility, but it does increase it. This it does in two ways: (1) by weakening or banishing all inhibitory tendencies, and also (2) by increasing the dominance over attention possessed by the central idea or impulse. These are, of course, but two aspects of the same thing, but for the purposes of exposition it may be well to consider them separately.

There are many ways in which the presence of a crowd tends to break down the inhibitions both of action and of belief which ordinarily influence the minds of its members. One of the less important of these ways is to be found in the limitations of the individual's voluntary movements produced by the close proximity of many others.[14] As the control of one's muscles and the consciousness of moving them as one wills is an important factor in the sense of personality and of freedom, the loss of this power in a closely packed throng diminishes the sense of independence, produces a feeling of helplessness, and thus diminishes to some extent the force of those inhibitions which in freer physical conditions might oppose the suggestions

this suggestion upon their very primitive minds that one man after another felt compelled to dive into the water, until finally they begged that no more stones should be thrown.

[13] Professor Dewey has well pointed out the absurdity of the older view of suggestion and consciousness, which made individual and social psychology almost antithetic. "As a concrete illustration of the absurd results to which this antithesis led, it is perhaps sufficient to refer to those bizarre writings on the psychology of the crowd in which it was assumed that the psychology of the individual left to himself is reflective and rational, while man's emotional obsessions and irrationalities are to be accounted for by the psychology of association with others." ("The Need for Social Psychology," *Psy. Rev.* XXIV, July, 1917, 268.)

[14] A fact pointed out by Sidis, in "The Psychology of Suggestion " (New York, Appleton: 1909), p. 299.

of the crowd. Much more important than this loss of voluntary movement is the increased sense of power which one gets by being a member of a great throng. The consciousness of the force of united action makes obstacles seem slight which to the individual alone would seem insuperable. In the bright lexicon of the crowd there is no such word as *fail*. The sense of responsibility, moreover, is correspondingly weakened. The individual is hidden by the mob and therefore safe; no one can find and punish him. Only the crowd is responsible and the crowd is big and strong and need not fear. Hence the ordinary inhibitions of prudence and propriety are thrown off, and the individual may act as a primitive being who has not reached the stage of reflection.

But the crowd may intensify an idea or impulse in the mind of one of its members not only indirectly but directly. This it does by the large number of sources of suggestion which it brings to bear upon him. The normal individual may easily withstand suggestions from one or two sources if they be not too strong. But when these suggestions are multiplied by fifty, by one hundred, by ten thousand, many a man succumbs. This, as has often been pointed out, is one of the secrets of advertising. I can with equanimity and self-control read the sign " Use Sapolio. It Floats," and thereafter go my way undisturbed. I can see it displayed in shop windows and resist it. But when I find it impossible to enter a trolley car without being told that in Spotless Town nothing else is used, when I cannot open a magazine without being informed that hand sapolio is the only thing that will make me respectable, when I cannot walk the streets nor stroll into the country without being reminded by placards in large letters that I am really no gentleman because I have as yet failed to provide myself with that *sine qua non* of decency, my conscience finally speaks out, and I yield. In the words of Mr. Dooley, " I belave anything at all if ye only tell it to me aften enough." This principle of the force of repetition is of course seen to an immeasurable extent in the suggestions which the members of a crowd make to each other. A belief or impulse or emotion is propagated in a crowd by geometrical progression. Each member is influenced by each and influences each in turn, and so the contagion sweeps through the throng, the emotional impulse to action or to belief often becoming very nearly irresistible.[15]

The members of a crowd, therefore, tend to be more suggestible, more *primitive* in their reactions than they would be by themselves. The higher and more complex faculties are temporarily weakened by the influence of large numbers of like-minded fellows, and the more fundamental and simple reactions, no longer inhibited, have things their own way. As Le Bon has pointed out, men differ from each other most in intellect, morality, ideas, and least in animal impulses and emotions; hence the greater the power of the crowd the more do its members come to resemble each other, the things in which they differ being laid aside. Emotion and imagination become very prominent, while the critical judgment becomes weak. Hence the occurrence of collective hallucinations and the extreme impulsiveness and credulity of crowds, their lack of higher rational, moral, and prudential control, their cowardice and their courage, their cruelty, heroism, and self-devotion.[16]

The characteristics of crowds (in the psychological sense) which we have been discussing are all manifest in the religious crowd which one finds in every intense revival. The production of these characteristics is, in fact, the first condition of a successful revival, as is well known by every efficient evangelist. You cannot get up a revival in cold blood. It is not a thing to be done as you saw wood or write a sermon. You may collect a great throng of people — as you do in fact Sunday after Sunday — and still not have a " psychological crowd." The peculiar conditions of like mindedness, of great suggestibility, of emotional excitement, and of absence of inhibition which characterize a psychological crowd are not to be brought about *merely* by getting people together.[17] So long as your congre-

---

[15] Emotional and impulsive contagion of this sort is not confined to human crowds. Tennent gives an example of it in a herd of elephants (" Ceylon," London, Longmans: 1860; Part VIII, Chap. IV). A case of the same phenomenon among horses is cited by Sidis, op. cit., p. 314.

[16] Cf. Le Bon, " The Crowd " (London, Unwin: 1903), *passim.*

[17] It must be remembered, however, that the people who assemble to hear a revivalist are, as a rule, partly prepared in advance to be good " crowd " material, being chosen out from the community by a process of natural selection. Their very presence, moreover, in the church or auditorium or " tabernacle," with its many suggestions and influences does

gation is just a collection of individuals who retain all their inhibitions you may preach to them and reason with them and perhaps convince them of various facts, but you cannot have a revival. In the phrase of evangelical theology, the heart is not awakened and there is no overmastering sense of sin and no " conversions "; in psychological terms there is no increased suggestibility and loss of inhibition. Practical religious workers and " revivalists " know just as well as do the psychologists what is lacking and what must be done to bring about the desired result. The first condition is that a state of mental strain, expectancy, and subdued excitement should be induced throughout the community. This may come about naturally and without anyone's intending it, or it may be deliberately brought about through the initiative of individuals. It is the *sine qua non* of a successful revival. The community and the religious gatherings of the community must be transformed from mere collections of individuals into psychological crowds; the condition of like-mindedness must be induced. This is to be done in various ways. The thought of the community may be focussed on the one topic of the coming revival, and the mysterious and supernatural power which is expected to manifest itself therein. Thus a state of subdued excitement and intense expectation is induced which tends to inhibit critical reason, worldly ideas, and selfish purposes, and to prepare the mind for the unquestioning acceptance of wonderful things and for the complete surrender of purely individual aims.[18]

A beautiful illustration of this process is to be found in the very fragmentary account preserved in the book of Acts of the first Christian revival — the day of Pentecost. The little Christian community believed that Jesus had appeared to certain of their number and had bidden them assemble in Jerusa-

---

much toward changing the audience from a mere physical aggregate into a crowd. An excellent discussion of the influences here involved will be found in C. H. Woolbert's paper on " The Audience " (Psy. Monographs of the *Psy. Rev.* XXI, No. 4 June, 1916, pp. 37–54). See also Helen Clark's " The Crowd " in the same number.

[18] I do not wish to imply by the foregoing that preparation of the sort described is in any way improper. It is often the easiest means to a very desirable end. As Stanton Coit has pointed out, a religious movement need be none the less spiritual because organized. See his " National Idealism and a State Church," pp. 17–18.

lem and wait together until some mysterious token of His presence and power should come. Just what this should be they probably did not picture — it was quite vague; but the feeling was strong that some strange, supernatural event was to occur. As the days went by in mutual influence, the feeling increased by geometrical progression. Each one made the suggestion to his neighbor and received it back two-fold. They held constant meetings in which they talked the matter over with each other, prayed over it, and thus induced a state of like-mindedness and mutual suggestibility which transformed them (in all reverence be it said) from a collection of individuals into a genuine " psychological crowd." "And when the day of Pentecost was fully come they were all with one accord in one place." Notice the distinct assertion of like-mindedness. And then came the expected. The clouds somehow burst, the old inhibitions which may have bound them to their old lives were gone, everything was surrendered to the will of God, and a tide of emotion and devoted loyalty swept over them which they had never known before, the results of which will end only with human history.

The same sort of expectancy and suppressed excitement is the herald of most great revivals. This was notably the case with the revival of 1857 which grew out of the mental strain resulting from the financial crisis, a psychological condition utilized by the six persons who instituted the daily Fulton St. prayer-meeting.[19] The revivals of Edwards and Whitefield, and in more recent times of Moody and the great Welsh revival illustrate the same preparatory process. The early meetings in Billy Sunday's revivals, with their elaborate advertising and their sensational attractions, are deliberate attempts to prepare the community and the audience for efforts to be made later on to induce men and women to " hit the trail." The small group meetings held by local leaders before the arrival of the revivalist aim also at the same psychological result. The audience with which he is to deal must be transformed into a psychological crowd before he can really play upon it.[20]

[19] See Prime, " The Power of Prayer " (New York, Scribner: 1859), esp. Chap. II.

[20] In a little book called " Pentecost: or the Revival of the Work of

The methods used in the revival meeting itself are well known. Public prayer unless made by one who has the art of arousing emotion to an unusual degree is not very useful and may weary the audience; but the singing of hymns carefully chosen and in which all unite is exceedingly efficacious, and its value is not overlooked by those who know the technique of revivals.[21] The hymn has two great advantages. In the first place all can take part in it; the emotions which have been swelling up in the hearts of the individuals can thus be given vent. The man can sing as loud as he likes and thus express himself. Thus it comes that the hymn is especially valuable for both suggestion and auto-suggestion. By singing out at the top of his voice the sentiments and ideas which the revivalist desires to instill into him, each member of the audience suggests them to himself, in the technical meaning of that phrase. And he also at the same time passes on the suggestion to his neighbor. The whole audience thus acts upon each individual in the audience and so acts and reacts upon itself, thus spreading the desired suggestion by geometrical progression. Each in-

God," written in 1860 (Morgan and Chase: London) by the Rev. George Wilkinson, the reader will find a very clear-sighted presentation of the methods calculated to bring about the psychological condition requisite to a successful revival. The author of course writes purely as a theologian and practical religious worker, but shows much insight into the psychological principles concerned. See also Fryer's "Psychological Aspects of the Welsh Revival" (P. S. P. R. XIX, 86–87).

[21] Thus Wilkinson says: "As nothing relating to the proper conduct of the worship of God should be deemed unimportant or unworthy of regard, so attention should be given to the *singing*. Souls have been converted by means of the *hymns;* care therefore should be taken to select those which are suitable. Regard should also be had to the manner in which they are *given out*. They should be read with intelligence and feeling, that they may not be meaningless and unimpressive. The *tunes*, likewise, should be adapted to the words, and such as all can sing with ease." Op. cit., p. 68. The singing of hymns by the congregation was one of the most striking features of the late revival in Wales, and one of the chief instruments in rousing the desired religious enthusiasm. M. de Fursac who went over from France to watch the revival from the purely psychological point of view writes of the singing as follows:

"On a l'impression de quelque chose qui vous prend tout entier, vous étreint et vous pénètre: on éprouve le sentiment religieux par excellence, le sentiment d'une réalité supérieure depassant les réalités sensibles: il semble que la conscience affranchie de l'espace et du temps prenne contact avec l'absolu." ("Un Mouvement Mystique Contemporain," Paris, Alcan; 1907, p. 55.

dividual also feels the strength and power of the whole back of him, reinforcing his good resolves and his religious faith, and inhibiting all that opposes them. And secondly, the fact that the hymn involves music makes it a peculiarly fit tool for producing and communicating emotion. Music is essentially emotional and may often bring one into a mood which no amount of preaching could induce. Emotion is especially desirable at revival meetings, for it is one of the best tools for breaking down inhibitions, and filling the mind with some idea or impulse congruous to the emotion. The music of the hymns found in a revival hymn book, or chosen by the revivalist, is of an especially emotional nature. It is far from intellectual. It must not be melancholy though it may be sad, and it must not be gay though it may be joyful. Above all it must not be difficult and it must be catchy.[22] It must be of the kind that runs on in the head and sings itself. And it must be very decided in its emotional coloring, so that the mere music itself may alone arouse the particular emotions of awe, repentance, hope, etc., that the revivalist seeks to bring about. This heightening of emotion may often be a most worthy aim, and I speak of it not at all to bring reproach upon the singing of hymns. The impulse which the revivalist is usually seeking to induce is complete devotion to the will of God,— an impulse that is often inhibited in the individual by selfish and unworthy motives. If now the mind can be so filled with religious emotion that all these inhibitions shall lapse into the background or be clean forgotten and only the desire to do God's will remain, the result not only may be excellent, but may lead to further steps which shall mean genuine and lasting conversion.

The aim of the revivalist's sermon or address is seldom to convince the reason by logical arguments. As the revivalist knows perfectly well, most of his audience is already *convinced,* so far as intellectual acceptance is concerned, of all his doctrinal points, and if they were not he could hardly hope to make any great effect upon them by logic, and if he should do so it would have only a logical effect in changing their creed. The trouble with his hearers is not in their heads but in their hearts, not in their creed but in their emotions and impulses and actions.

---

[22] Cf. " Brighten the Corner "— the favorite hymn of all Billy Sunday's audiences

Somehow he must act upon their minds in such a way as to control the whole man, to give him emotions so intense that he shall never forget them and that he shall look upon life from a new point of view, and readjust his whole system of values. Hence it is not logic that the revivalist needs to know but psychology, and hence also he is quite justified in not making his address a cold logical argument.

And so every revivalist makes a large part of his address an emotional appeal, playing upon the hearts of his hearers, throwing in a bit of humor now and then to keep the attention of the less interested, introducing many a pathetic story to bring tears to the eyes, getting the audience more and more under his sway, and finally leading up to a well planned climax which brings things to a crisis.   Many emotions are thus induced, but the two most often used in revivals are fear and love.   In the days when belief in hell was much stronger than it is to-day fear was a very powerful instrument in the hands of the preacher.[23]   To depict the fate of the lost soul in terrific terms and to point out that undoubtedly some sitting there would in a very short time be suffering those eternal torments was an unfailing means, in the hands of men like Jonathan Edwards, of driving all inhibitions out of one's mind and making one cry out in despair, "What must I do to be saved?"   To-day it is rather love than fear that is emphasized — the love of the father for his prodigal son, the love of Christ on the Cross, the picture of God stretching out his arms to the sinner, etc.

Another means of suggestion besides this powerful appeal

[23] The use of fear in revivals together with threats of hell fire are by no means things of the past.   As all newspaper readers know, Billy Sunday is very generous with his brimstone and probably succeeds in terrifying some members of his audience.   An example of this sort of revival preaching from a less well known evangelist — the Rev. B. S. Taylor — seems worth quoting here.   It is taken from an address delivered in 1907 in northern New York: " I preach hell because God puts His special blessing on it, convicting sinners and sanctifying believers, arousing the Church to greater effort for the salvation of the perishing.   I preach hell because it arouses their fears, arrests their consciences, and causes them to reform their lives and habits . . . *Hell has been running for six thousand years.* It is filling up every day.   Where is it?   About eighteen miles from here. *Which way is it?   Straight down* — not over eighteen miles, down in the bowels of the earth."   (" Death, Hell and Judgment," God's Revivalist Office, Mount of Blessings, Cincinnati, O., 1900.   Republished in the *Life Line,* July, 1907, p. 4.)

to the emotions and the imagination, is affirmation and repetition. Perhaps no one in the audience would deny the truth of Jesus' words, " Ye must be born again," but this intellectual assent to them has no influence on conduct. When, however, the audience, by all the means thus far described, has become extremely suggestible and has come completely under the dominance of the preacher, his solemn affirmation and repetition of these words of Jesus throws a new light upon them, and they fill and dominate the mind as never before.

In what one might call the milder or more rationalistic type of revival meeting, the audience is at this point dismissed. But revivalists who wish to use all the weapons of psychology in saving souls are unwilling to let their hearers go home and make their decisions in the cold light of to-morrow's reflection. The iron that is now hot will not remain so long, and now is therefore the time to strike. If the repentant sinner can be got to put himself on record before his fellows by some overt act as being definitively on the Lord's side, he will find in the coming days all the forces of personal pride and of social encouragement reënforcing his weakening enthusiasm. Hence the use of the " mourner's bench," the " anxious seat," the " sawdust trail." Hence also the personal appeal at the close of the address or during the latter part of it, made either by the revivalist himself or by his assistants in the audience, to particular individuals who seem on the verge of surrender. The procession of these converts up the " trail " to the " mourner's bench " acts, of course, as a new and powerful suggestion upon all who see them. Hymns are now sung chosen specially for their suggestive effect — some of them seemingly written to produce auto-suggestion. What psychological means, for example, could be better adapted to the end in view than that hymn so commonly used at such meetings:

> " Just as I am without one plea
> But that Thy blood was shed for me
> And that Thou bidst me come to Thee,
> O Lamb of God, I come, I come."

Analyze this hymn and you will find it psychologically a masterpiece of auto-suggestion. In the first place, the very tune to which it is sung tends to arouse the desired feeling state and inspire ideas and impulses of self-devotion and love.   The verses describe exactly the feeling of sinfulness, hope, and love with which the revivalist wishes to fill the hearts of his hearers.   And most important and effective of all, each verse ends with the refrain "I come, I come."   Between the singing of the verses the speaker says in low and tender tones, "Won't you come? Come now!"   And then the audience sings "I come, I come." A more obvious case of auto-suggestion could not be found.[24]

It is of course the most suggestible who start the procession up the "trail," the most "primitive," the most impulsive, the least rational and responsible.   The appearance of slight abnormal nervous phenomena in some of the more unstable members of the audience may also have a similar effect in increasing the power of suggestion.   In our day, to be sure, these extreme expressions of emotion (of which more later on) are pretty generally deprecated and may have an inhibitory rather than a suggestive effect upon the beholders.   But in the palmy days of revivals they were used as powerful implements by the practiced revivalist who knew how to utilize them to the utmost. Thus Jonathan Edwards writes: "The unavoidable manifestations of strong religious affections tend to a happy influence on the minds of bystanders, and are found by experience to have an excellent and endurable effect; and so to contrive and order things that others may have opportunity and advantage to observe them, has been found to be blessed as a great means to promote the work of God." [25]

Probably the great majority of revivalists to-day deprecate the occurrence of such phenomena as those which Edwards and the men of his time welcomed; but there still are a few — or at least there were very recently — who make the most of every aid, normal or abnormal, and who "contrive and order things" with all the success made possible by their deep knowledge of psychology and their skill in applying it.   Professor Coe tells of one revivalist who practiced the most undisguised

[24] In a revival meeting in Mississippi a few years ago I found this hymn used in the manner described, and with great skill.

[25] "Thoughts on the Revival of Religion in New England" (New York, American Tract Society), p. 260.

and premeditated form of suggestion, calling out, when no one as yet had started for the mourner's bench, " See them coming ! See them coming ! "   And he adds, " Now if a professional hypnotizer should employ precisely the same means to bring subjects to the platform, he would probably succeed, though his power would go under some other name than preaching or oratory." [26]

The effects produced by so powerful a force as a revival of the sort we have been studying may be, and usually are, both good and evil.   The power of suggestion which it yields is simply enormous and in the past it has often swept through whole communities and countries with a force of contagion hardly to be resisted.   The most hardened sinners and scoffers often yield to this mysterious force of social suggestion, this overpowering form of ideo-motor action.   They come to scoff and remain to pray.   Innumerable cases of the sudden conversion of depraved men and women in revival meetings are recorded in the books, and not infrequently we are assured that a real and lasting reformation of life has followed.   Many a man whose selfish and vicious instincts are too strong for him to overcome by any amount of reasoning and good resolve has been set right once and for all by the tremendous power of a revival.   He has had a glimpse into a new realm of life of which he never dreamed before.   Mr. W. T. Stead writes as follows of the revival in which as a boy he was converted : " There is one point upon which I think I may fairly claim to speak at first hand, and that is as to the effect of that experience at Silcoats in 1861 upon my whole life.   It is forty-three years since that revival at school.   The whole of my life during these forty-three years has been influenced by the change which men call conversion which occurred with me when I was twelve. Other spiritual experiences I have had and hope yet to have. But the fundamental change came to me then.   My life has been flawed with many failures, darkened with many sins, but the thing in which there was good, which has enabled me to resist temptations to which I would otherwise have succumbed, to bear burdens which would otherwise have crushed me with

[26] " The Spiritual Life," p. 145.   Cf. also the case of Le Roy Sunderland, cited by Davenport, op. cit., p. 254–57.

their weight, and which has kept the soul within me ever joyfully conscious that, despite all appearances to the contrary, this is God's world, and that He and I are fellow workers in the work of its renovation — that potent thing came into my life then and abides with me to this hour,— my one incentive in this life; my sole hope for that which is to come." [27]

One who should fail to recognize the great service which revivals have done in stirring and reinforcing the religious and the moral life of many men and women, especially in the centuries before ours, would show little comprehension of the subject.   The revival is a center of enormous power and this power often works mightily for righteousness.   In the words of Mr. C. C. B. Bardsley, " well-known facts are seen transfigured with the new light; doctrines which have been mechanically professed for years suddenly appear as intimate realities and are invested with a new and wonderful wealth of meaning; worship becomes communion; prayer and praise, from being formal utterances on the lips, become the expressions of the overflowing desire and adoration of the heart." [28]

Unfortunately, the enormous power of the revival is not always directed wholly toward ends so desirable as those just described.   The power of suggestion which characterizes it, once let loose, may produce effects that hardly tend to edification.   These questionable and abnormal effects are, indeed, very much less common than once they were, and are steadily decreasing.   Yet they are by no means a thing of the past, and the danger of them is ever present once the psychical force of the revival has been induced.   They have formed, moreover, so striking a characteristic of the great historical revivals that they deserve some attention here.   For purposes of exposition they may be viewed under three heads,— namely as the breaking down of inhibition (1) to emotion, (2) to action, (3) to belief.

The letting loose of emotion is so obvious a result of the revival that we need not dwell upon it.   It is brought about by all the elements of the meeting — by the presence of others, by the prayers, especially by the hymns, and by the sermon.[29]

[27] " The Welsh Revival " (Boston, 1905) pp. 12–13.

[28] " Revival, the Need and the Possibilities " (London, Longmans: 1916), p. 21.

[29] Among more primitive communities, e.g., with the southern negro —

The value of this emotional incitement will depend on the nature of the emotion aroused and on the use made of it. It may be a decisive force in the struggle of higher ideals over lower tendencies, and may thereby carry the individual over some turning point in his life and thus largely determine his destiny and usefulness. On the other hand to appeal to the emotions upon questions where only reason and evidence are really relevant is to found one's house upon the sands. The immediate results may pile up fine figures of conversion and of increased church membership, but the seeming growth of the religious community, thus brought about, will be very unsound.

The breaking down of the ordinary inhibitions to action and the corresponding reinforcement brought to various motor impulses by the excitement of the revival needs no special treatment here, and many illustrations of it will probably occur to the reader — such as the preaching of Peter the Hermit, the "Children's Crusade," contemporary methods for raising money at church meetings, for inducing drinkers to sign the pledge and young men to promise to join the church or go upon missions. There is, however, one peculiar expression of the abnormal impulsiveness sometimes produced by revivals which deserves some consideration here, both because of its rather striking nature, and also because of its continual reappearance at various times in the history of Christianity, from the days of the Apostles down to our own time. I refer to glossolalia, or "speaking with tongues."

It consists in this: that under the pressure of great excitement one or more individuals begin to express their emotions by pouring out a broth of meaningless syllables, which they and those around them take to belong to some unknown language. This gibberish of syllables and new-made sounds is of course not all invented on the spur of the moment. Try to

the sermon is almost entirely an emotional affair. It contains practically no ideas, no attempt at reasoning; it is merely an excited endeavor to rouse the emotions. Thus in one negro revival meeting which I attended in Mississippi the preacher intoned his address,— sang it on one or two notes. What he said was merely a concatenation of misquoted and irrelevant Bible verses, quite detached; but the result was considerable. If he had spoken in Chinese and used the same intoning or singing method, his results would probably have been about as great.

talk nonsense for five minutes and you will see why. Some real words will now and then come out. Especially will this be the case with those who think they are speaking some language not their own and who happen to know a few words of some other tongue. In the volley of meaningless sounds which they pour forth they will be pretty sure to include specimens of whatever foreign tongue they know and now and then a word of their own language. This being the case, it naturally happens that by-standers who are thoroughly convinced that this collection of sounds really means something and is inspired by the Holy Ghost, will recognize a word occasionally and interpret the meaning of the whole accordingly. And the interpretation is of course still more due to intonation, gesture, the general expression of emotion, and the conventional ideas uppermost in the meeting.

The frequency of this peculiar phenomenon is apparently due to two things. (1) First the presence of an overpowering emotion altogether in excess of ideas. " Brethren," exclaims a brother in a New York camp meeting of whom Professor Coe writes, " Brethren, I feel — I feel — I feel — I feel — I feel — I can't tell you how I feel, but O I feel! I feel! " [30] Feeling, on the other hand, is notoriously incommunicable in words, and on the other it is essentially explosive and must be expressed somehow. So some brethren say " I feel," others, shout and sing, and others speak with tongues. No words of any known tongue will express their feeling, so to give it vent they use the words of an unknown tongue.— (2) The other cause of this peculiar phenomenon is the powerful suggestion derived from the Acts of the Apostles and the writings of St. Paul. To speak in an unknown tongue is Biblical, and probably most of those who indulge in it get the idea from the Bible. It is spoken of in the New Testament as a peculiar sign of the presence of the Holy Ghost. Hence when one is sure from the intensity of one's feelings that the Holy Ghost is within one, it comes into one's head to express one's emotions by speaking in an unknown tongue.

The first occurrence of the phenomenon of which we have any record was at Pentecost. It was a time of very intense

[30] " The Spiritual Life," p. 215.

religious excitement and suggestibility.   There had been days of oppressive strain and waiting, and at last the flood gates of emotion were opened and a great revival occurred.   Under the influence of this intense emotion some of the individuals started expressing their new-found joy either in some real language which they knew but which was not their own or else in the same sort of meaningless syllables that are used by their imitators to-day.   Jerusalem, it must be remembered, was a decidedly polyglot community, and nearly every individual in this first Christian revival knew a great many words of other languages besides his own — it was impossible to' walk the streets without hearing and learning them.   No great wonder then that the listeners, made credulous by emotional excitement and suggestion, should say, " We hear them speak every one in our own language." [31]   The fact that it was taken as a sign of the presence of the Spirit forced its acceptance upon the early Church as a recognized form of religious expression, and it is spoken of by St. Paul as on a par with other " spiritual gifts."   It seems to have been especially prevalent among the Corinthians. And in giving them directions as to their meetings St. Paul says: " If any man speaketh in a tongue let it be by two or at most three, and that in turn; and let one interpret: but if there be no interpreter let him keep silence in the church and let him speak to himself and to God."   It is interesting to note that Paul refers to speaking with tongues as a method of giving expression to the " spirit " (which I suppose one may understand, from a psychological point of view, to mean the feelings but not the understanding).   " For when I pray in a tongue my spirit prayeth but my understanding is unfruitful.— What is it then?   I will pray with the spirit and I will pray with the understanding also." [32]   The tone of this passage shows that Paul, with his usual keen insight and good sense, tolerated rather than urged this kind of expression,— a fact which is

[31] Weinel, who has studied glossolalia in the New Testament carefully, regards these words as an interpretative addition of the compiler of Acts, not based upon the sources but upon his false assumption that in " speaking with tongues " unknown but real languages were used.   " Die Wirkungen des Geistes und der Geister " (Freiburg, Mohr: 1899), p. 75.

[32] See 1 Corinthians, XIV, 14.   The feelings seem to have been regarded as inspired by the Spirit.

better seen in such a passage as I Cor. XIII and XIV where he discourages the custom, saying, " I had rather speak five words with my understanding that I might instruct others also, than ten thousand words in a tongue," (XIV. 19) ; and, " If I speak with the tongues of men and of angels and have not love I am become sounding brass or a clanging cymbal." [33]

The phenomenon, however, has persisted all through the Christian centuries and crops out now and then (among the more primitive) at times of great religious excitement — especially as a result of revivals. It seems to occur most often, as one might expect, in rather polyglot communities, where every one knows some words of some foreign language. I cite a few instances. Mr. W. T. Ellis, who was sent around the world in 1907 to investigate Christian missions, came upon the phenomenon in India (a very polyglot community) among Hindu Christians,— and in fact returned a convert to its supernatural genuineness, though apparently without any careful investigation. In the same year the phenomenon appeared in South America, Colorado, California, Maine, and several other states, and at about the same time in Norway, Germany, England, and Switzerland. As late as 1910 there was to my knowledge a considerable epidemic of it in Chicago and Zion City. And in fact the practice of speaking with tongues is probably to be found in some part of the United States nearly all the time.[34]

---

[33] For a careful study of the whole matter see Weinel, op. cit., pp. 71–101.

[34] See the *Literary Digest* for Feb. 1, 1908, p. 157, quoting from the *Presbyterian Standard* of Charlotte, N. C.; also F. G. Henke's " The Gift of Tongues and Related Phenomena at the Present Day," *Am. Jour. of Theol.* XIII, 193–95. For accounts of various recent cases see Zeitschrift für Religionspsychologie, I, 320, 392, 439–40, 470–71; The Open Court XXII, 492–98; *Die Christliche Welt* (Marburg) for Mar. 12, 1908, pp. 272–276; Die Heiligung (Steglitz), Heft Nr. 110; Rubanowitsch's " Das heutige Zungenreden " (Neumünster) ; and Dallmeyer's " Satan unter den Heiligen " (Neumünster). The most instructive case of glossolalia I have found is that of the German " Pastor Paul " (Editor of " *Die Heiligung* ") whose case is reported at length in his own monthly and also in *Die Christliche Welt*. He had read with great interest of the speaking with tongues in America and Norway, went to the latter country to see for himself and was deeply impressed, studied First Corinthians with care, and finally on Sept. 15, 1907, in a religious meeting the power came upon him also. Singing " in tongues " has become one of his accomplishments,

More striking and certainly far more undesirable than speaking with tongues are the so-called " bodily effects " of revival excitement.   They are of many sorts — and most of them thoroughly pathological and disgusting.   Suggestion and excitement here become positively abnormal, so that the man ceases to have control any longer of his own nerves and muscles.   The simplest form perhaps is the " powers," common in the religious meetings of the southern negro,— and sometimes among whites. The victim (for so we may call him) jumps about, or collapses into unconsciousness [35] through religious excitement.   Extremes

the tune of some familiar hymn getting itself filled out with new syllables in meter and rhyme.   Here is an example:

> " Schua ea, schua ea
> o tschi biro ti ra pea
> akki lungo ta ri fungo
> u li hara to ra tungo
> latschi bungo ti tu ta."

By a comparison of these hymns " in tongues " (" in Zungen ") with the German of the hymn usually sung to the given tune, Pastor Paul has been enabled to discover the meaning of some of the new words, and now rejoices that he has learned some of the language of Heaven (" *ich habe etwas von der himmlischen Sprache gelernt* ").

So far as I know there is nothing so elaborate as this in America.   In 1910 I was present at a religious meeting in Chicago in which the brethren and especially the sisters spoke in tongues, but in these cases the speaking was almost invariably confined to exclamations more or less long.   Never, so far as I know, has the American type of glossolalia ventured into verse, although singing in tongues is not uncommon.   By far the most detailed treatment of this subject is that by Emile Lombard, " De la Glossolalie, chez les premiers chrétiens at des phenoménes similaires " (Lausanne, Bridel; 1910).   A description of the Chicago type of glossolalia, together with an excellent psychological analysis, will be found in Dr. Henke's article.   An interesting case of glossolalia connected neither with revivals nor with Christianity was investigated by Prof. James in 1895, who communicated to the Society for Psychical Research the account of the phenomenon written by the subject himself.   It was diagnosed by Prof. James as " a decidedly rudimentary form of motor automatism analogous to the scrawls and scribbles of an ' undeveloped ' automatically writing hand." The meaningless words produced in this case were of course much like those ejaculated by a practiced speaker-with-tongues of the religious sort, and in fact (like Pastor Paul's) were in verse as well as prose.— (" A Case of Psychic Automatism, including ' Speaking with Tongues.' "   P. S. P. R. XII, 277–97.)

[35] Loss of consciousness was not uncommon in the revival in Wales in the middle of the 19th Century,— " sleeping cases " they were called.   A similar loss of consciousness took place occasionally under Finney.   See Davenport, pp. 192–200.

of this sort have been common in many revivals, an especially striking case being the "rolling exercises," "jerks," and "barks" of the great Kentucky revival in 1800. I cite in a note the account of them given by Richard M'Nemar in 1807.[36]

The Kentucky revival though extreme was by no means unique in its production of physical effects. Similar scenes were common in the revivals under John Wesley [37] and other

[36] "The rolling exercises consisted in being cast down in a violent manner, doubled with the head and feet together, and rolled over and over like a wheel, or stretched in a prostrate manner, turned swiftly over and over like a log. This was considered very debasing and mortifying, especially if the person was taken in this manner through the mud, and sullied therewith from head to foot. Still more demeaning and mortifying were the *jerks*. Nothing in nature could better represent this strange and unaccountable operation than for one to goad another, alternately on every side, with a piece of red hot iron. The exercises commonly began in the head which would fly backward and forward and from side to side, with a quick jolt, which the person would naturally labor to suppress, but in vain; and the more any one labored to stay himself and be sober, the more he staggered and the more rapidly his twitches increased. He must necessarily go as he was stimulated, whether with a violent dash on the ground and bounce from place to place like a foot-ball, or hop round, with head, limbs, and trunk twitching and jolting in every direction, as if they must inevitably fly asunder. And how such could escape injury was no small wonder to spectators. By this strange operation the human frame was commonly so transformed and transfigured as to lose every trace of its natural appearance. Sometimes the head would be twitched right and left, to a half round, with such velocity that not a feature could be discovered, but the face appear as much behind as before; and in the quick progressive jerk, it would seem as if the person was transmuted into some other species of creature. . . . The last possible grade of mortification seemed to be couched in the *barks*, which frequently accompanied the jerks; nor were they the most mean and contemptible characters who were the common victims of this disgracing operation; but persons who considered themselves in the foremost ranks, possessed of the highest improvements of human nature, both men and women, would be forced to personate that animal whose name, appropriated to a human creature, is accounted the most vulgar stigma — forced I say, for no argument but force could induce any one of polite breeding in a company to take the position of a canine beast, move about on all fours, growl, snap the teeth, and bark in so personating a manner as to set the eyes and ears of the spectator at variance." ("The Kentucky Revival: or A Short History of the Late Extraordinary Outpouring of the Spirit of God in the Western States of America," by Richard M'Nemar, published in 1807 and reprinted in New York by Jenkins in 1846.) The quotation above is from pp. 64–66.

[37] See his "Journal," *passim*, but esp., April to October, 1739. Cf. also Davenport, op. cit. Chap. IX. In the recent Welsh revival effects were noticed which seem to have been due to subconscious phenomena,— e.g., hallucinations, "photisms," etc. See Fryer, op. cit. pp. 94–97.

distinguished and venerated evangelists, and abnormal phenomena of much the same sort are still produced in certain American communities.[38] Nor were these unpleasant phenomena generally regarded as deplorable, or explicable by natural causes. Something supernatural was seen in them, and they were explained as the work either of God or of Satan. Three of the older authorities on revivals from whom I have quoted,—Jonathan Edwards,[39] Wilkinson,[40] and M'Nemar [41]— regarded them as the work of God, brought about for the purpose of saving souls. This explanation has been pretty generally given up by revivalists to-day,[42]— the Holy Spirit is no longer seen in the " jerks." But some evangelists still see in pathological phenomena of this sort some kind of supernatural power, attributing them, however, not to God but to the Powers of Evil. This seems, for example, to be the position of Evan Roberts, the great Welsh revivalist.[43] With the spread of psychological knowledge, however, evangelists are becoming more and more inclined to see in the abnormal phenomena that sometimes accompany revivals only the results of over-wrought nerves and great suggestibility.[44] It goes without saying that this is undoubtedly the true explanation. Great nervous excitement of any kind, but especially fear and joy, has to overflow into the muscles somehow. This is seen, as Davenport has pointed out, in the shouts and actions of children, and in

[38] E.g. the " holy rollers." An account of a phenomenon much like the " jerks " and occurring in a clergyman in 1907 will be found in Dr. Henke's article above referred to.

[39] Op. cit. pp. 258–59.

[40] Op. cit. pp. 116–117.

[41] Op. cit. pp. 33–34.

[42] Not altogether. The clergyman who had the jerks in 1907 (referred to in Dr. Henke's article), was very proud of them and regarded them as a mark of divine favor.

[43] See the Zeitschrift f. Religionspsy. I. 471. The 1907 revival in Kassel and other parts of Germany produced many of the common bodily effects. These were attributed by some to God, by some to evil spirits, one authority arguing learnedly for the latter hypothesis because Daniel, Paul, and John fell on their faces, while those who spoke with tongues in Kassel fell on their backs!

[44] So long ago as 1842 this view was taken by the very sensible anonymous author of a little book already once referred to —" Revivals of Religion in Scotland, Ireland, and Wales "— (published in Philadelphia by the Presbyterian Board), see pp. 13 and 14.

the expression of strong emotions generally in both animals and men. Emotions normal in amount and character find regular channels prepared for their escape, but when the emotion is too strong or too sudden for the usual channels it takes unusual ones. At such times the least suggestion, such as that of seeing some one else express himself by jerking or barking, takes possession of the individual and determines the outlet for the nerve excitement, especially in persons of more or less primitive disposition.

So much for the effect of revivals upon action and impulse. We turn now to the third general result — namely the abolition of inhibitions on belief, the banishing of the critical reason. The extreme results which the less admirable revivalists seek are of course impossible unless the critical reason be quite inhibited; and all evangelists alike seek (and quite rightly) to inhibit what they call the worldly reason, the counsels of selfish prudence and mere material welfare. When critical thought is in whole or in part put to sleep through the influence of an emotional atmosphere of suggestion, it is surprising to see how audiences of very high intelligence can at times be reduced to a state of relative primitive credulity. Examples are to be found in the meetings in which hundreds of young men and women are brought to believe absolutely in the "conversion of the world in this generation." Arguments of course are used but these are not the only tools nor the chief ones. The principal thing is to rouse what Leuba calls the "faith state," to put the audience into the emotional mood of belief. Make the individual *want* to believe with all his heart, make him feel that he *ought* to believe, and also that others around him are believing, and he will believe. "To doubt would be disloyalty, to falter would be sin." He simply shuts his eyes to the enormous and insuperable difficulties of the task proposed, the stubborn facts which make his inspiring dream only a dream after all. Not that I would deny the value of a daring faith,— a faith which while not shutting its eyes to the facts is willing to "take a long chance." Every year this kind of faith produces seeming miracles and regularly accomplishes the impossible. And revivals of the better sort have done a magnificent work in kindling this kind of faith — faith in God, in one's fellow men, in oneself, faith in the eternal laws of righteousness and the virtue that is its own reward, the faith that stops the mouths of lions, quenches the violence of fire, and endures without complaint the unheralded drudgery of the common day.

Unfortunately there are revivals of another sort and revivalists who seek other things, and these often succeed in changing man from a rational animal to an emotional animal, in breaking down all forms of reason and making him open to every idea the revivalist would suggest. The strength of inhibiting reason on such occasions is seen when the usual excitement of the revival meeting is dampened or suppressed by the presence of a few skeptics. These act as a break on the suggestions of the speaker and keep some rational inhibitions awake in the minds of the audience.[45] When there are no such inhibiting rational factors present, the audience may be reduced to a state of very great credulity and is ready to accept whatever ideas arise. All the opponents of the revivalist are *of course* wrong and their arguments must simply not be heard. The ideas present to the audience are so vivid that they must be true. What the speaker and community at large believe is accepted by the individual at such times as not to be doubted — even if it be quite out of the course of natural science and rational thought.[46]

The most extreme pathological result of revival methods is

[45] This has been noticed by several, e.g., in the recent Welsh revival — one of the ministers saying concerning it on one occasion, " I don't know what is the reason that this meeting and others I have noticed are so hard. The Spirit of God does not seem to work here to-night yet, but I know that after the *skeptics* and *lookers-on* have gone home, it is then that the spirit works among us." (Fryer, op. cit., p. 127.)

[46] It is in this anti-rational attempt to blind the audience to the facts of science and make them deaf to the appeals of cool thinking that the Rev. Billy Sunday is chiefly to be criticized. His revivals have, on the whole, been notably free from " bodily effects," and his reiterated emphasis upon the moral issue deserves warm commendation. His attempt, however, to base the religious faith of his converts upon the impossible dogmas of a naïve and outgrown theology must inevitably militate against the permanence of his results. It is another case of founding one's house upon the sands.— The reader will find a sympathetic presentation (possible over-sympathetic) of the better side of Mr. Sunday's work, in the *official* account of the revivalist by " Ram's Horn Brown " (Rev. Elijah P.

of course insanity. This, to be sure, does not occur often, but it does occasionally. Weak minds may be roused to such a state of emotional excitement that they simply go to pieces. Fortunately seizures of this sort usually last for only a short time. Under the influence of suggestion from the New Testament they sometimes take the form of demon possession. In Wesley's revival this was common.[47] Sometimes the insanity induced by revival excitement is more lasting, and it may take months or even a year to restore the weak and shattered mind to anything like a normal balance.[48] A few years ago I was told, by the physician in charge of a large asylum in the South, of a revival gotten up by the "Holiness" sect which had brought to the asylum three cases in one week; and one or two cases of temporary insanity, he said, were commonly to be expected after such a period of emotionalism. The proportion of persons affected in this way is, however, extremely small. According to Fryer, not more than one per cent of the increase of insanity in Wales in 1905 was due to the revival.[49] De Fursac would place it higher.[50] The increase in any case, however, is very slight. And one should set against this increase the fact that the number of cases of insanity in Wales due to alcoholism decreased at the same time (and probably as a consequence of the revival) from seventy-one to forty-two, or from sixteen per cent of the total number of cases in 1904 to twelve per cent in 1905. Thus as de Fursac says, " if one considers the number of those whom the revival saved from alcoholic insanity and the number of those whom the revival threw into religious insanity, society is seen to benefit by it. ' It is better,' as some

Brown, D.D.) — entitled "The Real Billy Sunday" (New York, Revell Co.: 1914).

[47] Cf. Davenport, pp. 158–162.

[48] De Fursac saw a student in the Asylum of Glamorgan (in Wales) whose mental health seemed to be permanently compromised as a result of the revival.

[49] This is based on figures from the Glamorgan County Asylum, but presumably holds roughly for the rest of the revival district.— Op. cit. p. 142.

[50] The director of the Glamorgan Asylum gave de Fursac the following figures; Number of cases resulting from religious exaltation in 1904 (the year before the revival), 5; in 1905, 21. In 1904 the religious cases constituted one per cent of the total number of cases received; in 1905 six per cent.

one has said, 'that one man should go mad through religion than that ten should go mad through alcohol.' " [51]

This quotation brings up the question of the relative good and harm wrought by revivals, a question too large to be exhaustively discussed in this place.[52] Here I can merely remind the reader of what I said at the beginning of this chapter as to the normal place of rhythm in all life, and of revivals in all religions. Revivals of religion, revivals of morality, of insight, of patriotism, of ideals, are necessary to the best and noblest living. This is recognized by institutions quite remote from evangelism. Every nation has its annually recurring seasons for the nurture of patriotism. The American college renews the loyalty of her sons at Commencement and at class reunions, and there they often celebrate revivals not only of college spirit but of human loyalty and aspiration. So long as human spirits are connected with human bodies, some kind of seasonal revival will be an important part of their spiritual food.

This does not mean that the old-fashioned emotional revival, gotten up to save souls by means of the power of suggestion, is an immortal institution. Its day is fast going — is practically gone. But while the harmful methods of the old revival are being given up, all that was best in it, by the process of natural selection, survives and will live on. And in a very general way

[51] Op. cit., pp. 124–125. De Fursac adds that the police records of Glamorgan County show even greater results in the repression of alcoholism. The number of cases of drunkenness recorded in 1904 was 10,686; in 1905, 8,422. This improvement, moreover, did not stop at the close of the revival: in 1906 the number of cases was only 5,673.— See pp. 126 and 127, note.

[52] The reader will find this discussed by the following authors:
Cutten, " The Psychological Phenomena of Christianity " (New York, Scribner's: 1908), Chap. XIV.
Davenport, op. cit., Chaps. XIII and XIV.
Dike, " A Study of New England Revivals." *Am. Jour. of Sociology*, XV, 361–78.
Janes, " Religious Revivals, their Ethical Significance " (*Internat. Jour. of Ethics*, XVI, 332–340).
Moses, " Pathological Aspects of Religion " (*Am. Jour. of Religious Psy. and Ed.*, Supplement I. September, 1906, pp. 47–59).
Prime, op. cit., pp. 150f, 178f, 256f.
Sprague, " Lectures on the Revivals of Religion " (N. Y., Appleton: 1833).
Starbuck, " The Psychology of Religion," pp. 165–179.
Stead, " The Welsh Revival."

it is not hard to indicate which parts of it were evil and which were good. The positive elements in it, one may say, constitute its real value, the negative elements its harmful limitations. That doubtless is a rather abstract way of putting it, but what I mean is this: The inhibition of reason, the inhibition of free and responsible individual action, the forcing of emotions and convictions and physical reactions upon relatively passive recipients through the use of semi-hypnotic methods, these things dwarf the personality and belittle the man, these things bring about few if any results of real and permanent value. It is from the recruits of these hypnotic methods that the subsequent " back-sliders " come.[53] On the other hand, a revival adds to the values of life when it emphasizes the positive things, leaving the individual in full command of his reason and free to choose and to act, but giving him new insights and wider glimpses of the truth, opening up to him undreamed-of worlds of possible experience, revelations of new value, arousing in him larger inspirations, purer emotions, and higher aspirations and ideals. These things cannot be given by the methods of hypnotic suggestion and emotionalism. But neither are they to be brought about by conventional morality or " cold " logic. And the church which understands human psychology and wishes for lasting results, will both refrain from the methods of the religious hypnotist and also make some special efforts to obtain " seasons of refreshment from the hand of the Lord."

[53] See Starbuck's comparison of the permanence of conversions made during revivals and of those independent of them — op. cit., p. 170.

CHAPTER X

THE BELIEF IN A GOD

PROBABLY the three most important phenomena in the religion of average men and women are communal worship, private prayer, and belief or faith. It is pretty evident that all of these must have originated and developed together, inasmuch as each of them may almost be said to presuppose the other. There could be no religious cult unless there were some implicit though vague belief on the part of the participants; and every serious and genuine form of religious belief among primitive peoples must almost certainly have worked itself out into some sort of expression — an expression which, from all that we know of early religions, seems pretty surely to have been some form of communal cult. Cult and belief, moreover, through all their development have been mutually influencing each other, so that one who should attempt to write a history of the two would seem to be under obligation to describe both at once. This of course is hardly possible, and in fact the tendency of very many writers on this subject is to neglect the fact of the common birth and parallel development of cult and belief, and to make one of them fundamental and the other derivative. Up till fairly recent times it was belief that was usually made primary, cult being regarded as merely its expression. During the last few years, however, the trend has been all the other way. Primitive societies performed certain rites in common — this is the more recent doctrine — and as a result beliefs arose to interpret the rites. While so extreme a position seems to me quite unjustified by either anthropology or psychology, it is, perhaps, a needed antidote to the older view which saw in primitive men lonely theologians; and certainly there is this much of truth in the newer conception, namely that perfectly definite cult did probably precede definite and explicit religious belief. For this reason I should have preferred to treat communal worship before religious belief. For purposes of exposition, however, there are certain advantages in treating belief first; and since the two are really twins it makes little difference which is first described.   Especially is this true for us, since our question is not the anthropological one: How did religious belief originate; but rather the psychological question: Why does it continue, and what is its nature as a mental phenomenon? — It is to these questions that the present chapter is to be directed.

And first of all we must consider briefly the nature of belief as such.   That this question has certain initial difficulties was made evident by some of the earliest psychologists who undertook to answer it.   St. Thomas defines belief thus, "*Credere est cum assensu cogitare.*" [1]   This is admirable as far as it goes: but it is unsatisfactory as a complete definition both because of the peculiar distinction which the learned saint makes between belief and knowledge, and also because of the lack of any psychological analysis of *assent*.   Some advance is made by David Hume who points out in his Treatise, that "the idea of an object is an essential part of the belief of it but not the whole.   We conceive many things which we do not believe. . . . 'Tis evident that the idea of existence is nothing different from the idea of any object, and that when after the simple conception of anything we would conceive it as existent we in reality make no addition to or alteration on our first idea. . . . When I think of God, when I think of him as existent, and when I believe him to be existent, my idea of him neither increases nor diminishes.   But as 'tis certain there is a great difference betwixt the simple conception of the existence of an object and the belief of it, and as this difference lies not in the parts or composition of the idea which we conceive; it follows that it must lie in the *manner* in which we conceive it."

So far Hume's analysis seems persuasive enough: belief differs from mere ideation " in the *manner* in which we conceive " our object.   But it is hard to be completely satisfied with Hume's description of what this " manner " is.   " Our ideas," he tells us, " are copy'd from impressions [i. e. sense perceptions] and represent them in all their parts.   When you wou'd any way vary the idea of a particular object, you can only

[1] " Summa Theologiae," Part II, II.   Quest. II, Art. I.

increase or diminish its force and vivacity.   If you make any other change on it, it represents a different object or impression. . . . As belief does nothing but vary the manner in which we conceive any object, it can only bestow on our ideas an additional force and vivacity.   An opinion, therefore, or belief might be most accurately defined, *A lively idea related to or associated with a present impression.*"   Or, as Hume defines it again in a foot-note, belief is " only a strong and steady conception of any idea, and such as approaches in some measure to an immediate impression." [2]

Surely there is more in belief than this.   And yet the element in belief which Hume has singled out is deserving of great emphasis.   Sense perception is the stronghold and the ultimate source of reality feeling.   Our earliest beliefs all come from it — in some sense all our beliefs do — and our most highly wrought and sophisticated propositions about the real seek inforcement and demonstration by some indirect relation to sensuous experience.   In the last analysis nothing else brings about the " sentiment of conviction " quite so easily or nearly so universally as actual presence to sense.   " To see is to believe "; and the tangible is often considered very nearly synonymous with the unmistakably real.   At every remove from sense perception our representations enjoy less and less of reality feeling. A memory image feels to us more real and inspires us with more unquestioning belief than does a mere imagination; and other things being equal imagination more easily produces belief than does conception, while between several imagined objects the most vivid (and therefore the most akin to sensation) will seem the more real.   It is extremely difficult for us to believe strongly in anything which we can in no wise imagine.

Yet, true as all this is, it is not the whole story.   A very vivid imagination may often fail to arouse the belief which (especially among us sophisticated moderns) some abstract concept may inspire.   At times, in fact, even a sense perception may fail to bring with it full reality feeling or belief. This is seen in many cases of illusion, particularly of the auditory type.   The voice of a friend whom we know to be absent we interpret away as purely " subjective " — we persuade our-

[2] " A Treatise of Human Nature," Book I, Part III, Chap. 7.

selves that we didn't really hear it after all. Even a visual illusion will fail to dominate our belief as soon as we have discovered that it does not fit in with the rest of our visual field and particularly if it be inconsistent with our tactual world. We test sight by touch, and if the visual object is not congruous with the tangible we put it down as subjective and unreal. But not even the touch sense is altogether beyond criticism. An isolated tactual experience if incongruous with the rest of our perceptual system will be judged illusory.[3] It is evident, therefore, that congruity with our already accepted perceptual world is prerequisite to our belief in the reality of even a sensuous object. And this characteristic of congruity with the great mass of our already accepted reality is, of course, no less a condition of our belief in images and concepts as truly representative of the real. Other things being equal, vividness of imagination is more likely to bring with it reality feeling than is an abstract concept; but other things are not always equal. And as men grow more sophisticated and come to think more in general and abstract terms, the world they really live in becomes increasingly one of concepts; so that congruity with an accepted conceptual system gains enormously in importance in determining belief. As a correlate of this process, sense perception and vividness of imagery steadily lose in relative importance. The conceptual thinker has learned to believe in many things which he can neither perceive nor vividly picture. We children of modern civilization are brought up to feel ourselves surrounded by and living in a certain kind of world which transcends our immediate sense perceptions and in fact all our possible sense perceptions but which we consider quite as real as they. Our real world — the world we think about and act in — is largely one of representations and concepts. If, now, a new concept or image is proposed and set up within our conceptual world and fails to harmonize and fit in with it, it will lack reality feeling and fail to arouse our belief. Our sense of its incongruity with the whole background of our ac-

[3] Cf. the seemingly enormous size of a new tooth cavity explored for the first time by the tongue; the illusion (first noted by Aristotle) of the duality of an object placed between the first and the second fingers when they are crossed; or, for that matter, almost any of the stock tactual illusions of psychology.

cepted reality will not so much prove it unreal as in truth *be* the very feeling of its unreality. We may be perfectly able to imagine it, and as vividly as you like. Indeed, if for a moment we succeed in isolating it from our accepted world this vividness will bring with it for the time the sense of reality. Some people have partitions in their minds, so to speak, and are able to isolate certain systems of ideas from others, so that though really incongruous they are never felt to be such. But once the incongruity is felt, the sense of reality oozes out from the less massive of the two systems. The vividness of the lesser image may still remain, but we can no longer believe it truly representative of the real. Nor can argument in favor of an incongruous concept, any more than vividness, produce the sense of reality,— unless, indeed, it succeed in revolutionizing our whole system of accepted truth. Unless this be done, or unless the proposed object be shown, after all, to be quite congruous with our universe, arguments will be vain. We may be silenced by the arguments but in two minutes we shall go back to our old view, because the whole of our conceptual real world fights against the new-comer. Berkeley may answer all our criticisms of his idealism which fits in so ill with our instinctive beliefs; but, as Hume said, his exposition will be really quite as unpersuasive as it is unanswerable. The trained scholastic, if you are so ill-advised as to enter into argument with him, will break down all your miserable modern criticisms of St. Thomas and will prove to you logically the existence of all his mediæval entities. You remain speechless — and unconvinced. For his entities, no matter how logical, will not fit in with our modern view, and in spite of logic we can no longer get from them any sense of reality.

And now, if the reader's patience be not exhausted, we come at last to the question of religious belief. The objects of religious belief are, as every one knows, as numerous as the choir of heaven and the furniture of earth and it would be a hopeless task to undertake even an inventory of them. But there are two great objects of faith which stand out with such prominence above all others in the long history of religion that no keenness of analysis is needed to bring them to light nor any persuasiveness required to prove their importance. I refer to the belief in a God and the belief in a future life.   These two great dogmas of religion will occupy us in this and in the following chapter.

We are not at all concerned, let me remind the reader, with the origin of the belief in a God or gods.   That we leave to the anthropologists and the historians, not to mention the theologians, the sociologists, and the philologists.   Our questions are the less speculative and more hopeful ones, Why do people continue to believe in God, and what are the psychological factors that influence or determine the meaning of that term?

I am inclined to think the second of our questions the more difficult of the two.   It would indeed be easy enough to collect from the creeds of Christendom and the dogmatic theologies of the theologians and from the sermons of the clergy many clear-cut and elaborate definitions of the deity; but no one can for a moment suppose that these represent with any accuracy the living conviction of the mass of Christian people.   Such definitions are almost invariably forms of words put together for the purpose of answering questions.   They have a proper and important place in theology and philosophy; they may express what we ought to believe; they have their influence, no doubt, on what we do believe; but most of them are very far from expressing what God really means to us in our inner and practical living.   Their chief fault *as representations of actual belief* is, in fact, their very definiteness.[4]   The notion of God which most religious men and women carry around with them when not repeating the Creed, is far less clear-cut than are the definitions of the theologians.   At a prayer meeting in a small village not far from where I live, the pastor asked those present to describe their idea of God.   One good and very candid deacon, when it came his turn, responded that his idea of God was " a kind of an oblong blur."   The answer probably represented fairly well the state of mind of most of his less candid neighbors.

The influences determining the idea of God as actually held by living individuals are sociological and psychological as well

---

[4] This is, of course, no criticism of the credal and theological definitions, for they were never meant as descriptions of what most Christians really have in their minds, but of what the formulators conceived God to be.

as logical. The great general sociological influence — and indeed the greatest of all influences — in determining the form of the belief is of course the traditional view of the society into which one is born. More specifically, as was pointed out long ago by Robertson Smith, the social and political organization does much to determine the idea of God held by the members of the social group.[5] Monarchical societies are likely to have monarchical gods — a fact shown plainly by ancient history, and indeed amply illustrated by *der alte Gott* of some of our recently monarchical contemporaries. Ames has suggested that democratic institutions have an equally strong influence on the God-idea, making it practically equivalent to the conception of a kind of imminent justice.[6] Moreover, the social factor in worship is itself an influence toward making the idea of God anthropomorphic. The abstract God of the philosophers — the great First Cause, the Absolute, the Unknowable or what you will — may well enough be the cherished belief of the lonely thinker, but it can hardly be the common object of all sorts and conditions of men brought together for common worship. Inasmuch as the God who is to be worshiped by the community must be expressed in common terms, He necessarily comes to be described anthropomorphically. This description may be regarded by thinkers as symbolic, but hardly so by the rank and file; and since this symbolic expression is the only thing all the members of the group have in common, it comes to be considered sacred and hence tends to be taken with unchanging literalness.[7]

[5] Cf. "The Religion of the Semites" (3d Ed. London, Black: 1901), Lecture II.

[6] "The Psychology of Religious Experience," p. 312.

[7] An influence which may be considered in part sociological, in part psychological, is the effect of the cult in formulating belief. The very activity of the cult puts the worshiper into a certain attitude toward the deity, and he naturally, therefore, finds himself entertaining certain views which are none the less real because implicit only. In one of his typically clever illustrations, Professor Royce suggests that if the pigeons which we feed were to formulate their ideas after the fashion actually used by primitive men, they would express themselves concerning the man who feeds them somewhat as follows: "Behold do we not cluster about him and beg from him, and coo to him; and do we not get our food by doing thus? He is, then, a being whom it is essentially worth while to treat in this way. He responds to our cooing and our clustering. Thus we compel him to feed us.

There are psychological as well as social influences at work tending toward anthropomorphic ideas of God. Probably the greatest of these is the important place in belief held by the senses and the imagination. As we saw in the earlier part of this chapter, sense perception and vivid imagination are influential factors in most strong popular beliefs. In nearly all religions the idea of God is inculcated and enforced for each rising generation by means of actual sensuous representations — images, pictures etc. — or by vivid descriptions in which the appearance or activity of the Most High is presented in sensuous terms. Judaism and Mohammedanism forbid the use of pictures and images; but the Old Testament and the Koran are full of verbal pictures which make Jehovah and Allah almost as capable of visualization as is Shiva or Jupiter. For many centuries the anthropomorphic tendency of the mind had pretty full sway — as, indeed, it still has with a large number of people. But as men come to live more and more in a conceptual world, they feel the necessity of a less anthropomorphic and a more abstract God-idea, pictured no longer according to tradition alone but largely influenced by what the individual happens to know and accept from science and philosophy. It might be supposed that when this new idea is formed, the older picture — so inconsistent with it and with the common modern *Weltanschauung* — would lose all its reality-feeling and fade into the realm of Santa Claus and Jack Frost. So indeed it does with some, and so it would with all if the logical incongruity were universally and invariably felt. But, as I have pointed out in a previous connection, many people — probably most people — have water-tight compartments within their minds, and are able to retain as genuinely real two inconsistent systems of ideas, going from one to the other almost at will and carefully shutting the door behind them. Hence we shall find in many people, and, as I believe, in a great many people, two inconsistent and alternating ideas of God, each dominating consciousness in its turn according to the varying demands

Therefore he is a worshipful being. And this is what we mean by a god; namely, some one whom it is practically useful to conciliate and compel by such forms of worship as we practice." ("William James and Other Essays." New York, Macmillan: 1911, pp. 105–106.)

of action, emotion, and thought.[8]   Consider, for example, the following typical responses reported by V. R. Robinson in the *Journal of Religious Psychology* for November, 1908:

" God is a presence daily near, yet always where reason comes in far away beyond reach."   Another defines God as personal and then adds: " In melancholy moments when I think hardest, God loses all personality and becomes an indefinite force." A third describes her two conceptions of God as (1) an impersonal Being arrived at logically and (2) a person, " the God to whom I go for help."   Another writes: " Ordinarily the image of God is gray and formless.   In prayer, the face of Doré's Christ, which does not speak but prompts something in me to words." [9]

This dual God-idea — imaginative and conceptual — is probably to be found to some extent in almost every one who can be said to have any God at all.[10]   In different individuals, how-

[8] Professor Leuba sums up his results from the responses of nine hundred and thirty college students thus: " Two-thirds of the men, and nearly half of the women disclaim any mental picture of God.   The larger number of the remainder distinguish between image or symbol, and reality. In a remarkably large number of cases, however, a description in sensory terms is held to represent God adequately.   That young people having reached the mental development of college students should think of God as ' actual skin and blood and bones, something we shall see with our eyes some day,' is almost incredible; but the evidence is compelling.   Seven per cent. hold apparently to a thoroughly anthropomorphic conception of God." (" The Belief in God and Immortality."   Boston, Sherman, French: 1916, pp. 205–06.)   The college students investigated by Professor Drake (from Harvard, Illinois, and Wesleyan) were not so naïve in their conceptions. Although all but four of the total 249 who responded to his questionnaire believed in God, less than 35 per cent. felt assured that God was a conscious person.   (" The College Graduate and the Creeds," *Independent* for Sept. 25, 1913, pp. 755–58.)   A survey of various views on the nature of God as expounded by recent writers will be found in Professor Drake's paper: " Seekers After God."   (*Harvard Theol. Rev.*, XII, 67–83.)

[9] " The Conception of God of College Students," loc. cit., pp. 247–57.   The author adds: " Frequently the student has not thought about the matter sufficiently to be aware of the contradiction in his ideas.   It is not uncommon to find God imaged as a King in Heaven with bodily form, yet when use is made of him he is described as ' near me.'   Let me insist upon the fact that where there is a contradiction in the concept, whether or not it is observed by the student, it seems a matter of little concern.   There is seldom any attempt to reconcile the two views or to decide which is the true one " (p. 249).

[10] In Mahayana Buddhism it is, in fact, explicitly provided for, in the contrast between the Dharmakaya and the Sambhogakaya — the two forms under which the Supreme Buddha may properly be thought.

ever, the relative importance of the two factors will vary.   This variation, moreover will hold true of the same individual at different ages, the imagination decreasing in relative importance with maturing years.   Different sects, different religions, and different races also lay different degrees of emphasis upon imagination and conception in their ideas of God.[11]

A little more must be said of the conceptual element of the God-idea.   Having warned the reader (quite unnecessarily I am sure) against over-emphasizing this definite and rational part of religious belief, I feel it equally important to warn him against underestimating it.   Seldom, probably never, does it constitute the entirety of any religious man's idea of God; yet it does contribute and for thousands of years has contributed a very important part of that idea.   If the history of religions can be trusted to teach us anything at all upon the subject, it shows clearly that the development of rational thought, seeking to make its world consistent and to avoid the consciously incongruous, has played a more important rôle than any other one thing in making older ideas of God incredible and in developing new and genuinely vital beliefs.   The whole story of the development of monotheism and the growth of the moral conception of the deity has been largely determined by a kind of implicit logic,— a sense of dissatisfaction with the incongruous.[12]   The ideas of God cherished to-day by the majority of

[11] This is a point well brought out by Professor Stratton.   "The serious imagery of Protestant Christianity is far less rich and vivid than that of the Roman Church.   The Catholic Church, the patron of art and the imagination, has found little toleration for its images either physical or mental among the colder minds of the north, which from early times seem to have had distrust of too definite representations of the gods. . . . The freedom of the imagination, so characteristic of childhood and of youth, may continue into later years.   But with maturity the fabric of the imagination often ceases to interest, and falls into decay. . . . And so religion as it grows to be a zeal for good works to one's fellows, or for emotional submission and awe before the gods, or for an intellectual grasp of the divine and a rational justification of God's ways to men — as it develops thus, there appears a reticence, a hemming-in of the pictorial representation of the central objects of worship."   ("The Psychology of the Religious Life."   London, Allen & Co.: 1911, pp. 225 and 226.)   See also the excellent twenty-third chapter on "The Idealizing Act."

[12] Cf. Chapters III, IV, and V of my "Psychology of Religious Belief." While the influence of reason in religious belief has usually favored monotheism, this is not always the case.   In the *Hibbert Journal* for October,

intelligent Christians are more indebted than is, perhaps, generally realized to Aristotle, Spinoza, Kant, and Darwin. This is not to say, however, that the rationalistic element is itself a unitary influence. In minds of different sorts — and within the same mind under different circumstances — it leads in very diverse directions. Two tendencies in particular stand out with marked prominence as one views the development of religious thought in history and within our own generation. Both these tendencies are characterized by the search for congruity, but one is dominated by a partly rational, chiefly æsthetic desire for a monistic conception and finds satisfaction only in an all-inclusive Absolute; the other is guided by a demand that the divine shall be congruous with our moral sense, and therefore finds the Absolute essentially unsatisfying as a God-idea.

The imaginative and the conceptual elements of most men's idea of God may dodge each other within the mind, each coming to the center of attention only at the call of certain conditions, and thus the incongruity between them may never be deeply felt. When the incongruity is squarely faced an effort is sometimes made to throw off one of the two views, and perhaps more often the attempt is made to retain both and regard one as symbolic of the other.[13] The symbol acts in two ways. It makes one's belief more concrete and thereby more vivid, comforting, and efficient. It also has a peculiar psychical effect, which religion has always loved, in suggesting the indefinable, the illimitable, the ineffable. It acts upon the inner vision in a way analogous to that in which the rich and storied windows of a cathedral effect the outer sense, bathing the mind in a kind of dim religious light. Even non-religious symbolism has much of this half-magical influence. The reader of Tagore's

1912, the reader will find an elaborate argument by a native Fijian Christian, to prove that the decrease of the birth-rate in Fiji is due to the neglect of the ancient gods of the land and the substitution of the One God of Christianity. The same type of argument was used by the Jews of the Old Testament as late as 586 B. C. against the exclusive worship of Yahveh. See Jeremiah 44.

[13] Cf. Robinson's results. "Usually the student distinguishes between reality and image, and states that the image probably does not correctly represent reality. Of the cases quoted above only ten seem to think that the image corresponds to reality, for the rest it is merely a convenient symbol." Op. cit., p. 250.

Gitanjali and Fruit Gathering, of Hauptmann's *Versunkene Glocke,* and of other poems of the same indefinite symbolic sort, closes the book with the feeling that unutterable thoughts have been dimly adumbrated to him, though just what thoughts he cannot tell; and if he be not provoked at the author for his lack of clarity he will be likely to feel a strong emotion half way between the æsthetic and the religious. The really great power of Tagore's " King of the Dark Chamber " is due entirely to the symbolic form in which he has half expressed yet half concealed India's noble conception of the relation of God to the soul. He who has overlooked the tremendous emotional power of the symbolic expression of a religious truth has failed to understand much of the hold that religion has over a very large number of the men and women round about him.

But not only may the imaginative be regarded as symbolic of the conceptual; the concept itself — the credal definition, the exact theological exposition — may be held by a certain complex type of mind as itself only a symbol — a symbol of a Reality too great ever to be truly expressed in any form of words. A friend of mine, a Catholic priest, writes me thus: . . . . " You see what I think about dogmas. They are a kind of intellectual sacrament — that is intellectual and imaginative signs of realities that are supra-intellectually cognized by the deep, dim, intuitive apprehension of faith; and they well may be called a kind of sacrament, for they are effectual signs — that is they tend to generate or elicit in the mind which receptively apprehends them that very vision of faith which they so inadequately express and attempt to communicate."

Here, surely, is a most important point. The dogma as well as the pictorial representation is of value to the religious mind largely (though not entirely) because it " generates a vision of faith," because it arouses a certain emotion and satisfies a certain demand of the heart. The God-idea which most persons carry around with them and live by is to be described not only in terms of imagination and conception but in terms of human need. The dominant feature in most religious people's working idea of God is practical rather than theoretical, and is to be found not in what God is conceived to *be* but in what He is relied upon to *do*. On the basis of the responses to his questionnaire

Mr. Robinson writes: "God is described as 'directly interested in me,' as 'Friend,' 'Comforter,' 'Sympathetic Father.' It is in this class of attributes, which marks not the nature of God himself, but his relation to the individual, that the value of the religious concept lies." [14]   And Professor Leuba, commenting upon similar responses collected by him, writes in an oft-quoted passage: "The truth of the matter may be put this way: *God is not known, He is not understood; He is used —* used a good deal and with an admirable disregard of logical consistency, sometimes as meat purveyor, sometimes as moral support, sometimes as friend, sometimes as an object of love." [15]

That the idea of God contains, thus, a large "pragmatic" element is indubitable.   And in this it is by no means unique. The same is true of most ideas.   My notion of a house is not exhausted or fully described when I have detailed its visual and geometrical characteristics.   The most important constituent in my idea is the fact that a house is a place to *live in*.   Very central to our idea of anything you like is the answer to the question: What can I do with it? or what may I expect of it?   As Royce has somewhere said, I have a very inadequate notion of a lion if I think it a kind of beast whom I can pat on the head, saying, "Nice little lion!"   Similarly there is no vitally religious idea of God which does not include to some extent an answer to the question, What may I expect of Him?   We must surely go with James and the pragmatists at least so far as to say that the meaning of "God" is to be found largely in those consequences in our experience which may be expected if God exist which could not be looked for in a universe without Him.

Our idea of God is therefore largely the result of our practical demands and attitudes, and an important element in it consists in the differences within human experience which are anticipated because of it.   But a number of thinkers who seek to carry pragmatism into the psychology of religion go so far as to identify the idea of God wholly with this attitude and these expected consequences.   "The highest religious conception, that of the deity," writes Dr. Irving King, "is an expression of personal attitude rather than a statement of an existence of some

---

[14] Op. cit., p. 251.
[15] "Contents of the Religious Consciousness." Monist XI, 571.

sort which may reveal itself by various interpolations within the natural order of phenomena." [16]   In similar pragmatic vein Professor Ames insists that the difficulty in understanding the idea of God in the past has been due to the fact that it has been taken out of relation to the social experiences and genetic processes in which alone it has meaning.   " Perhaps the case is analogous to the experience of a child who looks behind the mirror for the reality answering to the image which he sees. Before he can solve the puzzle of the reflected image he must seek for it in another place and by a different method.   The reality to which the image leads is not within the image alone, as phenomenism might say; neither is it behind the mirror as the realist and the absolute idealist might say, but it lies on this side of the mirror, within the actual world of men and things.   The idea of God, when seriously employed, serves to generalize and to idealize all the values one knows. . . . The reality answering to the idea of God, it may be said, must include, at its best, all that is involved in the deep instinctive historical and social consciousness of the race.   It signifies the justice which government symbolizes, the truth which science unfolds, and the beauty which art strives to express.   The attributes in the conception of God are as numerous as the ideal interests of those who use it, for it signifies the totality of our purposes and values." [17]

If the idea of God be what Professor Ames has here described and no more, the religious consciousness should welcome his book as the final and complete refutation of all possible atheism. For if by God we mean merely our human values then not even the fool will venture any longer to say in his heart, There is no God.   By one clever stroke of pragmatic logic and functional psychology Professor Ames seems to have accomplished what all the long line of philosophers and theologians have attempted in vain.   But I fear the religious reader of " The Psychology of Religious Experience " will find cold comfort after all when he learns that the only God who exists is just human society's longings and ideals and values, and that He cannot even *mean* anything more than that.   And even after Professor Ames and

[16] " The Development of Religion," p. 12.
[17] " The Psychology of Religious Experience," pp. 317–18.

Dr. King and their colleagues have made use of all the appliances of the latest structural psychology in the analysis of the God-idea and found in it only personal and social attitude and various human values, the religious soul, I fear, will remain stupidly unconvinced. "I know," he will say, "what I mean by the justice which government symbolizes, the truth which science unfolds, and the beauty which art strives to express. And I know that while these may be included within my idea of God, I mean by God something besides these things. I mean by God 'an existence of some sort' (in spite of Dr. King), a real Being who dwells not only 'within the actual world of men and things,' but, if you will, 'behind the mirror.'"

I feel convinced that such a response to Professor Ames and his school would be quite justified. Important as is the pragmatic element in the God-idea it is not the only element. And the attempt to prove it such is both bad psychology and bad epistemology. Bad psychology because it neglects altogether certain real elements in the religious consciousness, whether found in philosopher, priest, or humble worshiper,— men who through all the ages have truly meant by "God" something more than the idea of God, something genuinely transcendent. Bad epistemology because based ultimately upon a viciously subjective view of *meaning,* a view which would identify our objects with our ideas of our objects, and which, carried to its logical conclusion, would result in solipsism.[18]

So much for the nature of the God-idea and the psychological factors at work in determining it. We turn now to our other question: Why do people believe, or continue to believe, in God; What are the psychological bases and the leading types of this belief? There are of course many types of religious belief, and for various purposes various different divisions might be devised, all equally true. For the purposes of this chapter, however, we shall make use of a four-fold division,[19] sug-

[18] For a statement of what seems to me the real relation between the knower and his objects. see my papers, "The Confessions of an Old Realist" and "A Defense of Dualistic Realism" in the *Journal of Philosophy,* XIII, 687f and XIV, 253f respectively: also "Essays in Critical Realism," *passim.*

[19] It would ill become me to insist that there are just four types of religious belief, namely those described in this chapter. In 1906 I published

gested by Bain's classical treatment of the psychology of belief,[20] — a division which has here the added advantage of corresponding exactly with the four-fold division of religious attitudes elaborated in our first chapter.   Our four types of religious belief may then be styled (1) authoritative or habitual,
(2) reasoned, (3) emotional, and (4) volitional, according as
the belief is based upon the natural credulity of the mind, upon
some form of argument explicit or implicit, upon an emotional
experience, usually of the mystic sort, or finally upon the will
to believe.

Our first class is a very large one and includes several kinds
of people.   Some of these believe in God because when children
they were taught to believe, and have continued doing so ever
since, not because of any new experience or appealing argument
of strong desire, but simply from the force of habit.   Their
first belief in God as children — and that is true of all of
us — was a simple case of primitive credulity, the original
tendency of the mind to accept whatever is presented to it; and
a kind of mental inertia combined with the common dislike of
changing things once regarded as settled, has merely prolonged
the original belief of childhood on into mature life by the
simple process of inhibiting all incipient efforts of the critical
faculty.

Closely connected with this type of believer is the man who,
though not contented with merely habitual faith, naturally tends
to avoid all serious thinking on his own part, preferring that
others should do it for him.   " I believe in God," writes one
of my respondents, " because my father does and did when I
was young."   Of many of us is Professor James's oft quoted sentence very true: " Our faith is faith in some one else's faith."

a study of the subject in which I divided religious belief into five types
(" Types of Religious Belief," *Am. Jour. of Relig. Psy.*, March, 1906, I,
76–94) ; while the following year, in my " Psychology of Religious Belief,"
I reduced the number of types to three.   In 1877 C. S. Peirce enumerated
four methods of fixating belief, certainly quite as important and undeniable
as the four-fold division I have borrowed from Bain — namely the methods
of tenacity, authority, inclination, and scientific verification.   My division
is, of course, no *truer* than Peirce's, but it is better adapted to the purposes of our study.

[20] " The Emotions and the Will " (3d Ed.   London, Longmans: 1888),
p. 511.

A much more earnest and truly religious sort of conviction is to be found in the believer who pins his faith not to some other man's faith but to some great and widely recognized source of authority, such as the Bible, the Church, the words of Jesus, or the great mass of the community.   " I believe," writes one man to me, " because I feel that so many people have believed and so long."   Among Catholics the authority appealed to is, of course, the Church, while among Protestants the authority most quoted is the Bible.   One respondent writes: " I believe from the argument of the Scriptures (see Col. I 16–21) and the authority of the Bible — the detailed account of Creation, His dealing with Sin and Satan, the Prophets, Isaiah 53 more than any other."   This man likes to think his belief is based on an " argument " and evidently fails to see that as an argument his appeal to Scripture goes in a circle, presupposing its infallible inspiration by God in order thereafter to prove the existence of God.   As a fact, of course, his belief has little enough to do with any reasoning processes; the " argument," such as it is, being devised *after the fact,* to justify what he believes on authority and through habit.   In this connection, however, it should be said that the appeal to the Bible as a binding authority is relatively rare; the tendency in almost every Protestant denomination and sect being decidedly away from the almost servile attitude toward the letter of Scripture which orthodox Christianity is often accused of inculcating.

Eighty-nine out of three hundred and sixty-seven respondents of mine [21] — i. e. just under twenty-five per cent — must certainly be classed under this habitual or authoritative type; and I feel very sure the number should be considerably larger.   The faith of most people, of course, finds its psychological roots in all four of the sources mentioned; and the principle of classification in our four-fold division is merely that of singling out the *predominant* source in each case; but it is inevitable that in

[21] Seventy-one of these 367 responses were used in preparation of my " Psychology of Religious Belief " in 1907. Since that time I have collected 296 additional answers to the question, " Why do you believe in God? " through questionnaires distributed by my students. In preparing this chapter I have gone over the responses used in my earlier book and reinterpreted them, a procedure which has resulted in a few slight changes in my figures.

figures based on questionnaires the authoritative source should receive much less than its due emphasis, since nearly all persons with whom it is really the chief determinant like to persuade themselves that their belief is based on something quite different.

For this reason our second class of believers — those who rest their faith chiefly on some form of reasoning — undoubtedly bulks larger in the results of a questionnaire than it has really any right to do.[22]   One hundred and thirteen of my respondents — i. e. about thirty per cent — insist that their faith is based chiefly on some form of reasoning.   Many of them probably really belong to our first type; but just how many it is impossible to say.   The exact percentage, therefore, is of little significance; the important thing for us to notice being the nature of the type under consideration, not its chance numbers in my small and haphazard collection of respondents.

All the members of this second class start out with some general conception of the universe which is taken for granted — such as its obedience to the causal law, its moral nature, etc. — and the arguments made use of are really efforts to show explicitly that the non-existence of God would be incongruous with such a Reality.   The arguments referred to are sometimes the stock arguments for theism to be found in so many books and formerly heard in so many sermons.   It is particularly the cosmological and the teleological arguments that seem vitally to affect belief.   A goodly number of my respondents say they believe in God because they cannot imagine how the universe could ever have been started or could be kept going without a " Master Mind " to make and run it.   Sometimes these arguments are expressed conventionally and glibly, sometimes with a good deal of evident feeling.   It would certainly be a great mistake (if I may judge by my respondents) to suppose that

[22] The fact that belief very often rests much less upon rational considerations than the believer supposes is an important and indubitable fact, to which psychologists have often called attention.   This, for example, is the central theme running through Professor Joseph Jastrow's " Psychology of Conviction " (Boston, Houghton, Mifflin: 1918), and specially expounded in the leading essay of the volume.   Professor Jastrow makes emotion and convention the chief determinants of belief, giving reason a third place. As he includes under " emotion " what I have treated under that head and also under the " will to believe," his classification agrees essentially with the one given in the text.

the cosmological argument has been dead since Kant's time or that Darwin gave the *coup de grâce* to the argument from design. Whatever we may think of these venerable forms of reasoning from a philosophic point of view, the student of the psychology of religion must admit that with very many earnest men and women they are exceedingly vital still.— Perhaps not so vital as they used to be, certainly not so important as their upholders like to think; probably never the sole support of any real faith; but still very real *aids* to belief in God.

Another type of argument which seems quite as important as the more philosophic sort — and which is probably more genuinely efficient in producing conviction — is derived from the effect of Christian belief upon human life. " My belief in God," writes one man, " is from the argument of the lives of those whom I have known to have believed in Him, the strength of whose lives seemed to lie in that fact." And another: " I believe in God from the proof of His ability to help me." A very real kind of argument of this pragmatic type is sometimes made in favor of the authority of Christ or of some prophetic person, and belief in God is then based upon this authority. Cases of this sort should be distinguished sharply from those of our Class I; for the foundation of the belief here is not authority but some form of reasoning,— as in the following: " The process is more or less one of reasoning. I am much helped by the mystics — by the experiences of men like Dr. Bucke (see James's ' Varieties '). A good deal by the steadfast conviction of the Father which appears in the words of Jesus." In many cases, however, reasoning and authority blend in such fashion as hardly to be distinguishable — belief beginning in primitive credulity, later basing itself on arguments, and finally continuing through the force of habit after the arguments have been half forgotten. " Everything in nature seems to prove there is a God," writes one woman; and having said this to justify her faith by logic, she continues: " I cannot tell why I believe in God, but think argument and Bible reading have helped me to feel sure there is a God, and now I believe without proof or reason."

Class III is composed of those whose belief in God is based chiefly on some form of the affective consciousness. To avoid unduly technical phraseology I have called this type "*Emotional Belief*," though strictly speaking I should have used the word *affective* rather than *emotional,* since I mean to include in it more than belief based on emotion alone, in the technical sense of the word. It is often said that religion is a matter of feeling; and so of course to a considerable extent it is; but when this expression is properly used it must be remembered not only that religion has other elements besides the affective ones, but also that "feeling" when thus applied has at least three distinguishable degrees of complexity, and that religion partakes of all three. The simplest of these is to be found in the pleasant and unpleasant affective tones that accompany nearly all — if not quite all — mental processes. Higher than these in the scale of complexity come the emotions. An emotion is no simple thing like a feeling and it includes or at least involves some elements by no means affective in their nature. Whether or not we accept the James-Lange theory, a full-fledged emotion always involves an ideal element. It is a complex of feelings crystallized about an explicit or implicit meaning — which may be in part the cause or in part the effect of the feelings and their bodily expressions — and tending always to some form of activity. Finally, following Mr. Shand [23] and Mr. McDougal,[24] we may use the word sentiment to denote those complexes of emotional tendencies which are enduring and largely *potential* rather than actual forms of immediate experience. A sentiment has a more explicitly ideational element than emotion, and includes, usually, a number of emotions which may be summoned into action at any time by the idea of the object about which the sentiment centers. A religious belief of the affective type is, therefore, much more closely related to sentiment than to emotion in the stricter sense of the term. It does not depend for its existence upon the actual excitation of the emotion; nor (in most cases, at any rate) is there any one emotion upon which it rests. Rather is the affective conviction of God's existence bound up with a whole system of potential emotions, whose past activity

[23] See his "Character and the Emotions" in *Mind* for April, 1896. (N. S. V.), esp. pp. 214–24.
[24] See his "Social Psychology," Chap. V.

THE BELIEF IN A GOD 215

and whose possible activity are kept constantly in the dim background of the mind, and which may at any moment be called into play by the idea of the Divine. But the most important thing to recognize in this connection is that this affective type of faith as well as every other has necessarily a good deal of ideational content. It is not merely *felt*: it possesses meaning. The attempt to interpret faith as merely a form of feeling, and thus to deny it any intellectual element, is merely a new illustration of the force of momentum; anti-intellectualism having got a tremendous start is unable to stop. In the words of Professor Armstrong: "The sentimental theory is almost as one-sided as the intellectualism which it seeks to supplant. If it lays stress on factors in belief which need to be emphasized, over-emphasis involves both theoretical and practical dangers." [25] Feeling is important for religious belief not in supplying its content — or supplanting its content — but in lending it strength.

If we may trust the outcome of my questionnaire, this third type of belief includes a larger percentage of the religious people in the community than any of the three others. Thirty-two out of seventy-one of my earlier cases,[26] and one-hundred and four out of two-hundred and ninety-six of my later cases — in all one-hundred and thirty-six out of three-hundred and sixty-seven — seemed from their answers to belong to this class. Two comments, however, must be made upon this fact. In the first place it seems probable that a number of the respondents really misinterpreted their own belief and that a truer insight would have attributed the chief influence to authority or to the will to believe. The line between our third and our fourth classes — between "feeling" and wish — is notably hard to

[25] "Is Faith a Form of Feeling?" (*Harvard Theological Review*, IV, 79.) Cf. also the following very wise words of Erich Warschauer: "Wissen und Glauben sagen aus dass etwas ist. Oder: 'ich weiss' und 'ich glaube' heisst zunächst weiter nichts als: ich halte für wahr. Wie sehr man auch mit recht den Glauben von Wissen trennen will, es muss ohne weiteres zugegeben werden, dass beides keinen anderen Sinn haben kann, als die positive Setzung eines Inhalts mit dem apodiktischen Auspruche: Diese Aussage soll objective Gültigkeit haben, soll wahr sein." ("Zur Psychologie der Entstehung und Entwicklung des Glaubens," Zeitschrift f. Religionspsychologie. January, 1911, p. 340.)

[26] That is, those reported in the "Psychology of Religious Belief."

draw,[27] and many a believer whose faith is really based on strong desire undoubtedly succeeds in persuading himself that it is due to mystic feeling or some other form of " inner experience." And secondly I must point out to the reader the very obvious fact that even if we were to trust all my respondents' introspection it would be a great mistake to consider them entirely representative of the community at large. For every person who answers a questionnaire there are six or seven who throw it into the waste basket. And probably no class of believers is so likely to answer a questionnaire on religion as those who belong to our third type.

Still I cannot but consider it of some interest and significance that thirty-seven per cent of those who did answer my questionnaire insisted — and usually with a good deal of vehemence — that their belief in God was based not on authority, argument, or wish, but upon some form of feeling or " inner experience." So far as I can judge — by my own personal knowledge and my students' knowledge of them — my respondents are fairly representative of the religious portion of the community; and my study of the subject during the last fifteen years confirms me in the opinion expressed in my " Psychology of Religious Belief " that the source of a large part of the most living faith in our country is due to a mild type of mystical experience.[28]

The emotional or affective experience from which the members of our third class draw most of the strength of their faith is of several kinds. Perhaps the most common — if we may trust the replies — is an incipiently mystic " experience of God's presence." This comes out repeatedly in the responses, sometimes in conventional language but often also with a freshness and sincerity of expression that leaves no room for doubt of the reality of the experience,— however the experience should be interpreted. I shall not give any examples of it here, for we shall study the question at considerable length when we take up the subject of mysticism.

---

27 Höffding even goes so far as to say, " The belief which cannot be proved is a wish that what we believe may be true." " The Philosophy of Religion," p. 341.

28 While this is true, I have come to the conclusion that in my former book I somewhat overestimated the spread of the mystic consciousness.

Many of the respondents who lay claim to no such experience still refer their faith to something that is essentially affective,— using such expressions as "instinct," "direct consciousness," "intuition," "the feeling within that there is a God," etc. "I believe in God," writes one, "not from argument but from something within that tells me there is one. I think nothing could shake that faith." Another: "I have never seen a high mountain or the ocean or any other vast and beautiful sight, without a strengthening of my belief in God. But it is also true that I have never seen a miserable child, a suffering, abused animal or a fallen woman without the same effect. There *must* be some One by whom all these creatures shall be avenged — ' all tears wiped away.' "

As the reader will see, this last case is on the line between our third and fourth types. This fourth class — whose faith is based on the will to believe — makes a small showing in the results from my questionnaire — only twenty-nine of the three-hundred sixty-seven, that is about eight per cent, belonging to it. As I have previously indicated, however, my figures are here presumably untrustworthy; and many of my respondents pretty certainly belong to this class who maintain (and doubtless fully believe) that their faith is based on mystic feeling or, still more likely, on argument.[29] The immediate influence of a questionnaire is to put the respondent into a *theoretical* frame of mind and to induce him to formulate arguments for beliefs which he holds from quite other causes. Nor do we have to go to the respondents of a questionnaire to see how natural it is for the will to believe to go unrecognized by the believer, while various arguments, more or less extraneous, get the credit for the faith. In a sense the whole history of philosophy and of theology is an illustration of this. How easily, for example, does Descartes's firm determination to doubt everything doubtable capitulate to the God of theology after the exposition of an argument which, to the modern reader at any rate, seems less a proof than a lengthy excuse elaborated by

[29] According to Freud, wish is always at the bottom of belief; but this wish is often masked or hidden from the believer. One of the commonest of the mechanisms for hiding this fundamental wish is rationalization. We persuade ourselves that our belief is based on reason when, as a fact, it is only an expression of desire.

the philosopher for giving in his assent. And much the same surely could be said of many another defender of the faith. Saint Evremond says of the Orthodox Catholics of his day (about 1650): "With most of them the wish to believe takes the place of actual belief. Their will assents to what their intellect desires." [30] This is not true of 17th Century Catholics alone. Many a modern Catholic bases his faith in the authority of the Church ultimately upon his wish to believe in the Church. A striking and rather melancholy illustration of this is to be found in the long struggle of that rare spirit, George Tyrrell, who with all his love for Catholicism was too clear in self-analysis and too ingenuous in expression to pretend that it was reasoning that led him to Rome. "I felt," he writes, concerning his conversion to Catholicism, "I felt it would be Rome or nothing. I knew dimly that I had not any real *faith* in Rome — only a great wish that I could believe — a wish that some of the grosser obstacles were non-existent; I was tempted to do what I knew or suspected would be internally dishonest." And looking back at his long attempt to be a good Jesuit he confesses: "Sometimes I think it must be said that, in the deepest depths of my self-consciousness, I believe nothing at all, and am self-deceived in the matter; and the recognition of the manner in which I have, all along, allowed the 'wish to believe' to play upon me rather confirms this melancholy hypothesis." [31]

With Protestants no less than among Catholics, the will to believe often unites with authority, each reinforcing the other — as poor Tyrrell tried to make them do in his own life. A very representative picture is given by the following from one of my respondents: "I have been taught to believe in God from childhood, and I can see no object in *not* believing. A trust in a higher divine power makes my life seem more than if I believed there was nothing to live for but the present." And here are two more typical responses in which appeal is made

[30] Quoted by St. Cyres in his "Pascal" (New York, Dutton: 1910), p. 177.

[31] "Autobiography and Life," Vol. I, pp. 155, and 133. The wish to believe which led Tyrrell to Rome was not strong enough to keep him there, and the latter part of his life was one long revolt of intellect and heart against the strong wish, which had never been fully satisfied.

only to the will: "I believe in some divine power but know not whether it is a remote 'God' or my own soul. I hold the former belief in time of despondency; the latter in time of self-confidence." "I believe in God because of the need of my moral nature. I need Him as a child needs its parents."

The fact that belief can be actually brought about by wish and nourished by systematic acts of will is the foundation of all the methods of faith-culture within one's self. One may sometimes produce faith in others by means of authority and argument, but all attempts at inducing faith in one's own mind rest ultimately upon the will-to-believe. And the self-culture of belief is often most effective, as is known by all skillful persuaders of souls. If a strong wish for faith can be induced, a little faith will follow, and a little faith once started can be systematically cultivated by voluntarily attending to it, enjoying it, acting upon it, and inhibiting all ideas that tend to negate it. So the skillful evangelist urges the skeptic who is approaching the melting mood to pray, "Lord, I believe; help Thou mine unbelief." He has his congregation sing the hymn,

"Only believe and thou shalt see
That Christ is all in all to thee."

And he reiterates in his sermons the admonition that his hearers whose faith is small and weak should live on their belief and act as if it were true, and he promises that if they will fulfill this injunction systematically they will find their faith constantly growing. I have heard it expressed in the following words from the pulpit: "By constant prayer to Christ, by acting and living on your faith, you will find your faith made strong; so that the longer you live the more you will see your faith has a strength superior even to the certainty of a mathematical demonstration." The method here involved is obviously auto-suggestion. The skeptic who *wishes* that a certain religious doctrine were true is induced to suggest to himself constantly that it is true, and so comes at last to believe.

The will may be used to induce something like our first type of belief:— a kind of habitual faith or primitive credulity; or (in rare cases) it may even bring about the emotional and mystic type of belief. The former process is excellently illustrated by the following words from Pascal's " Pensee " in which he prescribes a method by which a merely cold intellectual assent may be turned into a vital belief through the voluntary production of a habit:

" We have a body as well as a mind; and therefore we are not swayed by proof alone. Intellectual convictions are worth little if the mechanical side of our nature is set in the opposite direction; we must gain over our whole self. So soon as we know where truth lies we must ask custom to soak and steep us in that belief. For we cannot be always carrying proofs around in our minds; it is much easier to believe by force of habit. This uses neither violence nor artifice nor argument; but all unconsciously it brings a certain bias into play, and into that our mind falls naturally."

In commenting upon this passage St. Cyres adds: " Pascal will advise his free-thinker, at a certain stage in his conversion, to live as though he already were a Catholic. ' Have masses said and take holy water; naturally that will stupefy you and make you believe.' This famous passage does not mean that a man may lawfully hocus himself into accepting a creed which he knows to be untrue; all Pascal maintains is that our ' machine ' — our instincts, habits, associations — will never keep pace with our brain unless we call in custom to get them out of an old groove into a new one." [32]

A rather remarkable case in which something like a mystical experience and its correlative belief were brought about by a deliberate process of willing to believe in God is reported by Miss Amy E. Tanner in the *Psychological Bulletin* for Feb., 1907. The case is that of a woman, who in youth found much comfort in " communion with God " and then, through some trying personal experiences, completely lost her faith. For twenty years she remained in this skeptical state of mind, far removed from any sort of religious belief, when, through some new conditions, she found her own ideals and her own strength insufficient to carry her through a moral crisis, and she began to long for the old sense of the divine presence and divine help. " Then came the question whether I could use the concept of a personal God without belief in its objective existence. Could

I try it as a mere working hypothesis and expect to get any valuable results? Anyhow I saw nothing else to do, so I said to myself that it does not in the least matter whether God exists outside of the minds of men. . . . Therefore I deliberately set to work to recognize the sense of God's presence which I had not had for nearly twenty years. I reinforced my reason by reiterating my reasons for assuming such a personality, and I prayed constantly after the fashion of the old skeptic: ' O God, if there is a God, save my soul if I have a soul.' Then one night after a week of this sort of thing, the old sense of God's presence came upon me with overpowering fullness. I cannot express the sense of personal intimacy, understanding, and sympathy that it gave to me. I felt the thing — whatever it was — so close to me, so a part of me, that words and even thoughts were unnecessary, that my part was only to sink back into this personality — if such it were — and drop all worries and temptations, all the straining and striving that had been so prominent in my life for years and years. Then as I felt consolation and strength pouring in upon me, there came a great upwelling of love and gratitude toward their source, even though I was all the time conscious that that source might not be either personal or objective. It *felt* personal, I said to myself, and no harm would be done by acting as if it were so. . . . On the practical side the value of this experience up to now — after a period of three months — has been permanent. I find my thoughts falling back upon the idea of this presence as soon as I get into any sort of trouble or perplexity; and the invariable effect is to calm me and to enable me to take a wider outlook." [33]

That the deliberate cultivation of belief may develop, or degenerate, into veritable malpractice upon one's own mind is evident enough without any words of mine. But that fact should not hide from us the really great value of the will to believe when properly used and in the proper place. Just

[33] Loc. cit., pp. 33–36. I should add, however, not only that this case is very unusual and not at all typical, but also that even in this case the induced " faith state " does not seem to have been permanent. Miss Tanner writes me that " After the stress and strain of the situation, there was a distinct tendency to revert again to the condition of doubt or disbelief in an objective God."

what the proper place and the proper method are I shall not here discuss, as the whole question has been so admirably presented in Professor James's famous essay.   Where reason and evidence can reveal to us the truth they certainly should be relied upon to do so.   But in questions upon which they cannot give a decision yet toward which we must take some attitude, surely the question of the practical results of belief and of disbelief is revelant; and the faith venture while not logically required may be morally demanded.   " The wise shall live by postulates," says Professor Royce; and surely there is at least this much of truth in St. Paul's words, " The just shall live by faith."

The questions of religion are too vast for any of us to settle with perfect demonstration, and the will to believe will always form an integral part of normal, healthy faith.   And the same may be said of each of the psychological elements of belief we have been considering.   Reliance upon authority and tradition is perhaps the least intellectual of the four, yet the strength which it can lend will ever be needed — and probably demanded — by every great religion.   If the weight of tradition were not overmastering — in religion and in other things too — each individual would have to begin all over again for himself the long journey for the pursuit of knowledge and of helpful opinion which the race has accomplished through so many weary ages. As it is, the universal tendency to believe on authority makes each of us, in a true sense, the intellectual heir of all the ages. The individual is too small to walk alone, his life is too short and his mental grasp too slight for him ever to throw aside the assistance of the community's faith.   All the great religions lend to their believers to-day a strength of accumulated tradition which no new creed or sect could gather n hundreds of years.   Nor should reason — in our days so derided — be left out from the ideal faith.   The *Credo quia impossibile* of the Middle Ages has been weighed in the balances by human history and found wanting.   No belief can long stand which is inconsistent with reason, and he who leaves reason out of his reckoning in rearing his faith edifice is building upon the sands.   In the words of Professor James — who surely was no advocate of intellectualism — " weak as reason is, it has this unique advantage over its antagonists that its activity never lets up and that it presses always in one direction, while men's prejudices vary, their passions ebb and flow, and their excitements are intermittent." [34]   At the very least, reason must be able to show the possibility of the religious object and thus give one the right to believe.   And while the mystic sense is not essential to faith there is probably nothing else that lends to faith such invincible energy.   Finally, lest all else should fail, the man who through thick and thin is to maintain both his belief in the realm of spirit, and his loyalty to the truth as he sees it, must have in his heart the courage to make the faith venture.   In short the highest and healthiest type of faith in the spiritual world, a faith that is warm but without fanaticism, reasonable but not coldly abstract, courageous yet never self-deceived nor disloyal to truth, calmly confident but never blind, and neither slavishly servile to authority nor yet lonely and separatist,— such a faith must draw its strength from all four of the sources indicated in this chapter.

[34] " Remarks at the Peace Banquet "; in " Memories and Studies " (New York, Longmans: 1911), p. 300.

CHAPTER XI

THE BELIEF IN IMMORTALITY

THE individual's attitude toward the Determiner of Destiny, which is religion, has always an essentially practical coloring. It involves a belief, to be sure, but this belief is never a matter of pure theory, but bears a reference, more or less explicit, to the fate of the individual's values. Hence in nearly every religion which history has studied or anthropology discovered, the question of the future in store for the individual believer has been of prime importance.[1]

Fortunately we are not called upon in this place to consider the various ideas of a future state which the various religions have devised; such a subject would require a chapter, if not a volume, by itself. Nor is much to be gained by an investigation of the ideas of the future life as held by men and women round about us. I have nearly a hundred responses to questions about the soul, heaven and hell, etc., but on reading them over find little in them that is either instructive or interesting, beyond the fact that the old ideas of golden streets and of fire and brimstone seem to have been pretty generally given up. Heaven is spoken of as a " state " rather than as a place, and is characterized by moral progress and opportunity for service quite as much as by joy and rest. Only a small proportion of my respondents believe in anything like the old-fashioned hell.[2]

[1] I mean by this that the question here referred to is of prime importance among the beliefs of every such religion. A few societies have been reported in which cult seems to be very much more important than any belief.

[2] For some years I have amused myself by collecting, from my friends and students, descriptions of the " soul." I cannot call the answers very instructive but the experiment has often proved interesting. One lady describes the soul as " a sort of round haze a little larger than a baseball, somewhere in the body near the heart." Another makes it the size of a football and locates it in the air back of the left shoulder. Some say it is conscious, some not; but nearly all agree that it is that which goes to heaven when you die.

Much more important for our purposes is the question *why* people believe in a future life. What are the psychological sources from which this belief springs, and what are the leading types of this belief? In other words our question here is quite parallel to that discussed in the preceding chapter concerning belief in a God. And I think we can hardly do better than make use again of the four-fold division of belief which was there our guide. In fact it would not be difficult to show in purely empirical fashion that (however else one may treat the subject) faith in a future life is always based either (1) on primitive credulity, habit, and authority, (2) on reason, (3) on some form of feeling, or (4) on will.

There is, however, one peculiarity of this belief which differentiates it from belief in the existence of God. We begin believing in God because we are taught to do so. But in one sense it is hardly true to say we begin believing in the uninterrupted continuation of conscious life because we are taught it. Rather is this the natural though by no means explicit attitude of the young mind. The child takes the continuity of life for granted. It is the fact of death that has to be taught. Almost every child, I believe, learns only with a good deal of astonishment that he is going to die,— *that* surely cannot be! Hence the explicit idea of a future life comes to him as the most natural thing in the world, provided he is going to die at all. It quite fits in with the tendency of the young life to believe in its own perpetuity.

With this understood, we may say truly enough that the *explicit* belief in a life after death begins with nearly all of us as a matter of teaching and of primitive credulity. And with many a pious soul untroubled by a disturbing critical faculty, the belief continues to be based chiefly on authority to the end of life. As nothing disturbs it and as it is nourished rather than weakened by the only intellectual atmosphere to which it is exposed — namely the sermons of the pastor and a few religious books — it grows into a habit which finally becomes too strong to fear any attack. Very typically of this class, a woman of nearly seventy writes me, " I believe in personal immortality because I have been taught it." The authority appealed to is of course often the Bible, Christ, or the Church. Sometimes the appeal is of a less "orthodox" variety and partakes more nearly of the nature of reasoning. Many draw their faith largely from what one of my respondents calls "the expert authority of men of all ages." With some the authority — say of the Bible or of Christ — is inextricably bound up with a kind of mystic sense; as in the following: "My feeling of oneness with Christ lies at the basis of my assurance of my blessed personal existence with him forever." "I believe because my Lord tells me so and because that word of His rings true in my own heart." — As I pointed out in the last chapter, belief based on authority and habit is stronger with nearly every one than he is usually willing to admit. It forms the background of the faith in immortality with many a man and woman who likes to think that some argument is the really decisive factor. At times of mental alertness the argument may stand forward as the great champion of faith; but when the mind grows weary it is usually the tradition and the habit of childhood — always there in the background — which comes forth as the truly decisive forces. Even with men of the highest intellectual culture this is often the case. Amiel, for example, writes: "What is my real faith? Has the universal, or at any rate the very general and common doubt of science, invaded me in turn? I have defended the cause of the immortality of the soul against those who questioned it, and yet when I have reduced them to silence, I have scarcely known whether at bottom I was not after all on their side. I have tried to do without hope; but it is possible that I have no longer the strength for it, and that, like other men, I must be sustained and consoled by a belief, by the belief in pardon and immortality — that is to say by religious belief of the Christian type. Reason and thought grow tired, like muscles and nerves. They must have their sleep, and this sleep is the relapse into the tradition of childhood, into the common hope. It takes so much effort to maintain oneself in an exceptional point of view, that one falls back into prejudice by pure exhaustion, just as the man who stands indefinitely always ends by sinking to the ground and reassuming the horizontal position." [3]

[3] *Journal Intime* (for Jan. 25, 1868). Eng. translation by Mrs. Humphry Ward. (New York; A. L. Burt.)

I am inclined to think that belief in a future life is less often based upon argument than is belief in God. Certainly this second source of faith in man's survival of death contributes far less of strength than any of the other three,— at least if we take into account only its *direct* contribution.   The arguments that men offer in defense of their faith are in most cases of a negative sort, aiming merely to show that those who deny the eternal life are no more justified by logic and evidence than are the believers, and thus leaving open the door to faith if one wills to make the faith venture.   More positive arguments are sometimes given.   To those who start out with the view that this is a moral universe or that there is a just God, the idea of death ending all seems incongruous and therefore untenable; the evils of this life must be righted somewhere and sometime, the good rewarded and justice done.   So far as I can judge, however, this argument is less generally impressive than it was a generation ago.   It is very seldom mentioned by any of my respondents — in explicit form, at any rate — nor do I find in conversation with various people that it is often seriously relied upon as an argument.   The believers who answered my questionnaire, so far as they refer to reasoning at all, usually make their arguments much more indefinite.— " My reason demands such a belief to rationalize present existence."   " Because of the evident purpose behind the laws of the universe, and of the manifest evolution of all things toward perfection, which development does not appear at all complete in the human life by death."   A few mention the results of psychical research as the basis of their faith.   The Proceedings of the Society for Psychical Research, and the books by Sir Oliver Lodge, Professor Hyslop, Frederick Myers and others of their school, together with the influence of a few more or less respectable mediums in each of our large cities and the occurrence of " psychic phenomena " here and there in the community have had some effect in resuscitating belief in the survival after death, though probably less than most of us would have predicted. Since the beginning of the recent war, however, so-called communications from the other side and popular books upon the subject have notably increased not only in number and variety but in influence as well.   Added to this, as a reinforcement to faith, has come the striking confidence in the soul's life with which thousands of our young men have marched almost gaily to their death. How long the effects of this war-born faith will last, now that the war is over, it is impossible to predict, but no observer of the times can fail to see that, temporarily at least, the future life has been made distinctly more real to a large portion of the community. "Whatever our personal beliefs," writes Winifred Kirkland, "we are strangely stupid if we are not startled by the overwhelming evidence of the present centering of the general attention upon the possibility of survival." "Myriads of people are to-day ordering their lives on the hypothesis of immortality. For one man four years ago who lived in accordance with this hypothesis, to-day a thousand do." [4]

Probably the argument for immortality that is both most generally persuasive and logically the soundest consists in pointing out the essential difference between consciousness and its processes, on the one hand, and the material world and its laws on the other. This is, of course, the essence of the Platonic arguments, and nothing better is likely ever to be suggested. "Since the life in us is not material," writes a woman, "it cannot perish as a material thing." Surely a great deal could be said for this position and there is no doubt that it or something like it, in explicit or in implicit form, has much to do with the quiet confidence in which many thinking people face death. Yet, after all, its chief value lies in opening up the road so that the more deep-lying influences may have free play. I find, in fact, that most of my respondents who name some argument for their faith end by adding — "And then it *must* be so," or "my mind *demands* it," or something of like tenor which shows plainly enough where the real strength of their faith lies. Emerson, who was one of the most ardent defenders of the faith in immortality, at the close of a careful exposition of the reasons for his confidence, adds: "There is a draw back to the value of all statements of the doctrine, and I think that one abstains from

[4] "The New Death" (Boston, Houghton, Mifflin: 1918), pp. 7–8, 21–22. Miss Kirkland, of course, never meant her figures to be taken literally. While she is very much in earnest, her eloquent little book is better classed as poetry than under statistics.

writing or printing on the immortality of the soul, because, when he comes to the end of his statement, the hungry eyes that run through it will close disappointed; the listeners will say, That is not here which we desire; and I shall be as much wronged by their hasty conclusions as they feel themselves wronged by my omissions.   I mean that I am a better believer, and all serious souls are better believers in immortality than one can give grounds for.   The real evidence is too subtle, or is higher than one can write down in propositions." [5]

The more deep-lying influences productive of this faith in immortality are to be found in the realms of feeling and will.   At first sight it may seem odd that feeling can give strength to a belief about the future; but on further reflection it will be plain that there is nothing at all strange about this.   For the belief in question is not one of reasoning but of immediate reality feeling; and as we have seen, if an object of thought is vividly and warmly presented and is felt to be congruent with one's background sense of reality, it is *ipso facto* felt as real.   Belief of this emotional type as applied to a future life is of various sorts.   Many persons who feel it strongly are unable to analyze it, and can describe it only as a " feeling " or an " instinct " or by some other word which in its non-technical sense is sufficiently vague.   " Instinctively I feel that I am not to be obliterated," is a typical response.   Sometimes the belief is of a more plainly mystic type.   The individual who feels himself " united with God " often feels — rather than argues — that his life is therefore safe and eternal.   " To be conscious of the divine life within," writes one of my respondents, " is to know that life cannot die."   A somewhat different type of mystic belief one finds in writers like Walt Whitman.   "And again lo! " he writes in one of many characteristic passages, " the pulsations in all nature, all spirit, throbbing forever — the eternal beats, the eternal systole and diastole of life in things — wherefrom I feel and know that death is not the ending as was thought, but rather the real beginning — and that nothing ever is or can be lost, nor ever die, nor soul nor matter."   This is not argument

[5] " Immortality," Vol. VIII of his complete works.   (Boston, Houghton, Mifflin: 1890), p. 328.

nor is it the will to believe; it is a statement of an immediate apprehension, deeply felt, and one which borrows its sense of reality from nothing else. It is its own authority.

If we analyze the emotional form of conviction concerning immortality we shall, I think, find that in most cases it is based upon a direct apprehension of the essential worth of the self; [6] going back, I suppose, to the instinct of self-assertion — if indeed it do not go back farther than any instinct. The individual is conscious of inherent powers and purposes too great to be exhausted here, and feels that his own nature is such that the death of the body is irrelevant to its life. This is not an argument nor a demand but an immediate sense that the death of the spirit is intolerably — almost ludicrously — incongruous with what one feels of indubitable reality within. " I believe in immortality," writes one woman, " because I feel that I cannot live out all that is in me in one life time." Another: " My mind refuses to believe that its existence can be destroyed." " Only this I feel warranted in holding fast to," writes Felix Adler, " that the root of my selfhood, the best that is in me, my true and only being, cannot perish. In regard to that the notion of death seems to me to be irrelevant." [7] Some such inner assurance as this seems to have been the source of Goethe's belief in immortality. Speaking of death he said, " The thought of it leaves me in perfect peace, for I have a firm conviction that our spirit is a being of indestructible nature; it works on from eternity to eternity: it is like the sun which though it seems to set to our earthly eyes, does not really set but shines on perpetually. Do you think a coffin can impose upon me ? " [8]

[6] Stratton has pointed out the influence of this factor in belief. " The sense of personal worth or worthlessness is reflected in the belief in immortality or in the final extinction at least of consciousness. A readiness to believe in ultimate extinction is a sign of self-depreciation; while the opposite feeling — that in some way this self of mine is treasured, is essential to the world — supports the idea that death is but a superficial experience, and that in spite of it the individual soul lives on." (" The Psychology of the Religious Life," p. 30.)

[7] " Life and Destiny," p. 39, quoted in Leuba's " Belief in God and Immortality."

[8] Quoted by Lowes Dickinson in the Notes to his Ingersoll Lecture on Immortality — " Is Immortality Desirable ? " (Boston, Houghton, Mifflin: 1909), p. 55.

Some of the answers to one of the questions asked in my questionnaire are of interest here. The question ran: "When are you most impressed with the reality of a future life? In sickness or in health? Please describe your circumstances and feeling states when the belief is most strong." The number of answers to this question was very small, and those that I received seemed at first confusing and contradictory. Besides several scattering responses which were not significant, twelve asserted that their faith was strongest when in health, seven at times of sickness, and ten when confronted with the thought of their own death or when present at the death of a friend. Contradictory as these responses seem, I believe, on careful examination, that they are all to be explained on the same principle — the principle, namely, we have just been considering. The same person, in fact, might well find both health and sickness and the thought of death strengthening to his faith,— just as each of these conditions, for other reasons, may detract from it. These reasons for detraction may be mentioned before considering the more positive influences in question. Some find their belief less strong in health because their attention is then most commonly turned away to other things. In sickness belief may wane with other mental functions from sheer fatigue. "My faith is weakest," writes one respondent, "when I'm tired out." But it is the positive influence of health and sickness that are of most interest. When one is enjoying life to its full and is in the complete possession of all his faculties which are working at their best, the thought of death often seems incongruous to an extreme. "My belief in a future life," writes one man, very typically, "is merely my belief in life." With Goethe such a man would ask, "Do you think a coffin can impose upon me?"

But it is to the same sense of the uniqueness and value and inner strength of the life of the spirit, that those refer who find their faith strongest in sickness or in the presence of death or at the thought of death. "Very often," writes a friend of mine, "when I stand in the presence of death, I feel as if the immortality of the one who is gone is perfectly clear. Furthermore, I feel that if death should plainly present itself as a near possibility for myself or for some one especially near to me I would not in the least fear it or feel that it offered a barrier to the truest development of anything good in me." At such a time

> " The soul secure in her existence smiles
> At the drawn dagger and defies its point."

And here I have in mind nothing poetic nor metaphysical but the plainest and prosiest of psychological facts. To the man who has developed to any considerable degree the sense of inner worth and of strong spiritual life, the thought of death is likely to come as a kind of challenge and to rouse within him that impulse to break down all impediment and to defy one's opponent to come on and do his worst, which psychology terms the instinct of pugnacity and popular speech calls the sporting blood. It is thus that the aged poet defies the coffin to impose on him and that the ancient philosopher drinks off the hemlock " right blithely," ordering with his last breath an offering to the god of health.

Belief of the kind I have just been describing is usually very strong, and has the added advantage of being at its strongest at exactly the times when it is most needed. It is not, however, for all, and I cannot say that those in whom it is the dominant type of faith form a very large class. Far and away the largest of our four classes is the fourth — those, namely, whose faith is based chiefly on will. It hardly needs to be said that the great majority of people desire a future life — whether intensely or slightly. Three of my students have issued questionnaires on this subject and between them have collected sixty-five answers to the question: " Do you desire a future life ? " Of these sixty-five respondents, fifty-eight answered Yes, seven No. Of Mr. Simeon Spiddle's one hundred and seven respondents, ninety-five preferred immortality, while twelve were indifferent.[9] Professor Leuba reports that 83.8% of the less eminent, and 67.7% of the more eminent physical scientists, among whom he circulated his recent questionnaire, desired immortality; and that 70.7% of the " lesser " and 68.4% of the " greater " biologists desired it. The percentage among the historians and sociologists who an-

[9] " The Belief in Immortality." *Journal of Relig. Psy.*, V, 5–51.

swered his questionnaire did not differ materially from those just cited. Among the psychologists the desire for immortality was found at its lowest, only 53.8% acknowledging it.[10] The first question on the questionnaire gotten out a few years ago by the American Branch of the Society for Psychical Research reads, " Would you prefer to live after death or not ? " Out of 3218 replies 2993 were in the affirmative, 225 in the negative.[11] These figures from Dr. Schiller's questionnaire are not so significant as they seem; for the answers to later parts of the questionnaire reveal the fact that in many cases the affirmative answer to the first question did not necessarily imply any strong desire for continued existence. Question IV read " Do you now feel the question of a future life to be of urgent importance to your mental comfort ? " To this the answers were " No," 2007; " Yes," 1314. Among the 2007 who voted No, however, were included practically all those who did not believe in a future life and those who felt skeptical about it; hence we may fairly conclude that a large proportion of the earnest believers voted Yes. Certainly this is the case with my students' respondents, and I think we shall be safe in concluding that the desire for a future life, though not always strong, is fairly general; and that among earnest believers the question of its reality is of urgent importance.

As our present interest is concerned altogether with the believers, we may dismiss from consideration the unbelievers and the skeptics; for our present question has to do only with the source of the belief of those who do believe. If I may judge by the sixty-five responses to my students' questionnaire and the sixty-nine to my own,[12] we may conclude (as already indicated above) not only that the great majority of believers in a future life desire it, but that the largest class of believers is

[10] " The Belief in God and Immortality." Chap. IX.

[11] This is not stated explicitly in the report, but comes out on p. 431.— See F. C. S. Schiller: " The Answers to the American Branch's Questionnaire, regarding Human Sentiment as to a Future Life." P. S. P. R., XVIII, 416–53.

[12] The only question on my questionnaire referring to this subject read: " Do you believe in personal immortality? If so, why? " There was no question concerning the *desire* for a future life. The responses that I received, however, showed plainly that desire was the principal cause of the belief.

made up of those whose faith is based chiefly on their desire. The word " chiefly," however, must not be left out; for it would be a mistake to suppose that the desire for a future life can often by itself produce belief. One cannot genuinely desire what one genuinely believes impossible and out of the question. Hence desire must be helped out either by authority or by reason or by some sort of intuition or feeling.

The nature of this desire varies with different people. The fundamental as well as the most wide-spread and influential form of it is simply the love of life as such, the instinctive impulse which normally makes men cling to life, however wretched they may be. In the words of Wijnændts Francken, " The demand for self-preservation is one of our most powerful instincts; it transcends the tomb itself, for the desire for immortality is nothing else than one form of the search for self-preservation." [13] This sometimes expresses itself in the instinctive horror at the thought of death and the longing to avoid it. One of the earliest recorded expressions of desire for a future life is of this naïve type. It was written many thousands of years ago by some Egyptian, to whom the hope of personal immortality was somehow bound up with the hope that his body might avoid the horrors of disintegration. In contrast to the usual coldly conventional tone of the Book of the Dead, this cry of a longing soul comes to our ears to-day, through no one knows how many millenniums, with a note of earnest human appeal and a touch of nature that makes us feel him truly our kin. " Grant thou," he prays to the God Osiris, " that I may enter into the land of everlastingness, according to that which was done for thee, whose body never saw corruption. . . . Let not my body become worms, but deliver me as thou didst thyself. . . . Let life come from the body's death and let not decay caused by any reptile make an end of me. Homage to thee, O my divine father Osiris, thou hast thy being with thy members. Thou didst not decay, thou didst not become worms, thou didst not diminish, thou didst not become corruption, thou didst not

---

[13] " Psychologie de la Croyance en l'Immortalité." Rev. Philosophique, LVI, 278. While it is hardly correct to speak of the " *instinct* of self-preservation," there is a certain truth behind the phrase. For a discussion of this matter see Hocking, " Human Nature and Its Remaking," Chap. X.

putref*y*, thou didst not turn into worms. I shall not decay, I shall not rot, I shall not putrefy, I shall not turn into worms. I shall have my being, I shall have my being; I shall live, I shall live!" [14]

Horror at the destruction of the body of course plays no part in the desire for immortality to-day. But dread, or at least dislike, of annihilation and the instinctive clinging to life that Mr. Francken refers to, are with many still as strong as was fear of the tomb with the ancient Egyptian. Twenty-two per cent. of Schiller's respondents asserted that they preferred a future life of *any* sort to annihilation. Three very typical answers to the question (in my students' questionnaires), " Why do you want a future life? " were the following: " Because I do not like the thought of empty nothingness beyond the grave." " To ask if I want a state after death is much such a question as, Do you want life? — I think it is fair to say, Certainly I want life after death as well as before — an after life not as a reward, etc., but because this inner spiritual life is the greatest thing in the world." " Because I decidedly dislike the idea of leaving the world and things to go on without me, rather than because life is so pleasant. I do not care to be snuffed out like the light of a candle." This last response is typical both in the love of life it shows and also by its negative reference to the expected happiness of the next world. Very few of my respondents made much of the prospect of eternal bliss; and Schiller reports the same fact as true of the responses to the S. P. R. questionnaire. Possibly I should mention one kind of happiness as an exception to this statement; for the hope of reunion with one's friends is certainly one of the very largest factors in the desire for immortality. One respondent writes: " I desire future life partly because extinction is a horrible thought. Above all, however, it is *love* that leads me on. I have always felt the most burning love for my absolutely devoted mother, and when she was so prematurely taken from me, it became the cry of my life to be with her." [15] This,

[14] " The Book of the Dead," translated by E. A. W. Budge (Chicago, Open Court: 1901), Chap. CLIV.

[15] This factor in the desire for immortality might be illustrated by an almost endless number of examples. I take one at random from Arreat's

indeed, can hardly be called the desire for happiness, nor do most of the other descriptions of what my respondents desire and hope to do in the next life imply a hedonistic basis for the demand. The desire for moral progress, for enlarged service, and for a better opportunity for those who have had no chance here are mentioned not infrequently among the reasons why immortality is wished for.[16] But quite as common as this desire for a future life on its own account is the demand that it shall exist in order to give meaning and purpose to this. One thoughtful woman writes: "I believe in personal immortality because I cannot think in any other terms. Life to have any meaning or reason for being must continue, and (whether partly from training and continual habit I am not sure) I find it impossible to think at all in any other way. It is a postulate; not arrived at by any course of reasoning, and without it life would be horrible." In a less extreme form this same attitude is expressed by Mr. Lowes Dickinson in his own personal confession embedded in his Ingersoll Lecture: "I find then that, to me, in my present experience, the thing that at bottom matters most is the sense I have of something in me making for more life and better. All my pain is at last a feeling of the frustration of this; all my happiness a feeling of its satisfaction. It governs all my experience, and determines all my judgments of value. . . . The Goods we have here are real Goods, and we may find the Evil more than compensated by them. But what I do maintain is that life here would have indefinitely more value if we knew that beyond death we should pursue, and ultimately to a successful issue, the elusive ideal of which we are always in quest. The conception that death ends all does not empty life of its worth, but it destroys, in my judgment, its most precious element, that which transfigures all the rest: it

"Le Sentiment Religieux en France" (Paris, Alcan: 1903), which is typical of many: "J'ai besoin de croire que les êtres que nous avons tant aimés ne nous sont pas arrachés brutalement pour toujours. Sans religion, la vie ne vaut pas la peine d'être vécue: elle est notre seule raison d'être" (p. 123 — in the Appendix).

[16] One respondent (who surely is *not* typical) writes that he wants a future life "to carry on the great missionary plans of God to millions of spirits who need to know the story of redeeming Love! To preach and testify this to myriads of angels will keep them from falling from holiness forever."

obliterates the gleam on the snow, the planet in the east; it shuts off the great adventure beyond death." [17]

These testimonies bring us back again to that inherent demand for conscious life as such, for an endless continuation of spiritual opportunity, which is at the bottom of so much of the earnest desire for immortality. As we have seen, it is based upon an instinct — if, indeed, it be not ultimately based on something deeper still — and it manifests itself through all grades of spiritual development, from the unthinking, organic fear of death, up to the longing of the artist, the philosopher, and the mystic. "Feeling one's exquisite curiosity about the Universe fed and fed, rewarded and rewarded" in an unending life, would be, in the opinion of Henry James, the greatest artistic delight, the highest conceivable good — "a million times better than not living." [18] The scientific desire to know and to *keep on knowing* is another form of the same demand for life. Many a scientist, in order to attain a pure objectivity, seeks to kill out this desire so far as it relates to a continuation of the knowing process after the death of the body — though the position of earnestly desiring and eagerly delighting in the knowing process, and at the same time being perfectly willing that it should cease altogether on the occurrence of some perfectly irrelevant physical accident seems, to say the least, highly artificial and something closely resembling a pose. But though many scientists seem to hold this attitude as an ideal, not all succeed in realizing it. One of the most "objective" of scientists — Thomas Huxley — toward the close of his life wrote to his friend Morley: "It is a curious thing that I find my dislike to the thought of extinction increasing as I get older and nearer the goal. It flashes across me at all sorts of times and with a sort of horror that in 1900 I shall probably know no more of what is going on than I did in 1800. I had sooner be in hell a good deal — at any rate in one of the upper circles where the climate and company are not too trying." [19]

This demand for unobstructed life, for life in the fullest sense

[17] Op. cit., pp. 30–33.
[18] See the *Literary Digest* for March, 1910, p. 303.
[19] "Life and Letters of Thomas Huxley" (New York, Appleton: 1901), Vol. II, p. 67.

that the individual can conceive, which is seen in the common man, the artist, and the scientist is seen again in the longings of the saint and mystic. "If to any man," writes Augustine, "the tumults of flesh be silenced, if fancies of the earth and waters and air be silenced also; if the poles of heaven be silent also, and if He speak alone; not by them but by Himself, that we may hear his own word; not pronounced by any tongue of flesh, nor by the voice of angels, nor by the sound of thunder, nor in the dark riddle of a resemblance; but that we may hear Him whom we love in these creatures, Himself without these; could this exaltation for ever continue and ever ravish us and swallow us up, and so wrap up their beholder among these more inward joys as that his life might be forever like to this very moment of understanding which we now sigh after; were not this indeed to Enter into Thy Master's joy?" [20]

Before concluding this chapter it will, I think, be worth our while to supplement our study of belief with a short study of unbelief. Having seen some of the psychological sources of belief in a future life, we may now ask, What are the psychological influences involved in the doubt or denial of a future life? In a general way, of course, the answer is to be found in the absence of those causes which our study has shown us lead to belief. In the first place we must recognize that a fairly large number of persons have no real desire for life after death.[21] The causes of this indifference are not easy to ascertain with any degree of completeness or exactitude. Possibly some guidance may be found in a comparison of our times with the Middle Ages. The apparent loss of desire for a future life in the last 500 years is due in part to the greater attractiveness of this world in our times and the increase of interests of all sorts which keep one's attention too firmly fastened here to allow of much thought being spent on the other world. As people cease to think about a future life it becomes less vivid to them and hence less an object of desire. The shattering of authority and the weakening in popular estimation of the arguments in its favor have also had the same tendency of making

[20] " Confessions," Bk. IX, Chap. X.
[21] Leuba cites many examples of indifference and even of dislike to a future life. (Op. cit., pp. 297–311.)

it seem less real and hence less genuinely longed for. For desire and belief are *mutually* helpful; not only does desire tend to beget belief, but some sort of belief in at least the possibility of the object is a condition of any real desire for it. In the 15th and 16th centuries men so desired the spring of perpetual youth that they were willing to risk all they had in the search for it. Youth is no less loved to-day, but it can hardly be said that any one ardently desires to discover a spring whose magical water would make it perpetual. We do not desire it as our ancestors did because we no longer harbor it in our thoughts as a genuinely possible object of discovery. Other causes for the loss of desire for immortality besides its lessening vividness are of course at work in various individuals — and always have been. Distaste for life in general, weariness, and dread of responsibility, tend to make one look forward to death as the definitive end with carelessness or even with longing.[22] Cases of this sort, however, are not common, and are probably little commoner to-day than in previous ages. The great cause of the loss of desire is the indifference described above, due to the disappearance of the vitality of belief.

I have no idea to what extent the change in the intellectual atmosphere of modern society has undermined emotional belief, but there can be no doubt that it has been the great factor in weakening belief from authority. And here the various arguments against human survival of death have been reinforced by all the rationalistic influences of every sort that have been steadily wearing away the authority of Bible, Church, and tradition these many years. Hence from several sides is borne in upon us the immense influence of thought in determining belief.[23] This influence as it comes to bear upon the individual

[22] Leuba sums up the causes for this loss of desire as he views them in the following words: "A weariness of existence, temperamental or the fruit of age or of other circumstances; a disposition to enjoy the mood that informs Bryant's noble poem, Thanatopsis; and especially, perhaps, an inability to picture in intelligible and acceptable form a future life, suffice to make of a death that ends all a satisfactory, even a desirable goal." (Op. cit., p. 301.)

[23] Dr. E. Griffith-Jones, in an excellent little book on "Faith and Immortality" (New York, Scribner's: 1917), brings out one intellectual influence — a theological one — which I have not mentioned, but which has probably had some effect in weakening the faith of certain classes of

is largely indirect and largely negative, and for that reason when one studies the particular positive beliefs of individual men and women, thought seems to have a very second rate — or fourth rate — position.   But when we take into consideration the movement of society during several centuries we see that the influence of thought (directly upon society and indirectly upon the individual) is of prime importance — something too often forgotten by the enthusiastic anti-intellectualism of our day.   In fact it would be a mistake to say that thought modifies the individual's belief only indirectly; for if we take into account its negative and destructive influence, its action is certainly direct enough; Spiddle reports that nearly all of his respondents whose belief concerning immortality has passed through a period of radical change, ascribed this change to the study of science and philosophy,[24] and in this his responses were surely very representative.   Among the college students who responded to Leuba's questionnaire there was a steady loss of the belief with academic advance.   " Only fifteen per cent of the freshmen reject immortality and four per cent are uncertain; while nearly thirty-two per cent of the juniors have given it up, and eight per cent more are uncertain.   The cause of this Leuba finds not so much in increased knowledge as in increased individualism and freedom from the authoritative creeds that dominate childhood.   That both the intellectual and the indi-

society.   He attributes the loss of belief in a future life to the coöperation of three factors: (1) the spread of natural science with its rationalistic and skeptical tendencies, (2) the centering of the modern man's interest in this world, (3) the inability of contemporary theologians to agree on any doctrine as to the nature of the next life, with the resulting conflict of rival theories which utterly bewilder the layman and make him feel that there is no definite doctrine of immortality in which he can rest.   Especially has this been the result of recent discussion by Biblical critics of the eschatological passages in the New Testament.   " Science and theology during the last quarter of a century have thus coöperated from different points of view in disturbing the sure foundations of the earlier belief in a future state; the first by making it difficult to believe that the ' soul ' can survive the body, or whether there was a ' soul ' to survive at all; and the second by bringing the scriptural evidence as to what follows death into uttermost discord and confusion.   It is no wonder that in face of these contrary winds of doctrine the light began to flicker and burn dimly on the altar of the Immortal Hope " (p. 30).

[24] " The Belief in Immortality," p. 47.

vidualistic factors continue their negating influence after graduation from college seems to be indicated by Leuba's figures concerning American scholars, whose belief in a future life (according to the results of his questionnaire) are represented by the following figures: among physical scientists 50.7% believe in immortality; biologists 37%; historians 51.5%; psychologists 19.8%. It is especially significant that the percentage of believers among the more eminent psychologists was only 8.8.[25] These figures are, of course, quite exceptionally low; yet in the case even of those who do not go into any scholarly profession, an increased individualism guided by certain destructive arguments leads not indeed to the complete loss of belief in immortality, but to the placing of it upon a shelf in the mind, among those things which are merely and abstractly possible.

This happens more frequently and more easily to-day because of the psychological atmosphere that has been produced by the successive triumphs of natural science. Students of science are less likely to believe in immortality than others, not because the arguments against it are stronger than those for it, nor yet because they see the logical difficulties in the way of immortality more clearly than do those whose thought has been engaged chiefly in other lines, but largely because their training has produced in them a habit of regarding the scientific laws of the material world with the same sort of reverence that the old-fashioned Christian feels toward the teaching of Scripture. Leuba's figures, just quoted, illustrate this point rather nicely. While scientists as a class are less likely to believe in the survival of bodily death than others, there are, as we have seen, significant differences between different classes of scientists. If the reader will look back at the statistics on the subject, he will see that over fifty per cent of the historians and physical scientists believe in immortality, while among the biologists and psychologists the percentage of belief is notably lower. This fact is undoubtedly due to the constant effort made by both the latter classes to view the phenomena of life and mind in terms of something like mechanical sequence; an effort which

25 " The Belief in God and Immortality," Chaps. VIII and IX.

with some has become a habit, and by some is regarded as a presupposition of scientific procedure.

The truth is, non-belief, like belief, draws its strength not only from reason but from authority; in fact, for many enthusiastic students of science the will to believe has a good deal to do with the result. In certain scientific circles it is not good form to believe in a future life; and the ascetic ideal which would sacrifice selfish interests for the personal values of science also comes into play. Moreover non-belief, like belief, is a product not merely of logical argument, authority, habit, and volition, but is largely influenced also by the imagination; and the peculiarly objective point of view which natural science inculcates and the habit it produces of considering causation and the laws of matter universal and invariable give a certain cast to the imagination which makes the idea of the survival of bodily death increasingly difficult.

This question of the imagination is most fundamental to the understanding of belief and disbelief. In the early part of our last chapter, when discussing the psychology of belief in general, we saw the enormous part played by the imagination in producing the vividness of reality feeling. It is very difficult to believe earnestly in anything that we can in no way image to ourselves; and this general fact finds ample application and illustration in the field under discussion. Though no doubt there are exceptions, it is still a very general truth that those who deny a future life are those who find it impossible to imagine it in vivid and persuasive fashion; while they have few doubts on the subject who find little difficulty in imagining it and who perhaps would find it difficult to imagine death ending all. Belief and disbelief would therefore seem, in one sense, to be correlative to two types of imagination or two points of view from which the imagination regards the future life.

We can best get at these two types of imagination by contrasting two classes of person who are known to have quite different views on the subject of immortality. Perhaps no large class of men are more given to a skeptical or even materialistic view on this subject than physicians; and probably none have more genuine faith in a future life than clergymen. Doubtless differences of opinion on authority and on the logic of various arguments has much to do with this difference of belief; but these things do not fully explain the contrast. The physician finds it hard to imagine, with any reality-feeling, life after death, while the clergyman finds it easy to do so. The reason for this is largely to be found in the fact that the physician tends to think of death from the point of view of the body, and that death means to him usually the death of some one else; whereas the clergyman views death more subjectively and from the point of view of the "soul." The physician takes the objective view of death. All his experience, his training, his daily work, his professional habits of thought, lead him to this. Inevitably death means to him the ceasing to function of certain vital organs. Thus it comes about that even when he thinks of his own death he pictures it also objectively — externally; he sees his body lying on a bed, his heart ceasing to beat, his respiration stopped. Those manifestations of life in which he is professionally interested he pictures at an end; and that *means* to him that life has ceased. As dies the beast, so dies the man — literally true from an external view point certainly. As this habit of thought grows upon the physician or scientist he finds it increasingly difficult to hold alongside with it the old view, taught him in childhood, that conscious life continues beyond the grave. To believe it might be logical enough, but he finds it very hard to imagine with any lively sense of reality.

The clergyman, on the other hand, thinks of death, as I have said, from the point of view of the "soul." Death means to him primarily *his* death; that is the type of death for him. He thinks of other people's death as meaning what his own death would mean. That is, he views death from the subjective, or, rather, the inner point of view. Very likely he knows little enough about the physiology of death: or if he is versed in this aspect of the case it is not this primarily that he thinks about. Death means to him a form of subjective experience, not a physiological phenomenon. His whole training and his daily work enforce this view. As a result it is very easy for him to imagine a continuation of conscious existence after death; in fact, it may be difficult for him to imagine the contrary. And of course not only is this true of ministers but it holds frequently of many other men whose thoughts are habitually occupied with the spiritual and inner side of life.   Goethe is quoted as saying, " It is, to a thinking being, quite impossible to think himself non-existent, ceasing to think and live."   This, as I have pointed out, is the natural attitude of the untaught mind.   It is with a tremendous shock of surprise that the child learns he must some day die; and for a considerable time most children probably refuse really to believe it.   The belief that life as a matter of course will not end seems to be almost as natural as the desire that it should continue.   The idea that life will end may be logical but it is an acquired and secondary product.

> " All men think all men mortal but themselves."

There are several reasons for this.   For one thing, it is hard to think of the world continuing to run along and we not here to witness it.   We are all incipient Berkleyans, at least to the extent that in our images of various external events there is usually, in the background of our minds, an implicit recognition of the relation or possible relation of the event to us.   We picture ourselves as the hidden beholders of all that we imagine. More important than this is the fact that the thought of oneself ceasing to exist is most difficult for the natural man, quite aside from his relation to the external world.   Our past experience of consciousness is of a stream which, in spite of its temporary breaks in sleep, still seems to us really continuous and without conscious beginning or end.   We have gone to sleep many times, but always to wake once more.   *We have got into the habit of being alive.*   Hence the association of non-being with ourselves is unnatural and difficult.   Nor do past experience and the laws of association and habit explain the whole matter.   Life somehow *feels* itself and *wills* itself to be endless — not explicitly, but by a violent reaction against the idea of extinction.   To look at oneself objectively, from an exterior point of view, as one of those things which may cease to be, requires a considerable degree of sophistication, and both in the individual and in the race [26] it is learned only with difficulty.

[26] In this native difficulty of imagining one-self really dead is to be found,

The two types of imagination that I have been describing —
the external and the inner — are to be found not only in different individuals with different kinds of training; they may alternate within the same individual under varying circumstances.
If I may take myself as an example, I find my own belief in
a future life at its strongest when thinking of my own death.
As such a time it is unnatural for me to take any but the subjective and inner point of view; so that the thought often gives
me a kind of secret exhilaration such as one feels who sees
his enemy in the distance and cries, " Come on ! "   But when I
see a person die I am sometimes very skeptical.   I remember
seeing a man run over by a train, and being surprised to find
how hard it was for me to believe that the man's consciousness
still existed or would ever exist again.

But difficulties connected with the imagination are responsible for another source of weakness in the belief in immortality,
in addition to this objective and external mode of representation.   Belief in an abstract truth, a truth which can be conceived but not imagined, is usually cold and lacking in that
vividness which is the primitive touch-stone of reality.   The
more concrete details that can be added to our mental picture,
the more real does it become to us.   This increased sense of
reality through imagined details is the effect which the historical
novel has — or should have — upon the reader.   It makes
Louis XI or Richard I real and living to us by supplying a
host of concrete details which add the very warmth of life
to characters that had been but names before.   Now it is the
impossibility of surrounding the idea of the next world with
any concrete details which are not themselves almost impossible,
that makes the belief in question so hard for many to retain.
If the departed really still have conscious existence, what are
they doing?   What are the conditions of their life?   What
are their employments and their pleasures?   If we allow ourselves to ponder over these questions most of us will find our
notion of a future life taking on the color of a fairy tale.   The
questions, if we face them steadily, demand some kind of answer; and yet almost any conceivable answer put in vivid detail

in my opinion, one of the original sources of the belief in a future life at
least as important as seeing ghosts in dreams.

will make the belief all the more difficult. The historical attempts that have been made to picture the next world so as to
give it the reality-feeling that comes from vivid images, have
all had but very moderate and temporary success. From the
Book of the Dead, through Virgil, Dante, Milton, down to *Gates
Ajar,* and the descriptions in our hymn books, they all seem
either mythical or puerile, so far as they are given in terms of
detailed imagination. And the same thing surely is true of the
Book of Revelation. The Bible elsewhere on this point is
wisely reticent. Jesus had no descriptive phrases for the life
of heaven which were anything more than plainly symbolic.
And his immediate followers perceived the wisdom of his example. " Eye hath not seen nor ear heard, neither hath entered
into the heart of man the things that God hath prepared for
them that love Him."

For from the nature of the case, all the material for the
details of another life must be drawn from this; and yet it is
plain that if there is a future life (unless we adopt the conception of reincarnation) it must be in many of its details and
surroundings very different from this. Hence the ascription
to it of images drawn from this life strikes us as inharmonious
and incongruous. The idea therefore never gets dressed out in
the details which are so helpful in imparting reality-feeling, and
for most of us it remains always largely abstract and verbal.
Hence the large number of people who, while not denying it,
and even willing to say that they suppose they believe in it,
are quite indifferent to it and never give it a thought. The
imaginative difficulties in it are such that it resembles one of
those small stars which can be seen only by indirect vision, and
which disappear when looked at directly. Many people find
that their belief in immortality is strongest when they think
least about it.

There are two or three classes of people whose faith in a
future life is not greatly affected by the difficulties we have
been discussing. These are, in the first place, that small class
of thinkers who have trained themselves to live so constantly in
a world of concepts that lack of imaginative vividness is no loss.
Much larger is the class of uncritical believers, whose faith is
based upon authority, and who either find no difficulty in ac-

cepting the pictures in the *Revelation,* or else possess so strong a faith that difficulties in imagining a future life are powerless against it. A smaller but in many ways more interesting class are the mystics. For them the difficulties which others feel are not overcome but quite lacking. They will tell you that they can not only conceive but imagine — or rather directly experience — what the future life will be, at least in its most important aspect. For them the most significant feature of that life will be its union with the Divine; and this is for them, they insist, no mere verbal phrase nor abstract idea nor pious hope, but a genuine and very real experience of this present life. People such as these need no detailed descriptions of how the dead are raised up or with what body they shall come. The details they can leave with perfect confidence for the future to reveal. The substance they already possess.

For the great majority who are not mystics, however, the difficulty of giving the future life any imaginative reality must always be a source of real weakness in belief. If they cling to the hope, they usually avoid any serious attempt to picture the details of the future life, either dodging the question altogether or refusing to take any suggested answer seriously. One of my respondents — a student of natural science, who yet hopes for and believes in immortality — writes, " To hold this faith without picturing the nature of the future life I find impossible, but I manage with ease and naturalness to keep those mental pictures in a flux, as it were, making them the poetry of my faith without giving them the definiteness which would challenge my own scientific criticism." This man's position is the wise one for most people who desire to keep their faith. Belief in a future life, like belief in God, is usually an *attitude,* a way of holding oneself in relation to the future, quite as much as a definable concept, and certainly more than a detailed picture. To try to turn it into the latter, either in oneself or in others, is surely unwise. " How are the dead raised up and with what body do they come? Thou fool! "

These then are some of the psychological influences tending to weaken the belief in a future life. Having considered this general question, it may be of some interest to consider briefly the more special question of the weakening of this belief within

Christianity. For that it is being weakened I suppose there is little doubt,[27] and that it is being weakened more rapidly in western Christendom than in other parts of the world seems probable. One of the things that strikes one most forcibly on a visit to India — at least if I may trust my own experience — is the vitality of the belief in immortality among all classes of society except those that have come under western influence. Not only does there seem to be comparatively little theoretical skepticism on the subject; the belief seems to hold a vital place in the lives of a surprisingly large proportion of the people. The chief cause for this contrast is undoubtedly the fact already pointed out, that modern western science tends both to destroy authority, undermine various ancient arguments in favor of immortality, and also induce a form of imagination distinctly hostile to this belief. I think, however, there are several additional factors which give Hinduism a certain advantage over Christianity in nourishing a strong belief in immortality. One of them is connected with the question of the

[27] Leuba has shown, from his statistical report, how surprisingly small a proportion of the classes of people he investigated really care deeply for another life. Dr. Schiller, in the report upon his questionnaire, writes: "On the whole the answers to this question seem distinctly unfavorable to the doctrine that the interest actually taken in the matter of a future life is commensurate with its spiritual importance, or that the question looms as large on our mental horizon as tradition had assumed" (p. 429). Cf. also Schiller's Essay on "The Desire for Immortality" in *Humanism* (London, Macmillan: 1912). The loss of interest in the future life is summed up by a professor of Divinity in the University of Cambridge in the following trenchant words: "Among all the changes which have come over religious and theological teaching within living memory, none seems to be so momentous as the acute secularizing of the Christian hope, as shown by the practical disappearance of the other world from the sermons and writings of those who are most in touch with the thought and aspirations of our contemporaries." (Quoted by Dr. R. F. Cole in the *Auburn Seminary Record* for July, 1911, p. 175.) It should, however, be remembered that the opinions quoted in this note were expressed before the great war; and that since then a very deep-lying and wide-spread interest in the possibility of a future life has been revealed. Indifference to the nature of the future life, moreover, must not be taken as evidence of disbelief in it. Carrington and Meader, in the responses to their questionnaire on the nature of Death, found quite as striking an amount of indifference as is ever met with in circulating a questionnaire on immortality: yet one could hardly conclude that their respondents failed to believe in death.— See their "Death: Its Causes and Phenomena" (New York, Funk and Wagnalls: 1912). Chap. VIII.

imagination already discussed. The Hindu finds no difficulty whatever in imagining the next life, for his belief in reincarnation teaches him that it will be just this life over again, though possibly at a slightly different social level. I am inclined to think, moreover, that the Christian and the Hindu customs of disposing of the dead body may have something to do with this contrast in the strength of their beliefs. Is it not possible that the perpetual presence of the graves of our dead tends to make Christians implicitly identify the lost friend with his body, and hence fall into the objective, external form of imagination about death that so weakens belief in the continued life of the soul? We do not teach this view to our children in words, but we often do indirectly and unintentionally by our acts. The body — which *was* the visible man — is put visibly into the grave and the child knows it is there; and at stated intervals we put flowers on the grave — an act which the child can hardly interpret otherwise than under the category of giving a present to the dead one. And so it comes about that while he is not at all sure just where Grandpa is, he is inclined to think that he is up in the cemetery. Much of our feeling and of our really practical and vital belief on this subject, as on most others, is of course derived from our childhood impressions. And so it comes about that this attitude toward the body and the grave is not confined to children. Says Agnes in Ibsen's " Brand " of her dead boy Alf, when her husband has reproved her for thinking tenderly of the little body in the grave:

> " ' What thou sternly call'st the corse,
>   Ah, to me, my child is *there!*
>   Where is body, there is soul:
>   These apart I cannot keep,
>   Each is unto me the whole;
>   Alf beneath the snow asleep
>   Is my very Alf in heaven.' "

The Hindu is not likely to make this identification. The body of his lost friend is burned within a few hours after death, and the ashes swept into the river and forever dispersed. There is no body left and no grave around which he may center his thoughts of the departed. If he is to think of him at all it cannot be of his body and must be of his soul. The Christian decks the tomb of his departed one with flowers: the Hindu instead performs an annual Shraddha ceremony to the spirits of those gone before.

But there is, I believe, one further reason for the greater strength of the Hindu faith over the Christian, and that is to be found in the contrast between the two conceptions of immortality. In the Christian view the soul's survival of death is essentially miraculous. The soul is conceived as coming into existence with the birth of the body, and the thing to be expected is that it should perish when the body perishes. This is prevented through the intervention, so to speak, of God, who steps in and rescues the soul and confers upon it an immortality which, left to itself, it could never attain. Thus it comes about that when the idea of supernatural intervention has been generally discarded, and even the belief in God as an active force outside of nature has been weakened — as is the case all over western Christendom — there is little left to support the belief in the continued existence of the soul after the death of the body. In India all this is changed. The soul's immortality has there never been thought dependent upon any supernatural interference or miraculous event, nor even upon God Himself. There are atheistic philosophers in India, but they are as thoroughly convinced of the eternal life of the soul as are the monist and the theist. For in India the soul is *essentially* immortal. Its eternity grows out of its very nature. It did not begin to be when the body was born, and hence there is no reason to expect that it will cease to be when the body dies. Existence is a part of its nature. If you admit a beginning for it, you put it at once out of the class of the eternal things, and are forced to hang its future existence upon a miracle. But for the Hindu " the knowing self is not born; it dies not. It sprang from nothing; nothing sprang from it. It is not slain though the body be slain." [28]

But while it is hardly to be questioned that the belief in immortality is less widespread with us than it is with the Indians, it would be a great mistake to regard it as a secondary

[28] Katha Upanishad I. 1. 2. (S. B. E. Am. Ed., New York, Christian Lit. Co.: 1897.) Vol. I, Part II, pp. 10–11. I have discussed this question at greater length in my " India and Its Faith," pp. 105–07.

and unimportant part of Christianity as Christianity is actually believed and felt and lived to-day. Christianity, like Hinduism, has always considered faith in immortality one of the essential aspects of religion. Not all historical religions have done this. The Old Testament made little of personal immortality, as did also the classical form of Paganism, while orthodox Buddhism of the " Southern " type seems to deny it altogether. But Christianity has persistently and steadily put its emphasis upon this larger human hope.[29] And if we base our judgment as to what Christianity believes not on the aggregate of persons who inhabit Christendom but upon those Christians whom popular thought singles out easily as religious people, we shall find that the hope of eternal life is still one of the essential and characteristic elements of Christianity.[30] The difficulties in the conception which I have pointed out are undoubtedly present, and the faith of many Christians is plainly weaker because of them. Yet in spite of these things faith in immortality is still a living and most important part of the Christian conviction.

I am aware that this is not the opinion of all who have studied the subject. Thus Dr. G. Stanley Hall writes: " As to *immortality* in the orthodox sense of the word, if men really believed that there was another life vastly better and more desirable in every way than this, the world would soon be depopulated, for all would emigrate from it, unless fear of the mere act of dying deterred them. At least all the strong and enterprising souls would go. But in fact even those surest of Heaven

[29] Professor T. C. Hall is so struck by this contrast of Christianity to Judaism that he attributes the emphasis on immortality to the Egyptian influence which came in by way of Egyptian-Christian monasticism in the early centuries of our era. (See his " Ethics within Organized Christianity." New York, Scribner's: 1910, pp. 216–17.) But surely one has only to read the history of the early church — or for that matter *The Book of the Acts* — to see that the enthusiastic emphasis upon the future life long antedated this Egyptian influence.

[30] The figures from Schiller's questionnaire do not in the least refute this view. For though the general impression which his results give is that the community is relatively indifferent upon the question, it must be remembered that only a small proportion of his respondents were what one would call essentially religious people. They were representative neither of the community at large (the proportion of the scientific class being much too high) nor of modern Christianity.

stay here to the latest possible moment, and use every means at their disposal not to graduate into the *Jenseits,* even though their lives in this world be miserable. Does not this show that belief in post-mortem life is a convention, a dream-wish ? " [31]

The fallacy of the argument used in this quotation is presumably plain enough. The fact that people do not commit suicide is no proof that they do not believe in a future life; it shows merely that the instinctive impulse for self-preservation, combined with the reiterated teachings of the Christian Church that suicide is a great sin, has strength enough to keep those who believe the other life is best still on this side, until it is God's will to take them. But aside from this psychologically sound explanation of the matter, and even if we were dealing with the (psychologically quite impossible) cold intelligences that President Hall for the moment seems to believe in, the utmost that his test proves is that religious people prefer one life at a time; that no matter how fair the next life may prove to be, they prefer to postpone it till the hour comes and they are ripe for it.

The question of the intensity of belief in what Dr. Hall, in characteristic phrase, calls the " postmortem perduration of personality," [32] is not to be settled in so simple a fashion. For many indifferent people it may be what Dr. Hall calls it — " a kiosk in Kamchatka, which believers have invested something in and fitted out with such comforts as they can " — " better fifty years of earth than a cycle of Heaven." But for many a religious soul — and for many more of them than Dr. Hall evidently supposes — the hope of the eternal life is something truly vital and fundamental, something too sacred and profound to be treated intelligently in Dr. Hall's flippant phrases. It may be that my experience is untrustworthy, but certainly it has been my observation that among religious people the hope and belief in a future life are very central to their religion. The results of my questionnaire show the same fact, if they can be trusted to show anything at all. Among one hundred and forty-seven respondents, one hundred and thirty-one believed in

[31] " Thanatophobia and Immortality," *Am. Jour. of Psy.*, for October, 1915, p. 579.
[32] " Educational Problems," Vol. I, p. 144.

a future life, as against sixteen who were agnostic. Of fifty-seven respondents to a question concerning the growth or decay of the belief, forty-five insisted that their faith in immortality was increasing, seven noticed no changed, and five found a decrease. I should claim no value for these figures were it not that I believe my respondents to have been fairly representative religious people, and that the tone of their answers is quite in accord with what the figures indicate. The faith in immortality may be less wide-spread than the belief in a God, though this is doubtful. Leuba's figures would, in fact, indicate the contrary. All the different classes of American scholars whom he investigated, except the psychologists, were found to include a larger percentage of believers in immortality than of believers in a personal God.[33] Whether this be true of the majority of mankind or not, certainly there is one sense in which the belief in immortality *means* more than the belief in a God. It is less a matter of theory and, when strong, is more personal and practical in its nature. It is far from being merely the continuation of a childish superstition, but, like the belief in God when this is normal, it changes and grows with the growing mind. My respondents may have exaggerated the increase of its strength with their maturing and advancing years, but their testimony is, I believe, trustworthy in so far as it indicates the steady increase of value that this faith has for life. To the religious man and woman this hope-faith becomes increasingly a part of his existence, a secret source of new courage and strength, as the years go by.

It is this essentially pragmatic value of the belief in immortality that I would stress in closing this chapter. As the belief in miracles and special answers to prayer and in the interference of the supernatural within the natural has gradually disappeared, almost the only *pragmatic* value of the supernatural left to religion is the belief in a personal future life. In many advanced religious circles the Absolute is climbing the throne of Jehovah, and the idealistic universe which has taken the place of the old one, when examined closely turns out to be just the materialistic universe with a new set of labels. In

[33] Op. cit., Chap. IX.

such a world only a minimum of pragmatic value is left to "God," and only the belief in human immortality remains from all the ancient faith which taught that the religious universe was really different and had appreciably different consequences from the non-religious one.

If we should affirm with Höffding that, from one point of view at least, " the essence of religion consists in the conviction that value will be preserved," [34] then surely the belief in human immortality would be found very central to it. In a very real sense, moreover, one may say that this faith is psychologically deep-rooted and psychologically justified. For it is based on the clear apprehension of a great truth and a great postulate. The truth is that value and conscious life are correlative terms, and that each is impossible without the other. The postulate is that the spiritual life is different in kind from and essentially independent of the world of matter and its laws and operations. Intimately intermingled the two are, but the human spirit has always insisted that they are not identical, and demanded that they shall not be utterly inseparable. The faith in the immortality of man's spirit is the great expression of this postulate, and of the inherent idealistic demand of human nature that the values of the universe shall not wholly perish. In one sense, therefore, this faith is even more fundamentally human — as it has in fact been more wide-spread both in space and in time — than the belief in a personal God. For it is essentially humanity's belief in itself, its faith in the highest form of the spiritual life that it has known. The particular forms of this faith have varied with man's changing circumstances through the ages and inevitably will vary. But the fundamental demand for the continuance of conscious and rational life, somewhere and somehow, will pretty certainly last as long as men have ideals and hopes and continue to take any attitude toward the Determiner of Destiny.

[34] " The Philosophy of Religion," p. 14, *et passim.*

CHAPTER XII

For one whose knowledge of public worship is limited to what goes on of a Sunday in his own Protestant meeting-house, it is hard to understand what can be meant by the *problem* of worship, or how there can be anything puzzling about it. It is all so simple and natural that the church-goer only wonders why any one stays at home; while the man at home is usually too busy with his Sunday paper to ask why any one goes. Church-going, either on our own part or on the part of others, is one of those commonplace, customary things which, unless our attention has been especially drawn to them, we take quite for granted. But put your average church-goer (or your average home-stayer) on a ship and pack him off to the East; land him at Calcutta near the Kalighat, or lead him inland to some temple on a hill-side overlooking a secluded village; and religious worship will no longer seem to him quite so self-explanatory. The drums are beating violently, as he approaches, and wild music of strange sorts is issuing from the equally strange building before him. He is admitted (after he has taken off his shoes) and beholds a sight as extraordinary as is the noise that accompanies it. On the walls of the rooms are hideous images, carved in stone and daubed with red paint, one representing a monkey, one a creature with a fat human belly and an elephant's head, each with an offering of yellow marigolds before it; while in the most prominent place is a stone pillar, rounded off on the top, wet from the pouring of much Ganges water, bedaubed with spots of paint, and surrounded with green leaves, uncooked rice, a few coins, and more yellow marigolds. There are two priests in the corner, beating tom-toms, and by the pillar stands a third, daubing it with more paint, pouring water over it, placing leaves upon it, and all the while mumbling words,— many of them mere repetitions of names — to which no one seems to listen. The noise becomes louder, and the old priest seizes a lighted lamp and brandishes it about in front of the much-bedaubed pillar, while the audience follow his motions with obvious excitement; and at the close of the hocus-pocus he distributes to them some of the rice which has been collected at the foot of the sacred object. The perform-ance has been utterly unintelligible to our visitor, but the most astonishing thing about it all is the attitude and aspect of the worshipers. For worshipers they indubitably are. Some of them have been standing, some kneeling, some prostrate on their faces. Each one has made an offering before the be-drenched pillar or at the feet of the grotesque figures on the walls, and though some seem indifferent, many give unmistak-able signs of reverence, and a few show in their faces, as they start homewards, that they have found in that preposterous transaction the same sort of inner treasure which our Protestant church-goer has occasionally carried home with him on a Sun-day from his American meeting-house.

" What under the sun do these people get out of this devilish performance ? " asks our friend. " Why do they go through these absurd actions ? How did the thing ever start and why do they keep it up ? "

If our friend continues his travels he will see stranger things than these — candles, bells, incense, bloody animal sacrifice, communal eating of sacred food, repetition of lengthy formulæ, twisting of fingers and wriggling of limbs, elaborate ceremonies of purification, imitation of the actions of animals, obscene rites, wild dances, painful self-torture. And as he travels more widely he will find many of these strange performances repeated by religion after religion, in continent after continent.[1] If, on returning home, out of curiosity he goes (probably for the first time) to the little Catholic Church around the corner, he will find again the candles, the bell, the images, the incense, the muttered words, the twisted fingers, the communal meal — and again also the reverence, the elation, the comfort, the inner re-ward of the worshipers. Such experiences as these may throw a new light even on his own Protestant " service." If instead

[1] One will find an interesting (though quite incomplete) table illustrative of this striking recurrence of seemingly improbable observances in W. B. Stover's " India: A Problem " (Elgin, Ill., Brethren Pub. House: 1903), pp. 165–168.

of coming from Asia, he had come from Mars, and had never seen any form of cult, how (he may now ask himself) would he have been affected by the Sunday doings which he has always taken for granted? Is it not a bit surprising that once in every seven days a great city should stop its work, and that half the population should turn out in their best clothes to hear one of their number read from a big book passages which most of them have long known almost by heart, that they should partake of bread and wine together, and (most astonishing of all) that they should all shut their eyes and listen while the man in the pulpit talks to some one who obviously is not there? Why do the people do these things? What is it all for? How did the custom ever originate and why does it continue?

The question last suggested is obviously a double one. Doubtless some of the psychological factors at work in both the origin and the continuation of the cult have been identical; yet origin and continuation are in one sense separate facts and each needs its own explanation. Many an institution has ceased to exist; why does religious cult, or public worship, still continue? The psychological explanation for each of these things,— so far as one can find any explanation for them — must, like other explanations, be of two sorts, causal and functional. We must, that is, seek to discover what are the influences external to the cult itself, which helped originate it and which tend to preserve it, and also what are the functions performed by the cult in the life of the individual and of society which have made it so valuable to generation after generation that the race has never been willing to give it up, but has clung to it, sometimes passively, often passionately, but always tenaciously.

Whatever may be the true theory of the origin of cult, it seems to be pretty plain at any rate, that one of the theories most commonly held not long ago must be given up. This was the view that man, starting with a belief in supernatural spirits, devised or hit upon various ways of placating their wrath and of gaining their favor, and that these more or less deliberate methods, arising subsequent to religious belief and dependent upon it, formed the origin of cult. " A sentiment of kinship with the superhuman powers," wrote Professor Tiele, " as well as a sense of entire dependence upon them, impels the religious man to seek communion with them, or at least to enter into some kind of relation towards them, and to reëstablish such communion when he thinks it has been broken off through his own fault.   From this impulse spring all those religious observances which are usually embraced in the term worship." [2]   Something not very different from this seems also to be the view of Tylor, who explains the various forms of the cult on the basis of a preëxisting animism.[3]   Such an hypothesis has the merit of simplicity and in fact it was, seemingly, its simplicity rather than anything decisive in the evidence that suggested it in the first place.   It owes its origin to a period, only a few years behind us, when the social nature of religion was but partially understood, and when (in spite of rapidly accumulating anthropological evidence) much greater confidence was felt than we feel to-day in the powers of *a priori* cogitation to think out the nature and origin of religion from what *must have been* the mental state of the *lonely individual.* Although contemporary investigators are far from agreed on the various questions relating to the origin of religion and of cult, two things seem fairly well established: first, that cult did not arise subsequent to belief, but in close connection with it, if indeed it was not the older of the two; and also that cult was not merely an individual but chiefly a social product.[4] Over thirty years ago W. Robertson Smith pointed out the close relation between a seemingly individual rite, namely sacrifice (in at least one of its forms), and that most central social act, the communal meal.[5]   More recently Dr. Irving King, Pro-

[2] "Science of Religion," Vol. II, p. 127.

[3] See his "Primitive Culture" (Fourth Ed. London, Murray: 1903), Vol. II, Chap. 18.

[4] This is well expressed by Professor Toy: "In early man there is little individuality of thought and of religious experience, and there is no observable difference between public and private religious worship. Ceremonies, like language, are the product of social thought, and are themselves essentially social." ("Introduction to the History of Religions," Boston, Ginn: 1913, p. 49.) The subject is dealt with at some length by Dr. F. G. Henke in his "Study in the Psychology of Ritualism" (University of Chicago Press, 1910), who argues at length against the distinction (maintained by Brinton and others) between individual and social rites, maintaining that all rites are social. (See, especially chapters 1 and 2 of his monograph.) The question at issue in Dr. Henke's study seems hardly worth much discussion as it is largely a matter of terms.

[5] "The Religion of the Semites." See especially Chap. VIII.

fessor E. S. Ames, and Dr. F. G. Henke have proposed a theory of the origin of cult which generalizes the suggestion made by Robertson Smith, and certainly does, at last, full justice by the social aspect of religion. According to these writers, the various ceremonies of the cult grow out of social activities, performed by the group in unison or coöperation, these social activities themselves having their origin in practical needs and fundamental instincts. " The forms of social life," writes Professor Ames, " are determined in their main outlines by reactions upon the environment under the stress of the nutritive and sexual impulses. These forms of social life — occupations, relations of the sexes, various ceremonials, and folkways — tend to become fixed, and to secure themselves against change by many natural safeguards." " Religion in its first form is a reflection of the most important group interests through social symbols and ceremonials based upon the activities incident to such interests." [6] Dr. King expresses the same thought. " The religious acts are themselves an organic part of the activities of the social body. They are, in fact, social acts. Under certain circumstances, customs become religious, or acquire religious values. It may be said that religious practices are social habits specialized in a certain direction." [7] To the practical and vital group activities which Professor Ames regards as the source of cult, Dr. King would add such further influences as the play impulse (which may well account for the dance) and even various chance occurrences, too obscure and varied for further analysis. But diverse as are these sources, they are all social, and require no antecedent religious belief to account for them. " If a social group tends naturally to express itself in various practical ways and in various social and playful forms, then that process which is seen to consist of one or more of these natural methods of activity does not require the introduction of any additional explanation, such as an original religious motive. A social group is sure, in any case, to have its practical problems, its sports, and its festive occa-

6 " The Psychology of Religious Experience," pp. 51 and 49. Dr. Henke adds the instincts of fear and anger to the list of original sources of the rite — though on questionable grounds. Op. cit. Chap. III.
7 " The Development of Religion," p. 88.

sions; we may more easily comprehend how these phases of action could be productive of a consciousness of higher values than that these values might have been given offhand, that is, that they should possess no antecedents or natural history." [8]

It would be a mistake to regard this theory of the social origin of cult as completely refuting the older view of Tiele and Tylor; for undoubtedly a very large part of the ceremonials of all developed historical religions is due to some more or less explicitly formulated belief. On the other hand, the origin of the very earliest and most primitive cults is pretty certainly to be sought among the social activities of primitive groups, such as those suggested by Dr. King and Professor Ames. I can hardly feel, however, with Professor Ames that when we have discovered the source of group activities, we have answered the question as to the origin of cult. " It would be no exaggeration," he writes, " to say that all ceremonies in which the whole group coöperates with keen emotional interest are religious, and that all religious acts are distinguished by this social quality." [9] Such a view makes no distinction between religious ceremonial and any other emotional group activity, such as the war dance. Dr. King sees that some distinction is here required, but though he labors it through several pages in an attempt to discover what this distinction may be, nothing very definite emerges. [10] Professor Ames's failure to distinguish religious ceremonies from other social ceremonies is in fact, for him, quite inevitable, since he makes no distinction between the religious and the social as such. As we saw in the first chapter, he defines religion as " the consciousness of the highest social values," making it identical with early group feeling and late social morality. Hence he is under no obligation to explain how the purely social activities of primitive societies came to be differentiated into religious cult. They never were so differentiated, since to be social is to be religious.

For us, however, who have a different view of religion, no such simple solution of the problem is permissible. Religion in our view is not merely the consciousness of the highest social

[8] Op. cit. p. 102.

[9] Op. cit. p. 72.

[10] Op. cit. Chap. V. See also his " The Differentiation of the Religious Consciousness," Psy. Rev. Monograph Supplement for January, 1905.

values, but an attitude toward the Determiner of Destiny; and it is exactly the religious part of the cult ceremonies which Ames and even King have failed to explain. The external part of the most primitive cult — so much as an onlooker might see and describe — may well enough have arisen in the way suggested by them; but how was the relation established in the minds of the participants, or in the mind of the group itself, between these activities and the Determiner of Destiny? Whence came into the cult that cosmic sense which (if our view be correct) must somehow be connected with an act if that act is to be genuinely religious?

The most influential group of modern writers on the sociological aspects of religion — namely M. Durkheim and his followers — will answer this question by insisting either that there is no truly cosmic sense connected with primitive religious cult, or that what passes for such is in reality simply a feeling for the social group. This is not the place for a lengthy discussion of this question, and I must content myself by pointing out that Durkheim's view stands or falls with the proposition that " Nature as such cannot inspire religious emotion." Dr. Goldenweiser (to whom I owe this formulation of Durkheim's position) points out, in refutation of this view, that " our familiarity with man, modern, ancient, and primitive, leaves no room for doubt that at all times and places man was strongly susceptible to the impressions produced on him by the phenomena of nature, and that such impressions assumed in his consciousness the form of quasi-religious sentiments." [11] We have, in short, no conceivable reason to suppose that the earliest men were *merely* social; that while enormously sensitive to the influences of their fellows and the group they were entirely obtuse to the tremendous forces of nature. Doubtless the interpretation which the individual gave to these forces was determined for him in large part by the attitude of the group; but that the group itself and all its members had an attitude toward a non-human and non-social source of power is hardly to be denied. It is, moreover, becoming increasingly probable that the earliest form of this cosmic sense (if so I may call it)

[11] " Religion and Society. A Critique of Émile Durkheim's Theory of the Origin and Nature of Religion." *Jour. of Phil.*, XIV (March, 1917), p. 116.

was not a belief in definite and man-like " spirits," but rather a feeling for that indefinable, impersonal, all-pervading power, which the Iroquois called *orenda,* the Algonquins *manitou,* the Sioux *wakonda,* the Melanesians *mana,* but which, under whatever name, is conceived as the ultimate source of power, the controller of happiness, the determiner of destiny.[12]

If modern anthropology is right in seeing in this mysterious power the earliest religious object, there is no reason to doubt that individuals as well as social groups, even in very early times, maintained an attitude toward it which we may properly call religious, and that many, though by no means all, of their individual activities were influenced by it.   For great as is the influence of society upon the individual, especially among early men, the evidence of anthropology bears out what one might naturally expect, in showing that there are individual as well as social religious feelings and activities even among primitive races — though of course the individual act is always directly or indirectly influenced by the social *milieu.*   " Within every culture," writes Dr. Goldenweiser, " religious experiences occur which are but weakly institutionalized, while some of these, although likewise provided with a traditional background, remain almost altogether unsupported by similar experiences of other individuals." [13]   The activities (but " weakly institutionalized ") of individual men and women which aimed at getting into touch with this non-human source of power, constituted the first appearance of what, in more developed stages, are known, on the one hand, as private worship, on the other as private magic.   Neither of these subjects will be discussed in this place, for magic is no concern of ours, and private worship particularly in the form of prayer will be the subject of a later chapter.

If one examine the group activities of various primitive peo-

[12] The reader who cares to study this very early concept in detail will find numerous excellent discussions of it in the works of recent anthropologists and psychologists, for example the following: Brinton, " Religions of Primitive Peoples " (New York, Putnam: 1898), pp. 60–64; Marett, " The Threshold of Religion " (London, Methuen: 1909), pp. 1–32; King, "The Development of Religion," Chap. VI; Leuba, "A Psychological Study of Religion," Chap. IV; Hartland, " Ritual and Belief" (New York, Scribners: 1914), pp. 26–66.

[13] Op. cit. p. 118.

ples one finds that they fall into two divisions, which indeed shade into each other but are yet sufficiently distinct. One of these classes of activities takes cognizance only of the forces of human society; the other is not merely social (in this sense) but has some more or less obvious reference to the non-human force — *orenda, mana,* or what you will — which we have been discussing. Plainly enough the public ceremonies of all the more developed races are susceptible of such a division (that is if we substitute "*the Divine*" for "*mana*"); but even among the most primitive peoples known to anthropology this distinction is still fairly clear. Thus the *Intichiuma* ceremonies of the Central Australians (the purpose of which is to secure the increase of the tribal totem) are permeated with ideas of *mana,* while the ceremonies connected with the knocking out of teeth, etc., and a large part of the rites of initiation are purely social and have no reference to anything or any power outside of the human circle.[14] What is true of Australian initiation ceremonies holds even more completely of initiation ceremonies in many other parts of the world. The "puberty institution" and the rites celebrated on the admission of youth into it are found among widely scattered peoples; and though here and there some magical or religious element has been introduced, the central part of the custom is obviously purely social, with no reference to any non-human influence.[15] Several other group activities or ceremonies (such as certain forms of the dance) might be mentioned which, from earliest times, have been quite distinguishable from those social activities possessed of extra-human significance. Not all ceremonies, therefore, "in which the whole group coöperates with keen emotion," can (from our point of view) be called religious. And the truly religious ceremonies thus owe their origin to two quite distinct influences,—(1) the social sense, and (2) the feeling for a power which is neither social nor personal. The external form of the cult may, to be sure, in some cases, be due almost exclusively to the practical activities of the group;

14 See Spencer and Gillen, "The Native Tribes of Central Australia" (London, Macmillan: 1899), Chaps. VI, XII and VII.

15 The whole subject is well presented in Professor Hutton Webster's "Primitive Secret Societies" (New York, Macmillan: 1908). See especially Chaps. II and III.

the inner meaning of the activity, both for the individual and for the group as a whole, will be changed when the performance in question comes to be used as a means of obtaining *mana,* or of influencing in some way its action.

The particular forms of the cult in this, its earliest phase, will of course depend in part upon the social activities from which it arises, in part upon the local ideas of *mana* which will vary from tribe to tribe.   Each new rite, moreover, that is added as religion develops will owe its explanation to some new belief or to some old social custom, while many a myth will grow up to rationalize ancient ceremonies which originated long before the stage of myth was reached.   Thus faith and cult will mutually influence each other.   For each of the strange details of cult referred to on page 256 and others like them, special local explanations must be sought; but the fundamental principles at work in the origin of cult, though variously applied, will be everywhere the same.

At the earliest level of culture there plainly can be, for us, no distinction between religious ceremonies and magic rites; what we have been describing is the matrix out of which both grew.[16]   As the social group advanced to higher levels of intelligence, religious conceptions developed, and the impersonal force was supplanted or supplemented by supernatural spiritual beings who themselves possessed great stores of *mana;* and hand in hand with these developing ideas the old ceremonies slowly changed and took on new meanings.   In these higher stages of religion (whether animistic, polytheistic, or theistic), religious

---

[16] This view is admirably presented and defended by Dr. Hartland, in his illuminating book, " Ritual and Belief," (see esp. pp. 26–89).   Professor Wundt's view differs from this more in terminology than in essence. For him there was a pre-religious stage, which he gives over to magic; but its character does not greatly differ from what I have been describing.   The development of the cult from this earliest phase to religious ceremonial in the full sense of the word was marked, according to Wundt, by three gradually emerging characteristics: (1) " die Gebundenheit an eine engere oder weitere Gemeinschaft " (a characteristic which, in our view, it possessed from the beginning), (2) " der umfassendere, die allgemeinsten von der beginnenden Kultur getragenen Lebensbedurfnisse in sich schliessende Zweck der auf die Gewinnung übermeschlicher. Wesen gerichteten Handlungen," (3) " die Beziehung der Kultushandlungen nach ihren Motiven wie nach ihren Gegenständen auf eine übersinnliche Welt " (" Völkerpsychologie," Vol. II, Part III [i. e. really Vol. V]), pp. 595–602.

cult, though still more or less closely intertwined at times with magical rites, is at last fairly distinguishable from magic; not indeed because it is social and magic individually [17] (for the very opposite is often the case), but because the religious ceremony seeks to gain its end through the assistance of the spirits or gods, while magic aims at its goal through no such indirect channel, but by the immediate control of the mysterious powers of the universe.[18]   In other words, as our definition of religion suggested, the religious attitude is always in some faint degree social, whereas the attitude of magic may be purely mechanical.

So much for the general principles underlying the origin of cult,— a problem which belongs rather to anthropology than to the psychology of religion.   We turn now to an investigation much more germane to the general subject of this book — the question, namely, of the retention and continuation of religious ceremonies and public worship.   Why, we ask, has religious cult, begun in the dark days of man's early ignorance, been continued into our own time, and by what forces of human nature are we to account for the modern man's adherence to it?

The answer to this question must take into account both the causal action of external influences upon the retention of the cult, and the function performed by the cult which makes it desirable and desired.   Prominent among the former must be reckoned the tremendous and unescapable influence of custom and of habit.   From the earliest times the social group has seen to it that the individual should perform the approved ritualistic acts.   The word *custom,* in fact, fails to express the force of the influence which society here brings to bear upon its members.   " Ritual," says Sumner, " is not easy com-

---

[17] This is the theory supported by Hubert and Mauss (" Théorie Génerale de la Magie," L'Année Sociologique 1902–03) ; Durkheim (" Elementary Forms of the Religious Life," Book I, Chap. I) ; Jevons (" Introduction to the Study of Comparative Religion," Lecture III) ; King, (" Development of Religion," Chap. VII).

[18] This view is held by Hartland (op. cit. pp. 85–89) and Leuba (op. cit. Chaps. III and VIII).   McDougal makes the essential distinctive one of psychological attitude: " the religious attitude is always that of submission, the magical attitude that of self-assertion."   (" Social Psychology," p. 306 note.)

pliance with usage; it is strict compliance with detailed and punctilious rule. It admits of no exceptions or deviations." [19] Although the influence of society upon the individual in matters of belief has been very considerable, it has been but slight in comparison with the compelling force it has almost invariably exerted to insure the observance of the rite. The Greek philosophers as a rule might believe what they liked; but the religious observances of their land they carried out like every one else, and, in fact, they seem hardly to have conceived the possibility of refusing to do so.[20] The force of social disapproval stamped upon any offender against the recognized forms of religious behavior in all ancient and many modern societies is as irresistible as the veto which our own society puts upon the indecent custom of the eating of dog flesh.[21] Something distantly like it is experienced when in war time some one conscientious pacifist. alone of all the community, refuses to display the flag.

[19] " Folkways," (Boston, Ginn; 1907), p. 60.

[20] " Aristote ne professa pas un moindre respect que Socrate et que Platon pour la religion traditionelle. Poser la question de savoir s'il faut ou s'il ne faut pas honorer les dieux de la cité lui parait aussi étrange que de demander si la neige est blanche; celui qui ose la soulever mérite la bastonnade tout aussi bien que celui qui discute sur l'amour filial." (Louis, " Doctrines Religieuses des Philosophes Grecs." — Paris, Lethielleux; 1909 — p. 150. See also pp. 154–55, and Arst. Topica VI 105.)

[21] Cf. Boas, " The Mind of Primitive Man," Chap. VIII. " Supposing an individual accustomed to eating dogs should inquire among us for the reason why we do not eat dogs, we could only reply that it is not customary; and he would be justified in saying that dogs are tabooed among us, just as much as we are justified in speaking of taboos among primitive people. If we were hard pressed for reasons, we should probably base our aversion to eating dogs or horses on the seeming impropriety of eating animals that live with us as our friends. On the other hand, we are not accustomed to eat caterpillars, and we should probably decline to eat them from feelings of disgust. Cannibalism is so much abhorred, that we find it difficult to convince ourselves that it belongs to the same class of aversions as those mentioned before. The fundamental concept of the sacredness of human life, and the fact that most animals will not eat others of the same species, set off cannibalism as a custom by itself, considered as one of the most horrible aberrations of human nature. In these three groups of aversions, disgust is probably the first feeling in our minds, by which we react against the suggestion of partaking of these kinds of food. We account for our disgust by a variety of reasons, according to the groups of ideas with which the suggested act is associated in our minds."

But not only does society, especially in its less sophisticated stages, demand conformity to the approved cult; the individual human being, even when withdrawn from social influence, finds the adoption and crystallization of some form of ritual both natural and almost unavoidable. This is due of course to the law of habit. Whatever we do several times we tend to repeat in the same fashion. We dress and undress in the same way day after day; in putting on our coats one of our arms invariably takes precedence, as of sacred right, over the other; in all the minutiæ of our daily life the established paths of the nervous system determine the order of our doings. So it is inevitably with our religious reactions. Given a man with religious beliefs and emotions and let him rebel against ritual as much as he likes, he will throw off the traditional forms only to invent and follow out a new ritual of his own. If the reader has ever regularly said "Grace" at meals, or has observed the procedure of those who do, he knows how quickly the "blessing," even in the most ultra-Protestant families, becomes a rite; how almost inevitable it is that the most obstinate effort at spontaneous and varied expression yields at last to the adoption of some approved and habitual form of words. The same phenomenon is noticeable in our most Protestant and anti-ritualistic churches. Stanton Coit has pointed out that even the religious service of the Friends, with their long silences, is a "most dramatic and eloquent ceremonial";[22] and Dr. Henke writes: "The churches that started out with a lively protest against the dead ritual of the liturgical churches have manifested a constant tendency to adopt definite forms of worship. We may with propriety speak of the ritual of non-liturgical churches. The members of the worshiping group think it strange when the regular order of service is not adhered to. They expect the singing of hymns, the prayer, the anthem by the choir, the announcements, the sermon, and whatsoever else there may be, to follow the habitual order and adhere to customary usuages. Strange though it may appear, revivalism itself has been ritualized. In camp-meetings and revival meetings the methods and arrangement of services are the same year after year, and the group consciousness that is developed at these

[22] "National Idealism," p. 317.

gatherings is no less in evidence than in primitive man's great ceremonial occasions." [23]

Thus it may come about that a given form of ritual is retained with little thought either of pleasing God or of affecting the audience, not merely as a result of habit but from the desire that things shall be done decently and in order, combined with the notion (due of course to habit) that the traditional way is the only orderly and decent way. Not only in religion but in various other activities many people feel a kind of duty toward form in the abstract. The New England house-wife considers it a moral obligation to keep all her rooms dustless, even though no one ever sees them; it is a duty she owes to the *house*. Many a teacher has a feeling that each day the lesson must be properly recited,— the approved form of words audibly pronounced in the class-room — no matter by whom and quite regardless of its effect on any one in particular. The reader could doubtless add many similar instances, and it is plain that in each case we should have an incipient but very real ritual, preserved for its own sake.

The use of ritual is natural to man not only because it is forced upon him by society and because his own nervous system tends to act in crystallized forms, but also because it appeals to two of his primitive instincts. One of these is the instinct of gregariousness. Man is a social animal; he cannot keep away from his fellows; and to act in unison and coöperation with them is one of his fundamental desires. Especially does he feel impelled to perform in company with them actions which are related to his strongest sentiments. Hence the native satisfaction in group expressions and patriotism and religion. The other instinct to which I referred as helping to explain the hold of ritual upon human nature is the impulse for self-expression (combined with the law of ideo-motor action). Whatever man believes and whatever he feels is bound to work itself out through his nerves and muscles in some form of activity; and for most men the form of action which is to express their emotion will be something of which others may take note: it will be some kind of *celebration*. Not only do we *have* to express ourselves somehow; nearly all of us like to express at least

[23] Op. cit. p. 87.

our more fervent emotions and beliefs in obtrusive forms. " I love anything ostentatious," exclaims one of the New Poets, with the naïve truthfulness that has made them the *enfants terribles* of our over-sophisticated modern life. For nearly all of us find times when our inner feelings demand expression by something a bit primitive and sensuous. The delicate tints will not do for our flags; and in national celebrations we want brass bands, drums, and fire crackers. Our religious emotions seldom express themselves so blatantly; but the strictest Puritan likes to hear the parson thump the desk, and most of us are fond of church bells and organ music, and have at least a sneaking interest in the smell of incense. The absence of a court and of a powerful aristocracy has, in Professor Stratton's opinion, been one of the causes for the simpler and more colorless ritual of Protestant and democratic America. " But," he adds, " after all, some violence has evidently been done to human nature that must be avenged. For the love of noble ceremony, cheated at its rightful place, appears in the tawdry ritualism of ' fraternal ' bodies, which in America has had such an unparalleled popularity. Here the staunch republican, renouncing the crown and pageantry of kings, can again rejoice in dazzling regalia and stilted phrase. The ceremonial side of these organizations shows an almost pathetic attempt to appease the natural craving for action unhindered, orderly, and gracious — a craving which in other countries finds its satisfaction in the scenes that go with military pomp, with royalty, and the service of great cathedrals." [24]

In the early part of this chapter I tried to show that the external cult in its origin was not dependent upon religious belief of any explicit sort. While this is probably true it is necessary to add that the particular forms of every cult and the continuation of cult in general are largely dependent upon explicit religious beliefs. Ritual and belief have influenced each other mutually for ages; and in all the more developed religions the kind of ritual which one finds is largely determined by the kind of God believed in. As religion becomes more self-conscious and more ideational, the attempt to influence the deity or to please him becomes more explicit. This is so obvious

24 " The Psychology of the Religious Life," p. 150.

that it needs no argument nor illustration — although it is a fact astonishingly unrecognized by many a contemporary anthropologist and psychologist. You cannot fully explain the fact that people worship God without referring to the fact that people believe in God.

So much for the more or less external causes which originated the cult, and have tended to keep it going. They have always had, and they still retain, a considerable strength. If they had been unsupported by other and internal influences, however, it is doubtful whether religious cult would have survived the infancy of man. What these inner forces are which have so strongly reinforced the practice of the cult we shall see in the following chapter.

CHAPTER XIII

HOW THE CULT PERFORMS ITS FUNCTIONS

THE retention of worship both by the individual and still more by society is to be accounted for (as I have more than once insisted) not only through the influence of relatively external causes, such as those considered in the last chapter, but also by the function which worship itself performs. People continue to practice the cult not only because society insists and because they believe that their God is pleased by it, but also because they find it pleasant or profitable or both, in its immediate effects upon themselves. This useful function of the cult may be more or less explicitly conscious but in some form or other it is to be found in most stages of development, high or low. As we have already seen in another connection, it brings a sense of social solidarity which appeals to the gregarious instinct, and at the same time gives pleasant vent to the instinctive impulse for self-expression. But its chief function is to reinforce religion and thus to realize and conserve the values which religion mediates. The nature and relative importance of these values is a large subject, and for our present purposes we need only note that they consist chiefly in the moral control of life and in the production of a kind of peace, joy, and hope for which no other surety can be found. The cult aids in doing these things for the individual and for society by keeping religious beliefs lively and vivid, by stimulating religious emotions, and in general by fastening the attention upon religion in such fashion as to make it real and vital for the worshiper.[1]

[1] A fact noted by Montesquieu in his " De l'Esprit des Lois." — " Une religion chargée de beaucoup de pratique attache plus à elle qu'une autre qui l'est moins; on tient beaucoup aux choses dont on est continuellement occupé." (Quoted by Arnold in " The Preaching of Islam " — New York, Scribners: 1913 — p. 417.) The very great influence of both Hinduism and Catholicism upon their worshipers, due largely to the great detail of their ceremonial, bears out this observation.

The ways in which the cult performs its function of enlivening religious faith and feeling are various.   One of the simplest
and most direct of these consists in bringing to religion the great
reinforcement of reality-feeling which comes from sensuous presentation.   We saw in chapter X how large a part the senses
play in belief; how, in fact, sensation is the primitive source
and the ultimate test of the real.   Now one of the things that
the cult does, in both very primitive and very advanced stages,
is to present to the worshiper's senses some object intimately
connected with his faith, in such fashion that the object of his
faith shall have almost the immediacy and concreteness and
tangibility of material things.   The earliest example of this
reinforcement of belief by sense perception is, of course, to be
found in the direct cult of natural objects — trees, animals,
streams, the heavenly bodies, " stocks and stones," [2] and other
men.[3]   A development and elaboration of this nature worship
is seen in fetichism.   The psychological effect of the fetich
upon the faith of the " heathen " is admirably shown in the
following sentences from Nassau, a missionary who spent many
years in West Africa: " The heathen armed with his fetich
feels strong.   He believes in it; has faith that it will help him.
He can see it and feel it.   He goes on his errand inspired with
confidence of success. . . . The Christian convert is weak in
his faith.   He would like something tangible.   He is not sure
that he will succeed in his errand.   He goes at it somewhat
half-hearted and probably fails. . . . The weak ask the missionary whether they may not be allowed to carry a fetich only
for show." [4]   Fetichism is a very wide-spread form of cult, and
the psychological function which it serves in lending reality feeling to religious ideas, and strength to religious emotion, is at
the bottom of many other religious practices which go by other
names.   The *churinga* of the Australian Arunta [5] — pieces of

[2] See my " Psychology of Religious Belief," pp. 47–50; also Frazer,
" Folk-Lore in the Old Testament " (London, Macmillan: 1919), Vol. II,
Part II, Chap. IV.

[3] The importance of the senses in man-worship in antiquity is notable.
Cf., for example, Wiedemann's " Religion of the Ancient Egyptians " (London, Grevel: 1897), pp. 174–77.   Frazer's " Golden Bough " (2nd Ed. London, Macmillan; 1911) Vol. I, Chap. VII.

[4] " Fetichism in West Africa," (London, Duckworth; 1904), pp. 112–113.

[5] Spencer and Gillen, op. cit. Chap. V.

wood or stone inscribed with the design of the totem, and used in most of their ceremonies — perform the same function as the fetich of West Africa. In the native temples of Samoa, according to Turner, there was " generally something for the eye to rest upon with superstitious veneration." This was not a fetich, nor was it regarded as the habitation of a God, but it was placed in the sacred shrine because a need was felt for some sensuous object in which one's faith in the unseen might find the needed support.[6] An example of this utilization of the senses among a much more intelligent people is to be found in the " Shintai " of Japan — objects such as a mirror or a sword which have become associated with the deity and whose use arose, according to Aston, out of " a greater necessity for some visible token of the presence of God." [7] In most of these cases the end actually subserved is not explicitly recognized as an aim by the worshiper; yet it is probably the function which it plays that, more than anything else, keeps the custom a'going from generation to generation.

The purpose of producing a subjective effect on the mind of the worshiper rises to a more self-conscious level in the case of the Hindu officer " of great shrewdness and very fair education " with whom Sir Alfred Lyall was personally acquainted, and who " devoted several hours daily to the elaborate worship of five round pebbles, which he had appointed to be his symbol of Omnipotence. Although his general belief was in one all-embracing Divinity, he must have something symbolic to handle and address." [8]

But the form of cult which most strikingly utilizes the support of the senses is idolatry. The need of an idol is often taken as a matter of course. The Chinese women of Sze Chuan, quoted by Mrs. Bird Bishop, were " quite unable to understand how people could pray ' unless they had a god in the room.' " [9] No one who has, with any degree of intelligent sympathy, watched the practice of idolatry in its more earnest form, as for example in India, can have failed to recognize the

[6] Turner, " Samoa " (London, Macmillan: 1884).

[7] " Shinto, the Way of the Gods " (London, Longmans: 1905), pp. 70–71.

[8] " Asiatic Studies " (2nd Ed., London, Murray: 1884), p. 10.

[9] " The Yangtze Valley and Beyond " (London, Murray: 1900). Vol. I, p. 257.

real help which it seems to bring to many of those who make use of it.   The Hindu widow who goes to the shrine of Mahadev with her little offering of yellow marigolds and Ganges water, and who, after placing the flowers before the *lingam* of the "Great God" and pouring the sacred water reverently upon it, pauses for a moment in silent prayer, goes out of the temple and back to her sad home and the weary monotony of her life with renewed hope and comfort.   If there were no image present, if the temple were empty like a Protestant Church, would she find the same degree of comfort there?   With different upbringing and education she might.   With a different religion and a wider outlook she might.   But then she would not be the woman of our illustration.   Repugnant as idolatry seems to us, there can be no doubt that as a fact this Hindu widow, and many like her, finds a reinforcement for her faith in the sensuous presence of a physical object,— a reinforcement of faith which she at any rate, being what she is, could not find without it.   Doubtless the "Great God," Mahadev, is present everywhere; but what is that abstract doctrine compared to the sense of the closeness of the deity and to the realization of his presence which come to the poor soul when she sees the sacred symbol of the mystery of life directly before her, and when she pours her offering and lays her flowers upon this concrete object in which the Great God has consented, for the moment and for her sake, to take up his miraculous abode?

Presumably the majority of those who in the lower religions make use of images have no thought of the subjective effect of the image upon their own faith and feeling; while on the other hand, thousands of relatively intelligent men continue the practice with little belief in the supernatural quality of the image before them, chiefly because they find their religious sense stimulated by the presence of a physical object which they have from infancy been trained to associate with the Divine.[10]   One very unintelligent Hindu whom I met in India showed me his idols and told me they were not images of his gods but the very

[10] "An image may be, even to two votaries kneeling side by side before it, two utterly different things; to the one it may be only a symbol, a portrait, a memento, while to the other it is an intelligent and active being, by virtue of a life or spirit dwelling in it and acting through it."   (Tylor, "Primitive Culture," Vol. II, p. 154.)

gods themselves. Another, rather higher in the intellectual scale, said to me, when I asked him about the image of Shiva which he was worshiping, " The image is not Shiva; Shiva is in heaven. But I want to worship Shiva, so I make a picture or image as like Him in appearance as I can, and then I pray to Shiva in front of it because it helps me to pray." By a third Hindu — this one a learned Bengalee Brahmin who gave me a long dissertation on the religion of his country — the subjective aspect of the cult and its retention explicitly for the sake of its psychological effects, was clearly recognized and emphasized. " The idol," he said, " is useful in aiding visualization and concentration. It is a sensuous symbol, just as the word G-O-D is. Both are symbols, one tangible and visible, the other audible; and both are helpful to our finite minds in standing for the Infinite. The man who worships before an idol in effect prays: ' O God, come and dwell in this image before me for the moment that I may worship thee here concretely!' " [11]

The need felt by less cultivated minds for something objective, visible, tangible, about which to crystallize their religious belief and feeling, is seen in the popular development of even those most subjective religions, Buddhism and Jainism. For some time, to be sure, after the death of the Founder, Buddhism seems to have continued its almost cultless form of religion (though some form of ceremonial there was from the beginning); but archæological research shows that somewhere between the first and fifth centuries A. D. the use of images of the Buddha and the worship of them was introduced and became widely popular.[12] So prominent a place do they hold in the popular religion of Buddhists in all parts of the

[11] It is, perhaps, of some significance in this connection that the earliest use of images in India seems to have been in the worship of the one Vedic deity who was invisible — namely Indra. (Cf. Rig Veda, IV, 24, 10, and VIII 1, 5.) It certainly is significant that when the Aryans admitted into their religious community the low-born Shudras, they adopted the latters' use of images; and that this new form of cult, in virtue of the greater satisfaction it gave to the psychical needs of the worshipers, soon supplanted the ancient and venerated Vedic cult — a worship of intangible and distant and often abstract deities.

[12] See Ferguson's " History of Indian and Eastern Architecture " (London, Murray: 1876), p. 125.

world to-day, that it is impossible to think of modern Buddhism without them. A parallel development is to be traced in the development of Jainism. A religion whose professed aim has always been of an almost purely subjective sort has covered large sections of India with elaborately carved temples, and has everywhere filled its temples with images of its twenty-four mythical [13] Tirthankaras,— for the very good reason that through centuries of experience its devotees have found their religious faith and feeling strengthened by the presence of these visible and tangible symbols.

Much more may thus be said in defense of the practice of " idolatry " than most of us have been brought up to suppose. It is based upon a perfectly sound psychological principle, and it appeals to a widely felt human need; and it is this fact that has given it so wide-spread and enthusiastic adoption through so many centuries.[14] Nor is the psychological principle in question limited to fetichism and idolatry. It explains a large part of the appeal to the senses of any and every sort, so common in the higher as in the lower religions. The miracle play in the Middle Ages as well as the temple processions of Egypt and India, the use of images of the Saints in Greek and Roman Catholicism, the cult of relics in Christianity and Buddhism, depend for much of their effectiveness upon the vivifying reinforcement which religious belief and feeling receive from contact with the visible and tangible. And no part of Christian worship owes more of its psychological effect to its connection with the physical than does its crowning sacrament, the Eucharist. This is of course especially true of the Catholic form of the Eucharist, combined as it is with the belief in transubstantiation.[15] The good Romanist, or the good

[13] This is hardly exact, as one of the twenty-four (and possibly a second) was an historical person.

[14] For further discussion of the merits and demerits of idolatry, especially in India, see Farquhar, " The Crown of Hinduism " (*Oxford University Press:* 1913), Chap. VIII; Howells, " The Soul of India " (London, Clark and Co.: 1913). pp. 416–21; Mrs. Besant, " In Defence of Hinduism," (Benares; T. P. S.) pp. 1–5; and my " India and Its Faiths," pp. 28–33. I would not leave the impression that I am an advocate of idolatry. Doubtless it has certain decided psychological advantages; but with equal certainty it has certain grave dangers. It makes religion easy — and sometimes cheap.

[15] The history of the development of the belief in transubstantiation in

high-churchman who believes he has partaken of the very body of God or of something spiritually equivalent thereto, has the same sort of advantage over the Protestant that the African fetich worshiper has over the converted African, as described by Nassau.[16] But even the modified form which the Eucharist assumes in the Protestant Church is not wholly devoid of the unique power which sensuous objects exert upon faith. If I am not mistaken, an analysis of the state of mind of the average Protestant who partakes of the Communion would show that its value to him lies largely in the increased vividness of faith which it produces, by connecting the concept of God and Christ with elements which are visible and tangible and which may be tasted and smelled.

What has been said of the senses applies only in less degree to the imagination; and the cult or ritual in every historical religion adds to the strength of the worshiper's faith by presenting him with vivid mental images which lend their reality-feeling to the abstract and unreal dogmas of theology.[17] More

the early church is a rather striking illustration of the need felt for a visible and tangible embodiment of faith. " Die Christologie," says Harnack, in summing up the forces that tended to produce the new dogma, " forderte ein immer gegenwärtiges christologisches Mysterium, das empfunden und genossen werden kann " (" Dogmengeschichte." Freiburg, Mohr: 1898) — p. 286). Already by the close of the Sixth Century it was definitely settled that the body of Christ was " as truly present on the altar of the church as it once was on the altar of the cross " (Schaff, " History of the Christian Church.— New York, Scribner: 1867 — Vol. III, p. 508).— Hand in hand with this doctrine came the custom of reserving the sacred elements within the Church at all times, that the divine presence might ever be assured and that believers might be able to strengthen their faith by the evidence of their senses. The comfort and assurance that this visible presence brings to the faithful is a fact of common recognition among all deeply religious Catholics and high churchmen. " Thus the sons of faith might go to be near Him and adore Him, for his ' delight is with the sons of men '; and His loving condescension has made Him the ' prisoner of the tabernacle,' and leads Him to give Himself to be ' exposed ' for worship, and in the service of the Benediction to bless His people with a blessing like that of His uplifted hand, behind the veil, so to speak, of the enshrining wafer." (Gore, " The Body of Christ "— New York, Scribner: 1901 — p. 137).— The desire of every Catholic Church to possess and keep under its altar the relic of some saint has much the same psychological explanation as that of the sacrament just discussed. An Italian priest, in explaining the custom to me, remarked: " *Il popolo deve avere una cosa sensibile.*"

16 See p. 272 of this book

17 This is plainly seen in the efforts of the Christian cult to bring home

will be said of this means by which the cult fulfills its functions when we come to deal with symbolism.

The appeal made by the forms of public worship to the æsthetic sense is too obvious to need much emphasis in this place, but too important to be left wholly unmentioned. The ritual and the surroundings of the cult are made beautiful in all stages of human society (and according to the taste of each stage), not only of direct purpose but also through the spontaneous impulse for self-expression. Both the religious and the æsthetic tendencies of man have something in common with the play impulse — namely, a certain freedom from the restraints of the actual, a joyful liberty to dwell in the realm of the imagination, and a consequent reaction which expresses itself in forms that delight the sense and which are ends in themselves.[18] The feelings, beliefs, and impulses which we call religious, like all other mental contents, have their motor tendencies and inevitably work themselves out into action; and the action in which they result is just the cult. It is, therefore, natural that the cult should have an intrinsically æsthetic element of its own. " One exposes oneself to grave misunder-

to the worshiper the image of the human Christ, in concrete imaginable form. The importance of this was felt as early as the time of the writing of the Fourth Gospel. The Logos of Philosophy and of the Greek philosophers, though accepted in one sense by the Evangelist, was felt to be too abstract to be humanly helpful, hence the writer proclaims, " The Logos became *flesh* and dwelt among us, and we *beheld* his glory." And the writer of the Epistle of John says, " That which we have heard, that which we have seen with our eyes, that which we beheld and our hands handled concerning the Logos, . . . that declare we unto you."

[18] The question is occasionally raised whether religious emotion and æsthetic emotion be not identical. From the point of view assumed in this book the answer must, pretty plainly, be that they are not identical, but that they have much in common. There is, of course, no specifically religious emotion, but all emotions are religious which include a consciousness of one's relation to the Determiner of Destiny. In all theistic religions and in most of the higher polytheistic religions the thought of the deity is suffused with or at least associated with the more or less dim notion of the Beautiful. Hence religious emotion is likely to contain, explicitly or implicitly, a reference to some kind of beauty — though this is by no means essential or universal. And, on the other hand, certain beautiful objects which excite the æsthetic emotion are likely to rouse religious emotion as well, particularly if these objects are associated in the individual's experience and training with religious ideas, or if in themselves they be such as to suggest the Determiner of Destiny, through their sublimity or some other *cosmic* quality.

standings," says Durkheim, " if, in explaining rites, he believes
that each gesture has a precise object and a definite reason
for its existence.   There are some which serve nothing; they
merely answer the need felt by worshipers for action, motion,
gesticulation.   They are to be seen jumping, whirling, dancing, crying and singing,— though it may not always be possible to give a meaning to all these actions.   Therefore religion
would not be itself if it did not give some place to the free
combinations of thought and activity, to play, to art, to all that
recreates the spirit that has been fatigued by too great slavish-
ness of daily work; the very same causes which called it into
existence make this a necessity.   Art is not merely an external ornament with which the cult has adorned itself in order
to dissimulate certain of its features which may be too austere
and too rude; but rather in itself, the cult is something
æsthetic." [19]

But though æsthetic in itself quite spontaneously, very early
in its history the cult is also deliberately adorned by added
efforts of self-conscious art; and this purposeful beautifying of
the forms of public worship continues to characterize it, except in unusual cases, throughout its history.   The purpose for
which this is done is twofold — sometimes it is in order to
glorify the deity in whose honor the cult is performed; sometimes it is for the sake of the psychological effect that beauty
is calculated to make upon the participant.   The objective aim
of pleasing and glorifying the Lord is of course most often seen
in the more primitive and less sophisticated stages of culture,
and the subjective aim of affecting the worshipers comes out
most plainly among more intelligent and self-conscious peoples;
yet both motives are to be found, with varying emphasis, in
nearly all communal worship except the most primitive and
the most sophisticated.   The objective moment is the dominant
one in most ancient cults, for example in the worship of the
Hebrews as portrayed in the Old Testament.   The Temple at
Jerusalem was adorned chiefly in order that Yahve might be

[19] Op. cit. pp. 381–82.   Professor Yrjö Hirn has worked out in detail
the contributions made by architecture, sculpture, painting, decorative art,
music, and especially poetry and the drama to the effectiveness of the
Roman Catholic ritual.— " The Sacred Shrine " (London, Macmillan:
1912).   Chaps. V–IX.

glorified, and its builders made it as gorgeous as their some-what barbaric taste could devise.   So, looking back at an earlier time, their historian draws a realistic picture of the contempor-aries of Moses contributing for the construction of the Ark in which Yahveh was to dwell " gold and silver and brass and blue and purple and scarlet, and fine linen, and goats' hair and rams' skins dyed red and porpoise skin and acacia wood, onyx stones and stones to be set." [20]   Our modern Christian churches are also made glorious with architectural design, sculptural adornment, the light of many-colored glass, and the fragrance of flowers; but the aim is quite consciously to produce a cer-tain desired effect upon the minds of the worshipers.   Dr. Müller-Freienfels has pointed out that this subjective influence wrought by art is brought about in two ways;— namely by increasing the strength of the emotional life in general, and also by changing its quality and redirecting it into new channels. " Religious exaltation requires a certain intensity of the en-tire emotional life, otherwise the religious sense remains dry and weak.   But in art there is found an excellent means for rousing and enlivening all the feelings, without putting to sleep the higher sentiments as alcohol and other stimulants do." Especially does music possess this stimulating effect upon the emotions.   " Experimental psychology shows us that the respir-ation and circulation are especially influenced by rhythm, all sorts of associative influences are added to this, and the in-fluence of music as a whole acts as a continual excitant, making all the feelings stronger and deeper.   If now in such an emo-tional condition, the thought is directed toward the Divine, whether by the words of the song or the following address of the preacher, it finds the soil already prepared and recep-tive.   In its power of intensifying the feelings lies the great significance of music for religion." [21]   The other arts, accord-ing to Dr. Müller-Freienfels, have also some influence of this general nature upon the emotional life; but their chief value in bringing about the desired religious state of mind is to be found in their ability to transform the quality of emotion and

[20] Exodus XXV, 3–7.

[21] " Die psychologische Wirkung der Kunst auf das religiöse Gefühlsle-ben."   (Ztsft. f. Relspsy, IV, 369–75.— Feb., 1911.)

lead it into new channels. "For in art is to be found the most potent means of transferring to others the feelings of men of fine and deeper natures." Music has this power to a great extent, but it is in poetry that is to be found the most efficient source of this refining influence. Its power is seen especially in its tendency to enlarge the religious conceptions and to raise the mind from the narrow and concrete to the more-inclusive and universal.[22]

But while the ritual by its beauty may often create for the observer the religious atmosphere, it produces its greatest effect when the observer becomes a participant as well. For then a new and powerful psychological mechanism is set in motion for the production of the religious sentiment. The law of "association" holds not only of "ideas" but of various mental states of a more general and less sharply defined nature, including such things as feelings, will attitudes, emotions, and moods. And just as one can call up the last half of a verse of poetry better by beginning with the first half and getting a start, so to speak, than by trying to recall it without preliminary or associate, so one can induce a mood more easily by summoning first some fairly common associate in the form of an act. For acts are directly under voluntary control, while moods can be induced or driven off only by indirect methods. It must be remembered, moreover, that the relation between acts and emotions is not one merely of association; but that (if there be any truth at all in the James-Lange theory) the kinæsthetic sensations and the other psychical correlates of activity constitute an integral part of emotion. Now with most religious persons certain bodily acts and attitudes have, since earliest childhood, been associated with religion, and the feeling of them has become a part of that psychic complex which one knows as religious emotion. I refer to such things as the bowed head, the folded

[22] "Während die bildende Kunst im allgemeinen die Gefühle durch Uebertragung ins Anschauliche konkreter und intensiver macht, lösen Musik und Pœsie die Gefühle eher von Irdischen los und heben sie in abstraktere geistigere Gebiete empor. Es ist darum verständlich, wenn in den romanischen und katolishen Ländern stärkere Beziehungen zu den bildenden Kunst sind, während die gewaltigsten und tiefsten religiösen Chorwerke und Dichtungen auf germanischen und protestantischen Boden erblüht sind." Op. cit. p. 375.

hands, the kneeling posture, the constraint of the motionless and silent attitude, the repetition of familiar and sacred words, the singing in unison with others of the hymns of the faith. The repetition of these bodily acts not only induces by association the religious sentiment with which they have been connected since childhood; the feeling of these acts *is* a considerable part of the religious emotion.

One of the most important ways in which public worship strengthens the faith of the individual is by bringing powerfully into his mind the sense of social confirmation. It is hard to believe anything which everyone else doubts, hard to cherish a feeling which everyone else ridicules, and hard to resist a feeling or a belief which everyone else cherishes. To a considerable extent the ritual even if repeated alone would have this power of forcibly suggesting faith and feeling; for it summons into the marginal region of the worshiper's consciousness the sense of a long line of past and venerated generations, of whose faith the ritual is a kind of crystallization. So great is the force of confirmation from the authority of the past, that it is unlikely any ritual can ever attain its full effect until it has reached a considerable age.[23]   And when the voice of the

[23] Many of the leaders of the Church of England are so well aware of this psychological fact that they oppose every slight change even in the wording of their ritual. In the opinion of the Rev. Percy Dearmer, (who here expresses the views of a large number of his colleagues) " The English Church does not now press doctrinal conformity to her own distinctive formulæ beyond the point of a general acceptance or ' assent '; in the second place, she does require an undertaking as to ritual that admits of no compromise. Freedom to think, freedom to discuss, freedom to develop, are necessary to the very existence of life and truth in a Church; but for the priest to omit or to alter the communion services of that Church is fatal to Christian fellowship, and robs the people of their rights." (Quoted from the " Parson's Handbook " by Stanton Coit, in " National Idealism," p. 113.) Such a hard and fast rule will seem to most of us a rather absurdly rigid application of a sound psychological principle; and, what is more important, it leaves out of account the fact that in the course of centuries an act of ritual may cease to express anything really vital in the belief of the worshipers, and that when this comes about it loses something even of its emotional hold over them and nearly all of its justification. On the other hand it would probably be flying in the face of psychology to go to the other extreme, suggested by Mr. Coit, and make a new ritual that should be completely up-to-date. The wise course would seem to be a gradual and continuous modification of the ritual, so that it may still retain most of the strength that comes from antiquity, without

past as heard in the ritual becomes the voice of our living fellows too, when one hears other worshipers on all sides repeating in tones of conviction the doctrines which one has always thought one believed, the force of social confirmation becomes, at least for the moment, too great to be resisted, and faith marches triumphant over doubt.[24] The recitation in unison of the Creed is thus recognized by a large portion of the churches of Christendom as an important part of the service, and its purpose is obviously and consciously subjective. The recitation in unison of the Apostles' Creed by all the congregation, as found in so many of the Protestant churches, is as much an implement of worship and a direct stimulus to faith as is the use of images in many a less sophisticated religious community. And in the Catholic Church the psychological effect of similar methods is surely not less. The triumphant sweep of the Nicene Creed when effectively sung —

> " Credo in unum Deum,
> Patrem omnipotentem,
> Factorem coeli et terrae "—

with the audience falling upon their faces as one man at the words,

> " Et homo factus est "—

this is enough to make, for the moment, a good Catholic of the most tough-skinned heretic and doubter who is willing to give

demanding too much re-interpretation on the part of the modern-minded worshiper. One must also remember that there are various kinds of people in the world, and that what holds for one sort may be untrue of some other. For the great majority ritual seems to need the reinforcement of tradition; yet in many of our large cities will be found little groups of radical thinkers who are able to find satisfaction in a ritual invented or put together by themselves.

[24] The enormous influence of cult upon belief is strikingly illustrated in the death of Roman Paganism. The old religion had indeed been in a state of decrepitude for centuries, but long after the wide spread of Christianity it still clung to life with surprising tenacity and numbered hundreds of thousands among its devotees. But when the Emperor Theodosius forcibly closed the temples and forbade the cult, the old religion very quickly disappeared in nearly every part of the empire. It was evidently the practice of the cult that kept the old religion alive for the last century or more of its existence, by placing it constantly before the attention and maintaining the habit of belief. An instructive account of the matter will be found in Chapter 28 of Gibbon's " Decline and Fall."

rein to his imagination and feelings; while the true believer goes away with reinforcement to his faith sufficient to last at any rate till the next high mass.

One very interesting thing about the religious utility of the public recitation of the creed is the peculiar fact that it loses but little of its psychological power for the strengthening of faith and feeling by being recited in an unknown tongue or even by containing certain details which the audience does not believe. Every student of the religions of the East must have been struck with the enormous importance there assigned to the letter of the sacred texts, an importance that increases rather than decreases as the language of the text is forgotten and its meaning nearly lost. Nor is this phenomenon confined to the various non-Christian religions. No doubt a large number of Roman Catholics, even among the ignorant, have a fair understanding (thanks to the instruction given by the Church) of the Latin prayers which they recite; but not the most ardent Romanist would deny that to many of his fellow religionists the prayers which they piously repeat convey no meaning and are merely a collection of sounds which one has revered since childhood. It is the syllables themselves that are hallowed and the pious reciter will often object strenuously to any change in them, regarding all attempts at revision or rationalization as a kind of shocking heresy. Trevelyan, describing the religious condition of England under James I, recounts that " in 1608 a clergyman, who was more alive to his duties than most of his fellow-laborers, complained that his flock ' superstitiously refuse to pray in their own language with understanding,' and contented themselves with such wreckage of the old religion as the following:

Creezum zuum patrum onitentem creatorum ejus amicum, Dominum nostrum qui sum sops, virgini Mariæ, crixus fixus, Ponchi Pilati audubitiers, morti by Sunday, father a furnes, scerest ut judicarum, finis a mortibus." [25]

Doubtless the retention and repetition of meaningless formulæ in the public worship is in part to be set down as a case of superstition and to be classed either as magic or at best a kind of irrational offering to God,— the syllables being consid-

---

[25] " England Under the Stuarts " (New York, Putnam: 1904), p. 63.

ered somehow powerful in themselves, or somehow pleasing to the Deity. But in nearly all such repetition there is also a subjective element, a recognition that the creed or prayer or formula thus recited, even though not understood, brings with it a certain religious atmosphere, a sense of reverence or dependence, or a renewed and strengthened faith. This is true both of the ignorant man who recites the creed in an unknown tongue, and of the intelligent man who knows perfectly well what the creed means but cannot assent to some of its details. Of course the ignorant worshiper must know something about the general meaning of the creed which he hears or recites, and the intelligent worshiper must be able to accept (and with some enthusiasm) the general position for which the creed stands, and the details with which he disagrees must not rouse in him a feeling of hostility. But no more exact understanding or acceptance is needed for the creed to produce very considerable effects in reviving faith and rousing religious feeling. The reason for this is to be found in the fact that it is the " emotion of belief " rather than intellectual assent which the recitation of the creed as an instrument of public worship seeks to induce. It aims to put the worshiper into a certain mental attitude, rather than to dominate that very small portion of his mind known as the cold intellect. Viewed in this light the creed is not so much a scientific statement as a *symbol*.

Symbolism covers a wide field. All forms of communication belong here, including such things as flags, uniforms, signs, gestures, written language, spoken language. But religious symbolism is not of the ordinary sort. It is more than a conventional means of communicating ideas. Before an object or an action can become a religious symbol it must have become so intimately associated with the religious object as to be itself permeated in the mind of the worshiper with the sacred feeling, the faith, the volitional attitude which *is* his religion. One may know perfectly well how to translate a given symbol into words, but that knowledge alone is far from enough to make the symbol in question a religious one. Your learned Hindu may know all you can ever tell him about the meaning of the cross; but it is no more a religious symbol to him than Shiva's lingam is to the Christian orientalist. Before an object or act can become a religious symbol to a man it must have entered into the emotional texture of his religious life. As a fact, therefore, nearly all the religious symbolism that ever becomes really potent in an individual's experience comes into his life in childhood. It is seldom after those formative years that the close association between object and emotion can be wrought which is essential to religious symbolism. It requires moreover, as a rule, the whole force of the child's social surroundings — the suggestive influence of parents, teachers, older playmates, and of the people in general in whose actions he is interested — to suffuse the material object or the spoken word or the external act with the religious feeling that shall make it truly and deeply symbolic. Hence it follows that it is quite impossible for the social group to make for itself a new religious symbol except by long years of gradual habitu- ation, or through the force of some emotional crisis. The cross might very well have become a truly religious symbol to the first generation of Christians, because of the terrible yet glori- ous event on Calvary. To an Indian villager converted by "Mass methods" it may be an excellent new kind of magic implement; but it can hardly take the place in his emotional and religious life previously held by the lingam of Maha Dev. And, it should be noted, for the Christian missionary or tourist or student to understand the real inner and emotional meaning of the lingam in the religious life of the devout Hindu is just as impossible as it is for the latter to understand in any but a coldly intellectual fashion what the cross means to us.[26]

To the Jews the cross of Christ was a stumbling block, to the Greeks it was foolishness; but to the man born and brought up in a Christian home it is often "the power of God and the wisdom of God." Under the influence which centuries of past faith and devotion can bring to bear upon the sensitive soul of the growing child, a religious symbol can gain a power over the mind which can quite defy the forces of reason and of doubt. It brings religion home to "that great multitude of sinful men who cannot apprehend spiritual truths except as em- bodied in some visible form," [27] and to the spiritual and intel-

[26] Cf. "India and Its Faiths," pp. 12-14.
[27] Tyrrell, "External Religion" (London, Longmans: 1906), p. 35.

ligent believer it may be the very concentration of thoughts and feelings whose depth and variety would tax all the resources of language to express. " The Crucifix," says George Tyrrell, " is the collective sin of the world made visible." [28]

The earliest material symbols seem to have originated from objects which were not symbolic but were regarded as sacred in their own right as the immediate embodiment of the mysterious or divine; and in like manner the first symbolic acts probably developed out of ceremonial activities which were thought to be of direct efficacy either by getting control of *mana* or by working upon the will of the deity. As the god retires from the image, and the concept of him becomes more abstract and more inclusive, the statue which has ceased to be his peculiar dwelling-place ceases also to be his likeness, and becomes merely his symbol. Even this form of representation in time becomes, for many a thoughtful worshiper, unacceptable, and God is conceived as indescribable and in no wise to be even symboled forth by any material thing.[29] The final step in this direction, as we saw in the chapter on Belief in God, consists in the making of the abstract concept itself only a symbol;— or the concept may be almost given up and only the *feeling* retained. " It comes about," writes Wundt, " that exactly where religious representations are vague and uncertain, or where they are felt to be merely inadequate symbols which at last resign all attempt at symbolism, there the religious feelings can be of special strength. In truth we come here upon the striking phenomenon that the feeling itself becomes a symbol — i. e. it is the only remaining sign in consciousness which represents a realm of religious thought [eine religiöse Gedankenwelt] standing behind it." [30]

This is an extreme situation, however, which holds only for the few. For the great mass of worshipers symbolism in the form of objects or at least of acts and of vividly represented images is very helpful. Material objects, to be sure, tend to become less frequently used as symbols, but the ritual is more

---

[28] Op. cit. p. 33.

[29] Cf. Wundt, " Völkerpsychologie," Vol. V (*called* Vol. II, Part III), op. 740.

[30] Op. cit. Part III, pp. 740–41.

firmly founded.   For the ritual itself is a symbol.   The admirable and oft-quoted definition of a sacrament as an outward
and visible sign of an inward and spiritual grace applies to all
deeply religious ritual.   As Stanton Coit has pointed out,[31]
the ritual is an outward expression of the inner state of the
worshiper, and hence is as truly symbolic as language.   We
have seen, however, that the religious symbol differs from
the ordinary sign in being more than a conventional means of
communication; it must possess a certain depth of emotional
meaning.   Mr. Coit has pointed out another though closely related characteristic of the ritual as a truly religious symbol;
it must be regarded by the worshipers as a token of a real
event actually taking place here and now, within, or in relation
to, the persons who perform it.   " Always his own will and his
own heart are committed by the person making a ritualistic
sign and are received and accepted by those to whom it is
made.   Participation in an act of ritual is a personal commit-
ment or pledge, and therefore is an act in the moral and social
history of the participants.   The woman who assumes the role
of bride in the marriage ceremony is actually thereby becoming
the wife of the man who stands by her side.   She is not simply
symbolically illustrating in fantastic manner some general principle of monogamy. . . .   The marriage ceremony is infinitely
removed in its nature from a show or a symbolical representation of some real event which took place elsewhere. . . .   The
little child baptised may never afterwards wholly escape from
the real moral and social effects of the fact that his parents
and the priest committed him to the Roman Catholic or to the
Anglican communion." [32]   In like manner, the Catholic mass
and the Protestant celebration of the Lord's Supper, the repetition of the creed and the recitation of the prayer would be unthinkable hypocrisies if performed by people who did not believe that in these acts something very real was actually happening within or in relation to their own souls.   " A great
event," says Coit, " is always taking place in the life of the
persons who are participating in any religious ritual. . . .
There is no such thing as a ' mere ceremony ' of ritual: for

[31] Op. cit. pp. 320–21.
[32] Id. pp. 329–30.

the moment it ceases to be an indispensable sign in the eyes of the community, it is not the sign at all." [33]

The most sophisticated of all the functions of cult or public worship is direct and explicit instruction. That this ever forms a part of the cult is sometimes denied;[34] but such a denial both involves a narrow definition of the cult which would rule out from it a large part of modern public worship, and also dogmatically shuts its eyes to certain features of ancient and primitive ritual. The initiation ceremonies of many primitive peoples, which are as truly religious in their nature as are the Christian sacraments of confirmation and baptism, include both indirect and direct attempts at instruction; and the same more or less explicit effort to impart information on religious matters is to be seen in the Mysteries of the Greeks and in some of the ceremonies of religious pilgrimages in various religions. It is true, however, that only in the more highly developed and sophisticated religions does direct instruction become a relatively important factor in public worship. It is seen in most explicit fashion, of course, in public scriptural reading and comment and in the sermon, as found to some extent in Southern Buddhism, and with greater emphasis in Mohammedanism and Christianity. It is here, of course, that the subjective aim of worship becomes most explicit; for hardly the most zealous advocate of the importance of the sermon will claim that it is preached for the benefit of the Almighty. The religious community which insists upon the sermon as a part of its " service " knows perfectly well that the only reason for it is to be found in its effects upon the hearers.

I make no claim to having exhausted in this chapter the methods used by the cult for the fulfillment of its religious functions. The ground, however, has been covered in sufficient detail to show the general nature of those methods. Further light will be thrown on the whole question by the more concrete considerations of the following chapter.

[33] Id. pp. 330–331.
[34] E. g. by Sumner, " Folk Ways," p 61.

CHAPTER XIV

In the two preceding chapters I have had occasion more than once to distinguish between two types of worship, one of which aims at making some kind of effect upon the Deity or in some way communicating with him, while the other seeks only to induce some desired mood or belief or attitude in the mind of the worshiper. The former of these types I shall refer to, for the sake of brevity, as *objective worship,* and the latter I shall call *subjective worship.* The distinction between the two seems to me so important that I doubt whether a thorough understanding of the various cults found in the different religions be possible unless this distinction be quite explicitly recognized. It is the key to many a ceremonial which without it must remain for most of us obscure, strange, and even ridiculous or shocking. This is true within the bounds of our own Christian religion. Consider, for example, the impressions of the Protestant on first being present at a Catholic Mass, or the feelings of the Catholic on first attending a Protestant service. To the Protestant the mass seems fantastic; to the Catholic the evangelical worship appears godless. Each can understand the other only by appreciating the difference in aim: the leading purpose of the mass is the worship of God, that of the Protestant service is the subjective impression upon the minds and hearts of the worshipers.

Perhaps the most notable instance of objective worship is the Chinese official cult of Heaven, which can be performed *only* by the Emperor (or President), who does it on behalf of all the people. The same purely objective purpose stands out with equal directness in the Hindu temple ceremonials, especially in the regular daily "*puja*" of the officiating priest. Quite frequently there is no audience at this ceremony,— no one is present but the priest who anoints the lingam, or strews flowers before the image, muttering certain sacred words of whose meaning he often has no notion and going through the ritual with the obvious single purpose of *gratifying the god*.[1]   Even when an audience is present the chief aim of the ceremony is plainly the adulation of the deity.   The worshipers come because their god wishes their adoration and they can, perhaps, move him to grant their requests by prostrating themselves before the throne where, in his sacred image, he is seated.   For the Hindu temple is in no sense a " meeting house."   It is not built for the benefit of the human worshipers, but for the greater glory of God.   The thought of going to the temple for the sake of the subjective effect which the *puja* might have upon one's own feelings is an idea that probably never enters into one Hindu head in a thousand.   Occasionally, indeed, as I pointed out in the last chapter, there is a self-conscious attempt to gain this end, but it is relatively rare; and unquestionably the subjective effect is in innumerable cases attained even when the thought of it is quite absent from the mind.   One need only watch the faces of the long line of heavy-laden humanity — especially of the widows — pouring quietly but steadily out of some temple of Shiva on the banks of the Ganges, to feel convinced that these dumb worshipers are taking home with them something of the same religious comfort and uplift which their sisters are finding in some little white meeting-house in far New England.

But the subjective benefits of cult and ritual which though often present in the less sophisticated forms of Hinduism remain almost unrecognized, come out quite explicitly in some of the very self-conscious Hindu reform movements.   An excellent example of this is to be found in the *Havan* ceremony of the Arya Samaj.   The Aryas are an exceedingly rationalistic group of religious thinkers who are bent on the moral and intellectual reform of Hinduism, and who never lose an opportunity to attack and ridicule idolatry and the popular temple worship, as well as polytheism in all its forms.   But from the very be-

---

[1] For the details of Hindu temple worship see Monier Williams, " Brahmanism and Hinduism " (4th Ed.   New York, Macmillan: 1891), pp. 93–94, 144–45, 438–41; Farquhar's " Crown of Hinduism," pp. 313–14; Bhandarkar, " Vaishnavism, Saivism, and Minor Religious Systems " (Strassburg, Trübner: 1913), p. 81; and my " India and Its Faiths," Chap. II.

ginning of their reform movement they recognized so clearly the human need of a ritual, for the sake of its effects upon the worshipers, that the founder of the church, Swami Dayanand, in part invented, in part adopted from the Vedas, a ceremony remarkably well adapted in more ways than one to bring about the state of mind which the Samaj desires in its members. The audience gathers around a small pit, prepared for the occasion, and there the leaders make a sweet-smelling fire, pouring into it from time to time ladles of *ghi* or liquefied butter, to the accompaniment of a steady chanting of Sanskrit verses. This, Dayanand assured his followers, was an ancient Vedic rite, handed down for ages in the holy days when only the one God was worshiped, and practiced by the Rishis who wrote the Rig Veda. Here, then, we have visible and tangible elements brought into direct association with the religious belief; and a sacramental offering of them by the community and its representatives in such fashion as to symbolize the faith of all, and thus to bring social confirmation to the individual's religion, and to bind the whole of the group to the great and revered Past whose authority thus becomes a perennial spring of fervent religious sentiment. There is no thought whatever of the ceremony being a sacrifice to God or a way of pleasing Him. If you ask the Aryas why it is performed they will tell you it is for the sake of emphasizing their connection with Vedic times, and as a symbol of their devotion to all the world.[2] It forms the central part of their daily and weekly religious meetings, and the earnest religious feeling which it arouses among them is patent to every visitor.[3]

But the extreme examples of subjective worship are to be found in two other of the religions of India, namely Jainism and Buddhism. In their popular forms, both of these cults are fairly objective; but always in theory (at least in their original theories), and among their more intellectual followers in prac-

---

[2] I should add that the chief function performed by this ceremony in the opinion of the Arya Somajists is the *purification of the air*. This notion originated with Swami Dayanand, who expounds it at length in the passage of his authoritative book, the "Satyarth Prakash," in which he lays down the rules for the Havan ceremony. See Durga Prasad's translation of the "Satyarth Prakash" (Lahore, Virjanand Press: 1908), pp. 101–103.

[3] For further description see my "India and Its Faiths," pp. 208–210.

tice, they carry subjectivity to an extreme from which the professors of every other religion, eastern or western, would probably shrink. For the Jaina there is no God; instead, there is a mechanically moral but unconscious universe, and there are also twenty-four Tirthankaras or ideal beings who once lived and have long since passed into Moksha. These are conceived as still conscious, but they are quite unconscious of human affairs and can never be reached or in any way affected by human prayers or offerings. One might conclude from this that worship of them would be out of the question, at any rate for the more intelligent. This is by no means the case. At the ceremonies in Jaina temples you will find, at least occasionally, very intelligent and educated men, who are firmly convinced that nothing they do or say or think will reach the Tirthankaras, and yet who are as enthusiastic in making offerings and intoning Sanskrit verses before a Tirthankara image as are any of their less enlightened brethren. I have talked with more than one of these men concerning their worship and they have insisted that they keep up the cult in this strict and scrupulous fashion because they find that its subjective effects upon them are decidedly beneficial — and this, in fact, is the orthodox Jaina theory upon the subject. Eight kinds of offerings are made to the images, and each of these has a symbolic meaning. Thus white rice represents knowledge, saffron rice beauty, etc.; and the presentation of these symbols, together with the Sanskrit verses chanted and the thought of the moral ideal for which the Tirthankara stands, all tend to bring new comfort and hope, new aspirations, and greater strength for the moral life.[4]

Buddhist theory, and to some extent Buddhist practice, carries this subjective worship if possible one step further. For in the religion as formulated by the Founder, and as still believed and practiced by a number of intelligent monks in Burma and Ceylon and also by some of the laity, there is not even

[4] See the chapter on the Jainas in my "India and Its Faiths," in which I have dealt in greater detail with this subject. For further descriptions of Jaina worship see Mrs. Sinclair Stevenson's "Notes on Modern Jainism" (Oxford, Blackwell: 1910), pp. 85–105, and her larger work, "The Heart of Jainism" (Oxford U. Press, 1915) Chap. XIII.

so much to pray to as a conscious but unreachable Tirthankara. Buddhism, like Jainism, has two substitutes for God; one of them this miraculously moral but quite unconscious Cosmos with its inescapable Law of Karma; the other the ideal being, Gautama, the Buddha. But the Buddha has long since sunk into Nirvana, which in the opinion of the majority of the more learned and intelligent monks seems to be equivalent to nothingness. Not only is he beyond all our prayers and offerings; he is not even conscious. In the words of many of the monks with whom I talked in Burma and Ceylon, "Buddha finish!" Yet these good atheists have by no means given up the cult. Morning and night, if they be monks, do they assemble in the hall of their monastery around the image of the Founder of their Faith, and offer fresh flowers and ancient praises in his honor. And most of them sometime during the day will go, together with little groups of faithful lay brothers, to some near-by pagoda, and there place a candle within the great shrine, and recite more verses and more praises. "Thus reflecting," says the Dina Chariyawa, in recital of the duties of the novice, "he shall approach the dagoba, or the bo-tree, and perform that which is appointed: he shall offer flowers, just as if the Buddha were present in person, if flowers can be procured; meditate on the nine virtues of the Buddha with fixed and determined mind; and having worshiped seek absolution for his negligences and faults just as if the sacred things [before which he worships] had life." [5] In short the enlightened Buddhist is to act "*just as if*" he believed various things which he does not believe, because the performance of these acts has been found to be helpful in the production of a desirable inner state of mind. A Burmese Buddhist book says plainly, "It is bootless to worship the Buddha; nothing is necessary but to revere him and the memory of him. Statues are useful only in so far as they refresh the memory; for as the farmer sows the seed and gathers in the grain in due season, so will the man who trusts in the Buddha and holds fast by his sacred

[5] Quoted in Hardy's "Eastern Monachism" (London, Partridge and Oxford: 1860), p. 25.

Law, obtain deliverance and pass into Nehban.   The earth and the Buddha are alike in themselves inert." [6]

When we turn from India to Christendom we find again both objective and subjective worship — sometimes standing out from each other quite obviously, sometimes inextricably intermingled.   Although both forms have been found many times over in both the great western branches of the Christian Church, objective worship comes out the more distinctly in Roman Catholicism, and subjective worship in Protestantism.   The Catholic Church seems to consider the direct worship of God as much a part of its duty as the salvation of souls.   In certain orders of nuns systematic efforts are directed toward making sure that the Blessed Sacrament is being constantly adored by pious sisters,[7] prostrate before it at every moment of the day and night. By a widespread custom in various parts of the Catholic world, laymen join with the " religious " once a year in consecrating " Forty Hours " to the adoration of the Sacrament.[8] A very considerable part of the day of every priest is occupied in saying the " Office." [9]   This rather heavy requirement is but distantly if at all connected with the purpose of saving souls or of producing a subjective effect upon anyone.   It aims primarily and chiefly *ad majoram Dei gloriam*.   The conception is that God is pleased with this chorus of prayers and praises rising to Him in unison from all quarters of the globe. The same objective character of much of Catholic worship is to be seen in the very buildings themselves which we know as Catholic churches.   As Henry Adams puts it, the nave was

[6] Quoted by Shway Yoe (J. G. Scott) in " The Burman " (London, Macmillan: 1882), Vol. I, p. 221.

[7] Four Orders have been founded and continued for this special purpose: — the " Religious of Perpetual Adoration " of Belgium, an order of the same name in Einsiedeln (Switzerland), the " Sisters of the Perpetual Adoration " (of Quimper, France), and the " Perpetual Adorers of the Blessed Sacrament,"— see Catholic Encyclopedia.

[8] " Questa divozione consiste nell'esporre il Santissimo Sacramento alla dorazione dei fedeli per tre giorni di seguito e per tredici o quattordici ore del giorno " (" Tutto con Me,"— Milano, Tipografia Santa Lega Eucaristica: 1908 — p. 847).

[9] The Office varies on different days, but in general it may be said to consist of about one-seventh of the Psalter — the entire Psalter being thus recited once each week — plus certain liturgical formulas and responses, with special additional material for saints' days.

made for the people but the choir for God.[10]　Especially noticeable is the arrangement for objective worship in the cathedrals of Spain, where the central portion of the nave is blocked up with the *coro* or choir, whose walls, rising on three sides, make it almost a separate building in the midst of the cathedral. Thus the view of the high altar is quite cut off from all parts of the church except the *coro,* the small space between it and the altar, and a minute section of each transept.　The result is that only a few worshipers in the whole cathedral can see the altar,— a commentary in stone upon the purpose of the cathedral and of the services performed within it.　The important thing is not that the worshipers should be able to behold and follow the service or be impressed by it, but *that God should be properly and gloriously worshiped.*

But it is not only in great cathedrals that the objective nature of Catholic worship is felt.　The Catholic church in every part of the world, and no matter how humble in architectural design, means to be (as the Hindu temple means to be) not a meeting house for worshipers but a place where in a peculiar sense God dwells.　The heart of Catholicism for its most spiritual children is its belief in the peculiar presence of God within the Sacrament; and it is this that makes the Catholic church mean so much more to the good Catholic than the Protestant meeting house can ever mean to anyone.　To some minds the contrast is enormous.　George Tyrrell tells us that at an early age he felt that " the difference between an altar and a communion table is infinite." [11]　When a Catholic goes into a Protestant church he has an immediate sense that something is lacking.　Involuntarily he looks for the altar with its hidden but ever present Host, and, not finding it, he realizes that the building is merely a place for people to meet together and think about God — not a temple in which one meets with God

---

[10] " The choir was made not for the pilgrim but for the deity, and is as old as Adam or perhaps older. . . . The Christian church not only took the sanctuary in hand and gave it a new form, but it also added the idea of the nave and transepts, and developed it into imperial splendor.　The pilgrim-tourist feels at home in the nave because it was built for him; the artist loves the sanctuary because he built it for God " (" Mont St. Michel and Chartres," Washington: 1912, p. 161).

[11] Autobiography," Vol. I, p. 98.

Himself in a peculiarly close and objective way.   To be sure God is believed to be present in the Protestant church, but nowhere in particular and no more in the church than elsewhere. God is present everywhere in general, and nowhere in particular.   In the Catholic belief, too, He is present everywhere in general, but He is also present in one place in particular.   He is there in the wafer, mysteriously transformed in " substance " into His very body, upon the altar.   Hence the glorious robes of the priest to do honor to the heavenly guest; hence the acolites, the incense, the music, the candles.   The objective nature of Catholic worship is plain in all these things; and especially when contrasted with the corresponding adornments of the Protestant service, notably its flowers.   The Protestant church decks its buildings with flowers solely and admittedly for the congregation to see.   They make the church pleasanter, possibly attract a few more people by their touch of color and beauty, and perhaps help to put some in a more spiritual frame of mind.   The candles of the Catholic church are placed there not for man but for God.   This is true of them whether publicly and officially or privately contributed.   The woman who places her candle before the shrine of the Madonna has no thought in her mind of the effect it may have on other worshipers.   The Madonna will see it and that is enough.   It would be placed there just the same were no one expected to enter the church.

The same contrast between the objective and the subjective is seen again if we compare the acts and bearing of the minister with those of the priest in conducting the service.   The minister as well as the priest may mean that God shall hear the words of the service, but he certainly also means that the congregation shall hear,— both in order that they may pray with him and also in order to produce upon them, by his prayers and their prayers, the desired psychological effect.   He not only prays; he " leads in prayer."   His prayer he utters in a loud voice, that all may hear, as he stands facing the audience.   And too often his prayer is of the sort intended in the oft-quoted description:— " the most eloquent prayer ever addressed to a Boston audience."

Instead of this, the priest turns his back on the congregation, faces the altar where God is, and whispers his prayer in a voice too low to be heard by anyone and in a tongue unknown to all but his fellow priests.   During most of the service he seems utterly oblivious to the presence of other worshipers.   The Protestant clergyman on a rainy Sunday, when the church is cold and only twenty or thirty are present, may dismiss his hearers and give up the service.   To the Catholic priest, the size of the congregation and the temperature of the building make no apparent difference.   He comes into the church from the sacristy carrying the chalice and followed by his attendant, looking neither to the right hand nor to the left for his audience, with his eyes fixed only upon the altar where the body and blood of Christ are shortly to be seen; and he says his mass in exactly the same way whether the Church be thronged or he and the boy be the only human beings in the building.

For the mass is viewed by the Church not as a means for producing an effect but as something objectively worth while in itself — the mysterious sacrifice on the cross of God to God, miraculously repeated upon the altar.   In the words of Frederic Harrison, "the Mass is a reality — if one admit its scientific extravagance — and for religious and moral efficacy the most potent institution that any religion in man's history can boast — 'the most admirable of the Catholic institutions' — at once a tremendous drama, a searching discipline, an entire creed transfigured in a visible presentment of a spiritual doctrine." [12] The mass is the very center of Catholic worship and the heart of Catholic belief; and leading up as it does to the miracle upon the altar and the tremendously dramatic climax of the elevation of the Host, it has no rival in the whole round of religious ceremonial for impressiveness and for the production of deep but controlled religious emotion.   To the unsympathetic and ignorant beholder it seems bizarre, but whoever enters sympathetically, intelligently, and imaginatively into the feelings of the worshipers kneeling around him, and for the moment takes their "objective" point of view of the peculiar and miraculous presence of the Divine, can hardly fail to find in it a new and unique and deeply religious experience.   It was this

[12] "The Positive Evolution of Religion" (New York, Putnams: 1913), p. 129.

almost unreplaceable stimulus to the religious sentiment that was left behind when our Protestant fathers went out from the old historic Church. And when this is understood one sees how hopeless it must ever be to fill the place of this lost sense of the peculiar immediacy of the Supernatural and Divine by any use of candles or incense, intoned service and ringing of bells, or the voices of violins, cellos, and opera singers.

In other words, the subjective effect of the objective methods used by the Catholic Church is very considerable, even though aimed at only indirectly,— in fact largely because it is aimed at only indirectly. To the reverent Catholic it makes little or no difference that he cannot hear the priest's words, and that if he could hear them they might be to him unintelligible. He may if he likes follow the service by means of the translation in his prayer book; but this he does not need and seldom tries to do. It is of no importance that he should. For he finds — and this sums up the subjective value of the mass — that a church in which mass is being said is an *excellent place to pray,* that the service gives him an intense realization of the closeness of God to human life, and that he goes away from it with a sense of spiritual refreshment.

So excellent in producing subjective effects are the objective methods of the Catholic Church that a benevolent atheist might conceivably do his best to forward the interests of Catholicism. If he were a wise as well as a benevolent atheist, however, he would probably keep his views of the truly subjective nature of worship entirely to himself. For once let the cat out of the bag, the desired result might become almost unattainable. And here we find both the strength and the weakness of purely objective methods. Given a body of worshipers who accept implicitly the belief back of the cult, and the effect of it upon their religious sentiments will be stronger than that which any direct attempt at influencing them could ever bring about. But the number of those for whom this is possible is likely to diminish steadily with the loss of respect for authority and the spread of modern education, free thought, and rationalism. The Catholic Church has always shown remarkable insight into the psychology of the mystic and of the uneducated. Its whole history shows also an almost equally remarkable failure to understand the minds of the rationalistic and the lovers of free thought. For Protestants the mass fails of its subjective religious effect because they cannot share the Catholic belief in transubstantiation, and hence the direct Catholic kind of objective worship is for them impossible. And something like this loss of subjective impressiveness in the mass holds true for an increasing number of the more intelligent Catholics themselves. In Italy and France, for example, there are a great many good men — nominally Catholics — to whom the mass is simply foolishness. To them, the Latin mumbling of the priest is a useless repetition, and the incense and candles are a kind of earnest nonsense. Not believing strongly or at all in the real presence, and not being of the emotional or mystical type, they fail to get anything out of the service — and hence stay away. For men of this sort, the reading of fairly long and consecutive and well-chosen passages of Scripture, followed by an intelligent sermon on some moral problem, with the singing of a few good hymns, might be the ideal form of public worship. But this is, of course, very nearly the Protestant and " evangelical " form.

While, therefore, the Protestant worship can probably never minister to the religious feelings of people of the mystical and traditional type as can the more objective worship of the Catholic Church, to persons of the intellectual and moral type it probably furnishes the best solution. I speak of it as a solution, for the worship which is to appeal to these two types of mind is indeed a problem. On the one hand it must not demand of them a faith which is for them no longer possible, hence must include much frank and self-conscious effort to influence their faith and feeling directly; and on the other hand it cannot afford to leave out entirely the objective aspect of worship, for to do so would be implicitly to surrender certain essential parts of the faith upon which much of the subjective effect of worship is ultimately based. The problem of the Protestant Church has therefore been to find a combination of objective and subjective worship that will plant and nourish the religious sentiments, enliven the moral emotions, and at the same time will not antagonize the reason of its members. It will be noticed that I have mentioned here one aim very prominent in Protestant worship which receives but little stress in the public worship of the Catholic Church — namely the enlivening of the moral emotions.   The Protestant Church seeks, quite self-consciously, so to construct its services as to reinforce the moral tendencies of its members with the strength which comes from deep religious sentiment.

The methods by which the Protestant Churches seek to solve their problem and to make their worship best fulfill its religious functions, are too well known to need description.   Objective methods have by no means been completely discarded.   There are presumably many congregations and individuals who still intend the hymns of praise which they sing — notably the Doxology — to be heard by the Deity.   " The office of song in the sanctuary," writes Dr. Snowden in a recent book, " is to praise God.   Worship seeks the highest form of expression which is poetry wedded to music, the rhythm of speech and song.   Music is one of the art-paths to God." [13]   An examination of our modern hymn-books, however, will show that the proportion of what we might call *objective* hymns is not large, and a study of older hymnals in comparison makes it plain that the percentage is decreasing.[14]   The chief function of the hymn is decidedly subjective.   The leading form, and for many people the only form of objective worship left in the Protestant service is prayer.   By nearly every religious Protestant this is regarded as truly objective in its nature — a direct address of the soul to the Deity ; and it seems most unlikely that more than a very few have any thought when they pray of the subjective effects prayer may have upon them.   Here, then, we find worship in the simple, direct, ancient sense.   We find it, that is, wherever the people actually do pray.   How many of the congregation are

[13] " The Psychology of Religion," p. 245.

[14] Cf. super, " The Psychology of Christian Hymns," *Am. Jour. of Relig. Psy.*, III, 1–15.   The history of the use of hymns in the Christian service gives an interesting example of the change from purely objective to largely subjective worship.   In the mediæval church the hymns were all in Latin and were sung not by the congregation but by the choir alone — the obvious purpose being to praise God.   The practice of writing hymns in the vernacular and having them sung by the congregation began with the Reformation — especially through the influence of Luther, Gerhardt, the Moravians, and the Methodists.— See Hewitt, " Paul Gerhardt as a Hymn Writer and His Influence on English Hymnody " (Yale University Press: 1918).

praying in any real sense of the word during the "long prayer" is a question which only He who hears prayers could answer. If I may trust my own observation, and the expressions of those whom I have questioned upon the subject, no very large portion of the congregation "follow" the long prayer, and fewer still find it really helpful in producing even the prayerful attitude of mind.

Nearly all the details of the Protestant service, then, and also the service as a whole, are planned out with the deliberate purpose of producing certain psychological effects upon the congregation. "The minister," writes Dr. Hartshorne, "has a definite purpose and a definite plan. He wishes to bring the congregation to a new point of view or to a new resolve. To this end he selects music, hymns, prayers, Scripture, and address, and weaves all into a harmonious whole which shall, in its total effect, induce the desired change in the minds of the audience. And consciously or unconsciously he makes use of the psychology of feeling and emotion." [15]   How successful the average minister is in this aim, the reader will probably decide for himself. Dr. John P. Hylan issued a questionnaire on this subject, a few years ago, and the responses showed that the service, the church building, and even the day itself — the Sabbath — shed upon most of the respondents a certain subjective influence of a rather mild sort.[16]   The success of different ministers and different churches in this effort of course varies enormously.

The tools, so to speak, by which this subjective effect is brought about are well known to us all.   The architecture and its decorations help, and so does (to those who attend the same church all their lives) the close association between the familiar church interior and the religious impressions and aspirations of childhood.   The creed, recited by the congregation in unison, has the effect already pointed out of reinforcing individual faith by social confirmation.   Especially is the congregational singing of hymns productive of considerable religious feeling;[17] while

[15] "Worship in the Sunday School" (New York, Columbia University: 1913) pp. 115–16.

[16] "Public Worship" (Chicago, Open Court: 1901).   Chap. III.

[17] Dr. Müller-Freienfels, in the article already once referred to, reports the result of a statistical investigation of his own to the effect that hymn singing in which the worshiper himself takes part has a much greater emo-

the rendering of selections by the choir at times aids in producing the desired religious atmosphere — provided the selections be really religious and the rendering of them be sincere.[18]   The " Scripture lesson " is usually too short to be of much influence. The aim of the sermon, the central part of most Protestant worship, seems to be threefold: to increase or correct the faith of the hearers, to nourish their religious sentiments, and to arouse, fortify, and redirect their moral convictions and emotions.   It is here that the Protestant Church finds its great weapon in liberalizing and deepening religious thought and in directing the forces of the Christian community toward purity of private life and toward aggressive actions in the great struggle for social righteousness.   The responses collected by Mr. L. W. Kline from various types of church-goers to the question, " Please state in what way sermons affect and benefit you," indicate plainly (so far, at any rate, as his respondents were typical) that it is the moral appeal of the sermon, especially when delivered with unmistakable earnestness and sincerity, that produces by far the greatest effect the preacher can hope for.[19]

But while the Protestant Church has done well in laying great emphasis upon the sermon, it is a question whether it has not laid too little emphasis upon the rest of the service. A recent contributor to the *Atlantic* asserts, in half-earnest, that " nothing would be so beneficial as to have our pulpits silenced for a year. . . . The other phases of worship would be restored — the worship of prayer, confession, praise, and enlightened faith.   Some of them are entirely gone from the churches.   The people no longer pray but listen to the minister

tional effect upon him than music to which he merely listens.   This is, of course, what we should naturally expect.— Op. cit., p. 371.

[18] All music tends to rouse some kind of emotion, but the state of mind incited by certain kinds of emotion may be almost inhibitory to the religious sentiment.   Indeed according to President Faunce, " in most churches the task of the preacher is rendered vastly more difficult by the intrusion of incongruous or impertinent music.   After the choir by elaborate performance has brought the congregation into the concert-mood, the preacher is expected to remove that mood and replace it by the temper of devotion."   (" The Religious Function of Public Worship," *Am. Jour. of Thol.* XIV 5.— Jan., 1910).

[19] " The Sermon: A Study in Social Psychology."— *Am. Jour. of Relig. Psy. and Ed.* I, 288–300.

as he prays.[20] Worship has become a passive matter. The congregation has become an audience — a body of listeners." [21] In short, the Sunday morning church service, while often appealing quite admirably to the moral emotions and convictions of the worshipers, seems to many of its best disposed critics and lovers to be lacking exactly on the religious side. The reality of the more-than-human, the relation of the individual to the Determiner of Destiny, the intense emotional realization of the Cosmic,— these things are no longer suggested to us in Church as they used to be to our fathers. Somehow in our smug security we seem armed against them, even when the preacher tries to bring them home to us. And the enormous throngs who never enter a church door are seldom reminded of them.

There is one kind of religious service which almost every one attends occasionally, no matter how skeptical he be, and one which seldom fails of producing upon all present a very deep effect. Strangely enough, moreover, it is seldom enumerated among the religious methods of the church. For an increasingly large number of people in our days the only form of religious service left is an occasional funeral. With the rarest of exceptions, the funeral is always a religious ceremony. Other former functions of the Church, such as marriage, education, the care of the poor, etc., are being taken over by the civil authorities; but the disposal of the dead almost everywhere still remains in the hands of religion. And though the religious value of the funeral is seldom recognized, or at least seldom mentioned, it is very considerable. For in the presence of Death we find ourselves face to face with the dreadful and silent forces which lie beyond our control — the Cosmic Reality, our conscious relation to which *is* religion. Here we stand on the very edge of the mystery. The curtain for a moment is partly drawn and we get a glimpse of the cosmic process. We return to our little tasks, to be sure, all the more mystified, but with at least a renewed sense of the reality of the mystery. Compared with the savage or with the mediæval Christian, we moderns spend our lives almost entirely in the light of common

---

[20] Query: Do they?

[21] G. P. Atwater, "The Ministry: An Over-crowded Profession." *Atlantic Monthly* for Oct., 1911, pp. 483-84.

day, in a world which science has made safe and common-place. It takes something like Death to startle us out of our complacent scientific and practical attitude, and to reveal to us the vista of cosmic mystery which (in cruder forms) was ever present to our less scientific forbears. It is this sense of the Unknown, this realization of our own dependence, this inti-mation of a Power not to be exhausted by the study of science, this questioning of the Why, the Whence, and the Whither, this placing of ourselves for once in a cosmic setting — it is this that the funeral brings, and to this that it owes its uniquely religious value. It seems, indeed, almost an irrational celebration of our own defeat, yet so commanding is its position in the spiritual economy of our lives that we may feel fairly sure of its retention as a religious ceremony to the end of human time.

But whether our Protestant Sunday service needs more of the solemnity and of the cosmic quality which the funeral possesses, or whether its chief need be more moral earnestness, more ritual, more preaching or no preaching at all, there seems at any rate to be a pretty general feeling that it needs something. Our various denominations are showing a very commendable dis-satisfaction with their present methods and a willingness to experiment on new lines in the hope of finding some type of worship more generally satisfactory. We see them fumbling about, groping for light, trying new plans of popular appeal which range all the way from vested choirs to moving pictures. A fairly large body in many of the denominations feels the need of more ritual — a need which, as we have seen, is deeply founded in human psychology. New rituals are therefore be-ing rapidly produced, but none of them seem quite to fill the need — a fact which might indeed have been anticipated con-sidering the importance of a traditional sanction if the ritual is to be felt as appropriate and fitting. The problem of re-shaping the Protestant worship is in fact pecularly difficult. For it means discovering a method of nourishing the religious sentiments of people most of whom are of the intellectual and active types. And it must do this without the aid of the two most powerful means which other churches and religions make use of for the purpose — namely the kind of belief which makes elaborate objective worship easy and natural for large groups, and a ritual which has the authority and sanctity of generations behind it.[22]

Fortunately it is not the task of a writer on the psychology of religion to devise a solution for this problem. I shall therefore content myself here by pointing out one or two things. In the first place we must remember that no one solution is possible. The variations in human temperament and taste are so great that a very considerable diversity in ritual among Christian churches — even among those who *believe* exactly the same things — will always be not only desirable but necessary if the Church is to feed the needs of all. The union of Christian churches in their various philanthropic and missionary undertakings is doubtless very desirable; but a union of the Churches which should banish or even decrease the present diversity in ritual would be a real misfortune.[23]

[22] The Protestant Episcopal Church has a much less difficult problem; for it has inherited a ritual which not only is beautiful in itself, but is rich in the sanctity and authority of an age-long tradition. Such a ritual is peculiarly adapted to the production of the religious atmosphere; and the individual brought up within the Episcopal fold almost invariably finds his church an excellent place in which to pray. The problem for the Episcopalian is simply to make his ritual elastic and adapted to the growing and ever new needs of the times, while keeping it also conservative and ancient. He must, if he can, strike the golden mean between the old and the new, he must retain enough of the traditional to appeal to the religious sentiment and yet surrender enough and add enough to conform to the demands of modern thought and modern needs. Changes, therefore, should be made from time to time in the ritual, but such changes should be gradual and for the moment always slight. If an outsider might make one further suggestion, I would add that the Episcopal Church would at any rate make a much greater appeal to stray visitors from other folds if her clergymen would pay more attention to the intellectual content of their sermons and the moral significance of their themes. There are many excellent preachers within the Episcopal Church, but the clergyman too often appears to be satisfied with a deadly conventional treatment of an insignificant or antiquated subject, seeming to be under the impression that the banality of his remarks may be hidden under a large use of the " chancel voice."

[23] The diverse ritualistic needs of men sharing practically the same beliefs is well illustrated by the case of those two good friends and excellent Christians, John Bright and William E. Gladstone. In his journal under date of September, 1873, while on a visit to Gladstone, Bright comments: " To Church. Service *high*. Three parsons. Mr. Gladstone most earnest in the singing, etc. To me much of the service seemed only fitted for very ignorant people." (Quoted in Trevelyan's " Life of John Bright," London, Constable: 1913, p. 415.)

No solution, moreover, seems to be possible which relies wholly on what I have called subjective methods. The attempt to produce merely subjective religious effects is always in danger of defeating itself. For religion, as we have seen, involves a belief which means to have objective validity; and if worship neglects this and directs all its efforts openly to the production of changes in social and psychical conditions, it may indeed remain a moral force, but it ceases to be religious and it loses all the emotional reinforcement that comes from the religious sentiment. I cannot, therefore, think that anything of much importance will be brought about by the adoption of prayer books or the processionals of vested choirs or anything else of a merely superficial sort. The difficulty with Protestant worship goes deeper than the surface, and until some more fundamental change is wrought, its mode of worship will remain always unsatisfactory. The worshiper in the Protestant Church must be made to feel, as the Catholic feels at the mass, that *something is really being done* — something in addition to the subjective change in his own consciousness. Let him understand that you wish him to come to church in order that you may make a psychological impression on him, and he will be increasingly likely to stay away. Or he may come to hear your opera singer, but his religious sentiment will remain untouched. If public worship is to be profitable to him he must find in it something more than that. In other words, what the Protestant service needs more than anything else is the development of the objective side of its worship. As we have seen, the principal objective element left in the Protestant service is prayer. Here, then, a beginning of the solution of the Protestant problem may be sought. The worshiper may be made to feel as he does not to-day that *in prayer something really happens*. This need not and should not mean that answer to special prayers and the influence of prayer upon war and weather is to be inculcated from the pulpit. It does mean that if the Protestant Church desires to make its worship more vital it should take great new pains to train its members, and especially its children, in the habit of prayer, and in the belief that somehow in prayer one puts oneself in touch with a supersensible world. The church should see to it that whatever else its Sunday service may neglect to do, it should bring to its worshipers an atmosphere of prayer, and a sense of the real presence of the Divine. Of course Protestantism has always made some effort in this direction, but when one compares the training in prayer and meditation which most of its young people receive with the best of the religious training given by the Catholic Church, one understands that there is a kind of *inwardness,* a sense of the vital reality of spiritual things, a feeling of need for spiritual reinforcement, which Protestantism has failed to foster.

But we must go deeper than this and ask ourselves the question whether we really believe that worship is any longer possible in the modern world at all. Plainly if objective worship be impossible for the intelligent, and if subjective without objective worship is self-delusion, there is an end of all worship for the modern man. Plainly also the second of the above hypothetical propositions is true,— subjective worship without some objective worship cannot stand. The question, therefore, narrows down to this: Is any kind of objective worship possible for the man of our age? In answer to this it must be said plainly and first of all, that objective worship of the sort that aims to please the Deity is a thing of the past. The modern man cannot even attempt to participate in it without conscious hypocrisy. That is not the end of the matter, however. There is a kind of worship that is perfectly objective and sincere and that is quite as possible for the intelligent man of to-day as it was for the ancient:— namely that union of awe and gratitude which is reverence, combined perhaps with consecration and a suggestion of communion, which most thoughtful men must feel in the presence of the Cosmic forces and in reflecting upon them. Such was the attitude of Spinoza and Herbert Spencer. Such was the genuinely objective worship of the ancient philosophers of Greece and India, and of many of the Hebrew Psalmists and Prophets. In this act of instinctive self-abasement there is no aim of producing an effect upon oneself; the attitude is as objective as it is natural. Worship is therefore not something to be outgrown. Its forms change with the changing symbols, the changing robes with which men seek to deck out the Determiner of Destiny. The thing itself is as eternal as is man's finitude.   The task of the Church is to stimulate and direct this fundamental human impulse, with what wisdom it can supply.

CHAPTER XV

PRAYER AND PRIVATE WORSHIP

In the chapter on the Cult and Its Causes we saw that the earliest religious object was in all probability that impersonal and superhuman power which the Melanesians called *mana;* and that individuals as well as social groups from a very early period must have felt characteristic emotions and taken characteristic attitudes in relation to it. This felt relation of the individual to the cosmic power, and the responses to which it led, developed (after the conception of supernatural conscious beings had arisen) into two interlocking though distinguishable phenomena, which we may call private magic and private worship. The distinction between magic and religion which for our purposes shall here be adopted, has already been indicated. We shall, namely, follow Hartland and Leuba, who use the word *magic* to include those supernatural devices employed to gain one's end without the help of spirits or gods, reserving the words *religious cult* and *worship* for those acts which depend upon the aid of the gods for the realization of the ends desired. The interrelations of the individual's magic with his private religious expressions is of some interest and importance. Not many anthropologists are willing to hold with Frazer that religion is simply "the despair of magic," [1] and that it merely succeeded it in time. A view which has place for more of the facts is that held by Marett and Wundt, that religion *grew out* of magic. On this general question little need here be said, unless it be to refer the reader back to the brief discussion of the subject in Chapter XII. It is possible that magic preceded the rise of belief in definitely anthropomorphic spirits or gods, but there is small reason to suppose that the two were related as source and outgrowth. No objection can well be found to the view that both magic and the belief in spirits grew, together

[1] "Golden Bough," Vol. I, Chap. 4, esp. pp. 237–40.

but independently, out of the original concept of *mana*. But the point that is here of special interest is the question of the relation of the magical spell to the (religious) prayer. As the title of his well-known essay indicates, Marett's view is that the course of religious development was " From Spell to Prayer." [2] The spell, in Marett's opinion, may have originated as a descriptive accompaniment of various magical acts,[3] but its real nature is seen only when it becomes an integral part of the performance and acts as an imperative utterance, a projection of the will, which in some supernatural fashion (through the action of *mana*) produces the desired effect. As disappointing experiences come to produce the conviction that the mere projection of will by means of a spell will not always achieve the end desired, and as the magician also comes to personify the instrument or symbol which he uses in his magical performance, " the imperative passes into the optative " and the spell becomes a prayer.[4] Wundt's view is not very dissimilar. Prayer originates from spell (*Beschwörung*), which is altogether a matter of magic.[5]

It is quite possible and in fact very likely that spell antedated prayer. There is, indeed, no decisive evidence on the matter, though there may be some significance in the fact that among the Australians of to-day the use of spells is well developed, while their prayers are hardly more than embryonic.[6] But to say that the spell antedated the prayer is one thing; to say that it produced it, that prayer came from spell, is quite another. One cannot logically argue from the chronological to the causal connection. The reasons given for such a view are far from conclusive. Wundt gives no reason at all, but simply states

[2] Published first in *Folk Lore*, for June, 1904, and later reprinted in his " The Threshold of Religion."

[3] " The Threshold of Religion," p. 54. Ames adopts this suggestion and makes more of it than does its author. See his " Psychology of Religious Experience," p. 142.

[4] Op. cit. See also Marett's article " Prayer " in the Encyclopedia Britannica (11th Ed.).

[5] Völkerpsychologie. Vol. II, Part III (i.e., really Vol. V), pp. 656–62.

[6] See Spencer and Gillen, op. cit. *passim*, and especially Chap. XVI. The spells used by the ancient Babylonians were evidently much older than the prayers and hymns to which they were (later on) attached.— See Jastrow, " The Civilization of Ancient Babylonia and Assyria " (Philadelphia, Lippincott: 1915), pp. 239–40.

his view in typically Teutonic and dogmatic fashion. Marett gives two arguments,— the natural tendency of the savage to personify the instrument of his magic, and the frequent failure of the spell as a command.[7] But the tendency to personification is of too wide an influence to appeal to here. It may be called the source of the development of anthropomorphic gods out of the primeval and impersonal *mana;* but with this personification surely the spell has nothing to do. Moreover, given such gods, no special personification of the magical instrument is needed to account for prayer. Mr. Marett's second reason is surely not different from Frazer's " despair of magic," which Marett sees clearly is no reason at all.[8] In short there is, in my opinion at least, no good reason for supposing that prayer *came from* spell, although it is very probable that many of those who despaired of spell betook themselves to prayer. There is a possible origin for prayer so natural and obvious that it is hard to understand the learned and laborious efforts made by so many scholars to explain its rise in some intricate and unexpected fashion. Granted that out of the original feeling for the impersonal *mana* the belief in personal powers arose, direct appeal to them was surely the most natural thing in the world. And if we are to consider the matter causally rather than chronologically, surely this is the most obvious and probable explanation of the rise of prayer.

I would not, however, be understood as implying that prayer and spell stand in only a chronological relation to each other. There can be no question of their mutual influence. Certain spells undoubtedly passed over into prayers, as the belief in powerful spirits or gods became more dominant. A great deal of primitive prayer was magical in spirit, and some of its magical nature has been inherited by the prayers of even the most spiritual religions. Thus the almost universal practice of closing Christian prayers with some such formula as, " In the name of Jesus Christ," or " For Jesus's sake," etc., is regarded by

[7] The latter appears only in his Encyclopedia article.

[8] As a third argument it may be urged that in some cases we actually find the spell passing over into the prayer; to which one may reply that quite as often we find the prayer passing over into the spell. These facts will be discussed a little later on.

anthropologists as a survival of the magical custom of using the names of powerful spirits as spells. But the history of religion gives us also many instances of the influence running in the other direction, instances which can only be described by the words, *from prayer to spell.* The earliest human records legible, the Pyramid Texts of Egypt, contain many a prayer, quoted from a period far more ancient even than they, and used in the texts as a magical formula.[9] The whole history of prayer in early India, from the Vedic to the Brahmanic period, is another illustration of this tendency, the spontaneous prayers of the early Rishis becoming hallowed and crystallized into magical formulas by which the gods themselves could be coerced.[10] This tendency, in fact, is by no means limited to Egypt and India, but is to be found in almost every religion. Spontaneous prayer tends to get itself repeated under recurring similar circumstances, according to the law of habit. Every one who observes the custom of " saying his prayers " at night or in the morning must have noticed how inevitably one's prayers become stereotyped and how unavoidably one formulates a kind of private ritual. Thus prayer, private as well as public, tends to become formal. Formal public prayers the individual learns from his elders, by imitation or direct instruction, and coming as most of them do with the authority of several generations behind them they are learned with reverence and regarded as sacred. The very form of words itself has a kind of sanctity, is peculiarly *religious,* and is naturally regarded as especially pleasing to the deity. Hence these formal prayers finally come to be viewed as possessing a virtue of their own, and as producing some kind of good result — even if they be in a language quite unintelligible to the one who uses them.

---

[9] So at least Breasted interprets them. See his " Religion and Thought in Ancient Egypt " (New York, Scribners: 1912), p. 95.

[10] The most primitive people of modern India, the Todas, present in their prayers a curious instance of much the same thing. Prayers, indeed, these still are in a sense, but they are in the very process of breaking down and turning into spells. What there is left of them shows that they were once simple petitions, but at present the petitional part " is often slurred over hastily and is less strictly regulated than the preliminary portion of the prayer," which consists in reciting various names, for whose sake the prayer is said to be offered. (Rivers, " The Todas," London, Macmillan: 1906, Chap. X.)

Hence the magic nature of the prayer-wheel for the Tibetan, of the Sanskrit prayer to the illiterate Hindu, of the Pali prayer to the Chinese Buddhist, and of the Latin Pater Noster to the European peasant.   When the ritualistic prayer comes thus to be considered as possessing power in itself, regardless of the mental state of him who says it, it ceases of course to be a prayer at all and becomes exactly a magic spell.

There is no doubt that all ritualistic prayer is open to this danger; but to say that is not to imply that the danger is unescapable nor that ritual is without its great counter advantages. Even the external aids of ritualistic prayer, the bent knee, the closed eye, and other bodily postures commonly used in worship, have on many a worshiper a decidedly helpful effect in bringing about the religious attitude of mind.[11]   This is partly due to the fact that most of the postures in question tend to the concentration of attention,[12] and many of them have been chosen quite naturally with nothing arbitrary or fortuitous about them, having developed directly from human nature and its instinctive expressions.   Nearly every one feels the helpfulness of closing the eyes in prayer, as this shuts out all irrelevant visual impressions.   The concentrated gaze of the Indian Yogin does much the same thing and also aids in concentration of thought; while the attitudes of kneeling or lying prostrate are the natural expressions of humility, or of what McDougal calls the instinct of self-abasement [13] and hence are real helps to

[11] Not all feel this influence.   The respondents to a questionnaire of mine upon prayer are almost evenly divided on this question, one half testifying to the helpful influence of bodily posture, the others insisting that bodily posture has no noticeable effect upon them.   Catholics are probably more susceptible to external influences of this sort than Protestants, and with them the influence of bodily posture is often considerable.   Professor Segond writes: "Les mouvements que l'on fait, dans le cult catholique, selon les divers moments des offices, les agenouillements, les prosternements, les relèvements, l'immobilité que l'on impose au corps, la fixation des regards sur l'autel, toutes ces conditions ont pour fin encore d'amener les fidèles à se recueillir; et toutes déterminent une certaine tonalité des rythmes vitaux; toutes, dès lors, règlent la conscience coenesthésique, et font ' rentrer en lui-même ' le fidèle par le sentiment de ce qui se passe en lui."   ("La Prière," Paris, Alcan: 1911, pp. 72–73.)

[12] Cf. Stolz, "Autosuggestion in Private Prayer" (published by the author, 1913), pp. 24–25

[13] "Social Psychology," pp. 62–66.

bringing about the humble attitude of the mind before God. Association also plays its part. If, as is the case with so many millions of human beings, the experience of kneeling, closing one's eyes, and clasping one's hands has from earliest childhood been associated with the emotions of reverence and religious awe, it is but natural that they should continue to suggest and incipiently to produce these emotions throughout life.

The articulation of a definite form of religious words, provided it has not become a *meaningless* form of words, acts even more forcibly in the same direction. Only for the mystically inclined is wordless prayer valuable or even possible; and as many a man, especially of the less religious or even of the less educated type, would find himself quite speechless if he depended for prayer upon his own spontaneous expression, it is well that society should furnish for all who need it some form of words expressive of universal human need and aspiration, sanctified if possible by the authority of past generations, "rich with the diction of ages."

For expression, it must be remembered, is an integral part of most comprehension. Whether or not imageless thought be possible, we make, at any rate, all our finer discriminations of meaning by the help of various real or imagined (i. e. incipient) sensuous experience and actions. The most natural and habitual of these activities and sensations are those connected with language. We think chiefly in words; and if there is any obstacle to our thought, we tend to speak the words. When we meet with a particularly blind sentence in some book, we are often helped by reading it aloud. The same assistance which this vocal expression gives us in grasping the meaning of an ambiguous sentence or of an illusive suggestion, many a mind of relatively simple organization seeks for and needs in order to realize fully the meaning of his own dumb religious aspirations. If the prayer is not given him in words, and if he does not at least incipiently mumble the words, he cannot intelligently pray. Unless there be some sort of articulation, of definite words, his prayer loses half its meaning.

Of course not only half, but all the meaning of the prayer is lost if by repetition it has become a *mere* form of words. Yet there may be a certain psychological and religious value even in prayer which has thus lost its meaning, a value seldom recognized but one that probably is an important factor in the vitality of Buddhism, Mohammedanism, Catholicism, and in fact of all really living religions that make large use of ritual. The form of words recited may act upon the mind of the worshiper in almost the same way as the bodily posture, the influence of which was recently discussed.   The verbal recitation may be associated, by the force of long-standing habit, or of deliberate effort, either with the prayerful attitude of mind in general, or with some specific line of pious meditation or prayerful aspiration.   That the Pali prayers act thus upon many an illiterate Buddhist and the Arabic prayers do the same for many an illiterate Moslem, I feel convinced.   A Buddhist monk in Mandalay said to me, "Prayer repeated by one who does not understand any of it — for instance, a Pali prayer recited by one who knows no Pali — may have some value; for it keeps the man's mind from evil thoughts for the time being, and also because the man at least *knows that he is praying* and *means* these unintelligible syllables as a prayer, and this puts him into the prayerful state of mind.   For this reason our sacred books assign *some* value even to prayers which one does not understand."   Nor is this spiritual use of prayer formula confined to the East.   The Catholic Church sometimes aims deliberately at this effect.   One is instructed while saying the ten "Hail Marys" of each decade of the Rosary to fasten the attention not upon the words repeated, but upon one of the mysteries, then upon another during the repetition of the next ten, and so on to the end.   In like manner the repetition of many of the other (Latin) prayers of the Church is used as an aid for fixing the thoughts on some religious theme not found in the prayer and for preventing them from wandering.[14]

A ritual of prayer, whether public or private, is therefore helpful to very many worshipers.   There are also, however, many persons who find public ritual disturbing and positively harmful to their devotions.   Some of these object to the ritual, some to the publicity.   Objection to ritual as such arises largely

[14] Dr. Stolz suggests that this automatic recitation of the rosary also aids in concentration of attention by providing "an outlet for distracting impressions."   ("Autosuggestion in Private Prayer," p. 38.)

from some particular conception of what prayer should be, while objection to praying in public most often comes from persons of the mystical temperament, who, having found in prayer something so inexpressibly more precious than anything which public ritual at its best can give, see in the latter a poor exchange for what they might experience in private. "I have no hesitation in saying," writes the anonymous author of "An Aspect of Prayer," "that to persons of my own disposition public prayer presents considerable difficulty; and I think that such must be the case with all those who, like myself, are keenly sensitive to their surroundings. It is very rarely indeed that I can attain to any concentration of thought when in company with others, and hence it is seldom that I take part in public worship." [15] Some mystics find even the use of definite words in prayer harmful or quite impossible. "What surprises me most," writes Mme. Guyon, "is that I had great difficulty in saying my spoken prayers which I had been in the custom of saying. As soon as I opened my mouth to pronounce them, the [divine] love seized me so strongly that I remained absorbed in profound silence and in a peace which I cannot express. I made new attempts, and passed my time in beginning my prayers without being able to finish them." [16]

It would be interesting, were it possible, to know what proportion of the community pray; but with our present data a discussion of this subject would be idle,[17] hence I turn to the more hopeful query, *Why* people pray. As was the case with the

[15] "An Aspect of Prayer," by "Digamma" (Oxford, Blackwell: 1908), p. 15.

[16] Quoted by Segond in "La Prière," p. 185. The *bienheureuse* Marguerite-Marie confessed to the same difficulty. (Id., p. 183.) St. Teresa had a similar experience and warns against the danger of *saying* fixed prayers. See Lejeune, "Introduction à la Vie Mystique" (Paris, Lethielleux: 1899), p. 87.

[17] Out of 193 respondents to questionnaires on this subject, issued a few years ago by me and my students, all but eight report that they pray. All of Mr. F. O. Beck's respondents pray (see his "Prayer: A Study in Its History and Psychology," *Am. Jour. of Relig. Psy.*, II, 107–12). One hundred out of 126 college students who replied to the questionnaire issued by Messrs. Morse and Allen report that they pray ("The Religion of One Hundred and Twenty-six College Students," *Am. Jour. of Relig. Psy.*, VI, 175–194). Owing to the selective nature of questionnaires on religion, however, these statistics seem to me to be worth but little.

parallel question in regard to public worship, we shall find that the answer to this query is two-fold: both external causes and the functions actually performed by prayer must be taken into consideration. The great external cause of prayer is, of course, the instruction which children receive and the example of others which they follow. Prayer begins in childhood as a matter of obedience and is continued for many years through the force of habit. But while some individuals keep it up through life only because of physical inertia, probably the great majority of people, when they reach late adolescence, either give it up altogether or continue to pray not only because of habit, but also because they *believe* it to be helpful and because at times they cannot help praying. Thus the prayers of praying people in their mature years are of two sorts; prayers which they " say " (largely from habit), and *real* prayers. If I may trust the evidence of the respondents to a questionnaire of mine, issued a few years ago, habit plays no large part in the prayers of mature life,[18] the explanation of the prayers of the great majority being found in two common responses, which are made repeatedly; " I pray because I can't help it," and " I pray because God hears." [19]

[18] Only five out of 185 mentioned habit as the predominant factor in their prayers. Similarly 2 per cent. of Beck's respondents pray from habit, 98 per cent. because they " feel the need of prayer."

[19] The change of feeling about prayer, its nature and value, which commonly takes place as the child develops into the adolescent is fairly well represented in the following reply of one of my respondents: " As a child I prayed as a *duty: * I *must.* I had *certitude* of God's presence and help because instructed so by parents. Prayer now, therefore, means *more* and *less.*" The sense, however, in which prayer means more than it did in childhood is of far greater importance than that in which it means less; and I find twenty-five out of the thirty-two who answered my question upon this subject insisting that prayer means much more to them than it did in childhood. Of the seven others, five reply that prayer to them means neither less nor more than formerly, while only two (and these both under twenty-seven) say that it meant more to them in childhood than it does now. It may be of interest to note some of the things in respect to which the prayers of my respondents have changed as they have grown older: and I here jot them down in abbreviated form for the benefit of any who may care to read: development of prayer from habit to a real source of strength; more universal things asked for; greater earnestness; greater desire to pray; more confidence in answer to prayer; greater realization of the limitations of prayer and fewer things, consequently, asked for; communion substituted for petition; need substituted for duty; shorter and

People who *can* help praying and who do not believe that God hears, are likely to stop praying. Morse and Allan report that of their twenty-four respondents who had ceased to pray, five stopped praying because of "negligence or indifference," nineteen because of "disbelief in the power of prayer."[20] Perhaps twenty influences are named by my respondents which in their experience have made prayer difficult or impossible, but they all may be reduced to the following three: (1) ill health, or exhaustion; (2) the sense of sin; (3) discouragement and skepticism. The last of the three is probably the one most commonly at work during the adolescent period. Seventy-nine per cent. of Morse and Allan's respondents who had ceased to pray had done so because of their disbelief in the efficacy of prayer.[21] One-third of my respondents testify that there have been times in their lives when they were convinced that prayer was useless, and in all of these cases this conviction was dated somewhere between the thirteenth and the twenty-first years. The cause of it is regularly some form of adolescent doubt,[22] either as to the existence or nature of God, or as to the reasonableness of prayer, and this skeptical view in many cases has its source in some antiquated teaching as to the nature of God or the purpose of prayer.[23] Another of the causes referred to above for the abandonment of prayer has its source also largely in theological teachings which should long ago have been outgrown. I refer to the sense of sin. And by this I do not mean actual sin, but the feeling of guilt, often of the Bunyan type, which makes the young man or woman regard himself as "lost" and too vile to come into the divine presence.[24]

less formal prayers. Sixty-six per cent. of my respondents pray more than they did as children, twenty per cent. pray less, and fourteen per cent. neither less nor more. Beck's figures are interesting in this connection: sixty-eight per cent. of his respondents prayed more, eight per cent. less, and twenty per cent. neither less nor more. What the remaining four per cent. do we are not informed.

[20] Op. cit., p. 180.

[21] Op. cit., p. 184. It must be remembered that all of Morse and Allan's respondents were adolescents.

[22] This of course does not necessarily imply a period of distress and *emotional* doubt.

[23] In the case of at least ten of my respondents the practice of prayer was abandoned because of some such unfortunate instruction.

[24] This had been the case with twenty of my respondents.

Skepticism and the sense of sin are the chief obstacles to prayer during the adolescent years. In mature life the leading deterrent seems to be nerve fatigue, exhaustion, and ill health of body and of mind. Confidence in the spiritual forces of the universe and love for them is one of the chief factors in earnest prayer, hence anything that tends to make affection less warm and the emotional life less strong tends to weaken prayer. Most people feel more affectionate when well and happy and less so when tired and ill, and these conditions can hardly fail to have their effect upon prayer. " I have done my best praying when in health," writes one woman. " My long severe illness left me too weak and full of pain to make the exertion required to make earnest prayer. In greatest pain I am passive." " When very tired at night," writes another, " it is hard to pray earnestly — it seems a matter of form." " When I am in good health and have much to be thankful for I feel like praying. I simply have to thank God for all the good things He gives." Some people, to be sure, pray most when in ill health, but the prayers made at such times seem to have, relatively, but little zest. " I think I pray more in poor health," writes one respondent, " perhaps a groaning prayer." [25]

It goes without saying (yet here *pro forma* it must be said) that one of the great reasons why adolescents and adults continue to pray is because they have needs, and they either believe that prayer will aid them to get what they need, or else they simply cannot help expressing their needs in some kind of prayer form — if it be but an ejaculation — quite regardless of theory. Petitional prayer is of course not the only kind, but it was the original form of prayer and it still is

[25] The whole question of the conditions of real as opposed to merely verbal prayer, and to the methods best adapted to produce a kind of prayer that shall be unquestionably worth while, is worthy of careful investigation. It is not a subject upon which the usual questionnaire method would be of much value unless the respondents were carefully chosen from the rather small class of *virtuosos* in prayer — if such a phrase may be permitted. Most of us know a few men and women who seem to have great " power in prayer," and in whose lives prayer is unquestionably a source of genuine efficiency. If a fair number of such persons could be induced to analyze their psychological methods and their experience in prayer, the results might be very enlightening. For an admirable discussion of this question see Eleanor Rowland's " The Right to Believe " (Boston, Houghton, Mifflin: 1909), Chap. VI.

and very likely always will be an important form,— for many people probably almost the only conceivable form. Out of sixty-five respondents who answered my question concerning the nature of their prayers, forty-two described them as "consisting largely of petitions," the twenty-three others saying that petition was in their prayers a very subordinate matter. It is interesting in this connection to note that seventeen of my respondents believe God's actions are changed by their prayers as against twenty-six who feel sure that this is not the case. A comparison of the different answers shows that about half of those who believe that God's actions are in no way affected by their prayers continue to make prayers which are "largely petitions," either because the felt need is so strong that it breaks forth into words regardless of all theory, or because (in rare cases) the benefit experienced from the formulation of one's desires is too great to be dispensed with. In the words of Emerson, "What we pray to ourselves for is always granted." [26]

As to the content of petitional prayer, it seems plain that among the more intelligent appeals for "spiritual blessings" largely predominate, and that "material blessings" and particular ends play a relatively subordinate rôle. An exception, indeed, must be made to this for times of crisis, such as grief, danger, etc.; for then the strong wish within the mind will force itself into the form of a prayer, if the individual is in the habit of praying at all. But at normal times the blessings asked for seem to be chiefly of a general and "spiritual sort." Only thirty-four of Morse and Allan's one hundred and twenty-six college students prayed for "definite and temporary ends." Seventy-three per cent. of Beck's respondents characterized their prayers as "prayers for spiritual blessings, i. e. for better disposition, firmer resolution, and redeemed inward nature." Seventy-five per cent. of them considered it a mistake to pray for a change in the weather; and twenty-nine out of ninety-three of my respondents state specifically that there are things for which they would not pray, several others implying the same thing. The tendency to limit petitional prayer in normal

[26] The mental attitude of those holding these diverse views about prayer is illustrated by citations from their responses in my article. "An Empirical Study of Prayer" (*Am. Jour. of Rel. Psy.*, 1V, esp. pp. 50–51).

times to general and spiritual ends is probably on the increase, as the belief in the invariability of natural law spreads throughout the community.[27]   Yet it must not be supposed that the belief in and the practice of praying for almost anything and everything has been by any means universally given up.   Over half my respondents believe in praying for pretty much everything one wants,— evil things, of course excepted.   The *Messenger of the Sacred Heart* publishes monthly a list of "Thanksgivings" for various favors and answers to prayer sent in by good Catholics from all parts of the United States. The list includes such things as recovery from various illnesses, marriage, "a successful party," "increase of salary," "cow recovered," "five deals made," "preserved from active duty," etc., etc.   The *Messenger* for August, 1919, announces, "Total number of Thanksgivings for the month, 4,876,932."   The "Pittsburgh Bible Institute" conducts a daily prayer meeting the purpose of which is to concentrate the prayers of a number of godly persons upon various petitions, which are sent in to them from all over the world with a request for their prayer. These petitions are systematically recorded and numbered, and those answered are regularly announced in the semi-annual publication of the Institute.   In August, 1919, the number of

[27] The feeling that there are things for which one should not pray is not very old.   In an oft quoted passage, Emerson refers, on the authority of Ezra Ripley, to a minister of Sudbury "who being at the Thursday lecture in Boston, heard the officiating clergyman praying for rain.   As soon as the service was over, he went to the petitioner and said, 'You Boston ministers, as soon as the tulip wilts under your windows, go to church and pray for rain, until all Concord and Sudbury are under water'" (Lectures and Biographical Sketches.   Boston, Houghton, Mifflin: 1891, p. 363).   Nor are the prayers of the fervent limited to things like the weather.   A rather dreadful instance of what prayer may be used for is to be found in Maitland's "Life of Anna Kingsford."   She was, at one time, greatly opposed to vivisection and was especially wrought up against Claude Bernard, the distinguished French physiologist, as one of the leaders of it.   She felt, in fact, it would be well if the earth could be rid of him.   Hence "with passionate energy she invoked the wrath of God upon him, at the same time hurling her whole spiritual being at him with all her might, as if with intent to smite him then and there with destruction."   Claude Bernard died suddenly soon after and she considered it a direct answer to prayer, saying: "It has been strongly borne in upon my mind that he has indeed come to his death through my agency." Quoted from Maitland's "Life of Anna Kingsford," by Tuckett, "The Evidence for the Supernatural" (London, K. Paul: 1911), p. 144.

petitions thus presented in public prayer had reached nearly 80,000. The blessings asked for are largely "spiritual" but also include such things as passing examinations, winning lawsuits, the healing of a sore finger, getting good servants, securing a good tenant, getting rid of undesirable boarders, etc.[28] If an emergency arises and one is in need of immediate help one telephones, and the requisite prayer is expedited.[29]

The question of the objective answer to prayer for particular things need not detain us here,[30] the point of chief interest with us, who are studying the religious consciousness, being the fact that very many people believe firmly in such special answers

[28] This belief in praying for all sorts of personal benefits is, of course, quite as common among European Catholics as among American Catholics and Protestants. The walls and columns of the church of Notre Dame de Lourdes, for example, are silent witnesses to this belief, covered as they are with chiselled inscriptions of prayer or of thankfulness for answered prayers of this special sort. The following examples taken almost at random from scores, are typical:

"Notre Dame de Lourdes, benissez notre union. Protegez notre famille et donnez nous le travail dans notre commerce."

"À notre Dame de Lourdes temoignage de profonde reconnaisance offert par la famille B de Constantinople comblée de bienfaits par le gain d'un important procès recommandé à son intervention."

[29] A lady in Pittsburgh recently diverted a fire from her house in this way, it being sent (in answer to prayer) in another direction. See "The Record of Faith" (Pittsburgh), V, 64.— Confidence in the almost mechanical action of prayer is not confined to Catholics and "evangelicals." Many of the "New Thought" groups have quite as firm a faith in the efficacy of prayer as has the Pittsburgh Bible Institute. One of these groups whose headquarters is in Kansas possesses a prayer-organization similar to that in Pittsburgh. A case has recently come to my knowledge in which one of its members made use of its advantages in a way not mentioned even in the "Messenger of the Sacred Heart" or the Bible Institute's "Record of Faith." The member in question is a lady of wealth and culture and of high social standing. She was spending the winter of 1917 in Washington, and had planned to give a large reception, but when the day arrived found it almost impossible to carry out her plans because of an extremely bad cold in her head. Fortunately at 11 A. M. she remembered her principles and telegraphed to the Kansas prayer center. By two in the afternoon her nose had ceased running and she was able to receive her guests without the aid of endless handkerchiefs.

[30] The reader will find a discussion of this subject in the article of mine already referred to, "An Empirical Study of Prayer," pp. 53–61. I might note here that sixty out of ninety of my respondents both believe in special answer to prayer and are convinced that they have had such answers in their own experience. See also Chapters IV and V of Dr. Stolz's monograph.

and that this is one of the great reasons why they pray. Most religious people, however, would pretty certainly continue to pray even if they lost all faith in special answers. This is shown by the fact that a very large number of religious people no longer cherish that faith yet continue to pray (and not merely out of habit), and by the further fact that most even of those who retain the belief in question find in prayer something of very much greater value than an easy means of satisfying particular wants. For there are other kinds of prayer beside the habitual and the petitional. Intense joy and thankfulness, for example, express themselves as naturally, and for some persons as inevitably, in prayer, as does the sense of crying need.[31] Such an expression of thankfulness, which does not ask for anything but simply longs somehow to get into communication with the great source from which " all blessings flow " is incipiently a " prayer of communion." If all prayers were classified into two or three leading types, the " prayer of communion," in which the presence of a higher Power is felt, would have to be made one of the chief subdivisions. How generally this type of prayer is shared in the community it would, of course, be impossible to say. Seventy per cent of Beck's respondents feel the presence of a higher power while in prayer, and sixty-five per cent of mine (110 out of 170) testify to the same thing. By no means so large a percentage of the adolescents who answered Morse and Allan's questionnaire claim to have had this experience;[32] but the difference may be in part due to the difference in age. While many good people who regularly pray know little or nothing of this experience, there can be no doubt that it, or something sufficiently like it to go by the same general name, is the leading characteristic of the prayers of nearly all more deeply religious persons.

The experience known as communion with God is one of the most interesting things in the psychology of religion.[33] So far

[31] Seven of Morse and Allan's respondents say that one reason why they pray is because prayer " is a way to glorify God." This is another illustration of what, in our last chapter, was called " objective worship."

[32] Only forty-five out of one hundred and twenty-six said they had a sense of communion; thirty-nine answering " No " to the question, and forty-two giving no answer at all.

[33] An analysis of this experience is to be found in W. S. Ranson's " Stud-

at least as I can judge, it is neither negative in its nature nor purely imitative in its origin. It is a very positive — sometimes almost a violent — experience. It is indigenous to every religion and to every social class, and *seems* to arise spontaneously among all sorts and conditions of men. Of course, like most other things which are worth cultivation and imitation, it is often transplanted by deliberate effort into lives which, but for the effort, would never have known it. Described, as it always is, in glowing terms by those who have experienced it in its freshness, it has become a thing to be desired, and its nurture is inculcated as a duty, and its appearance watched for. Many a good man to whom it is native in only slight degree longs for it, expects it, and at length persuades himself that he too has felt it. Thus it has come as near to being a social convention as so purely private and personal an experience can come to be. And as, in its induced and cultivated form, it contains so large an element of imitation and auto-suggestion, the temptation to the psychologist is strong to explain it *all* by means of those light-bringing terms.

This imitative element does beyond all doubt explain a good deal of the " sense of communion " in the case of many of my one hundred and ten respondents who testify to having felt it. This is shown by some of their answers to the following question: " In praying do you consider that you are communing with the Being to whom you pray? Is there any evidence of this? If so, what? " I shall set down some of the answers: " I endeavor to do so. At times a certain awe and quietness not felt at other times." " I consider so, but can give no evidence." " At times it seems as if God is very near, but more often there is an absence of that quickening of the heart one has when talking to one he loves." " Yes, to a slight extent. No evidence except my own feelings or rather faith." " Perhaps I do not commune with Him directly. I try to exclude all other thoughts." " To some extent, but it is possible that it is imagination. Or it may be that my strong faith in

ies in the Psychology of Prayer " (*Am. Jour. of Relig. Psy.*, I, 129–42). Mr. Ranson finds the essential elements of the experience in the " unification of consciousness through æsthetic contemplation of God." This is an excellent description of many cases of the phenomenon, but is hardly of universal application.

a spiritual world may increase the feeling of actual spiritual communion."

In spite of the imitative factor plainly present in all my respondents upon this subject it is perfectly plain to me that there are other factors also at work.[34] All speech originates through imitation, yet all speech *is* not imitation. The experience of "communion" to which my respondents testify doubtless had its origin in part through the influence and example of others; but once it comes, it is a perfectly real experience of a very definite sort, and by no means merely an imagination or a form of pious words. And when we turn from my very humble and commonplace respondents to the saints and mystics, we shall of course find the spontaneous element of this experience amply verified. This, however, is a question which belongs not here but in the consideration of mysticism.

Prayer of the "communion" type often presents itself under the form of an incipient conversation. The individual praying talks to the Great Listener and feels at times some faint suggestion of a response. That prayer should be of this conversational nature is not surprising; for, as Cooley has so well pointed out, "the mind lives in perpetual conversation." [35] In the prayerful individual this universal tendency to talk to oneself is modified into a longing to talk with God. And, as I have indicated, for the more mystically minded, the result may be not a monologue but something like a conversation. The spiritual directors of the Catholic Church often make a point of instilling this conception of prayer as an ideal upon their pupils.[36] And many a soul not mystic enough to catch

[34] This subject will be dealt with at greater length in the chapters on mysticism.

[35] "Human Nature and the Social Order," p. 54.

[36] "La forme concréte, vivante, que doit prendre le recueillement en général, mais que doit révêtir surtout le receueillement que nous déscrivons ici, c'est la forme d'un entretien avec Dieu. Or, dans un certain entretien, la parole n'est pas toujours à la même personne: chacun des interlocuteurs doit parler à son tour. Savoir parler et savoir écouter sont deux preceptes de la conversation également importants. Eh bien, n'arrivet-il pas, dans nos entretiens avec Dieu, que nous laissions dans l'oubli l'un de ces préceptes? Et lequel? Ce n'est certes pas celui qui nous autorise à parler: nous parlons assez, nous parlons même souvent beaucoup trop. Mais écoutons-nous suffisament Dieu qui parle? N'étouffons-nous pas sa voix par nos interruptions indiscrètes, par un flux de paroles qui absorbe

God's response, finds in the mere confession of his sins and needs and longings a kind of peace that comes in no other way. Here, indeed, is one of the great pragmatic values of the God-idea. For many a man God is not so much Creator or Giver of specific things, as the Great Confessor, He who sees us as we really are, and with whom alone of all beings we may be utterly frank. The need of confession, of pouring out all that is most pressing in one's mind, is with impulsive temperaments almost universal, and prayer is the great outlet for this urgent longing.

With temperaments of the more philosophic type, the prayer of communion takes on a more cosmic aspect. It is the moment of larger views, the vision of the Whole of things in their cosmic setting, the means of gaining the true perspective in which small things that had loomed large resume their appropriate and petty place, and hence it is a way of liberation from the tyranny of little worries. With the more mystical, it is a conscious union with the All.[37] In Professor Hocking's phrase, it is the recovery of the " natural vigor of the whole-idea." It is an act by which we free ourselves, moreover, not merely from worries but from the many-sided provincialisms which practical life and social life force upon us. Thus it is a winning at length to the purity of selfhood. " We must," writes Hocking, " know how to shake off the prepossessions of our theoretic wills; to regard all ambitions and duties for the time as non-existent; to reduce all reality to the primitive terms of self, universe, and the present moment (wherein everything begins from the beginning). In this stark, original selfhood, detached from action and from the warping of the interests of action, we view all that active career as in a drama, as the life of another, in the light of what we can then and there mus-

notre attention au point de nous rendre sourds à la parole divine? Cette surdité n'est-elle pas même chez nous à l'état chronique? Soupçonnons-nous seulement que Dieu ait sa façon de parler à l'âme? Comme son langage, dit Courbon, est tout spirituel, intérieur et sans bruit, il n'y a que ceux qui sont fidèles à l'ecouter qui ont le bonheur d'entendre cette divine voix quoiqu'il parle à tous et qu'il frappe souvent à la porte de nos coeurs." (Lejeune, " Introduction à la Vie Mystique," pp. 127–28.)

[37] This is the type of prayer which Miss Strong calls the " æsthetic "— one of the two tendencies in the " completely social type " of prayer. See Chap. V of her " Psychology of Prayer " (Chicago University Press: 1909).

ter of the whole. Its loves and hates rise up before us in a more universal frame. We must recall especially whatever is still to us of effortless value, whatever we do still sincerely enjoy and love, and we must pray for the vision of the whole of which these various goods are fragments, and upon which they depend as their absolute. I use the word ' pray,' because, in the end, there is no other word which conveys that attitude of will in which effort is so combined with non-effort, and self assertion with consciousness of absolute dependence. Nor do I know why this word should be translated into anything more scholastic. The insight we require is both a right and a gift, the justest gift in all experience; we dare not be too proud to comply with its evident conditions. We must know that in doing these things, we are already using a degree of mystic insight; we are relying upon an attachment to the whole which is too deep in us to be lost or overcome; we are striving to ' enter into ourselves,' to recognize this attachment for what it is, the love of the God of that alienated world. This is prayer." [38]

An experience and an activity such as is suggested here is plainly a very different thing from the prayer which one " says." It is not a petition for anything at all, nor can it even fairly be classed as in any ordinary sense a conversation. As Frederic Myers put it, "If we ask to *whom* to pray, the answer (strangely enough) must be that *that* does not much matter." [39] Nor need a prayer of this sort have anything to do with words. St. François de Sales compares the prayer of the mystic to the communion of lovers. " Love speaks not merely by the tongue, but by the eyes, the posture, the sighs; yes even silence takes the place of words." [40] And many a Catholic director recommends this wordless prayer, which is called " *colloque de silence.*"

It is evident that prayer of the sort we have been describing shades off imperceptibly into mysticism on the one hand, and into a kind of meditation and self-realization on the other. To mysticism we shall revert in the following chapters, but a word must here be said concerning the kind of contemplation

---

[38] " The Meaning of God in Human Experience " (New Haven, Yale University Press: 1912), pp. 438–39.

[39] Quoted in James's " Varieties," p. 467.

[40] Quoted by Lejeune, op. cit., p. 133.

which is midway between prayer and self-analysis or philosophic thought.   Intense spiritual aspiration, the emotional contemplation of an ideal, is a kind of prayer.   " Prayers," says Stanley Hall, " are paraligms of aspiration for the higher life and for unity with the great all." [41]   Another illustration of what I have here in mind will be found in the following citation from Dr. Cabot's " What Men Live By."   " We often advise each other to think it over and see what *on the whole* seems best; or we say, ' *All things considered,* I have decided to go.'   Anyone who did this would be near to prayer. . . . ' Considering all things ' is turning from part to whole, from brilliant near-seen views, all foreground, no perspective, to a vision like that from a mountain top.   Whoever tries to ' see life steadily and see it whole,' by retiring to a viewpoint detached from the current quotations and the latest news, has moved in the direction of prayer." [42]

It was largely this process of meditative self-realization that the Stoic philosophers meant by prayer.   " When you happen to be ruffled a little by any outward accident," wrote Marcus Aurelius, " retire immediately into your reason, and do not move out of tune any further than needs must; for the sooner you return to harmony, the more you will get it into your own power." [43]   Professor Segond, who in his learned work " La Prière " seems to identify prayer as such with this inward-turning self-realization (with, to be sure, a certain mystic tinge), connects the experience with cœnæsthesia and the feeling of the bodily rhythms.   Self-concentration of the sort found in prayer — " *de rentrer en soi,*" " *de prendre conscience de soi* " — he therefore identifies with the fading away of external and practical considerations and the " evaporating of the individuality." [44]   But while this is a true description of the experience of some, it will hardly hold for all.   It is doubtless

<hr />

[41] " Educational Problems," Vol. I, p. 145.

[42] " What Men Live By " (Boston, Houghton, Mifflin: 1914), pp. 275–76.   An admirable and extensive discussion of prayer from this point of view will be found in Drake's " Problems of Religions " (Boston, Houghton, Mifflin: 1916), Chap. XII.

[43] " Meditations," translated by Jeremy Collier (London, Scott), Bk. VI, 11 (p. 86).

[44] Op. cit., pp. 70–82.

true that psychological analysis will find cœnæsthesia in the content of the prayer-experience, but this fact should not be regarded as over important or illuminating. And while it is also true that in certain types of ecstatic mysticism the individuality tends to evaporate, the chief characteristic of prayer as self-realization lies in the fact that it is an attempt to find more and more explicitly just what one's true individuality really is and what is involved in it. "The simplest rational account of prayer," writes Hocking, "would probably be this: a voluntary recollection of those deepest principles of will, or preference, which the activities of living tend to obscure." [45] Professor Royce quotes from one of his former students the following description of what prayer means: "When things are too much for me," the student said, "and I am down on my luck, and everything is dark, I go alone by myself, and I bury my head in my hands, and I think hard that God must know it all and will see how matters really are, and understands me. And so I try to get myself together. And that for me is prayer." [46] One of my former students writes me as follows: "It is a good thing to formulate definitely one's desires and ideals, and by examining into their motives decide whether or not they are worthy. In asking for anything I always try to make up my mind why I want it and what will be the result of my obtaining it, and in consequence prayer sometimes leads me to give up cherished schemes. My conception of God is at present rather abstract than personal, and so my prayers are not often petitions for definite things. I incline to believe that petitions do not affect God. Still I think it best to make petitions for no other reason than for the stimulus that they give me in the quest of that for which I have asked. Most of my prayer is a seeking after what is best for me or for others and therefore to be asked for and striven after. By determining to strive after it, I bring into play a better self within to aid in obtaining it. . . . For several years before I came to the conception of prayer which I now hold I had convinced myself of the uselessness of a great deal of what is called prayer,

[45] Op. cit., p. 376.
[46] "Sources of Religious Insight" (New York, Scribner's: 1912), p. 133.

though I still clung to early habits of formal petitions, till, when I was about twenty or twenty-one (three years ago) my present ideas, which had long been growing, were fairly well formulated and I felt justified in discarding a worthless custom. The subjective benefits of prayer are sufficient to make it very much worth while. In fact, if such earnest self-examination and meditation as I have described is to be considered prayer (and I so consider it) it is indispensable." [47]

Cases such as those just cited illustrate the obvious fact that prayer of the sort we have been discussing may be of considerable benefit in a purely subjective fashion. Nor are the subjective benefits of prayer confined to any one type. The immediate value of the prayer of confession has already been indicated: it relieves the pent-up feelings, clarifies the conscience, and strengthens the will; and that it does so can no more be denied by the atheist than by the believer. The fact that it does these things is dependent upon no theory, but is a purely empirical observation. Its *modus operandi,* in fact, is constantly better understood. The methods used by Freud, Jung, Prince, Sidis, and other psychiatrists, of curing various psychic and neurotic disorders through the unearthing of some buried psychic complex, have demonstrated the great therapeutic value of confession. Further study in recent years has, moreover, shown that prayer can be of great assistance in the healing of disease not only in the way just indicated but also very largely through its power of suggestion. The value of the prayer of communion has been sung by many a mystic; but one does not have to go to the mystic to hear its praises. So unmystical a psychologist as Stanley Hall can write of it as follows: " The culmination of prayer is psychologically very analogous in the moral sphere to the hedonic narcosis that Scho-

---

[47] In a case that has recently come to my knowledge, a man prayed for light in the midst of a political crisis when his tired brain refused to work from the strain of toil and worry; and in the calm that succeeded his prayer, there came into his mind a course of action which, indeed, was perfectly reasonable (as, in fact, the successful issue showed), yet which he might probably never have thought of had he not had recourse to some such mental sedative as prayer. Mere meditation would not have done it. The religious element was essential, as it brought the quiet confidence and reliance on a greater Power which alone could disperse the weariness and worry.

penhauer ascribes to the moment of the most intense æsthetic
contemplation with surcease of all pain.   This is why mystic
prayer is sometimes so regenerating.   ' He prays best who loves
best,' and the acme of the communion of love is a transport
which usually leaves the soul permanently changed because
it has been caught up by the oversoul and received a higher
potentialization.   The soul has reopened the original well-
spring of life and perhaps glimpsed its own final destiny, augmented every higher motivation.   This makes prayer the opener
of new and higher ways, the purest psychic expression of the
evolutionary push-up in us." [48]

The influence of prayer upon the general hedonic consciousness is a fact of almost universal observation among praying
people.   It would be safe to say that there is no other method
comparable to it, either in simplicity of application or in certainty of result, for turning sorrow into resignation, fear into
courage, turmoil into peace.   An example of its power, given by
the anonymous author of " An Aspect of Prayer," is worth
quoting here:

" About the age of twenty-one I was involved in a set of circumstances which seemed as if they must inevitably lead to
the ruin of my career in life. . . . Thus it befell that during
these years I resumed the habit of regular prayer.   There was
a certain blindness and despair about the prayer.   I hoped for
little: I expected nothing.   The circumstances themselves
seemed to kill my faith in the beneficent ordering of nature.
Yet I prayed despite it all,— mainly, I think, because it seemed
impossible for unaided human nature to surmount the difficulties which faced me.   But there gradually dawned upon me the
fact that these prayers, blind though they were, were not without avail.   It is somewhat difficult to describe the actual nature of the phenomenon,— for as such it soon presented itself
to my mind, and as such I have since noted instances of it.   The
circumstances of which I have spoken tended to produce extreme mental depression.   A cloud had, as it were, descended
on my life.   But I noticed that after earnest prayer this depression was greatly relieved, and at times completely vanished.

[48] " Jesus, the Christ, in the Light of Psychology " (New York, Double-
day: 1917), Vol. II, p. 496.

That which struck me most with regard to the phenomenon was its irrationality. What I mean is that the relief was experienced again and again without any consciousness of its cause. I could not attribute it to a feeling of satisfaction at having performed a religious duty, for I noticed that the relief came in many cases when no such feeling of satisfaction was or had been present in my mind. The importance of the phenomenon in respect to one's life was such as to lead me to further observation of it; and this process of induction has with me extended over a period of more than twenty years. I am, of course, well aware of the tendency of the human mind to fail to notice negative instances in such a process, and I know how peculiarly one is exposed to the temptation of ignoring them or explaining them away in the case of a series of instances when the positive elements point to a conclusion such as one would desire to be true. In my own case this tendency is corrected by the fact that a forced or faulty induction would not convey any comfort to me. In watching this phenomenon therefore I have carefully checked by observation, and have excluded all instances in which some intermediary cause intervened between prayer and the mental happiness resulting from it. In the thousands of instances which have come under my observation, for the phenomenon is at least of daily occurrence, I have never observed any case in which earnest prayer has not been ' answered ' (to use the ordinary word) by an increase of mental happiness. I have spoken of this as ' irrational,' because it does not arise from any physical or external cause, nor indeed from any of those internal causes to which such feeling can be ascribed. Its irrationality consists in the fact that, if my induction be valid and correct, it is connected with the phenomenon of earnest prayer by a chain of causation which may be explicable by conjecture but is not determinable by reason." [49]

This case is, of course, in some respects unusual, but the same kind of help to which " Digamma " here testifies is being constantly found by an innumerable number of common-place people all around us. A considerable majority of Morse and Allan's respondents report that after prayer they feel a burden

[49] Op. cit., pp. 11–13.

of some sort removed from their minds; they feel " peace,"
" tranquillity," " renewed strength," " spiritual uplift."   Beck
says of his respondents, " Almost every answerer feels the manifestation of unusual power [from praying] which gives ability
to accomplish ends."   My respondents speak of prayer as having a calming influence upon the nerves; as resulting in " spiritual uplift," self-confidence, the substitution of love for hate
and of courage for fear, an increase of strength both physical
and moral, help in resisting temptation and in clear thinking,
joy, relief from care, and the sense that " all's well."   It is,
indeed, impossible to read over the responses to a questionnaire
on this subject without being impressed by the vital part which
prayer plays in the lives of the respondents.   This is the most
striking thing about the answers taken as a whole.   On other
points the language used is frequently conventional enough, but
when the question of the value of prayer in one's actual experience is raised, the words and expressions often take on a freshness and spontaneity which bear unmistakable witness to the
genuineness of the experience of which they speak.

The subjective benefits of prayer are so unmistakable that
one who had lost all belief in any objective relation between
the praying individual and a higher power, might very wisely
continue to pray (if he could) purely for the sake of the reflex
effects of prayer upon his own mind and character.   The case
cited a few pages back of a former student of mine who continues the use of petitional prayer merely for its subjective
influence shows that this deliberate use of prayer as self-culture
with no reference to any Being who shall hear and answer, is
not only possible but (at least in rare cases) actual.   The classical example of this sort of thing is, of course, to be found in
Jainism and Buddhism.   Though the more " advanced " Jaina
monks have given up prayer altogether for meditation, very
many of them, as well as many of the intelligent laymen, continue to pray, because experience has shown them that prayer,
though inconsistent with their theory, is helpful in practice.
Similarly the Buddhist monk in Mandalay quoted a few pages
back, said to me: " The intelligent Buddhist does not pray
for wealth nor health nor anything.   He repeats certain phrases
to the Buddha because of their good influence upon him.   The

whole thing is subjective and the effects to be expected are spiritual only. Of course the value of prayer in this sense is dependent on the state of mind of the man who prays."

The question whether prayer is nothing more than a mind state having a certain subjective value, such as auto-suggestion or the enjoyment of music, or whether it is also an objective relation between the prayerful soul and some sort of " Higher Power " above or " Spiritual World " round about, from Whom or from which new influxes of spiritual life may actually come,— this is for metaphysics rather than for psychology. Psychology may and should point out, however, that the subjective effects of prayer are almost invariably due, directly or indirectly, to some real faith in the objective relation. A few Jaina and Buddhist monks, and a few earnest " emancipated " minds the world over, may succeed in reaping some subjective benefits from prayer after they have given up the belief in any external influence; but a large part of this effect they can reap only because of an early faith in some external influence, and also (probably) because at the moment of prayer they put themselves back temporarily into something like the believing state of mind. Except in so far as this is true, their " prayer " is merely meditation. That meditation may have excellent subjective effects is not to be denied, but no one with any knowledge of the psychology of religion will claim for it an influence equal to that which results from the earnest prayer of the man of faith. The subjective effects of prayer, in fact, seem to be roughly proportional to the strength of the faith of him who prays. The benefits which the Jaina and Buddhist monks reap from prayer are probably insignificant compared with those which come to the earnest believer in prayer as an objective means of communicating with the Divine. The number of persons, moreover, who would be able to get any beneficent results from prayer once they had lost their faith in its objective nature, is exceedingly limited. Few people possess the histrionic ability and the volitional control over the imagination requisite for any notable effects from prayer without faith, and few even of those who possess these abilities would think it worth while to make use of them in such prayer for the sake of possible subjective benefits. For every case like that of the unbelieving student quoted above who still continued to pray, probably fifty cases could be cited of those who had completely given up prayer because of loss of faith in it as an actual relation between man and God.

This being the case it is interesting to note the fervor with which certain psychological writers extol the value of prayer and in the same breath either state or imply that its value is due entirely to subjective conditions. These writers seem to have forgotten what Dr. L. P. Jacks has well called the " alchemy of thought," " to interpret experience is to change it." [50] For since the subjective value of prayer is chiefly due to the belief that prayer has values which are *not* subjective, it will with most persons evaporate altogether once they learn that it is *all* subjective. Hence if it be true both that the subjective value of prayer is very great and also that it is the only value which prayer possesses, this latter fact should be assiduously kept secret. The psychologist who knows it and publishes it broadcast is like the physician who should disclose to his patient the great value and the true nature of bread pills. " Take these," the doctor may be conceived as saying; " take three of these after each meal and seven after Sunday dinner, and they will completely cure you. They contain nothing but bread and have no value in themselves, absolutely none; but since you don't know this fact and are unaware that you are being fooled, their subjective effect upon you will be invaluable."

No, if the subjective value of prayer be all the value it has, we wise psychologists of religion had best keep the fact to ourselves; otherwise the game will soon be up and we shall have no religion left to psychologize about. We shall have killed the goose that laid our golden egg.

[50] " The Alchemy of Thought " (London, Williams and Norgate: 1911), p. 108.

CHAPTER XVI

THE MILDER FORM OF MYSTIC EXPERIENCE

THERE is probably not another word in the English language so overworked and so ill-used as mysticism. It would not be difficult to produce some two dozen, more or less well known definitions of the term, each differing in something besides words from all the rest, and every one representing some fairly common usage.[1] To a considerable extent, the difference in purpose and in point of view is responsible for this wide divergence; and one's point of view must of course largely determine one's choice of a definition. Our point of view being here psychological we must seek for a definition which shall take mysticism as a psychological concept and make use of purely psychological differentia. And so far as I can see, if we are to do this — if we are to regard mysticism as a peculiar form of experience differing *psychologically* from other forms — we must give it a definition broad enough to include many things which are not specifically religious. One of the best short definitions of mysticism that have been suggested is " the consciousness of a Beyond." This is, of course, indefinite, but by making it somewhat more elaborate and explicit we can construct a definition which though clumsy will, I think, fill all the essential requirements. I propose, therefore, that for our purposes, mysticism be defined as the sense of the presence of a being or reality through other means than the ordinary perceptive processes or the reason. It is the *sense* or *feeling* of this presence, not the belief in it, and it is not the result of sight or hearing or touch, nor is it a conclusion one reaches by thought; it is, instead, an immediate and intuitive experience. The words " being " and " reality " as used in the definition must also be taken in a very broad sense. They may refer to a very definite individual, but they must also be allowed to have all the vagueness of the word

[1] Cf., for instance, Pacheu, " Introduction a la Psychologie des Mystiques " (Paris, Oudin: 1901), pp. 26–43.

" the Beyond," as used in the short definition quoted above.
Taken in the sense now defined, mysticism may, I think, be regarded as a psychological concept.   And as so defined it is, of
course, much too broad to be confined to purely religious phenomena.[2]   It includes the experiences called telepathic, the intuitive sense which the lover says he has for his love, which the
mother says she has for her child, the " possession " of the Shaman, the cosmic consciousness of the poet, as well as the ecstasy
of the " mystic."

But it is only with religious mysticism that we are here
concerned.   And, of course, religious mysticism differs from
other forms in that it has a religious object.   In other words,
the being or reality whose presence is felt is here regarded as
" divine."   Perhaps it is the personal Jesus, perhaps it is
the vague cosmical and pantheistic " Beyond," but so long as
the mystic directly feels the presence of what he regards as the
Divine we have religious mysticism.   I make no pretense that
this distinction is a psychological distinction, but I think it is
at least perfectly plain and simple.   And as the non-religious
forms of mysticism do not here concern us, I shall as a rule use
the term mysticism without modifying adjective to denote the
more limited form of experience which I have just described
as " religious mysticism."

But religious mysticism itself is no simple matter.   To be
sure all the mystics of every land and century may in one
sense be said to speak the same language; they understand each
other and no one else fully understands them.   And yet among
themselves they differ very considerably, and religious mysticism in general might well be divided into a large number of
distinct types.   If, for example, we should make our classification on the basis of the divine object whose presence the mystic
claims to " feel," we should have more kinds of mysticism than
there are religions.   No such elaborate subdivision, however, is
needed or desirable; for, in fact, if we examine even superficially the cases of religious mysticism they fall of themselves
into two quite distinct types, which indeed blend into each other
but are in principle quite distinguishable, and thus form a clas-

[2] Cf. Coe, " The Mystical as a Psychological Concept," *Jour. of Philosophy*, VI, 197–202.

sification which is both natural and illuminating. The two classes I have in mind might be called the mild and the extreme types. The former is common-place and easily overlooked, it is to be found among perfectly normal persons, and is never carried to extremes. The other type is usually so striking in its intensity and in its effects that it attracts notice and is regularly regarded as a sign either of supernatural visitation or of a pathological condition. Cases of this sort are generally found among intensely religious persons whose nervous systems are in a state of somewhat unstable equilibrium. And in these more intense cases of mysticism the simple " sense of a Beyond " develops into the ecstasy and the vision.

I cannot too strongly emphasize the importance of making and keeping clear this subdivision within religious mysticism. No just idea can be formed upon the subject and no sound conclusion as to the nature and place and value of mysticism can be reached unless one constantly keeps in mind the distinction between these two kinds of mystic states. A great deal of otherwise very valuable work on the subject has become exceedingly misleading for the incautious reader because of a failure to make this distinction. It is a common thing for a writer to make some general statement about mysticism as such which really applies to only one of the two types and not at all to the other. And the failure to make the distinction in question is particularly unfortunate because when either type is taken alone and by itself to represent mysticism the choice is not likely to fall on the mild and unobtrusive sort. Murisier is not the only writer who tells us that mysticism is the heart of religion, and then proceeds to examine the most extreme cases of the most extreme type, identifying these with mysticism and proving thereby that the heart of religion is rotten.[3]

Thus it has come about, quite naturally, that the pathological side of mysticism has been greatly over-emphasized, and that mysticism, and with it religion, is beginning to get a bad name. Several things have worked together to bring about this over-

[3] Cf. also Charbonier: " En fouillant la vie des mystiques, je vis claire-ment qu'ils avaient tous été malades " (" Maladies des Mystiques." Bruxelles, Manceaux: 1875, p. 5). Marie: " Saintes ou possedées, peu importe. Nous savons qu'elles sont tout simplement des malades." (" Mysticism et Folie," Paris: 1907, p. 131.)

emphasis on the abnormal aspects of mysticism. In the first place it is very striking and hence naturally interesting. The milder type is very commonplace, usually shrinks from expression and publicity, and in fact is often regarded as not worth being expressed. The more extreme type easily gets itself expressed and described (in some fashion) and inevitably attracts attention. Moreover the Church has throughout its long history regarded the trances and visions of its obedient and orthodox mystics as supernaturally inspired, and hence as of infinitely greater value than cases of the milder type, where no supernatural agency seemed to be involved. And the modern psychologist, naturally, has (for once) agreed with the Church in singling out just these extreme cases, though for a very different reason, namely because they offer such good illustrations of various kinds of mental pathology, and are so beautifully interpretable in terms of monoideism, autosuggestion, aboulia, etc., etc.

In writing as I have just now done, I do not mean to imply that the more intense and extreme form of mysticism is always pathological, nor that the frankly pathological cases are therefore necessarily entirely devoid of ultimate significance and on a par with every other kind of pathological mental condition. The explanation and value of the mystic ecstasy and revelation is a question which we need not here discuss and which I do not wish to prejudge. All that I mean to point out at present is the importance of distinguishing the two types of mysticism and of treating them separately. Whenever one uses the word mysticism he should ask himself first whether he means to refer to both types, and if not which of the two he has in mind. In order to make my own meaning perfectly clear, therefore, I shall treat of the two kinds of mysticism in separate chapters, dealing with the milder type here and reserving the following chapters to the more extreme form. In the present chapter, then, I shall seek simply to describe — not to explain — the less intense and commoner kind of mystic experience and to trace out some of the conditions that help bring it about, and some of the results that it produces.

The exact nature of this milder form of mystical experience is for the non-mystical psychologist a rather baffling question.

It is, of course, the sense of a Beyond, the feeling of the presence of the Divine. But direct and careful descriptions of this feeling are difficult to find. The expressions of the milder type of mystics when analyzed often seem to be hardly more than affirmations of their belief in the intercourse between God and man, or in some other theological or philosophical position. Very seldom, even in the best of the mystical writings, does one come upon a direct and analytic description of the experience which is the basis of the whole. Difficulties, however, must not daunt us; nor should we give up the attempt to understand mysticism because of the unfortunate fact that most mystics are not psychologists. Something may be done with the expressions of religious people though they be not expressed in psychological terminology. And I propose therefore to lay before the reader a rather heterogeneous collection of such expressions from which we may be able to make out with some degree of clearness what the milder form of the mystic experience is like — or, in short, " how God feels."

My collection of descriptions of the mystic experience is, as I have said, rather heterogeneous; and my arrangement of them has been purposely unsystematic. For in selecting my data I have sought to avoid the local and the provincial in order to make the resulting impression not that of American or of mediæval religious experience but of the milder mysticism as such, in its more general aspect. The data I shall present are therefore gathered from no one century and no one land. They come from persons of very different degrees of intelligence and education. They are not even confined to any one religion. And yet, as the reader will notice, though differing in many details, they show a rather remarkable (and I fear, to the reader, monotonous) agreement in essentials. Without further comment, then, I shall let the mystics speak for themselves, and tell (in their unfortunately rather indirect fashion) what is the experience of the " consciousness of the presence of God."

Let me begin with the expressions of some of my respondents. " I have experienced God's presence so that I felt the lack of nothing and feared nothing. It is hard to describe the feeling, but everything seems bright and clear ahead, and I feel as if I had the support of some great unimpeachable authority behind me for everything I may do then.   It feels as though I were not standing alone."   " I mean by this presence a peaceful consciousness of this support and indwelling. It is distinct.   In the face of struggle, hardship, or test it says, ' I am with you.'   That is strength.   It stands where all the world fails.   It is *sufficient* always — not half-way assistance but definite."   " For eleven years I have never for a moment lost the blessed sense of the Presence and indwelling of God.   God is as real as He is dear to me, and His nearness and dearness are unspeakably rich and indescribable, save in the most exaggerated terms.   I know the presence and the voice of my Beloved.   When I talk with Him it is as natural and as simple but far more delightful, than speaking to a dear one close at hand.   I know what it is to love God and let Him love me actively.   This continued state is my very life.   There have been times when for a little while I have lost the *experience* of the presence of God, as the Master did when His flesh cried out on the cross.   But I have never lost the knowledge of God's presence, and when I have come back into the realization of it, it has always been with a richer inflow of His holy love." " At times God is very real to me.   At such times He seems nearer and more real than any human being could be.   At other times He seems real but more or less remote.   There have been times in my life, beginning in early childhood, when I have believed myself to come consciously into the presence of God.   Sometimes this has occurred when I have been in great sorrow or in great fear and dread.   But sometimes I have felt His Presence without any special reason for it — for example, when I have been alone out of doors or reading something that has touched me by its beauty and truth, I have felt a quick, glad sense that He was near, ' closer to me than breathing, nearer than hands or feet.'   Such experiences while they last make me feel that I have come to my true self.   I seem to understand life better for them.   They are accompanied by no emotional excitement, only by a deep peace and gladness.   I have never spoken of them to anyone.   These experiences are not habitual with me, that is, they do not occur very frequently. They afford me my strongest ground for belief in God."

A witness to the same experience is found in Mr. H. G. Wells. In his " First and Last Things " he writes:

" At times, in the silence of the night and in rare lonely moments, I come upon a sort of communion of myself and something great that is not myself. It is perhaps poverty of mind and language obliges me to say that this universal scheme takes on the effect of a sympathic person — and my communion a quality of fearless worship. These moments happen, and they are the supreme fact of my religious life to me; they are the crown of my religious experience." [4]

" The sense of the presence of God," says St. Alphonse Rodriguez, " is not gained through the imagination; it is a spiritual and experimental certainty." [5] In similar strain, St. François de Sales writes, " The soul which is in quietness before God drinks in insensibly the sweetness of that presence without reasoning about it. . . . In this quietness she has no need of memory, for her Beloved is present. She has no need of imagination, for why need she present in an image Him whose presence she enjoys?" [6]

" Several persons," writes Poulain, " accustomed to the mystic union, have told me that the following comparison describes very exactly the inner possession of God: " We feel *the presence of our bodies* equally well with our eyes open or closed. If we know that our bodies are there it is not, then, because we see them nor because someone has told us of them. It is the result of a special sensation, of an interior impression which makes us feel that our souls penetrate and vivify our bodies. It is a very simple sensation which we try in vain to analyze. It is thus that in the mystic union we feel God within us, and in a manner quite simple." [7]

These quotations, I trust, will give the non-mystical reader some slight idea of the nature of the mystical experience. And yet it must be admitted that as descriptions they leave much

[4] " First and Last Things " (London, Constable: 1908), p. 60.
[5] St. Alphonse Rodriguez, quoted by Poulain, in " Des Graces d'Oraison " (Paris, Victor Retaux: 1906), p. 77.
[6] Quoted by Poulain, op. cit., p. 76.
[7] Op. cit., p. 91.

to be desired. It is extremely seldom that a mystic of this milder type gives or even attempts to give a detailed and exact description of his experience. There are several obvious reasons for this. One is that the mystic is not usually interested in exact description and never thinks of taking the psychological point of view. Poor introspection on the part of many is another reason. Most fundamental of all is the fact that exact psychological description of an emotional experience must necessarily be in sensuous terms, while the mystic often feels that sensuous terms are unworthy to be applied to his purely " spiritual " experience. He recognizes indeed that there is a sensuous element in his experience but this he regards as merely a chance accompaniment, and hence he tries to describe his exprience in terms that have no relation to sense. The result is the usual theological explanation put in place of a psychological description. And if the mystic really does begin to describe he often stops abruptly on discovering the inevitably sensuous nature of his description. One of my respondents puts it naïvely and excellently: " When I try to describe such an experience in words the terms are terms of sensation and they should not be."

A number of the most famous Christian mystics, however, especially those best endowed with introspective power, have no such scruples, and frankly analyze their experience — or at least parts of it — into the organic sensations that help to make it up. And though the great majority of those who have known the mystic experience only in its milder form give us only vague and inexact descriptions with no analysis, there is occasionally one here or there who recognizes the fact that religious emotion like every other emotion has a large sensuous element, and who frankly refers to this in his expressions. Thus St. Augustine, who though a mystic of the less intense type was gifted with unusual powers of introspection, writes as follows:

" Not with uncertain but with assured consciousness do I love Thee, O Lord. . . . But what is it that I love in loving Thee? Not corporeal beauty, nor the splendor of time, nor the radiance of the light, so pleasant to our eyes, nor the sweet

melodies of songs, nor the fragrant scent of flowers and oint-
ment and spices, nor manna and honey, nor limbs pleasant to
the embracements of the flesh.   It is not these things I love
when I love my God; and yet I love a certain kind of light,
and a certain kind of sound, and a certain kind of fragrance
and food and embracement, in loving my God, who is the light,
the sound, the fragrance, the food, the embracement of my inner
man; where that light shineth unto my soul which no place
can contain, where that soundeth which time snatcheth not
away, where there is a fragrance which no breeze disperseth,
where there is a food which no eating can diminish, where
that clingeth which no satiety can sunder.   This is what I
love when I love my God." [8]

Occasionally, but very rarely, one who has had the experience in question tries to put his description in purely sensational terms — one of my respondents, for instance, writing as
follows: "With me the physical effects begin usually with a
quivering and upheaving of the diaphragm which starts a wave
of sensation upward through the chest region and into the
pharynx, and results in incipient yawning.   This in turn is
followed by an excitement of the lachrymal glands and tears
sometimes fill my eyes.   All these physical sensations, considered as such, are mildly pleasing.   After they are over comes
a sense of great refreshment."

Such a purely sensational description as this when taken
by itself is certainly quite as incapable of giving us a just idea
of the nature of the experience as are the more "spiritual"
descriptions given above.   Both kinds are needed to supplement
each other.   For though sensation forms an important part in
every emotion and though emotion must be analyzed into sensational terms before it can be accurately described, the elements thus analyzed out *are* not the emotion, and the analysis
comes very near to destroying the experience.   When water
has been analyzed into hydrogen and oxygen it is no longer
water.   As Professor Royce puts it, "consciousness is not a
shower of shot."   An experience is what it is immediately
"known as," not what it might be analyzed into.   "The ele-

<hr>

[8] Confessions, X, 6.

ments that analysis detects exist, as consciousness states, when they are detected and not before." [9]

Hence, in one sense, the mystic is justified in his constantly reiterated assertion that his deepest religious experiences are indescribable — ineffable. This is of course true to a considerable extent of every emotion. Every emotion, that is, must undergo a certain amount of distortion and transformation if it is to be put into such a form as to be communicable. But different emotions involve different degrees of such transformation and distortion, according to their relative complexity and to the varying amounts and kinds of ideation and organic feeling that analysis would be able to detect in them. And the almost universal assertion of the mystics is that their religious experience is the one most difficult of all to be thus analyzed and described. In fact the ineffability of the experience is one of its most prominent characteristics. Tauler, after speaking at some length of the mystic experience, says, " What this is and how it comes to pass is easier to feel than to describe. All that I have said is as poor and unlike it as a point of a needle is to the heavens above us." And the author of the Theologia Germanica writes: " Now, it may be asked, what is the state of a man who followeth the true Light to the utmost of his power? I answer truly, it will never be declared aright, for he who is not such a man can neither understand it nor know it, and he who is knoweth indeed, but he cannot utter it, for it is unspeakable. Therefore let him who would know it give his whole diligence that he may enter therein; then will he see and find what hath never been uttered by man's lips." [10]

" It is in the personal or individual part of our experience," writes a modern mystic, " that we are disturbed by intermissions and that we have need of words. I believe that neither words nor variations have any place in the innermost Sanctuary. . . . The deeper we go the fewer will be our words, and the less will any need of them be felt. As we enter the innermost chamber of our own hearts, words, and it may be

[9] Royce, "Outlines of Psychology" (New York, Macmillan: 1904), pp. 108, 109. See the whole passage.

[10] "The Theologia Germanica," translated by Sussana Winkworth (London, Macmillan: 1907), p. 69.

even thoughts, are left behind. In the innermost Sanctuary itself nothing is known but the Light. Those who are permitted to dwell much in that Light of Life become suffused with a radiance more powerful than words to convey to others the knowledge of the place whence cometh our help. Where that radiance is, words and silence are alike living and blessed." [11]

A pupil came to one of the great masters of the Vedanta and said to him, " Reverend sir, teach me Brahman." The master responded by keeping silent. And the pupil said again, " O reverend Sir, teach me Brahman." He, however, still remained silent. When, now, the pupil asked him the third time, he said: " I do teach thee Brahman, but thou understandest it not. This Atman is silent." [12]

The ineffability of the mystic experience, however, by no means lessens the mystic's certainty that in it he somehow comes into touch with the " Beyond." " God is as real to me as myself," writes one of my respondents. " My recognition of Him is an *indistinct* but *real* presence." " I speak to Him with as much confidence as to a friend at the end of a telephone, and with no more doubt that He hears." This response is representative of the overwhelming majority of all those in whom the " mystic germ " (as James used to call it) is at all well developed. It would be a mistake, however, to suppose that the less intense forms of mystic experience bring with them always this same sense of irrefutable certainty. The man in whom the " mystic germ " is still but incipient may and often does question the authority or the significance of such moments. One of this type writes to me thus: " Perhaps I have experienced God's presence, but I am not sure. It may have been merely an emotional expression of my own nature. It came from a sudden realization of the glories of certain phases of nature. Its connection with God was extremely vague and may have come merely from my habits of thought. It cannot really be called an experience." This man, of course, cannot be classed as a mystic, so very faint and questionable was the experience of

---

[11] Caroline Stephen, in " Light Arising " (Cambridge, Helfer: 1908), p. 91.

[12] Quoted by Deussen, " Das System des Vedânta " (Leipzig, Brockhaus: 1906), p. 227.

which he speaks. When the mystic sense is more intense, though it may still be questioned, the individual usually comes in the end to a recognition of its objective significance. One quasi-mystic writes me thus: " Under great spiritual uplift I have stopped and asked, Is it possible that this intense feeling, this spiritual joy, is subjective? But I could not believe it possible to extemporize the peculiar experience without a divine presence." And almost without exception so far as I can discover, as the mystic life progresses and becomes either more constant or more intense, its authority for the subject of it becomes more and more irresistible and unquestionable.

" The man who truly experiences the pure presence of God in his own soul knows well that there can be no doubt about it," writes Tauler. By " devout prayer and the uplifting of the mind to God " there is " an entrance into union of the created spirit with the uncreated Spirit of God " so that the human spirit " is poured forth into God and becomes one spirit with Him." This knowledge comes only through experience of " entering in and dwelling in the Inner Kingdom of God, where the pure truth and the sweetness of God are found." [13]

This last sentence of Tauler's suggests the two-fold aspect of mysticism. For ineffable as this experience undoubtedly is for the mystic, we, the on-looking psychologists, may analyze his statements and make out from them some of the characteristics of the mystic state. Tauler, then, speaks of two things, namely *" pure truth "* and *" the sweetness of God "* as characteristic of the " Inner Kingdom." And while he may have written this with no idea of technical exactness, a study of the mystical writings as a whole shows that the two most prominent aspects of mysticism are just the two indicated by his expression. In other words, mysticism is in part emotional, in part ideational and cognitive. Only in its most extreme form (if indeed even then) is it a mere feeling state without farther content. Feeling indeed there is, usually in great richness; but this feeling is invariably crystallized about some central idea, some intellectual certainty, which comes to the mystic as a revelation of truth, and which he usually has no difficulty in

[13] Quoted from Tauler by Jones in " Studies in Mystical Religion " (London, Macmillan: 1909), p. 281.

defining and communicating. It does not come to him, to be sure, in the form of a clearly expressed judgment, but rather as an immediate intuition of a reality, which only later on he is able to formulate into a perfectly definite proposition.

The cognitive and emotional elements of mysticism are mutually influential. Strong emotion not only intensifies conviction but determines to some extent the nature of the intellectual content. Thus an intense sentiment of love will tend to make the mystic's God more personal and less cosmic. The process works in the other direction equally well. Emotional mysticism is almost invariably associated with belief in a personal God not only for the reason just suggested but also because belief in a personal God tends to rouse and increase the sentiment of personal love. An impersonal God, on the other hand, is seldom associated with the emotional type of mysticism. This is noticeable in a comparison of the theology of intellectual mystics such as Eckhart and that held by the emotional type, such as St. Teresa and John of the Cross. The contrast is equally striking in India. The earlier Upanishads, with their impersonal Brahman, show much less emotional intensity than the later theistic Upanishads, or than the Bhagavad Gita and the Puranas, which got their inspiration from belief in the personal deities of the great Sects. There is little warmth of mystic emotion in the attitude of the philosophical followers of Shankara to-day; and the mystical exercises of the atheistic Buddhists led to trance rather than to joyful ecstasy.

When we come (in a later chapter) to discuss the ecstasy of the great mystics and its noetic character, we shall consider at some length the nature of the cognitive element in mysticism. For the purposes of this chapter it will suffice to say that the one great truth of which the mystic of the less intense type always feels an intuitive certainty is the presence of the Beyond. Many insist that besides this (or almost as a part of it) they are intuitively " conscious " of the certainty of a future life, or of the optimistic world-view that ultimately " all is well." These deliverances of the mystic consciousness however, though sometimes present as a realization of the supreme worth of spirit, are by no means universal. The one thing, therefore, to which all the mystics of the less extreme form invariably witness is the presence of a greater Life which somehow comes in touch with theirs.

An attempt to analyze and describe the mystic sense of presence should begin with a consideration of ordinary perception. Perception, as contrasted with sensation, has two elements: (1) an immediate sensational or ideational and logical content, and (2) an outer reference. It means more than it is. External objects, as Professor Stout puts it, are " cognized as existing independently of us, just as we exist independently of them." " The external thing does not consist for us merely in the sensible features by which it is qualified. There must be something to which these sensory contents are referred as attributes." [14] In other words, an important part of perception is the implicit recognition of the presence of an object which is more than just our psychical content. It is this same sense of *objectivity* which the mystic feels; the experience brings with it an implicit certainty that the object or Being which he experiences is more than the experience itself.

As to the content of the mystical sense of presence we may again get light by considering the normal experience of perceiving and " feeling " the presence of other people. For a considerable number of cases are cited in James's " Varieties " [15] and in Leuba's " Belief in God and Immortality " [16] which link up the mystical experience with quite non-religious instances in which some invisible being is felt to be present without any suggestion that this being is God or any other religious object. This experience, moreover, seems to be much the same as that of the ordinary realization of a person's presence, minus the sensory causes which normally give rise to it. " The essential constituents of the experience of the presence of a person," writes Professor Leuba, " in a case of ordinary perception are neither sight nor sound nor even touch; but the very com-

[14] " The Groundwork of Psychology " (New York, Hinds Noble: 1903), p. 90. See also Titchener, " A Textbook of Psychology," p. 367; Pillsbury, " Fundamentals of Psychology " (New York, Macmillan: 1916), pp. 268–69; Ward, article on " Psychology " in the Britannica. I have discussed the matter at some length in a paper on " Realism and Perception " in the *Jour. of Phil.*, XVI, 596–603.

[15] Lecture III.

[16] Pp. 47–48.

plex sensory-motor activities which commonly follow upon these perceptions.   When we see some one and feel his presence, our whole psycho-physical attitude is modified; the facial and bodily expressions are altered, feelings and emotions are generated, and in addition thought is given a new direction; it centers about our relations with the person of the presence of whom we are aware." [17]

Both the characteristics of the ordinary realization of personal presence here described — the objective reference and the group of sensory-motor activities — are to be found in the mystical sense of presence.[18]   But the fact that the being thus felt is regarded as the Divine adds to the mystical experience an emotional intensity seldom found in the non-religious cases. This Divine Being may be sensed as a merely vague Presence, or as a perfectly definite personality, all but visible and audible.[19]   The nature of the emotion involved varies, moreover, from calm and joyful peace to violent love and intense adoration.   A triumphant sense of certitude, a swelling confidence in the power of the spirit, a reverent but trustful laying of hands upon the Invisible and the Infinite, make up, for many, a large part of this experience.   The mystical sense of presence, in fact, is so complex, and varies so considerably from subject to subject, that an exact and full description of one case would probably hold in its entirety of no other.   In this sense at least the mystic is justified in insisting that his experience is *sui generis*.

So much for the cognitive, or semi-cognitive, side of the milder form of mysticism.   The other aspect of the mystic experience is its emotional character.   Yet it is only for purposes of analysis and exposition that this can be called an " other " aspect, for in the experience itself the cognitive and the emotional elements are almost indissolubly blended.   The joy and sweetness of this experience is something to which the mystics universally testify with such unanimity that I need hardly make use here of any of their testimony — for no one

[17] Op. cit., pp. 48–49.

[18] See, for example, two very admirable descriptions of the experience given by a modern mystic with excellent psychological ability, in Flournoy, " Une Mystic Moderne," *Arch. de Psychol*, XV, 42–45.

[19] See the many examples given by Segond in Chapter III of " La Prière."

who has done any reading in the mystic literature can have failed to come upon numerous references to this joy. Three short quotations from three far-separated lands and centuries will here suffice. " The bliss of Brahman! " exclaims the Taitteriya Upanishad. " Speech and mind fall back baffled and ashamed. All fear vanishes in the knowing of that bliss." St. Augustine, who was only very moderately favored in this respect, speaks of the experience as " a most rare affection," " an inexplicable sweetness, such that, if it should be perfected in me, I know not to what point my life might not arrive." [20] One of my respondents writes, " God is very real to me, as real as an earthly friend, though with a more purely spiritual reality. I have experienced His presence. It touches the whole being into a warm and living but inexpressibly high and noble love of the universe and each dear thing in it, and makes one feel over all a wonderful and inexpressible power, which is God. Material things are unreal, then, or at least not distinct from the spiritual. This does not express it all — it is beyond expression."

For some — and I think especially for mystics of the milder type — the mystic experience is always one of joy and calm, and is unconnected with pain of any sort. It would be a mistake, however, to suppose that this is the case with all, or to regard mysticism as always a joyous thing with no heavier and sadder side. Mysticism has its pains as well as its delights. Especially is this the case with the more extreme type, but it is also true occasionally of the milder type studied in this chapter. Such mystic pains are of two sorts, positive and negative. The negative kind is the milder of the two and is due simply to the fact that the individual has, perhaps, overemphasized the importance of religious joy, or at any rate wishes for and expects its return at a time when, for some unknown reason, it cannot come. For, as we shall see, religious emotion of this kind is not at the beck and call of any one. It is impossible to remain ever " on the heights," and the person who expects to do so will experience and perhaps grieve over what the greater mystics know as periods of " dryness." This state of things is well depicted by Thomas à Kempis, who knows both

[20] " Confessions," X, 40.

what the experience is and how it should be treated.   " My son, thou art not able always to persist in the higher pitch of contemplation; but thou must needs sometimes by reason of original corruption descend to inferior things, and bear the burden of this corruptible life, though against thy will and with wearisomeness. . . . It is expedient for thee, then, to flee to humble and exterior works, and to refresh thyself with good actions; to expect with a firm confidence My coming and Heavenly visitation; to bear patiently thy banishment and the dryness of thy mind, till I shall again visit thee and set thee free from all anxieties." [21]

The more positive sort of mystic pain consists not merely in lacking the joyous sense of communion but in a rather intense feeling of being deserted by God and separated from Him. This is usually connected with a sense of sin and unworthiness and contrition,— some of the more intense pre-conversion phenomena belonging here.   God is still *felt* (in one sense at least) — that is, He is not merely believed in — but He is felt as far away or as separated from one by a barrier.   The experience seems to be comparable to that of the mother who sees her child but cannot get to him nor take him in her arms,— or, better still, perhaps, it is like that of the child who sees his mother and longs for her embrace but cannot reach her.   So the mystic sometimes " wrestles in prayer " seeking in vain to regain the lost sense of peace and to escape the ache and hollowness of a life that longs for God and apprehends Him, yet cannot come to Him.   " As the hart panteth after the water brooks so panteth my soul after Thee, O God.   My soul thirsteth for God, for the living God; when shall I come and appear before God ?   My tears have been my meat day and night, while they continually say unto me Where is thy God ?   These things I remember and pour out my soul within me." [22]   This is no intellectual assent to the proposition that God is far away; it is a genuinely mystic experience, an immediate *sense* of separation from a Being who yet is felt as in some way present.   It belongs not to the theological but to the psychological category.

These mystic pains do not come to all the mystics.   To bor-

21 " The Imitation of Christ," III, 51.
22 Psalm 42, 1–4.

row an expressive word from Professor James, they belong to the "sick soul." The "healthy minded" mystic knows little about them. Yet few of us are healthy minded or sick of soul all the time, and hence both the joyous and the painful types of emotion are to be found at least incipiently in most intensely religious persons. In fact with many people the two tend to induce and replace each other, according to the almost universal rhythmic law of human nature. Moods and emotions are particularly unstable things and are constantly swinging backward and forward in pendulum fashion. So it comes about that the man whose interest and thought are largely centered on the religious life often finds moments of intense religious joy giving place to periods of "dryness," and still more often does the sense of sin and separation from God drive him back into the experience of communion and the "joy of the Lord."

But though the mystic life has its shadow as well as its sunshine, it is the latter which gives it its dominant tone; the joy of the Lord is much more typical of it, taken as a whole, than is the pain of separation. And it is by the light and in the hope and memory of these moments of joyous communion that many a mystic lives. What determines the return of these moments is a question that the mystic often asks himself. And his usual conclusion is that in their more intense form they are in large measure beyond his control. Something may indeed be done to prepare oneself for them and to break down moral conditions which would inhibit their occurrence; but (as the very existence of the periods of "dryness" shows) beyond that the experience is not to be forced,— it bloweth where it listeth. A number of conditions over which the individual has no control play a large part in determining the recurrence of the mystic state. Prominent among these are age and health. There is, to be sure, no narrow span of years that can be called the mystic age. Yet the last years of adolescence seem more productive of the mystic state than either extreme youth or age. This is due, of course, to the absence of the disturbing conditions of early adolescence and of the weakening effects of advanced years.[23] And while individuals vary greatly and no minute

[23] Some of the great saints have become ecstatic in childhood, according to the belief of the Catholic Church. On this point Poulain, quoting

laws can be discovered which will hold for all, it seems clear that for any given individual there are certain conditions of health and of mental and bodily vigor which *for him* are best adapted to the mystic experience and largely influence it. These conditions vary, as I have said, with different individuals. For some a condition of rather poor health seems to be most propitious. "Health draws us toward external objects," says Maine de Biran, "sickness leads us back to ourselves." [24] Even extreme sickness and the hour of death itself — especially if recognized as such by the subject — are often accompanied by the sense of presence. For the more intense forms of this experience, however, either a fair degree of health or the stimulus and excitement of a great hour seem to be requisite. And for probably more than half of those who know the kind of mysticism dealt with in this chapter, health is a more suitable condition than sickness,— for, other things being equal, intense emotion of any kind is most likely to arise when bodily vigor is at its height. And though health draws us toward external objects and away from self, it often is just the thought of self that most inhibits the enlargement of consciousness which the mystic experiences. This explanation in fact is suggested by one of my respondents: "I feel the presence of God most intensely when feeling 'fine'— when out in the air, on a mountain, or bathing in the ocean at night. To generalize, I think the feeling is most intense when in the presence of something infinite enough to eliminate totally all thoughts of self or of finite things."

As this last quotation indicates, and as, in fact, every one knows, the influence of beautiful natural scenery, and of music or poetry,— of anything, in short, that tends to arouse æsthetic emotion — is likely in religious persons to induce, in-

from Dr. Imbert, cites four who had their first ecstasy at four; four at six; one at seven; one at eleven; one at fourteen; one at eighteen; one at forty; and one (St. Teresa) at forty-three. The ecstasy of a child of four or six years is, however, something which may well be questioned. And of course even if we accept these figures at their face value there is nothing in them inconsistent with the view expressed above that the mystic life is at its highest in late adolescence, for the precocious mystic usually continues his mysticism through the rest of his days.

[24] "Maine de Biran, Sa Vie et ses Pensées," edited by Naville (Paris, Didier: 1874), p. 7.

directly, religious emotion.   For many there is almost no line between the æsthetic and the religious; for others the emotion simply shifts its center, the idea of the divine forcing its way into the mind and the feeling elements which were already present simply crystallizing about it.   " I have experienced God's presence," writes one of my respondents; " and by that I mean that in a state of contemplation or under the influence of music or of superb natural scenery I have been lifted out of myself in a state of pure and ecstatic joy.   Not one of oblivion to the external world, but where it receded into the background of consciousness or fell into harmony with my feeling state and became a unified part of it."   Maine de Biran writes thus in his Journal: " May 17, 1815.   I felt this evening in a lonely walk, with wonderful weather, momentary flashes of that ineffable delight which seems to snatch us completely away from all that is earthly and to give us a fore-taste of heaven. The verdure had a new freshness and was glorified with the last rays of the setting sun; all the objects were animated with a soft luster; the trees gently waved their majestic tops. . . . Over all the impressions and the vague and varied images that rose from the presence of the objects and from my feelings, there hovered that sense of the infinite which sometimes transports us toward a world superior to phenomena, toward that world of realities which is in touch with God, the first and sole reality.   It seems that in this condition, where all the external and internal sensations are calm and joyous, there is a peculiar sentiment adapted to celestial things and which is destined, perhaps, some day to develop, when the soul shall have quitted its mortal vesture." [25]

Thus for many a mystic the joy of nature and the joy of the Lord are hardly distinguishable, and neither one would be complete without the other.   Of course this would not hold of all. The mystic brotherhood may be divided into two bands on the basis of their delight in the beautiful or their lack of it; the followers of Francis of Assisi, and the followers of Thomas à Kempis we might call them.   But every mystic who finds and approves of delight in this good world is likely to regard the experience as a very part of his religion.   " Your

[25] Op. cit., p. 171.

enjoyment of the world," writes Thomas Traherne, " is never right till every morning you awake in Heaven; see yourself in your Father's Palace; and look upon the skies, the earth, and the air as Celestial Joys; having such a reverend esteem of all, as if you were among the Angels. . . . You never enjoy the world aright till the Sea itself floweth in your veins, till you are clothed with the heavens and crowned with the stars." [26]

When both outer and inner conditions are favorable the joyous sense of the presence of the divine often comes quite unsought and unexpected, with a spontaneity and suddenness that at times almost astound the subject of it.   The following somewhat lengthy response will illustrate both this and several other of the conditions already referred to:

" It is always hard to analyze our deepest experiences and put the result into words which cannot be misunderstood. Some day when I am busy at work a dear friend enters the room without my hearing the footstep.   Before I am aware that any physical sense has registered an impression and while my friend is still out of my range of vision, her personality breaks into my consciousness.   Perhaps this may illustrate very faintly the feeling of God's presence that has sometimes come. It was in this way that He came after the dark two years. . . . To please those dear to me, I had finally gone to church one day.   It was a little country church with none of the modern accessories to worship.   Dr. A. J. Gordon preached that day, but no word of the sermon helped at all, for ' my heart was hot within me ' in rebellion against what I conceived to be the existing order of things.   Mrs. Gordon, a stranger to me, that day had the Sunday school class into which I felt obliged to go.   The words of the Scripture lesson came to me with a good deal of force, I suppose because I had not seen them for so long, but I do not remember paying much attention to the explanation.   When the class went, Mrs. Gordon detained me to ask two or three questions.   I must have given very vague and unsatisfactory answers, for I certainly would not then have told anyone what I was thinking, although I wanted the truth more than anything else in the world.   At last she knelt beside

[26] " Centuries of Meditation," I, 28 and 29.   (Edited and published by Bertram Dobell, London, 1908.)

me and began to pray. I remember thinking it all something of a bore, but staying because I did not want to be discourteous. I cannot now remember one word of the prayer, and do not think I could even then have had a very distinct idea of what she was saying, because it all seemed to have very little to do with me; but in the midst of it there came an overwhelming sense of a Presence infinitely pure and true and tender, a presence that broke through all preconceived notions and revealed itself to my consciousness in such beauty and power that after more than twenty-five years it seems to me the one real thing in my whole life. There was no physical manifestation or physical sensation. I was simply a soul in the presence of the Soul of souls. I made no sign and spoke no word of this to Mrs. Gordon, but said good-by and went my way; nor have I ever before attempted to put the experience into words, yet it has been the strongest influence of my whole life.

" This is not, however, the only time I have felt sure of His presence, but the definiteness of the impression varies under different conditions. And indeed all my impressions vary greatly in distinctness according to the state of my physical health and the urgency of other matters occupying my mind at the time. Even the impression of the presence of a person known to be in the room varies in this way. Sometimes, then, when I am away on the hills or in the woods alone, God seems very near; yet even then there is not the sense of physical nearness, but of something closer, something that goes deeper and means more. It is then that my soul goes out to Him most fully, and that I am nearest to freedom from the limitations of time and space and matter, nearest to gaining a true sense of relative values, nearest to knowing what things are real and lasting. I do not then arrive at conclusions through any process of reasoning,— I simply *know* for the time."

Any emotion which like the æsthetic is free from self tends in religious persons to lead into religious emotion and get itself interpreted in religious terms. And for a somewhat similar reason sorrow and despair often tend in the same direction. Here, to be sure, the self is not forgotten, as is the case in æsthetic delight, but it is negated, defeated, overwhelmed. The man can no longer trust in his own strength nor in the various finite sources of help on which he had usually relied; yet trust he *must*. Help must come from somewhere — the instinct for life demands it. And so the despairing soul turns to what it hopes may be an infinite source of help. Sometimes it fails to find help there too. But if the sufferer has a natural tendency toward mysticism, help is pretty sure to come in the sense of the presence and love of the Divine, and in a new trust that *somehow* all is well. In another place [27] I have quoted the words of one of my respondents who writes thus: " I shall never forget the feeling of the presence of God with me on that night when all alone in a stranger's house on the hill I worked over my precious child, realizing as I worked that I could not save his life and that nothing could. I could almost hear the words, ' When thou passest through the waters I will be with thee,' — and in the dreadful loneliness and anxiety and grief there came a wonderful peace and a feeling of God's presence that I am very certain of."

The influences mentioned thus far which condition the coming of the mystic sense are largely beyond the control of the individual's will. But while it is true that this experience cometh where and when it listeth and can never be forced, there are still several things within one's power which tend to bring about positively a favorable mental condition or to inhibit antagonistic tendencies. One of these modes of " waiting on the Lord " commonly urged and tested by mystics of many centuries is the practice of solitude and silence. " Seek a convenient time to retire into thyself," says Thomas à Kempis, " and meditate often upon God's loving kindness. . . . He that intends to attain to the more inward and spiritual things of religion must with Jesus depart from the multitude and press of the people. . . . In silence and in stillness a religious soul advantageth herself and learneth the mysteries of the Holy Scripture. There she findeth rivers of tears, wherein she may every night wash and cleanse herself; that she may be so much the more familiar with her Creator, by how much the farther off she liveth from all worldly disquiet. Whoso, therefore, withdraweth himself from his acquaintance and friends, God will draw near unto him with His holy Angels." [28]

<hr />

[27] " The Psychology of Religious Belief," p. 250.
[28] " The Imitation of Christ," I, 20.

" The inward silence and stillness," writes Miss Stephen, " for the sake of which we value and practice outward silence is a very different thing from vacancy. It is rather the quiescence of a perfectly ordered fullness — a leaving behind of hurrying outward thoughts and an entering into the region of central calm. And let us remember that it is a condition to be resolutely sought for, not a merely passive state into which we may lapse at will. In seeking to be still, the first step of necessity is to exclude all disturbances and commotion from without; but this is not all, there are inward disturbances and commotions to be subdued with a strong hand. There is a natural impulse to fly from the presence of God to a multitude of distractions, which we must resolutely control if we would taste the blessedness of conscious nearness to Him. I believe it often is the case that the way to achieve this resolute self-control is through thought — through a deliberate act of attention to our own highest conceptions of the nature and the will of Him with Whom we have to do." [29]

In similar vein the abbé Lejeune, in his " Introduction à la Vie Mystique," urges on those who would cultivate the mystic life, the regular practice of prayer and the attempt to realize constantly the presence of God — " to see Him by the eye of faith " always present, or better still to feel Him always within one.[30] One may go about one's work thinking of other things and actively engaged; yet the thought of God's presence may be continually in the background on one's mind guiding one's impulses and coloring one's feelings. But though this is quite possible — at least for many people — let no one think it an easy matter.[31] It goeth not forth save by fasting and prayer,— to gain this constant sense of the indwelling of God one must go through a course of careful self-training. It can no more be attained without preliminary effort than can skill in piano playing or the ability constantly to see double images. Like any other mental habit it must be cultivated in accordance with the regular laws of the mind, and this cultivation requires both effort and persistence.

In addition to silence and meditation, repentance and con-

[29] Op. cit., p. 65.
[30] Op. cit., Chaps. II and III.
[31] Cf. Lejeune, op. cit., pp. 83–90.

trition and effort for moral purity should also be mentioned as means frequently used by the more determined mystics for bringing themselves into the desired mental state. " Give thyself to compunction of heart," says Thomas à Kempis, " and thou shalt gain much devotion thereby." [32] As sin in any form is (at least while being indulged in) extremely antagonistic to the religious mood, the struggle against it is a prime requisite. Prayer, religious music, and reading from the Bible and devotional literature are also found helpful for gaining and retaining the " joy of the Lord." Several of these means are illustrated in the following account from one of my respondents of the way she sought to regain and keep her new-found experience of inner happiness:— " I think I was just thirteen when one night for a moment there came a feeling of great peace or rest. I almost held my breath, hoping to keep it, but it was gone, and left only the memory, which became an ideal for whose realization I began to hope and work. . . . It may have been Miss Havergal's word about ' the permanence of the joy of the Lord ' that gave me the assurance that such a feeling of peace ought to be constant instead of coming in flashes. It came to me only in that last way at first and I could not find a cause that would always produce them, and yet I remember feeling that they must be governed by some law, and that if I could only find that law I could reproduce them at will. . . . One day I found in an old commentary a description of my experience, and it gave me as its cause absolute obedience to God. I had already felt that study of His Word and prayer had a great deal to do with the coming of the peace. . . . Gradually by spending some time alone each day the experiences became longer and perhaps less intense. They were best expressed by the word *peace,* and I began to know that I might always have the feeling if I would instantly do the right as I saw it and would save time for quiet study. I found that when actual necessity interfered with that, the peace would not go; but carelessness would always drive it away." [33]

It will be noticed that as the " peace " came more and more under the control of my respondent's will, it changed in type,

[32] " Imitation," I, 21.
[33] Quoted in my " Psychology of Religious Belief," pp. 225–26.

becoming " longer and perhaps less intense." The more intense experience is probably never at the individual's command. But the constant peace, the certainty that God is near, that underneath are the everlasting arms, and that one's life is under His continued guidance,— this is for many men and women an actuality, conditioned only upon their following the moral guidance which their consciences give, and keeping their ears always open for the divine voice. By living *as though* God were present they have and keep the constant assurance that He *is* present.

This mild and constant sense of the Divine is consistent with great activity and can abide with many people through a large part of the working day. The ability to retain it while thinking intently on other things will of course vary with the individual. One of the chief ways in which individual minds differ is in the relative amount and importance of the fringe region. With the extreme rationalistic type whose thought is always clear and for whom everything has its definite and neat place, the margin is very narrow and has but little influence. The opposite type of mind has less power of concentration and a correspondingly broader field, running out into a wide background. The former of these types seldom produces mystics, and for it the business of life will, at least during the working day, crowd out the sense of the Divine. The mind with the wider margin, however, will have room for both things at once. Thus practical activity and the mystic sense prove by no means incompatible.

So much for the milder form of mysticism. In our next chapter we must attack the more difficult problem of the great mystics and their experience.

CHAPTER XVII

THE "MYSTICS" AND THEIR METHODS

In that great fountain-head of mysticism, the Enneads, Plotinus writes of his own experience as follows:

"Now often I am roused from the body to my true self, and emerge from all else and enter myself, and behold a marvelous beauty, and am particularly persuaded at the time that I belong to a better sphere, and live a supremely good life, and become identical with the Godhead, and fast fixed therein attain its divine activity, having reached a plane above the whole intelligible realm; and then after this sojourn in the Godhead I descend from the intelligible world to the plane of discursive thought. And after I have descended I am at a loss to know how it is that I have done so, and how my soul has entered into my body, in view of the fact that she really is as her inmost nature was revealed, and yet is in the body."

"The soul has naturally a love of God and desires to be united with Him. . . . In the higher world we find the true Beloved with whom it is possible for us to unite ourselves when we have seized and held it, because it is not clothed with flesh and blood. He who has beheld this Beloved knows the truth of what I say, how the soul then receives a new life when she has gone forth to it, and come to it and participated in it, so that in her new condition she knows that the giver of true life is beside her and she needs nothing else. Such a one knows also, however, that we must put all else away, and abide in the Beloved alone and become only it, stripping off all else that wraps us about; and hence that we must hasten to come forth from the things of this world and be wroth at the bonds which bind us to them, to the end that we may embrace the Beloved with all our soul and have no part of us left with which we do not touch God. It is possible for us even while here in the body to behold both Him and ourselves in such wise as it is lawful for us to see. Ourselves we see illumined, full of the

363

light of the intelligible, or rather as that very light itself, pure, without heaviness, upward rising. Verily we see ourselves as made, nay, as being God Himself. Then it is that we are kindled. But when we sink to earth again we are, as it were, put out.

"It is a bold thing to say, but in the vision a man does not see, or if he sees he does not distinguish what he sees from himself nor fancy that there are two — the seer and the seen. On the contrary it is by becoming as it were another than himself, and by neither being himself nor belonging to himself that he attains the vision. And having surrendered himself to it he becomes one with it, as the centers of two circles might coincide. For these centers when they coincide become one, and when the circles are separated there are two centers again. And it is in this sense that we too speak of a difference. It follows that the vision is hard to describe. For how could a man report as something different from himself that which at the time of his vision he did not see as different but as one with himself?

"Now since in the vision there are not two, but the seer is made one with the seen, not as with something seen but as with something made one with himself, he who has been united with it may, if he remembers, keep by him some faint image of the divine. He himself was one (in the vision), with no distinctions within himself either as regarded himself or outer things. There was no movement of any sort in him, nor was emotion or desire of any outer thing present in him after his ascent, no, nor any reason or any thought, nor was he himself present to himself, if I may so express it; but as wrapt and inspired he rested isolated in his unmoved and untroubled essence, inclining nowhere and not even reflecting upon himself, at rest in all respects, yea as if he had become rest itself. Nor did he concern himself with the beautiful, but had passed beyond beauty and had transcended the series of virtues as one might penetrate into the holy of holies, leaving behind in the temple the statues of the Gods. And these he would not see again till he came out after having had the vision of what lay within and communion there with what was no statue or image but the divine itself — of which the statues were but secondary images. Or perhaps his experience was not a vision but some other kind of seeing, ecstasy and simplification and self-surrender, a yearning to touch, and a rest and a thought centered upon being merged in the divine." [1]

I have quoted this passage at length both because of its historical position and its influence upon the mystic tradition,[2] and also because it is in itself an admirable description of the mystic experience of the more intense sort; and thus puts before us at the very outset a classical example of the thing we are to study in this and the following chapters. There is, of course, no hard and fast line separating the milder from the more intense forms of the mystic experience, although the distinction between the two is (as I have tried to show) a useful one. The intense mysticism of the great saints is merely an extension of the kind of experience studied in the last chapter. All truly religious men love God after some fashion or other; and, as Joly puts it, "the 'mystic' *par excellence* is a man whose entire life is enveloped and penetrated by the love of God." [3] "The saint," says Father Tyrrell, "differs from the ordinary Christian not in his mysticism but in the degree of his mysticism. . . . The difference is that between the seed and the flower. But because there is real continuity and sameness of kind, the saint is intelligible to us in that which is the very essence of his sanctity." [4]

Yet although the transition from the experience of the ordinary religious man to that of the saint is gradual and involves no leap, it is convenient to make the distinction; and the distinction becomes not only convenient but essential to a real understanding of mysticism when the experience of " the mystic *par excellence* " is carried to its extreme — for then we are

<hr/>

[1] Quoted from the fourth and sixth books of the Enneads in Bakewell's "Source Book in Ancient Philosophy" (New York, Scribner's: 1907). pp. 386, 389–92.

[2] Plotinus's description is obviously based upon his own personal experience; and this experience seems to have been (so far, at least, as we can see) uninfluenced by imitation but quite spontaneous in its nature. As such it set an example for all Neoplatonic mysticism and served as a text for Neoplatonic writers. Through " Dionysius the Areopagite " and Scotus Erigena, his translator, the torch was passed on into Christianity; so that Plotinus may in some sense be called the father of Christian mysticism.

[3] " Psychologie des Saints " (Paris, Gabolda: 1908), p. 43.

[4] " The Faith of the Millions " (London, Longmans: 1902), p. 261.

faced with a difference in degree so great as to become a positive difference in kind. The milder form of mysticism is shared by a very large number of people and is quite possible though latent for a great many more. As the experience becomes more intense, however, it is found in constantly decreasing measure. It is not for every one; and a somewhat uncommon disposition or temperament to start with is, for the more extreme forms of mysticism, quite essential. This disposition is in part the result of education but is chiefly congenital.

The religious mystic of the more intense type carries to an extreme two characteristics which have often been noticed and pointed out not only in the mystic of the milder sort but in various kinds of non-religious mysticism. I refer to the mystic's demand for immediacy and his love of the romantic. For him the mediate, the merely reasoned, the conceptual and discursive is relatively valueless. He regards conceptual knowledge as ever unsatisfying or meaningless, and immediate experience as the only trustworthy guide and the only solid satisfaction.[5]

It is for him the only trustworthy guide *because* it is the only solid satisfaction. And this brings us to the second of the two characteristics of the mystic to which I have referred. The mystic is essentially a romanticist. By saying this I mean that he exhibits in a large degree that confidence in emotion and imagination which are at the bottom of romanticism. He is

[5] This characteristic of the mystic has been frequently expounded,—perhaps best by Royce in " The World and the Individual," Vol. I, Lectures IV and V. The attitude of the mystic, with his love for immediacy, towards all sorts of discursive thought and mere conceptual knowledge has seldom been better expressed than in Walt Whitman's poem,

" When I heard the learn'd astronomer,
  When the proofs, the figures were ranged in columns before me,
  When I was shown the charts and diagrams, to add, divide, and
      measure them,
  When I sitting heard the astronomer where he lectured with much
      applause in the lecture-room,
  How soon unaccountable I became tired and sick,
  Till rising and gliding out I wander'd off by myself
  In the mystical moist night air, and from time to time,
  Looked up in perfect silence at the stars."

usually gifted with more intense feelings and more vivid imagination than are most people, and as is natural the two run together in most indistinguishable fashion. Not only are his feelings and imaginings intense but his confidence in them is usually considerable, and he often makes a deliberate effort to cultivate both.[6] Their intensity and his confidence in them mutually reinforce each other, and the result is what psychologists call a "circular process" — his emotional life and his faith in it increasing with the years.

In the greater religious mystics the emotional temperament common to mystics of every school expresses itself (partly as a result of early training) in an intense love for the Divine, the Perfect, the Absolute, conceived perhaps clearly, perhaps very vaguely. This love felt by the mystic, with its accompanying aspiration, is of course a gradual growth. Its starting point, says Boutroux, "is a state of the soul which it is difficult to define, but which is characterized well enough by the German word *Sehnsucht*. It is a state of desire, vague, and disturbed, very real, and liable to be very intense as a passion of the soul; very indeterminate, or rather very inexplicable, as regards both its object and its cause. It is an aspiration towards an unknown object, towards a good which the heart imperatively demands and which the mind cannot conceive. Such a state may indeed be found in men of very different characters, and may have very different degrees of significance. In the mystic it is profound and lasting; it works in the soul, which gradually forms for itself an idea of the object of its aspiration. This revelation is not direct. But, more or less suddenly, according to the individual experience, the things amongst which we live, things about which we thought we had formed stable judgments, appear to us in another light. The things that charmed us lose their color; the things we had admired seem debased; our dearest affections cease to fill our hearts. The things of the world no longer hold us; each of them now awakens in us the idea of its opposite. In all the objects presented to our sight we see only the distortion, the empty image, wan and dead,

[6] The spiritual exercises of Loyola, for example, and the systematic meditations of the Indian Yogin, are scientific methods of cultivating both imagination and emotion.

of the living idea perfect and definite, which sensible realities are powerless to express. We conceive, as the supreme object of our desires, the infinite, the eternal, the perfect — God. And reflecting upon the feeling which was the starting point of this conception, we can understand why the desire was tinged with disquiet, why we could neither escape from this feeling nor satisfy it. It was the still unconscious idea of an infinite object, which was creating an indefinable dissatisfaction in our consciousness with regard to the possession of all finite objects. It is in the passing of this idea from the region of the unconscious to that of distinct consciousness that the first phase of mystical development consists." [7]

This love for God becomes at last an intense longing for union with God. No barrier must be allowed to remain between the soul and its Master; oneness with Him comes to be regarded as the supreme goal of all life and all effort. The pleasant tone of the milder form of religious experience with which the mystic began now fails to satisfy, or only intensifies his thirst for deeper draughts of the Divine. He learns from the Church or from older mystics that actual union with God is possible, and nothing short of that will now satisfy his eager love.

This love for God, though resulting in keen desire for union with Him for its own sake, is in most respects essentially unselfish. The typical mystic is filled with an almost fanatical moral earnestness. As a rule he cherishes the ideal of service to God for its own sake, regardless of reward and blind to dangers, with the passionate cry, "Though He slay me yet will I trust in Him." Leuba [8] has well pointed out that although the mystics seek the joyous experience of the ecstasy, it is less for its own sake than because they regard it as a means of advancement in the moral life and the service of God. They love God and righteousness for their own sakes, not for the joy that comes from the love. Their strenuous effort for holiness in themselves and in others is impulsive rather than delibera-

---

[7] " La Psychologie du Mysticisme," in the *Revue Bleue* for March 15, 1902, and translated by Miss Crum for the *International Journal of Ethics*, XVIII, 182–195.

[8] " Tendences Fondamentales des Mystiques Chrétiens." *Revue Philosophique*, LIV, 1–36.

tive; they struggle against evil not in order to obtain some future joyous condition but *because they must.*

In addition to this emotional and moral ardor, which is characteristic of most of the Christian mystics, there is to be found in the more extreme cases, at least, a somewhat uncommon if not incipiently pathological condition of the nervous system, which manifests itself sometimes in physical disturbances, sometimes in a tendency toward mental dissociation. St. Teresa, in many respects a very typical mystic of the more extreme sort, was throughout her life in wretched health, and was subject to recurrent attacks of illness, all of which were evidently augmented by her state of nervous instability.[9] The same peculiar psycho-physical organization is apparent in most of the ecstatics.[10] The bodily pathological conditions of the mystics vary considerably, and a careful study and comparison of them might prove interesting.[11] They do not, however, bear upon our problem. Much more important for our pur-

[9] Her autobiography is full of such things as the following: " To dispose me toward the profession which was best for me the Lord sent me a great illness. . . . My health continued poor and I had great weakness as well as fever. . . . The change in my manner of life and nourishment affected my health; my weakness increased and my heart trouble was extremely great. Thus I passed the first year [in the convent]. My illness was so great that I was only partly conscious much of the time and sometimes lost consciousness altogether. . . . In the month of August I was taken with a fainting fit which lasted four days without any return of consciousness; and they were so sure I was dead that when I regained consciousness I found on my eyes the wax of the candle which they had used to see if I were living." Etc., etc., etc.

[10] Cf., e.g., Baron von Hügel's account of St. Catherine of Genoa — " The Mystical Element in Religion." Part II. See also his treatment of Ezekiel, St. Paul and other mystics, Vol. II, pp. 42–47.

[11] Duprat regards mysticism as originating from a sense of the mysterious which comes with a physical or psychological transformation of the self, and hence as having always a psychopathological origin. " Dans tous nous trouvons comme point de départ, un trouble profond de la personalité. 'Troubles physiologiques, troubles de la connaissance des choses et des hommes, conscience vague de ces processus anormaux, voila dit, avec raison, M. Revault d'Allonnes, les matériaux du sentiment morbide du mystère!' Il faut aller plus loin; voilà les *causes du sentiment mystique primitif.* . . . Il faut, donc, pour que le sentiment mystique prenne naissance, qu'un désarroi psycho-physiologique survienne chez des êtres en voie d'intégration mentale, en équilibre instable surtout au point de vue de la conception du monde et de ses relations avec le moi." " Religiosité et Mysticisme," Revue Philosophique, LXVIII, September, 1909, pp. 276–83.

poses is the mental state which is common to so many of the more extreme mystics.[12]

It would be dangerous to attempt to generalize very far on the mental conditions of the mystics. If any general statement could be found which would be exactly true of all the mystics it would probably have to be so broad as to be quite uninstructive. The majority, however, *of the ecstatic type* of mystic do possess certain common mental traits which it will be worth our while to examine. If all mankind should be divided into two classes, the mystical and the non-mystical, one of the chief distinctions that could be made out between them would probably be based upon the relative importance of the margin and the center of consciousness. The non-mystical type, as I pointed out in the last chapter, seems, on the whole, to have a narrower marginal region than has the mystical, and consequently in it the immediate object of attention is of greater relative importance. In the mystic ecstasy, to be sure, consciousness is narrowed to a small point, as we shall see, but this narrowness of the conscious field is not the usual state of the mystic in his non-ecstatic condition. In this latter state, (so far at least as I can make out) the marginal region is relatively broad and particularly influential. The working of his mind is largely guided by feeling and by ideas rising out of the fringe, while his non-mystical brother lives a life, perhaps, of clearer thought,— passing rapidly from one concentrated field of attention to another,— or, it may be, merely a life of dull routine and customary action, in which the content of consciousness is determined almost entirely by sense impressions and habitual associations, unenliv-

[12] The more extremely pathological cases merge, of course, into actual insanity, so that it would be hard to draw a clear line between pathological mysticism and mystical pathology. Religious paranoia sometimes results in phenomena quite comparable to those of extreme mysticism. Cf. the following description of this variety of insanity from Kraft-Ebbing: "Sometimes feelings of the sinful body being permeated by the divine breath come into consciousness, and in these states remove the individual from earthly interests and cares. A feeling of beatitude invades the patient as if the Holy Ghost had come over them; in women at the same time there is very frequently sexual excitement even with feelings of coitus, which find their expression later in delusions of immaculate conception. In these states of ecstasy cataleptiform symptoms may occur" (p. 404) "Text Book of Insanity" (Philadelphia, Davis: 1904).

ened by any of the surprises that come from the products of the marginal region.

This breadth of consciousness, which is characteristic of mysticism of both the mild and the intense kind, is sometimes associated, especially among intense natures, with a painful lack of inner unity and a great longing for it. To be sure we all lack perfect unity and we sometimes long for it — this is a characteristic of the moral struggle everywhere. But in the individual of mystic tendencies it is more pronounced than in the relatively simpler and more concentrated type of mind. Hegel finds in it one of the leading characteristics of the awakening religious consciousness.[13] In another connection we saw it illustrated in a man so far removed from the extreme form of mysticism as Maine de Biran. And in those individuals who are destined to become ecstatics this lack of unity is often very pronounced and is sometimes described as a state of distraction. Murisier, although misleading if his descriptions are taken to apply to the ordinary forms of mysticism, gives a fairly accurate idea of the mental state of the more extreme type, writing of it as follows:

" It is an exaggerated state of incoherence and instability, a perpetual conflict of psychic elements which never succeed in getting into harmony. Hence comes a feeling of *malaise* and a constantly growing desire to join oneself to a superhuman power capable of assuring one, in place of external protection and material advantages, repose, inner peace, deliverance." [14]

Connected with this state of distraction, and perhaps only an outgrowth or exaggeration of it, is a tendency in the more extreme ecstatics toward mental dissociation. It can hardly be doubted that many of the mystics have been at least incipiently hysteric. Either the marginal region or the subconscious or unconscious processes have so developed as to function in part independently of the normal center of consciousness and hence give the mystic the impression of an external power which he cannot recognize as in any sense his own. The extreme condition, however, of a split-off consciousness is by no means uni-

---

[13] " Die Phänomenologie des Geistes," IV, B.
[14] " Les Maladies du Sentiment Religieux " (Paris, Alcan: 1903), p. 20.

versal with the mystics; and it is, in my opinion, an absurd exaggeration to identify mysticism (even of the more intense type) as Murisier and Duprat seem to do, with a disintegration of the personality. If the temptation of the theologian is to interpret mysticism as a supernatural phenomenon, the temptation of the psychologist (no less strong and no less dangerous) is to be over-influenced in his interpretation by the charms of the pathological.

The antecedent physical and mental conditions which I have sketched may be sufficient to produce quite spontaneously some of the more intense mystical phenomena. But whether they do so or not, the mystic who longs for a more intimate sense of the divine usually takes all the means in his power to cultivate and deepen the experience. Various methods for the cultivation of the mystic life have been devised and practiced by individuals of various religions, in many lands and in as many centuries. In spite of their separation in time and place, however, and their independence of each other, these methods are strikingly similar the world over, although the similarity can hardly be called surprising, since it is based on the common laws of the human mind. It must not be supposed that these methods can by themselves assure the result desired. The Christian mystics and the systematic writers upon mysticism constantly protest that the means taken by the individual, no matter how carefully planned and exactly carried out, can never make the attainment of the goal a certainty.[15] There is always an incalculable element to be reckoned with, say the Catholic writers, a supernatural and direct gift of God,— which may be interpreted to mean some obscure but important psychical conditions which lie too deep to be induced by any methods as yet devised. These particular conditions are connected with those larger and more obscure general conditions which we call temperament and mood. It is not every one that can become a mystic, nor can the genuine mystic always force his moods. Yet, given an individual of the proper temperament, the methods approved by the long mystic tradition for training the moods may, if patiently practiced, result in the production of the desired men-

[15] Cf. Ribet. "La Mystique Divine" (Paris, Poussielgue: 1895), Vol. I, pp. 18 and 19; Lejeune, "Introduction à la Vie Mystique," p. 2.

tal state, and may even be one of the conditions *sine qua non* of its production. For the methods in question may well be termed ways of training one's moods, of inhibiting some and cultivating others;— in short, they are essentially cases of *applied psychology*. Protestant mysticism, which is of a very amateur sort, is often, indeed, unwilling to admit the propriety of applying psychology to the culture of the religious life, and would feel half ashamed to admit that it made use of any psychological methods in the production of its desired ends. And indeed when psychological methods are used to coerce the mind, to bring about a species of self-deception, to transform the thinking man into the hypnotic subject and substitute emotion for volition and sentiment for morality, then one may well oppose and fear them. Yet it must be remembered that at least one of the most important goals aimed at by religion and morality alike is, from the psychological point of view, a *state of mind;* and that states of mind follow psychological laws and are brought about by psychological means. If the means used have no accompanying evil effects such as weakening the will or clouding the intellect, there is no good reason why they should be feared. Protestantism in fact makes use of them constantly, though not always consciously, systematically, or wisely. Roman Catholicism, on the other hand, recognizes plainly that psychological means are requisite for bringing about psychological effects, and hence applies frankly and carefully and, one might almost say, scientifically, all the knowledge of the human mind which her long experience has gathered. The mysticism of India and of the Sufis is naïvely open in its application of psychological methods for bringing about the desired mental conditions.

There is much in common between the methods used by the mystics of whatever creed the world over. The religious enthusiast who wishes for the more intense form of the mystical experience usually begins with the methods described in the last chapter and carries them on consistently until he has felt to the full the milder form of mysticism. From reading the descriptions of former mystics, however, he knows that what he has thus far experienced is pale and cold compared with their ecstasies, and he enters, therefore, upon a more systematic self-

training.   This course of training, as outlined by the long tradition of Christian mystics, consists of two parts or stages, one
negative, the other positive.   The negative part is technically
known as the " purgative " stage, while the positive part is
called the " meditative " or " illuminative " stage.[16]   The negative part of the training is for the sake of the positive part,
hence is prior to it logically, though not necessarily so in point
of time.   The purgative and meditative " stages " thus are to
a great extent contemporaneous, although for purposes of exposition it is invariably found expedient to treat of the negative
methods or the purgative stage first.

The simplest and most obvious form of the negative method,

[16] These two are regularly regarded as the first and second steps of the
mystic life, the third or " unitive " stage being the goal at which the
others aim.   This three-fold division is the authoritative view of Catholic mysticism.   Cf. Suarez: " Distinguere solent mystici theologi tres
vias, purgativam, illuminativam, et unitavam."   Cf. also Scaramelli:
" Nel cammino della perfezione si va per tre vie al termine della nostra
celeste patria; la prima della quali chiamasi purgativa, la seconda illu-
minativa, e la terza unitiva; distinzione giusta e convenevole ammessa
da tutti gli Scrittori ascetici e Dottori mistici, che senza grave temerità
non può disapprovarsi."   Quoted by Ribet, op. cit., Vol. I, p. 17, notes
2 and 3.   The author of the " Theologia Germanica " accepts the same
three traditional stages as the more typically Catholic mystics.   See Miss
Winkworth's translation, Chapter XIV.   The " illuminative " and " unitive " stages, however, are not always interpreted in the same way.   The
" illuminative " stage is often taken to cover both the meditative part of
the preparatory course and also the ecstatic experience; while the term
" unitive " stage is sometimes used to mean only what I shall refer to
(following Delacroix) as the " mystic life."   This, for example, is Miss
Underhill's usage.   She, however, interpolates a new and distinct stage
between the " illuminative " and the " unitive," namely the " Dark Night
of the Soul."   See her "Mysticism " (London, Methuen: 1911), pp. 205–
07, and " The Mystic Way " (London, Dent: 1913), pp. 52–55.   Delacroix
has a somewhat similar four-fold division, though more truly psychological in character, " Études d'Histoire et de Psychologie du Mysticisme "
(Paris, Alcan: 1908), p. 346.   Boutroux makes five stages (see the Revue
Bleu for March 15, 1902, p. 7).   Professor Jones and Mrs. Herman have
very sensibly protested against taking any of these systematizations too
seriously; all of them are partial and most of them conventional; none
are capable of universal application or based upon any really general
psychological principle.   See Jones, " Mysticism in Present Day Religion " (Harvard Theological Review for April, 1915, especially pp. 163–
65); and Herman, " The Meaning and Value of Mysticism " (Boston, Pilgrim Press: 1915), pp. 13, 40, 162–63.   Miss Underhill's attempt to fit
the religious development of Jesus, Paul, and John into her four-fold
division is clever rather than persuasive.   (See " The Mystic Way," Chapters II, III, and IV.)

and in fact the very beginning and presupposition of all the rest, is common-place negative morality. Moral purity is the necessary condition of the mystic life. The soul that is filled with the love of sin will have no room for the love of God. The mind that is burning with hot lusts, that is the prey of tempestuous passions and worldly desires of any kind, can never give to the thought of God that quiet contemplation which is the condition and the beginning of " God's presence "—" Dieu sensible au coeur." [17] " He that committeth sin is the servant of sin " — and no man can serve two masters.

But moral purity of the ordinary kind is not sufficient for him who aspires to an extraordinary mystic life. The flesh lusteth against the spirit and the spirit against the flesh, and in this deadly conflict it will not do for him who aims at complete mastery to remain merely upon the defensive. The war must be carried into the enemy's country. One must not only resist the encroachments of the old Adam; one must crucify the flesh with the affections and lusts. The mind must be freed from the interruptions and distractions of the body at any cost. Hence the common expedient of what is known as " mortification " or asceticism.

The aim of asceticism is not ultimately negative, nor is it based upon an essentially pessimistic view of human nature. It would tame or even destroy certain normal human impulses, but only for the sake of the moral and spiritual freedom which it prizes higher than the things it sacrifices. Much in human nature it regards as evil, but the spiritual part of man is, for it, supremely good, and the life of the spirit supremely worth while. The view of human nature which it usually implies is thus patent,— namely the dualistic view so generally held in ancient India and during the Christian Middle Ages when the tradition of Catholic mysticism was formed. This view regards soul and body as distinct " substances " joined together temporarily in rather external fashion, and carrying on constant warfare with each other.[18] In a larger sense, however, asceti-

[17] Pascal's definition of mysticism.

[18] Cf. Lejeune, " Introduction à la Vie Mystique," p. 188: " Pour bien comprendre le phénòmene auquel il est fait ici allusion, il faut se rappeler qu'il y a chez l'homme deux substances, qui ne se ressemblent ni par leur nature, ni par leur fonctions. Qui ne connâit les noms consacrés par

cism transcends any particular theory and is confined to no one class such as the mystics. It is, in fact, the effort of the earnest soul to repress and destroy all that militates against the spiritual life. It is the expression of the conviction common alike to Hinduism, Buddhism, and Christianity, that the lesser self must die if the larger self is to live. It is voiced in the teachings of Gautama and of all of his disciples, whether Hinayana or Mahayana, who have grasped most fully the spirit of their master. It looms large in the Upanishads and the Gita, in the words of mediæval seers like Shankara and Kabir, and modern Hindu teachers like Ram Mohun Roy and Ramakrishna. It was at the heart of the teachings of Jesus, and is echoed in such typically Christian books as the Imitation of Christ, the Theologia Germanica, and the sermons of Tauler. The necessity of denying and crucifying the smaller self appears in fact to be one of the two or three fundamental insights upon which all the more deeply spiritual religions are agreed. This understood, asceticism is a much larger thing than mysticism. But the mystics as a class have had a quicker sense of its value than others could attain, and have tried to apply it with a system, a courage, and at times a rash fanaticism at which the rest of the religious world has been able only to gasp.

It would, however, be a mistake to say that asceticism as practiced by the mystics is entirely based even upon a general conviction. As Mrs. Herman [19] and M. Pacheu [20] point out, one great force in the self-inflicted pains of the Christian saints was their intense and unreasoning longing to suffer with Christ, and one might add, their desire to show thereby their love for Him.[21] Various other motives have doubtless also been at work.

l'usage pour exprimer cette dualité et cette opposition? C'est la chair et l'esprit. . . . Ces deux substances, bien qu'unies pour former le composé humain, n'ont pas cependant les mêmes aspirations et ne donnent pas naissance aux mêmes œuvres." etc., etc. The Yogins of India also based their ascetic practices in part on a dualistic psychology, distinguishing sharply between the purusha or soul and those " conformations " of qualities which are really due to our ignorance and illusion.

[19] " The Meaning and Value of Mysticism," pp. 182–86.

[20] " L'Experience Mystique et l'Activité Subconsciente " (Paris, Perrin: 1911), p. 207f. The ascetic practices prompted by love he distinguishes from moral mysticism as " l'ascétisme mystique."

[21] This has been common to many mystics, but is perhaps most notable among the Jansenists. Cf. St. Cyres' " Pascal," pp. 243–44.

In fact asceticism has to a considerable extent been built up by a process of trial and error, and its long retention by the mystics of Christendom and India and Islam is explicable only by the fact that it has produced the results desired.

The great aim of mortification is freedom — freedom from the things of this world and the distractions of the body. Hence the constant use of methods calculated to produce indifference.[22] The Buddhist who seriously seeks salvation must cut all the ties of family and friendship and worldly possession and either live with a band of monks or " wander alone like a rhinoceros." " The sensual pleasures which are various, sweet, and charming, under their different shapes agitate the mind; seeing the misery originating in sensual pleasures, let one wander alone like a rhinoceros. Having left son and wife, father and mother, wealth and corn and relatives, the different objects of desire, let one wander alone like a rhinoceros." [23] The great aim of the Buddhist training is thus to kill out desire and dependence upon it. And in similar vein Krishna, in the Bhagavad Gita, holds up as the ideal for imitation him " who being without attachments anywhere, feels no exultation and no aversion on encountering the various agreeable and disagreeable things of this world "; " who is self-contained; to whom a sod and a stone and gold are alike; to whom censure and praise of himself are alike; who is alike toward friends and foes." [24] Probably no religious sect has carried out this kind of training

[22] Perhaps the most obvious method for protecting the soul against the distractions of the body and the assaults of the world is to keep a strict watch upon its portals, the senses. Hence " the mortification of the senses is the chief part of bodily mortification." (Lejeune, op. cit., p. 210.) The books of direction to the young mystic are full of exhortations to avoid falling under the power of any of the senses. Alvarez de Paz takes up each sense specially and points out in detail the dangers to which it exposes the soul. In the case of sight and hearing, these are evident enough, but taste too is a great danger, and so is even the sense of odor. " Among the foods which are offered you, choose those which most mortify your taste." " Eat in such a way as not to be altogether given over to your action, but be attentive to a pious thought or to a book which is being read to you." Even perfumes should be avoided. (Alvarez de Paz, " De Exterminatione Mali et Promotione Boni,"— Lugduni, 1613 — Liber II, Pars II, Cap. II.)

[23] Sutta Nipata. S. B. E. Vol. X, Part II, pp. 8 and 9.

[24] Bhagavad Gita, II, 70, and XIV, 21. S. B. E. Vol. VIII, Part II, pp. 50 and 110.

in self-control through self-denial with such nicety of detail as have the Jainas. Of the twelve vows taken by every monk and by every earnest layman, seven deal with the limitation of desire in all sorts of things, little and big.[25] In this way the Jaina seeks to free himself from the imperious cravings of the flesh and from the domination of a world of things.

The Catholic Church in its encouragement of the monastic life has sought and cultivated this same freedom from the domination of the world. But one can cultivate it without actually leaving the world behind him, and even when still surrounded by the distractions of society. The systematic refusal to take delight in the good things, little and big, which one still retains is a refinement of asceticism which the Buddhist Bhikkhu never seems to have thought of. It is, nevertheless, say the Catholic writers, one of the best methods for gaining true and lasting independence of spirit. To deny oneself good things to eat is a crude (though for beginners often a necessary) form of asceticism; to eat what one likes but to take no pleasure in it is, when it can be done, a much more useful means, for it not only leaves the desire unsatisfied but tends to root it out altogether. It is particularly in connection with little things that one may cultivate this indifference to the world; for, as St. Dorotheas says, little things present opportunities for victory over self at every moment. The following illustrations are suggested by the saint just referred to: "You take a walk and curiosity makes you desire to look at something; you resist the desire and turn your eyes away. You feel an impulse to take part in a conversation concerning unimportant things; you impose silence on yourself and go your way. The thought comes to you of going to your cook and telling him to prepare your dinner; you don't go. You see an object and are filled with desire to ask who brought it; you do nothing and keep quiet. By mortifying yourself in little things you contract the habit of mortifying yourself in all things; and whatever happens to you, you are just as satisfied as if it had happened as you wished. Thus you see how useful these little things are to

[25] For details see Mrs. Stevenson's "The Heart of Jainism," pp. 209–21, and 165–68.

your perfection and how they aid you in controlling your will." [26]

For the control of the will is, after all, the chief thing. Nothing more impedes the spiritual life than self-will — hence the value of constant self-denial as a means of mortification. And the most important method devised by the Catholic Church for the ceaseless denial of self and the humbling of the will consists in " the three virtues of the religious life," — poverty, chastity, obedience. The vow of perpetual poverty cuts all the bonds that make one subject to material things, forbidding, as it does, not merely legal possession but any form of attachment to the things of the world. If a monk, for instance, finds himself becoming fond of a particular book he must get rid of it. He must not even take delight in the possessions of his order. The vow of perpetual chastity, which aims at purity of thought as well as of action, seeks to free one from all dominance of passion by renouncing once and for all every possibility of sexual satisfaction and training the mind and even the sense organs to avoid every slightest suggestions that might furnish fuel to the natural instinct of reproduction. Finally the vow of perpetual obedience to a superior attacks not merely the expression of the will but the will itself in its central citadel.[27] It means complete renunciation to the will of God as one understands that will — nothing of the little self shall be allowed to remain and impede the inflowing of the divine spirit.

All of the means for dominating the body and its impulses thus far described, even when combined, have not always been sufficient to bring about that complete crucifying of the flesh with the affections and lusts which the most eager of the mystics have desired; hence more heroic methods still have been devised and regularly practiced. I refer, of course, to what are known as " austerities." The Catholic writers consider these extremely important. " To lead us to the practice of austerities," writes Alverez de Paz, " nothing more is necessary than the example of all the perfect men. For who is there

[26] Quoted by Lejeune, op. cit., p. 201.

[27] Cf. Lejeune: " Par la vertu de pauvreté il immole à Dieu ses biens extérieurs; par la chasteté il immole son corps; par l'obéissance il complète son sacrifice et il donne à Dieu tout ce qu'il possède encore, ses deux biens les plus précieux, son esprit et sa volonté," p. 277.

among them who has not (unless prevented by severe illness) given himself over to austerities? Who is there among them that has not conquered his flesh by hair cloth, by the scourge, by fasting, by watching? If we run through the history of the saints we shall not find one who has not used this kind of mortification against his body." [28]

Foremost among the austerities comes fasting. In the attack upon the flesh it is comparable, says Surin, to the method of siege, cutting off the supplies of the enemy, sapping his forces, and thus patiently overcoming him.[29] The same writer gives the following suggestions for its practical application: "The man who wishes to conquer himself and his vices may follow this rule: to decrease his nourishment as much as he can without diminishing the strength which is necessary for him to perform his duties; and it is certain that by abstinence he will advance as much in the spiritual life and weaken the power of the enemy as by anything else that he can do." [30]

The extent to which abstinence has been carried by many mystics of many lands seems almost incredible. As Charbonier points out, the mystics of warm climates are more successful at it than are their northern fellows; yet in all latitudes it is practiced to some extent. The Indians have, perhaps, carried it farthest; [31] though many Christian saints have by gradual training learned to go for many days at a time with little food or none at all. St. Catherine of Genoa, according to von Hügel, in the great middle period of her life when her activity and usefulness was at its height, fasted regularly for long periods twice a year. Von Hügel tells us — basing his assertion upon the somewhat legendary "Life" of the saint — that for twenty years "she evidently went for a fairly equal

[28] "La Preparation à la Contemplation," Liber II, Pars II, Cap. V.

[29] Quoted by Lejeune, p. 226.

[30] This, though probably the chief aim of fasting, is not the only one with all the mystics. Galton points out that in many cases investigated by him fasting, and also sleeplessness and loneliness, have tended to induce visions; and this fact was known long before Galton's time to the whole mystic fraternity, from the Shaman to the saint.

[31] Especially the Jainas, with whom it has always been regarded as a great merit to starve oneself to death — a merit, moreover, still occasionally attained by extreme devotees. See Mrs. Stevenson, op. cit., pp. 221 and 163.

number of days — some thirty in Advent and some forty in Lent, seventy in all annually, with all but no food; and was, during these fasts, at least as vigorous and active as when her nutrition was normal." [32]   Louise Lateau for nineteen years took each day only a piece of apple and a piece of bread with a little beer; and this finally proved too hearty a diet and had to be reduced.[33]   Cases more or less similar could be cited almost *ad libitum.*

The universality of this practice is sufficient evidence of its usefulness in inducing the mental and bodily state which the mystic desires.   The body is considerably weakened, and has no superfluous force to spend upon the various buoyant impulses of the Old Adam.   Constant training reduces the amount of food actually required and enough food is taken to keep the body alive and give some additional strength which the will of the mystic uses in meditation and ecstasy, but no margin is left which might act as fuel to the slumbering fires of passion.[34]   The result is that the mind is left undisturbed to fasten its attention upon God, its superfluous energy is reduced, and the wandering of " discursive thought " (so feared by the mystic) is inhibited.   Thus both body and mind are brought to such a condition that the unity of the ecstatic trance is but one step distant.

Yet, great as is the importance of fasting it is a mistake to consider it (as Charbonier does) the source of all the phenomena of mysticism and the stock from which all the other austerities grow.   It is a decided misconception to suppose that any one austerity is the sole source of the mystic phenomena; there are in fact several kinds of austerities quite as fundamental as is fasting.   Sleeplessness,[35] for example, though

[32] Von Hügel, " The Mystical Element in Religion," Vol. II, p. 33.

[33] Charbonier, " Maladies des Mystiques."

[34] Cf. Alvarez de Paz: " The ardors of passion are cooled in the man who deprives himself of superfluous and delicate food.   To throw wood on the fire and at the same time pray that the fire may go out is to ask of God a miracle.   In like manner you tempt God, you ask an unnecessary miracle when you gorge yourself with food and in your prayers long for chastity."   " De Castitate," Cap. XIV.

[35] Pierre d'Alcantara, according to St. Teresa, went for forty years with but one and one-half hours of sleep out of the twenty-four.   " Vie," (French translation by Bouix, Paris, Lecoffre: 1907), p. 294.

less common, is a favorite means of subduing the flesh.   As used by the mystics it is at first artificially induced, after which it grows into a habit, and results in much the same bodily and mental conditions as lack of food.   Its specific effects are to make the mystic less susceptible to distraction and at last to bring about what Professor Haynes describes as the " smothering " of the attention.[36]   Besides sleeplessness and fasting there are many other forms of austerity, all aiming at the same goal: victory over the flesh by the spirit and the resulting freedom of the mind.   To illustrate them I need cite only one case, in which nearly all are included,— namely that of the famous German mystic of the early Fourteenth Century, Heinrich Suso.   I quote from Preger's account, which follows very closely Suso's own description in his autobiography, and is, in fact, hardly more than a condensation of certain passages in it: " From his eighteenth year on for twenty-two years he sought to break his ' wild spirit ' and his ' pampered body ' by an unintermitting series of painful practices.   For the first ten years (1313–1323) he shut himself up in absolute seclusion in his cloister.   A chapel which he had built for himself, his cell, and the choir of the church constituted his narrowest circuit, the cloister a wider one, and the walk as far as the gate his widest circuit, between which he chose according to rule.   For a long time he wore a hair shirt and an iron chain, later a hair undershirt with nails, which pierced his flesh at every motion and whenever he lay down.   In order not to be able to avoid the bites of the vermin (for he did not bathe during the twenty-two years) he put his hands in slings during the night.   He bore a cross a span long, with thirty nails and seven needles, bound upon his bare back; every day he lay upon it or threw himself upon it.   For a long time a door was his bed.   The pains of cold, hunger, thirst, and bloody flagellation he inflicted upon himself for so long a time and with such severity that he came near dying."   He says of himself (speaking in the third person) : " His feet came to be full of sores, his legs swelled as though dropsical, his knees were bloody and wounded, his hips covered with scars from the hair shirt, his back wounded with

[36] Cf. his paper on " Attention, Fatigue, and the Concept of Infinity " in the *Journal of Philosophy*, IV, 601f.

the cross, his body exhausted by endless austerities, his mouth and his tongue dry from thirst, his hands trembling from weakness." [37]

It must not be supposed from what I have said that the aim of these austerities, or of asceticism in general, is chiefly the joyous thrill of the mystic trance.   Often this joy comes not at all and is hardly expected, and when it does come it is usually regarded (at least by the great mystics) as being, after all, of only secondary importance.   The mystic feels driven on *a tergo* by the very force of his moral earnestness to root out the sins of the flesh; or if he be led on from before it is in order that he may the better walk with God and serve Him.   The true place of asceticism in religion must, therefore, not be judged by the place given it in this chapter.   For purposes of exposition I have found it most convenient to treat of it here as one of the modes of preparation for the mystic experience, but it has other relations and functions than this.   And the mystic regards it only incidentally as a means toward a particular kind of experience, and chiefly as a kind of spiritual training undertaken for the sake of greater moral purity and increased efficiency.   In the words of de Montmorand: " Asceticism from the Christian point of view is nothing but a collection of

[37] " Geschichte der deutschen Mystik," three volumes (Leipzig; Doerffling; 1874, '81, '93).   Vol. II, pp. 350 and 351.   The literature of mediæval penance is very large, and no special reference is here needed, for the lives of almost all the saints and mystics are full of it.   A systematic account of one important aspect of it — flagellation — will be found in a curious book by the Rev. William Cooper, entitled " The History of the Rod " (London; Reeves).   Self-inflicted torture of various sorts has been common among many primitive races.   Among civilized races the Indians have carried it to the greatest extreme — as nearly every book on the religions of India will show.   The classical account, I suppose, is that given by Dubois, in his " Hindu Manners, Customs, and Ceremonies " (Third edition, Clarendon Press, 1906), esp. pp. 517f, 529f, 535, 597.   It should be added, however, that Dubois's account though doubtless trustworthy so far as it goes is lacking in sympathy and vision.   A more sympathetic account will be found in Chapter VII of Farquhar's " Crown of Hinduism."   Both the Hindu and the Christian ascetic are prompted in their self-torture by love of God or desire of reward from Him.   It is therefore interesting to note that the atheistic Jainas also make use of similar penitential practices, with the purpose of conquering the flesh for the sake of the spirit.   See, e.g., the directions given in the Akaranga Sutra I, 7, 8 (translated by Jacobi in the Sacred Books of the East); also Mrs. Stevenson's " Heart of Jainism," p. 163.

therapeutic methods tending toward moral purification. Asceticism comes from the Greek 'ασκεῖν, to exercise, to combat; who says ascetic says athlete. The Christian ascetic struggles to transform his corrupted nature, to beat a path for himself toward God, against the obstacles which his passions and the world create for him. And he struggles not solely for his own sake, but still more for the welfare and the salvation of society as a whole." [38]

It is in this larger sense that the value of asceticism and its proper place in life must be judged. Its aim, as expressed in the passage just quoted, is indeed admirable; the real question, therefore, is: To what extent does it fulfill its aim?

It is easy to dispose of asceticism by calling it abnormal and unnatural in all its forms, a product of mediæval superstition, thus relegating it to the Dark Ages. But such a course is rather too easy and simple. Asceticism has had too wide a practice and is even now too prevalent, in one form or another, to be regarded as essentially abnormal. While its extreme cases doubtless are " against nature " the feeling which prompted these and which runs through them all cannot be accounted for by reference to any theological doctrine or local custom. The essential thing in asceticism — the systematic denial of the personal self and its individual desires — is profoundly normal, and in all those who have a touch of the heroic it is as natural as self-preservation or self-pleasing. The moralists have been telling us for several centuries that altruism is as native to humanity as egoism; but it has not been so often nor so clearly pointed out that the love of the strenuous, the difficult, the self-denying life is a " spring of action " coördinate with, if not equal to, the love of pleasure. There is something in most of us that rises up and says Amen to Browning's brave words:

> " Poor vaunt of life indeed
> Were man but formed to feed
> On joy, to solely seek and find and feast;
> Such feasting ended, then

[38] " Ascétisme et Mysticisme," *Revue Philosophique*, LVII, 244. Cf. also Joly's " Psychologie des Saints," pp. 183–85. Dr. Moerchen defines asceticism as " das Streben nach einer Erziehung der körperlichen Funktionen im Sinne einer absoluten Unterordnung derselben unter das Geistige." " Die Psychologie der Heiligkeit " (Halle, Marhold: 1908), p. 22.

As sure an end to men;
Irks care the crop-full bird?   Frets doubt the maw-crammed beast?

" Then welcome each rebuff
That turns earth's smoothness rough,
Each sting that bids nor sit nor stand but go!
Be our joys three parts pain!
Strive, and hold cheap the strain;
Learn, nor account the pang; dare, never grudge the throe! "

The response which our hearts make to exhortations like this,
and the sense of dissatisfaction that would come to most of us
with a life of mere enjoyment from which all the pain of self-
sacrifice had been excluded, will perhaps explain to some extent
the more extreme case of the mystic who exclaims, " Suffering
alone, from now on, can make life supportable to me.   My dearest wishes all lead to suffering.   How often from the bottom of
my heart have I cried out to God, O Lord to suffer or to die is
the only thing I ask." [39]

Some degree of asceticism seems to be essential in most lives.
It is a kind of stimulant without which the individual cannot
work to best advantage.   There can be no doubt, moreover,
that the steady practice of self-denial in purely selfish and unnecessary things is of considerable effect in the upbuilding of
character and the development of the spiritual life.[40]   The greatest authority on this subject gave as preliminary directions for
spiritual living the denial of self and the taking up of one's
cross.   And if the value of the ascetic method was overrated
in the Middle Ages, it is as certainly underrated in our times.
Amid our eagerness for universal amusement, our royal roads
to learning, our patent methods for " getting rich quick," and
our constantly growing habit of pampering ourselves and our
children, the uneasy question can hardly be avoided whether we
would not do well to cultivate some of the sterner virtues of the
Mystic and the Puritan, and whether the practice of a little systematic and gratuitous self-denial is not worthy at least of
our serious consideration.

[39] St. Teresa.   Quoted by Joly, p. 183.
[40] Cf. James's excellent exposition of this view in his " Psychology,"
Briefer Course (New York, Holt: 1893), p. 149.   See also the "Varieties,"
pp. 296–325.

But I fear much of what I have been saying is rather far removed from the subject of this chapter. To return, then, to asceticism as a means of preparation for the mystic life, it must be granted, as it seems to me, that when practiced very moderately and with care, the denial of our less important desires may be and often is a very real assistance in the cultivation of spirituality. But if asceticism is to be what its defenders claim it is — a course of training for the moral athlete — it must in no way injure the man in health of body or health of mind. This in fact is taught by the majority of the Roman Catholic writers. Thus Lejeune: "Austerities which prevent one from fulfilling the obligations of one's charge or vocation are by that very fact condemnable and opposed to the will of God." [41] In like manner St. François de Salles urges the young mystic when in doubt as to the proper amount of austerity to lean always to the side of indulgence rather than to that of asceticism.[42] Yet that this has not been by any means the universal course advised or pursued is shown by the many extreme cases like that of Suso and by the admonitions of mystics like Teresa who urge the beginner to throw to the winds all considerations of health and even of life, and to conquer the body at any cost. And it must be admitted that the asceticism which in any way makes the mystic in body or mind less of a man, the asceticism which transgresses the limits set by health, is harmful and always to be condemned. It is a sort of malpractice upon one's self and tends to put one into a state of physical and mental weakness and self-delusion. In so far as this extreme form is used to bring on the mystic state it drags the latter down with it into the region of pathology, and thus robs it of much of its significance and importance. It is a dangerous thing to lop off any of one's mental powers or reduce to any extent the mind's normal activity; and so far forth as the ecstatic trance is induced by this kind of mental malpractice it is in a real sense pathological and stands on a par with hypnosis.

Mortification of the body and even of the spirit are at best but negative methods of reaching the mystic's goal. The posi-

[41] Op. cit., p. 220.
[42] See Lejeune, p. 277. Cf. also Tauler's saying: "We must lop and prune vices, not nature, which in itself is good and noble."

tive methods which he uses for gaining it come under what is officially known as the "meditative" or "illuminative" stage of the mystic's progress.   As I pointed out some pages back, this second stage is not necessarily second in time, but comes logically after the purgative stage in the course of exposition.   As a matter of fact the negative and the positive methods are carried on side-by-side, and the mystic as long as he lives is perpetually practicing both.

The value of the negative methods and their psychological explanation may be summed up in the word *inhibition.*   Their aim is to keep out from the mind the undesirable and to leave it free from all that is irrelevant and distracting.   The value of the positive methods may be expressed by another common psychological term :— *auto-suggestion.*   They are the means which the mystic uses to get his attention under the control of the proper ideas and emotions, so that these may dominate his whole mind and his whole activity.   To say that inhibition and auto-suggestion sum up the aim and the result of all the preparatory methods, both negative and positive, may seem like undue simplification ; but if these terms be taken in a large sense they do cover the whole ground.

The positive methods of the "meditative" stage consist, then, in a long continued course of suggesting to oneself, by direct and indirect means, that God is present.   Probably the most important of these methods is the "practice of the presence of God," — the habit, diligently cultivated, of keeping constantly either in the fringe or in the center of one's mind the thought that God is present or that He is even within one.   If the latter is found difficult of attainment, Catholic writers recommend that the novitiate begin by training the imagination to picture Christ present at our side in the flesh.   When the ability to do this with some ease has been attained, one should go on to realize the presence of God about one — to *see* Him by the eye of faith.   Thus finally one will be able to realize (and constantly suggest to oneself) the presence of God *within* one.[43]

Meanwhile, the mystic is seeking by the constant practice of prayer to come to a closer and closer union with God and a

<hr>

[43] Cf. Alvarez de Paz, "La Preparation," Lib. V, Pars I, Chap. VIII, IX, and X, quoted and summarized by Lejeune, Chapter III.

deeper experience of His presence. And knowing that even
small matters and the environment are of importance, he sees
to it that at the time when he makes orison all the conditions are
favorable.   Solitude he knows is almost an essential and he
sees to it that he is alone.   Even the bodily posture may help
the concentration of the mind on the sacred theme which
should dominate it; for by long continued habit certain attitudes and gestures, such as kneeling, clasping the hands, making the sign of the cross, etc., have become associated with
the religious mood.   Hence, especially if he finds difficulty in
keeping his mind fixed upon the subject chosen for his meditation, the mystic tries various devices of posture and bodily
activity until he finds one that proves helpful.[44]

It is probably the mystics of India who have most refined
upon the art of influencing mental states by physical and physiological conditions.   One device which they have practiced for
centuries as a means of cultivating the religious attitude of
mind is the control of the breath.   This practice originated,
I suspect, in some long-outgrown animistic theory, but there is
probably more than theory in its continuation.   The religious
mood, like every other, being largely dependent upon the condition and the activities of the body, it is possible to control it
to some extent by controlling them.   Many of the organic activities which affect mood are not controllable by the will, but
breathing is.   The rate of breathing, moreover, affects directly
the excitement-calm " dimension " of feeling — rapid breathing being associated with the former, deep and slow breathing
with the latter.   By controlling the breath the Indian devotee
is therefore able to do at least something toward determining
the nature of his religious emotion.   What more there may be
in it I do not yet see, but it seems probable that there is a

[44] " ' S'il vous arrive, Philothée, dira saint François de Sales, de n'avoir
point de goût ni de consolation en la meditation, . . . piquez quelque fois
votre coeur par quelque contenance et mouvement de devotion extérieur,
vous prosternant en terre, croisant les mains sur l'estomac, embrassant un
crucifix. . . .' Écoutons maintenant saint Ignace : ' Je commencerai ma
contemplation tantôt à genoux, tantôt prosterné, tantôt étendu sur la
terre, le visage vers le ciel, tantôt assis, tantôt debout. . . . Si je trouve
ce que je désire à genoux ou prosterné je ne chercherai pas une autre
position.' " De Montmorand, " Ascétisme et Mysticisme." (*Revue Philosophique*, LVII, 249.)

good deal more. Until some western psychologist, however, shall take a long course under an Indian guru and finally turn *Sadhu* we shall probably remain in the dark as to the full explanation of the breathing methods. Many other devices besides that of controlling the breath have been regularly used by Indian holy men, some of them skillfully adapted to the concentration of attention and the gradual narrowing of its scope, as well as for the production of certain religious emotions. A classical example of these psychological methods will be found in a note — a passage from the Gita in which Krishna gives directions to his worshiper.[45]

The Moslem Sufis and Dervishes have devised methods for inducing desirable forms of religious emotion only less elaborate than the Indian. The Dervishes have learned the influence of breath-control over feeling, and in their exciting religious exercises make use of it and of rhythmic and violent swaying of the body, at the same time controlling their attention by the enthusiastic repetition of the sacred phrase *La ilaha illa llah* (There is no God but God).[46] It is, however, the Sufis who

[45] "A devotee should constantly devote himself to abstraction, remaining in a secret place, alone, with his mind and self restrained, without expectations and without belongings. Fixing his seat firmly in a clean place, not too high nor too low [in order, evidently, that the mind should not be distracted by anything in the bodily attitude] and covered with a sheet of cloth, a deerskin and kusa grass, and there seated on that seat, fixing his mind exclusively on one point, with the workings of the mind and the senses restrained, he should practice devotion for purity of self. Holding his body, head, and neck even and unmoved, remaining steady, looking at the tip of his own nose, and not looking about in various directions, with a tranquil self, devoid of fear, he should restrain his mind and concentrate it on Me and sit down engaged in devotion, regarding Me as his final goal. Thus constantly devoting himself to abstraction, a devotee whose mind is restrained attains that tranquillity which culminates in final emancipation and assimilation with Me." Translation by Telang, in S. B. E. American Edition, Vol. VIII, Part II, pp. 68–69. For other classical descriptions of Indian methods see the Kshurika Upanishad, translated by Deussen in his "Sechzig Upanishads des Veda" (Leipzig; Brockhaus; 1905), pp. 634–36; and "The Yoga System of Pantanjali," translated by Woods (Harvard Univ. Press; 1914), especially books I and II. The various kinds of Yoga practiced to-day in India are largely elaborations upon the ancient methods. For an interesting account of an attempt made by a European to follow out the bodily and mental exercises of the Hatha Yoga, see James's address on "The Energies of Men," published in *Science*, XXV, 326–29.

[46] For an excellent and sympathetic account of the dervish *zikr* see Mac-

have made the subtlest use of psychological devices to induce the mystic state, and I therefore embody in a note Macdonald's account of the methods used by the school of al-Ghazzali.[47] I should add that some of al-Ghazzali's followers have introduced into it elaborate methods of breath control similar to the Indian.

These external methods whether used by Indian, Moslem, or Christian, of course are indirect and are valuable only in so far as they aid in mental concentration. A more direct means is the purely mental one of "meditation." The mystic here seeks to concentrate his attention on purely religious themes. Perfect concentration is not yet possible; the mind is still subject to the law of constant change and cannot fix its attention for any length of time upon any single object, hence some changing and developing subject is chosen and the attention closely follows its course. Ignatius Loyola, one of the great systematizers and directors, recommends to beginners that this form of meditation should invoke the imagination,[48] the

donald's "Aspects of Islam" (New York; Macmillan; 1911), Lecture V. Some years ago I attended one of these exciting exercises and can testify to its emotional effect.

[47] "The course which is advised is as follows. Let the seeker sever all the ties of this world and empty it from his heart. Let him cut away all anxiety for family, wealth, children, home; for knowledge, rule, ambition. Let him reduce his heart to a state in which the existence of anything and its non-existence are the same to him. Then let him sit alone in some corner, limiting his religious duties to what are absolutely incumbent, and not occupying himself with reciting the Quran or considering its meaning, with books of religious traditions or anything of the like. And let him see to it that nothing save God most High enters his mind. Then as he sits alone in solitude, let him not cease saying continuously with his tongue, 'Allah, Allah,' keeping his thought on it. At last he will reach a state where the motion of his tongue will cease, and it will seem as though the word flowed from it. Let him persevere in this until all trace of motion is removed from his tongue, and he finds his heart persevering in the thought. Let him still persevere until the form of the word, its letters and shape, is removed from his heart, and there remains the idea alone, as though clinging to his heart, inseparable from it. . . . Nothing now remains but to await what God will open to him. If he follows the above course, he may be sure that the light of the real will shine out in his heart." ("Religious Attitude and Life in Islam." University of Chicago Press; 1909, pp. 255–56.) The student of Indian religions will be reminded of the use by Indian mystics of the repetition of sacred names, such as *Om*, Krishna, etc.

[48] Which he calls the "memory."

understanding, and the will. One, for example, may choose a theme in the life of Christ and depict it to oneself in sensuous imagery. Or one may consider some religious truth and its bearings and relations. And in connection with both of these one should exercise one's will and one's affections, arousing, in connection with each sacred scene or theological truth, the appropriate emotion.

Let no one think the exercise of meditation an easy matter. Saint Teresa says of it, " For years I occupied myself less with useful and holy reflections than with the desire to hear the clock announce the end of the hour consecrated to prayer. Often, I confess, I should have preferred the rudest sort of penance to the torment of meditation." [49] For the beginner, especially if he be chiefly an imitator who is seeking the mystic state as described to him by others and by means of rules laid down for him by others, there are indeed many difficulties and many discouragements. It is no easy thing to become a mystic by rule. And here let me add that the systematic training prescribed by such writers as Loyola [50] presents the practice of the imitators rather than that of the great mystics. While these have indeed been diligent in the use of both the negative and the positive methods of purgation and meditation, and while they have carefully followed the advice of their spiritual directors, they have to a large extent been a law unto themselves, each working out by a process of trial and error the method most useful for him, and many of them coming to the goal of

[49] Vie. p. 78.

[50] See Loyola's " Exercitia Spiritualia " (Romæ, 1615). This gives a series of most elaborate and systematic meditations, for the training of the imagination, to be gone through on successive days at various stated hours. That St. Ignatius knew the value of the sensuous in bringing about reality feeling is shown by his repeated admonitions to direct the imagination toward each of the senses in turn as it seeks to conjure up the scene which is the subject of the particular meditation. Thus in the " Contemplatio de Inferno," " Punctum primum est spectare per imaginationem vasta inferorum incendia, et animas igneis quibusdam corporibus, velut ergastulis inclusas. Secundum, audire imaginarie plāctus, einlatus, vociferationes, atque blasphemias in Christum, et Sanctos eius illinc erupentes. Tertium, imaginario etiam olfactu fumu, sulphur, et sentinæ cuiusdam feu fæcis, atque putredinis graveolentiam persentire. Quartum, gustare similiter res amarissimas, ut lachrymas, rancorem, conscientiæque vermen. Quintu, tāgere quodomodo ignes illos, quorum tactu animæ ipsæ amburantur " (pp. 39–40).

their longing quite suddenly and sometimes spontaneously.

The kind of meditation on many sacred themes which has just been described, if faithfully followed, is likely to lead at last to a new kind of experience which the French mystics call the "oraison affective." At this stage reasoning and argumentation and discursive thought are no longer needed and give way to an emotional conviction; and in like manner imagery becomes less important and its place is largely taken by a succession of appropriate and corresponding emotions. Finally the constant change of mental content which usually characterizes waking consciousness becomes less pronounced and less swift, and the multiplicity of ideas and even of emotions less varied. The field of consciousness is limited and the attention is able to cling longer to one object than before. Of course this object — which is almost invariably some form of the idea of God — is not a stark and changeless unity. Even in extreme forms of ecstasy, as the descriptions of the mystics show, there is constant change of mental content. Normal attention to a single unchanging object lasts from five to eight seconds, with a maximum of perhaps forty; and there is no reason to suppose that the mystic goes beyond this. But when he has reached this last preparatory stage which I have just described — the "oraison de simple regard" or "d'attention amoureuse à Dieu present," as the French call it — the changing object of consciousness has a peculiar unity, and its variations are confined to a small circle.[51]

When the mystic has reached this utmost achievement of "meditation" (which here, indeed, deserves the name "contemplation") he is on the very verge of the full realization of the mystic experience. "There comes a day," says Lejeune, "while the soul is making its orison, that it feels its spiritual sense suddenly awakening; it becomes conscious of the presence of God in a way quite new. It is but a flash that lasts only a moment, but it is enough for the soul to be sure that a chasm separates this way of feeling God, of being united to God, and all the usual modes of meditation. It is enough to assure

[51] Cf. Lejeune, op. cit., pp. 302–06, 325–27. Poulain, "Des Graces d'Oraison," pp. 7–10.

it that it has been transported for a moment into a new world." [52]   It is this new manner of feeling God and of being united to Him that we are to study in the following chapter.

[52] Op. cit., p. 327.

CHAPTER XVIII

THE ECSTASY

In the preceding chapter we studied the two preliminary stages of the more extreme form of mysticism — the "purgative" and the "illuminative" or "meditative" stages as they are called by the systematizers — and at last we have reached the third or "unitive" stage, the goal of all the mystic's painful preparation. This third stage is both a kind of experience and a kind of life. In this latter sense it is described thus by Ribet:

"Finally, love becomes dominant and is unified with the divine good will. The soul cares less about avoiding hell and gaining heaven and more about pleasing her well-beloved. Her desire is to free herself from all that is not God, and even to quit the world and life in order to enjoy the presence of God fully and indissolubly." [1]

While the third stage of the mystic progress is for many a mystic, and especially for the greatest, a life rather than a particular experience, it involves for all mystics a special type of experience which because of its striking character is regarded as the mystic state *par excellence* and which distinguishes it more, perhaps, than anything else from the life of the ordinary moral and religious but non-mystical individual. This experience is commonly known as the ecstasy, and I shall regularly use this term to designate it. [2] It usually makes its first appearance at the beginning of the "mystic life" and reappears from time to time, being perhaps both partial cause and partial result of that new way of living. This, however, is not the universal rule; some attain to the mystic life with no such extreme experience, and many taste the experience but are unable to fill their lives with the mystic spirit and let it domi-

---

[1] "La Mystique Divine," Vol. I, p. 16.

[2] The term is limited by various Catholic writers to a particular phase of the mystic experience.

nate them.   The ecstasy, being the more striking phenomenon
of the two, has naturally attracted most of the attention of the
psychologists and has even been regarded as constituting the
whole of mysticism.[3]   But if the great mystics themselves
should be consulted I fancy they would put the emphasis in
quite a different place.   For most of them the essential thing
has been the life, the ecstatic experience being extremely important indeed, but after all secondary to the constant sense of
the divine guidance and the complete submission of the self
to the will of God.   Both ecstasy and the mystic life, however,
are of importance and must be studied separately.   And as the
ecstasy is most characteristic of the earlier part of the mystic's
life we shall begin with it.

Ecstasy differs from "meditation" — the stage that preceded it — both in character and in development, both in the
mental content found at any one moment and in the law of
the change of that content from moment to moment.   Perhaps
the most marked difference in character, according to most
Catholic writers, is the substitution of passivity for activity.
In all the long preliminary training of the mystics — and most
of all, perhaps, in meditation — a constant exertion of the will
is required.   But when at length the new and long-desired experience comes "like a flash" into the heart, the mystic knows
that he has nothing more to do but wait and accept what is
given him.   Thus, at any rate, say the literary mystics and
systematizers.   His work is done, and from now on what happens in his soul must be the work of God.   Substituting psychological for theological terms, we might say that by long exertion of the will certain obscure psycho-physiological processes
have been started, and that these now continue to function of
themselves, in such a way that further volitional effort not
only would be of no assistance but might even tend to inhibit
the process.   This is by no means peculiar to mysticism but
has numerous analogies in other mental processes.   The case
of habitual and instinctive action, for instance, is quite parallel.
Once the habit is gained (or the instinct inherited) and the
proper stimulus received, the action works itself off mechanically, and any attempt at guiding it throws the mechanism out

[3] This, e.g., is Murisier's view.

of gear or even inhibits the action altogether. The process of putting oneself to sleep is similar in principle, and offers a closer analogy to the inducing of ecstasy. By a long and painful process of picturing sheep jumping over fences, or saying our multiplication table up into the thirteens, or counting backwards in German, we may inhibit the disturbing ideas, narrow the conscious field, and thus at last (by considerable effort of will) get the mind started in a suitable direction and at a promising pace. If then, just at the right moment, we know enough to take our metaphorical hands off, the mental mechanism will carry us safely into the land of sleep, and thought turn into dream. But if we interfere and try again to guide the process, alas, we are wide awake and the sheep and the numbers must begin jumping and multifying once more. The similarity between this common experience and the oncoming of the ecstasy will be seen from the following directions of Mme. Guyon:

During meditation, " it is best to pause softly upon some substantial idea, not with argumentation, but merely as a means of fixing attention." " When at length the soul begins to perceive the odor of the divine perfumes . . . it is of great importance to put an end to one's own activity in order to let God act. Keep yourself in repose. . . . [At first] it is necessary to blow the fire gently; but as soon as it is lighted, cease to blow, for by blowing you may extinguish it." [4]

Besides the passive nature of the ecstasy another characteristic of its content is its relative unity and the narrowness of its conscious field. To a considerable extent the outside world is shut out and the senses are closed — in the extreme form completely so. The variety which ordinarily characterizes the object of consciousness is considerably reduced, and in fact nearly everything is pushed out of the mind but the idea of God and the congruent emotions of joy and love. These fill the mind to the exclusion of almost everything else, and are themselves blended into a single whole. It is not that the mystic *believes* God to be present; he *feels* God united with his soul, so that this immediate awareness and its strong emotional accompaniment leave no room in his consciousness for anything else.[5]

[4] From the " Moyen court et facile de faire Oraison," quoted by Leuba in " Tendances religieuses chez les Mystiques Chretiens," *Rev. Phil.*, LIV, 453.
[5] Cf. Poulain's two " theses " by which the mystic union is to be distin-

The ecstasy, moreover, (as I have already said) has not only its own characteristic content but its own characteristic course of development as well. For of course the content has to change; otherwise the oncoming of ecstasy would mean the immediate oncoming of sleep. This development may be summed up very briefly as a gradual process of substituting emotional for ideational content, and a corresponding process of constantly narrowing the field of consciousness. More and more the mind becomes shut off from the outer world, " retiring into itself " and shutting the doors of its senses (to use a common figure); the inner unity becomes more intense; the object of consciousness possesses constantly less variety and its change is at a slower rate; the ideas that remain become more vague and give place to emotion; and while the emotion itself does not *absolutely* grow and may even diminish (so far at least as we can speak of any absolute measure here), it gains greatly in relative importance. The ideal limit toward which this variation tends is of course a state of almost pure emotion which itself gradually vanishes away and yields to complete unconsciousness.

What I have just described is the course which the ecstatic process takes (in psychological theory, at least) when carried to its extreme limit. But it must be noted that as a fact the process is seldom completed. Most mystics go only a little way in the ecstasy and then return to the ordinary form of consciousness. I have here sketched an outline of the whole process in its theoretical completeness in order that we may have it all before us as an aid in our more careful study of its various details. Much more elaborate and systematic descriptions of the development of the ecstasy are given by some of the great mys-

guished from all lower forms of orison are: (1) " Les états mystiques qui mettent en rapport avec Dieu attirent tout d'abord l'attention par l'impression de recueillement, d'union qu'ils font éprouver. De là le nom d'union mystique. Leur vraie différence avec les recueillements de l'oraison ordinaire, c'est que dans l'état mystique Dieu ne se contente plus de nous aider à *penser* a lui et à nons souvenir de sa présence; mais il nous donne de cette présence, une connaissance intellectuelle expérimentale." (2) " Ce qui constitue le fond commun de tous les degrés de l'union mystique, c'est que l'impression spirituelle par laquelle Dieu manifeste sa présence, le fait sentir à la manière de quelque chose *d'intérieur*, dont l'âme est pénétrée; c'est une sensation *d'imhibition*, de *fusion, d'immersion*." " Des Grâces d'Oraison," pp. 66 and 90.

tics and by various Catholic directors; for since the time of Hugo of St. Victor mysticism has been treated analytically by the Church and systematized into various stages.

There would be little purpose in reproducing here all of these various (and somewhat varying) systematizations, but it may be well to have one of them before us, as the systematizers who made them have often been gifted with rare powers of introspection and psychological analysis. Probably the best of these orderly expositions of the mystic development, and the one that has had the most influence, is that of St. Teresa in her last great work, the "Château Intérieur." According to her there are four degrees of the mystic union with God,[6] namely (1) the incomplete mystic union, or "oraison de quietude," (2) complete or semi-ecstatic union; (3) the ecstatic union; or ecstasy in the stricter and more limited sense; (4) the transforming union or spiritual marriage. Only the first three of these belong to what I have referred to as "ecstasy" (in the broader sense of the word), the fourth being no transitory state but an almost constant condition, and representing, in fact, the highest type of what (following Delacroix) I have called "the mystic life."

The first three of St. Teresa's stages are in most essentials alike, differing from each other chiefly in intensity. What difference there is between them Poulain (who interprets St. Teresa admirably) expresses as follows:

"The mystic union is called (1) Quietude when the divine action is still too feeble to prevent distractions, that is, when the imagination is still free. (2) Complete Union when it has the two following characteristics: (a) its intensity is so great that the soul is completely occupied with the divine object, i. e. it is not turned aside by any other thought; (b) on the other hand, the senses continue to act, in such a way that one can still, by more or less effort, put oneself in touch with the outer world by speaking, walking, etc., and can arouse himself from his orison. (3) Ecstasy, when the divine action has considerable force and

[6] This four-fold division must not be confused with the four-fold division of *oraison* given by Teresa in Chapters XI to XXI of the *Vie*. The *Château Intérieur* describes seven "demeures" of the soul, but the first three cannot be called "union." (See French translation by Bouix. Paris, Lecoffre: 1907.)

when all communication of the senses with the outer world is broken off or nearly so; and when, likewise, one cannot make voluntary movements nor leave his orison at will.

"It is evident," continues Poulain, "that these definitions are not vague. Each stage differs from that which precedes it by a new fact, and this fact is directly and easily observable. 'Complete union' differs from 'quietude' in the absence of distractions, and 'ecstasy' differs from 'complete union' by the alienation of sense." [7]

This systematization of the mystic experience into definite stages which follow each other regularly must not be taken too seriously. Even the Catholic systematizers recognize that there is nothing sacred in their divisions, and that almost any amount of irregularity in the process is possible.[8] The variations in these descriptions are sufficient evidence of this; and much of the uniformity that is left is doubtless due to more or less conscious imitation. It is hardly safe to give a more elaborate picture of the development of the ecstasy than the rather vague and general one presented on page 397. Without delaying longer over the order of the various mystic phenomena it will be well for us to turn at once to a closer study of the phenomena themselves.

The more intense kind of mystic experience, like the milder type, has two aspects which (though they must always be taken

---

[7] Op. cit., pp. 56–57. St. Bonaventura has "seven degrees of contemplation," Gerson three, St. François de Sales six, Alvarez de Paz fifteen, Scaramelli eleven, Ribet (a recent Catholic writer whose four-volume work on the Mystic Life is scholarly and valuable, although without the psychological insight of Poulain) finds seven stages in "Contemplation"—namely the following: (1) "Le Recuiellement passif," the passive concentration of the thought upon God, a "supernatural" condition which may come suddenly and should be greeted with an attitude of expectancy; (2) "Quietude" (practically the same as St. Teresa's first stage of mystic union; (3) "Transports"—this is of four different kinds and has no exact counterpart in Teresa's and Poulain's scheme; (4) "L'Union Simple"—the identification of the will with God's will plus the consciousness of union with Him; (5) "L'Union Extatique," which differs from the preceding stage in inhibiting the senses and concentrating the attention on the divine so completely that one sometimes becomes unconscious of what is happening to the body; (6) "Le Mariage Spirituel,"—an habitual and permanent condition of ecstasy, of intense but calm joy; (7) "La Vision Beatifique," a supreme stage which has been experienced in this life fully only by Jesus.—See Vol. I, Chapters X–XXII.

[8] Cf. Ribet, op. cit., Vol. I, p. 98.

in connection with each other) may be studied most conveniently apart. I refer, of course, to the noetic and the emotional elements, each of which forms a necessary part of every ecstasy. It is only in a very special sense, however, that the ecstatic experience can be called noetic. And to understand clearly what the mystic means when he speaks of his revelation we must recall the distinction between the two kinds of knowledge to which reference was made in the early part of the preceding chapter. To make the matter perfectly plain I can probably do no better here than quote from James's " Principles of Psychology " : [9]

" There are two kinds of knowledge broadly and practically distinguishable; we may call them respectively *knowledge of acquaintance* and *knowledge-about*. Most languages express the distinction: thus γνῶναι, εἰδέναι; noscere, scire; kennen, wissen; connaître, savoir . . . I know the color blue when I see it and the flavor of a pear when I taste it . . . but *about* the inner nature of these facts or what makes them what they are I can say nothing at all. I cannot impart acquaintance with them to anyone who has not already made it himself. I cannot *describe* them, make a blind man guess what blue is like, or tell a philosopher in just what respect distance is just what it is, and differs from other forms of relation. At most I can say to my friends, Go to certain places and act in certain ways and these objects will probably come."

" Knowledge of acquaintance " is, then, the immediate and direct experience itself, standing for itself and not taken as pointing to or representing something else. It is our sensation, or better still our feelings, that are typical of it. " Knowledge-about," on the other hand, is seen in ideas and abstract thought. It is conceptual, descriptive, representative, communicable. All general propositions, descriptions of things which make them communicable to other minds, all " universals," scientific formulas, and the like, come under this heading.

Now while each of these kinds of knowledge implies and requires to some extent the other, the mystic experience, so far as it is noetic at all, is characterized by the *immediate* kind of knowledge, and has relatively little to do with *knowledge-*

9 Vol. I, p. 221.

about; and the mystic, so far as he comes to theorize about the nature of knowledge usually glorifies the former kind and depreciates the latter. Conceptual, representative knowledge is always pointing you elsewhere, it is always saying, Reality is not in me. Hence, think the mystics, it can never give complete satisfaction. It is only the beginning of one's search and can help one only a little way toward the Truth. Only in an immediate experience which stands for itself alone, can one find true reality; and most certainly of all, there alone can one find the ultimate Reality which is God. Thus Plotinus says, " Our apprehension of the One does not partake of the nature of either understanding or abstract thought as does our knowledge of other intelligible objects, but has the character of presentation higher than understanding. For understanding proceeds by concepts, and the concept is a multiple affair, and the soul misses the One when she falls into number and plurality. She must then pass beyond understanding and nowhere emerge from her unity." [10]

The noetic element of the mystic experience may therefore be said to have both a negative and a positive aspect.[11] It is characterized, that is, by the relative lack of conceptual knowledge and abstract judgments, on the one hand, and, on the other, by the presence of a relatively intense immediate experience, which indeed necessarily includes some ideation, but in which immediacy is much more prominent than representation. Both of these characteristics, for instance, are emphasized by such typical expressions as the following:

" But thou, O dear Timothy," writes Dionysius in his " Mystic Theology," " by thy persistent commerce with the mystic visions, leave behind sensible perceptions and intellectual efforts and all objects of sense and of intelligence, and all things being and not being, and be raised aloft unknowingly to the union, as far as attainable, with Him who is above every essence and knowledge. For by the resistless and absolute ecstasy in all purity, from thyself and all thou wilt be carried on high to the

---

10 " Enneads," VI, 9, quoted from Bakewell's " Source Book in Ancient Philosophy," p. 367.

11 Cf. Ribet: " Selon les mystiques, on s'élève a la connaissance de Dieu par un double procédé, savoir: par affirmation et par négation." Op. cit., Vol. I, p. 86.

superessential ray of the divine darkness, when thou hast cast away all and become free from all." [12]

In like manner Plotinus, in a famous passage, asks: "How, then, are we to speak of the One? How can we speak of it at all, when we do not grasp it as itself?" That is, if God, or the One, is not to be known by any of the ordinary, conceptual, descriptive ways of knowledge, how can we even speak of Him? And Plotinus's answer is based upon the fact just pointed out that there is a positive as well as a negative side to the mystic experience. In his own words, "The answer is that though the One escapes our knowledge, it does not entirely escape *us*. We have possession of it in such a way that we speak of it, but not in such a way that we can express it. . . . We are like men inspired and possessed who know only that they have in themselves something greater than themselves — something they know not what — and who therefore have some perception of that which has moved them, and are driven to speak of it because they are not (wholly) one with that which moves them. So it is with our relation to the Absolute One. When we use pure intelligence we recognize that it is the mind within the mind, the source of being and of all things that are of the same order with itself; but we see at the same time that the One is not identified with any of them but is greater than all we call being, greater and better than reason and intelligence and sense, though it is that which gives them whatsoever reality they have." [13]

Perhaps the most striking and yet the least important characteristic of the mystic experience so far as it is positively noetic is the occasional phenomenon of visions and "locutions." Christ and various saints are seen, the Trinity is presented symbolically but visibly under the form of a diamond,[14] or truths

[12] "The Works of Dionysius the Areopagite," translated by Parker (London, Parker: 1897), p. 130.

[13] "Enneads," V, 3, 14. I have here used Caird's excellent translation in his "Evolution of Theology in the Greek Philosophers" (Glasgow, Maclehose: 1904), Vol. II. pp. 218–19.

[14] St. Teresa saw it thus. She also frequently had visions and locutions. Her description of one of the former I will quote here as a sample of the whole class. The Savior appeared to her in glorious light which " surpasse infiniment celle d'ici-bas, et auprès de ses rayons qui inondent l'œil ravi de l'âme, ceux du soleil perdent tellement leur lustre, qu'on ne

are heard inwardly but quite clearly expressed.   These visions
are rarely true hallucinations but are what psychologists distinguish as pseudo-hallucinations;— the subject even during the
experience knows that it is a vision that he sees.   In psychological structure and causation many of these visions are not
essentially different from dreams.[15]   Sometimes, in fact, they
are mere normal dreams, sometimes they are dreams occurring
in abnormal fashion while the dreamer is half awake, in what
Sidis would call a hypnoidal state, sometimes they are probably
mere hypnagogic hallucinations, common to most of us on the
approach or at the close of sleep;[16] sometimes they are no more
than vivid memories of former experiences.[17]   The visions of
the mystics are determined in content by their belief, and are
due to the dream imagination working upon the mass of theological material which fills the mind.   It is probable also that at
times the vision, like the normal dream, originates from some
sensational stimulus which the imagination proceeds to interpret and elaborate.   If there be any truth [18] in Freud's insistence upon the symbolic nature of normal dreams, it is the
less surprising that the dream imagination of the Christian
mystic should work up visions of a symbolic sort.   Symbolism
is a striking characteristic of the visions of the mystics, as every-

voudrait seulement pas ouvrir les yeux pour les regarder. . . . Cette lumière est un jour sans nuit, toujours éclatant, toujours lumineux, sans
que rien soit capable de l'obscurcir.   Enfin elle est telle que l'ésprit le
plus pénétrant ne pourrait, en toute sa vie, s'en former une idée.   Dieu
la montre si soudainement que, s'il était besoin pour l'apercevoir d'ouvrir
seulement les yeux, on n'en aurait pas le loisir, mais il n'importe qu'ils
soient ouverts ou fermés."   "Vie," p. 301.   The chapter (XXVIII) in which
this description occurs is devoted to a discussion of these visions.

[15] Some mystic visions are less complex in content but less normal in
cause — cf. a recent case of vision of light which occurred repeatedly during prayer through a period of six weeks and considered "God's Light."
Dr. Denby, who reports it, calls it a case of association neurosis.   (Journal of Abnormal Psychology, II, 56.)

[16] Cf. N. S. Yawger, "Hypnagogic Hallucinations with Cases illustrating these Sane Manifestations," Jour. of Abnormal Psychology, XIII, 73–
76.

[17] This fact was noticed by Teresa among the young mystics of her
convents.   See her "Le Livre des Fondations" (French translation by
Bouix.   Paris, Lecoffre: 1907), p. 81.

[18] Personally I think there is a little truth in it, but a truth which he
and his followers have enormously exaggerated.   Some dreams are probably symbolic; the great majority I believe are not.

one knows who has dipped into the subject. The classical instance is, of course, that of Ezekiel; but many mediæval mystics
such as Elizabeth of Schonau and Hildegard of Bingen had
visions almost as elaborately symbolical as his.[19] Our modern
tendency to consider visions quite extraordinary and pathological is probably mistaken. According to Galton's investigations,[20] visions (of a fragmentary sort) are common with many
normal persons. Every good visualizer has at times visual
images quite comparable in intensity with dreams or actual per-
cepts. Such persons in their childhood, in fact, not infrequently fail to distinguish between the real and the imagined.
As Galton suggests, in a community where belief in the appari-
tion of the supernatural is unquestioned, even such fragmentary
visions as normal people of good visual imagery often experience
may well be made objects of great attention and regarded as
visions.[21]

Visions and other hallucinatory phenomena I have called the
least important part of the ecstasy because they are so considered by the mystics themselves. At best they are but unnecessary accessories to the ecstasy and are by no means always
present. At their worst they are often considered by the mys-

[19] For descriptions of some of these visions see Taylor's "Mediæval
Mind" (London, Macmillan: 1911), Vol. I. Chap. XIX.

[20] "Inquiries into Human Faculty," pp. 125–28.

[21] The Catholic mystics, and more especially the mystic systematizers,
distinguish three kinds of visions: corporeal, imaginary, and intellectual.
The third class is regarded as of special value and thought to come from
God alone, and to have the peculiar quality of being without images.
Scaramelli defines it as "a clear and certain apprehension of some object
by the intellect without any form or figure of any kind being seen, and
without any actual dependence on the fantasy." "Handbook of Mystical
Theology" (London, Watkins: 1913), p. 108. Teresa analyzes such a vision in her "Relations au P. Rodrigue Alvarez" (p. 590 of the French
translation of the "Vie"), and several of the more introspective mystics,
such as John of the Cross and Alvarez de Paz, have done the same.
Suarez did not believe the visions could really be without images, and the
probability is that the descriptions and assertions of the mystics are due
to their lack of interest in the subsidiary images which were what Professor Strong would call the "vehicles" of the intuited essence. The
nature of these visions is of some psychological interest to-day because of
the recent theory of "imageless thought." (See, for example, Woodworth,
"A Revision of Imageless Thought," *Psychological Review* for 1915, XXII,
1–27.) The subject is discussed at some length from the orthodox Catholic point of view by Pacheu, "L'Expérience Mystique," pp. 135–49; Poulain, op. cit., Chap. XX; Scaramelli, op. cit., pp. 108–12.

tics essentially pathological — or, in theological terms, the work
of Satan.[22]

Much more important than sensuous hallucinatory phenomena of this sort is the ideational element which forms the core
of the ecstasy and is inseparable from it. For the affective elements of consciousness, in the mystic state as elsewhere, are always associated with some central idea, around which they
cluster and which in fact to a considerable extent determines
their nature. The mystic ecstasy, therefore, in spite of its emphasis on immediacy, means to be (to some extent) *noetic* or
cognitive. I am using the word cognitive here in a psychological rather than in an epistemological sense. Whether the mystic in his ecstasy really *knows* any genuine *truth* or merely
seems to himself so to do is not our question. The point I wish
to make here is that the ecstasy is *cognitive in form;* it seems
to reveal reality to the mystic quite as much as does his sight or
his hearing. His experience does not consist of mere feeling,
but is largely also one of intuition. It is the sense of being
face-to-face with reality. It is the same sort of cognition that
one has on seeing a color or smelling an odor. Moreover the
mystic intuition is seldom mere immediacy; it is seldom unaccompanied by some degree of " knowledge about " — it not only
is but it has a message or makes an assertion about some reality
or truth.[23] Says Professor Ewer, in dealing with intuition,
" its fundamental character is what is frequently called ' self-
transcendence,' the direct cognition of reality other or larger
than the cognitive state of consciousness itself. That is to
say, the proper epistemological conception of intuition makes
of it, not an absolutely peculiar kind of cognitive process, occult
and totally different from the processes of ordinary experience,
but rather a commonplace character without some measure of
which no consciousness would be truly cognitive. No less important, however, is the accompaniment, permeation, and modification of this character by the correlative character of inter-

[22] That they are pathological phenomena quite on a level with other
hallucinations, and resulting from an hysterical condition is, of course,
beyond doubt. They are paralleled by many purely pathological cases.
Cf. Marie, " Mysticisme et Folie," pp. 140ff and 267ff.
[23] Compare what was said in Chapter XVI of the outer reference in perception and in the milder form of the mystic experience.

pretation. Intuition is seldom if ever pure, but it may be genuine even when partial, imperfect, biased by apperception. This is not the most popular or the best-known historical concept, but it is the only one which is worth upholding or criticizing." [24]

Whatever may be our technical definition of intuition, then, the mystic experience is "known as" objective — not merely as subjective. The mystic returns from it with the certainty of having there come into contact with a reality other than his own consciousness and with a new revelation of some "truth" (for so he calls it) which the experience has impressed upon his mind. In illustration of this let me quote here from three mystics cited by Poulain. First, Angela da Foligno: "All that the soul conceives or knows when it is left to itself is nothing in comparison with the knowledge that is given it during ecstasy. When the soul is thus raised aloft, illumined by the presence of God, when God and it are lost in each other, it apprehends and possesses with joy good things which it cannot describe. . . . The soul swims in joy and knowledge." Ribadeneira in his Life of St. Ignatius describes one of his visions as follows: "Absorbed in contemplation of divine things, the saint seated himself for a time by the road looking at the stream which crossed it. Then the eyes of his soul were opened and were inundated with light. He perceived nothing that fell under his senses, but he comprehended marvelously a great number of truths pertaining to the faith or to the human sciences. They were so numerous and the light was so bright that he seemed to enter into a new world. The abundance of this knowledge and its excellence were so great that, according to Ignatius, all that he had learned in his life up to his sixty-second year, whether supernatural or through laborious study, could not be compared to that which he gained at this one time." St. Francis Xavier once said to a distinguished scientist and philosopher: "I too, in my youth, pursued knowledge with ardor, and I even prayed God to help me attain it to make me more useful to my Congregation. After this prayer I found myself inundated by divine light; it seemed

[24] "Veridical Aspect of Mystical Experience," *Amer. Jour. of Theology*, XIII, 578–9.

to me that a veil was raised before the eyes of my spirit, and the truths of the human sciences, even those which I had never studied, became manifest to me by an infused intuition, as to Solomon of old." [25]

The " truths " which the mystics carry away with them from the ecstasy, or hold more firmly because of the ecstasy, differ with different individuals. Their general tendency, as Professor James points out,[26] is towards optimism and monism. Professor Ewer enumerates several of them as follows: " That reality is unitary and divine; that ordinary experience is merely phenomenal, its content only imperfectly known; that its limitations and contradictions are transcended in true knowledge; that in such knowledge the soul, which is the key to reality, rises to identity with God and infinite vision; that the Divine Presence may be found hidden in the midst of daily life; that the real is ultimately good, and sin only negative, a privation, unreal." [27] The list of " truths " which the mystics would teach us as a result of their insight might be made still longer.[28]

We must, however, be careful to distinguish between the content of the intuition which takes place during the ecstasy, and the truths which the mystic comes to believe as a result of reflecting upon his experience. By later reflection and interpretation he may arrive at any number of conclusions; but he does

[25] These three (and several other citations like them) are quoted by Poulain, op. cit., pp. 271-73.

[26] " The Varieties of Religious Experience," p. 416.

[27] Op. cit., p. 576.

[28] An interesting example not indeed of new ideas but of new conviction gained through the mystic experience is furnished by the contemporary mystic of whom Professor Flournoy has given us an account. Her idea of God, prior to her mystical experiences, had always been extremely personal, identified usually with Christ, and possessing little of the cosmic. She had but little of the common mystic view of the identity of God and the soul,— the relation to her had been a personal and external one. Her ecstasies changed all this. She writes: " La notion du divin que me fait entrevoir cette Expérience divine dépasse en grandeur et en immediateté tout ce que j'ai pu imaginer jusqu'a à présent. C'est un Dieu qui m'enveloppe et me soulève, m'illumine et me purifie, mais me brise aussi, et n'entre en contact avec moi qu'au prix de ce ' lâchez tout ' de ma conscience de moi-même." (" Une Mystique Moderne," p. 77. See also pp. 87 and 134.) Prof. Flournoy summarizes the conception of God resulting from her ecstatic experiences under three heads —" incomparable mystery," " necessary being," " vital energy " (pp. 184-85).

not do this *as mystic*.   It is not by his processes of thought that he differs from the non-mystical person; hence the conclusions he comes to in this manner are not themselves mystic and should not be confused with the truly mystic intuition experienced during the ecstasy.   And if I am not greatly mistaken, a large number of the " mystic truths " so called — as, for instance, several of those quoted above from Dr. Ewer — are due to secondary reflection rather than to immediate intuition.

In fact many of the descriptions given by the mystics themselves would seem to point in this direction.   For on returning from that ecstatic condition where the greatest amount of truth is seen, the mystic seems least able to bring with him any of these truths to the light of common day.   Thus St. Francis Xavier finishes the description of his vision of all knowledge, from which I recently quoted, as follows: " This state of intuition lasted about twenty-four hours; then, as if the veil had fallen again, I found myself as ignorant as before."   In like manner it is related of Herman Joseph: " Suddenly God enlarged the field of his insight; He showed him the firmament and the stars and made him understand their quality and quantity, or to speak more clearly, their beauty and immensity. When he returned to himself he was not able to explain anything to us; he said simply that this knowledge of creation had been so perfect and so intoxicating that no tongue could express it." [29]   This seems to have been rather disappointing to his expectant friends; and indeed it is surprising that if the mystics have the revelations of which they write they should be unable to communicate them — or apparently even to remember them — on their return to this world.   Poulain, who admits the fact, would explain it by the nature of the truths thus revealed.   All the ecstatics, he says, affirm that during the stage known as " ravishment " one experiences a widening of the in-

[29] Cited by Poulain, op. cit., p. 272.   St. Teresa had repeated experiences of this kind.   Thus she writes at one time, " Il m'est arrivé, et il m'arrive encore quelquefois, que Notre Seigneur me découvre de plus grands secrets. . . . Le moindre de ces secrets suffit pour ravir l'âme d'admiration. . . . Je voudrais pouvoir donner une idée de ce qui m'était alors découvert de moins élevé; mais en cherchant à y parvenir, je trouve que c'est impossible." (" Vie," p. 482.)   In similar vein Ramakrishna testifies to the impossibility of putting into words the knowledge of Brahman attained in Samadhi (" Gospel of Ramakrishna," pp. 106–09).

telligence. " Noble scenes, profound ideas are offered to their spirits. But they are unable to explain what they have seen. This results not from any lethargy of their intelligence, but because they have been elevated to the vision of truths that the human spirit cannot attain to, and for which they have no terms. Will you ask a mathematician to express the profundities of the infinitessimal calculus with the vocabulary of a child ? " [30] With all the good will in the world for the Church's view of Mysticism, and in spite of the deep respect I feel for Father Poulain's usual insight, I cannot take his explanation very seriously. His own citations, in fact, confute him. For, according to the expressions of the mystics, the " truths of human science " are revealed and then lost quite as readily as " divine truths," and the descriptions imply quite plainly that it is usually lack of memory rather than lack of terms that makes it impossible for the mystic to communicate to others the truths revealed to him in his ravishment.

Leuba, in fact, carries his criticism of the mystic revelation (based on much the same grounds as those taken above) to the extent of asserting that there is really no " revelation " at all, no apprehension of any truths in the ecstasy, but that the persuasion of the mystic that he has had a revelation is wholly illusory and is due to a combination of the four following causes: " (1) The feeling of intimacy coming from the bond of love and from the disappearance of desires opposed to the divine will. (2) An illusory illumination quite common in sleep, due to the exclusion of mental oppositions and to a feeling of ease and of power. (3) Visual hallucinations and especially directing auditory hallucinations. (4) The clearer apprehension of the divine will on coming out of the ecstasy." [31] The second of these is perhaps the most important, and is based on the analogy of a phenomenon fairly familiar to most of us. We sometimes awake from a dream feeling that in it we have solved some difficult problem, but alas cannot remember the solution. This, says Leuba, is due to the fact that the objections and contradictions which our logical waking thought

[30] P. 253.
[31] " Tendances Religieuses chez les Mystiques Chrétiens " (*Rev. Philosophique*, LIV), 480.

sees have disappeared and in the narrowed field of consciousness there remains only the problem with a sense of ease and
mental mastery. In like manner the mystic in the narrowed
field of the ecstasy has present only the name of some theological
doctrine, such as the Trinity, freed from its logical difficulties,
and colored by a sense of ease and power. Returning from his
" intellectual vision," he is convinced that he has in it perceived
plainly how the three Persons are one God, etc., etc., although
now he is still quite as unable to explain it as before his revelation.

An additional explanation for the mystic's sense of knowledge
is to be found in the emotional intensity of the ecstasy. An
analysis of many of the descriptions given by the mystics makes
it probable that the sentiment of conviction with a minimum
of intellectual content often plays an important part in the experience. Thus Prof. Flournoy's patient, who combines a remarkable mystical experience with great powers of self-analysis
and of psychological description, writes concerning her inability
to describe the new insight gained in ecstasy: " All the traditional ideas about God and His action in us seem to me now
so weak, insufficient and limited. And yet if I try to analyze
what I know of God in addition to these ideas, I find nothing.
I could weep over my inability to describe that which I feel
again and again. The content is at a minimum." [32]

While these various explanations of the mystic's conviction
of insight go a long way, I do not think they show his sense of
revelation to be entirely illusory. In the first place, the mystics are by no means always unable to communicate the truths
which they have intuitively perceived during their ecstasy, although it must be noted that the " revealed " truths which they
can communicate are always old truths which they knew (though
in a much less living form) before. Most of us have experienced at rare intervals those unique moments of insight when
we seem to see into the totality of things with a strange freshness and clearness.[33] These moments indeed bring us no new
ideas, they discover to us no new facts (unless it be this fact
about ourselves), but they seem to give us a sense for the whole,

[32] " La matière y tient le minimum de place "—" Une Mystique Moderne," p. 72.
[33] Compare the oft-quoted lines from Wordsworth's " Tintern Abbey ":

and to throw around the old truths a new light that makes them living and vital to us as they never were before. It is a new union of idea with emotion, which gives the former a burning life and a moving power it never before possessed. This experience which many of us share at times, intensified to a very considerable degree, makes up probably a large part of the mystic's revelation. And many of the "mystic truths," such as those quoted from Ewer, are doubtless in this fashion the object of the mystic intuition.[34]

It would, however, as we have seen, be a mistake to regard all of the "truths" referred to as essential deliverances of the mystic consciousness as such. While many of the Christian mystics agree on most of the religious or philosophical positions which I have named and may even regard them as genuine mystical revelations, there is only one of them which is really essential to mysticism as such and a genuinely universal asser-

> "that serene and blessed mood
> In which the affections gently lead us on
> Until, the breath of this corporeal frame
> And even the motion of our human blood
> Almost suspended, we are laid asleep
> In body, and become a living soul;
> While with an eye made quiet by the power
> Of harmony, and the deep power of joy,
> We see into the life of things."

[34] St. Teresa furnishes a rather illuminating example of this. In the course of an ecstasy she heard the words "Tous les malheurs qui arrivent dans le monde viennent de ce que l'on n'y connait pas clairement les vérités de l'Ecriture." To this she made very frank reply (apparently in the ecstasy itself) that both she and all the faithful had always believed this. Whereupon the voice replied: "Sais-tu ce que c'est de m'aimer veritablement? C'est de bien comprendre que tout ce qui ne m'est pas agréable n'est que mensonge." This thought, surely not really new to a mystic like St. Teresa, immediately surrounded itself with such an emotional tinge that it seemed to her a great discovery, and one which she describes as "une vérité qui est la plénitude de toutes les vérités." ("Vie," pp. 519–20.) At another time she writes, "Sortant de cette oraison, et me preparant à écrire sur ce sujet, je cherchais dans ma pensée ce que l'âme pouvait faire pendant ce temps. Notre Seigneur me dit ces paroles: 'Elle se perd tout entière, ma fille, pour entrer plus entimement en moi. . . .' Ceux que Dieu a élevés à cet état auront quelque intelligence de ce langage; ce qui se passe alors est si caché qu'on ne saurait en parler plus clairment. J'ajouterai seulement ceci; l'âme se voit alors près de Dieu, et il lui en reste une certitude si ferme, qu'elle ne peut concevoir le moindre doute sur la vérité d'une telle faveur" (p. 174).

tion of mysticism everywhere and always. This pronouncement is, of course, the constantly reiterated assertion that in the mystic experience one comes into immediate touch with the Divine. Possibly *all* the mystical " revelations " may be accounted for as being first carried into the ecstasy by the mystic, and derived originally from social education, and all except this sense of presence may possibly be mere conclusions which the mystic comes to after reflecting upon his experience by a process of ordinary discursive thought; a number of mystics will be found to admit this in the case of each of these subsidiary and accessory deliverances. The " immediate knowledge of God's presence," on the other hand, is the one thing which the mystics universally consider directly experienced in a peculiar way during the ecstatic condition.[35]

If the mystic experience, then, is really cognitive this is what it " knows." This I say, let me repeat, from a psychological not an epistemological point of view. The mystic's consciousness, so far as it is something more than merely emotional, is an intuition of the " Beyond." After our study in Chapter XVI of the sense of the Beyond in the less intense forms of mysticism a few more examples of it, in the ecstatics, will suffice to put before the reader's mind the testimony of the mystics upon this point. Says Gerson: " It must be explained how one *experiences* this union (with God). We may say that this *experimental union* is a simple and actual *perception* of God." Antoine du Saint-Esprit writes thus: " God manifests Himself to pure spirits in such a way that they perceive and enjoy immediately and experimentally this presence by the knowledge and embracements of love." Father Maynard: " The union is a living and profound sense of *God present within us.* . . . The soul knows that God is there, and knows it by its sweet experience." [36] St. Teresa: " God establishes Himself within one's soul in such a manner that when the soul returns to herself *it is impossible to doubt that God has been in her and she in Him.* And this certainty remains so firmly imprinted

---

[35] This universality of the mystic's testimony must not be taken as necessarily possessing metaphysical significance. It is, however, a striking fact.

[36] These citations I have quoted from Poulain's excellent collection. See pp. 74–86 and 98–109, op. cit.

on one's mind that if one should go for many years without being raised again to this condition, one could neither forget the favor that has been received nor doubt of its reality." [37]

The analysis given in Chapter XVI of the sense of presence as found in the milder form of mysticism seems plainly to hold of the more extreme cases as well, if we bear in mind the fact that the experience is here accompanied with much more intense emotion. It is not surprising, therefore, that the great mystics vehemently insist that their sense of God's presence is unique and ineffable. This conviction, when combined (as it is in certain schools of mystic theology) with a negative conception of the Deity as ultimately indescribable, may lead the mystic down the "*via negativa.*" A negative conception of God, such as that found in Dionysius and some of the Upanishads, and the steady narrowing of the field of consciousness induced by the ecstasy and trance mutually reinforce each other and add their influence in persuading the mystic that he has become one with the Infinite Blank.

The negative way of defining God is based upon the principle that no quality known in human experience can worthily be attributed to Him. As say the Upanishads, He can be described only by " Neti, Neti," — or " No, No." Even the highest attributes we men can picture are unworthy of Him and incompatible with His (or Its) absolute unity. Thus according to Plotinus neither purpose nor thought nor self-consciousness can be ascribed to the One. For purpose of course implies want, and " everything which wants stands in need of well-being and preservation. It follows that for the One, nothing can be good, nor can it wish anything. It is rather super-good, a good not for itself but for other things. Nor can the One be thinking, lest there be difference and motion in it. It is prior to motion and to thinking. For what shall it think? Itself? In that case, before it thinks it will be ignorant, and what is self-sufficient will need thought in order to know itself. . . . The Only One will neither know anything nor have anything to be ignorant of. Being One and united with itself it does not need to think of itself. You cannot catch a glimpse of it even by ascribing to it union with it-

37 " Chateau Interieur," Œuvres, Vol. III, p. 459.

self. Rather you must take away thinking and the act of being united and thought of itself and of everything else." [38]

In like manner the mystic's scorn of conceptual knowledge and discursive thought sometimes leads him (especially if he hold the negative view of God just described) to insist that emptiness of mind is the only road toward union with the "Divine Gloom." "It is during the cessation of every mental energy," says Dionysius, "that such a union of the deified minds toward the superdivine light takes place." [39]. "The Divine Gloom is the unapproachable light in which God is said to dwell. And into this gloom, invisible indeed on account of surpassing brightness, and unapproachable on account of the excess of the superessential stream of light, enters every one deemed worthy to know and to see God, by the very fact of neither seeing nor knowing, really entering into Him who is above vision and knowledge." [40] "The emptier your mind," says Meister Eckhart, "the more susceptible are you to the working of His influence." "Memory, understanding, will, all tend toward diversity and multiplicity of thought, therefore you must leave them all aside, as well as perception, ideation, and everything in which you find yourself or seek yourself. Only then can you experience this new birth,— otherwise never." [41]

The logical result of this conception of God and of this view as to the means of communing with Him would be, if carried to the extreme, the deliberate and systematic attempt to "simplify" one's conscious field till nothing should be left. Murisier, who regards this "simplification" as the typical mysticism, has described it so well that he has almost succeeded in getting his description accepted by some psychologists as the norm of all mystic phenomena. [42] The mystic seeks simplification of the

[38] Enneads, VI. Bakewell's Source Book, p. 370. Cf. also Lao-tze's famous sentence: "The reason that can be reasoned is not the Eternal Reason; the name that can be named is not the Eternal Name." (Tao Teh King, 1.)

[39] "Divine Names" (Parker's translation), p. 8.

[40] "Letter to Dorotheus," p. 144.

[41] Meister Eckhart's "Mystische Schriften" put into modern German by Landaur (Berlin, Schnabel: 1903), pp. 20, 23.

[42] His description holds properly only of the quietist, a type of mystic recently studied by Ribot ("L'Idéal Quietiste," Rev. Philosophique for

heterogeneous elements of his mind and life by a process of elimination. This is Murisier's formula for the whole process from beginning to end, and certainly it is extremely illuminating and useful in aiding us to understand many of the phenomena involved. Asceticism the mystic has used only as a tool for lopping off the rougher outer elements of diversity and sources of distraction; and the processes of meditation and contemplation are for the purpose of reducing the mind itself to unity. One idea after another is done away with, the rapidity of thought is stopped, and gradually the mystic approximates a condition of monoideism where one idea alone remains with its accompanying feeling tone, dominating the mind. " This is sometimes an abstract idea, analogous to the idea of the Good, or to the law of the ' cause of sorrow,' knowledge of which conducts the Buddhist to the repose of Nirvana. It is more frequently a vague and confused image drawn from former representations, or rather it is the residue of these representations after they have been impoverished and simplified by the gradual effacement of their differences and their contours. . . . Sometimes visions still remain but if so they are visions without images, sudden illuminations of the soul which at last comprehends how all things are in God. Monoideism, the absence of simultaneity and of succession, is incompatible with the ordinary notions of space and time. ' To know ' in this manner is therefore to free oneself from extension and duration, to prolong the perception of the present beyond every assignable limit, to enjoy an ' eternal now,' to lose oneself in an immensity without bounds, in a word, to become identical with God." [43]

This phenomenon of monoideism, let me repeat, is a height of supernatural power, or a depth of pathological weakness (as you choose), to which not many mystics attain. The ecstasy is usually terminated before this stage is reached. But we are here considering the extreme cases and Murisier's description is probably excellent for them.

1915, pp. 440–54). Ribot's treatment is not essentially different from Murisier's; the quietist he describes as a mystic in whom the instinct of self-preservation is inverted, so that he seeks the destruction of the self.

[43] " Les Maladies du Sentiment Religieux," pp. 61–62.

While ideation has been decreasing, emotion (at least in its relative proportion) has been increasing; and in fact throughout the ecstasy the emotional element predominates and is of an intensity which seems far to exceed that of any emotion known to the mystic in any other condition. Mme. Guyon exclaims: "O my God, if thou wouldst make the most sensual persons feel what I feel they would quickly quit their false pleasures to enjoy so true a joy." [44]

This ecstatic joy is the joy of love in the realization of the unity of the soul with its "Well Beloved." "It is," says Therese Couderc, "a sweet feeling of the presence of God and of His love, which gives the soul so great delight and so unites it with Him, that it can scarcely be distracted. . . . All other pleasure beside that of enjoying God seems to me insipid." [45] In like manner Richard of St. Victor says of this joy, "It is so great that no natural delight can be compared to it, and it fills the soul with disgust for all the external sweets of pleasure and vanity." [46]   And the other Victorine, Hugo, describes the ecstatic experience as follows: "What is this sweet thing which at the thought of God sometimes comes and touches me? It affects me so keenly and with such sweetness that I begin to be separated from myself and to be carried I know not where. Suddenly I feel myself transformed and changed; it is joy un-

[44] Quoted by Leuba, "Tendances Fondamentales des Mystiques Chrétiens" (*Rev. Phil.*, LIV, 1–36), p. 6. The descriptions of the ecstatic joy given by one of Janet's patients are particularly good: "J'ai ressenti comme une joie intérieure qui s'est répandue jusque dans tout mon corps . . . l'air que je respire, la vue du ciel, le chant des oiseaux, tout m'a causé des jouissances inexprimables, j'ai vu des beautés inaccoutumées, en marchant je me suis sentie soutenue et j'ai éprouvé dans l'air véritable volupté. . . . J'ai des jouissances que, en dehors de Dieu, il est impossible de connaître. . . . La terre devient vraiment pour moi le vestibule du ciel, mon coeur jouit à l'avance de la félicité qui lui est réservée, . . . mes impressions sont trop violentes et j'ai de la peine a comprimer mes transports de bonheur." Bulletin de l'Institut Psychologique, I, 229–30.

[45] Cited by Poulain, p. 79.

[46] Quoted by Ribet (Vol. I, p. 132) from the Benjamin Major, 18. In another passage Richard compares the delight to that of a maiden suddenly overcome with wine and not knowing its nature: "Cogitemus modo puellam quandam teneram et delicatam, utpote in multa deliciarum affluentia educatam, sed in multo vino jam madidam, utpote in cellam vinariam introductam et torrente voluptatis potatam, et quasi prae nimia teneritudine vix posse incedere, et prae nimia ebrietate viam quam tenere debeat nullo modo posse discernere."

speakable. My mind is exhilarated, I lose the memory of my past trials, my heart is inflamed, my intelligence clarified, my desires satisfied. I feel myself transported into a new place, I know not where. I grasp something inwardly as with the embracements of love. . . . I struggle deliciously not to lose this thing which I desire to embrace without end." [47]

The reader will probably have noticed the emphasis which Hugo of St. Victor, in this last quotation, puts upon " *embracements.*" In this his language is very typical. The writings of the Christian mystics in description of the joy of ecstasy are teeming with expressions drawn from human love. As Leuba has put it:

" Whoever has read the mystics must have been struck and perhaps scandalized by the erotic character of their language and of their images. . . . The commerce of God with man is by the mystics put entirely in terms of profane love. The terms ' Lover ' and ' Spouse ' designate by turn Jesus Christ and sometimes God who is often confused with His Son. The Virgin is ' the incomparable Love,' ' the daughter of delight,' ' the unique dove.' In the course of one page Ruysbroeck accumulates the following terms : ' amorous embracements,' ' bonds of love,' ' ecstatic beatitude,' ' amorous immersion.' " [48]

Expressions like these could be quoted from a large number of the ecstatics.[49] As Leuba says, the effect is sometimes

[47] Cited by Poulain, p. 105. For similar expressions from Ruysbroeck see Hebert, " Le Divin," pp. 17–18.

[48] " Tendances Religieuses chez les Mystiques Chrétiens," p. 459. Cf. also the following passage from this article of Leuba's: " Saint Thérèse goûtait habituellement d'enivrantes delices dans la compagnie de son Seigneur. Tous les plaisirs de la terre pâlissaient devant ceux-là; ils n'étaient plus que de la fange. Voici un passage tout à fait frappant dont nous tirerons instruction tout à l'heure, en discutant la possibilité de l'origine sexuelle d'une des jouissances qu'ils disent ' spirituelles.' Elle avait parfois des visiteurs angéliques. Un jour elle vit un très petit et très bel ange. Il avait dans les mains ' un long dard qui était d'or et dont la pointe en fer avait à l'extrémité un peu de feu. De temps en temps il le plongeait au travers de mon coeur et l'enforçait jusqu'aux entrailles; en le retirant, il semblait me les emporter avec ce dard et me laissait tout embrasée d'amour de Dieu. La douleur de cette blessure était si vive, qu'elle m'arrachait ces faibles soupirs . . . mais cet indicible martyre me faisait goûter en même temps les plus suaves délices." For a full discussion of the subject one should read all of Leuba's article and the paper by de Montmorand cited below. See also Hebert's " Le Divin," pp. 17–24.

[49] Nor are they by any means confined to the ecstatics. So non-ecstatic

startling. One should not, however, make too much of it —
on second thought many of these expressions cease to be surprising and seem natural enough. For there are several excellent reasons why the mystics almost inevitably make use of
the language of human love in describing the joy of the love
of God. The first and simplest is this: that they have no other
language to use.[50] The emotion of the ecstasy is before all
else a burning love for God and a joyous consciousness of this
loving presence. It is evident then that the mystic must make
use of expressions drawn from earthly love to describe his experience, or give up the attempt of describing it at all. It is
the only way he has of even suggesting to the non-mystical what
he has felt. Even Plotinus — who blushed at the thought of
having a body — says: "Those to whom this heavenly love is
unknown may get some conception of it from earthly love, and
what joy it is to obtain possession of what one loves most." [51]

A special reason for the amorous language of the mediæval
Christian mystics is to be found in the nature of the book which
they constantly used as their model, the Song of Songs.[52] This
book which is really a naïve and straightforward glorification
of natural and proper sexual love, was regarded by the Christian
Fathers from Origen down as having really nothing to do with
sex, but as symbolic of the love between Christ and the Church,
or between God and the soul. Here then, the mystics thought,
was a divinely inspired treatment of exactly the experience
which they themselves so prized. Hence it was their favorite
book and its language inevitably influenced their own.

Much of the amorous language of the mystics must undoubtedly be explained as due to one or both of these two causes.
But when all is said there remains a good deal that is not yet explained; and we can hardly believe that so much erotic language
can have been used to describe experiences which in themselves

and literary a mystic as Coventry Patmore uses expressions of much the
same sort as those found in the erotic mystics of India. See "The Rod,
the Fruit, and the Flower" (London. Bell: 1914), pp. 106. 216; and
"Religio Poetæ" (1907), especially the closing essay, "Dieu et Ma
Dame."

[50] Cf. De Montmorand, "L'Erotomanie des Mystiques Chrétiens." *Revue
Philosophique*, LVI, 382–93.

[51] Bakewell's "Source Book," p. 389.

[52] Cf. again, De Montmorand, op. cit.

had no touch of anything but " Platonic " love. This is made
the more evident when we turn from Christian to Indian mysticism, for while much of the erotic language to be found in
India's religious literature is certainly due to the lack of any
other suitable expression for so intensely an emotional experience, the mystical and the sexual life of many Indian devotees are frankly recognized as being closely united. The
three great Sects of modern Hinduism — Vaishnavas, Shaivites,
and Shaktis — have in the past openly encouraged a mingling
of the erotic and the mystical which seemed to the worshipers as
natural and exalted as it seems to us strange and degraded.[53]
There is no reason to suppose that this mingling of seemingly
divergent tendencies is confined to India. The various passages from the Christian mystics already cited can hardly be
interpreted without recognizing the fact that here too the sexual
has been mingled with the religious, although the mystics themselves regularly fail to realize it.[54] The more sophisticated but
no less earnest contemporary Christian mystic investigated by
Professor Flournoy gives plain evidence of sexual influences in
some of her ecstasies. These to be sure are confined to the parts
of the experience preceding and following the central stage, and
they are rare even at that; but in one of the ecstasies the erotic
forces broke out into such open self-assertion as to be undeniable,
and resulted in a terrible night of conflict.[55] Her experience
throws light on that of many a Christian saint, and Professor
Leuba is probably right in pointing out that in some of the more
extreme Christian cases positive sexual delight is involved, although the mystic himself is usually quite unaware that this is
so. It is certainly true that sexual desires and sexual pleasure

[53] The (innocent) expression of divine love in terms of human love is
to be found repeatedly in the Bhagavad Gita, the Puranas, the Tantras,
and in much popular Shaivite and Vaishnavite poetry. Erotic mystical
practices are (or at least *were*) not uncommon among subjects of Vaishnavism and Shakti.

[54] Not invariably. The Fioretti of St. Francis, for example, informs
us that friar John of Alvernia was uplifted " to amorous and immoderate
embracings of Christ, not only with inward spiritual delights but also
with manifest indications and corporeal pleasures."

[55] See pp. 81–82, 93–96, 189, 192. It should be added, however, that
in only one out of thirty-one recorded ecstasies did the erotic forces become recognizable, and that in nearly every other case the influence of the
ecstasy was to banish all sexual ideas.

of a mild and disguised sort permeate most of our life, quite without our knowing it. All our emotions have some "bodily resonance"; they are due in part to the tension or relaxation of some muscles, to the functioning of some gland, or to some other physiological activity. The various joyous emotions have their foundation in various parts of the body; and the emotion of intense love, even in its purest form and quite divorced from every sexual idea, is usually connected with the incipient excitation of the sexual organs. This seems to be the case with the intense love of God and the joy in his love felt during ecstasy. But while this is doubtless true, no one would be so surprised to hear it even suggested as the mystic himself; for so far as his mind and will are concerned he is essentially pure from all sensual taint. What is going on in his body to color his emotions is of no interest to him, though it is of interest to us as psychologists. Our realization of this fact, therefore, must not be allowed to influence our valuation of him from the moral point of view.

While we are considering the emotional side of ecstasy we may as well take up the phenomenon known as "ravishment," for though it, of course, includes ideational as well as affective elements, it is the emotional crisis of the whole process. "Ravishment" is usually classed by the systematizers as one aspect of the third stage of mystic experience, or the "ecstatic union." [56] Its particular characteristics that differentiate it from the rest of the ecstasy and mark it out for special consideration, are its intensity, its suddenness, and the peculiar experience often connected with it known as "levitation." It comes upon the mystic with a great rush of emotion and (apparently) some inner bodily change, so that it often causes sudden fear and overcomes all resistance. The outer world is more completely shut out than ever. "The body retains the attitude in which it was surprised; thus it remains on its feet or seated, the hands open, or closed; in a word, in the condition in which the ravishment found it." [57] The mystic can sometimes

[56] St. Teresa, on the other hand, insists (in Chapter XX of the "Vie") that she recognizes no difference between "*ravissement*" and "*extase*." She distinguishes sharply, however, between "*ravissement*" and "*union*." (Cf. p. 190 of the "Vie.")

[57] St. Teresa, Vie, Chapter XX. Janet's ecstatic in the Salpetrière often exhibited this immobility during her attacks.

neither speak nor move. The attack, if so we may call it, may interrupt the course of one's thought or conversation like a fainting fit and after it is over the broken thought or sentence may be taken up where it was left.[58] It is usually of short duration — a few minutes or seconds only, but may last an hour or more.[59]

In connection with ravishment, as I have said, frequently comes the phenomenon of levitation. This is due to the sensational disturbances already referred to in ravishment. For not only sight and hearing but also the more fundamental and less easily inhibited sensation of pressure, together with muscle and joint sensations, apparently are to some extent deranged, parts of the body becoming anæsthetic. Visual imagery, fairly vivid yet not due to present sensory stimuli and therefore suggesting a new situation in space, may also at times have some influence. According to Lydiard H. Horton, who has investigated the phenomenon in a number of subjects in the process of inducing sleep, the most important cause is to be sought in the vaso-motor relaxation which is brought about by the approach of sleep, by "æsthetic repose," religious concentration, and other forms of relaxation.[60] The result is that the ecstatic either gets a new combination of sensations, or else gets almost none at all. In the former case he sometimes feels that his body has been lifted from the ground and is suspended freely in the air; in the latter case he may feel freed from his body altogether. "My body became so light during ravishment," says St. Teresa, "that it no longer had any weight, so that in fact sometimes I could not feel my feet touch the ground." [61] It is interesting to compare with this the description of much the same phenomenon experienced by one of my respondents during prayer: "It is a singular feeling or sensation which comes to me when I pray, that while I pray I feel my body

[58] Poulain, p. 245.

[59] This is Ribet's opinion, based upon that of several good authorities. Poulain says it may last even for days; but this is probably with intervals. Scaramelli says it "may last for several hours or even for several days, but during this period there may be fluctuations of intensity." (Op. cit., p. 80.)

[60] "The Illusion of Levitation," *Journal of Abnormal Psychology*, XIII, 12–53, 119–27.

[61] "Vie," p. 200, and other parts of Chapter 20.

is lifted up from the floor and I feel light and floating, so to speak, in the air. Though my eyes are shut I see objects far below and yet I feel my arms on my bed (as I usually kneel down beside the bed). . . . I feel no weight of body and my body becomes as light as a feather." It will be noted that the sense of pressure in the arms is referred to but not in the legs and feet, and that visual images contribute to the sense of floating in the air. It seems likely enough that the vaso-motor relaxation to which Mr. Horton refers may also have supervened.[62] So common is this experience to those who attain to the stage of ravishment that the good Father Ribet, who accepts piously what the Church teaches him, remarks, " There are but few ecstatics who have not been seen, at one time or another, during their ravishment elevated in air without support, sometimes floating and swinging in the slightest breeze " ! [63]

Before going on to the question of trance I should perhaps deal with certain other pathological phenomena sometimes found in the extreme type of ecstasy. As early in the development of the mystic experience as the *" oraison de quietude "* (St. Teresa's first stage, as the reader will remember) there may develop a loss of will which the technical writers of the Church have named " ligature." In this state one feels *bound,* and is unable to carry out various small activities of body or mind. As prayer is the principal voluntary activity in the mystic state, the mystics' attention has been chiefly struck by the fact that they often find it impossible to pray — either aloud or even inwardly; they cannot tell the nature of the interdiction but feel themselves quite passive and powerless. At deeper stages of the ecstasy (especially in the ravishment, as has already been said) control over the voluntary muscles is sometimes lost. And parallel with this impairment of the will goes a weakening of various non-voluntary bodily functions and a gradual and

[62] Cases of levitation are not uncommon. Another case besides that of the student referred to above has come to my notice, the experience coming suddenly while the individual was walking about a cathedral. In Mr. Horton's opinion it is common to many of us on going to sleep, but is unobserved and forgotten. Eight out of thirty subjects in whom he induced sleep reported the experience. Op. cit., p. 50.

[63] Vol. II, p. 639.

partial loss of sense perception.[64] Respiration is in part arrested, the heart beats very faintly, the circulation becomes sluggish, and as a consequence the bodily heat is largely lost. The eyes may remain open, but if they do they see surrounding objects (if at all) as through a veil or smoke.[65] Hearing is not so much affected as sight, and pressure apparently still less. The pain threshold is probably considerably raised during the ecstasy — as is likely to be the case at all times of concentrated attention and narrowed consciousness. Whether the senses of smell and taste are affected is obviously a question on which data would not naturally be furnished by the mystics,— although as pointed out in a previous note, Scaramelli insists that they too quite cease to function. This passive condition, according to St. Teresa, never lasts longer than half an hour, seldom so long; although counting the alternating states of more wakeful and active consciousness it may last several hours.[66]

It seems probable that will and sensation are but seldom as completely inhibited in "ligature" as many of the mystics themselves have believed. Professor Janet's interesting study of a modern ecstatic, whom he was able to have under careful observation in the Salpêtrière, shows that she was really in much closer touch with the outer world and much better able to react upon it during her ecstatic state than she herself supposed. "If there is [during the ecstasy] some good reason for it, either in her ideas or in external events, Madeleine can very well decide upon action." She could even converse with Janet and follow him to the laboratory. "It is the same with the physiological disturbances. She supposes that her lips are glued together and that she does not breathe at all during the ecstasy, but if one measures the respiration one finds it slight

---

[64] Scaramelli is the systematizer most quoted as authority in this matter. He writes thus of the bodily effects of ecstasy: "Quasi sono un'impotenza totale nei sentimenti esterni a produrre le loro operazioni sensitive; sicchè non possa l'occhio rimirare; nè l'orecchio ascoltare; nè il tatto, benchè tormentato da ferro e fuoco, sentire dolore; nè l'odorato sentire la fragranza; nè il palato sentire il sapore; nè possa alcun membro con minimo suo moto dar segno alcuno di vita." Quoted by Ribet, Vol. II, p. 438, note.

[65] See Poulain, p. 165, who says that several mystics have told him this in describing their experience.

[66] "Vie," p. 173.

indeed (12 a minute) but sufficiently normal. . . . These observations show us well enough that sensation also is not suppressed, and that it is not altogether the death of sense as the patient supposes. All sorts of experiences which I cannot indicate prove that Madeleine perceives very well the objects which I place in her hand during the ecstasy, that she recognizes them, that she hears and sees if she consents to open her eyes. It is for sensation, as for movement, only a sluggishness of the subject, who has only to turn her attention in order to do whatever one asks of her." [67]

Madeleine's was, of course, not one of the most extreme cases,— although had we been dependent for our knowledge on her own description, based on introspection and memory, we should undoubtedly have considered her much more cut off from the world of sense than she really was. But while we cannot accept the descriptions of the ecstatics themselves as absolutely reliable in this matter, there is no doubt that in the condition of " ligature " the voluntary control of the muscles is considerably weakened and the sensations become very dull and dim. The higher centers of the brain seem to be partially split off from the incoming sensory currents, on the one hand, and from the motor centers, on the other. Thus the mystic becomes more and more cut off from the outer world.[68] While this is happening, be it remembered, the mental state itself is usually becoming narrower and more " simple," and the many objects of normal consciousness gradually tend to give way to a state of monoideism. And in those rare cases where the ecstasy is continued to its extreme and the psychological tendencies which have characterized its progress are carried out to the end, the state of monoideism gives place to a condition of almost pure emotion. That there can be such a thing as absolutely pure emotion with

[67] Op. cit., pp. 228, 229.

[68] St. Teresa describes her own experience as follows: " L'âme tombe dans une espèce d'évanouissement, qui, peu à peu, enlève au corps la respiration et toutes les forces. Elle ne peut, sans un très pénible effort, faire meme le moindre mouvement des mains. Les yeux se ferment, sans qu'elle veuille les fermer; et si elle les tint ouverts, elle ne voit presque rien. Elle est incapable de lire, en eût-elle le désir; elle aperçoit bien des lettres, mais comme l'ésprit n'agit pas, elle ne peut ni les distinguer ni les assembler. Quand on lui parle, elle entend le son de la voix, mais elle ne comprend pas ce qu'elle entend."

no central idea seems to me exceedingly doubtful, and one certainly not to be demonstrated by the somewhat indefinite descriptions of the mystics. That some of them, in the ecstasy, do attain to a condition approximating to pure emotion as nearly as is possible we may however accept. This is especially true of the Quietists, and Mme. Guyon in particular is cited by Murisier in illustration of the pure emotional condition which is, according to him, a regular stage of the ecstasy when carried to its extreme form. Mme. Guyon's description is as follows:

" The whole occupation of the soul is a general love, without motive, without reason for loving. Ask of her what she does in the orison and during the day; she will tell you that she loves. But what motive or what reason have you for loving? She knows nothing about that. All that she knows is that she loves and that she burns to suffer for that which she loves. But is it, perchance, the vision of the sufferings of your Well-beloved, O soul, that make you thus long to suffer? ' Alas,' she responds, ' they do not even enter into my mind.' But is it, then, the desire to imitate the virtues which you see in Him? ' I do not even think of them.' But what, then do you do? ' I love.' But is it not the sight of the beauty of your Lover which rouses your heart? ' I do not see that beauty.' " [69]

When this exceptional state of consciousness is reached " the intellectual elements of belief are lost, the soul is nothing but ardor and love. God manifests Himself still, but without the intermediation of any concrete or abstract representative, in an incomprehensible manner, in complete darkness. . . . The emotion itself probably has diminished in intensity at this point; but it seems very intense because of its isolation." [70]

The usual laws of psychic regression would, as Murisier has also pointed out,[71] demand that the intellectual elements should

[69] Quoted from "Torrents Spirituels," by Murisier, "Les Maladies du Sentiment Religieux," p. 64. Cf. also the following from the " Beguines " of Ruysbroeck: " Le quatrième mode d'aimer est un état de vide, où l'on est uni à Dieu par un amour nu, et dans une lumière divine, libre et vide de toute pratique amoureuse, par delà les œuvres et les exercises de la piété; simple et pur amour, qui consume et anéantit en lui-même l'âme humaine, de telle sorte que l'on ne songe plus ni a soi-même, ni à Dieu, ni à quelque chose de créé. Rien qu'aimer! " Quoted by Hebert, " Le Divin," p. 44.

[70] Murisier, pp. 62–63.

[71] P. 65.

give place to the affective elements, that the emotion itself should pale into indifference, and that finally consciousness, thus narrowed to a point, should at length go out altogether and be replaced by the complete unconsciousness of the trance.[72]

[72] This way of reducing consciousness to the minimum and inducing trance is by no means peculiar to religious mysticism. The proper psychological methods will bring it about without involving any "sense of presence" or any "union with the divine." The last two stages of the "Noble Eight-fold Path" of Buddhism—"Meditation" and "Contemplation" lead up to it, though the ideational element in them is on a perfectly atheistic basis. One of the sermons of Gautama, preserved for us (in probably something very like its original form) in the Majjhima-Nikaya describes the process with real psychological exactness. The reader will note the order of regression: sensual pleasures, reasoning, joy, perception of diversity, and at last consciousness itself going out one by one.

"The monk, having isolated himself from sensual pleasures and de-meritorious traits, and still exercising reasoning and reflection, enters upon the first trance which is produced by isolation and characterized by joy and happiness. . . . Then through the subsidence of reasoning and reflection, and still retaining joy and happiness, he enters upon the second trance, which is an inner tranquillization and intentness of the thoughts, and is produced by concentration. But again, through the paling of joy, indifferent, contemplative, conscious, and in the experience of bodily happiness, he enters upon the third trance. . . . But again, through the abandonment of happiness and misery, through the disappearance of all antecedent gladness or grief, he enters upon the fourth trance which is neither misery nor happiness, but is contemplation as refined by indifference. . . . But again, through having completely overpassed all perceptions of form, through the perishing of the perceptions of inertia, and through ceasing to dwell on perceptions of diversity, the monk says to himself, ' Space is infinite,' and dwells in the realm of infinite space. . . . But again through having completely overpassed the realm of infinite space, the monk says to himself, ' Consciousness is infinite ' and he dwells in the realm of infinite consciousness. . . . But again . . . he says to himself ' Nothing exists,' and he dwells in the realm of nothingness. . . . But again, having completely overpassed the realm of nothingness, he dwells in the realm of neither perception nor yet non-perception. [That is he has ceased to *say anything to himself*, ceased to formulate the content of consciousness in any way.] . . . But again, through having completely overpassed the realm of neither perception nor yet non-perception, he arrives at the cessation of perception and sensation." Warren's "Buddhism in Translations" (Cambridge; Harvard Univ. Press; 1896), pp. 347–349. Hinduism has made more of the mystic trance than Buddhism, connecting it, as the neoplatonists did, with the immediate intuition of the Absolute. The Kshurika Upanishad gives careful directions as to the psychological methods by which it may be attained; see Deussen's translation—"Sechzig Upanishad des Veda," pp. 634–36. Under the name *Samadhi* it is still the aim of the Hindu mystic, though there are few if any of the present generation who claim to have attained it. Rama-

In the mysticism of the Indian specialists this in fact is what we find, and occasionally also in a few extreme mediæval Christian mystics. It is a mistake, however, to consider this typical of Christian mysticism; its real home is India.

The complete loss af consciousness is a more natural aim of the Indian, whether Buddhist, Yogin, or Vedantist, than of the orthodox Christian because of their contrasting views of the supreme good. The extinction of what we know as consciousness in Nirvana, the freedom of the " purusha " or soul from all content of consciousness, the identification of the " atman " or self with Brahman or the pure perceiving subject who perceives nothing in particular — these are the ideals of many of the Indian mystics, and hence the unconsciousness of the trance is deliberately sought. When Agatasatru wished to teach his pupil what it was to know Brahman, he " took him by the hand and rose and the two together came to a person who was asleep." [73] The ideal of the orthodox Christian mystic, on the other hand, is very different; his goal is always some form of consciousness or activity. Hence it is only the exceptional Christian ecstasy that ends in trance. That this sometimes happens, cannot, of course, be denied. Sometimes, as says St. François de Sales, " the soul ceases even to hear her Well-beloved, or to perceive any sign of his presence. On awaking she may say truly, I have slept in the presence of my God and within the arms of His providence, and I knew it not." [74] The practices of many of the heretical Christian mystics, such as the Quietists on Mt. Athos,[75] approached rather closely to those of the Indians. And the protests of St. Teresa against the "*longs evanouissements*" [76] practiced in many orthodox mon-

krishna, the Hindu saint who died in the year 1886 attained it many times. See, for example, " The Gospel of Ramakrishna," pp. 189, 209–10; also Max Müller's " Ramakrishna, his Life and Sayings," pp. 34, 112.

[73] Brihadaranyaka Upanishad. Max Müller's translation. S. B. E. Vol. I, Part II, p. 103.

[74] Quoted by Leuba, op. cit., p. 451.

[75] Cf. Reckenbergius, " Exercitationum in N. Testamentum." (Lipsiæ, 1707), pp. 388–389.

[76] This sort of " spiritual sensuality " is in fact recognized as such and heartily discouraged by the Church and by the orthodox mystics. " One does very ill," says St. Teresa, " in employing in the service of God long hours lost in this kind of drunkenness." And she advises the strict elimination from all monasteries of these " *longs evanouissements.*"

asteries in her day, and similar protests by other sensible saints, show that ecstatic conditions bordering on trance were by no means unknown, though never approved, within the Church. The ecstasies of Professor Flournoy's "modern mystic" regularly ended in a short lapse of consciousness, or possibly in a dream forgotten on awaking.[77] Of her tenth ecstasy (which was quite typical) she writes as follows: "It seemed to me that I was only *soul,* drawn irresistibly by the universal soul, by the luminous reality, the sum of all partial realities. I tried to collect my thoughts and to pray, but could not; that would have been to return, to fall back into the visible. Finally the sense of floating became less and less conscious and I perceived the inner light [a regular experience in her ecstasies]. I had the impression of plunging into it with a cry of joy, of finding again the source of life itself — — —[These dashes she uses regularly to indicate the lapse of consciousness]. I emerged on the other side of the Experience with a sense of great spiritual wellbeing, of having renewed my strength, of having communed with God without intermediary, without language nor formula."[78]

Leuba has pointed out that the mystic trance does not differ psychologically in any essential from other kinds of trance; and that it very closely resembles hypnosis. This too begins with a narrowing of consciousness, a "simplification" of the mental field, and is characterized by a gradual loss of control over the voluntary muscles and by hallucinations,— these things being suggested by the hypnotist. The deliberate methods of some of the Indian mystics, in fact, are almost identical with those of the scientific hypnotist. The Yogin chooses a quiet place, seats himself in a position that will not attract his mind to bodily sensations, murmurs the mystic word Om, fixes his attention on his thumb or his navel, or on successive parts of his body, thus narrowing his attention, or, deliberately fixing his mind upon the self alone, seeks to "think of nothing," until at last he falls into unconsciousness.[79]

[77] This is suggested in her account of her eleventh ecstasy. See op. cit., p. 89.

[78] Op. cit., p. 83.

[79] Cf. the Kshurika Upanishad (Deussen's translation), esp. vv. 2-7,

The mystic trance differs from the hypnotic trance, however, in that it lacks the final stage of somnambulism, in which the hypnotized person performs various actions at the suggestion of the hypnotist. What is the explanation for this? Leuba's answer is (and in this he seems to be quite in the right) that throughout the earlier stages of the mystic trance the idea of God is substituted for the hypnotist;[80] and that when the mystic has reached the extreme form of his ecstasy where all ideas, even that of God, vanish, there remains no source of further suggestion, and hence the mystic either returns to ordinary consciousness or lapses into normal sleep.

11–12, 21–23. Also the Bhagavad Gita, VI, 18, S. B. E. Vol. VIII, Part III, pp. 68–70.

[80] Sometimes, however, the confessor or director seems to play a part corresponding somewhat to that of the hypnotist. Thus it is related of St. Francesca Romana that during ecstasy he could hear the questions of his confessor but not those of others. See Poulain, p. 165. Cf. also Scaramelli, " Mystical Theology " (English translation), p. 76.

CHAPTER XIX

THE MYSTIC LIFE

THE amount of space I have devoted to the various aberrations of the ecstatic condition must not be taken as indicating the amount of importance belonging to this unfortunate side of mysticism. As I have several times pointed out, these pathological extremes are by no means characteristic of all the mystics; and when they do occur they are seldom regarded even by those who experience them as of the first importance. Of course, there have been, even in the Christian Church, a large number of individuals who have induced the ecstatic condition for the sake of its pleasure and indulged repeatedly in this spiritual drunkenness (as St. Teresa calls it) for its own sake. This, however, has not been the practice of the majority whom posterity has recognized as "the great mystics"; and to emphasize the ecstasy and its accompanying abnormal phenomena as if it were the whole of mysticism would therefore be a misleading (though it is unfortunately a common) way of treating the subject. To understand mysticism aright one must take into consideration the whole life of the mystic, including both the recurring states of ecstasy and the periods intervening between them or subsequent to them.

Herbert Spencer has sought to show that the "Rhythm of Motion" is one of the fundamental laws of the material universe.[1] However this may be, it is certain that rhythm is one of the fundamental characteristics of human life. The pendulum swing of our moods, each giving place to its opposite, has been noted over and over again by most observers of human nature. Disgust follows undue indulgence, depression follows great elation, sleep follows activity. And like the pendulum, moreover, the farther we go to one side the longer is likely to be our swing in the opposite direction when the time for it comes. The mercurial temperament knows both the keenest delight and the deepest (temporary) depression; while the man of phleg-

[1] "First Principles," Part II, Chapter X.

matic disposition is less influenced by either. It was in part upon this psychological law that the Buddha founded his great principle for the destruction of sorrow; give up the intense and passionate joys of life and you will avoid most of its intense suffering; keep the pendulum from swinging to the right and there will be no danger of its swinging to the left.

Now the Christian ecstatic though in some respects strikingly Buddhistic, is in this matter at the very antipodes of the Buddhist ideal. He longs for and patiently cultivates the intense joy of the ecstasy; and by the law of rhythm he usually has to pay for it by periods of suffering and " dryness " which bring him as much depression as the ecstasy brought elation. His is merely an extreme case of what we all experience, and it is based ultimately on what is perhaps a purely physical law.[2]

It would be a mistake to suppose that the ecstasy is an experience of mere sweetness. For many mystics it is what Browning describes as the ideal of joy — " three parts pain." [3] It is, however, a very real and intense joy. This cannot be said of the periods of dryness. The sufferings of the ecstatics during these times are of many sorts. St. John of the Cross classifies them as of three kinds: loss of delight in any creature, the

---

[2] The ecstatics themselves have their own theological explanation for this: the favors of God in the ecstasy if unaccompanied by pain might be sought too exclusively for their own sakes, or fill the soul with pride; the soul needs further purifications besides those which the mystic can actively inflict upon himself, hence these " passive purifications "; and then God comforts, encourages, and rewards him again by the " consolations " of the returning ecstasy. Cf. Montmorand, " Les Mystiques en dehors de l'Extase," *Rev. Phil.*, LVIII, 621–22. Cf. also the following from the " Theologia Germanica ": " Christ's soul must needs descend into hell before it ascended into heaven. So must also the soul of man. . . . Now God is not forsaking a man in this hell, but He is laying His hand upon him that the man may not desire nor regard anything but the Eternal Good only, and may come to know that that is so noble and passing good that none can search out or express its bliss, consolation and joy, peace, rest and satisfaction. . . . Again: this hell and this heaven come about a man in such sort, that he knoweth not whence they come; and whether they come to him or depart from him, he can of himself do nothing towards it. . . . And when a man is in one of these two states, all is right with him, and he is as safe in hell as in heaven, and so long as a man is on earth it is possible for him to pass ofttimes from the one into the other; nay even within the space of a day and night, and all without his own doing." Chapter XI (translation by Susanna Winkworth).

[3] Cf. St. Teresa, " Vie," pp. 194–96.

feeling of one's distance from God and the memory of the joy of ecstasy which is no longer to be had, and thirdly inability to " meditate " or to excite oneself to pious emotion by the use of the imagination.[4]   This triad, however, fails to exhaust all the ills reported by many of the mystics during these times of dryness.   St. Teresa's chief source of pain seems to have been a recurrent doubt as to whether her mystic experiences were not after all the product of illusion and the work of the Wicked One.[5]   Another source of grief, especially with mystics less completely devoted than Teresa, is hardness of heart and a renewal of worldly temptations.   Causes of a similar sort could be cited for the pains and dryness of some of the Hindu mystics. As a rule, it may be said, the phenomenon is due to an impoverishment of the emotional life through its over stimulation during the periods of ecstasy.   The former joy is remembered and longed for but does not come; hence disappointment.   The methods that usually succeed in bringing one at least into a state of pleasant and pious calm are in vain.   The emotional nature being temporarily worn out and exhausted, the mystics can take no pleasure in anything, divine or human; all is vanity and vexation of spirit.   The sense of fatigue, like a mist, settles down over the earth and shuts out heaven.   Even the truths of theology, having lost their emotional tinge, appear as mere intellectual judgments and hence, seen in the cold light of logic, may be positively doubted — to the great dismay of the mystic.   And in like manner virtue itself may lose some of its luster, or the effort to strive after an almost unattainable goal may seem to the poor tired will hardly worth the while. " Sometimes," says St. Teresa, in describing the experience as she knew it, " I find myself in a sort of strange stupidity.   I do neither good nor evil; I go as I am directed by others, experiencing neither positive pain nor consolation, insensible to life as to death, to pleasure as to sorrow." [6]

These periods lasted with St. Teresa some two or three weeks. With Mme. Guyon such a period once lasted, with slight alteration, for five years.   St. Chantal suffered even more extremely in this manner for the last seven or eight years of her

[4] Cf. Ribet, Vol. I, pp. 374–75.

[5] See, e.g., the " Vie," pp. 328–29.

[6] " Vie," Chapter XXX.

life — though the last two months before her death brought her
" consolation " once more. Cases like the last two mentioned
are not usual. More frequently the periods of suffering are
more evenly interspersed with those of joy; though there is
certainly a tendency for them to be grouped largely in one
period of the mystic's life; and especially is this true of the
greater mystics.[7]

It must not be supposed, however, that the life of the mystic
consists chiefly in a succession of elated and depressed moods;
that it is nothing but " ecstasy " and " dryness." There is another rhythm more important in the life of the mystic than
that between pleasure and pain; it is, namely, the rhythm of
contemplation and activity. The life of the morally great mystic out of the ecstasy is not so much a life of depression as a
life of action. This of course is not true of all. Many in-
mates of the monasteries have spent their lives sucking the
sweets of ecstasy and paying for it by periods of emotional
and volitional fatigue. But many of those individuals who are
by common consent considered the great and typical mystics,
and upon whom the Church has set her stamp of approval, have
been noted for their activity as well as for their emotions. And
in their cases the rhythm between meditation on the one hand,
and active work on the other, has been essentially healthful and
desirable. The mystic of this active type often comes back from
his contemplation, and sometimes from his ecstasy, with a
heightened moral enthusiasm for the strenuous and the heroic.[8]
In like manner, activity prepares one the better for contemplation. The two are complementary and lend each other mutual
aid. Their rhythm is analogous not so much to that of elation
and depression as to that of exercise and rest. As Joly puts it

[7] Murisier points out (pp. 33–36) that this stage of " dryness " is analogous to the periods between hypnosis in the life of the mentally dis-
eased. As the hypnotic trance into which the patient is thrown for
therapeutic reasons corresponds to the ecstasy of the mystic, so the disquiet of the period of dryness corresponds to the longing which the patient
feels, after the immediate effects of the hypnosis have begun to pass away,
to be quieted and put to sleep again by the hypnotist. This is an excellent
comparison and throws light on the cases to which it applies. It must
again be noted, however, that this condition of affairs is true only of
the more pathological cases and is by no means typical of all mysticism
as such.

[8] Cf. Boutroux, op. cit., p. 186.

in his " Psychologie des Saints," " Contemplation is closely connected with love and *active* love; it is the effect of love already
exercised and already intense; it is the inspiration and the director of a love still more ardent." [9]

These three things, then,— (1) contemplation and ecstatic
joy, (2) suffering and dryness, and (3) active service guided
and inspired by the love of God — make up, together, the life
of the great mystic. The further question, therefore, naturally
arises, Are these three definitely related so as to make up one
general scheme with a logical or psychological development, or
are they separate and do they simply arise without special order and haphazard? Certainly this question is an important
one and has not been often enough raised. The mystic experience has been carefully studied by psychologists in *cross section*
but not enough *longitudinally*. The great mystics themselves
however and their theological expositors have often looked at
the matter as a unitary development; and recently a psychologist, Professor Delacroix of Caen, has made an elaborate " longi-
tudinal " study of the lives of five great mystics: St. Teresa,
Mme. Guyon, St. François de Sales, St. John of the Cross, and
Suso. His conclusion is that the three phases of the mystic
experience to which I have referred arise in a certain order of
development according to a regular law; that the life of the
mystic is not so well described by the word *oscillation* as by the
word *systematization*.[10]

The mystic begins, according to Delacroix, with the desire
for the ecstasy and finally attains it. In this stage he experiences a new and very intense joy which for a time seems worth

[9] P. 189. From what has been said it is evident that two distinct types
of rhythm are to be found in the experience of many mystics — (1) that
of ecstasy and dryness, (2) that of contemplation and action. The first
of these is plainly undesirable, usually pathological, and probably unnecessary. The second is both natural and necessary in any fully rounded
life, whether mystical or not. Hocking who discusses the second of these
rhythms very admirably seems to regard his position as incompatible with
that of Delacroix. The distinction I have indicated between the two kinds
of rhythm does away, in my opinion, with any real divergence between
these two most sympathetic interpreters of mysticism; for they are discussing different things. See Delacroix, " Etudes d'Histoire et de Psychologie du Mysticisme," Chapters II, VI, XI; and Hocking's " The Meaning of God in Human Experience," pp. 392–97.

[10] Op. cit., p. 424.

while in itself. The ecstatic condition, however, even when no painful periods intervene between the ecstasies, has its defects. In the first place if pursued for its own sake it becomes mere religious indulgence; God is *enjoyed* for the sake of the self. Secondly it induces a feeling of self-confidence and magnifies the personal self through the intimacy with God which it seems to bring about. And thirdly if cultivated exclusively it results in inactivity toward the outer world, the mystic's thought and action (so far as he is active) being centered on continuing his own ecstatic delights. The great mystics themselves have seen these defects and have, therefore, not regarded the ecstasy as the culmination of mysticism. Hence in their view the period of dryness and sorrow which often follows the period of ecstatic joy has an important though negative function, namely, to counteract the defects of the first stage. By means of the suffering and disappointment which the mystic goes through, the self-centerdness of the first period is effectively destroyed, and the mystic is filled with a dominating intuition of personal worthlessness. This period of dryness, Delacroix points out, is doubtless due to physiological and psychological causes, but it is *used* by the mystic for his own moral advancement. And when at last his little self, with its interests and joys have been killed out, the mystic finds himself entering into a new and final period, filled with a joy of its own, in which the personal consciousness is lost and his actions are guided by a power which he cannot recognize as his own will — in short the " transforming union " or " spiritual marriage " of St. Teresa's account. When this stage is reached the mystic looks back on his long course and understands it all at last. He has now the key to his former sufferings, he sees why it was all necessary, and he interprets the whole process in the light of its final term. The three periods thus form (although Delacroix does not himself point this out) a beautiful example of the Hegelian triad, with the simple joy of ecstasy as the thesis, the deeper pain of separation from God and self-despair as the antithesis, and the " apostolic life " of guided activity as the synthesis, in which all that was best in the other two is " *aufgehoben* " — taken up, transformed, glorified.

This theory of Delacroix's, excellent as it is, and based as it is on the views of some of the great mystics themselves, cannot be accepted without some reserve. The difficulty with it is that it is much too simple. The facts drawn from the lives of the majority of the mystics do not bear it out. Particularly is this the case with the relation between the first and second periods. In the lives of most mystics ecstasy and dryness are not periods or stages that come once each, but episodes which oscillate and give place to each other through long years. They are really only the intensified states of religious emotion and its opposite which all religious persons feel. And to say that only those who fill out the formula are mystics or " typical " mystics comes very near to begging the question. It must, however, be admitted that a large number of those who are generally recognized as the great historical mystics do approximate Delacroix's triadic formula — not indeed perfectly, but still with a fair amount of exactness.[11]   We may, in fact, go further and recognize this fundamental truth in Delacroix's view: the defects of ecstasy are those which he points out; the moral function of dryness has been that which he and the mystics claim for it. More important still, the " spiritual marriage " of automatically guided activity (in those mystics who have attained to it at all) has regularly come last and has crowned the whole, presupposing to a large degree both the antecedent stages.

This crowning phase of the mystic life is one of the most interesting things in mysticism. It is in the eyes of the great mystics themselves the supreme climax of the whole, the only part of their experience that is worth while entirely for its own sake. It is moreover (at least if we can trust their testimony) not subject to any very great change but is essentially permanent.[12]   It has, according to Poulain, three chief characteristics: first, the permanence just referred to; second, its transforming nature, the mystic feeling that his acts are not his own but God's; third, the continual vision of God or sense of His presence in the midst of and undisturbed by great activity.

Delacroix, whose analysis is much more careful than Pou-

[11] The experience of Flournoy's *mystique moderne* could also with a little good will, be shown to exemplify Delacroix's law fairly well — as could also the development of Ramakrishna's mystical life.

[12] *Within it*, of course, the rhythm between contemplation and activity — just as that between sleeping and waking — continues.

lain's and is from the psychological, rather than the theological point of view, enumerates four [13] characteristics. (I speak of this as Delacroix's analysis, but it is really, as he shows, Mme. Guyon's). The first characteristic is " the abolition of the personal consciousness and the substitution for the habitual self of a more ample personality. Before there had been a distinction between self and God; this opposition now ceases by the abolition of the self, which is driven out by God. Before this the soul possessed God in certain states; now it is possessed entirely and forever by God." The second characteristic is automatism. " For the action guided by the personal consciousness, which has its roots in the individual and is willed, is substituted an immediate and direct action, which seems to be the action of God Himself and which gives to the individual the sense of freedom and of infinite power.[14] He no longer desires, because he is above all desires, because he is no more attached to the objects of his action. . . . This feeling that it is God who acts assures the constant communion between God and the soul." The third distinguishing quality is a new kind of joy. It is something like the joy of ecstasy continued, but differs from it certainly in being only incidental, not essential, and probably differs in certain other ways as well. It is a feeling of energy and plenitude and exuberance, a sense of a mission to be fulfilled and the power to fulfill it. And though it is not sought for itself — perhaps for that very reason — it is very intense. Mme. Guyon says of it: " It is an immense but insensible joy, due to the fact that one fears nothing, desires nothing, wishes nothing." One is not thinking about it nor saying, " How ecstatic I am ! ", because one is not thinking of oneself at all. It is the direct result of the loss of self, referred to as the first characteristic of the " spiritual marriage." And in this connection it may be well to point out the similarity between the Christian mystic's experience in this stage and that of the Buddhist who has in this life attained to the destruction of desire, the annihilation of self, and the consequent joy of Nir-

[13] Delacroix really enumerates five, but two of them are hardly distinguishable.

[14] Cf. the last stages of the Boddhisattva's development according to the Mahayana theory; Suzuki, op. cit., pp. 322–28.

vana.[15]   Truly " 'Tis self whereby we suffer."   It would be a mistake, however, to suppose that the " mystic life " is one of unmixed happiness.   In Tauler's words, the state of those who are most nearly perfect " is one of mingled joy and sorrow whereby they are tossed up and down; for the Holy Spirit is trying and sifting them and preparing them for perfection with two kinds of grief and two kinds of joy and happiness which they have ever in their sight. . . . Thus all his being is swallowed up in sorrow and remorse for that he is still laden with his boundless infirmity.   But he hath delight and joy in that he seeth that the goodness of God is as great as his necessities, so that his life may well be called a dying life, by reason of such his griefs and joys which are conformable and like unto the Life of our Lord Jesus Christ, which from beginning to end was always made up of mingled grief and joy." [16]

The fourth characteristic of the mystic life, according to Mme. Guyon and Delacroix, is a seeming division within the personality; a dissociation between the bodily and earthly human self, and the real self who has become identified with God.[17] This seeming division within the personality of course varies greatly with different mystics.   Something like it is seen in many a non-mystical and perfectly normal individual whose life is divided between the prosecution of some great purpose and the fulfilling of the common duties of daily life.   And it is almost inevitable that some such doubling should occur in the case of one who believes himself to catch occasional glimpses into another world; a certain amount of absent-mindedness and mental abstraction and temporary confusion is a natural result.   The description which Browning has given us of Lazarus's state of mind after he was raised from the dead depicts so well this phase of the mystic consciousness that I shall quote a few lines from it:

[15] Cf. Scaramelli's enthusiastic description of the joy of the Spiritual Marriage, op. cit., pp. 88–89, which is strikingly like many a Buddhist description of the joy of Arahatship.

[16] From the Sermon on the Feast of St. Stephen, translated by A. W. Hutton in a collection of Tauler's sermons called " The Inner Way " (London, Methuen: 1909), pp. 38 and 40.

[17] Delacroix, op. cit., pp. 142–48.

> " He holds on firmly to some thread of life —
>   (It is the life to lead perforcedly)
> Which runs across some vast distracting orb
> Of glory on either side that meager thread,
> Which, conscious of, he must not enter yet —
> The spiritual life around the earthly life;
> The law of that is known to him as this,
> His heart and brain move there, his feet stay here.
> So is the man perplexed with impulses
> Sudden to start off crosswise, not straight on,
> Proclaiming what is right and wrong across,
> And not along this black thread through the blaze —
> ' It should be ' mocked by ' here it cannot be.' "

The mystic thus lives in two worlds and feels himself animated and guided by two powers. " I live," says Paul, " yet not I, but Christ liveth in me." The individual will is not lost — the man is not in a dream or trance; yet the individual will still present is present only to yield to what the mystic takes for the divine will, which in all matters dominates the life. The two wills have become so united as to be but one. This union, says the Theologia Germanica, " is such that we should be purely, simply, and wholly at one with the One Eternal Will of God, or altogether without will, so that the created will should flow out into the Eternal Will, and be swallowed up and lost therein, so that the Eternal Will alone should do and leave undone in us." [18] And again, " So that every enlightened man can say, ' I would fain be to the Eternal Goodness what his own hand is to a man.' " [19]

The mystic's life is therefore from the time of his attainment of the " spiritual marriage " onward a life of activity guided by a power which he cannot recognize as his own. This " apostolic life " is really only an intensification (sometimes to an almost pathological degree) of the " led life " which, as we saw in Chapter XVI, many commonplace Christians live. The difference is a matter only of degree; but the degrees are so different that with some of the great mystics action seems to be almost automatic. According to Delacroix's theory, their action is guided not by the conscious will but by the subconscious

[18] P. 98.
[19] Ibid., p. 32.

forces of the psycho-physical organism. This does not make their action any the less intelligent or purposive. It is in a sense impulsive,— that is the force comes *a tergo* — but it is still purposive; and this purposiveness makes it different from the impulses studied by the aliensists.

Of course there is sometimes an irrational element in the actions of the mystic — as he himself plainly sees and which, he attributes to the impulsions of the devil. But his action as a whole, though guided by habitual and in part subconscious forces, is, as I have said, essentially rational, purposive, and moral. If we accept Delacroix's theory of subconscious guidance (and with a certain amount of toning down we shall, I think, be justified in so doing [20]), we can understand why the mystic's life should be on so high a plane. In the first place the subconscious nature of the mystic is by no means the same as that of all other men, good and bad. His is essentially and by nature a moral subconsciousness. That is what we mean when we speak of a man who is naturally good: his unguided impulses and actions are on the whole of the right sort. Especially is this true of the intense religious natures of the mystics who (as a rule) from their childhood have loved virtue. And secondly the mystic's is a *trained* subconsciousness. It has been trained in the first place by the long years of his

[20] It is highly questionable whether the facts justify so large a use of the subconscious as Delacroix would have us believe. A large part of the "apostolic life" requires no more recondite explanation than does the activity of many a good man of settled character who is under the conviction that he is the subject of divine guidance; but Delacroix at least implies that the subconsciousness of the mystic is decidedly different from what one finds in "normal" persons. By looking for some unusual explanation of the facts of the mystic life and thereby admitting that they belong to a category different from that of ordinary living Delacroix has opened himself to the accusation which Pacheu brings against him, that he has manufactured a subconscious *ad hoc*, in order to explain facts which would otherwise demand a supernatural explanation, and that the subconscious which he has devised is one which psychology has seldom if ever come across elsewhere. (See "L'Experience Mystique," pp. 75–85, 285–96.) We shall, however, be justified in using the word subconscious in dealing with the mystic life if we mean by it no more than what we find in the life of every man of settled character, whose actions are guided largely by unconscious forces, whose psycho-physical mechanism is so predisposed in all habitual situations that he finds most decisions already made in advance and feels himself to be carrying out some unitary life plan.

social education. Society sees to it that the wilder and more indecent parts in the subconscious natures of us all are considerably subdued and tamed. The subconscious is constantly being influenced by the conscious personality as this reflects the demands and conventions of society. And, as Professor Coe has pointed out,[21] the subconscious is essentially conservative, and hence often acts as a storehouse for the generally accepted moral precepts of the community and uses them in restraint of the non-social desires of the individual. Furthermore, the mystic has taken particular pains through years of ascetic discipline to remold his subconsciousness (though he himself has never heard the term), and kill out from it all that he regards as evil. It is not surprising then that the automatically guided life of the mystic in this final stage should be essentially moral from the objective and conventional point of view.[22] So far indeed so good. Whether everything is explained by the use of the word " subconscious " is not so certain.

It must not be supposed from the last pages that all the mystics are active. Most of them never reach the heights of the " spiritual marriage," and many of them prefer to remain in the first stage and suck its sweetness. Yet though this is the case it still is true that activity forms an important part of the life of many of the greater Christian mystics. Moral earnestness and unselfish ardor for righteousness have been almost as characteristic of them as is the joy of ecstasy.[23] Whether the ecstatic experience and the other features of the extreme sort of mysticism are a help or hindrance in the life of active service, whether the saints have been strenuous soldiers in the cause of righteousness because of or in spite of their ecstasies, is a question for which there has been no place even in these three long chapters.

[21] " The Mystical as a Psychological Concept," *Journal of Philosophy*, VI, 201.

[22] Whether semi-automatic conduct (such as that of Mme. Guyon in her stage of " Apostolic life ") can be truly called moral from the subjective point of view, is another question.

[23] It must, however, be remembered that it is the ecstasy, not the activity, which singles them out as mystics.

CHAPTER XX

THE PLACE AND VALUE OF MYSTICISM

In the four preceding chapters I have tried to give a just description of mysticism as a psychological phenomenon. The description has necessarily been long, and, I fear, rather wearisome, and to avoid making it still longer 1 have had to leave out of account several related questions which naturally present themselves in this connection. The present chapter will, therefore, be devoted to the more important of these problems,— nearly all of which are concerned with the value of mysticism and its place in religion and in life. As a preliminary to this question, the origin or source of the individual's mystical experience naturally presents itself for our consideration. For if its source be what some think it, this would have an important, if not a decisive, bearing on the question of its value.

In general it may be said that there are three leading views as to the origin and nature of the mystic revelation. The first of these appeals frankly to the Supernatural. This is, of course, the view held by the Roman Catholic Church and the many learned writers on mysticism who represent it. More important still, this is the view of most of the mystics themselves. In the ecstasy, say they, the soul comes face to face with God and receives from God revelations, comfortings, assistance which it can carry back into the world for the help of all the faithful. This hypothesis is usually based upon a dualistic view of the universe as consisting of the two realms of Nature and of Grace, each with its own laws; and the contact of the soul with the Supernatural realm in the mystic union is regarded as more or less miraculous.[1]

Opposed to this view is the completely naturalistic interpre-

---

[1] For a serious attempt to present this view in scientific fashion see A. B. Sharpe's "Mysticism, Its True Nature and Value" (London, Sands: 1910), especially pp. 1–69, 113–21. Pacheu takes the same view in "L'Experience Mystique" but realizes fully that there is no room for ultimate explanation within psychology.

tation. This either denies altogether the existence of any supernatural realm, or if it admits its possibility, insists that it is quite separate from nature and must be kept strictly apart from it in our thought; the Supernatural never interferes with the natural, hence to explain the latter we must confine our hypotheses entirely to it. Mysticism, therefore, like everything else, is to be accounted for solely by the laws of a scientific psychology, and its source is to be sought in the individual mind and in society. Imitation, social education, and individual suggestion furnish a quite sufficient explanation for all the phenomena of mysticism.

Midway between these opposing explanations stands the third view, which seeks, in a sense, a compromise or combination of the two. Natural law everywhere holds; but what we formerly knew as the Supernatural is not ruled out, because it is really a part of nature. In other words, the dualism which both the other views accepted (so far as they admitted anything besides "this world") it rejects, and hence it is able to maintain that if explanation is forced to look beyond "this world" of "Nature," that does not imply a miracle. What the theologians call the Supernatural is merely *more* of the natural,— a farther part of it about which, indeed, we know little, but which we conceivably might come to know in the same way that we now know this part. For the supposition is that in that case we should find it too a world of laws, and that its laws are in some ways related to and continuous with those laws of nature which we already know. There is then, according to this view, really no supernatural; there is merely an as yet Unknown,— an Unknown which it would be cowardice to call an Unknowable. The upholders of this general view do not fully agree as to details — in fact none of them has tried as yet to work the theory out into particulars. But it may in general be said that they find, or hope to find, a bridge between the known and the unknown parts of reality in the constitution of the mind and the laws of its workings. Boutroux puts the suggestion (for with him, as with most of those who propose it, it is as yet only a suggestion) in this way:

"Is there for us, as conscious beings, besides the individual life, a universal life, potential and already in some measure real? Is our reflective and individual consciousness, according to which we are external to one another, an absolute reality or a simple phenomenon under which is concealed the universal interpenetration of souls within a unifying principle?"[2]

Miss Underhill, whose position is not unlike that of Boutroux, is more explicit, or at least more detailed. A large part of her argument in favor of the view that the mystics are in direct touch with Reality, consists in an attempt to break down the naïve confidence in common sense and natural science. Neither of these, she insists, though they be practically useful as guides to action, can give us any true insight into the nature of the real. Sensuous knowledge is always relative, and scientific knowledge is merely symbolic.[3] For conventional and practical purposes we have agreed to put tags upon reality, and these tags we take for the things they should merely signify. "It is notorious that the operations of the average human consciousness unite the self, not with things as they really are, but with images, notions, aspects of things. The verb 'to be,' which he uses so lightly, does not truly apply to any of the objects amongst which the practical man supposes himself to dwell." "Because mystery is horrible to us, we have agreed for the most part to live in a world of labels."[4] Thus we make reality over in conventional form, according to our practical needs and the artificial categories of language; and these conventions we take for reality. Even the practical man, however, occasionally has glimpses or intuitions of the Reality behind the sense world. To the mystic these intuitions are habitual. He lives in the direct apprehension of this "One Reality," since he perceives that the sense world is only symbolic of It. He alone lives in close touch with Reality and when he speaks he gives us not conventions but immediacy. There is, then, no dualism of Natural and Supernatural. Nothing, in Miss Underhill's opinion, is more profoundly natural than mysticism; and her world is too completely monistic to admit of any such rift as that implied in the naïve doctrine which would divide it into two realms. If

[2] "The Psychology of Mysticism," *Internat. Jour. of Ethics*, XVIII, 194. Eucken's position is not dissimilar. See, e.g., his "Meaning and Value of Life" (London, Black: 1910), p. 79ff.

[3] See her "Mysticism," Chap. I.

[4] "Practical Mysticism" (New York, Dutton: 1915), pp. 5 and 7.

dualism there be it is a dualism of the real and the conventional.

Professor James's point of view is naturally very different from that of Miss Underhill; yet his conclusions are in many ways similar to hers. Mystical states, he suggests, may be " windows through which the mind looks out upon a more extensive and inclusive world." Through the doorway of the subconscious, in his opinion, the mystic comes into touch with " an altogether other dimension of existence " in which most of our ideals originate.[5] This view is James's " *over-belief* " merely; neither he nor any other really scientific upholder of it would as yet regard it as anything more than a working hypothesis.

In seeking to decide between these three explanations of mysticism — the supernatural, the naturalistic, and the reconciling position of Boutroux, Underhill, and James — we must first make up our minds whether we really wish, so far as possible, to stick to science. For our attitude toward the first of the three hypotheses at least will be largely, if not entirely, determined by our answer to this question. Not that science dogmatically denies the existence of the Supernatural. It neither knows nor pretends to know anything about this. It merely points out that if the Supernatural can and does interfere with the natural then there is, at the spot where the interference takes place, no longer any room for science. If the supernaturalists are right in maintaining miraculous breaks in natural law, science must, at the very least, modify her pretensions, and speak no longer in universal terms but in the more modest diction of mere probability, imitating mathematics hardly more than history.

It would seem only just for every one who is pursuing an investigation in any sense scientific to make up his mind at the start to give science a fair chance; to let it explain the facts in question if it can, and to accept its explanations if they do explain. A scientific " law," like a political law, if really deserving of being discarded, can best be proved so by strict enforce-

5 " The Varieties of Religious Experience," pp. 428, 515f. Here also should be mentioned James's last suggestion on the subject, namely that in the mystic revelation the threshold of consciousness is lowered, and what is usually in the subconscious region comes suddenly into full consciousness.— *Jour. of Phil.*, VII, 85–92.

ment. Nor should one easily be driven, by the temporary failure of science, into the arms of the Supernatural — "that refuge of ignorance," as Spinoza calls it. And so great have been the achievements of science in the past, so repeatedly has she brought forward explanations of the seemingly inexplicable for those who waited patiently upon her, that the burden of proof is certainly on those who would urge us to flee to the Supernatural,— the burden, namely, of showing us that no scientific explanation is possible.

If we accept this point of view — and the very undertaking to study religious psychology forces it upon us — we shall find our attitude toward the supernatural explanation of mysticism already settled. For certainly the facts of mysticism are not such as to drive us out of the realm of all possible scientific knowledge. There is nothing, surely, in the mystic's revelation or experience so striking or extraordinary as to lead us to despair of ever understanding them by the laws of the human mind. To say this is not to deny the Supernatural. It may indeed exist outside of nature; or, as the Absolute, it may include all nature. The laws which science knows may be only the Absolute's thoughts, or God's ways of doing things. But supernatural interference cannot be introduced into the chain of natural law and substituted for one or more of its links to account for phenomena. The Absolute may explain *everything;* it cannot explain anything in particular.

Nor can Miss Underhill's view of mysticism be fully reconciled with the strictly scientific attitude. The "One Reality" which, according to her, is directly apprehended by the mystic, is, after all, apprehended by means of the mystic's interpretation of his experience, or through a symbolic rendering of sense perception. The emotions, visions, beliefs, apprehensions of the mystic are not themselves the "Real"; they merely point toward or indicate it, and they, not It, are the objects which a scientific psychology must study. Miss Underhill may be right in her view that they are good evidence of an encircling spiritual world; but this hypothetical encircling world is not an object for psychology. The mystic experience is perhaps one end of a chain which binds the human consciousness to the divine: but science, in the nature of the case, can never get beyond

this end.   The " Presence " which the mystics claim to apprehend is, on their own showing, of such an indefinite, incommunicable, " ineffable " a nature as to preclude it from being
seriously considered as a scientific object; while their reiterated
insistence that the mystical experience is unrepeatable through
any discoverable devices makes it impossible to verify their assertions concerning the objectivity of this " Presence," and
hence prevents us from regarding its existence as a scientific
fact.[6]   Nor does Miss Underhill's critique of scientific categories and common sense terms make her own symbolic interpretation of the given world any more trustworthy.   If conventional thought is at fault in putting " labels " on things, is mysticism therefore any nearer the truth by substituting symbols ?
Is it questionable whether symbolism is much truer to the immediacy of fact than is the much reviled common sense.   The
truth is, we all reconstruct our world out of the materials of
mere immediacy — all of us, at least, but the invertebrates.
The mystic is no exception.   Much that is indubitably real he
leaves out of his account because he fails to find it interesting,
while, on the other hand, he reads into it much that no mere
immediacy could possibly give.   He differs from the plain man,
not by refusing to reconstruct his world, but in the manner of
his reconstruction; substituting some theological conception or,
it may be, the poetical imagination and its symbols, for the
principle of utility and its labels.— Not that this is the only
difference between him and the plain man.   Equally important
with this contrast in the method of remaking the world of mere
immediacy, is the fact that the mystic has experiences which the
non-mystical never shares.   But that these experiences are experiences of the " One Reality " is an hypothesis which no
amount of immediacy can ever verify, and which, even if perfectly true, can never be a fact of science.[7]

[6] I have expounded this view more fully in a paper entitled " Can Theology Be Made an Empirical Science? " in the *Am. Jour. of Theol.* for
April, 1920.

[7] I have said nothing of Miss Underhill's hypothesis of a " mystic sense,"
which, though it has " attachments to emotion, to intellect, and to will,"
" differs from and transcends the emotional, intellectual, and volitional
life of ordinary men."   I say nothing of it in part because Miss Underhill herself seems to be utterly uncertain as to what she means by it.   So
far as she uses it to mean a heightening of the ordinary mental powers,

Criticism of this general nature does not at first seem applicable to the mediating view of James and his followers who appeal only to natural laws.   A more detailed study of the facts on which this view is based is requisite before we can form an enlightened judgment upon it.   Such a study is to be found in James's " Varieties of Religious Experience "— particularly in the Lectures on Mysticism and in his " Conclusions."   James points, namely, to the sense of indubitable authority and immediate certainty of the mystic intuition, and to the unanimity with which the mystics of all lands testify to the common mystic creed.   This mystic creed is the belief, or the immediate sense, that " the limits of the individual self are transcended through some kind of mingling in, or other realization of, a larger world of the spiritual order; that this larger reality is good, and that in it the contradictions and the mystery of existence are solved." [8]   Or, in James's own words, mystical states " break down the authority of the non-mystical or rationalistic consciousness, based upon the understanding and the senses alone.   They show it to be only one kind of consciousness.   They open up the possibility of other orders of truth, in which, so far as anything in us vitally responds to them, we may freely continue to have faith." [9]   The religious man with a touch of mysticism " becomes conscious that the higher part of him is conterminous and continuous with a MORE of the same quality which is operative in the universe outside of him, and which he can keep in working touch with, and in a fashion get on board of and save himself when all his lower being has gone to pieces in the wreck. . . . Let me propose that, whatever it may be on its *farther* side, the ' more,' with which in religious experience we feel ourselves connected, is on its *hither* side the subconscious continuation of our conscious life. . . . Disregarding the over-beliefs, and confining ourselves to what is common and generic, we have in the fact that the conscious person is continuous with a wider self through

there is nothing to be said; so far as she means by it literally a different and special faculty, I need hardly point out that psychology knows absolutely nothing about it.

   [8] Coe's formulation of James's conclusion —" The Sources of the Mystic Revelation," *Hibbert Journal,* VI, 360.

   [9] The " Varieties," p. 423.

which saving experiences come, a positive content of religious experience which, it seems to me, is literally and objectively true as far as it goes." [10]

As I said above, Professor James's own "over-belief," or working hypothesis, is that the farther side of the " MORE " is the spiritual world with which the mystics insist they have come in contact in trance and similar states of non-rational consciousness.   Such an interpretation James regards not as demonstrated, indeed, but as, all things considered, more reasonable and more consistent with the facts of experience than is the purely naturalistic explanation.

Perhaps the most systematic critique of this view is to be found in a paper by Professor Coe which appeared in the *Hibbert Journal* for January, 1908, under the title, " The Sources of the Mystical Revelation." [11]   The seeming unanimity of the mystics to which James appeals is due, according to Professor Coe, to the fact that the cases used in the " Varieties " are *selected,* and selected almost necessarily from those individuals who are most suggestible.   The very conditions of trance, moreover, are such as to explain, in perfectly natural and naturalistic fashion, the content of the mystic revelation.   " The typical mystical process, which culminates in trance, is, formally considered, nothing else than partial or complete hypnosis. . . . Therefore the most direct method of examining the formal conditions that now interest us is to make the experiment of self-hypnosis."   The characteristics of such an experiment when tried, with no religious ideas in mind, were found to be the following: " First, the bodily sensations were modified.   A sense of strangeness came on, and it increased until the mind seemed to be *there* rather than *here* — alive, yet not ' mine ' in the old intimate way. . . . Second, the self-feeling underwent an equally marked change.   It seemed as if the self melted into its object, or as if two fluids were poured together.   The result was like a generalization without particulars, or a sort of pure being.   Attention had been narrowed to such a degree that

[10] Pp. 508, 512, 515.   A similar view, largely adapted from James, is to be found in Dr. C. M. Addison's " The Theory and Practice of Mysticism " (New York, Dutton: 1918), pp. 88–101.

[11] Cf. also Leuba on " Professor James' Interpretation of Religious Experience," *Int. Jour. of Ethics,* XIV (1904), 322–39.

the usual contrasts and antitheses by means of which we define our world had grown dim. Consciousness was absorbed, as it were, in the bright object at which the eyes gazed, and this one object seemed somehow to become a One-All, at once subject and object, and yet neither one. Here is a counterpart of the absorption into deity of which mystical saints speak, a parallel to the realization of a larger life continuous with our own and of the same quality, of which Professor James speaks. . . . Third, the feeling-tone of the whole was agreeable. . . . It is indeed obvious that muscular relaxation was in this case a chief ground of the agreeable feeling-tone. Moreover, it is easy to see how, from this beginning, if religious auto-suggestion had been active, or even if the strange experiences of the hour had been met with naïve wonder instead of scientific coldness, pleasurable motion of any degree of intensity might have developed. Here, evidently, is the root of the mystical feeling of attainment, of the resolution of discords, of the goodness of the All.

"In short, the mystical revelation can be traced down to the formal conditions, physiological and psychological, of the mystic himself. . . . The mystic acquires his religious convictions precisely as his non-mystical neighbor does, namely through tradition and instruction grown habitual, and reflective analysis. The mystic brings his theological beliefs to the mystical experience; he does not derive them from it." [12]

This last sentence is especially well put. The particular theological beliefs which the mystic carries away from his trance he first brings to it, usually in the form of dogmas explicitly held, sometimes as ideas up to that time buried in the unconscious or subconscious regions of his mind. The former of these are simply glorified and reinforced by the emotion of belief through the intense joy of the trance; while the latter, never having been held consciously by the mystic, seem to him obvious revelations. And certainly, now that we have learned from the investigations of Freud, Prince, Sidis, and others how much may come into the subconscious through the regular door of the every-day consciousness and remain there for years without its presence being suspected, we should hardly be justified in seeking to explain the particular deliverances of the mystic

[12] Op. cit., pp. 364, 365, 366, 367.

trance as due to anything else than social education and suggestion.

I am not sure that the general sense of presence, which we may perhaps regard as the peculiar characteristic of all mysticism, is to be so easily accounted for. Professor Coe's analysis of the trance form, which proved so useful in explaining the emotions and revelations of the ecstasy, will not greatly help us here; for the sense of a Beyond, and the resulting strength that often comes from it, is by no means dependent upon trance, and occurs in innumerable cases when the trance conditions are absent.

The explanation which naturally presents itself first is the hypothesis that the experience is due entirely to social education, imitation, auto-suggestion. This probably accounts for a very great deal that passes under the name of the sense of presence. I quote here from one of my respondents who is certainly typical of a great many religious people. " I have many experiences that to me mean God's presence, although I cannot describe them. One Sunday I was discouraged thinking no one cared for a beautiful bouquet I placed on the altar. As I turned to walk away a light seemed to descend on my head, filling my soul with sweetness. God was there and accepted my offering. I wept, feeling unworthy, yet so glad of God's love." Perhaps one ought not to be dogmatic about even a case of this sort. And yet it seems clear enough that no further explanation here is needed than that to be found in an emotional, simple, and suggestible nature molded since childhood by the common idea that religious feeling is always a sign of the presence of God.

But while imitation and suggestion will explain a large part of the experience in question, they fall short, in my opinion at least, of being a complete and adequate explanation. The case just cited, while typical of a large class of religious people, is very far from being typical of mysticism as a whole. The reader of this book will recall many cases in which the sense of presence was, to say the least, very much less easy of explanation than in that of the woman and the bouquet. And even if it be granted that the mystic's *idea* of God's presence is always due to social education, the intensity of the *experience* that

God *is* present is hardly to be accounted for so easily. If we may trust the mystic's word at all, the experience is a very different thing from the idea; and while, very possibly, the idea must be there before the experience can come, something else must be there too.   As Delacroix puts it:

" The mystic tradition explains the search of the mystics, but it would not suffice to transform it into experience if the search itself had not been the sign of a particular aptitude.   For it is not a question of understanding a doctrine but of experiencing a certain condition; and whatever be the power of suggestion in the case of a doctrine, it certainly is not able to create out of nothing a psychical nature which shall transform the doctrine into a state of the soul."   This psychical nature, this state of the spirit, the mystics call intuition, in contradistinction to meditation.   " The appearance of spontaneous intuitions which occupy and dominate the consciousness and may by repetition form almost a habit, and by linking themselves with each other form almost a continuous intuition, characterize the mystics very exactly; and no external tradition could pass into them if they did not already possess this mode of consciousness, which is in fact at the very basis of the mystic tradition itself." [13]

Education and suggestion, then, constitute a partial, but only a partial explanation of the mystic consciousness.   For a full and complete explanation we must go deeper than this.   I do not think that psychology is yet ready to give this explanation in any detail.   But if it is ever to be fully made out it must be sought pretty far down in the less superficial parts of our psycho-physical being.   Intuition and instinct are closely allied, and the mystic sense is in some respects similar to both.   It is the expression of the religious attitude and demand of the race.   And the full explanation of it, if it is ever found, will involve not merely the acceptance of suggested ideas, but much of our emotional and volitional nature, the fringe region of consciousness, and perhaps also the unconscious and instinctive regions of our being.   It is hardly to be expected that such a complete explanation will be made out for several generations at the earliest.   For various lines of psychological investigation bear

[13] Op. cit., pp. 359 and 361.

upon it. If, for instance, the existence of telepathy could be demonstrated and its laws formulated, it is conceivable that a great deal of light might be thrown on our problem. And the various facts that are gradually being discovered about the subconscious, multiple personality, association, emotion, etc., may all have their contributions toward any possible answer. Our problem and our data are exceedingly complex, and no simple formula or phrase such as " auto-suggestion " and the like can be really satisfactory.

It is of course possible that even if all the relevant psychological facts were known we should still be unable to formulate the facts of mysticism into regular laws; or that even with some kind of formulation there would still remain evident gaps between the facts as formulated. From this we might conceivably be led to accept the hypothesis of Miss Underhill or of James (in some modified form) as the most probable metaphysical view. But be it noted that in the last analysis these attempts at a mediating position cannot be called scientific; they are hardly more scientific in the strict sense of the term than is the frankly supernatural view. For the appeal that they make is, after all, an appeal to hypothetical events that are essentially unverifiable in human experience. A position such as that of James or of Boutroux may indeed be a perfectly good metaphysical hypothesis and it might be put in such a way as to be consistent with a naturalistic description of the facts. The mystic experience may indeed be significant of something beyond itself, and the metaphysical question whether a materialistic or a spiritualistic *Weltanschauung* is most consistent with it and most satisfactorily explains it is still an open question. But it is a question upon which science cannot take sides. And since science as such is limited to the description and generalization of human experience, we are forced as psychologists to make use of the " naturalistic " view (which does *not* mean the *materialistic* view), no matter how firmly we may be convinced that an *ultimate* metaphysical explanation would quite transcend our naturalistic description.

But did I go too far in admitting, as I did a moment ago, that the mystic's experience may be significant of something beyond itself? May it indeed still be possible that, though psychology is bound to confine itself to the psychic state as such and its relations to other forms of human experience, the mystic's interpretation of his experience is still, in some respects at least, literally true? — that he actually does, in some sense, apprehend or come into contact with, an encircling spiritual world? — Some psychologists would certainly insist that we have no logical right to such an hypothesis. Professor Leuba, for example, as I understand him, insists that the only kind of God logically thinkable is an Absolute who never does anything, but merely always does everything and who, therefore is no more to be found in the workings of the mystic's consciousness than in the roaring of the sea. It is the purpose of that very able Eleventh Chapter in his " Psychological Study of Religion " to show that " inner experience " cannot be regarded in any sense as evidence of the existence or presence of God. " To make ' inner experience ' the only source of religious knowledge means," he insists, " a surrender to psychological science." [14] And by a surrender to psychological science he means a surrender of all transcendental reference. He quotes Ribot and Flournoy to the effect that when dealing with religious feeling psychology " is incompetent in the matter of its objective value," and he adds: " Professor Flournoy is right if the God of religion is really the Metaphysical God, Infinite, Impersonal. In that case science is certainly incompetent. But if, on the contrary, the object necessary to the religion of Professor Flournoy's auditors, and to religion generally, manifests himself directly to human consciousness, if he reveals himself in human experiences, and if faith in him is based upon these facts — then he is an empirical God and belongs to Science." [15]

In putting the matter thus I cannot think that Professor Leuba means his words to be taken literally. The God whom modern theologians consider demonstrated, or made probable, by religious experience, surely can in no sense be said to " belong to Science." For by hypothesis He could never be a scientific object, but only a proposed explanation of various psychological events.[16] Doubtless Professor Leuba's meaning, more exactly

[14] " A Psychological Study of Religion," p. 256.
[15] Ibid., p. 246.
[16] One might even go further and maintain with Pacheu that to insist

expressed, is that the supposed evidence for such a God should be dealt with, not by the theologian but by the psychologist, and that He could be argued to as an explanation of experience only on condition that all strictly scientific explanations of the experiences in question failed.   This, in fact, comes out clearly in more than one passage in the chapter referred to, as in the following: " Should God act in this manner [i. e. as a cause of particular ideas or emotions] nothing ought to be easier than to show in the life of feeling and of thought disturbances not depending upon known natural causes.   The student of the religious life would be in the position of the astronomer who knows that certain stars are affected by forces of which he does not yet understand the source.   The fact is that, in proportion as psychology advances, the apparent anomalies of the religious life are more and more completely explained according to known laws." " I trust it has become clear that the hope to lift a theology based on inner experience out of the sphere of science is preposterous: since whatever appears in consciousness is material for psychology. . . . A theology that should remain within the domain accessible to science would be limited to a mere description of man's religious consciousness and would be deprived of the right to any opinion on the objective reality of its objects and on the universal validity of its propositions." [17]

There can, I think, be little doubt that Professor Leuba, in most of his positions, is perfectly unassailable.   If the existence or presence of God is to be proved by an analysis of ' inner experience,' it is the psychologist who must do it; and it is vain to talk of any psychological or scientific demonstration of the kind until the psychologist acknowledges that it has been accomplished.   And if the psychologist can explain all the facts of the religious consciousness by scientific laws then there is no psychological proof of God's presence and influence in our lives.   To be sure, psychology is still a long way from any such universal explanation; and it seems likely enough that no such complete explanation may ever be attained.   Still, the

upon an atheistic explanation as at the same time scientific and ultimate is neither philosophical nor scientific but pure dogmatism. (See " L'Experience Mystique," p. 303.)

[17] P. 242.

possibility of such an explanation — at any rate in the present condition of our ignorance — should not be left out of account.

But neither should we leave out of account the sort of thing a psychlogical explanation is. It will not do to go back to the pre-Humian notion of science, which puts it quite on a par with mathematics. The universality and necessity of science to-day is rather a pragmatic postulate than an axiom or logical principle. And the only sort of explanation it can offer is, in the last analysis, merely a description of what it has regularly found. Particularly in psychology do we see the great chasm lying between mathematical principles and so called scientific laws." The "Laws of Psychology" can hardly be stated explicity without a wink, and I sometimes feel that modern psychologists are in much the same predicament as the augurs of Cicero's time. For there is an undeniable chasm not only between mathematics and the physical sciences, but also between physics and psychology. And there are many philosophers and psychologists — and it would seem a steadily increasing number of them — who believe that there is a reason for this chasm. For in the opinion of these thinkers the object which psychology studies is in nature essentially different from the object of the physical sciences. Psychology, in fact, seems to be a mixture of two sciences, or to have at least a two-fold subject matter. It is in part a description of certain psychical processes which are directly connected with certain physiological processes and which therefore obey the laws of the bodily mechanism; and it is also a *description of the way in which persons usually think and act.*[18] Such a view of the task of psychology is, I confess, not the orthodox view in most psychological circles, but it is a view held by many individual psychologists and philosophers, and one which (whatever else may be said of it) is essentially empirical, undogmatic, and close to the facts.

If this view be true, then the " explanations " of psychology

[18] Views of the nature of psychology similar to that here suggested will be found in W. McDougall's " Body and Mind " (London, Methuen: 1915), *passim*; in Calkins' " First Book in Psychology " (New York, Macmillan: 1910), and her various writings on the self; in Ogden's " Introduction to General Psychology " (New York, Longmans: 1916), Chap. XV; and in Coe's " Psychology of Religion," Chap. II.

will be only the most general sort of description, since the activities of personality, by their very nature, can be psychologized only in a most superficial way. This, however, by no means does away with psychology. Inasmuch as even free personalities are more or less alike, and since all human persons are compelled to make use of the same sort of physiological machine, their customary activities and experiences will be capable of description in generalized language. And this generalized description — which is psychology — would still hold even if these selves were surrounded by a non-human spiritual world with which they had actual commerce. This spiritual world from which " saving experiences come," could indeed never be the object of psychology and could never be scientifically proved to exist except through the complete failure of psychology in some one particular spot. But the real influence of such a world or such a God upon the minds of men is in no wise incompatible with any descriptions of human experience which psychology has as yet given us or seems likely ever to give.

Possibly I can make this clearer by an illustration. Let us imagine the human organism always played upon by light; or let us picture the human race as living always in conditions such as those that now obtain in the north arctic regions during summer. Let us suppose, moreover, that the majority of men are blind and that only a few see. When, now, the eyes of one of these seers are open, or he is not in some way shading his retina, he will be constantly receiving light sensations. In investigating these very interesting experiences your strict psychologist, who is seeking to frame an exact scientific account of the psychic life of one of these unusual individuals, would, of course, correlate the light sensations with raised eyelids, and their cessation with closed eyes. Light sensations, he would say, are the invariable accompaniment of open eyes; they are, in fact, a " function " of open eyes. The principle of single difference could be applied with exactitude to show that the opening of the eyes was the cause of the light sensations, and fully explained them (in the psychological sense),— no reference being needed to the sun or the ether waves or any other outer source. The naïve seer, innocent of the ways of science, might indeed insist that he saw the *sun,* and not merely his own sensations;

but the psychologist would assure him that he mistook his sensations for something objective, that, in fact, he was substituting interpretation for description, and that the only verifiable and scientific fact was his sensations of light. These, he would add, were fully described, generalized, and therefore explained, by the scientific law correlating them with a certain condition of the organism — namely raised eye-lids, stimulated retina, afferent impulse in the optic nerves, and stimulation of the visual centers in the occipital lobes. If the naïve seer were still unsatisfied, the psychologist could challenge him to see light with his eyes shut or to fail to see it with them open, or to point out a single element in his experience not accounted for by the psychological formula.

Both seer and scientist would be right. The psychological explanation would be complete (in its own way and within its self-imposed limits), and it would be vain to seek to prove the objective existence of the sun by breaking down the psychological correlation of light sensation and organic condition. And yet it would be true that the seer saw the sun.

May it, then, perhaps be that the mystics are the seers of our world, and that whenever they open the eyes of their souls, the Eternal Light pours in; and that though we blind ones learnedly describe, generalize, and explain their experience by regular psychological laws which take account only of the psycho-physical organism, still the light is really there and the mystic apprehends it directly, even as he says? This question is not for psychological discussion. But I think we may say at least this much: that while the psychology of religion must have a free hand, and while it is hopeless to look to it for a proof of anything transcendent, nothing that it can say should prevent the religious man, who wishes to be perfectly loyal to logic and loyal to truth, from seeing in his own spiritual experiences the genuine influence of a living God.

The question we have been discussing is certainly an important one and very worthy of study. Yet it must be confessed that our investigation of it has thrown but little light, except in a negative way, on the question with which we started out — namely the place and value of mysticism. We have indeed learned that mysticism is neither to be prized nor to be despised because of its origin, that its value is to be determined (to use James's phrase) not by its roots but by its fruits. Whatever its cause, it *is* (as the pragmatists would say) what it is *known as.* Hence to determine in more positive fashion its place in religion and its value in life we must take up a more direct consideration of its characteristics and its consequences.

And first of all, the question presents itself, To what extent is mysticism a pathological condition, and how far is it normal? On a question of mental pathology certainly no one can speak with more authority than Professor Pierre Janet, and we may, therefore, profitably consider first of all his opinion on this matter. Professor Janet formed his conclusions largely on the basis of his direct observations of the ecstatic whom he studied at the Salpêtrière. In her ecstatic phase " Madeleine " presented symptoms suggesting hysteria yet differing from it in some important respects; while in her periods of dryness she seemed much more closely allied to the *" scrupuleux."* In spite of her burning altruism she had a great dread of the world, a corresponding weakness of will and of the attention, and a consequent inability to attain to the full sense of certainty and reality. Like the historical mystics we have studied, she suffered frequently, in her periods of dryness, from doubts and the loss of the sense of reality. The question which presented itself to Professor Janet was therefore how to diagnose a case which seemed to be half way between hysteria and scrupulosity. His final conclusion made the latter the more fundamental of the two, the ecstatic condition being regarded as a temporary relief from the chronic sense of unreality, and its intense joy being due to the contrast between it and the patient's more habitual psychosis. The striking similarity between Madeleine's ecstasies and those of the historical mystics, and also that between her periods of dryness and theirs, led Janet to apply his diagnosis of her case to all the ecstatics; and he therefore concludes: " The ecstatic is a *scrupuleux* who tends toward hysteria, and who now and then approximates it without ever quite reaching it." [19]

In this view of mysticism Professor Janet is by no means

[19] " Une Extatique." Bulletin de l'Institut Psychologique International, I, esp. pp. 238–240.

alone. Murisier, from whom so much has been quoted in the preceding chapters, and who had a rather remarkable gift of keen psychological analysis, regards mysticism as essentially a process of pathological " simplification " and therefore as one of the two great " *maladies du sentiment religieux.*" The mystic at the very beginning of his course is somewhat abnormal; his conscious life is characterized by an exaggerated and distressing incoherence and instability and also by a great longing for unity. Unity he seeks by a process of *elimination.* One thing after another — impulse, thought, emotion,— is stripped off, till at last the poor consciousness is bereft of almost every natural human possession and a state of monoideism sets in, to be followed by a pure emotional state and the unconscious trance. Thus at last, and for a brief interval, is the pain of incoherence allayed and the peace of inner unity won. Thereafter this peace, which is found alone in the ecstasy, becomes the mystic's one goal and his constant thought.[20]

Much the same general view of the pathological nature of mysticism is held by numerous other psychologists and physiologists. In Maudsley's opinion, the mystic intuition, when not simple imagination and self-delusion, is ordinary delirium.[21] Charbonnier regards mysticism as an aberration of the digestive apparatus due to fasting.[22] Marie considers it of the same type as obsession and delirium, and explains it by an ingenious theory, borrowed from Meynert, according to which ancestral ideas and practices are inherited by all but lie dormant

[20] " Les Maladies du Sentiment Religieux," Chap. I.

[21] " Natural Causes and Supernatural Seemings " (London, Trübner: 1897), Part III.

[22] " Voyons ce que rapporte l'histoire des mystiques concernant leurs maladies. Causes prédisposantes: Les aliments, de la plus tendre enfance, sont tirés exclusivement du règne végétal. Le défaut de viande porte une atteinte fâcheuse non seulement aux activités physiques de l'homme, mais à ses facultés supérieures. Prodromes: appétit languissant; appauvrissement du sang; tendance à la melancolie et à la méditation. Symptomes: On remarque une perte complète d'appétit qui dure parfois un mois, des névralgies multiples et très rebelles. Les sécretions se font mal; la transpiration se supprime. La constipation, l'absence d'urine temoignent que les fonctions de nutrition sont arrètées. Souvent des hémorrhagies pulmonaires et cutanées, délire. Mille hallucinations apparissent. Le malade entend et voit des personnages invisibles." P. Charbonnier, " Maladies et Facultés Diverses des Mystiques: Mémoire presenté a l'Academie royale de medicine de Belgique," pp. 222–23.

in the subconscious of the normal mind, while in the mystic and other abnormal individuals they are roused from their unconscious slumbers by some derangement of the higher centers.[23] In like manner for Binet-Sanglé practically all the mystics are degenerates of one form or another, Jesus in particular being a paranoiac.[24]

In considering this question for ourselves we shall first of all recall to mind the distinction, so often emphasized, between the milder and the more extreme forms of mysticism. Of course none of the distinguished writers whom I have just quoted means to maintain that the mysticism of the common-place type, described in Chapter XVI, is pathological. Doubtless they would consider it a case of mild self-delusion, but self-delusion is, unfortunately, too common a thing to be called abnormal. It is only the mystics of the more intense type to whom these writers refer — the noted historical " mystics " and all others who display the characteristics described in the preceding three chapters. These they consider essentially pathological and as belonging to the same group as the hysterics, the *scrupuleux,* the *abouliques,* etc.

Now our study of mysticism in this more intense form has

[23] "Mysticisme et Folie," pp. 125–131. Cf., esp., the following: "Maigré la diversité apparente des déités invoquées par les délirants, on peut ramener à deux groupes des déités mises en cause selon que ce sont des ésprits malfaisants ou bien-veillants: dieux ou diables. Or, en somme, l'évolution de l'idée diabolique depuis le XVIIe siècle peut se résumer en un mot: Le diable a été vaincu. Il n'y a plus de possession par les mauvais anges. Mais il reste encore la possession par les bons anges. Ce qui au XVIIe siècle aurait fait brûler, aujourh'hui sanctifie. . . . Saintes ou possedées, peu importe. Nous savons qu'elles sont tout simplement des malades," pp. 130–131.

[24] This is the thesis of his most recent work, "La Folie de Jesus" (Paris, Maloine: 1910). His conclusion as to Jesus is as follows: "Ce dégénéré était donc atteint de paranoia religieuse, de théomégalomanie. Il sut, surtout dans la première période de son délire, des hallucinations de nature religieuse: hallucinations visuelles hautes et lumineuses, exoauditives verbales, kinesthésiques verbales avec automatisme, aéroplaniques, les unes consolantes, les autres terrifiantes, celles-ci se groupant de façon à constituer le syndrome de la démonomanie externe. En tout ceci Jésus ne différait point des théomégalomanes observés avant et après lui, de ces agités qui troublèrent le monde jusqu'au dix-neuvième siècle et qui ne se rencontrent plus que dans les maisons de santé et dans les asiles." Vol. II, pp. 509–10. No comment here is needed. The reader will probably judge for himself that the learned alienist is himself not altogether free from paranoia.

certainly indicated that there is a great deal of truth in this contention. In the first place it cannot be denied that many of the lesser ecstatics have been simple cases of mental pathology, differing from other unfortunates only in the fact that their particular kind of insanity had a religious tinge. The books on psychiatry are filled with reports of weak-minded and degenerate men and women who see visions, hear voices, and experience emotional thrills quite similar to those described by some of the mystics.[25] Nor can it be denied that there is something pathological in the experience of many of even the great mystics. So true is this that the mystics themselves, far from denying it, are the first to recognize and call attention to it. Many of their visions and locutions and impulsions they brand as temptations of the Evil One, or sometimes call them frankly hallucinations.

But to say that the great mystics are therefore to be classed as hysterics, etc., is a very different matter. Surely one may have an occasional headache without being an invalid; and not even a fever delirium and an hallucination should class one among the insane. Moreover, although a superficial view of some of the unusual experiences of these greater mystics reminds one of aboulia, *idee fixe,* hysteria, etc., a closer examination shows certain very important differences. Many of the mystics certainly have been subject to hallucination, and to a narrowing of consciousness similar to the initial stages of the hypnotic trance — as described in the previous chapter; but, as Leuba has so well shown, it is a mistake to regard them as cases of aboulia or *idée fixe,* or " simplification." [26] The great mystic is not troubled with the chaotic turmoil of ideas, from which the " *douteurs* " and the " *scrupuleux* " suffer. Murisier's description of the instability and incoherence of the mystic's consciousness, while it is applicable to some of the more abnormal cases, certainly does not apply to the majority. The mystic seeks to simplify not

<hr/>

[25] To seek to determine the exact mental disease to which the mystics are subject would be futile, both because different mystics show so many different kinds of symptoms, and also because it is so unsatisfactory to attempt any exact classification of mental diseases with hard and fast lines between them. Cf. Dubois, " The Psychic Treatment of Nervous Disorders " (New York, Funk and Wagnalls: 1907).

[26] " Tendances fondamentales des Mystiques Chrêtiens," esp. pp. 28–30.

his ideas but his impulses and to bring them all into harmony with what he regards as the will of God.

Nor can the mystics be written down as pathological because of their "monoideism" and their "suggestibility." In one sense, as Boutroux has pointed out, these two words characterize excellently the mystic's life. But in this sense they characterize every earnest life. "The man of genius, too, is possessed by one idea, suggests to himself to find it great and beautiful, and ends by acting, as it were, automatically according to that idea. Nor is it only the man of genius, himself somewhat akin to the mystic, who offers examples of auto-suggestion and mono-ideism. These two phenomena are to be met with in every man of action, in all who devote themselves to some one cause, mission, or task. I believe, indeed, that both of them are definite conditions of existence for every man who reflects." [27] Here the important thing to notice (which Boutroux does not make quite as plain as he might) is that the auto-suggestion and mono-ideism of the great mystic are more nearly related to those of the man of action, than to the pathological conditions of the same name found in degenerates. This will be clearer if we compare the mystic more specifically with the hysteric.

Some of the great mystics have probably had touches of hysteria at certain crises in their careers. But if we take their lives and activities — in short their mysticism as a whole — they present a very marked contrast to the hysteric. Both indeed are very suggestible; but the hysteric is subject to all sorts of haphazard suggestions, from without and from within, whereas the Christian mystic is dominated constantly by the *self*-suggestion of a determined will bent on the pursuit of righteousness. The flabbiness of will and the disintegration of the personality which are so characteristic of the hysteric are certainly the last things to be found in the great Christian mystics. In fact perhaps nothing more distinguishes them than just this strength of will, this determination to unify their lives and direct their activities according to the divine purpose. Their very physical and nervous weakness, when it appears,

[27] Boutroux, "The Psychology of Mysticism," *Am. Jour. of Ethics,* XVIII, 193.

only shows this in clearer light. Weakness of the body, exhausted nerves, a touch of hysteria, a " temptation of Satan," these they recognize as being there only to be overcome.[28] " These great conquerors of souls conquered themselves first of all. They discipline what Maine de Biran calls the mechanical or the organic, they overcome the wildness or the excess of their neurotic constitution; they inhibit or make use of the superabundance and the irrationality of their emotional excitability, they impose a rational plan upon their automatisms, they adapt nervous and psychical activities to an end which they pursue with all their zeal. The soul of the mystic has a richness of intuition and of action which sometimes goes to the extent of delirium; but the power of adaptation to life, and the intelligence which stands back of the intuition, distinguish the ordering of the mystic life from that of the really delirious." [29]

It is even possible that the ecstasies of the mystics, pathological as they seem to us, may not always have been altogether disadvantageous but may have added an insight or an inspiration which was needed for the full development of the mystic's life and activity. I do not say that these phenomena are on the whole desirable — in fact I am convinced they are not; but I am not sure that the question is altogether so simple as at first it may appear. It is easy to say without further investiga-

[28] Cf. Joly, "Psychologie des Saints," pp. 109–126. "Ainsi donc, les grands saints peuvent ressentir des phénomènes pathologiques dont un docteur en maladies nerveuses est fort tenté de s'emparer. Mais ces accidents ils en triomphent, et comment? Par ce qui leur reste d'une forte et saine organization? Peut-être! Mais beaucoup plus encore par leur volonté orientée sur le devoir, par l'habitude qu'ils ont prise de se vaincre at de tirer parti de tout ce qui leur arrive de plus douloureux ou de plus humiliant," p. 122.

[29] Delacroix "Études d'Histoire et de Psychologie du Mysticisme," p. 344. The marked development and importance of the mystic's will needs especial emphasis as it is so completely overlooked by the popular view of mysticism. The mystic is frequently pictured as a weak, sentimental creature with little will power, but excelling in intellectual abstractions. The use of the technical words "meditation" and "contemplation" by the mystics and the writers on mysticism has doubtless had much to do with this; and of course some of the mystics have been weak and some philosophic. But the great mystics, and many of the lesser ones, have been strong and (in their own way) practical; and as a rule their "meditation" and "contemplation" have been far from intellectual — as the preceding chapter shows. Cf., further, Montmorand, "Des Mystiques en dehors de l'extase," *Revue Phil.*, LVIII, 602ff.

tion, Ecstasy is abnormal and the abnormal is always and in every respect bad.   But a life-long student of mysticism like Baron von Hügel can ask, " Would that particular temperament and psycho-physical organism congenial to Sister Lukardis, to Catherine Fiesca Adorna, to Marguerite Marie Alacoque, and to Isaac Hecker, have — taking the whole existence and output together — produced more useful work, and have apprehended and presented more of abiding truth, had their ecstatic states or tendencies been absent or suppressed ?   Does not this type of apprehension, this incubation, harmonization and vivifying of their otherwise painfully fragmentary and heavy impressions stand out as the one thoroughly appropriate means and form of their true self-development and self-expression, and of such a showing forth of spiritual truth as to them — to them and not to you and me — was possible ? "

Von Hügel believes that during their productive periods the ecstasy was to the mystics a source of bodily strength.   And he adds " if after this, their productive period, some of these persons end by losing their health, it is far from unreasonable to suppose the actual alternative to these ecstasies and this breakup, would *for them* have been a life-long dreary languor and melancholy self-absorption, somewhat after the pattern of St. Catherine's last ten preconversion years.   Thus for her, and doubtless for most of the spiritually considerable ecstatics, life was, taken all in all, indefinitely happier, richer, and more fruitful in religious truth and holiness, with the help of those ecstatic states, than it would have been if these states had been absent or could have been suppressed." [30]

One cannot too constantly keep in mind the fact that there are several different kinds of people in this world, and that what for one would constitute ideal conditions of productivity would for another result in a cramping and deadening of all spiritual life.   We common-place people are always in danger of thinking that just because we are in the majority we are therefore the norm for all, and that what is best for us is best for the insignificant minority as well.   But it is certainly possible that for unusual personalities, like a St. Francis or a St. Teresa, unusual experiences may work the birth and unfolding of larger powers

[30] " The Mystical Element in Religion," Vol. II, pp. 58–59.

and the beginning of a deeper insight than we self-satisfied, "normal" people ever possess.

For the value of mysticism is hardly to be determined by pointing out that ecstasy is "abnormal." When an expression like this is used to settle everything, as the last word on the subject, one feels like responding: What of it? — or at least like asking what is meant by the "normal." If the normal is simply the usual, then doubtless ecstasy is abnormal; and so is genius and holiness. But if we seek some more illuminating and fruitful definition for our terms we shall probably be driven to the pragmatic view that the normal is that which produces desirable results. If this be so, then the extreme forms of mysticism are just as normal and just as abnormal as they are found to be. Like everything else they are to be judged by their fruits. This, in fact, is the test used by the great mystics themselves to distinguish the demoniac from the divine,— as the following very typical quotations from St. Teresa's autobiography indicate: "I found myself through these words [i. e. the words of the Lord] alone tranquil and strong, courageous and confident, at rest and enlightened: I felt I could maintain against all the world that my prayer was the work of God." "I could not believe that Satan, if he wished to deceive me, could have recourse to means so adverse to his purpose as this, of rooting out my faults and implanting virtues and spiritual strength: for I saw clearly that I had become another person by means of these visions." "I was in a trance; and the effects of it were such that I could not possibly doubt that it came from God." St. Teresa never tires of describing in enthusiastic tones the value for life of those ecstatic experiences which she regards as divine. "Often, infirm and wrought upon with dreadful pains before the ecstasy, the soul emerges from it full of health and admirably disposed for action. . . . After such a favor the soul is animated with a degree of courage so great that if at that moment its body should be torn to pieces for the cause of God, it would feel nothing but the liveliest comfort. Then it is that promises and heroic resolutions spring up in profusion in us, soaring desires, horror of the world, and the clear perception of our own worthlessness." [31]

[31] "Vie," p. 229.

In like manner St. John of the Cross writes of these mystic experiences: " They enrich the soul marvelously. A single one of them may be enough to abolish at a stroke certain imperfections of which the soul during its whole life had vainly tried to rid itself, and to leave it adorned with virtues and loaded with supernatural gifts. . . . Invested with an invincible courage, filled with an impassioned desire to suffer for its God, the soul then is seized with a strange torment — that of not being allowed to suffer enough." [32]

Testimony of this sort, coming as it does from those who know whereof they speak, must be given a good deal of weight in making up our final decision as to the value of ecstasy. It shows plainly that the great mystics have a very proper notion of the test of value. Does it also show that the value of the ecstasy is as great as they think it? Before accepting their view we should subject it to careful scrutiny. Are the " supernatural gifts " with which the ecstasy " adorns and loads " the soul of such a sort as to seem to us altogether desirable? Does the courage which is gained from the experience usually lead the mystic to the actual performance of socially valuable deeds, or does most of it evaporate in an *emotion* of courage? Doubtless Murisier's accusation that mysticism is antisocial is an extreme statement and could easily be refuted from the lives of certain carefully selected mystics such as Teresa and Tauler; but if we consider the rank and file of the ecstatics, is there not a great mass of evidence in its favor? And if Murisier and the pathologists have exaggerated, what shall be said of Miss Underhill and the romanticists? I trust I shall not be accused of lack of an initial sympathy for mysticism, but I must confess that the emphasis laid by many writers of our times upon the practical efficiency and the original insight of the ecstatics seems to me to go altogether beyond the facts. Mrs. Burr, basing her conclusions upon an unusually wide reading of mystical literature, insists that the ecstatics as a class are characterized by a lack of creativeness and a paucity of original ideas, and that what they did accomplish either in practical activity or in constructive thought was usually done in spite

[32] Quoted by James, " Varieties," p. 414.

of their mysticism rather than because of it.[33]   And if we study the subject of ecstasy in a truly empirical fashion and without prejudice, instead of confining our attention to a few brilliant and " typical " cases, I fear we shall be forced to agree in large measure with Mrs. Burr.

While Mrs. Burr's presentation of the matter is much nearer the truth than is that of many an enthusiastic defender of the mystics, however, it must be remembered that it is of the ecstatics she is writing, and that what she says of their experience and its consequences is by no means to be applied in its entirety to the less intense form of mysticism. This milder type of religious experience, amounting as it often does to no more than an emotionalization of the cosmic, may be and frequently is a stimulus to both thought and activity in a way that the ecstasy seldom is except among the very greatest of the ecstatics.

But something further, I believe, may be said even for the ecstatics. While, with a few prominent exceptions, their practical activity was slight and was probably hindered more than helped by their ecstasies and trances, and while they have contributed but little to the world's stock of ideas, they have contributed something, directly and indirectly, and the mystics in their entirety have contributed a very great deal, to the loftiest religious literature of nearly all the great religions. It is a mistaken view which regards the expressions of the mystics and of those who have been inspired by them as *philosophy,* and which attempts to judge them accordingly. Rather they should be taken as a kind of earnest poetry. One should add at once that while this poetry does not mean to be scientific, it does wish to communicate to the reader a certain cosmic sense, an apprehension of the ultimately real, a suggestion of a spiritual environment which though undemonstrable is also irrefutable — a poetry which has not been without its value — even its " pragmatic " value — in the life of the last twenty-five centuries. Scarcely even the most " hard-minded " philosopher could read over a well-chosen collection of mystical writings,[34]

[33] " Religious Confessions and Confessants," pp. 341–484.
[34] Such, for example, as Buber's " Ekstatische Konfessionem " (Jena, Diederichs: 1909), or the " Oxford Book of English Mystical Verse " (Clarendon Press: 1917).

and then study the subtle influences which such expressions as a whole have exerted upon the thought and feeling, the courage and happiness, the daring and the humility of the race, without recognizing that mysticism has contributed something which the world would miss.

Just how much of the indubitable value of mysticism is due to the ecstasy is a question which it is impossible to answer. Plainly the ecstasy has contributed something [35] — in part directly, much more indirectly. But by far the greater part of the contribution of mysticism has been made by the milder type and by persons who though gifted with a strong and emotional sense of cosmic values have never indulged in the excesses of the ecstatics. Even at its best the ecstasy is dangerous [36] and at its worst is altogether evil. While it is not the totally unproductive thing that Mrs. Burr considers it, I can have little doubt that its dangers are greater than its probable rewards, and that it is a form of experience which should be emphatically discouraged.[37]

I have said that mysticism is a kind of poetry. It is, however, at the antipodes from the mere musings of fancy. As we have seen, it has a message to give concerning the spiritual

[35] We have the direct evidence of Professor Flournoy's modern mystic to show that the ecstasy does contribute something to the conception of God. In her own words, the experience in question "a inauguré en moi une nouvelle conception du divin, à laquelle je ne suis pas arrivée d'un bond, mais qui me semble maintenant avoir consisté à dégager l'idée de Dieu de toute entrave dogmatique, de toute formule immuable. Avant cela, j'avais de Dieu une idée toujours la même (*cut and dried* comme disent les Anglais) ; et je sens bien, maintenant, combien limitée, étriquée, était cette conception. Puis parce que cela ne changeait pas, cela avait presque cessé d'être en moi le vivant, le réel par excellence. Là dedans, née je pense des profondeurs de ma détresse morale, a éclaté l'Expérience. J'ai essayé tant de fois de la décrire, je ne veux pas le tenter une fois de plus, tout ce que j'en ai dit n'a jamais pu en donner une idée adéquate. J'ai eu d'emblée la conviction triomphante et irraisonnée que c'était le contact avec *ce qui est*, l'approche de la Réalité essentielle. A chaque fois tout en moi a tressailli d'une émotion que je n'ai jamais éprouvée ailleurs. C'était comme l'attouchement immédiat, sans intermédiaire intellectuel, avec ce que je ressentais comme une force divine." (Op. cit., p. 147.)

[36] Cf. Mrs. Herman, "The Meaning and Value of Mysticism," pp. 134–38.

[37] It is interesting to note that Professor Flournoy's mystic gradually came to disapprove of the ecstasy, partly because it helped her in no way to help others, partly because the milder form of the experience seemed to her increasingly the more thoroughly satisfying.

environment of man about which it is very much in earnest.   In this connection it is at times faced with the question of personality, and its position on this subject is often uncertain and often misunderstood.   The intense conviction which all the mystics share, that at times man can come into touch with God, tends to bring many to the conclusion that in this communion the human self is lost or dissolved in the divine.   " The created abyss," says Tauler, referring to the human soul, " leads into the Uncreated Abyss, and the two abysses become a single unit, an unmixed, divine Being.   The human spirit loses itself in the Spirit of God, it is plunged in the Bottomless Sea." [38] And starting from some such view of the mystic experience some have gone still farther and concluded that there is really no human self to be dissolved, but that only the Divine exists — and this not as a personality but as an unknowable " Brahman " or a " *stille Wüste.*"

There is one type of mysticism (designated by Ribot [39] as Quietist) which certainly tends to inhibit the impulse for self-preservation and to produce a longing for the obliteration of the self.   This does not as a rule lead to or suggest suicide; it is self as a metaphysical entity which the Quietist seeks to be rid of.   While the name which Ribot has given this type is drawn from a small school of Christian mystics, it is most commonly met with in India, especially among the Buddhists; and its representatives are to be found in every religion and even outside of any recognized " religion."   Combined, however, with the desire " to be nothing, nothing," there usually goes, as Ribot has pointed out, a longing for union with the Suprapersonal which markedly modifies the purely negative desire for mere self-obliteration, and makes the Quietist really less the enemy of self than on the surface he seems.   It must be remembered, moreover, that this type is only one subdivision of mysticism as a whole.

This latter fact is often forgotten and mysticism as such is frequently represented as destructive of personality, either in the actual result upon the mystic or in the production of a pantheistic theory.   Thus with the usual disregard for two-

[38] Quoted by Preger.   Vol. III, p. 219.
[39] " L'Ideal Quietist," *Rev. Phil.* for 1915, pp. 440–54.

thirds of the facts and the love of sweeping generalization which seem to be the special dangers of writers on mysticism, the author of a recent book on the subject tells us, " The mystic knows no personal God.   Personality has limitations, therefore away with personality both in God and in man. . . . The true mystic refuses to think of himself as standing before his God as an *I* to a *thou* but rather as an I to a higher I.   Or better — he wants to be so absorbed, so made one with his God, that there exists no longer either *I* or *thou*." [40]

Statements of this sort are so absurdly general and so easily refuted by reference to the history of mysticism that they would not be worth noting were they not so common and so influential with those who have studied the subject but superficially.   It is true, as I have pointed out, that many mystics have been pantheistic and it is also true that the communion of the human with the divine, which all mystics claim in some degree to have experienced, tends to break down their belief in the sharp and eternal division of the two which the non mystical so often regard as essential to " orthodoxy." [41]   It is also true that certain great mystical schools, such as that of Neoplatonism and that of the monistic Vedanta in India, have been pantheistic or have denied the real independent existence of human personality.   But in Christianity mysticism has usually been of a personal nature; and it is not true — though it is so often thoughtlessly asserted — that even the mystics of India always leave out personality.   The majority of Indian mystics have not been adherents of Shankara's monistic Vedanta but have belonged to the great *bhakti* schools whose emphasis has always

[40] E. Lehmann, " Mysticism in Heathendom and Christendom " (London, Luzac & Co.: 1910), p. 8. A somewhat similar view, though much more guarded and better expressed, will be found in Professor Watson's " The Philosophical Basis of Religion " (Glasgow, Macelhose: 1907), pp. 434–440. In Professor Watson's case, however, this is due to his taking the term mysticism to denote a certain philosophical point of view. For a somewhat similar reason Professor Hall finds little religious or ethical value in Roman Catholic mysticism, identifying it, as he does, with a certain dualistic and pantheistic faith. See his " History of Ethics within Organized Christianity," p. 342ff. Miss Sinclair, while very sympathetic with mysticism, insists that it is essentially monistic and pantheistic — a characterization which in her view is, of course, laudatory rather than the reverse. " A Defence of Idealism," Chap. VII.

[41] Cf. von Hügel, Vol. II, pp. 328–29.

been upon personality. The probability is that the great majority of mystics, taken first and last, have been very far from pantheistic; and there is nothing in the nature of mysticism which logically involves, or necessarily results in, a loss of belief in personality, either human or divine.

Even in those cases where mysticism has been accompanied by a loss or dimming of belief in personality as a matter of theory, it is by no means the rule that there is a corresponding loss of individuality in practice. The mystic, in fact, is in religion the great individualist. He has for himself tasted and seen that the Lord is good; why then needs he any further witness? Firmly planted on his own irrefutable and immediate experience, he has an independence in religious matters which his neighbors cannot share, and which makes him relatively careless both of the authority of religious tradition and of the arguments and attacks of its critics. " What are antiquated Mythuses to me?" cries Carlyle's mystic philosopher. " Or is the God present, felt in my own heart, a thing which Herr von Voltaire will dispute out of me; or dispute into me? To the ' Worship of Sorrow' ascribe what origin and genesis thou pleasest, *has* not that Worship originated, and been generated; is it not *here?* Feel it in thy heart, and then say whether it is of God! This is Belief; all else is Opinion,— for which latter whoso will let him worry and be worried. Neither shall ye tear out one another's eyes, struggling over ' Plenary Inspiration,' and such like; try rather to get a little even Partial Inspiration, each of you for yourself. One Bible I know, of whose Plenary Inspiration doubt is not so much as possible; nay with my own eyes I saw the God's Hand writing it; thereof all other Bibles are but Leaves,— say in Picture-Writing to assist the weaker faculty." [42]

Repeatedly in the history of Christianity has this reliance upon first-hand experience led groups of mystics into more or less open disregard of ecclesiastical authority. And even those who have been obedient and loving servants of the Church and have accepted her dogmas and the scriptural revelations as authoritative, have reinterpreted them in the light of their own inner experience. Hence the frequent use of symbolism by mys-

[42] " Sartor Resartus," Book II, Chap. IX.

tical writers.   Believing himself to have known the Divine at
first hand, the mystic can never again be content with mere
second-hand reports, coming from without and unillumined by
the light within.   Even the Bible has for him a deeper meaning
than its merely historical and superficial aspect, and must be
interpreted in terms of his own spiritual life.   Unless God speak
in the soul it is vain to seek what others report of Him.   " The
outward word," says Thomas à Kempis, " even of Moses and
the prophets, is only *letter;* it cannot impart the spirit.   Speak
thou, God, Eternal Truth, speak Thou to my soul." [43]

The doctrines of the historical religion which the mystic pro-
fesses may gain in value to him through his very mysticism,
being touched into new life by the vitality of his own experience.   But they cannot be again as once they were.   Either
they must take on a changed and living aspect, becoming now
chiefly interpretations of the mystic experience, or else they will
be thrown aside as no longer relevant to the spiritual life.   For
the mystic has forever turned away from *mere* doctrines, *mere*
creeds, *mere* authorities, " as one might penetrate into the interior of the Holy of Holies, leaving behind in the temple the
statues of the gods.   And," Plotinus continues (for it is from
him I quote), " these he would not see again till he came out
after having had the vision of what lay within, and having communed there with what was no statue or image, but the Divine
itself — of which the statues were but secondary copies." [44]

When the mystic returns from the " Holy of Holies " he
speaks with a conviction and an authority quite unknown to
those who have gone no further than the temple and seen only
the statues of the gods.   It would be a mistake, indeed, to
affirm that the mystic experience invariably puts an end to all
doubt.   Occasionally it happens that a mystic comes to question
whether there was anything but delusion in what he had formerly considered the voice of God within him.   Thus even St.

[43] " Imitation," Book III, Chap. 2.
[44] " Enneads," VI, 9, quoted from Bakewell's " Source Book," p. 392.   It
is largely this refusal of Mysticism to base itself upon the historical which
has led the Ritschlians to their astonishing assertion that there is no
room for it within Christianity.   Cf. Hermann, " Der Verkehr des Christen
mit Gott " (Stuttgart, 1898), pp. 28–29; and Lehmann, " Mysticism in
Heathendom and Christendom," Chap. VI.

Teresa writes of herself: " She never undertook anything merely because it came to her in prayer. Although her confessors told her that these things came from God, she never so thoroughly believed them that she could swear to it herself, though it seemed to her that they were spiritually safe because of the effects thereof." [45]   Yet this attitude of suspended judgment is certainly rare among the mystics, and the passage just quoted from Teresa will hardly apply to the deeper of her mystic experiences.   Thus she says that in the " fifth Abode " of the " Interior Castle," — by which she means the more genuinely spiritual stages of the mystic life — " God establishes himself within one's soul in such a way that when the soul returns to itself it is impossible for it to doubt that it has been in God and God in it; and this conviction remains so firmly imprinted upon one that if one should go for many years without being raised anew to this blessed state he could still never forget the favor once received, nor doubt of its reality." [46]

A touch of mysticism may be quite enough to lend vitality to one's religion, even when in theological matters one has become skeptical.   The religious agnostic is by no means an uncommon type, and is more often met with every year; and it is in part the reality and the living force of the mystic experience which makes this type possible.   Many a man of culture and intellectual power who is well versed in the science and criticism of our day and as a result feels himself unable to subscribe to any creed or even to worship with any church, finds springing up within him a stream of inarticulate but genuine religious experience and intuition which is to him the very water of life. Let me here quote from one such instance,— the confession of a French agnostic:

" I seem to feel within the depths of my being an action, a presence; in short I seem to be the object, even prior to being the subject, of an action that is spiritual.   This is in part a rudimentary, half-conscious belief, in part it is simply the expression of a fact, the testimony to a sort of profound and vague sensation.   I tell myself that this sensation may itself be an illusion, that there may be nothing real about it apart from my

[45] " Vie," 413f.
[46] " Le Château Interieur."   Œuvres.   Vol. III, p. 459.

subjectivity; but it *is,* and that is enough for me to live by. . . .
It is a part of my being and has for the rest of my being an importance and a value that are supreme — that suffices me.   And
for the rest, I tell myself that the very fact that I possess this
experience called ' religious,' is a witness in me to the existence
of the inaccessible reality; of the union within my consciousness
of the me and the not-me; that in it I have in some measure an
immediate knowledge of the roots of my being, of a bond between me and something else, this ' something else ' being necessarily self-conscious since it passes within my self-consciousness. . . . And just because I have become agnostic, and because every intellectual formulation of the inaccessible is for me
simply a representation of the Reality, without any value in itself, I feel myself on solid ground.   I have the experience there
within that I have not to act but to receive; that I have not the
initiative but the duty of waiting and listening; that the source
of life is beyond the conscious self, for me, for all men." [47]

This man is perfectly capable of taking the naturalistic point
of view, of looking at his religious experience objectively and
seeing that it might quite well be classed as hallucinatory.   And
yet the experience for him loses none of its authority, none of
its certainty.   The naturalistic interpretation he deems quite
consistent and tenable; yet for his own part he is convinced that
the religious explanation is the true one, and his agnosticism on
most points of creed and theology in no wise interferes.   He remains a religious man in spite of his agnosticism, because this
religious experience of his is his very own, and because it has
for his life a value that is unique and supreme.

To those whose mystical experience has been of a more intense
sort, the accompanying certainty regularly rules out all questioning.   " I am as certain as that I live," says Eckhart, " that
nothing is so near to me as God.   God is nearer to me than
I am to myself." [48]   A modern mystic, Dr. Bucke, writes of
his own experience as follows: " The vision lasted a few seconds and was gone; but the memory of it and the sense of the
reality of what it taught has remained during the quarter of a

---

[47] Quoted from Flournoy, who reports the case at length.   See his " Observations de psychologie religieuse," *Archives de Psychologie,* II, 327–366.
[48] Meister Eckhart's " Mystische Schriften " put into modern German by
Gustav Landauer, p. 96.

century which has since elapsed.   I knew that what the vision showed was true, I had attained to a point of view from which I saw that it must be true.   That view, that conviction, I may say that consciousness, has never, even during periods of deepest depression, been lost." [49]

In similar vein another contemporary mystic, Mr. Benjamin P. Blood, says in reference to his own mystical insight:

" This has been my moral sustenance since I have known it. In my first printed mention of it I declared: ' The world is no more the alien terror that was taught me.   Spurning the cloud-grimmed and still sultry battlements whence so lately Jehovan thunders boomed, my gray gull lifts her wing against the nightfall, and takes the dim leagues with a fearless eye.' And now, after twenty-seven years of this experience, the wing is grayer, but the eye is fearless still, while I renew and doubly emphasize that declaration.   I know, as having known, the meaning of Existence; the sane center of the universe — at once the wonder and the assurance of the soul." [50]

There is no need of further quotation.   If there were, an almost inexhaustible amount of testimony, drawn from the mystics of every land and every age, could be easily adduced to show the supreme authority with which " the inner voice " speaks, the sense of certainty and infallibility which the mystical experience brings with it, to those who have known it directly.   The authority of tradition, of Church and Book, often — and in our day more and more — loses its force and yields its position before the attacks of rationalism; and reason is often at war with itself and results either in agnosticism or in an intellectual creed which may or may not stand, but which has within it little of the warm life and throbbing joy of genuine religion.   The authority of the religious intuition, the mystic experience, on the other hand, is seldom questioned, and it carries with it the very breath of life.   In spite of all that intellectual skepticism can say, it claims for itself an unfaltering credence, and an absolute authority, which is seldom challenged.

[49] Quoted by James from Dr. Bucke's privately printed pamphlet which preceded his " Cosmic Consciousness."   See the " Varieties," p. 399.

[50] Quoted by James in his last published article, " A Pluralistic Mystic," *Hibbert Journal*, VIII, 753, and reprinted in his posthumous " Memories and Studies."

And if it ever comes to argumentation at all, there is one argument in favor of the acceptance of this inner experience at its face value which, to him who has known it, is usually quite decisive: namely its value for life.   In the words of our French agnostic, quoted above, it is " enough to live by," " it is a part of my being and has for the rest of my being an importance and a value that are supreme, and that suffices me."   We outsiders may classify it learnedly as " *phénomène hallucinatoire* "; but the man himself knows that it is good to live by, life-giving,— and " *cela me suffit.*"

In our recognition of the new confidence which mysticism brings to religion we should be careful to avoid the not uncommon extreme of regarding it as the only form of the religious life.   There are many good people whose attitude toward the Determiner of Destiny, though central in their lives, can hardly be called mystical.   It is surely a mistake to say, with a recent and most admirable writer on mysticism, that " the man who has no mysticism in him is the abnormal man," and that " one cannot be really good without being, in some sort and degree, mystical." [51]   Many truly religious people are emphatically not mystical and mysticism is by no means *essential* to religion. One may indeed even question the propriety of the oft-heard assertion that " mysticism is the heart of religion " — unless, indeed, one be willing to admit that religion of a very real sort may get on without a heart.

To exaggerate the importance of mysticism is to do it no real service.   Nor will its good name, among thoughtful people, be greatly enhanced by the ardent advocacy it is receiving at the hands of many glib talkers and writers to whom philosophy means theosophy and whose " New Psychology " finds the solution of all problems in the " Subconscious."   Possibly another cause for the ill-repute into which mysticism is in danger of falling is the exaggerated importance that has sometimes

[51] J. W. Buckham, "Mysticism and Modern Life" (New York, Abingdon Press: 1915), pp. 163 and 165.   It is only fair to add that Professor Buckham does not seriously mean to identify religion with mysticism.   In fact he says, in another connection, " This by no means makes mysticism equivalent to religion.   One may be religious, earnestly religious, whose faith in God is — or is conceived to be — a rational inference or an accepted belief, not an immediate experience " (p. 18).

been attributed to feeling by various religious bodies and the consequent neglect which the other functions of the mind have suffered at their hands. Professor Coe, for example, has pointed out [52] that Roman Catholicism has usually emphasized in its typical saints the sentimental and emotional, while Protestantism as a whole has neglected the masculine as compared with the feminine virtues, and certain Protestant denominations have made feeling the one essential in religion. The word "spirituality," he insists, in its common use has come to mean the soft and passive, or even the unmanly; and it is therefore high time that a protest should be made against this sentimental view of religion.

That Professor Coe's words apply very accurately to a considerable amount of past and present religious talk is not to be denied. Yet I for one cannot feel that the danger of our becoming too emotional or too contemplative is really very great. Doubtless there was a time when this was the case,— when otherwordliness was taught and activity forgotten. But is this really the situation to-day? Will any one who has been to church in the last fifteen years seriously affirm that the importance of mysticism and of the "spiritual life" is really being over-emphasized in our pulpits? Do not the signs of the times point, in fact, quite in the opposite direction? Certainly it would seem that the chief trend of things to-day is toward practical efficiency and "cash value" results. The practical point of view whether known as Pragmatism or by some other title is still winning converts in the philosophic field, while Functionalism is having things all its own way in psychology. Thought and feeling, we are told, have at last been shown up in their true light as merely tools, means, instruments, while the great aim and the only value of life is *action*. As things are going at present, therefore, I apprehend that there will be little danger, in the immediate future at any rate, of too great emphasis on contemplation and mysticism.

The danger, in fact, seems to me to be chiefly on the other side. In our very laudable enthusiasm over action and social morality and class equality and hygienic conditions and international policies and tangible results, we are beginning to forget

[52] See his chapter on "Spirituality" in his "The Spiritual Life."

the inner life of the soul, the quiet turning of the spirit back upon itself, which in the rhythmic life of man is quite as important as is the outward-going impulse.   In our safe and sane and sober fear of emotionalism and sentimentality, we seem tempted to disown the spiritual nature which is part of our human heritage.   The glow of feeling, the sense of the Infinite, the intuition of a Beyond, the aspiration for the more than earthly, these are and always must be an important, if not an essential, part of religion.   And they are genuinely human as well,— as genuinely natural *ends* as are the biological processes of digestion, assimilation, and reproduction.   It is certainly of great importance that we should consider what we and our slum friends shall eat and what we shall drink and wherewithal we shall be clothed; but there are one or two other things which it is well to seek, and perhaps the " kingdom of God " is one of them.   And while many will respond that the " kingdom of God " consists just in the proper physical and social conditions, I cannot forget that one who spoke with some authority on this matter said, " The kingdom of God is within you."

In short every age has need of " the contemplative life," and ours is no exception to the rule.   It might, in fact, be maintained that our twentieth century stands in special need of it. When, indeed, could its importance be more properly emphasized than at a time when Activity is the shibboleth of theory and Efficiency the motto of practice, when we are brought up to feel that at every moment we must be working or else we must be amused, and taught to believe that most real values are to be appraised in terms of economic productivity?   Even social justice and college settlements and industrial democracy and international amity are not enough to satisfy the full warm life of the soul.   The soul needs a larger draft of air, a less circumscribed horizon, than even these excellent things can give.   It needs a chance for spreading its wings, for looking beyond itself, beyond the immediate environment, and for quiet inner growth, which is best to be found in that group of somewhat indefinite but very real experiences — aspiration, insight, contemplation — which may well be called the mystic life.

INDEX

481